4.95

8

1961

A Layman's Harmony of the Gospels

JOHN FRANKLIN CARTER

A
Layman's
Harmony
of the
Gospels

Based on the American Standard Version of the Bible

398

BROADMAN PRESS
Nashville, Tennessee

© 1961 • BROADMAN PRESS
Nashville, Tennessee

All rights reserved
International copyright secured

Third Printing

421-061

To

MATTIE

Charming Sweetheart of My Young Manhood

and

Loyal Helpmeet Through the Years

Preface

No other person in history has left such an imprint on the life of the world as Jesus of Nazareth. There has been wide difference of opinion about who or what He was, and about His authority as a teacher, His power as a miracle worker, and the nature of the benefits which His followers receive from Him. But there is no denying the impact of His life and teachings, and the effect of His death and His resurrection on the history of the world. A study of the life of Jesus, therefore, as it is set forth in the four Gospels, holds first place of importance among all possible biographical studies.

It has been my privilege and responsibility to lead a great many classes—more than two score—through a study of the earthly life of the Lord Jesus. For the most part, they were classes of freshmen and sophmores in college, and classes in a Bible School for preachers of limited educational background. During one three-year period, I was also asked to teach classes of eleventh and twelfth-grade high school students. I am convinced that every study of the life of Christ ought to be based on the Gospel records themselves, and that the student ought to have these records before him at all times. It is my judgment, therefore, that the indispensable text for such a study is a "harmony of the Gospels," a work in which the accounts in the Gospels are arranged in the order which, to the best of our knowledge and studied inference, was the order of the occurrence of the events in His life, and paralleled so that the accounts can be studied together. Any explanatory material should be in addition to the authentic records, and considered to be of secondary importance to them.

I realize that many harmonies of the Gospels have appeared through the centuries; and, from a perusal of publishers' catalogues, I am aware that still others are being made in our day. Yet, at the risk of appearing presumptive, I am adding this work to the list. My reasons for doing so are: First, although I realize that we cannot be sure at all times of the exact order of events related in the Gospel records, a study of those records through the years has led me to conclude that in a number of instances the order was different from that suggested in the harmonies of the Gospels or the works on the Life of Christ which I have been privileged to study. And an understanding of the words of Jesus, and in some instances of His actions, will be affected by the narrative background of those actions and words. Second, I have felt that the grouping of the material into sections here presented is most conducive to an earnest study of our Lord's life. Third, I believe that the information given in the notes is that which college students and many others will find most helpful. And finally, I have tried to write the notes in as simple language as possible, so that earnest Bible students generally can profit by them.

The version of the Scriptures used is the American Standard Version, given to the English-speaking world in 1901. I have used it for the following reasons: First, it makes use of the most significant results of the study that has been made of ancient manuscripts of the Bible which have been found since the appearance of the King James Version in 1611. I recognize that remarkable progress in understanding the grammar of first-century Greek and probably the significance of some of its words has been made since 1901. But much of this progress simply confirmed principles which the scholars a half century ago had already come to observe. Second, my own limited acquaintance with the Greek New Testament convinces me that the American Standard adheres more closely to the original text than does either the King James Version or any other of the recent translations which have been widely read. I am sure the King James Version will continue for a long while to be the people's Bible for devotional reading and the Scriptures read in the churches, but the sincere Bible student will certainly want a translation which, as nearly as possible, literally reproduces the sense of the sacred writers. Third, I have felt that the practice of printing in italics those words which the translators supplied to bring out the true meaning, but for which there was no equivalent in the Greek text, is of true benefit to the serious student of the Gospels, even though he may not know any Greek. And it is still more helpful to the student who has done a limited study in Greek. I believe that such a practice on the part of the translators is a matter of honesty with their readers. This practice is observed in the American Standard Version, just as it is in the King James Version; but is not observed in the other recent versions. I am grateful to Mr. C. R. Tate of Jackson, Mississippi, and his staff for their meticulous care in setting up the Scriptures for this work, which involved so many italicized words and still more marginal notations.

Since the Gospel writers wrote for readers more or less familiar with the history and the social and religious manner of life of the people with whom Jesus lived and taught, modern readers need to have many facts of history and geography and religious practice explained. Therefore I have given in the historical and religious background the explanation of those facts which most students need. I have also tried to make it possible for a student to follow the journeys of our Lord by a frequent reference to the maps. On each map the travels of Jesus are numbered consecutively, and there are not so many journeys on any map as to make following them difficult. In the explanations are references to the sections of the harmony in which the journeys were narrated. The material is outlined both at the beginning of each period and at the head of each section. At the beginning of periods Three, Five, and Six, the outlines have been abbreviated so as to give the student a general view of the periods in the shortest possible compass.

I cannot begin to name all the sources of ideas and information. They have been the teachers I have had, the lectures 'I have heard, and the books and articles I have read through the years. I want to express my sincere appreciation to the many friends and helpers who have contributed to the accomplishment of the work. My typists, Mrs. James Wood and Miss Nancy Lee, have been patient and cooperative. The members of the faculty and the office and library staffs at Clarke Memorial College have accorded me many favors through the months that have multiplied into years as I worked on the manuscript. My wife has proof-read all the notes—some of them many times—and has helped proof-read the Scripture passages as they came from the typesetter. Mrs. James L. Clark has rendered most valuable service in proof-reading and in preparing the manuscript for printing. The drawing of the temple is the work of Mr. Clayton Boyd of Southwestern Baptist Theological Seminary. The maps were first drawn by Mr. Robert Meyer and Mr. William Moote, students in Clarke Memorial College. I am under obligation also to the staff of the Broadman Press, particularly to Mr. Joseph F. Green, general book editor, to the art department for work on the drawings, and to Miss Oneta Gentry, manuscript editor, for detection of many errors and for valuable suggestions.

I hope that these pages may be instrumental in bringing students and readers into a clearer comprehension of our Lord's purpose of redemption. I am convinced that from the time of His baptism—probably earlier—there was in His consciousness the intention to offer Himself in death as a ransom for sinners (Matt. 20:28) and to achieve victory over sin and death in a mighty resurrection. These experiences were His life's aim; they were the climax of His teachings and His mighty works. To be sure, His teachings set forth the world's highest social and ethical standard; they were the perfecting of the law and the prophets (Matt. 5:17). But He did not come into the world to condemn the people of the world with a standard of life that they have never attained, but to save the defaulting sinners of the world (John 3:17). Throughout this work I have endeavored to recognize the centrality of this truth. I pray that the Comforter, the Holy Spirit of God, who has been promised to teach us, to testify to us concerning our Lord, to guide us into the truth, and to receive the things of Jesus and show them unto us, may be present with everyone who shall use this book and so fulfill His function of teaching and testifying and guiding and showing the marvelous truths about the Saviour.

John F. Carter

Clarke Memorial College
Newton, Mississippi

Contents

Introduction

In preparation for a study of the earthly life and the saving work of the Lord Jesus, three introductory matters ought to be briefly considered: (1) the historical background of the people among whom He lived and of whom He was an individual, (2) the religious background of His generation, and (3) at least a brief look at some of the characteristics of the four Gospels, which are the only authentic, original sources of our knowledge of His life. Because of limitation of space, inquiry into these matters must be brief.

I. THE HISTORICAL BACKGROUND

The Lord Jesus was, according to the flesh, a Jew; and His earthly life was spent among the Jews who were dwelling in their ancestral homeland of Palestine and were perpetuating their racial and religious traditions. He shared the historical heritage of the Jewish people of His day, and His earthly life was grounded in their history. That history naturally falls into two eras: (1) the era of the Old Testament and (2) the Interbiblical era.

1. The Old Testament Era of History. The Lord Jesus and the people among whom He lived, including His disciples, regarded the Old Testament as a revelation from God and the history recorded therein as true and authentic. They accepted the Genesis account of the creation of the universe, the origin of the human race, the entrance of sin into the world through the first man's disobedience of God's command, and the displeasure of God against sin. The people among whom Jesus lived prided themselves on being children of Abraham and of Israel. The fortunes of the patriarchs, the growth of Jacob's family in Egypt into the nation of Israel, the deliverance of this family-nation from Egyptian bondage, the divine care for it during the forty years in the wilderness, the giving of institutions of worship and a code of moral and civil law, the settlement in the land which had been promised to their fathers—these events along with the numerous miracles of those early ages were matters of common knowledge with the people among whom Jesus lived. And they were familiar with the exploits of the judges, the rise of the kingdom and the age of David, the erection of the first temple under the agency of Solomon, the division of the kingdom—permitted because of Solomon's sins, the continued sinfulness of the people and the preaching of the prophets to give warning, the captivity of the northern kingdom into Assyria and later of Judah, the southern kingdom, into Babylon, and the restoration of Judah, when Cyrus, the Persian who had conquered

Babylon, permitted Jews* under Zerubbabel to return to their homeland, to restore Jerusalem, and to build the second temple. Moreover, many of the reforms under Nehemiah, who was the last Old Testament political leader, persisted as social customs until the days of the New Testament.

Throughout the Old Testament national Israel is seen as a people separated from the rest of the world. Their advanced moral and civil code, the system of sacrifices given to them at Sinai—especially the sin offerings, the greater accountability in which they were held for waywardness from the high standards they had learned, the captivities into which they were permitted to go because of their lapses into idolatry, and withal the way in which the Jewish people were preserved—all these, as they are set forth in the Old Testament, make an important background of history for a study of the life and mission of the Lord Jesus.

2. The Interbiblical Era. But the New Testament is not just a continuation of the Old, as any thoughtful student of the Bible will notice. A political situation vastly different from that of the Old Testament era and a greatly changed social order are observed in the New Testament. An interval of more than 400 years came between the time of Nehemiah and that of John the Baptist and Jesus. Governmentally this era falls into four epochs: the Persian, the Greek, the Maccabaean, and the Roman.

a. The Persian Epoch. When the Old Testament era came to a close the Persians were ruling over the Jews who had resettled in Palestine; and their rule continued until the fall of the Persian empire to Alexander the Great, or at least until the entry of Alexander into Jerusalem in 333 B.C. During this epoch the High Priest began to exercise civil as well as religious functions, and there first appeared the jealousy and the cleavage between the Jews and Samaritans. Also, the scribes, who became influential interpreters and the teachers of the Mosaic law, made their appearance as a distinct class during this epoch.

b. The Greek Epoch. This era lasted from the conquest of the land by Alexander until the heroic exploits of the Maccabaean family, who achieved political independence for the Jewish community in Palestine. Under Alexander the Jews lived in comparative peace and prosperity. After the conqueror's death in 323 B.C., Judaea was first made a part of the Greek kingdom in Egypt whose capital was Alexandria, and whose kings are known in history as the Ptolemies. Their rule was sometimes tolerant and beneficient and sometimes cruel and tyranical. The second Ptolemy was interested in the Jewish sacred

*From about the time of the captivity of Judah, both the people who were taken as captives to Babylon and the remnant of the people left in the land of Judah came to be called "Jews" (cf. II Kings 25:22; Jer. 52:28; 40:11) and this name was applied to all those who returned from the captivity, cf. Ezra 4:12; and *Antiquities of the Jews* by Flavius Josephus, trans. William Whitson (Philadelphia: John C. Winston Company), XI.v.7, last sentence.

books and had the Old Testament translated from Hebrew into Greek, which translation is known as the Septuagint. After 125 years under Egypt, the Jewish people and their homeland were seized by the Greek kings of Syria whose capital was Antioch. This epoch was brought to a close in a series of most violent oppressions and persecutions with much bloodshed, inflicted by Antiochus Epiphanes, known as one of the cruelest tyrants in all history. Many thousands of Jews were slain, and other thousands were sold into the cruelest slavery. The temple at Jerusalem was polluted and closed, and the Jewish people were forbidden to worship Jehovah or observe their religious customs, but were commanded to offer sacrifices to the Greek gods.

c. The Maccabaean Epoch. The oppression and persecution inflicted on the Jews by Antiochus could not do otherwise than arouse resentment on the part of the faithful ones and inspire resistance at the first opportunity. In the little town of Modin,* Mattathias, an aged priest, dared to refuse to offer a heathen sacrifice, as the king's officers had ordered him, and in open defiance of the tyranical rulers, struck dead an apostate younger priest who volunteered to officiate. Then Mattathias and his five sons, aided by their fellow-townsmen, turned on the Greek officers and slew them all. Immediately the challenge went forth to all who were zealous for their traditions and the worship of Jehovah to rally to the hills around the brave old priest, with thousands responding. But Mattathias soon succumbed to the hardships of the camp and the infirmities of age; and leadership of the band of patriots passed to Judas, his third son, known in history as Judas Maccabaeus (Judas the Hammerer). Without doubt Judas was the most illustrious figure in Jewish history between David and Jesus. Against overwhelming odds this praying genius of battle won five of the most brilliant victories recorded in history. After one of these victories he led an army of rejoicing citizens into Jerusalem (165 B.C.) to reopen the temple, which had been closed for three years, to cleanse it and its furnishings from the defilement which Antiochus had put upon them, and to dedicate it anew to the service of the true God. At last Judas fell in battle with an overwhelming Syrian-Greek horde, but the fight for freedom went on, led by his undaunted brothers. Jonathan, youngest of the five, a shrewd diplomat, having taken the reins of leadership, secured important concessions for his people from a rival claimant to the throne in Antioch who later came into power. When Jonathan was treacherously assassinated, Simon, the oldest of the sons of Mattathias, took up leadership in the cause. In 144 B.C. he achieved for his oppressed people full freedom from the Greeks, both through his bravery in battle and by his wise statesmanship. As these heroes were of the priestly family, they served in a double capacity—as political rulers, and as high priests in the cleansed and restored temple. At length Simon, like his brother Jonathan, was

*Sometimes spelled "Modein."

betrayed and slain along with two of his sons; but a third son, John Hyrcanus, was quick to take the reins of leadership. After successful struggles to establish his power in the face of the Greek sympathizers, this ruler led a series of expeditions against hostile neighboring tribes, particularly the Idumaeans to the south and the Samaritans to the north. Later he suppressed the unfriendly activities of the tribes that lived east of the Jordan. By these operations he extended the boundaries of his country until they embraced all the lands of the Old Testament twelve tribes.

But succeeding generations were not always as unselfish in spirit or as genuinely patriotic as Mattathias and his sons. A son of Hyrcanus assumed the title "King of the Jews" with royal pomp, at the same time retaining the high priest's office and function. There were family jealousy and murder in the scramble for the throne and the high priesthood, and at times the people were sorely oppressed.

It was about this time that the sects, the Sadducees and the Pharisees, appeared. Fundamentally, the difference between these groups was religious (see pp. 17f); but during the Maccabaean epoch they became more or less political parties, the Pharisees being the party of the common people and the supporters of the revolution, and the Sadducees the party of the wealthy aristocrats and sympathizers with the Greeks.

d. The Roman Epoch. For centuries the power of the Romans in the west had been rising. Their victorious armies were subduing kingdoms and principalities around the shores of the Mediterranean Sea and far into the interior, bringing them under Roman rule; nor was the little kingdom of the Jews to escape. A quarrel between two brothers for the high priesthood and the Jewish throne was the occasion for the Romans to sieze the country and establish their power over it. When Pompey, the Roman general, came into the country, each of the brothers appealed to the invader for aid on his side of the quarrel. Before Pompey rendered a decision, the younger of the two brothers, who was the more aggressive and in many respects the stronger, siezed the city of Jerusalem and fortified it against the Romans. After a long and bloody siege the Romans entered the city. They took the ambitious younger brother and his two sons as prisoners, and making Judaea a Roman province, named the older of the brothers, and the more peace-loving, as high priest and "ethnarch." This latter appelation was an empty title, for the real ruler of the country was Antipater, a crafty Idumaean chieftain who never lost an opportunity to increase his own power or advance the interests of his family. He was soon given the title "procurator," that is, guardian of the country for the Romans.

Upon the death of Antipater by assassination in 43 B.C. his son Herod (known in history as Herod the Great) became the ruler. After six years of bloody war with the last claimant of the Maccabaean throne, and with invading Parthians, Herod was named "King of Judaea" by the Romans. His reign was marked by insane jealousy and ruthless bloodshed. He did not hesitate to put to death any who opposed him, or who

4

seemed to obstruct or hinder his rule or his purposes. Among those executed were three of his own sons, his favorite wife, Marianne, and her brother, whom he had shortly before appointed high priest. He was the king when Jesus was born; and his action in having all the young boys of Bethlehem put to death, in order to be rid of One who was reportedly born King of the Jews, is well known to Bible students. But Herod was a builder; he rebuilt many of the cities which had been ravished in the wars. Best known of his building projects was the replacing of Zerubbabel's temple, erected five centuries before, with the magnificent structure which was in use during the life of Jesus.

According to the provisions of Herod's will, his kingdom was to be divided among three of his sons: Archelaus was to be "king" in Judaea and Samaria, Antipas (the Herod who had John the Baptist beheaded) was to be tetrarch in Galilee and Peraea, and one Philip tetrarch in Ituraea and Trachonitis, a region east of the Sea of Galilee. When he died in 4 B.C., the Roman senate confirmed this arrangement, except that Archelaus was named "ethnarch" of Judaea instead of "king." Archelaus was a weakling, as cruel as his father, but not so efficient as a ruler (cf. Matt. 2:22). After ten years of misrule the Romans found it necessary to remove him; and at the request of many Jews, Judaea was put under a procurator—or governor—sent directly from Rome. Pontius Pilate, who gave the death sentence against Jesus, was the fifth such governor sent to Judaea.

<u>Political Situation During the Ministry of Jesus.</u> In Luke 3:1 there is a general, though not quite complete, statement of the political situation during the active life of Jesus. The territory ruled by Pilate embraced Judaea and Samaria, all of which lay between the Mediterranean Sea and the Jordan River; that ruled by Herod Antipas included Galilee west of the Jordan valley and Peraea east of that valley (spoken of in the Gospels as "the region beyond Jordan"). The tetrarchy of Philip lay east of the Sea of Galilee and the upper Jordan. Within the territory of Antipas and of Philip was a group of cities, inhabited mostly by Greeks, which were free from rule of the tetrarchs. Originally there were ten of those, joined in a loose league known as Decapolis; but their number varied from time to time. All of them were east of the Jordan except Sythopolis.

II. THE RELIGIOUS BACKGROUND

The Jewish people of our Lord's day were intensely religious. Their history, as it appears in the Old Testament had been written altogether from a religious viewpoint. Their most brilliant heroes of the Interbiblical period were priests, who led the revolt against foreign tyrants for religious reasons, and whose loyal followers were religious enthusiasts. In the years of oppression and bloodshed during the administration of Antipater as governor and the reign of Herod as king, many devout Jews, losing all hope that their nation would gain political

5

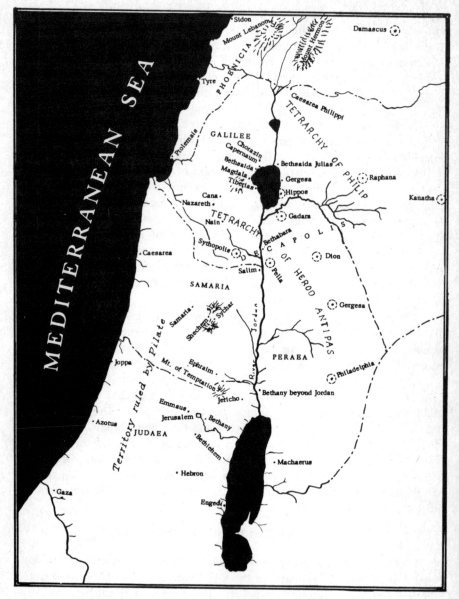

MAP SHOWING THE POLITICAL SITUATION DURING THE MINISTRY OF JESUS
(The cities of the Decapolis league are designated thus ⊙.)

6

freedom, gave themselves to a study of the prophecies in their Scriptures and fondly indulged the hope of a coming Messiah and His glorious kingdom. Their religious life was expressed in a system known today as Judaism, which had been developed during the Interbiblical period from the Mosaic law and the prophets and the interpretative comments of the scribes.

1. PLACES OF WORSHIP

In our Lord's day the Jewish people maintained two institutions of worship: the temple and the synagogue. There was one temple located at Jerusalem, in which the priests officiated at sacrifices and offerings. But there was a synagogue, in which the Scriptures were read and interpreted, in every town or village and even in many foreign cities.

(1) The Temple. In the Old Testament, worship was largely by sacrificial offerings and ceremonial rites. There was very little congregational worship—singing, public prayer, or public reading of the Scriptures; and formal preaching was unheard of. The first central place of worship was the movable tabernacle built in the wilderness under the supervision of Moses about 1497 B.C.;* it was followed by the temple of Solomon (1012—586 B.C.); and this in turn by the temple of Zerubbabel, which was erected in 516 B.C. and endured until Herod the Great dismantled it in 23 B.C. that he might erect a new one. In the new structure the temple proper was completed in a year and a half (22 B.C.), the cloisters eight years later, but the entire structure was not finished until A.D. 64,** just six years before it was totally destroyed by the Romans.

The exact plan on which it was built is not certainly known, though many restorations of it have been drawn from information found in Josephus and in the Talmud.*** The whole area enclosed by the outside porch was about twenty-six acres. It included a Court of the Gentiles, a Court of the Women, a Court of the Israelites, a Court of the Priests, and the temple building proper. That building was the heart of the whole institution, containing the holy place and the most holy place, or Holy of Holies, as did the tabernacle and the two temples before it.

As one "went up into the temple" (cf. Luke 18:10) from any direction, he first entered the Court of the Gentiles through a porch supported by marble colonnades, which surrounded the entire structure. The porch on the south end, which was known as the Royal Porch, had four rows of massive columns; those on the other three sides had only two. The colonnade on the east side, which was backed by the east wall of the city, was known as Solomon's Porch (John 10:23; Acts 3:11;

*These dates are taken from the *Dated Events of the Old Testament* by Willis Judson Beecher (New York: Harper and Brother, 1907). Many other authorities give later dates, but there is much uncertainty about them.
**W. Shaw Coldecott and James Orr, "Temple" in *International Standard Bible Encyclopedia*, Vol. V, p. 2937; T. W. Davis, "Temple" in *Hasting's Dictionary of the Bible*, Vol. IV, p. 712.
***The drawing on page 8 is a composite of plans found in Bible dictionaries, atlases, and other sources compared with the descriptions available.

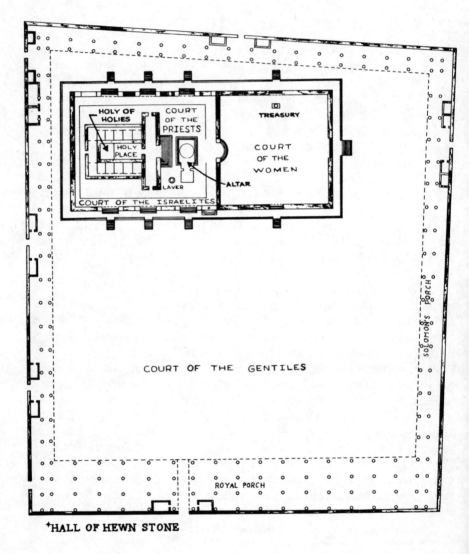

HOLY OF
HOLIES

COURT
OF THE
PRIESTS

TREASURY

HOLY
PLACE.

COURT
OF THE
WOMEN

LAVER

ALTAR

COURT OF THE ISRAELITES

SOLOMON'S PORCH

COURT OF THE GENTILES

ROYAL PORCH

†HALL OF HEWN STONE

8

5:12). The area immediately enclosed by these porches was called the Court of the Gentiles, because non-Jews might enter into it, but could proceed no farther into the temple. Without doubt, it was in the Court of the Gentiles that a market for sacrificial animals had been set up, along with tables for the money-changers (cf. Note 28), which operations Jesus drove out on two occasions. Four gates opened into this court from the outside on the west, one on the north, one on the east, and according to most authorities, one on the south.

Within the Court of the Gentiles was the sacred enclosure, entered by nine gates—one on the east and four each on the north and the south. That on the east, leading into the Court of the Women, was probably the "Beautiful Gate" of Acts 3:2, 10. At each of these gates was a stone with a carved inscription warning all Gentiles, on pain of death, not to enter. The eastern part of the sacred enclosure was the Court of the Women, on a level nineteen steps higher than that of the Court of the Gentiles. In this court, of which the area has been estimated at from one to one and three fourths acres, were the treasury and chambers for storing facilities for various temple operations. Into this court both Jewish men and women might come, but it was as near to the altar or the "House of God" as the women could approach. On the west of the Court of the Women, and on a higher level, was the Court of the Israelites. Before the gate between the two, within the Court of the Women were fifteen semicircular steps. The Court of the Israelites (men's court) was little more than a corridor surrounding the Court of the Priests, from which it was separated by a low stone wall. In the Court of the Priests, which contained the large Altar of Burnt Offerings and the laver, the ritual of animal sacrifices was conducted.

Within the Court of the Priests, on the peak of Mount Moriah, twelve steps higher than the surrounding court, was the "House of God," the temple proper. It had three parts: the porch and the chambers, which together surrounded the other two parts, the Holy Place, entered from the porch, and the Holy of Holies, behind the Holy Place. The walls, including those of the porch, were said to be 100 cubits (150 feet) high. The Holy Place contained the table of shewbread, the golden candlestick (or lampstand), and the golden altar of incense, just as the Holy Place of the tabernacle of Moses had done. But there was no Ark of the Covenant in the Holy of Holies; for that article, which had been the most sacred object in the tabernacle and in the temple of Solomon, was probably consumed in the flames that destroyed Solomon's temple in 586 B.C. In the Holy of Holies of Herod's temple (as of Zerubbabel's temple) there was only a flat stone, on which the high priest placed his censer and sprinkled the blood of the sin offering on the annual Day of Atonement, which was the only occasion on which that room was entered. It was separated from the Holy Place by a veil of very heavy material (according to an account in the Mishna, two

9

veils). It was this veil which was torn in two from top to bottom at the time of the death of our Lord. *

As a place of worship the temple was designed for sacrificial ceremonies. Only during the feast seasons did people gather in the courts in considerable numbers, and no provision was made in it for congregational worship. Individuals would come to the temple for private prayer whenever they felt the need of it (Luke 18: 10), and groups would gather in prearranged places for prayer meeting (Acts 3: 1). The teaching done in the temple usually took place when interested crowds would gather around a teacher to ask questions or to hear what he had to say (Luke 20: 1 et al.).

(2) The Synagogue. Not all of the worship of New Testament times was centered in the temple. During the Interbiblical Period the synagogue had arisen, a local institution to which the Jewish people of each community came to worship—not with sacrifices, but with prayers and eulogies and the reading and interpreting of the law and the prophets. No mention of the synagogue is found in the Old Testament, but in the time of our Lord there was one in every town in Palestine, and in foreign cities where there were as many as ten Jewish households. The officials of the temple were the priests, but those of the synagogue were: the synagogue-ruler, the elders, and the "attendant." The synagogue-ruler arranged for the services. He appointed the leader for each service and selected the one who would read the law and the one who would read the prophets and those who would recite the interpretations of these Scriptures. The elders seem to have formed a sort of advisory board to assist the synagogue-ruler. The attendant combined the work of sexton and teacher, and usually executed the decisions of the other officers. The order of the services seems to have been: eulogies, benedictions, reading from the law, interpretation of the law, reading from the prophets, interpretation of the prophets, sermon or exhortation, benediction. The interpretations were probably stereotyped translations of the Hebrew Scriptures into the current Aramaic; they were usually given by a scribe if one was present. Any man might be called on to read the different portions of the Scriptures or for a sermon or exhortation, or a man might ask for the privilege of preaching** (cf. Acts 13: 15). The benediction was usually pronounced by a priest if one was present; if not, by anyone. We learn from Luke 4: 16 that the Lord Jesus was accustomed to regular attendance at the Synagogue in Nazareth and could be depended upon to take a part in the worship.

2. TIMES OF WORSHIP

The important times of worship for the Jews of New Testament days were the weekly Sabbath and the annual feasts.

* See Matthew 27:51, #253 and Note 257.
**Paul Levertoff, "Synagogue" in *International Standard Bible Encyclopedia* (Chicago: The Howard Severance Company, 1915), Vol. V, p. 2879.

(1) The Sabbath. In the days of the Lord Jesus, and indeed throughout the Interbiblical Period, the Jews had great reverence for the Sabbath as a day of worship, particularly worship in the synagogues. Moses had delivered to the people of Israel rather stringent commandments concerning the Sabbath day (Exod. 20: 6—11; 31: 14—17; 35: 2—3; Lev. 23: 3; Num. 15: 32—36, et al.), but the emphasis in these commandments was on resting on the Sabbath day rather than worshiping. In actual practice, it seems that from the settlement in the land of Canaan until the Babylonian Exile people were lax, if not negligent, in observance of the Sabbath. But it is very probable that during the Exile groups would gather on the Sabbath day for Scripture study, Psalm singing, and prayer. After the restoration of the people to their homes in Palestine, the reforms under Nehemiah reemphasized the Sabbath as a day of rest (Neh. 13: 15—22); and with the institution of the Synagogue, it came to be a day of worship, also.

Before the time of the Lord Jesus many of the scribes, in emphasizing the law of the Sabbath, had gone to foolish extremes in the matter of burden bearing and laboring on the Sabbath, and had laid down many rigid rules, and then had provided ways of escape from their own rulings by means that were just as foolish.* One prominent cause of conflict between Jesus and synagogue authorities was the disregard on His part for those Sabbath regulations which had been set forth by the scribes, but which were not in the law given through Moses.

(2) The Feasts (and Fast). The Jews of New Testament times observed many religious feasts and fasts. We shall notice six feasts and one fast, of which four of the feasts and the fast had their beginning in the law of Moses (cf. Lev. 23: 4—44). The other two feasts were of later origin.

a. The Feast of The Passover. (Exod. 12: 1—20; Lev. 23: 5—8; Num. 28: 12—25). This was the oldest of the Jewish feasts, having been inaugurated in Egypt at the time of the Exodus. It celebrated the deliverance from Egyptian bondage. The people were commanded to meet from year to year in the city of the central place of worship (tabernacle or temple) and repeat the activities of the last night in Egypt. After making sure that no leaven was in the house where they were staying, they would kill the lamb on the fourteenth day of their first month (Abib, or Nisan), roast its meat, and as a group eat it that evening with unleavened bread and bitter herbs. By New Testament times the Jews had made changes in the details of observing the feast. The people would eat at ease rather than in haste, signifying that they were no longer in bondage to the Egyptians; they would pass a cup of wine arou̅d the table at intervals, and each one would take a sip from it; the sp̲ .ing of the blood on the door posts and lintels seems to have been scontinued;** and they would sing from Psalms 113—118

*Edersheim, Life and Times of Jesus, Vol. I, p. 136; Vol. II, pp. 56, 777ff.
**Nathan Isaacs, "Passover" in International Standard Bible Encyclopedia, Vol.

(continued on next page)

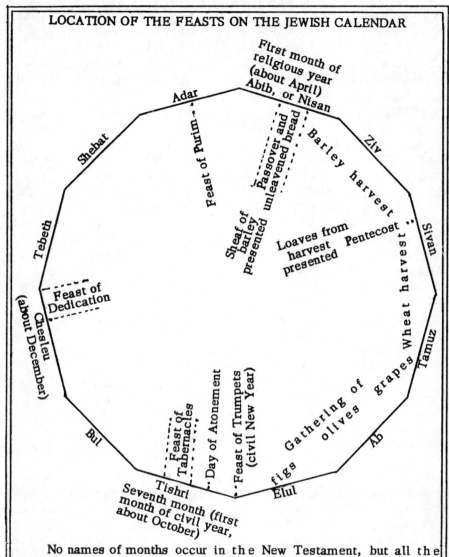

LOCATION OF THE FEASTS ON THE JEWISH CALENDAR

First month of religious year (about April) Abib, or Nisan

Adar

Feast of Purim

Shebat

Passover and unleavened bread

Barley harvest

Ziv

Tebeth

Sheaf of barley presented

Loaves from harvest presented

Pentecost

Sivan

Feast of Dedication

Chesleu (about December)

Wheat harvest

Tamuz

Feast of Tabernacles

Day of Atonement

Feast of Trumpets (civil New Year)

Gathering of grapes olives

Ab

Bul

figs

Elul

Tishri

Seventh month (first month of civil year, about October)

No names of months occur in the New Testament, but all the months except Ab are named somewhere in the Old Testament. In Exod. 12:2 Abib (Nisan) was designated as "the first month of the year," and later the other sacred occasions were dated by the number of the month after it. However, before the Exodus, people probably regarded the year to begin after the harvest of crops. Thus the Feast of Tabernacles, which was also called "the feast of ingathering," though in the seventh month, was said to be "at the end of the year" (Exod. 23:16), when the people had finished their harvesting (Deut. 23:13). For centuries the Jewish people have celebrated the Feast of Trumpets ("the first day of the seventh month," Lev. 23:24) as New Year's Day ("Head of the Year"). Apparently they had two calendars, one religious, from Nisan through Adar, and the other civil, from Tishri through Elul.

(the Hallel) during and after the meal. Since the Jewish day closed, and a new day began, at sunset, the actual eating was during the early hours of the fifteenth day of the month. The Feast of Unleavened Bread followed the Passover proper and lasted eight days, during which there were special sacred meals and sacrifices. The first day of that feast and the last day were "holy convocations" (special rest days), regardless of what day of the week they fell on. Sometimes the whole occasion was spoken of as "the Passover." The time of the year was March or April. Since Jesus was crucified at the time of the Passover and was raised from the dead on the third day thereafter, the Jewish Passover and the Christian Easter, which celebrates the resurrection, come at the same season of the year.

b. The Feast of Pentecost (Lev. 23: 15—20; Num. 28: 26—31). This was a feast of the first fruits of grain, coming fifty days after the Passover.* It was a thanksgiving for the crops ready for harvest, and a presentation of the first fruits of the harvest to the Lord and to His priests. It is sometimes called the "Feast of Weeks," because it came seven weeks—a week of weeks—after the Passover. The celebration was at the tabernacle or temple and lasted only one day. That day also was the anniversary of the giving of the law (the Ten Commandments) by the Lord God from Mount Sinai.** To Christians it is familiar because on the day of this feast the Holy Spirit came with power upon the group of disciples who were the nucleus of the early Jerusalem church (Acts 2: 1).

c. Feast of Trumpets (Lev. 23: 23—25; Num. 29: 1—6). Every time this occasion is mentioned in the Bible, it is said to be the first day of the seventh month, but it has long been observed by the Jewish people as the New Year's Day (Rosh Hashana, "Head of the Year"). Probably even before the time of the Exodus from Egypt it had been celebrated as the beginning of the crop year, because it came after the harvest of the previous year's crops and before the sowing of the crops for the coming year. According to their civil calendar it was the beginning of the year, but according to their religious calendar it was the beginning of the second half of the year. It was a one-day feast observed at home.

d. The Day of Atonement (Lev. 16: 1—34; 23: 26—32; Num. 29: 7—11). This great day, probably the most sacred of the year for a devout Jew, was observed the tenth day of the seventh month (in the religious calendar). The people remained at home, abstaining from food throughout the day (presumably occupied in confession, repentance,

(continued from preceding page)

IV. pp. 225f. I find no mention of the practice in the descriptions of the Passover in Alfred Edersheim's *Life and Times of Jesus, the Messiah* (Chicago: W. P. Blessing Company, 1886).

*Hence the name "Pentecost," from the Greek *pentecostos*, "fiftieth."
**William Owen Carver, *The Acts of the Apostles* (Nashville: Broadman Press, 1916), p. 25.

and prayer), while the high priest offered sin offerings to make atonement for the sins committed by the people during the past year. It was the only day during the year when he went into the Holy of Holies, taking the blood of the sin offering.

e. The Feast of Tabernacles (Exod. 23:16; Lev. 23:34—44; Num. 29:12—40; Deut. 16:13—15, cf. Neh. 8:13—18). This was an eight-day feast beginning the fifteenth day of the seventh month in the religious calendar. Thus the people generally had just enough time to go from their homes to the tabernacle or temple after the Day of Atonement. Its purpose was probably two-fold:

1) It was a thanksgiving for the crops already gathered. It was therefore sometimes called the feast of ingatherings (Exod. 23:16; 34:22). To this feast they would take the tithes of the previous year's harvest and increase of cattle.

2) It also celebrated God's care for the Israelites during the forty years of wandering in the desert. Three practices engaged in during the week commemorated the providential care for their fathers.

(a) During the week the people dwelt in booths in imitation of their fathers' dwelling in tents in the wilderness (Lev. 23:40—43; Neh. 8:14—15).

(b) Great candelabra with many lights were erected in the Court of the Women* in commemoration of the pillar of fire which guided the people in the wilderness by night.

(c) On the last day of the feast a pitcher of water was brought from the pool of Siloam by the multitude and poured out with great ceremony at the foot of the altar in the Court of the Priests, in commemoration of the water which the Israelites had received from the Lord out of the rock (Exod. 17:5—6; Num. 20:11).** John has given an account of one Feast of Tabernacles which Jesus attended (John 7).

f. The Feast of Purim. So far as we know this was the first feast to be instituted after Moses. It was first observed near the close of the Old Testament era—during the first half of the Persian epoch. It celebrated the deliverance of the Jewish people from the plot of Haman, an ambitious Persian official, which deliverance was brought about through the courageous action of Esther, the Jewish queen in the Persian Court (Esther 9:26—28). It was observed in their twelfth month (about our March).

g. The Feast of Dedication. This commemorated the reopening, the cleansing, and the rededication of the temple by Judas Maccabaeus after its horrible desecration by Antiochus Epiphanes three years before (cf. p. 3). The celebration occurred in their ninth month (our December), and lasted a week. Very probably all the events of John 9:35—10:39 took place during the week of this feast.

*Edersheim, *Life and Times of Jesus*, Vol. II, p. 165; Brooke Foss Westcott, *The Gospel According to St. John* (Grand Rapids: William B. Erdman Company, 1881), p. 128.

**Edersheim, *Life and Times of Jesus*, Vol. II, p. 158; Westcott, *The Gospel According to St. John*, p. 123.

All these feasts are mentioned or alluded to in the New Testament except the Feast of Trumpets and the Feast of Purim. The student will find the Jewish calendar with the feasts placed in their proper order represented by a circle on page 12.

3. THE SCRIPTURES

The Jews of New Testament times, including Jesus, regarded the Old Testament as the Word of God (John 10: 35). At that time they had come to think of their Scripture as composed of three groups of books: (1) the Law, five books of Moses, (2) the Prophets, including many books of history as well as most of the books of prophecy, and (3) the Writings, including the Psalms and many other books of our Old Testament (cf. Luke 24: 44). In their minds the books of the Law came from God through Moses (cf. John 7: 19, 9: 28—29, et al.). Moses was insistent that the commandments and the other things he wrote should be received and kept as coming from God (Deut. 6: 6ff; 31:9—13, 24—26), and from the time of the settlement in the land of Caanan these books of Moses were regarded as God's law (Josh. 1: 8; 8: 32, 36). But there were long periods of neglect of the law. At the time of the captivity the Jews must have been permitted to take with them to Babylon copies of the law and of other treasured books—history and prophecy and the Psalms and books of wisdom. A new interest in the study of the law was stirred during the Babylonian Exile. At that time the Jewish captives, being in a strange land, and deprived of their temple and their sacrificial system, would gather in groups for a study of the law, the singing of the Psalms, and prayer (cf. Ezek. 8: 1; Ps. 137).

Ezra, who lived first at Babylon and then at Jerusalem shortly before the close of the Old Testament period, is credited with bringing together the books of the Old Testament.* He was of the priestly family, and he also designated himself "a ready scribe" (Ezra 7: 1—6, 12). When he migrated to Jerusalem, he aroused a lively interest in studying the sacred books, so that from his days the Scriptures were the principal influence among the Jewish people.

The Old Testament was originally written in Hebrew, except small portions of Jeremiah, Daniel, and Ezra, which were written in Aramaic, a language closely resembling Hebrew. About 250 B.C. a translation into Greek was made at Alexandria, Egypt, known as the Septuagint (commonly written "the LXX") because of a tradition that the work was done by seventy scholars. The translation seems to have been made from a Hebrew text which differs slightly at many places from the text accepted by the scribes (the "Masoretic" text), but the

---

*In II Macc. 2:13 Nehemiah is credited with this work. Very probably it was done by Ezra and his associates (who may have been "the Great Synagogue") under the direction of Nehemiah, who was the governor at that time.

Septuagint was very influential in New Testament times. In making quotations from the Old Testament, Jesus and the apostles would sometimes quote from the accepted Hebrew and sometimes from the Septuagint, and that fact accounts for many differences between New Testament quotations from the Old Testament and the way those passages read in our Old Testament.

Many Jews of the days of Jesus had come to give to traditional interpretations of the law by the scribes equal weight of authority with the law itself. These are referred to in Matt. 15:2 and Mark 7:5 as the tradition of the elders. This tradition was gathered together in the third century A.D. in a work known as the Misha. By the end of the fourth century it had been enlarged with much other material into a voluminous work known as the Talmud, which has been authoritative for Jewish rabbis down to the present.

The fourteen books which we know as the Apocrypha were probably in existence in the days of Jesus, but there is no evidence in the New Testament that either Jesus or the apostles regarded these books to be of divine origin and authority. For the most part, they are inferior in content to the accepted books of the Bible. First Maccabees probably sets forth authentic history and portrays inspiring examples of courageous loyalty to true religion; but the other books of this collection are of little historical or religious value. It is possible that they influenced to some extent the thought of the people of New Testament times. The early Christians, though they permitted these books to be read for "edification," rejected them from the list of authoritative books. However, they were made a part of the Roman Catholic Bible by the Council of Trent in 1546.

4. RELIGIOUS SECTS AND CLASSES OF PEOPLE

Some of the influential groups or parties of the people mentioned in the Gospels were: the priests, the scribes, the Pharisees, the Sadducees, the Herodians, the publicans, and the Samaritans. Besides these, there were the Essenes and other similar groups, who are not mentioned in the Bible, but who are thought by some Bible scholars to have been influential among the people during New Testament times.

(1) The Priests. At the beginning of the history of Israel as a nation Aaron, the brother of Moses, of the tribe of Levi, was named high priest, and his sons were named priests with him. After that the priesthood and the high priesthood were hereditary in the family of Aaron. There came to be many priests, so that in the days of David they were grouped into twenty-four courses (I Chron. 23:1—10). Even so, a priest without special favor might serve in the temple only a few times in his life, and many who were of the priestly family never had an opportunity to serve. But apart from their function in the temple, there was doubtless an honor and dignity attached to priestly lineage

(cf. Luke 10:31; John 1:19; also, The Life of Josephus*). In Old Testament times one consecrated as high priest would normally serve for life, but during the Interbiblical Period the foreign powers exercising rule began to claim the prerogative of appointing the high priest—of course confining the appointments to members of the priestly families. During the Maccabean epoch, the high priest was also the king; and after the Romans seized the country, the high priest continued to exercise great influence, being ex officio president of the Sanhedrin. Consequently, the Roman rulers took to themselves the authority to appoint and to remove high priests. A high priest might (and many did) lose favor with a Roman ruler, so that he would be displaced by another after serving only a short time.

Mention is frequently made in the Gospels of "chief priests" who were members of the Sanhedrin (Matt. 16:21; 26:3 et al.). Broadus suggests** that the "chief priests comprised the high priest at the time, any person who had previously occupied that office, and probably also the heads of the twenty-four courses of priests."

(2) The Scribes. The scribes as a class probably first appeared during the Babylonian Exile (Ezra 7:6).*** At first they were professional writers who made copies of the law for those who desired them. Since they would naturally soon know more about the law than anyone else, they came in time to be teachers of the law and its interpreters. From among their number came the lawyers and the professional rabbis. The most learned among them were "doctors of the law" (cf. Luke 2:46; 5:17; Acts 5:34). The "tradition of elders," which was so highly regarded by the Pharisees, was composed largely, if not altogether, of the interpretations of the law which the learned scribes had made.

(3) The Pharisees. This group was doubtless the most influential of the religious sects of the time of Jesus. The roots of some of their practices may be seen in the reforms and the prayers of Nehen.iah (cf. Neh. 13:14), but they had their beginning as a group with the struggles against the heathenizing Greeks in the days of Mattathias and Judas Maccabaeus. At first they were called "Chasidim" (Separatists) because of their determination to keep themselves (and the nation, as much as possible) from contaminating foreign influences. During the time of Jesus their distinguishing characteristics and doctrines were: (a) They put great emphasis on keeping the law. By their selfish, credit-seeking conformity to legal requirements they sought to bring God under obligation to themselves (cf. the Pharisee's prayer, Luke 18:11—12). (b) They regarded the interpretations by the scribes (the "tradition of the elders") as equally authoritative with the written Law itself. (c) They

*Life of Flavius Josephus by himself included in Antiquities of the Jews.
**John A. Broadus, Commentary on Matthew in An American Commentary on the New Testament, Alvah Hovey, ed. (Philadelphia: American Baptist Publications Society, 1886), p. 18.
***Those mentioned before the time of the exile were likely official recorders, or chroniclers (for example II Sam. 8:17).

looked on themselves as righteous (and sometimes were so regarded by their fellows) and were highly critical of others (cf. Luke 18: 11—12; Matt. 5: 20). They called those sinners who lived in disregard of their rules and standards. (d) They believed in the existence of angels, in life after death, and in a future resurrection of the unjust and the just (cf. Acts 23: 6, 8; 24: 15). In general, they were the conservative element of Judaism.

(4) The Sadducees. Opposed to the Pharisees were Sadducees. For the most part, they were priests who were willing to compromise their Jewish principles for favors from the foreign rulers. Probably they began to appear as a separate class during the closing years of the Greek period. They took their name from Zadok, the priest who was faithful to David and Solomon when Abiather, the other priest, fell away to Adonijah (I Kings 1: 32—34). Their distinguishing doctrines and characteristics were: (a) They denied the existence of angels, the immortality of the soul, and any idea of a future resurrection (Matt. 22: 23; Acts 23: 8). (b) They rejected the "tradition of the elders" and the so-called oral law, accepting as authoritative only the written Old Testament. (c) They were severe in their judgment, and were not very popular with the common people.

(5) The Herodians. This group is mentioned in only two connections (Mark 3: 6; 12: 13; and parallels). Not much is known of them, but they were doubtless Jews who preferred to be ruled by one of the Herod family rather than by Roman procurators, and yet they professed a willing submission to the Roman government.

(6) The Publicans. When the Romans conquered Judaea and made it a part of the Empire, they imposed Roman taxes on the people. The publicans were Jews who collected those taxes for the Romans. Ordinarily, tax collecting was a lucrative employment, because the collectors paid a stipulated amount to the Romans and took from the people what they saw fit, or what they could. But the publicans were hated by the people generally because: (a) they were collecting the taxes for the foreign conquerors, and (b) they frequently extorted from the people more than was due, and consequently were rich. Of course, the publicans did not pretend to keep the Jewish law with any degree of exactness, and they were usually classed with the sinners. Jesus was called a friend of the publicans because He was willing to receive those that came to Him, and to accept the hospitality of those who invited Him into their homes; but of course He did not condone their extortion (cf. Luke 19: 7—9).

(7) The Samaritans. These were in reality a different race, or rather a mixed race, instead of just a class of the people. They were descended from those Israelites of the northern kingdom who were left in the country when northern Israel was taken captive by the Assyrians, and of the foreigners that came to live around the city of Samaria. They worshipped Jehovah, but in their worship they mingled many heathen

ideas (cf. II Kings 17: 24ff). During the Persian epoch they built a temple on Mt. Gerazim, in which their priests officiated for about 275 years. This temple was destroyed by John Hyrcanus (121 B. C.) and was never rebuilt; but the Samaritans continued to worship on and around Mt. Gerazim. The Jews despised them because of the impurity of their race and because of the readiness with which they made religious compromises with the Greeks and other foreigners. They are in existence today, but their number has dwindled to a few hundred. They possess a very ancient manuscript of the books of Moses, which is of great value in the study of the Old Testament.

(8) The Essenes and Other Similar Groups. Josephus, the historian, and Philo, the philosopher, tell in their writings of a sect of Jewish people known as Essenes, who lived during the first century. These people are not mentioned at all in the Bible, and in the descriptions of them that have been preserved there are confusing and even conflicting statements. Some of them lived in groups or quarters to themselves in many of the cities and villages of the land, but those about whom most has been written lived like inmates in a monastery, withdrawn from the world on the west shore of the Dead Sea, supposedly near the town of Engedi. In some matters the teachings of these people resembled those of the Pharisees, but they renounced worldly wealth and followed a rigid schedule of holy living. They did not practice animal sacrifices but sent gifts otherwise to the temple in Jerusalem. The greater part of them renounced marriage and all activities for pleasure. New members were put through three years of rigorous trial during which at intervals certain secret knowledge was imparted to them. In fact, in some respects, they resembled a secret order.

Interest in this group has been revived by the discovery of the "Dead Sea Scrolls" in 1947 and later, which have brought to light a similar group that lived at Qumran, a considerable distance north of Engedi but also near the Dead Sea. Some scholars maintain that these were the Essenes, and that Qumran was their place of residence rather than Engedi. But the customs and teachings of that group differ considerably from those related by Josephus and Philo. Some scholars have held that John the Baptist—and some, that even Jesus—came under the influence of these groups. But evidence for such a view is far from convincing—indeed, to me, some of the conclusions suggested seem to be arbitrary and unrelated to the evidence adduced.*

°Flavius Josephus, *Antiquities of the Jews* XVIII. i.5; *Wars of the Jews* II. vii.3; J. E. H. Thompson, "Essenes" in *International Standard Bible Encyclopedia,* Vol. II, p. 997; Bishop J. B. Lightfoot, *Saint Paul's Epistles to Colossians and to Philemon* (New York: The MacMillan Company), pp. 348-417. For the more radical view of the Dead Sea Scrolls, cf. Emil G. Kraeling, *Rand McNally Bible Atlas* (New York: Rand McNally and Company, 1956); for a more conservative view, cf. William Sanford LaSor, *The Amazing Dead Sea Scrolls* (Chicago: The Moody Press, 1956), especially chapters 14 and 16.

5. THE SANHEDRIN

The word Sanhedrin is not found in our English New Testament, but repeated mention is made of a council or court composed of "chief priests and elders and scribes." This council is not spoken of in the Old Testament; it doubtless arose during the Interbiblical Period, possibly in the Maccabaean epoch. It included seventy-one members chosen from the three groups most influential with the people. The high priest was always one of its two presidents. The place of its meeting is not certain; the Talmud indicates that it was the "Hall of Hewn Stone" in the temple, but Josephus mentions the meeting place as outside the temple. The membership included both Sadducees and Pharisees (Acts 23: 6). During New Testament times it had authority in religious and most civil matters, and limited authority in criminal matters. In cases involving capital punishment, approval of the Roman procurator, or governor, was required before execution of the sentence, except that the Sanhedrin might of its own authority impose and execute the sentence of death on a Gentile—even a Roman citizen—who had violated the sacred courts of the temple by going beyond the Court of the Gentiles, or on a Jew who had invited or escorted a Gentile beyond that Court. Regularly there were no sessions at night, or on a Sabbath day or a feast day. "A sentence of capital punishment could not be passed on the day of the trial. The decision of the judges must be examined on the following day, except in a case of a person who misled the people, who could be tried and condemned on the same day."[*]

6. THE MESSIANIC HOPE

Many prophecies about the coming of the Christ (or the Messiah[**]) are found in the Old Testament. Sometimes the prophecies are dim, but understandable to us when we view them through the New Testament records as glasses, as in Gen. 3: 15, where it is merely stated that the Seed of the woman would bruise the head of the serpent while that one would merely bruise the heel of the promised Seed; but in many of them the promise is clear and assuring. A great many of the prophecies promise a glorious kingdom presided over by a God-sent King who would deliver His people from their enemies and reign in righteousness (cf. Isa. 9: 6—7; 11: 1—10; Jer. 23: 5—8; Mic. 5: 2—5; Ps. 2; 72; 89: 3—4; 110; et al.); and repeatedly it was foretold that this king would be of the lineage of David (Ps. 89: 3—4; Isa. 11: 1—10; Jer. 23: 5—6; et al.). The Jews of the Interbiblical Period, suffering from misrule and oppression of the Greeks and the Romans, found comfort and inspiration in anticipation of the promised King and His Kingdom;

[*]Paul Levertoff, "Sanhedrin" in *International Standard Bible Encyclopedia* Vol. IV. pp. 2689f.

[**]Messiah is from the Hebrew word meaning "anointed one," and Christ is from the Greek word of the same meaning.

and many of the scribes gave themselves to a careful study of those prophecies. As a result of that study some of the scribes had outlined a program of the messianic age.* From Matthew 16:14 (and parallels) and John 1:21, it is evident that their program included the reappearance of an Old Testament prophet (Jeremiah or some other one besides Elijah), the reappearance of Elijah, and the appearance of the Messiah. Before the time of Jesus false messiahs had arisen (Acts 5:36—37), who, enticing multitudes of followers, came to disastrous ends. The scribes could readily inform Herod that the Christ would be born at Bethlehem (Matt. 2:5—6), and without hesitation they answered Jesus that the Christ would be a descendant of David (Matt. 22:42). At the time of the ministry of John the Baptist "the people were in expectation" (Luke 3:15), which was shared even by the Samaritans (John 4:25). There were many pious ones who were waiting for the redemption of God's people; notably Zacharias, father of John the Baptist, Simeon and Anna (Luke 2:25—38), Joseph of Arimathaea (Luke 23:52).

Besides those prophecies which promised a royal Messiah, there are others (Ps. 22:1—21; Isa. 53, and others) which portray a suffering One, who would bear the sins of the people. Christians confidently identify that One as the Christ, who was promised to be both King and Saviour. It is noteworthy also that Ps. 22:22—31; Ps. 110:2—3; and Isa. 53:10b suggest a spiritual Kingdom, in contrast with the glorious visible Kingdom pictured in the other prophecies. But the scribes did not see in Ps. 22 and Isa. 53 any reference to their Messiah. Therefore, the self-righteous Pharisees and the politically-minded Sadducees did not recognize Jesus as the fulfillment of their cherished messianic prophecies. Accordingly, they condemned Him to death, and thus they unknowingly fulfilled prophecies about the Messiah which they had overlooked. But Christians of the New Testament recognized Jesus of Nazareth to be the fulfillment of all classes of messianic prophecies— they trusted Him as Saviour, they acknowledged Him as spiritual Lord and King in their lives, and they looked for Him to return and inaugurate a glorious visible Kingdom.

III. THE GOSPELS

For authentic information concerning the earthly life of the Lord Jesus, we are dependent on the four Gospels written by Matthew, Mark, Luke, and John. The few other purported records of His words and His works are fragmentary and altogether untrustworthy. Yet no one of the four is a full biography of our Lord, nor are all of them combined. Except for a few incidents which occurred in connection with His birth and the account of one journey to Jerusalem when He was twelve years old, the Gospels do not have anything to say about the youth of our Lord.

*Charles B. Williams, *New Testament History and Literature*, pp. 37f; Henry C. Sheldon, *New Testament Theology* (New York: The MacMillan Company, 1922), pp. 11-25.

21

Indeed Mark and John begin their accounts with events in His public ministry.

The four Gospels do not all tell about the same things. There is material in each one which is not found in any of the other three. Nor do they give in the same order the accounts of those events which are recorded in more than one Gospel. The order of events in Mark and Luke, so far as they parallel each other, is very near the same; but this order is very different from that in Matthew especially for the events that occurred during the first two and one-half years of our Lord's public ministry. The material found in John, for the most part, is altogether different from that which is found in the other three. This difference is so great that John's Gospel is generally thought of in a class to itself, and Matthew, Mark, and Luke are named the Synoptic Gospels, because they are said to record the life of our Lord from the same viewpoint.

1. INSPIRATION OF THE GOSPELS

I take it that each of the Gospel writers wrote as he was inspired of God; and that the work of each one, as it came from his hand, was and is the Word of God. But the original works of the Gospel writers (that is, the parchment or papyrus manuscripts which they wrote) have been lost, and we must rely on copies of copies many times removed. It is not claimed that the scribes of the Middle Ages who made copies of the Bible, or portions of it, were inspired. Such a claim could not be supported if it were made, since the old manuscripts which were made before the invention of printing differ at many places among themselves. Where different readings occur in the old hand-written copies, students of the text of the New Testament have had to determine the best they could from the copies just what the inspired authors did write. This accounts for some of the differences in the various translations, because many old manuscripts of the New Testament which had been stored in old churches or monasteries have been discovered since 1611, when the King James translation was made.

The Lord God inspired each of the Gospel writers. He knew that there would be four—indeed He planned that there should be four and chose the four individuals for the work, though surely the Gospel writers were not conscious of being thus chosen. Certainly He must have chosen these four because He knew their personal characteristics and their peculiarities of style. This means that the Holy Spirit did not deprive the Gospel writers of their ordinary habits of expression when He inspired them to compose their records, but that He used those habits. We can, therefore, study the style of these writers just as we study the style of authors not so inspired. Each writer wrote under the guidance of the Holy Spirit in his own peculiar style such things as contributed to his own immediate purpose, so that the work of them all is exactly what God desired should be for all time His own word for all the world. It will therefore help us to understand the message which God has for us in the Gospels if we will study briefly something of the characteristics and peculiarities of the writers and the particular message of each.

2. THE FOUR GOSPELS

(1) MATTHEW

a. Author. Students of the New Testament are almost unanimously agreed that the apostle Matthew wrote the Gospel that comes first in our Bibles. About Matthew the Bible tells us six things: (1) that he was of the family of Alpheus, (2) that he was also called Levi, (3) that in his early life he was a publican, or Roman tax collector, (4) that Jesus called him to be a disciple, (5) that in appreciation of the Master's consideration of him he made a feast, inviting Jesus and some of his publican friends, and (6) that Jesus included him in the group of twelve whom He chose and ordained as apostles. His work as collector of Roman taxes doubtless required a familiarity with, and an easy usage of, the vernacular Greek language, as well as his native Aramaic. This certainly was a providential preparation for his work as a Gospel writer.

b. Purpose of Writing. Students of the New Testament are generally agreed that Matthew wrote his Gospel especially for the Jewish people. Christian writers of the second century (100—200)* make the assertion that Matthew first wrote the "logia" (saying, or oracles) of Jesus in Hebrew—probably meaning Aramaic. So far as anyone knows, no copy of this Aramaic work has remained to the present, and no one knows for sure what was in it. It may have been chiefly some of the impressive discourses of Jesus, but it certainly must have included some narrative material. But he wrote it in the native language of his fellow-Jews, evidently to convince them that Jesus was truly the Messiah who had been foretold in the Scriptures.

c. Noticeable Characteristics

(a) Quotations from the Old Testament. He frequently appealed to the Old Testament to show that the events in the life of Jesus were a fulfillment of prophecy, or at least in accord with it. Westcott and Hort** list 136 quotations or citations from the Old Testament which Matthew includes in his Gospel.

(b) Emphasis on the Kingdom. In a Gospel for the Jews, who were looking for a kingly Messiah, Matthew gave special emphasis to our Lord's kingly relations and activities. His favorite term for designating the rule of the Messiah was the phrase "Kingdom of Heaven." It is found thirty times in Matthew but nowhere else in the New Testament. A possible reason for its use is that in some Jewish literature "Heaven"

*Particularly Papias, quoted by G. H. Schodde, "Matthew, Gospel of," in *International Standard Bible Encyclopedia*, Vol. III, p. 2010. Cf. Charles B. Williams, *New Testament History and Literature* (Kansas City, Mo.: Western Baptist Publishing Company, 1917), p. 54.

**Brooke Foss Westcott and Fenton John Anthony Hort, *The New Testament in Original Greek* (New York: MacMillan Company, 1914), pp. 602f.

sometimes designated the Deity (cf. I Macc. 2:21; 3:17). But the phrase "Kingdom of God," which is the term used by the other Gospel writers, is found also in this Gospel five times. Matthew showed to his Jewish brethren that the Messiah did inaugurate His kingdom, all authority in Heaven and on earth being given to Him (ch. 28:18). For the present age, to be sure, that Kingdom must be seen in the loyal submission of His people to Him and their obedience to His rule, but the Messiah's kingdom is no less real because it is spiritual. Moreover, Matthew assured his brethren that the King will return, and during the age of the "Regeneration" will sit on the throne of His glory, at which time He will, through His faithful ones, rule over the twelve tribes of Israel (ch. 19:28). But he also warned his readers that the benefits of the Kingdom would extend beyond the limits of the Jewish race. Disciples are to be made during the present age from among all the nations (ch. 28:19), while the Kingdom grows as a mustard bush grows from a tiny seed (ch. 13:31). In the age to come all the nations will be gathered before the King and the faithful ones invited to inherit the Kingdom (ch. 25:32, 34), in which Kingdom people will come from the east and the west and the north and the south and sit down with the patriarchs, while the unfaithful "sons of the Kingdom" (the unbelieving Jews) will be cast out (ch. 8:11, 12). Matthew certainly had in mind also to impress his Jewish brethren that the mission of the King was to save the people of the Kingdom from their sins—therefore the King's name was Jesus, "Jehovah will save" (ch. 1:21). Matthew, himself was transformed from a despised publican into an apostle of the Kingdom. In order to save His people, the King gave His life as a ransom (ch. 20:28); His blood was poured out for the remission of sins (ch. 26:28). His power to deliver His subjects from their emeny (the Devil) was demonstrated, first by vanquishing him in all his temptations (ch. 4:1—11), and second by coming victoriously alive from the dead (ch. 28; cf. Heb. 2:14).

(c) Discourses of Jesus. One notable characteristic of Matthew's Gospel is the number and length of the discourses of Jesus which it records. Those who believe that the "Logia," which Matthew wrote first, was a group of the sayings of Jesus hold that these lengthy quotations were copied from the earlier work. If such be the case, the Lord guided him both in the first writing and in quoting from it in the permanent Gospel. However that may be, we observe the following: the Sermon on the Mount (chs. 5—7), the instructions to the disciples on the eve of their practice trip (ch. 10), eight of the first great group of parables (ch. 13), the discourse on humility and forgiveness (ch. 18), the oration against the scribes and Pharisees (ch. 23), and the prophecies of the destruction of the temple and of His return to earth (chs. 24 and 25), besides many other parables and sayings found only in this Gospel.

(d) Order of Events. Another characteristic is, that chapters 5 through 13 were not written in chronological order: that is, the order in which the events occurred. These chapters, embracing the Ministry to the Multitudes in Galilee (the third period), seems to be written in logical order, rather than chronological order. Comparing them with the records of the same events in Mark and Luke we conclude that some of the events recorded in chapters 8 and 9 occurred before the Sermon on the Mount, which is in chapters 5 through 7; and some of the others took place after speaking the parables of chapter 13. The events of 11: 2 through chapter 13 came before those of 9: 35 through 11: 1.

d. Date of Writing. Assigning dates to the writing of the Gospels is largely a matter of conjecture, based on meager evidence in the Gospels themselves, in Acts and the Epistles, and in the early Christian writings. In all probability, the Gospel of Matthew, at least in the Hebrew (Aramaic) version, was among the sources of information which Luke mentions in the preface of his Gospel (Luke 1: 1—4). In that case, that writer must have obtained a copy of Matthew's work, or have made copious notes from it, before he sailed with Paul for Rome from Caesaraea in the autumn of A.D. 60. This is on the assumption the Gospel was produced in Palestine of Syria. Evidently, then, that version was produced as early as 59 or 60. The Greek version, which we have, was surely produced before the outbreak of the Jewish-Roman War in 66, probably between 61 and 65.

(2) MARK

a. The Author. There is no doubt, to speak of, among students of the New Testament that our second Gospel was written by Mark, also called "John Mark" or "John whose surname was Mark." He is mentioned in Acts 12: 12, 25; 13: 5, 13; 15: 37—39; Col. 4: 10; Phile. 24; II Tim. 4: 11; and probably I Pet. 5: 13. Some New Testament students suppose that the upper room where Jesus ate the last Passover with His disciples and instituted the Memorial Supper was in Mark's home, and that he was the young man referred to in Mark 14: 51—52. Surely his home was in Jerusalem (Acts 12: 12).

b. Source of Information and Occasion of Writing. Early Christian writers* say that Mark went with Peter on many of his preaching trips and was interpreter for him; and that he thus learned from that apostle many of the things he recorded in his Gospel. It is stated by Clement of Alexandria, who wrote about A.D. 200, that, at the request of the Christians in Rome, Mark recorded the things that Jesus did and said as he had heard them from Peter.** We know that Mark was in Rome during the first imprisonment of Paul (Col. 4: 10; Phile. 24), at which time, or earlier, the Roman Christians probably made their request.

c. Characteristics. For his aggressive Roman readers Mark pictured Jesus as a Man of action and power, the Son of God as well as the Jewish Messiah. The miracles and the deeds are prominent rather

*Irenaus, Turtullian, Clement of Alexandria, cf. Charles B. Williams, *New Testament History and Literature*, p. 61.

**Ibid., p. 62.

25

than the teachings. One of Mark's favorite terms is the word that is translated "immediately" or "forthwith," which is found forty times in this, the shortest of the four Gospels. Thus Mark shows the Lord Jesus as constantly on the go.

Many New Testament students, including Dr. A. T. Robertson, regard the Gospel of Mark as the standard of the chronological order of the events in the life of our Lord.* In this Harmony I have deviated from Mark's order only at the account of the supper at Bethany, where it seemed best to follow the order of John (cf. #196 and Note 198).

d. Date of Writing. The Gospel of Mark was probably the first of the four to be produced in its present form; that is, in Greek. The Aramaic version of Matthew was probably produced as early as Mark, if not earlier. We have no New Testament account of Mark's activities after he accompanied Barnabas to Cyprus (Acts 15: 39) until we find him in Rome during Paul's first imprisonment—unless the mention of his name in I Pet. 5: 13 is to be dated between those incidents. At least part of his association with Peter might well have been during the ten or more years intervening. Mark may have been in Rome when Paul, as a prisoner, and Luke, as his companion, arrived there in the spring of A.D. 61; and Luke probably soon thereafter obtained a copy of this Gospel to add to the sources of information for his own Gospel. Most probably the date of writing was as early as 59 or 60.

e. Concluding verses. There is question among some students of the New Testament about what is the proper ending of this Gospel. In the oldest two of the known copies, or manuscripts, it closes with verse 8 of the sixteenth chapter. The Revised Standard Version brings the body of the book to a close with that verse and puts verses 9—20 in the margin. The manuscripts that do contain those last verses differ among themselves, and other manuscripts have a verse that is not in our English Bibles, except as part of the footnote in the Revised Standard Version. I recognize that there is difficulty harmonizing those verses with the other Gospels; but since for centuries the Lord God has seen fit to allow them to be regarded as part of His word, and since they do not contradict anything appearing elsewhere in the Bible, I am convinced that they are to be received as true and inspired, whether Mark wrote them or someone else (cf. Note 267).

(3) LUKE

a. The Author. The third Gospel in our Bibles and the book of Acts had the same author; and the unanimous conclusion of conservative students of the New Testament is that the author was Luke, Paul's companion in many of his travels and in his imprisonments. We can trace his labors with Paul (1) by the "we passages" in the book of Acts (16: 10—17; 20: 5—15; 21: 1—18; 27: 1—28: 16) and (2) by the mention of his name in the epistles of Paul (Col. 4: 14; II Tim. 4: 11; Phile.

*A. T. Robertson, *Harmony of the Gospels for Students of the Life of Christ* (New York: George Doran Company, 1922), p. 24.

24). From these we learn that he was with the Apostle for a short time during the Second Missionary Journey; and, beginning with the voyage to Jerusalem at the close of the Third Missionary Journey, he seems to have been his more or less constant companion until the close of the Apostle's life. Paul called him "the beloved Physician" (Col. 4: 14). It is generally thought that Luke was a Gentile, but there is no direct statement in the Bible to that effect; and for a Gentile, he had a rather thorough acquaintance with, and high regard for, the Jewish Scripture. It is not known where his home was, but it was not in Palestine. He probably remained at Philippi after Paul's departure from that city on the Second Missionary Journey until he rejoined the Apostle there at the close of the Third Missionary Journey. He was a man of high culture, and his usage of the Greek language is probably the best in the New Testament.

b. Source of Material. Luke gathered the material for the Gospel second-hand from those who had known the Lord Jesus (cf. ch. 1: 2). This was probably done while Paul was a prisoner at Caesarea. We wonder if during that time he talked with Mary, the mother of our Lord, and if she related to him the incidents recorded in the first two chapters of the Gospel. If she was still living at the time, he probably did meet her; if she was not living, he surely received that material from someone who had been a close friend to her. The account of the birth of Jesus in the Gospel of Luke is from Mary's viewpoint, and it contains elements that only Mary herself or her intimate friends could have known. During that period he probably gathered information also from many other eyewitnesses, and it is likely that he came in contact with the early version of the Gospel of Matthew. Probably also, the sources of his information included the Gospel of Mark, which he surely came to know after he arrived in Rome, if not before. The order of events agrees with that in Mark wherever those Gospels are parallel, except for a few details.

c. Characteristics. Luke showed the marks of a true historian in that he sought his material from "eyewitnesses and ministers of the word," and in that he "traced all things accurately from the first." Under the guidance of the Holy Spirit he obtained and has preserved for us in chapters 10 through 19 of his Gospel a wealth of material on the later teachings and works of Jesus which is not found in the other Gospels. This Gospel shows also the author's world-wide sympathies, his appreciation of deep spiritual experiences, such as the joy of forgiveness, prayer, and heartfelt praise, and his high regard for womanhood. It seems that Luke had in mind to set forth Jesus as the world's Saviour.

d. Date of Writing. We are on comparatively sure ground in fixing the date of the writing of Luke's Gospel. We know that it was written before Acts, because in Acts 1: 1 the author refers to it as the "former treatise" which he had made "of all that Jesus began both to do and to teach." Luke and Paul began their voyage to Rome in the autumn of the year in which Festus succeeded Felix as procurator of Judaea, which is usually said to have been A.D. 60; and they arrived the following spring (61). Luke remained with the apostle throughout his imprisonment at Rome and probably wrote Acts after two years of that confinement (Acts 28: 30—31), or A.D. 63. Therefore, the Gospel must have been written in late 61 or 62.

e. Dedication. Both the Gospel and Acts are addressed, or dedicated, to one called Theophilus. But who was Theophilus? The name means "Lover of God," and it was not an uncommon name during the first century. Many think that someone by that name was a personal friend of Luke's who encouraged him to write his books and sponsored the copying of them. But no other reference to a person by that name is found in the New Testament, and that fact makes one wonder whether Luke was addressing someone specifically by that name, or whether he used the name Theophilus as a sort of personal appellation to express his admiration for some outstanding Christian in his circle of friends. If the latter be true, we wonder to whom of his friends the "beloved physician" was more devoted, and to whom the appellation, "Lover of God," was more fitting, than to the Apostle Paul. Another possibility is, that he may have regarded anyone interested in reading an account of the life of Jesus or of the doings of the apostles to be a "Lover of God," and that in this way he was addressing each of his readers personally.

(4) JOHN

a. Authorship. The prevailing belief for centuries has been that the fourth Gospel in our Bibles was written by the apostle John, "the disciple whom Jesus loved" (cf. ch. 21: 20, 24, also 19: 35). But some modern scholars deny this conviction, holding that this Gospel was not written until sometime in the second century, after the death of John, who was the longest-lived of the apostles. However, conservative Bible students find no convincing reason for dating the fourth Gospel so late or for doubting that John the apostle was the author. A careful study of this Gospel reveals evidence that the writer was a companion of Jesus and an eyewitness of the events narrated, just as he claimed (cf. ch. 19: 35; 21: 24 cited above). The late Dr. Tidwell remarks: "The very vividness (of his narratives) points to one who was present. We can hardly see how he could make it so vivid if he had not been present."[*] The history of the Gospel (external evidence) points to the same conclusion. The fourth Gospel was certainly known and used early in the second century, and the earliest Christian writers who name anyone as author (Irenaeus and others, who wrote about the middle of the second century) ascribe it to John.[**] I am therefore convinced that there is no

*Josiah Blake Tidwell, *The Gospels and The Life of Christ* (Waco, Texas: Baylor University Press, 1921), p. 69, also Charles B. Williams, *New Testament History and Literature*, p. 78.

**James Iverach, "John, Gospel of," in *International Standard Bible Encyclopedia*, Vol. III, p. 1720.

good ground for rejecting the traditional belief that the apostle John was the author.

   b. About the Author. John is one of the best-known characters of the New Testament. He was a son of Zebedee, and brother of James, who was also an apostle. His mother was Salome (cf. Matt. 27: 56 with Mark 15: 40), who may have been a sister of Mary, mother of Jesus (cf. John 19: 25, also Note 16). In early life he was associated with his father and brother in the fishing business (Mark 1: 19—20), and with them Simon Peter and Andrew were associated as partners (Luke 5: 7, 10). The business certainly prospered, because, besides owning their boats and nets, they were able to employ "hired servants" (Mark 1: 20). He is generally thought to have been that disciple of John the Baptist who with Andrew left John (the Baptist) to follow Jesus—these two becoming the first disciples of Jesus. Along with James and Andrew and Peter, he readily accepted the later challenge of Jesus to follow Him constantly and learn the art of fishing for men. These four are named as the first of the three groups of four in all of the lists of the apostles (cf. Note 55, 3), and he and Peter and James seem to have been a sort of "inner circle" in the apostolic group, who on three occasions were asked to accompany the Lord on missions in which the others did not share. He and Peter were chosen to make preparations for observing the last Passover Supper for Jesus and the group; they were present at the Jewish trials of Jesus; and they visited His tomb together when Mary Magdalene informed them that it was empty. So far as we know, he was the only one of the disciples to see Jesus crucified (but cf. I Pet. 5: 11). Although he liked to refer to himself as "the disciple whom Jesus loved," he was on three occasions sharply rebuked by the Master—two times along with his brother James (cf. Mark 9: 38—40; Luke 9: 54—56; Mark 10: 35—40). After the ascension of Jesus he occupied a prominent place in the Jerusalem church, being a companion of Peter at the healing of the lame man and in the first experience of imprisonment for the gospel (Acts 3: 1 to 4: 21), and being sent with him by the church on an important mission to Samaria (Acts 8: 14). Paul named him as one of the pillars of the Jerusalem church (Gal. 2: 9). Christian writers of the second century (Irenaeus and others) relate that in the later years of his life John labored in and around Ephesus. From this city he was banished to the island of Patmos, where he was given to see the glorious visions described in the book of Revelation. John is also generally accredited with writing Revelation and the Epistles, I, II, and III John.

   c. Date of Writing. Most students of the New Testament hold that all the works of John were written late in the first century. Irenaeus has related that he lived until 97 or 98.* The Gospel, therefore, was probably written between 90 and 95. Revelation was probably written earlier. First John was surely written later, and there is no way of telling when the short Epistles, II and III John, were written.

   *Charles B. Williams, *New Testament History and Literature*, p. 80.

d. Style of Writing. The Gospel of John was written in the simplest Greek of the New Testament. In fact, all of John's writings, except Revelation, were written in comparatively easy Greek. It is possible that John learned to use Greek after he went to Ephesus, and that Revelation was written before he was as familiar with that language as he was in later years.

e. Distinctive Message. As has already been stated (page 22) the fourth Gospel is very different from the other three—different as to the events narrated, different in the viewpoint of the work and teachings of our Lord, and different in the manner of presentation. For the most part, the events related in the Gospel of John are not mentioned in the other three. Only three events which occurred before the last week of our Lord's life are related in both John and any one of the Synoptics: (1) the arrival in Galilee at the beginning of the ministry in that district, (2) the feeding of the five thousand, and (3) the walking on the water. The events related in John occurred, for the most part, in or near Jerusalem; most of those related in the Synoptics, except those of the last week, occurred in Galilee. Even the events of the Judaean and Perean ministry, related in Luke, are omitted from John. John mentions six feasts, the others mention only the last Passover.* In John are found many discussions, or arguments, between Jesus and His opponents, in which Jesus set forth some of His sublimest teachings. The picture of Jesus in John is that of the eternal Son of God, who was made flesh, but who is ever One with the Father. There is much about the relation of the Son to the Father, and about eternal life as a present possession of those who believe on the Son. These differences have led Bible students to regard the Gospel of John to be in a class to itself and to designate the other three as the "Synoptic Gospels"—that is, the ones that see the life of Jesus alike.

f. Purpose.

(1) To Emphasize the Deity of Jesus. The primary purpose of John in writing the Gospel is stated in chapter 20:31; "These are written that ye might believe that Jesus is the Christ, the Son of God; and that believing, ye might have life in His name." Many think that this was in answer to the teachings of the Gnostics, a heretical group of John's time who posed as Christians, but who included in their teachings some elements of Greek philosophy, some of the teachings of the Jewish philosopher, Philo, and elements of those pagan religions known as the "mystery cults," as well as some Teachings based on the Old Testament and some teachings about Jesus. The Gnostics held generally that the God of the universe was so high and holy that it was impossible for Him to create a material world or to have any dealings with persons possessed of material bodies, that there were innumerable intermediary beings or "aeons" (possibly angels), one of whom created the world; and another, called "the Logos" or Word of God, was the only channel

*Besides the Passover during the boyhood of Jesus (Luke 2:41-51).

30

through whom God could reveal Himself to the world. Some of them said Jesus was the "Logos" and therefore of an order of life somewhere between God and man. Any thinking student of the New Testament can see that such teaching would do great harm to true Christianity. John answered these and other wild claims of that sect by affirming: that the Word (Logos) who reveals God is as eternal as God, that He has fellowship with God, that indeed He is of the same essence as God. John affirmed also that He was "made flesh" (that is, took the nature of mankind, including a material body) and lived on the earth as Jesus, the only begotten Son of God; that life was in Him and light which overcomes darkness (just as He overcame death in His resurrection) and that salvation is to be had in consequence of faith in Him, rather than by acquiring a system of hidden knowledge. In setting out the purpose of his work, John declared: These things are written that people might have faith in Him as the anointed Saviour and the true Son of God, and that in consequence of this faith they "might have life through His name."

(2) To Tell Important Events Not in Other Records. I believe that John certainly had in mind a historical purpose also. It is possible, and I think probable, that he purposed to preserve an account of many incidents that were not mentioned in the other Gospels. Since the aged apostle wrote thirty years after the writing of the Synoptics, he was certainly acquainted with those works. In them no mention was made of the first miracle, of the discourse with Nicodemus, of the conversation with the Samaritan woman, of the repeated trips to Jerusalem and the controversies with the religious leaders in that city, of imparting sight to the man born blind, of the parable (or allegory) of the Good Shepherd, or of the raising of Lazarus, besides many other deeds and words of Jesus. Probably the old apostle, the last of his generation, had spoken of these things in his preaching or in conversation with younger Christians at Ephesus, and those Christians prevailed on him to put them in writing. If so, how glad we are that he chose to do so, and that the Holy Spirit inspired him as he wrote!

SEVEN PERIODS IN THE LIFE OF OUR LORD

I. BIRTH AND GROWTH TO MANHOOD
From the events' which heralded his birth until the preaching of John the Baptist

II. BEGINNINGS OF PUBLIC MINISTRY
From the preaching of John the Baptist until the arrival at Nazareth after the early Judaean ministry

III. MINISTRY TO THE MULTITUDES IN GALILEE
From the arrival in Nazareth until the sending forth of the twelve

IV. SPECIAL MINISTRY TO THE TWELVE DISCIPLES
From the sending forth of the twelve until the Feast of Tabernacles of His last year

V. CLOSING MINISTRY IN JUDAEA AND PERAEA
From the Feast of Tabernacles until the arrival in Bethany for His last Passover

VI. MINISTRY OF THE LAST WEEK OF HIS LIFE AND HIS SACRIFICIAL DEATH
Frequently called Passion Week

VII. MINISTRY OF THE RESURRECTION AND THE FORTY DAYS

Gospel Introductions
(## 1--3)

1. Prologue or Introduction to Gospel of John

#1

JOHN 1:1-18

1 In the beginning was the Word, and the Word was with God, and the Word was God. 2 The same was in the beginning with God. 3 All things were made through him; and without him [1]was not anything made that hath been made. 4 In him was life; and the life was the light of men. 5 And the light shineth in the darkness; and the darkness [2]apprehended it not. 6 There came a man, sent from God, whose name was John. 7 The same came for witness, that he might bear witness of the light, that all might believe through him. 8 He was not the light, but *came* that he might bear witness of the light. 9 [3]There was the true light, *even the light* which lighteth [4]every man, coming into the world. 10 He was in the world, and the world was made through him, and the world knew him not. 11 He came unto [5]his own, and they that were his own received him not. 12 But as many as received him, to them gave he the right to become children of God, *even* to them that believe on his name: 13 who were [6]born, not of [7]blood, nor of the will of the flesh, nor of the will of man, but of God. 14 And the Word became flesh, and [8]dwelt among us (and we beheld his glory, glory as of [9]the only begotten from the Father), full of grace and truth. 15 John beareth witness of him, and crieth, saying, [10]This was he of whom I said, He that cometh after me is become before me: for he was [11]before me. 16 For of his fulness we all received, and [12]grace for grace. 17 For the law was given through Moses; grace and truth came through Jesus Christ. 18 No man hath seen God at any time; [13]the only begotten Son, who is in the bosom of the Father, he hath declared *him.*

[1] Or, *was not anything made. That which hath been made was life in him; and the life. &c*
[2] Or, *overcame* See ch. 12. 35 (Gr.). [3] Or, *the true light, which lighteth every man, was coming*
[4] Or, *every man as he cometh*   [5] Gr. *his own things.*   [6] Or, *begotten*
[7] Gr. *bloods.*   [8] Gr. *tabernacled.*   [9] Or, *an only begotten from a father* Comp. Heb. 11. 17.
[10] Some ancient authorities read *(this was he that said).*   [11] Gr. *first in regard of me.*
[12] Or, *grace upon grace.*   [13] Many very ancient authorities read *God only begotten.*

Note 1. In this passage John called our Lord "the Word" (verses 1, 14). The same author spoke of Him as the "Word of life" in I John 1:1 and as the "Word of God" in Rev. 1:2; 19:13. For a probable significance of this term see page 30. This prologue expresses John's firm conviction concerning the eternal pre-existence of Jesus and his high appreciation of that truth.

2. Preface and Dedication of the Gospel of Luke

#2

LUKE 1:1-4

1 Forasmuch as many have taken 'in hand to draw up a narrative concerning those matters which have been [1]fulfilled among us, 2 even as they delivered them unto us, who from the beginning were eyewitnesses and ministers of the word, 3 it seemed good to me also, having traced the course of all things accurately from the first, to write unto thee in order, most excellent Theophilus; 4 that thou mightest know the certainty concerning the [2]things [3]wherein thou wast instructed.

[1] Or, *fully established*   [2] Gr. *words.*   [3] Or, *which thou wast taught by word of mouth*

Note 2. Four assertions about Luke and the Gospel he wrote which are of historical interest are observed in the foregoing verses: (1) Other accounts of the work and teachings of Jesus had been circulated before Luke produced this Gospel. Nothing is stated about the nature of those accounts, but two of them may have been the Gospel of Mark and that of Matthew—at least in its first ("Hebrew") edition, if not in its final writing in Greek. (2) Luke gathered his material from eye-witnesses of the events that he recorded and from such other sources as he considered trustworthy. (3) He combined the material into an orderly arrangement. This probably meant that he also carefully sifted the evidence in the material (the Lord inspiring him) so that his reader could rely upon ("know the certainty concerning") the matters he was recording. (4) The work was addressed to one whom Luke designated as "Theophilus," or a Lover of God. See page 28 in the Introduction for a possible identity of Theophilus.

3. Genealogies of Jesus
#3

<table>
<tr><td>MATT. 1:1-17</td><td>LUKE 3:23b-38</td></tr>
</table>

MATT. 1:1-17

1 ¹The book of the ²generation of Jesus Christ, the son of David, the son of Abraham.
2 Abraham begat Isaac; and Isaac begat Jacob; and Jacob begat Judah and his brethren; 3 and Judah begat Perez and Zerah of Tamar; and Perez begat Hezron; and Hezron begat ³Ram; 4 and ³Ram begat Amminadab; and Amminadab begat Nahshon; and Nahshon begat Salmon; 5 and Salmon begat Boaz of Rahab; and Boaz begat Obed of Ruth; and Obed begat Jesse; 6 and Jesse begat David the king.
And David begat Solomon of her *that had been the wife* of Uriah; 7 and Solomon begat Rehoboam; and Rehoboam begat Abijah; and Abijah begat ⁴Asa; 8 and ⁴Asa begat Jehoshaphat; and Jehoshaphat begat Joram; and Joram begat Uzziah; 9 and Uzziah begat Jotham; and Jotham begat Ahaz; and Ahaz begat Hezekiah; 10 and Hezekiah begat Manasseh; and Manasseh begat ⁵Amon; and ⁵Amon begat Josiah; 11 and Josiah begat Jechoniah and his brethren, at the time of the ⁶carrying away to Babylon.
12 And after the ⁶carrying away to Babylon, Jechoniah begat ⁷Shealtiel; and ⁷Shealtiel begat Zerubbabel; 13 and Zerubbabel begat Abiud; and Abiud begat Eliakim; and Eliakim begat Azor, 14 and Azor begat Sadoc; and Sadoc

LUKE 3:23b-38

23b being the son (as was supposed) of Joseph, the *son* of Heli, 24 the *son* of Matthat, the *son* of Levi, the *son* of Melchi, the *son* of Jannai, the *son* of Joseph, 25 the *son* of Mattathias, the *son* of Amos, the *son* of Nahum, the *son* of Esli, the *son* of Naggai, 26 the *son* of Maath, the *son* of Mattathias, the *son* of Semein, the *son* of Josech, the *son* of Joda, 27 the *son* of Joanan, the *son* of Rhesa, the *son* of Zerubbabel, the *son* of ¹Shealtiel, the *son* of Neri, 28 the *son* of Melchi, the *son* of Addi, the *son* of Cosam, the *son* of Elmadam, the *son* of Er, 29 the *son* of Jesus, the *son* of Eliezer, the *son* of Jorim, the *son* of Matthat, the *son* of Levi, 30 the *son* of Symeon, the *son* of Judas, the *son* of Joseph, the *son* of Jonam, the *son* of Eliakim, 31 the *son* of Melea, the *son* of Menna, the *son* of Mattatha, the *son* of Nathan, the *son* of David, 32 the *son* of Jesse, the *son* of Obed, the *son* of Boaz, the *son* of ²Salmon, the *son* of Nahshon, 33 the *son* of Amminadab, ³the *son* of ⁴Arni, the *son* of Hezron, the *son* of Perez, the *son* of Judah, 34 the *son* of Jacob, the *son* of Isaac, the *son* of Abraham, the *son* of Terah, the *son* of Nahor, 35 the *son* of Serug, the *son* of Reu, the *son* of Peleg, the *son* of Eber, the *son* of Shelah, 36 the *son* of Cainan, the *son* of Arphaxad,

---

¹ Or, *The genealogy of Jesus Christ*
² Or, *birth*: as in ver. 18.
³ Gr. *Aram.*   ⁴ Gr. *Asaph.*   ⁵ Gr. *Amos.*
⁶ Or, *removal to Babylon*   ⁷ Gr. *Salathiel.*

¹ Gr. *Salathiel.*
² Some ancient authorities write *Sala.*
³ Many ancient authorities insert *the son of Admin*: and one writes *Admin* for *Amminadab.*
⁴ Some ancient authorities write *Aram.*

Matt. 1

begat Achim; and Achim begat Eliud;
15 and Eliud begat Eleazar; and Eleazar
begat Matthan; and Matthan begat
Jacob; 16 and Jacob begat Joseph the
husband of Mary, of whom was born
Jesus, who is called Christ.
17 So all the generations from
Abraham unto David are fourteen
generations; and from David unto the
⁶carrying away to Babylon fourteen
generations; and from the ⁶carrying away
to Babylon unto the Christ fourteen
generations.

⁶ Or, *removal to Babylon*

Luke 3

the *son* of Shem, the *son* of Noah, the
son of Lamech, 37 the *son* of Methuselah,
the *son* of Enoch, the *son* of Jared, the
son of Mahalaleel, the *son* of Cainan,
38 the *son* of Enos, the *son* of Seth, the
son of Adam, the *son* of God.

Note 3. There are differences in the two genealogical tables which some students of the New Testament regard as discrepancies. Matthew's list of our Lord's ancestors contains twenty-seven names coming between David and Jesus, while Luke's list for the same period has forty-one. Furthermore, the names in the two accounts, except Shealtiel and Zerubbabel, are, different (verses 13 in Matt. and 27 in Luke). The best explanation of these differences seems to lie in the inference that Matthew gave the genealogy of Joseph, who was regarded by the neighbors in Nazareth to be the father of Jesus (Luke 4: 22 et al.) and sustained to Him the legal relation of father, and that Luke gave the genealogy of Mary. It is admitted by all that Matthew wrote the account of the birth of Jesus from Joseph's viewpoint while Luke wrote it from Mary's viewpoint. If this inference is true, Heli (Luke 3: 23) was in reality the father of Mary; but for some cause Joseph, his son-in-law was named as his son or heir. This was probably done regularly when a man's children were all daughters, in which case, according to the Mosaic law, sons-in-law, inherited as sons (cf. Num. 27: 1--11; 36: 1--13). Of course, we do not know that such was the condition in the home of Mary, but it might have been. Observe that in Luke's account, the words "the son," after the first occurence in verse 23, are in italics, indicating that the translators regarded it necessary to supply them for the understanding of the original.

A PREVIEW OUTLINE OF PERIOD ONE, ##4-16

I. Events heralding the birth of Jesus (ushering in the Messianic era), ##4—8
    1. The first annunciation—that to Zacharias promising a son who would be forerunner to the Messiah, #4
    2. The second annunciation—that to the virgin Mary concerning the coming birth of Jesus, #5
    3. The visit of Mary to Elizabeth, #6
    4. Birth of John the Baptist, the forerunner of Jesus, #7
    5. The third annunciation—that to Joseph, reassuring him of the purity and fidelity of Mary and affirming the coming virgin birth of Jesus, #8

II. The birth of Jesus at Bethlehem, #9

III. Reactions of the people at the birth of Jesus, ##10—13
    1. Three groups made happy, ##10—12
        (1) The Bethlehem shepherds, #10
        (2) Simeon and Anna, who saw Him in the temple when He was forty days old, #11
        (3) The Magi ("wise men") from the East, #12
    2. One person (Herod the King) made jealous, flight of the family into Egypt, #13

IV. Years of growth, ##14—16
    1. Settlement at Nazareth, growth of Jesus as a boy, #14
    2. Visit to Jerusalem to attend the Passover when Jesus was twelve years old, #15
    3. Summary of eighteen years of the growth of Jesus as a youth, contemporary growth of John the Baptist, #16

Birth and Growth to Manhood
(## 4 - 16)

I. Events heralding the birth of Jesus (ushering in the Messianic era), ## 4— 8

    1. The first annunciation—that to Zacharias, promising a son who would be forerunner to the Messiah.

#4

LUKE 1:5-25

5 There was in the days of Herod, king of Judaea, a certain priest named Zacharias, of the course of Abijah: and he had a wife of the daughters of Aaron, and her name was Elisabeth. 6 And they were both righteous before God, walking in all the commandments and ordinances of the Lord blameless. 7 And they had no child, because that Elisabeth was barren, and they both were *now* [1]well stricken in years.

8 Now it came to pass, while he executed the priest's office before God in the order of his course, 9 according to the custom of the priest's office, his lot was to enter into the [2]temple of the Lord and burn incense. 10 And the whole multitude of the people were praying without at the hour of incense. 11 And there appeared unto him an angel of the Lord standing on the right side of the altar of incense. 12 And Zacharias was troubled when he saw *him,* and fear fell upon him. 13 But the angel said unto him, Fear not, Zacharias: because thy supplication is heard, and thy wife Elisabeth shall bear thee a son, and thou shalt call his name John. 14 And thou shalt have joy and gladness; and many shall rejoice at his birth. 15 For he shall be great in the sight of the Lord, and he shall drink no wine nor [3]strong drink; and he shall be filled with the Holy Spirit, even from his mother's womb. 16 And many of the children of Israel shall he turn unto the Lord their God. 17 And he shall [4]go before his face in the spirit and power of Elijah, to turn the hearts of the fathers to the children, and the disobedient *to walk* in the wisdom of the just; to make ready for the Lord a people prepared *for him.* 18 And Zacharias said unto the angel, Whereby shall I know this? for I am an old man, and my wife [5]well stricken in years. 19 And the angel answering said unto him, I am Gabriel, that stand in the presence of God; and I was sent to speak unto thee, and to bring thee these good tidings. 20 And behold, thou shalt be silent and not able to speak, until the day that these things shall come to pass, because thou believedst not my words, which shall be fulfilled in their season. 21 And the people were waiting for Zacharias, and they marvelled [6]while he tarried in the [2]temple. 22 And when he came out, he could not speak unto them: and they perceived that he had seen a vision in the [2]temple: and he continued making signs unto them, and remained dumb. 23 And it came to pass, when the days of his ministration were fulfilled, he departed unto his house.

24 And after these days Elisabeth his wife conceived; and she hid herself five months, saying, 25 Thus hath the Lord done unto me in the days wherein he looked upon *me,* to take away my reproach among men.

[1] Gr. *advanced in their days.*   [2] Or, *sanctuary.*   [3] Gr. *sikera.*
[4] Some ancient authorities read *come nigh before his face.*
[5] Gr. *advanced in her days.*   [6] Or, *at his tarrying.*

Note 4. This was the first authentic account of a divine appearance, or voice of prophecy, after the days of Malachi—after an interval of more than 400 years. The stories of divine or angelic appearances contained in the Apocraypha and apocalyptic writings of the Interbiblical Era are not regarded by most Bible students to be authentic. The angel Gabriel is mentioned by name two times in the Old Testament (Dan. 8: 16; 9: 21) and only two times in the New Testament (Luke 1: 19, 26). The "angel of the Lord" who appeared to Joseph was not designated by name. The birth of John the Baptist was miraculous, but not in the same way as the birth of Jesus. It was similar to the birth of Isaac (cf. Gen 18: 10—14).

2. The second annunciation—that to the virgin Mary, concerning the coming of Jesus.

#5

LUKE 1:26-38

26 Now in the sixth month the angel Gabriel was sent from God unto a city of Galilee, named Nazareth, 27 to a virgin betrothed to a man whose name was Joseph, of the house of David; and the virgin's name was Mary. 28 And he came in unto her, and said, Hail, thou that art [1]highly favored, the Lord *is* with thee[2]. 29 But she was greatly troubled at the saying, and cast in her mind what manner of salutation this might be. 30 And the angel said unto her, Fear not, Mary: for thou hast found [3]favor with God. 31 And behold, thou shalt conceive in thy womb, and bring forth a son, and shalt call his name JESUS. 32 He shall be great, and shall be called the Son of the Most High: and the Lord God shall give unto him the throne of his father David: 33 and he shall reign over the house of Jacob [4]for ever; and of his kingdom there shall be no end. 34 And Mary said unto the angel, How shall this be, seeing I know not a man? 35 And the angel answered and said unto her, The Holy Spirit shall come upon thee, and the power of the Most High shall overshadow thee: wherefore also [5]the holy thing which is begotten [6]shall be called the Son of God. 36 And behold, Elisabeth thy kinswoman, she also hath conceived a son in her old age; and this is the sixth month with her that [7]was called barren. 37 For no word from God shall be void of power. 38 And Mary said, Behold, the [8]handmaid of the Lord; be it unto me according to thy word. And the angel departed from her.

[1] Or, *endued with grace*
[2] Many ancient authorities add *blessed* art *thou among women.* See ver. 42.
[3] Or, *grace*   [4] Gr. *unto the ages.*
[5] Or, *that which is to be born shall be called holy, the Son of God.*
[6] Some ancient authorities insert *of thee.*   [7] Or, *is*   [8] Gr. *bondmaid.*

Note 5. Joseph, the husband of Mary, was not the father of Jesus, nor was any other man. This is made clear by Mary's emphatic denial of any procreative relations with any man ("I know not a man," vs. 34) and by the statement of the angel Gabriel to her that conception of the promised child would be brought about by the coming of the Holy Spirit upon her and the power of the Highest overshadowing her. It is clear also from the words of the angel to Joseph as given in Matt. 1 : 20, #8. This fact is spoken of as the virgin birth of our Lord. In answering the doubts in her mind (and the objections in multitudes of modern minds) the angel imparted news of the pregnancy of her older cousin, Elizabeth, and added the eternal truth that "with God nothing shall be impossible" (vs. 37; cf. Gen. 18: 14, also spoken by a visitant from heaven, and in similar circumstances). It is presumed that the conception of Jesus occurred immediately after the annunciation by Gabriel, from which it is usually said that John was six months older than Jesus.

3. The visit of Mary to Elizabeth
#6
Luke 1:39-56

39 And Mary arose in these days and went into the hill country with haste, into a city of Judah; 40 and entered into the house of Zacharias and saluted Elisabeth. 41 And it came to pass, when Elisabeth heard the salutation of Mary, the babe leaped in her womb; and Elisabeth was filled with the Holy Spirit; 42 and she lifted up her voice with a loud cry, and said, Blessed *art* thou among women, and blessed *is* the fruit of thy womb. 43 And whence is this to me, that the mother of my Lord should come unto me? 44 For behold, when the voice of thy salutation came into mine ears, the babe leaped in my womb for joy. 45 And blessed *is* she that [1]believed; for there shall be a fulfilment of the things which have been spoken to her from the Lord. 46 And Mary said,

My soul doth magnify the Lord,
47 And my spirit hath rejoiced in God my Saviour.
48 For he hath looked upon the low estate of his [2]handmaid:
For behold, from henceforth all generations shall call me blessed.
49 For he that is mighty hath done to me great things;
And holy is his name.
50 And his mercy is unto generations and generations
On them that fear him.
51 He hath showed strength with his arm;
He hath scattered the proud [3]in the imagination of their heart.
52 He hath put down princes from *their* thrones.
And hath exalted them of low degree.
53 The hungry he hath filled with good things;
And the rich he hath sent empty away.
54 He hath given help to Israel his servant,
That he might remember mercy
55 (As he spake unto our fathers)
Toward Abraham and his seed for ever.
56 And Mary abode with her about three months, and returned unto her house.

[1] Or, *believed that there shall be*   [2] Gr. *bondmaid*   [3] Or, *by*

Note 6. There must have been a warm friendship and a close tie of kinship between Mary and Elizabeth—unusually so for cousins differing so widely in age. Note that Elizabeth was inspired to call Mary "the Mother of my Lord." This probably meant the mother of God's Messiah, and was certainly not equivalent to the phrase "Mother of God" as it appears in the Romish Creeds. The song of Mary is called "The Magnificat," since it begins with the verb magnificat in the Latin Bible. In it she spoke of God as "Saviour;" and although we cannot know in what sense she used the word "Saviour," there was likely some connection between her statement and the name she was directed to give her Son (vs. 31, #5).

4. Birth of John the Baptist, the forerunner of Jesus
#7
Luke 1:57-79

57 Now Elisabeth's time was fulfilled that she should be delivered; and she brought forth a son. 58 And her neighbors and her kinsfolk heard that the Lord had magnified his mercy towards her; and they rejoiced with her. 59 And it came to pass on the eighth day, that they came to circumcise the child; and they would have called him Zacharias, after the name of his father. 60 And his mother answered and said, Not so; but he shall be called John. 61 And they said unto her, there is none of thy kindred that is called by this name. 62 And they made signs to his father, what he would have him called. 63 And he asked for a writing tablet, and wrote, saying, His name is John. And they marvelled all. 64 And his mouth was

Luke 1
opened immediately, and his tongue *loosed,* and he spake, blessing God. 65 And fear came on all that dwelt round about them: and all these sayings were noised abroad throughout all the hill country of Judaea. 66 And all that heard them laid them up in their heart, saying, What then shall this child be? For the hand of the Lord was with him.

67 And his father Zacharias was filled with the Holy Spirit, and prophesied, saying,

68   Blessed *be* the Lord, the God of Israel;
    For he hath visited and wrought redemption for his people,

69   And hath raised up a horn of salvation for us
    In the house of his servant David

70   (As he spake by the mouth of his holy prophets that have been from of old),

71   Salvation from our enemies, and from the hand of all that hate us;

72   To show mercy towards our fathers,
    And to remember his holy covenant;

73   The oath which he sware unto Abraham our father,

74   To grant unto us that we being delivered out of the hand of our enemies
    Should serve him without fear,

75   In holiness and righteousness before him all our days.

76   Yea and thou, child, shalt be called the prophet of the Most High:
    For thou shalt go before the face of the Lord to make ready his ways;

77   To give knowledge of salvation unto his people
    In the remission of their sins,

78   Because of the [1]tender mercy of our God,
    [2]Whereby the dayspring from on high [3]shall visit us,

79   To shine upon them that sit in darkness and the shadow of death;
    To guide our feet into the way of peace.

[1] Or, *heart of mercy*   [2] Or, *Wherein*   [3] Many ancient authorities read *hath visited us.*

Note 7. Zacharias' words of praise and prophecy (vss. 68-79) are known in literature as the "Benedictus," because in the Latin Bible they begin with that word.

5. The third annunciation—that to Joseph reassuring him of the purity and fidelity of Mary and affirming the coming virgin birth of Jesus

#8
MATT. 1:18-25
18 Now the [1]birth [2]of Jesus Christ was on this wise: When his mother Mary had been betrothed to Joseph, before they came together she was found with child of the Holy Spirit. 19 And Joseph her husband, being a righteous man, and not willing to make her a public example, was minded to put her away privily. 20 But when he thought on these things, behold, an angel of the Lord appeared unto him in a dream, saying, Joseph, thou son of David, fear not to take unto thee Mary thy wife: for that which is [3]conceived in her is of the Holy Spirit. 21 And she shall bring forth a son; and thou shalt call his name JESUS; for it is he that shall save his people from their sins. 22 Now all this is come to pass, that it might be fulfilled which was spoken by the Lord through the prophet, saying,

23   [4]Behold, the virgin shall be with child, and shall bring forth a son,
    And they shall call his name [5]Immanuel;

which is, being interpreted, God with us. 24 And Joseph arose from his sleep, and did as the angel of the Lord commanded him, and took unto him his wife; 25 and knew her not till she had brought forth a son: and he called his name JESUS.

[1] Or, *generation:* as in ver. 1.   [2] Some ancient authorities read *of the Christ*
[3] Gr. *begotten.*   [4] Is. vii. 14.   [5] Gr. *Emmanuel.*

Note 8. Since Matthew relates the birth of Jesus from the viewpoint of Joseph, he does not say anything about the appearance of the

angel to Mary. If she told Joseph about it, he certainly found her story hard, if not impossible, to believe; and very naturally he was troubled—suspicious and deeply hurt—when, after her return from the home of Elizabeth, he could perceive that she was going to become a mother. Among the Jews betrothal was a sacred relation entered into in the presence of witnesses, and could be dissolved only by divorce proceedings. But that proceeding might be a private transaction if the man so desired,* and that was what Joseph was contemplating. However, to calm his troubled spirit the angel appeared to him in good time assuring him that the child which Mary would bear was "of the Holy Spirit," and that she was innocent of any act of unfaithfulness.

The Bible accounts of the virgin birth of our Lord are told with such simplicity and naturalness as to bear the mark of genuineness on their face—just as the Bible account of all the other miracles. And it is significant that Matthew was led by the Holy Spirit to see in this event the true fulfillment of Isa. 7:14, God's promise of a virgin-born One, who in reality would be "Immanuel" (God with us). But this assertion of Scripture has been hotly contested by many twentieth century Bible students. Those scholars who deny the divine inspiration of the Bible and the deity of our Lord and other cardinal truths of New Testament Christianity do not hesitate to assert that the accounts of His birth are fabrications of early Christians, possibly of second century Christians. Others, in an effort to take a "middle of the road" course, maintain that the virgin birth is a relatively unimportant question, claiming that no great doctrine of Christianity is dependent on it. In view of these contentions I make the following observations:

(1) Denying the virgin birth of Jesus, or admitting that it may be doubtful, involves a denial of the divine origin of New Testament Scripture. The two Gospel records which contain accounts of the birth of Jesus state the virgin birth as a fact; and all the references in the New Testament to His human origin are in harmony with this assertion (cf. Matt. 1:16; Luke 3:23; Gal. 4:4). It is true that Matthew, Luke, and John tell how the multitudes regarded our Lord to be the son of Joseph (Matt. 13:55; Luke 4:22; John 1:45; 6:42), but the Gospel writers merely recorded that popular supposition without giving approval to it. Naturally the fact of the divine conception was not discussed with the neighbors; thus it was not known by the people of Nazareth (cf. Luke 3:23 and Note 15). If He were not virgin born, we must conclude not only that Matthew and Luke were not inspired, but that they included a deliberate fabrication in their accounts. If this be granted, the way is open for any student of the New Testament to determine by rules of his own making whether any passage in the New Testament is truth or myth.

(2) To deny the virgin birth of Jesus Christ is in the last analysis to deny His essential deity. I do not see how He could be the Son of Joseph, or of any other man, and also be the eternal second person of

*Edersheim, *Life and Times of Jesus*, Vol. I, pp. 149f, 154.

41

the Trinity. If he had been a son of Jospeh, His life would have begun with His conception and His personal independent life would have begun with His birth—just as the life of every other human being since Adam and Eve has begun. If this be true, He was not pre-existent; He was not in the beginning with God; He was not God (John 1: 1—2).

(3) Denying the virgin birth leaves one facing other miracles just as difficult to account for, if not more so. Only on the ground of His essentially divine personality (which, as I have shown, necessitated a virgin birth) can we account for His sinless living, or His perfect use of the scientific principles of pedagogy which is ascribed to Him almost universally by writers on psychology, as well as the many spectacular miracles ascribed to Him in the Gospels. Certainly the account of His virgin birth is no more difficult for even a rationalist to believe than the account of His victorious resurrection from the dead.

(4) The importance of the virgin birth as a doctrine of Christianity may be judged from the effect that the acceptance or rejection of it has on one's attitude toward other doctrines which are fundamental to the Christian faith. In rejecting the virgin birth, one must not only reject the divine origin of the New Testament (or of the whole Bible) and the essential deity of Christ; but with these gone, the efficacy of His death as a sacrifice for sin must be rejected; and there would be no ground or reason for His victorious resurrection. These two events, the sacrificial death of Jesus and His resurrection, are at the heart of the Christian system; on them are based the Christian's hope for the future and his power for victory in the present.

II. The birth of Jesus at Bethlehem
#9
LUKE 2:1-7
1 Now it came to pass in those days, there went out a decree from Caesar Augustus, that all [1]the world should be enrolled. 2 This was the first enrolment made when Quirinius was governor of Syria. 3 And all went to enrol themselves, every one to his own city. 4 And Joseph also went up from Galilee, out of the city of Nazareth, into Judaea to the city of David, which is called Bethlehem, because he was of the house and family of David; 5 to enrol himself with Mary, who was betrothed to him, being great with child. 6 And it came to pass, while they were there, the days were fulfilled that she should be delivered. 7 And she brought forth her first-born son; and she wrapped him in swaddling clothes, and laid him in a manger, because there was no room for them in the inn.
[1] Gr. the inhabited earth.

Note 9. This journey was not "to pay their taxes," as some gather from the King James Version of this passage, but "to be enrolled" or to be counted in a census (Greek, apographesthai). However, the census was taken for the purpose of taxation.

When was the Lord Jesus born? It is a matter of common knowledge that our present system of dates was designed to begin with the birth of Christ. Then presumably Christ was born in the year 1. But it must be remembered that the present system was not begun as soon

42

as He was born, or during the time of His earthly life, or even during the lifetime of anyone who lived while He was on earth. Dionysius Exiguus, a monk of the sixth century, was the first to suggest that the Christian world date all events from the birth of Christ. About A.D. 525 Dionysius set about to determine the year of our Lord's birth, calculating it to have been in the year 753 of Roman history. But it has been proved that he made a mistake of at least four years, possibly five. Among the reasons for this conclusion, we know from the history of the times that Herod the Great died in the year 4 B.C., or 749 of the Roman era. But Herod was king when Jesus was born. That means that Jesus must have been born at least four years before the year 1 of our present era. Just when He was born has not been proved with certainty. After the mistake of Dionysius was discovered, all the records of the world were not changed; instead, we just say that Christ was born in 5 or 4 B.C., that He was baptized about A.D. 26, and that He was crucified and rose from the dead in A.D. 30.

It is well to remember also that neither Matthew nor Luke mentions the month or the season of the year in which He was born, and all conclusions as to the month and day must be based on an inference. The best that we can say is what the Holy Spirit led Paul to write to the Galatians: "But when the fullness of time was come God sent forth His own Son"—that is, in a time when He saw fit (Gal. 4: 4). It is a consolation that there are some things which we do not have to know.

III. Reactions of the people at the Birth of Jesus, ##10 - 13
    1. Three groups made happy, ##10 - 12
        (1) The Bethlehem Shepherds

#10
LUKE 2:8-20

8 And there were shepherds in the same country abiding in the field, and keeping [1]watch by night over their flock. 9 And an angel of the Lord stood by them, and the glory of the Lord shone round about them: and they were sore afraid. 10 And the angel said unto them, Be not afraid; for behold, I bring you good tidings of great joy which shall be to all the people: 11 for there is born to you this day in the city of David a Saviour, who is [2]Christ the Lord. 12 And this is the sign unto you: Ye shall find a babe wrapped in swaddling clothes, and lying in a manger. 13 And suddenly there was with the angel a multitude of the heavenly host praising God, and saying,
14 Glory to God in the highest,
And on earth [3]peace among [4]men in whom he is well pleased.
15 And it came to pass, when the angels went away from them into heaven, the shepherds said one to another, Let us now go even unto Bethlehem, and see this [5]thing that is come to pass, which the Lord hath made known unto us. 16 And they came with haste, and found both Mary and Joseph, and the babe lying in the manger. 17 And when they saw it, they made known concerning the saying which was spoken to them about this child. 18 And all that heard it wondered at the things which were spoken unto them by the shepherds. 19 But Mary kept all these [6]sayings, pondering them in her heart. 20 And the shepherds returned, glorifying and praising God for all the things that they had heard and seen, even as it was spoken unto them.

[1] Or, night-watches   [2] Or, Anointed Lord
[3] Many ancient authorities read peace, good pleasure among men.
[4] Gr. men of good pleasure.   [5] Or, saying   [6] Or, things

Note 10. The song of the angels (verse 14) is called "Gloria in Excelsis."

(2) Simeon and Anna, who saw Him in the Temple
when He was forty days old
#11
LUKE 2:21-38

21 And when eight days were fulfilled for circumcising him, his name was called JESUS, which was so called by the angel before he was conceived in the womb.

22 And when the days of their purification [1]according to the law of Moses were fulfilled, they brought him up to Jerusalem, to present him to the Lord 23 (as it is written in the law of the Lord, [2]Every male that openeth the womb shall be called holy to the Lord), 24 and to offer a sacrifice according to that which is said in the law of the Lord, [3]A pair of turtledoves, or two young pigeons. 25 And behold, there was a man in Jerusalem, whose name was Simeon; and this man was righteous and devout, looking for the consolation of Israel: and the Holy Spirit was upon him. 26 And it had been revealed unto him by the Holy Spirit, that he should not see death, before he had seen the Lord's Christ. 27 And he came in the Spirit into the temple: and when the parents brought in the child Jesus, that they might do concerning him after the custom of the law, 28 then he received him into his arms, and blessed God, and said,

29 Now lettest thou thy [4]servant depart, [5]Lord,
   According to thy word, in peace;
30 For mine eyes have seen thy salvation,
31 Which thou hast prepared before the face of all peoples;
32 A light for [6]revelation to the Gentiles,
   And the glory of thy people Israel.

33 And his father and his mother were marvelling at the things which were spoken concerning him; 34 and Simeon blessed them, and said unto Mary his mother, Behold, this *child* is set for the falling and the rising of many in Israel; and for a sign which is spoken against; 35 yea and a sword shall pierce through thine own soul; that thoughts out of many hearts may be revealed. 36 And there was one Anna, a prophetess, the daughter of Phanuel, of the tribe of Asher (she was [7]of a great age, having lived with a husband seven years from her virginity, 37 and she had been a widow even unto fourscore and four years), who departed not from the temple, worshipping with fastings and supplications night and day. 38 And coming up at that very hour she gave thanks unto God, and spake of him to all them that were looking for the redemption of Jerusalem.

[1] Lev. xii. 2-6.   [2] Ex. xiii. 2, 12.   [3] Lev. xii. 8; v. 11.   [4] Gr. *bondservant.*
[5] Gr. *Master.*   [6] Or, *the unveiling of the Gentiles*   [7] Gr. *advanced in many days.*

Note 11. The Lord Jesus was born under the law (Gal. 4: 4), and was therefore subject to the requirements of the law. Joseph and Mary faithfully carried out the following regulations in regard to the birth of a boy: (1) Circumcision of every male child was required on the eighth day of his life, in connection with which he was named (v. 21, cf. Gen. 17: 12). (2) If the oldest child in a family was a son, he must be presented before a priest and redeemed in recognition of the deliverance of the Israelites from Egyptian slavery at the price of the first born of Egypt (Exod. 13: 2, 34: 20). The redemption price was five shekels, worth about $3.10 (cf. Num. 3: 46—47). (3) Forty days after the birth of a son the mother was required to bring offerings to the temple for her purification (Lev. 12: 2—8). In the case of Jesus the presentation of the son and the purification of the mother were doubtless made on the same occasion. It was on this occasion that they encountered Simeon and Anna. The words of Simeon brought amazement to Joseph and Mary—

probably all the more because they knew about the supernatural conditions of the child's birth. Simeon's prayer (vv. 29—32) is known in literature as the "Nunc Dimittis," because in the Latin Bible it begins with these two words.

(3) The Magi ("wise Men") from the East

#12

Matt. 2:1-12

1 Now when Jesus was born in Bethlehem of Judaea in the days of Herod the king, behold, [1]Wise-men from the east came to Jerusalem, saying, 2 [2]Where is he that is born King of the Jews? for we saw his star in the east, and are come to [3]worship him. 3 And when Herod the king heard it, he was troubled, and all Jerusalem with him. 4 And gathering together all the chief priests and scribes of the people, he inquired of them where the Christ should be born. 5 And they said unto him, In Bethlehem of Judaea: for thus it is written through the prophet,
6 [4]And thou Bethlehem, land of Judah,
Art in no wise least among the princes of Judah:
For out of thee shall come forth a governor,
Who shall be shepherd of my people Israel.
7 Then Herod privily called the [1]Wise-men, and learned of them exactly [5]what time the star appeared. 8 And he sent them to Bethlehem, and said, Go and search out exactly concerning the young child; and when ye have found *him*, bring me word, that I also may come and [3]worship him. 9 And they having heard the king, went their way; and lo, the star, which they saw in the east, went before them, till it came and stood over where the young child was. 10 And when they saw the star, they rejoiced with exceeding great joy. 11 And they came into the house and saw the young child with Mary his mother; and they fell down and worshipped him; and opening their treasures they offered unto him gifts, gold and frankincense and myrrh. 12 And being warned *of God* in a dream that they should not return to Herod, they departed into their own country another way.

[1] Gr. *Magi*. Compare Esther 1. 13; Dan. 2. 12; Acts 13. 6, 8.
[2] Or, *Where is the King of the Jews that is born?*
[3] The Greek word denotes an act of reverence whether paid to a creature (see ch. 4. 9; 18. 26), or to the Creator (see ch. 4. 10).   [4] Mic. v. 2.   [5] Or, *the time of the star that appeared*

Note 12. The word which Matthew used to designate these men, (magoi), means magicians, rather than men of unusual wisdom. Hence they are generally called "the Magi." They seem to have been well versed in the supposed science of astrology. About this time there came from Mesopotamia and other countries east of Palestine many who "practiced magical arts" (cf. Acts 8: 9ff; 19: 19). Most of them were deceivers, but the men of this account were beyond doubt sincere worshipers of God, and most certainly the Lord God had given them a special revelation concerning the birth of our Lord.

2. One person (Herod the King) made jealous, flight of the family into Egypt

#13

Matt. 2:13-18

13 Now when they were departed, behold, an angel of the Lord appeareth to Joseph in a dream, saying, Arise and take the young child and his mother, and flee into Egypt, and be thou there until I tell thee: for Herod will seek the young child to destroy him. 14 And he arose and took the young child and his mother by night, and departed into Egypt; 15 and was there until the death of Herod: that it might be fulfilled which was spoken by the Lord through the prophet, saying, [1]Out of Egypt did I call my son.

[1] Hos. xi. 1.

16 Then Herod, when he saw that he was mocked of the [2]Wise-men, was exceeding wroth, and sent forth, and slew all the male children that were in Bethlehem, and in all the borders thereof, from two years old and under, according to the time which he had exactly learned of the [2]Wise-men. 17 Then was fulfilled that which was spoken through Jeremiah the prophet, saying,
18 [3]A voice was heard in Ramah,
Weeping and great mourning,
Rachel weeping for her children;
And she would not be comforted, because they are not.

[2] Gr. *Magi*. Compare Esther 1. 13; Dan. 2. 12; Acts 13. 6, 8.   [3] Jer. xxxi. 15.

Note 13. This was Herod the Great, the first of the Herods, who was an Idumaean, or Edomite, by race (cf. p 4).   At the time of the birth of our Lord he was nearing the end of his bloody reign of thirty-seven years.

IV. Years of growth, ##14—17
1. Settlement at Nazareth, growth of Jesus as a boy
#14

MATT. 2:19-23

19 But when Herod was dead, behold, an angel of the Lord appeareth in a dream to Joseph in Egypt, saying, 20 Arise and take the young child and his mother, and go into the land of Israel: for they are dead that sought the young child's life. 21 And he arose and took the young child and his mother, and came into the land of Israel. 22 But when he heard that Archelaus was reigning over Judaea in the room of his father Herod, he was afraid to go thither; and being warned *of God* in a dream, he withdrew into the parts of Galilee, 23 and came and dwelt in a city called Nazareth; that it might be fulfilled which was spoken through the prophets, [1]that he should be called a Nazarene.
[1] Isa. xi. 1 in the Heb.?

LUKE 2:39-40

39 And when they had accomplished all things that were according to the law of the Lord, they returned into Galilee, to their own city Nazareth.
40 And the child grew, and waxed strong, [1]filled with wisdom: and the grace of God was upon him.
[1] Gr. *becoming full of wisdom*.

Note 14. Archelaus, who had been named ruler in Judaea a n d Samaria by his father, and Herod Antipas, named ruler in Galilee and Peraea, were sons of Herod the Great by Malthace, a Samaritan woman. Archelaus was as unprincipled as his father, but he possessed none of his father's shrewdness for ruling. After ten years of misrule he was deposed by the Romans, and was suceeded by a line of governors or procurators sent directly from Rome. Pontius Pilate was the fifth such governor.

2. Visit to Jerusalem to attend the Passover when
Jesus was twelve years old
#15
LUKE 2:41-51
41 And his parents went every year to Jerusalem at the feast of the passover.

46

42 And when he was twelve years old, they went up after the custom of the feast; 43 and when they had fulfilled the days, as they were returning, the boy Jesus tarried behind in Jerusalem; and his parents knew it not; 44 but supposing him to be in the company, they went a day's journey; and they sought for him among their kinsfolk and acquaintance: 45 and when they found him not, they returned to Jerusalem, seeking for him. 46 And it came to pass, after three days they found him in the temple, sitting in the midst of the [1]teachers, both hearing them, and asking them questions: 47 and all that heard him were amazed at his understanding and his answers. 48 And when they saw him, they were astonished; and his mother said unto him, [2]Son, why hast thou thus dealt with us? behold, thy father and I sought thee sorrowing. 49 And he said unto them, How is it that ye sought me? knew ye not that I must be [3]in my Father's house? 50 And they understood not the saying which he spake unto them. 51 And he went down with them, and came to Nazareth; and he was subject unto them: and his mother kept all *these* [4]sayings in her heart.

[1] Or, *doctors.* See ch. 5. 17; Acts 5. 34. [2] Gr. *Child.*
[3] Or, *about my Father's business.* Gr. *in the things of my Father.* [4] Or, *things*

Note 15. Apparently Mary had never told Jesus the secret of His divine conception and birth, but had taught Him to regard Joseph as father. However, the answer He gave her in verse 49 reveals that even this early in His life He knew that God, not Joseph, was His Father.

3. Contemporary Growth to Manhood

Of John the Baptist

Of Jesus

#16

Luke 1:80

80 And the child grew, and waxed strong in spirit, and was in the deserts till the day of his showing unto Israel.

Luke 2:52

52 And Jesus advanced in wisdom and [1]stature, and in [2]favor with God and men.

[1] Or, *age* [2] Or, *grace*

Note 16. Jesus grew in wisdom as well as in body. This means that during His earthly life, although our Lord was fully divine, He did not independently exercise the divine attribute of knowing everything. According to Mark 13:32, He confessed just three days before His death that He did not know when He will return to earth. The best explanation of this is found in Phil. 2:7 where it is said that He emptied Himself to take the form of a servant and to be made (or born) in the likeness of men (American Standard Version and all other recent translations). Besides growing in wisdom, He also became increasingly popular with His neighbors and increasingly gratifying to God.

What do we know about the home life of Jesus?

1. His home town was Nazareth of Galilee, a town which had an unsavory reputation (John 1:46).

2. He was naturally regarded as the son of Joseph, the secret of the divine nature of His birth not being known by the public (Matt. 13:55; Luke 4:22; John 1:45; 6:42).

3. The family occupation was that of a carpenter (Matt. 13:55).

4. There were other children in the home. In Matt. 13:55–56 and Mark 6:3, (#111) the neighbors at Nazareth named four brothers (James, Joses, Simon, and Judas) and mentioned His sisters without

naming them or saying how many. On other occasions the brothers are mentioned in connection with His mother (John 2: 12, #24; Matt. 12: 46, #89, and others). The natural understanding of these passages is that these brothers and sisters were children of Joseph and Mary—all, of course, younger than Jesus. That would make them half brothers and sisters, children of the same mother but not of the same father. Some, particularly Catholics, in an effort to establish the perpetual virginity of Mary, have contended that the other boys and the girls were children of Joseph by a former marriage. As such they would have been only in the relation of step brothers and sisters, and all older than Jesus. There is nothing in the Bible to support such a contention, and the most natural understanding of the word "firstborn" in Matt. 1: 25 and Luke 2: 7 is that Mary bore children to Joseph after the birth of Jesus.

5. The family were surely regular attendants on the Sabbath synagogue worship. Jesus not only went regularly to the synagogue, but He also came to be depended on to take an active part in public worship (Luke 4: 16). His custom as a young man most likely reflects the custom of the home.

6. Very likely Joseph passed away before Jesus was thirty years old, since he is not mentioned in any of the references to the family after the incident in the temple when Jesus was twelve years old (cf. John 2: 12; Matt. 12: 46—50; Mark 3: 31,—35; John 19: 25f; Acts 1: 14). If that is true, Jesus being the oldest boy, would naturally take control of the family carpentry business on the death of Joseph (cf. Mark 6: 3).

7. Were Mary and Salome, the mother of James and John, sisters? Compare the list of women at the cross (John 19: 25; #251; Matt. 27: 56, Mark 15: 40, #253). If this be true, it would explain why Jesus at the time of His death committed His mother to John rather than to one of her own sons, His half brothers, especially since His half brothers did not believe on Him until after the resurrection (cf. John 7: 5).

8. Did Mary and Elizabeth keep up their intimate acquaintance as the boys, Jesus and John the Baptist, grew up? Of course, we cannot know for certain, but such would have been natural. If they did, it would account for the fact that John knew enough about Jesus to say that Jesus ought to baptize him, but at the same time he did not know that Jesus was the One mightier than he whom he had proclaimed to be coming after him (cf. Matt. 3: 15 with John 1: 33).

Some Bible students have held that John the Baptist spent some time, (possibly years), as an inmate of the monastic institution at Qumran, near the Dead Sea, and that he obtained his ideas about repentance and baptism from that group. Others have suggested that probably he came under the influence of the Essenes. They appeal to Luke 1: 80 to substantiate their assumptions, but that verse merely asserts that he "was in the deserts until the day of his showing to Israel." Since, however, the items of John's food were things obtainable in the wilderness, and his clothing was of the most primitive nature, the natural conclusion is that he spent the time in seclusion. He was probably acquainted with the group at Qumran and with the Essenes; but (under the guidance of the Holy Spirit) he certainly kept himself apart from these groups. There are wide differences between the preaching of John and the teachings of those groups.* According to Luke 3:2, the source of John's message was "the word of the Lord" (cf. also John 1: 33).

*LaSor, *Amazing Dead Sea Scrolls,* pp. 203-206.

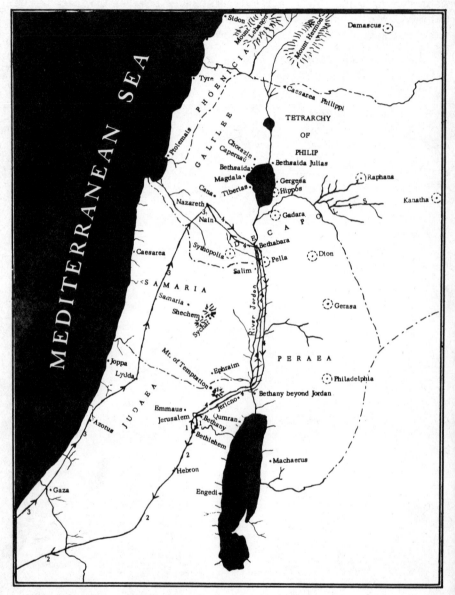

JOURNEYS OF JESUS IN THE FIRST PERIOD
1 - From Bethlehem to Jerusalem when He was forty days old and return to Bethlehem (#11). 2 - Flight into Egypt after the coming of the Wise Men (#13). 3 - Return to Palestine and settlement at Nazareth (#14). 4 - To Jerusalem for Passover when He was twelve years old and return to Nazareth (#15).
(• Traditional location. ⊙ A city of the Decapolis League)

I.   Preaching and ministry of John the Baptist, the forerunner, #17

II.   Baptism of Jesus, #18

III. A season of temptation of Jesus, #19

IV. John the Baptist's formal testimony to Jesus, ##20-21
     1. Before a committee from Jerusalem, #20
     2. Before the multitudes of his congregation (when he saw Jesus coming to him as He returned from the Mount of Temptation), #21

V.   Jesus attracting His first disciples (from among the disciples of John), #22

VI.   The first miracle—changing water to wine at Cana of Galilee, #23

VII. A brief sojourn at Capernaum, #24

VIII. The first Passover of His public ministry, ##25-26
     1. First cleansing of the Temple, #25
     2. The discourse with Nicodemus, #26

IX.   First Judaean ministry, repeated testimony of John the Baptist, #27

X.   Returning to Galilee through Samaria, ##28-31
     1. Leaving Judaea (imprisonment of John the Baptist), #28
     2. Ministry in Samaria, ##29-31
        (1) Winning the Samaritan woman at the well, #29
        (2) Winning the people of Sychar, #30
        (3) Departure for Galilee, #31

SECOND PERIOD

Beginnings of Public Ministry
(## 17 - 31)

Note 17. Jesus began His public ministry with His baptism at the age of thirty. Notice that Mark regarded that event as the beginning of the gospel. Until that time He had lived a normal life in Nazareth. If, as is generally supposed, Joseph passed away before that time, it would be expected that Jesus, as the oldest boy, would assume leadership in the home and the business. Thus, while in Matt. 13:55 His former Nazareth neighbors called Him the "carpenter's son," Mark quotes these neighbors as asking, "Is not this the carpenter, the son of Mary?" Meanwhile John was living in the desert, experiencing communion with God, and receiving in some way the revelation that would form the substance of his preaching. God caused him to know that the Kingdom was at hand, that the Mighty One who would be the King was coming after him, that repentance on the part of the people was necessary for a place in the Kingdom, and that the way to confess repentance was by being baptized.

I. Preaching and ministry of John the Baptist, the forerunner
#17

MATT. 3:1-12	MARK 1:1-8	LUKE 3:1-18
1 And in those days cometh John the Baptist, preaching in the wilderness of Judaea, saying, 2 Repent ye; for the kingdom of heaven is at hand.	1 The beginning of the ¹gospel of Jesus Christ, ²the Son of God. 2 Even as it is written ³in Isaiah the prophet, ⁴Behold, I send my messenger before thy face, Who shall prepare thy way;	1 Now in the fifteenth year of the reign of Tiberius Caesar, Pontius Pilate being governor of Judaea, and Herod being tetrarch of Galilee, and his brother Philip tetrarch of the region of Ituraea and Trachonitis, and Lysanias tetrarch of Abilene, 2 in the highpriesthood of Annas and Caiaphas, the word of God came unto John the son of Zacharias in the wilderness. 3 And he came into all the region round about the Jordan, preaching the baptism of repentance unto remission of sins; 4 as it is written in the book of the words of Isaiah the prophet,
3 For this is he that was spoken of through Isaiah the prophet, saying, ¹The voice of one crying in the wilderness, Make ye ready the way of the Lord, ¹ Isa. xl. 3.	3 ⁵The voice of one crying in the wilderness, Make ye ready the way of the Lord, ¹ Or, good tidings: and so elsewhere. ² Some ancient authorities omit the Son of God. ³ Some ancient authorities read in the prophets. ⁴ Mal. iii. 1. ⁵ Is. xl. 3.	¹The voice of one crying in the wilderness, Make ye ready the way of the Lord, ¹ Is. xl. 3 ff.

52

Matthew 3

Make his paths straight.
4 Now John himself had his raiment of camel's hair, and a leathern girdle about his loins; and his food was locusts and wild honey. 5 Then went out unto him Jerusalem, and all Judaea, and all the region round about the Jordan; 6 and they were baptized of him in- the river Jordan, confessing their sins. 7 But when he saw many of the Pharisees and Sadducees coming ²to his baptism, he said unto them, Ye offspring of vipers, who warned you to flee from the wrath to come? 8 Bring forth therefore fruit worthy of ³repentance: 9 and think not to say within yourselves, We have Abraham to our father: for I say unto you, that God is able of these stones to raise up children unto Abraham. 10 And even now the axe lieth at the root of the trees: every tree therefore that bringeth not forth good fruit is hewn down, and cast into the fire.

² Or, *for baptism*
³ Or, *your repentance*

Mark 1

Make his paths straight;
4 John came, who baptized in the wilderness and preached the baptism of repentance unto remission of sins. 5 And there went out unto him all the country of Judaea, and all they of Jerusalem; and they were baptized of him in the river Jordan, confessing their sins. 6 And John was clothed with camel's hair, and *had* a leathern girdle about his loins, and did eat locusts and wild honey. 7 And he preached, saying,

Luke 3

Make his paths straight.
5 Every valley shall be filled,
And every mountain and
hill shall be brought
low;
And the crooked shall
become straight,
And the rough ways
smooth;
6 And all flesh shall see
the salvation of God.
7 He said therefore to the multitudes that went out to be baptized of him, Ye offspring of vipers, who warned you to flee from the wrath to come? 8 Bring forth therefore fruits worthy of ²repentance, and begin not to say within yourselves, We have Abraham to our father: for I say unto you, that God is able of these stones to raise up children unto Abraham. 9 And even now the axe also lieth at the root of the trees: every tree therefore that bringeth not forth good fruit is hewn down, and cast into the fire. 10 And the multitudes asked him, saying, What then must we do? 11 And he answered and said unto them, He that hath two coats, let him impart to him that hath none; and he that hath food, let him do likewise. 12 And there came also ³publicans to be baptized, and they said unto him, Teacher, what must we do? 13 And he said unto them, Extort no more than that which is appointed you. 14 And ⁴soldiers also asked him, saying, And we, what must we do? And he said unto them, Extort from no man by violence, neither accuse *any one* wrongfully; and be content with your wages.
15 And as the people

² Or, *your repentance*
³ That is, *collectors or renters of Roman taxes.*
⁴ Gr. *soldiers on service.*

Matthew 3 | Mark 1 | Luke 3

were in expectation, and all men reasoned in their hearts concerning John, whether haply he were the Christ; 16 John answered, saying unto them all, I indeed baptize you with water; but there cometh he that is mightier than I, the latchet of whose shoes I am not [5]worthy to unloose: he shall baptize you [6]in the Holy Spirit and *in* fire: 17 whose fan is in his hand, thoroughly to cleanse his threshing-floor, and to gather the wheat into his garner; but the chaff he will burn up with unquenchable fire.

11 I indeed baptize you [4]in water unto repentance: but he that cometh after me is mightier than I, whose shoes I am not [5]worthy to bear: he shall baptize you [4]in the Holy Spirit and *in* fire: 12 whose fan is in his hand, and he will thoroughly cleanse his threshing-floor; and he will gather his wheat into the garner, but the chaff he will burn up with unquenchable fire.

There cometh after me he that is mightier than I, the latchet of whose shoes I am not [6]worthy to stoop down and unloose. 8 I baptized you [7]in water; but he shall baptize you [7]in the Holy Spirit.

[6] Gr. *sufficient.*
[7] Or, *with*

[4] Or, *with*
[5] Gr. *sufficient.*

18 With many other exhortations therefore preached he [7]good tidings unto the people.

[5] Gr. *sufficient.*
[6] Or, *with*   [7] Or, *the gospel*

Note 18. The Kingdom of God. In the section above is the first reference in the Gospels to the Kingdom of Heaven, or the Kingdom of God. This phrase was among the most frequently used in the teachings of Jesus, and the Kingdom it denoted was central in His mission on earth. The Jewish people of that day were awaiting the coming of the Messiah, who would be a God-sent King, the Anointed of God. Observe in Luke 3:15 above that "all the people were in expectation." For example, Simeon was "waiting for the consolation of Israel," (Luke 2:25) and Joseph of Arimathea "waited for the Kingdom of God" (Luke 23:51). When, therefore, John proclaimed that "the Kingdom of Heaven is at hand," it is no wonder that the people came in crowds to hear him. To understand the teachings of Jesus it is important to learn something of this phrase.

1. Prominence in the teachings of Jesus. The phrase, or some equivalent expression is used 107 times in the four Gospels, eighty-seven in quotations from Jesus. Deducting twenty-two duplications in parallel passages, we have record of sixty-five sayings of Jesus concerning the Kingdom. In addition to these, there were two or more other occasions when He spoke of the Kingdom without using the word "kingdom."

2. Terms used. The expression most frequently encountered is the phrase "Kingdom of God," used fifty-six times in the Gospels and sixteen times in the rest of the New Testament. The phrase "Kingdom of Heaven" is found thirty times in Matthew, and Jesus used the phrase "My Kingdom" three times and the phrase "Kingdom of My Father" one

time. Others in addressing Jesus said, "Thy Kingdom" three times; and the words "the Kingdom" without specifying modifiers are found six times. I assume that these expressions all denote the same group of people or the same condition of living.

Some interpreters have sought to find a difference between the Kingdom of God and the Kingdom of Heaven. "Kingdom of Heaven" occurs only in the Gospel of Matthew; but "Kingdom of God" is also found in that Gospel five times. To me, all efforts to point out a difference in their meaning are strained, and the difference claimed seems artificial. One very good reason for this conclusion is that in as many as eight parallel passages Matthew has "Kingdom of Heaven," and Mark or Luke or both of them have "Kingdom of God." (See ##32, 54, 81, 91, 96, 113, 186, 188). Unless the two phrases had the same meaning, it is hard to see why the Holy Spirit would inspire Matthew to write "Kingdom of Heaven" and inspire Mark and Luke, in telling the same incident, or quoting the same saying of Jesus, to write "Kingdom of God." Also it is noted that in Matt. 19:23, 24, both phrases are used manifestly to express the same meaning.

Possibly Matthew's use of the phrase "Kingdom of Heaven" is explained by the fact that he wrote primarily for the Jews, and in some Jewish circles it was not uncommon to use the term "Heaven" where we would use a word for "God." (cf. I Maccabees 2:21; 3:17; also the usage in the parable of the Prodigal Son, Luke 15:18,21).

3. What the Jews expected. It is easy to observe that the people were looking for a Messiah who would free them from their conquerors and oppressive rulers, and who would himself rule in justice and peace; and some expected him in turn, as the King of Israel, to be the ruler of other nations of the earth. It was natural that they should entertain such expectations, because many of the glorious prophecies on which they grounded their hopes of a Messiah apparently promised such a Kingdom (cf. Ps. 2:6, 8--9; all of Ps. 72; Isa. 9:4--7; all of Isa. 11; Mic. 4:1-5; 5:2; Zech. 14:9ff, et al.). An odd circumstance is that in the Gospels we have almost no statement from the enemies and critics of Jesus revealing their notion of the Kingdom; though Luke 14:15; 17:20 may be examples. Indeed the leaders of the Sanhedrin group seem to have been so cowed by the Romans that they feared for anyone to have much to say about the Messianic Kingdom or to aspire to inaugurate it (John 11:48; cf. Acts 5:36--37). They were glad to use against Jesus the wrath which the Romans exercised against those who entertained hopes of establishing a regime that would threaten Roman rule over the people cf. Luke 23:2ff in ##245, 247; cf. also Matt. 27:29, 42 in ##248, 251).
But it is probable that those passages revealing the hopes of the disciples and friends of Jesus in regard to the Kingdom reflect also the expectations of the people generally. (See John 6:15; Matt. 18:1; 20:21; Luke 23:42; Acts 1:6).

4. The Kingdom as Jesus taught it. All students of the New Test-

ament realize that Jesus never did intend to free the Israelitish people from Roman domination, or to set up at that time a visible rule over the people. His purpose of redemption certainly precluded such action during His life in the flesh.

(1) The Spiritual Kingdom. But John the Baptist in the section above, in proclaiming his God-given message, announced that the Kingdom "is at hand" (literally, has come near). Later Jesus proclaimed the same thing (Matt. 4:17), and still later He directed the disciples to preach the same thing (Matt. 10:7). He maintained before His critics that His casting out demons through the Spirit of God was proof that the Kingdom of God had come upon them (Matt. 12:28); and on a later occasion He said to the Pharisees, "The Kingdom of God is within you" (Luke 17:21). The Kingdom, therefore, was certainly inaugurated by the Lord Jesus during His earthly life. It began small like a mustard seed, but was destined to grow to tremendous proportions (Matt. 13:31—32). Some of those who stood with Him at Caesaraea Phillipi would see it come with power before they should taste of death (Mark 9:1). It is composed of the poor in spirit (Matt. 5:3), of those who come to Jesus, even little children if they come to Him (Matt. 19:14). To prepare for participation in the benefits of the Kingdom the people were admonished to repent of the evil in their lives (Matt. 3:2; 4:17 et al.). Before an individual can enter into the Kingdom, it is necessary for him to be born from above (John 3:5). Righteousness exceeding that of the scribes and Pharisees is required for entrance into the Kingdom (Matt. 5:20), but people are encouraged to seek the righteousness of God when they seek a place in the Kingdom of God (Matt. 6:33) with the promise that those who hunger and thirst after this righteousness will be filled (Matt. 5:6, cf. Phil. 3:9; II Cor. 5:21). I assume therefore, that the Kingdom of God is presently existing in reality, with God in the person of Jesus as King; and that those who have repented of their former manner of life and looked to Jesus in faith for the righteousness of God, submitting themselves to Him as their Lord and King, are the members or subjects of the Kingdom. This is the spiritual Kingdom of God, or the Kingdom in its spiritual manifestation.

(2) The visible Kingdom. But not all that Jesus said about the Kingdom can be interpreted as applying to the present spiritual Kingdom. On two occasions He said to His Jewish hearers that many will come from all directions to sit down with the patriarchs of old who have died, but who will have been restored to life, in the Kingdom of Heaven (Matt. 8:11), or the Kingdom of God (Luke 13:28). He said that the righteous shall shine as the sun in the Kingdom of their Father (Matt. 13:43). After the Passover which He observed just before His arrest and death, He said that He would not drink any more of the fruit of the vine until the Kingdom of God shall come (Luke 22:18). In these sayings He speaks of the Kingdom in the future in a different manifestation from that of the present spiritual Kingdom. He indicated that this manifestation

of the Kingdom will be inaugurated at the time of His bodily return to the earth (Luke 21: 31). He called the time for this Kingdom "the regeneration," when His faithful followers will be rewarded with high honor and responsibility in service (Matt. 19: 28). It is to be noted that Luke in relating the popular expectations of the visible Messianic Kingdom apparently indicated that he, an inspired Gospel writer, still expected such a Kingdom (Luke 19: 11). That will be the visible Kingdom of God, or the Kingdom in its visible manifestation. When it shall be realized, Jesus will be visibly present as the reigning Monarch.

5. Definition. What does the phrase, Kingdom of God, denote? Possibly the most satisfactory definition is: The rule of God exercised through Jesus Christ over those who willingly submit themselves to His authority and power. During this present age this rule is spiritually exercised in the heart of each individual Christian so that his prevailing manner of living is affected. Neither Jesus nor the Gospel writers say how it will be exercised during the visible Kingdom. But we are assured that those in the Kingdom in its present manifestation will be in it in its future manifestation. It will be noticed, therefore, that in the larger number of scriptures by far referring to the Kingdom of God no distinction is made between the spiritual and visible manifestations. Usually they state conditions or facts that are true of the Kingdom and its subjects in both eras. It is well in studying the words of Jesus about the Kingdom for the student to try to decide whether the passage being studied refers to the spiritual Kingdom or the visible Kingdom, or whether it states a condition or fact true of both manifestations.

Note 19. Baptism. In the foregoing section is the first mention of the practice of baptizing found in the Bible. It is not mentioned in the Old Testament, nor apparently in the literature of the Interbiblical Period. The Mosaic law often prescribed a sacred bath for the cleansing of those who were regarded as ceremonially unclean—as in Leviticus, chs. 15, 16, 17; Numbers, ch. 19. The so-called "proselyte baptism," which is known to have been practiced after sometime in the second century of the Christian Era, and which many scholars suppose to have been practiced even before the time of John the Baptist, was probably developed from the sacred bathing of the Levitical law. But it is not likely that John got his idea of baptizing people from these sacred baths for two reasons: (1) There was a difference in administration—the unclean person of the Old Testament times and the proselyte (that is, a Gentile convert to the religion of the Jews) immersed themselves, but John the Baptist was the active administrator of the ordinance to his converts. (2) There was a difference in meaning—to the Old Testament character who bathed himself and to the proselyte of a later era it signified a cleansing from defilement, but to the person whom John baptized it meant a confession of sins (Matt. 3:6) and a profession of repentance (Matt. 3:8).*

Certainly John was the first to practice baptism as an ordinance, and he maintained that he was commissioned directly from God in this practice (John 1:33). With this claim Jesus was in agreement when He taught by inference that the baptism of John was from Heaven (Matt. 21:21-27). For a short time Jesus took up the practice, having His disciples to administer the ordinance (John 3:21; 4:1-2), but apparently He discontinued it at the beginning of the Galilean ministry. Yet in His commission to the disciples who met Him on the appointed mountain in Galilee, the risen Jesus enjoined baptizing of those who should be made to be disciples, and it has been practiced by the churches through the centuries.

II. Baptism of Jesus
#18

MATT. 3:13-17	MARK 1:9-11	LUKE 3:21-23
13 Then cometh Jesus from Galilee to the Jordan unto John, to be baptized of him. 14 But John would have hindered him, saying, I have need to be baptized of thee, and comest thou to me? 15 But Jesus answering said unto him, Suffer ¹it now: for thus it becometh us to fulfil all righteousness. Then he suffereth him. 16 And Jesus, when he was baptized, went up straightway from the water: and lo, the heavens were opened ²unto him, and he saw the Spirit of God descending as a dove, and coming upon him; 17 and lo, a voice out of the heavens, saying, ³This is my beloved Son, in whom I am well pleased.	9 And it came to pass in those days, that Jesus came from Nazareth of Galilee, and was baptized of John ¹in the Jordan. 10 And straightway coming up out of the water, he saw the heavens rent asunder, and the Spirit as a dove descending upon him: 11 and a voice came out of the heavens, Thou are my beloved Son, in thee I am well pleased.	21 Now it came to pass, when all the people were baptized, that Jesus also having been baptized, and praying, the heaven was opened, 22 and the Holy Spirit descended in a bodily form, as a dove, upon him, and a voice came out of heaven, Thou art my beloved Son; in thee I am well pleased. 23 And Jesus himself, when he began to teach, was about thirty years of age.

¹ Or, me
² Some ancient authorities omit unto him.
³ Or, This is my Son; my beloved in whom I am well pleased. See ch. 12. 18.

¹ Gr. into.

Note 20. Why was Jesus Baptized? This question has been often raised and variously answered. I will first suggest three answers which I hold to be wrong, and then the one which I regard to be correct.

(1) Certainly it could not have been in confession of sins on His part. John demanded such confession and a profession of repentance by all others whom He baptized, but Jesus was not guilty of any sin (cf.

*For the same two reasons it is certain that he did not get the idea from the Essenes or the Qumran group.

John 8:46; II Cor. 5:21; Heb. 4:15), and certainly John recognized that fact (Matt. 3:14).

(2) Nor does it seem fitting to regard the baptism of Jesus as a confession on His part of the sins of mankind with whom He purposed to identify to Himself. To be sure, Jesus was going to assume in His death the guilt of the sins of the race—make it His own, as it were, so that He could justly pay the penalty for the sins of humankind; but there was no reason at this time for Him to confess for mankind its sins. Indeed during His life it became Him as the world's High Priest to show Himself to be "holy, guileless, undefiled, separate from sinners" (Heb. 7:26).

(3) Nor was being baptized in itself the fulfilling of righteousness. Jesus was, indeed, subject to the law (Gal. 4:4), but being baptized was not required in order to fulfil the demands of the law. Nor did He merely regard submission to the ordinance a good thing for anyone to do, so that He submitted as an example to the people of that day or of succeeding generations. Being baptized was not, and is not, a good thing for any one except for the person who by it proclaims the truth which the ordinance is designed to set forth.

(4) When he said, "Thus it becometh us to fulfil all righteousness," the word "thus" refers to those experiences of which His baptism was a picture; that is, to His burial (following His death) and His resurrection. In baptism, therefore He solemnly dedicated Himself to the mission of redeeming people by dying for them and then victoriously overcoming death in a resurrection. It was through these experiences that he was destined to fulfil righteousness. In response to this solemn self-dedication, both the other persons of the Godhead expressed their approval and good pleasure—the Father by the heavenly voice, and the Holy Spirit by visibly descending upon Him. Jesus knew, therefore, at the beginning of His ministry that a sacrificial death and a victorious resurrection awaited Him, and His words repeatedly, even in His early ministry, reflect this knowledge.

Did John know Jesus? How can we reconcile the words of John in Matt. 3:14 (I have need to be baptized of Thee, and comest Thou to me?) with his assertion in John 1:33 (and I knew Him not; but He that sent me to baptize in water, He said unto me, Upon whomsoever thou shalt see the Spirit descending, and abiding upon Him the Same is He that baptizeth in the Holy Spirit)? John had been given to proclaim that a "Greater One" would come after him, whom he certainly understood to be none other than the Messiah; and he had been given the sign of the descending Spirit by which to identify that One. Therefore he did not know Jesus to be that "Greater One" until Jesus was coming up out of the water after being baptized. But we remember that his mother and the mother of Jesus were cousins, and it is very probable that the families occasionally saw each other while the boys were growing up. John surely had opportunity to observe the character of Jesus as being above all suspicion of wrong. However, John, being human, was not free from the stain of sin in his own life, and in the presence of Jesus he was keenly conscious of his own shortcoming. Therefore, when Jesus presented Himself for baptism, which John regarded to involve confession of sin, the baptizer set in to hinder his cousin in His purpose, asserting that it would be more proper for him to receive baptism at the hands of Jesus. But being assured by Jesus that it would be altogether proper, John proceeded to administer the ordinance, and immediately afterward he received the fulfillment of the sign which had been given him.

III. A season of temptation of Jesus
#19

MATT. 4:1-11	MARK 1:12-13	LUKE 4:1-13
1 Then was Jesus led up of the Spirit into the wilderness to be tempted of the devil. 2 And when he had fasted forty days and forty nights, he afterward hungered. 3 And the tempter came and said unto him, If thou art the Son of God, command that these stones become ¹bread. 4 But he answered and said, It is written, ²Man shall not live by bread alone, but by every word that proceedeth out of the mouth of God. 5 Then the devil taketh him into the holy city; and he set him on the ³pinnacle of the temple, 6 and saith unto him, If thou art the Son of God, cast thyself down: for it is written, ⁴He shall give his angels charge concerning thee: and, On their hands they shall bear thee up, Lest haply thou dash thy foot against a stone. 7 Jesus said unto him, Again it is written, ⁵Thou shalt not make trial of the Lord thy God. 8 Again, the devil taketh him unto an exceeding high mountain, and showeth him all the kingdoms of the world, and the glory of them; 9 and he said unto him, All these things will I give thee, if thou wilt fall down and	12 And straightway the Spirit driveth him forth into the wilderness. 13 And he was in the wilderness forty days tempted of Satan; and he was with the wild beasts;	1 And Jesus, full of the Holy Spirit, returned from the Jordan, and was led in the Spirit in the wilderness 2 during forty days, being tempted of the devil. And he did eat nothing in those days: and when they were completed, he hungered. 3 And the devil said unto him, If thou art the Son of God, command this stone that it become ¹bread. 4 And Jesus answered unto him, It is written, ²Man shall not live by bread alone. 5 And he led him up, and showed him all the kingdoms of ³the world in a moment of time. 6 And the devil said unto him, To thee will I give all this authority, and the glory of them: for it hath been delivered unto me; and to whomsoever I will I give it. 7 If thou therefore wilt ⁴worship before me, it shall all be thine. 8 And Jesus answered and said unto him, It is written, Thou shalt worship the Lord thy God, and him only shalt thou serve. 9 And he led him to Jerusalem, and set him on the ⁵pinnacle of the temple, and said unto him, If thou art the Son of God, cast thyself down from hence: 10 for it is written, ⁶He shall give his angels

¹ Gr. loaves. ² Dt. viii. 3.
³ Gr. wing. ⁴ Ps. xci. 11, 12.
⁵ Dt. vi. 16.

¹ Or, a loaf   ² Dt. viii. 3.
³ Gr. the inhabited earth.
⁴ The Greek word denotes an act of reverence, whether paid to a creature, or to the Creator (comp. marginal note on Mt. 2. 2).
⁵ Gr. wing.   ⁶ Ps. xci. 11, 12.

Matthew 4	Mark 1	Luke 4
⁶worship me. 10 Then saith Jesus unto him, Get thee hence, Satan: for it is written, ⁷Thou shalt worship the Lord thy God, and him only shalt thou serve. 11 Then the devil leaveth him; and behold, angels came and ministered unto him.	and the angels ministered unto him.	charge concerning thee, to guard thee: 11 and, On their hands they shall bear thee up, Lest haply thou dash thy foot against a stone. 12 And Jesus answering said unto him, It is said, ⁷Thou shalt not make trial of the Lord thy God. 13 And when the devil had completed every temptation, he departed from him ⁸for a season.
⁶ See marginal note on ch. 2. 2. ⁷ Dt. vi. 13.		⁷ Dt. vi. 16. ⁸ Or, *until*

Note 21. The Temptations of Jesus.

1. How was it possible for Jesus to be tempted? When our Lord emptied Himself that He might be made in the likeness of men (Phil. 2:7, see Note 16), he became subject to human limitations, and it was therefore possible for the Devil to assail Him with real temptations. Jesus exposed Himself to the capability of sinning in order that He might be our Saviour.

2. What did these temptations involve? The temptations described in this section were certainly neither the first nor the last that Jesus encountered, but in them the Devil sought: (1) to induce Him to prostitute His divine power for personal ends, (2) to influence Him to seek popularity by deception and to dare God to perform an unnecessary miracle, (3) to persuade Him to turn aside from His purpose of dying for the redemption of sinners, promising Him the world as a kingdom if He would compromise with evil.

3. What was the significance of our Lord's victories over these and other temptations? (1) Overcoming the Devil in temptation was assurance of power for the greater victory over the same enemy in the resurrection, which Jesus expected to win. In that victory He would through death "destroy him that had the power of death; that is, the Devil" (Heb. 2:14). (2) The victories of our Lord over temptation and over death are an assurance to the Christian of power for victory over the same evil forces, since His mighty resurrection power is made available "to usward who believe" (Eph. 1:19-20).

IV. John the Baptist's formal testimony to Jesus
##20 - 21
1. Before a committee from Jerusalem
#20
JOHN 1:19-28

19 And this is the witness of John, when the Jews sent unto him from Jerusalem priests and Levites to ask him, Who art thou? 20 And he confessed, and denied not; and he confessed, I am not the Christ. 21 And they asked him, What then? Art thou Elijah? And he saith, I am not. Art thou the prophet? And he answered,

No. 22 They said therefore unto him, Who art thou? that we may give an answer to them that sent us. What sayest thou of thyself? 23 He said, I am the voice of one crying in the wilderness, Make straight the way of the Lord, as [1]said Isaiah the prophet. 24 [2]And they had been sent from the Pharisees. 25 And they asked him, and said unto him, Why then baptizest thou, if thou art not the Christ, neither Elijah, neither the prophet? 26 John answered them, saying, I baptize [3]in water: in the midst of you standeth one whom ye know not, 27 *even* he that cometh after me, the latchet of whose shoe I am not worthy to unloose. 28 These things were done in [4]Bethany beyond the Jordan, where John was baptizing.

[1] Is. xl. 3.　　　　[2] Or, *And* certain *had been sent from among the Pharisees.*　　　　[3] Or, *with*
[4] Many ancient authorities read *Bethabarah,* some *Betharabah.* Comp. Josh. 15. 6, 61; 18. 22.

Note 22. Without doubt the work of John the Baptist was attracting more and more attention. Assuming that Jesus presented Himself for baptism six months after John began to preach, and allowing for the time of the temptations, we conclude that the wilderness campaign had been in progress seven and a half months or longer when the Jerusalem deputation came to inquire about John's claims for himself.* Earlier the Pharisees and Sadducees had sought to participate in the Messianic program that John was heralding, on the chance that it might be a true one; but they had been rebuffed because they showed no evidence of genuine repentance (Matt. 3: 7). Now they desired to know what character in the Messianic program John claimed to be.

In the program, as they had outlined it, the central person was, of course, the Messiah; but before the Messiah they expected Elijah, the Old Testament prophet, returning in person to herald the coming of the Messiah (Matt. 17: 10, #134; cf. Mal. 4: 5—6). Also, some of them expected the reappearance of Jeremiah in person, or one of the Old Testament prophets (Matt. 16: 14; Luke 9: 19, #130; cf. Deut. 18: 15—18). John was not any one of these personally, although Jesus twice asserted that the prophecy about Elijah was fulfilled in him (Matt. 11: 14; 17: 10—13). Their inquiry about his practice of baptizing stemmed from the thought that even one of priestly parentage would not presume to inaugurate a new ordinance or program of purification (John 3: 25) without the authority of one connected with the Messianic age. However by identifying himself with the voice of Isaiah 40: 3, John did lay claim to Messianic connection, and he further informed his inquisitors that the "Great One" of whom he often spoke had already appeared and was among them (verse 26; cf. Matt. 3: 11—12, 17).

2. Before the multitude of his congregation (when he
   saw Jesus coming to him as He returned from the
   Mount of Temptation)

#21

JOHN 1:29-34
29 On the morrow he seeth Jesus coming unto him, and saith, Behold, the Lamb

*Broadus, *Commentary on Matthew,* p. 54; Alvah Hovey, *Commentary on John,* also in *An American Commentary on the New Testament,* ed. Alvah Hovey (Philadelphia: American Baptist Publication Society, 1885), p. 10.

of God, that [1]taketh away the sin of the world! 30 This is he of whom I said, After me cometh a man who is become before me: for he was [2]before me. 31 And I knew him not; but that he should be made manifest to Israel, for this cause came I baptizing [3]in water. 32 And John bare witness, saying, I have beheld the Spirit descending as a dove out of heaven; and it abode upon him. 33 And I knew him not: but he that sent me to baptize [3]in water, he said unto me, Upon whomsoever thou shalt see the Spirit descending and abiding upon him, the same is he that baptizeth [3]in the Holy Spirit. 34 And I have seen, and have borne witness that this is the Son of God.

[1] Or, *beareth the sin*   [2] Gr. *first in regard of me.*   [3] Or, *with*

Note 23. Without doubt Jesus returned after the season of temptation to the place where John was preaching and baptizing, arriving the next day after the visit by the deputation from Jerusalem. This was probably John's first opportunity to point out Jesus as the One mightier than himself of whom he had been preaching for months.

V. Jesus attracting His first disciples (from among the disciples of John)

#22
JOHN 1:35-51

35 Again on the morrow John was standing, and two of his disciples; 36 and he looked upon Jesus as he walked, and saith, Behold, the Lamb of God! 37 And the two disciples heard him speak, and they followed Jesus. 38 And Jesus turned, and beheld them following, and saith unto them, What seek ye? And they said unto him, Rabbi (which is to say, being interpreted, Teacher), where abidest thou? 39 He saith unto them, Come, and ye shall see. They came therefore and saw where he abode; and they abode with him that day: it was about the tenth hour. 40 One of the two that heard John *speak,* and followed him, was Andrew, Simon Peter's brother. 41 He findeth first his own brother Simon, and saith unto him, We have found the Messiah (which is, being interpreted, [1]Christ). 42 He brought him unto Jesus. Jesus looked upon him, and said, Thou art Simon the son of [2]John: thou shalt be called Cephas (which is by interpretation, [3]Peter).

43 On the morrow he was minded to go forth into Galilee, and he findeth Philip: and Jesus saith unto him, Follow me. 44 Now Philip was from Bethsaida, of the city of Andrew and Peter. 45 Philip findeth Nathanael, and saith unto him, We have found him, of whom Moses in the·law, and the prophets, wrote, Jesus of Nazareth, the son of Joseph. 46 And Nathanael said unto him, Can any good thing come out of Nazareth? Philip saith unto him, Come and see. 47 Jesus saw Nathanael coming to him, and saith of him, Behold, an Israelite indeed, in whom is no guile! 48 Nathanael saith unto him, Whence knowest thou me? Jesus answered and said unto him, Before Philip called thee, when thou wast under the fig tree, I saw thee. 49 Nathanael answered him, Rabbi, thou art the Son of God; thou art King of Israel. 50 Jesus answered and said unto him, Because I said unto thee, I saw thee underneath the fig tree, believest thou? thou shalt see greater things than these. 51 And he saith unto him, Verily, verily, I say unto you, Ye shall see the heaven opened, and the angels of God ascending and descending upon the Son of man.

[1] That is, *Anointed.* Comp. Ps. 2. 2.   [2] Gr. *Joanes:* called in Mt. 16. 17, *Jonah.*
[3] That is, *Rock or Stone.*

Note 24. The testimony about Jesus which John the Baptist bore on the day Jesus returned from the place of temptations (#21) was doubtless public and general. The repetition of the essential part of that testimony on the next day was directed personally to two of his followers and must have been intended to induce them to do just what they did do: that is, to seek an audience with Jesus. The companion of Andrew is not named, but Bible students generally suggest that he was John the son of Zebedee, who became an apostle and the author of this record. It is significant that this author never refers to himself by name.

John likely used the Roman civil system of time throughout his Gospel; that is, he counted a day as running from midnight to midnight as we do (cf. John 19: 14).* The Synoptic writers used the Jewish system, regarding a day as from sundown to sundown (cf. Mark 15: 25). The tenth hour here, therefore, was our ten o'clock in the morning, not four in the afternoon.

Why did Philip call Jesus the son of Joseph? His statement here and that of the multitudes on other occasions (Matt. 13: 55; Luke 4: 22; and John 6: 42) indicate that the public did not know about the virgin birth of Jesus (cf. Note 16 (2); also the words of Mary in Luke 2: 48). Nathaniel's question about Nazareth (vs. 46) is more suggestive when we observe that he was from Cana (John 21: 2) which was not far from Nazareth. In calling him "an Israelite indeed," Jesus doubtless implied that Nathaniel represented the true meaning of the name Israel—"a prince with God" (cf. Gen. 32: 28).

These five were the first of the multitudes who were attracted to Jesus during His earthly ministry. He did not at this time invite or challenge them to be his constant followers; but for some months probably before such a challenge was issued, they or some of them, accompanied Him on His journeys and were His loyal adherents.

VI. The first miracle - changing water to wine at Cana of Galilee

#23

JOHN 2:1-11

1 And the third day there was a marriage in Cana of Galilee; and the mother of Jesus was there: 2 and Jesus also was bidden, and his disciples, to the marriage. 3 And when the wine failed, the mother of Jesus saith unto him, They have no wine. 4 And Jesus saith unto her, Woman, what have I to do with thee? mine hour is not yet come. 5 His mother saith unto the servants, Whatsoever he saith unto you, do it. 6 Now there were six waterpots of stone set there after the Jews' manner of purifying, containing two or three firkins apiece. 7 Jesus saith unto them, Fill the waterpots with water. And they filled them up to the brim. 8 And he saith unto them, Draw out now, and bear unto the ¹ruler of the feast. And they bare it. 9 And when the ruler of the feast tasted the water ²now become wine, and knew not whence it was (but the servants that had drawn the water knew), the ruler of the feast calleth the bridegroom, 10 and saith unto him, Every man setteth on first the good wine; and when *men* have drunk freely, *then* that which is worse: thou hast kept the good wine until now. 11 This beginning of his signs did Jesus in Cana of Galilee, and manifested his glory; and his disciples believed on him.

¹ Or, *steward*   ² Or, *that it had become*

Note 25. Notice how John, the author, dates these events: first day in this series of events, the coming of the deputation from Jerusalem (#20); second day, the return of Jesus from the wilderness of temptation and identification of Him by John the Baptist as the Lamb of God and the One of whom he had been telling the people (John 1: 29);

*Westcott, *The Gospel According to St. John*, p. 282; Hovey, *Commentary on John*, p. 377.

64

third day, the second designation of Jesus as "the Lamb of God," attracting the first three disciples (John 1:35ff); fourth day, the departure for Galilee, call of Philip and that one's bringing Nathaniel (John 1:43ff); on the seventh day (third after the call of Philip) the marriage at Cana (John 2:1). An interesting coincident is that Nathaniel's home was at Cana (cf. John 21:2). We wonder why Mary, mother of Jesus, was present and what responsibility she had in serving the feast. Could either the bride or the groom have been a special friend or relative of the family of Jesus? At any rate observe the following points of interest:

(1) Why did Mary come to Him with this problem? And what did she understand about His "hour?" Is it possible that He had at some time intimated to her something of His power and His mission on earth? At any rate Mary was not offended at an answer which at first seems disrespectful and a refusal to help. Instead she instructed the servants to obey whatever orders He should give. His words indicate that at this early date He had in mind an hour which would be both an hour of suffering and an hour of glory (cf. John 12:23; 17:1).

(2) The question has been frequently asked: Was the wine that Jesus made intoxicating? Sometimes we wonder if the motive behind the question is a sincere desire to know the truth. Any answer given must of necessity be only an inference. As such for two reasons, I would answer, probably it was not. (a) Since it was a miracle, and since there is available to the Lord God unlimited means for producing a beverage of greatest delight to the user which was not intoxicating, I maintain that it did not need to be such. The wine made from water was better than that served at the beginning of the feast, which because of custom was supposed to be of superior quality; and probably it was different from, and better than, any that the feast-ruler had ever tasted. And whatever its chemical formula, it would probably have been called by Greek-speaking people oinos ("wine"). (b) He who came to be of service (Matt. 20:28), who through His life went about doing good (Acts 10:38), would certainly have had no part in putting before others that which contained an enticement to evil, and which might result in the downfall of the user.

Note 26. MIRACLES
(1) Definition: A miracle is an event in the external world in which the power of God operates immediately, superceding the forces that are regularly at work in the universe, which attests the presence of God with, and His approval of, the person through whom the work is wrought. A miracle is not a violation of a law of nature nor the temporary suspension of law; but it is the bringing to bear of a new force immediately on the case at hand, which force is greater than the forces that regularly operate in nature.
(2) Words Used in the New Testament to Describe Them:
a. "Wonders" (terata), emphasizing the state of mind produced on those observing them (Acts 2:19, 22).

65

b. "Signs" (sēmeia), signifying that the miracles attested God's presence with, and approval of, Jesus—or the miracle-working agent, whoever he was (John 2: 11).

c. "Powers" (dunameis) emphasizing divine ability, usually translated "mighty works" (Matt. 11: 20), but in Mark 9: 29 the King James Version has "miracles."

d. "Works" (erga) emphasizing the products of His busy activity; it frequently occurs with this meaning in John 5: 36; 14: 11—12).

(3) Nature of Bible Miracles.

a. They reveal God's power and authority over all the realms of His creation. It is significant that in the creation account Moses (or whoever the inspired writer was) used the word for "create" (Hebrew bara') in connection with the work of God on three days. On the first day He "created," or brought into existence, the material universe and light, representative of all energy (Gen. 1: 1, 3); on the fifth day He "created" living animals, bringing life into existence (Gen. 1:21); and on the sixth day He "created" persons, imparting spirituality to the race (Gen. 1: 27). And the miracles of God show His power of control over the realms in which His creative power was exercised. And corresponding to the three acts of creation, the miracles may be classified: (a) those in which He exercised His power of the material world, as turning water into wine or stilling a storm at sea, and others, (b) those manifesting His power over the biological world, as the many miracles of healing or bringing the dead to life, and (c) those which show His power over the spirit world, as casting demons out of their victims or the experience of regeneration, changing the purpose and outlook of a person.

b. They reflect the character of God as well as His power. Some extra-Biblical accounts of miracles are rejected, not because those "miracles" would be impossible for God, but because they misrepresent His character.

c. For the most part, they were beneficient rather than punitive; that is, they were generally performed for the good of the people affected, rather than as a punishment on someone for wrong doing. However, some of the miracles recounted in the Bible were punitive, among them: the plagues of Egypt (Exod 7:19--12:30), the leprosy of Miriam (Num. 12: 10), the death of Korah and his confederates (Num. 16: 31—35), the tearing of the children who mocked Elisha (II Kings 2: 23--24), the leprosy of Gehazi (II Kings 5: 20—27), the dumbness of Zacharias (Luke 1: 18--20), the death of Ananias and Sapphira (Acts 5: 5, 10), the blindness of Elymas (Acts 13: 11). It is significant that none of the miracles performed by the Lord Jesus was punitive (cf. Luke 9: 54--55).

d. They were performed by personal agents of God, and not by the magical power of an inanimate object. Three seeming exceptions to this statement were the resuscitation of the man buried in Elisha's tomb (II Kings 13: 21), the healing of the woman who touched the hem of Jesus' garment (Matt. 9:20), and the healing of those who obtained handkerchiefs and aprons from the body of Paul (Acts 19:11—12).

e. They were free, never charged for or wrought for pay. On the other hand, compare the punishment of Gehazi, who accepted a reward from Naaman for himself and Elisha (II Kings 5:20—27).

(4) Value of Miracles as a Testimony to the Claims and Teachings of Jesus:

a. They attested God's approval of Him and a commission to bear a message from God. This was true also of others who performed miracles.

b. They thus confirmed His claims about Himself and the gospel and teachings which He proclaimed. They did not prove His deity directly; but since He claimed divine sonship and accepted this appelation from others, the miracles in confirming the claim did prove His deity indirectly.

c. They reveal the nature of His mission, a mission of self-giving rather than self-exaltation (cf. Acts 10:38).

d. They were doubtless performed in power granted to Him by the Father or the Holy Spirit rather than in His own power as God the Son. He confessed that it was by the Spirit of God that He cast out demons (Matt. 12:28); and it is probable that He performed all other miracles in the same power of the Spirit or of the Father (cf. Luke 4:14; Acts 10:38; John 11:41—44; 14:10). This conforms to the statement that He "emptied Himself" when He "was made in the likeness of men" (cf. Phil. 2:7, ASV).

(5) Miracles Since the Earthly Life of Jesus:

a. He promised His disciples that they would do greater works than those which He had been doing. The account of some of those "greater works" is found in the book of Acts.

b. Doubtless there have been many miracles since the days of the apostles, wrought in answer to prayer, especially when such working of God's power would serve for the advancement of His cause.

c. In the experience of Jesus the suggestion to challenge God to perform an unnecessary miracle was from the Devil (cf. #19), and it is well to remember that we are warned in the words of the Lord Jesus, in the inspired writings of Paul, and in the Revelation of John (Matt. 24:24; II Thess. 2:9; Rev. 13:13—14) that Satan will in time perform "lying wonders." Careful discrimination must be used, therefore, in giving credence to "miracles," which serve no useful purpose, or which are manifestly "performed" for publicity, or which are "performed" by one whose teaching or preaching is in conflict with the truth revealed in the Bible.

d. Today the miracle of regeneration, followed by consistent Christian living, may be seen in victory over former habits of, and disposition toward, sin. This is a more effective testimony of God's presence and the working of His power than are the spectacular "miracles" often so widely publicized.

67

VII. A brief sojourn at Capernaum
#24
JOHN 2:12

12 After this he went down to Capernaum, he, and his mother, and *his* brethren, and his disciples; and there they abode not many days.

Note 27. Our Lord had probably already determined to make Capernaum the headquarters for His ministry in Galilee. It was a busy commercial center near "Bethsaida, the city of Andrew and Peter" (John 1: 44). The sojourn related here was likely to arrange for removal from Nazareth to Capernaum. His mother and half brothers apparently decided not to move, but to remain at Nazareth.

VIII. The first Passover of His public ministry
##25 - 27
1. First cleansing of the Temple
#25
JOHN 2:13-22

13 And the passover of the Jews was at hand, and Jesus went up to Jerusalem. 14 And he found in the temple those that sold oxen and sheep and doves, and the changers of money sitting: 15 and he made a scourge of cords, and cast all out of the temple, both the sheep and the oxen; and he poured out the changers' money, and overthrew their tables; 16 and to them that sold the doves he said, Take these things hence; make not my Father's house a house of merchandise. 17 His disciples remembered that it was written, [1]Zeal for thy house shall eat me up. 18 The Jews therefore answered and said unto him, What sign showest thou unto us, seeing that thou doest these things? 19 Jesus answered and said unto them, Destroy this [2]temple, and in three days I will raise it up. 20 The Jews therefore said, Forty and six years was this [2]temple in building, and wilt thou raise it up in three days? 21 But he spake of the [2]temple of his body. 22 When therefore he was raised from the dead, his disciples remembered that he spake this; and they believed the scripture, and the word which Jesus had said.

[1] Ps. lxix. 9.   [2] Or, *sanctuary*

Note 28. At this, the first Passover feast of His public ministry, our Lord cleansed the temple of the sellers of animals for sacrifice and the money changers. We shall see Him repeat this action during the last Passover He attended (#202). Notice that this occasion is recorded only by John; the latter one by the Synoptics. Observe that on this occasion His charge against the traffickers was desecration of the temple; at the later cleansing it was both desecration and thievery, or extortion.

At first thought, it might seem that these traffickers were doing the worshipping public of that day a service in supplying animals for sacrifice and for Passover observance and thus relieving them of the necessity of driving their own animals the long distance from their homes. But consider the following facts: (1) Those who controlled the temple were the priests and the Sanhedrin. (2) The priests had to pass on all animals offered for sacrifice as to whether they were without blemish or not. (3) The Sanhedrin gave or sold the concession in the temple for the selling of animals for sacrifice. Indeed, Annas, head of the high priestly family at this time, is said to have controlled this market and to have grown wealthy from it.[*] (4) This made it easy for

[*] D. Miall Edwards, "Annas" in *International Standard Bible Encyclopedia*, Vol. I, p. 137.

some sort of agreement to be reached between the priests and dealers in sacrificial animals by which these dealers would have an absolute monopoly and could therefore charge extortionate prices.

The money-changers were likewise driven out for their extortion. Consider the following: (1) There was a temple tax of half shekel a head (cf. Matt. 17: 24--27, #137). This was likely based on the requirement of Moses for the building of the tabernacle (cf. Exod. 30: 13--16; 38: 26. cf. also Neh. 10: 32). (2) This had to be paid in Jewish money; but for about one hundred years no Jewish money had been coined, and the supply of half shekels at that time was limited. (3) Those who made change from Roman money to Jewish money charged for their services and usually charged their own prices. After a worshiper obtained his half shekels he deposited them in the treasury box in the temple. Later they were brought out and turned over again to the money-changers to be exchanged for more Roman money.

The Lord Jesus, being enraged at these extortionate practices in the name of religion, drove the guilty ones from the temple.

2. The discourse with Nicodemus

#26
JOHN 2:23—3:21

23 Now when he was in Jerusalem at the passover, during the feast, many believed on his name, beholding his signs which he did. 24 But Jesus did not trust himself unto them, for that he knew all men, 25 and because he needed not that any one should bear witness concerning [1]man; for he himself knew what was in man.

1 Now there was a man of the Pharisees, named Nicodemus, a ruler of the Jews: 2 the same came unto him by night, and said to him, Rabbi, we know that thou art a teacher come from God; for no one can do these signs that thou doest, except God be with him. 3 Jesus answered and said unto him, Verily, verily, I say unto thee, Except one be born [2]anew, he cannot see the kingdom of God. 4 Nicodemus saith unto him, How can a man be born when he is old? can he enter a second time into his mother's womb, and be born? 5 Jesus answered, Verily, verily, I say unto thee, Except one be born of water and the Spirit, he cannot enter into the kingdom of God. 6 That which is born of the flesh is flesh; and that which is born of the Spirit is spirit. 7 Marvel not that I said unto thee, Ye must be born [2]anew. 8 [3]The wind bloweth where it will, and thou hearest the voice thereof, but knowest not whence it cometh, and whither it goeth: so is every one that is born of the Spirit. 9 Nicodemus answered and said unto him, How can these things be? 10 Jesus answered and said unto him, Art thou the teacher of Israel, and understandest not these things? 11 Verily, verily, I say unto thee, We speak that which we know, and bear witness of that which we have seen; and ye receive not our witness. 12 If I told you earthly things and ye believe not, how shall ye believe if I tell you heavenly things? 13 And no one hath ascended into heaven, but he that descended out of heaven, *even* the Son of man, [4]who is in heaven. 14 And as Moses lifted up the serpent in the wilderness, even so must the Son of man be lifted up; 15 that whosoever [5]believeth may in him have eternal life.

16 For God so loved the world, that he gave his only begotten Son, that whosoever believeth on him should not perish, but have eternal life. 17 For God sent not the Son into the world to judge the world; but that the world should be saved through him. 18 He that believeth on him is not judged: he that believeth not hath been judged already, because he hath not believed on the name of the only begotten Son of God. 19 And this is the judgment, that the light is come into the world, and men loved the darkness rather than the light; for their works were evil. 20 For every one that [6]doeth evil hateth the light, and cometh not to the

[1] Or, *a man; for . . . the man.*　　[2] Or, *from above* See ver. 31; ch. 19. 11; Jas. 1. 17; 3. 15, 17.
[3] Or, *The spirit breatheth.*　　[4] Many ancient authorities omit *who is in heaven.*
[5] Or, *believeth in him may have*　　[6] Or, *practiseth*

69

light, lest his works should be [7]reproved. 21 But he that doeth the truth cometh to the light, that his works may be made manifest, [8]that they have been wrought in God.
[7] Or. *convicted*   [8] Or, *because*

Note 29. What do we know about Nicodemus?

(1) He was a Pharisee, which meant that he was careful to keep the law (cf. page 14). (2) He was a ruler, which surely meant that he was a member of the Sanhedrin court at Jerusalem (cf. John 7:50). (3) He was a teacher (verse 10), possibly in one of the two Rabbinical colleges in Jerusalem. (4) He was probably wealthy, since at the burial of Jesus he brought "about a hundred pound weight" of myrrh and aloes (John 19:39). (5) He was among those who began to believe on Jesus because they saw the signs (2:23), but Jesus trusted him more than He did the others of that group and made known to this Pharisee some of the cardinal truths of Christianity, namely: (a) Natural man is lost beyond repair—he must be born over (vss. 3, 5). (b) God's concern for man led Him to provide means and method of man's new birth even at the cost of God's only begotten Son (vs. 16). (c) In order to make the rebirth of a man possible, it was necessary for God's Son to be lifted up in death (vss. 14—15). (6) He was probably convinced of the Messiahship of Jesus through this conversation, because in John 7:50f he took Jesus' part before the Sanhedrin, and after the crucifixion he braved the displeasure of the other Sanhedrists to help in putting away the body of Jesus.

What did our Lord mean by being "born of the water?" At least five interpretations have been suggested:

(1) Many say that He was referring to the act of baptism. I reject that idea because: (a) Baptism is not mentioned by name at any point in this conversation, and to speak of baptism in this connection would be bringing in foreign matter. (b) Our Lord never at any other place made spiritual blessings depend on conformity to physical ritual. (c) He repeatedly in other connections gave promise of salvation without mentioning baptism as a condition.

(2) Others say that the expression refers to the cleansing process in salvation (justification), while being born of the Spirit refers to the renewing process (regeneration). (3) Others say that water is used as a symbol of the part played by the Word of truth in salvation, reminding us that "sanctification of the Spirit and belief of the truth" are both necessary (II Thess. 2:13. cf. also James 1:18). (4) Others say being "born of the water" and being "born of the Spirit" mean the same thing, that the Lord Jesus would emphasize the importance of the regeneration experience by expressing it in a twofold figure.

(5) But to me, it seems most natural to understand it as referring to the natural or physical birth. Nicodemus spoke of the physical birth in the preceding verse, and Jesus spoke of it in the following verse. It

seems natural to regard Him to be speaking of the same birth in this verse. Why He used "water" as a symbol of the physical birth we cannot say with certainty.

IX. First Judaean ministry, repeated testimony of John the Baptist
#27
JOHN 3:22-36

22 After these things came Jesus and his disciples into the land of Judaea; and there he tarried with them, and baptized. 23 And John also was baptizing in Aenon near to Salim, because there [1]was much water there: and they came, and were baptized. 24 For John was not yet cast into prison. 25 There arose therefore a questioning on the part of John's disciples with a Jew about purifying. 26 And they came unto John, and said to him, Rabbi, he that was with thee beyond the Jordan, to whom thou hast borne witness, behold, the same baptizeth, and all men come to him. 27 John answered and said, A man can receive nothing, except it have been given him from heaven. 28 Ye yourselves bear me witness, that I said, I am not the Christ, but, that I am sent before him. 29 He that hath the bride is the bridegroom: but the friend of the bridegroom, that standeth and heareth him, rejoiceth greatly because of the bridegroom's voice: this my joy therefore is made full. 30 He must increase, but I must decrease.

31 He that cometh from above is above all: he that is of the earth is of the earth, and of the earth he speaketh: [2]he that cometh from heaven is above all. 32 What he hath seen and heard, of that he beareth witness; and no man receiveth his witness. 33 He that hath received his witness hath set his seal to *this*, that God is true. 34 For he whom God hath sent speaketh the words of God: for he giveth not the Spirit by measure. 35 The Father loveth the Son, and hath given all things into his hand. 36 He that believeth on the Son hath eternal life; but he that [3]obeyeth not the Son shall not see life, but the wrath of God abideth on him.

[1] Gr. *were many waters.*
[2] Some ancient authorities read *he that cometh from heaven beareth witness of what he hath seen and heard.*   [3] Or, *believeth not*

Note 30. This is called the "First Judaean Ministry," because, in the fifth period of His life our Lord journeyed in that province, teaching and healing, approximately three months—from the Feast of Tabernacles until the Feast of Dedication (#151—161). All the record that we have of this ministry is found in John 3: 21, 26, and 4: 1—2. We know none of the details of His labors nor how long this ministry lasted. If the words of Jesus in John 4: 35 mean that there would be four months until the next harvest season, the visit in Samaria (which was made at the close of the Judaean ministry) was in December, and this ministry occupied seven or eight months. But there are grave doubts on the part of the interpreters about the implication of that statement by Jesus. It is possible, if not probable, that the Judaean Ministry did not last more than two or three months.

Jesus had not yet challenged the disciples to follow Him constantly (cf. #36); but disciples had accompanied Him to Jerusalem for the Passover (John 2: 17), and during the ministry in Judaea they were His agents in administering baptism (John 4: 2), and they were with Him in Samaria as He was returning to Galilee (John 4: 8). These probably were, or included, some (if not all) of those who had been attracted to Him at Bethany beyond Jordan. At this time they were following Him because of personal interest in the things He taught and did.

X. Returning to Galilee through Samaria
##28—31

1. Leaving Judaea (imprisonment of John the Baptist)
#28

MATT. 4:12	LUKE 3:19-20	JOHN 4:1-3
	19 But Herod the tetrarch, being reproved by him for Herodias his brother's wife, and for all the evil things which Herod had done, 20 added this also to them all, that he shut up John in prison.	
12 Now when he heard that John was delivered up, he withdrew into Galilee;		1 When therefore the Lord knew that the Pharisees had heard that Jesus was making and baptizing more disciples than John 2 (although Jesus himself baptized not, but his disciples), 3 he left Judaea, and departed again into Galilee.

Note 31. John the Baptist was imprisoned by Herod Antipas just before the close of our Lord's "first Judaean ministry" (probably A. D. 27) and remained in confinement until he was beheaded a short time before the third Passover. The place of his imprisonment is usually taken to be Machaerus, east of the Dead Sea, where Herod maintained a palace.

Matthew sets forth that the imprisonment of John was the reason why Jesus at this time removed from Judaea to Galilee; but in the Gospel of John it is stated that this removal was because He (Jesus) knew that the Pharisees had learned that He was more successful than John in making disciples. Very probably both reasons had weight in the decision of Jesus.

2. Ministry in Samaria ##29--31
a. Winning the Samaritan woman at the well
#29
JOHN 4:4-29

4 And he must needs pass through Samaria. 5 So he cometh to a city of Samaria, called Sychar, near to the parcel of ground that Jacob gave to his son Joseph: 6 and Jacob's [1]well was there. Jesus therefore, being wearied with his journey, sat [2]thus by the [1]well. It was about the sixth hour. 7 There cometh a woman of Samaria to draw water: Jesus saith unto her, Give me to drink. 8 For his disciples were gone away into the city to buy food. 9 The Samaritan woman therefore saith unto him, How is it that thou, being a Jew, askest drink of me, who am a Samaritan woman? ([3]For Jews have no dealings with Samaritans.) 10 Jesus answered and said unto her, If thou knewest the gift of God, and who it is that saith to thee, Give me to drink; thou wouldest have asked of him, and he would have given thee living water. 11 The woman saith unto him, [4]Sir, thou hast nothing to draw with, and the well is deep: whence then hast thou that living water? 12 Art thou greater than our father Jacob, who gave us the well, and drank thereof himself, and his sons, and his cattle? 13 Jesus answered and said unto her, Every one that drinketh of this water shall thirst again: 14 but whosoever drinketh of the water that I shall give him shall never thirst; but the water that I shall give him shall become in him a well of water springing up unto eternal life. 15 The woman

[1] Gr. spring: and so in ver. 14; but not in ver. 11, 12.
[2] Or, as he was Comp. ch. 13. 25.
[3] Some ancient authorities omit For Jews have no dealings with Samaritans.
[4] Or, Lord

72

John 4

saith unto him, ⁴Sir, give me this water, that I thirst not, neither come all the way hither to draw. 16 Jesus saith unto her, Go, call thy husband, and come hither. 17 The woman answered and said unto him, I have no husband. Jesus saith unto her, Thou saidst well, I have no husband: 18 for thou hast had five husbands; and he whom thou now hast is not thy husband: this hast thou said truly. 19 The woman saith unto him, ⁴Sir, I perceive that thou art a prophet. 20 Our fathers worshipped in this mountain; and ye say, that in Jerusalem is the place where men ought to worship. 21 Jesus saith unto her, Woman, believe me, the hour cometh, when neither in this mountain, nor in Jerusalem shall ye worship the Father. 22 Ye worship that which ye know not: we worship that which we know; for salvation is from the Jews. 23 But the hour cometh, and now is, when the true worshippers shall worship the Father in spirit and truth: ⁵for such doth the Father seek to be his worshippers. 24 ⁶God is a Spirit: and they that worship him must worship in spirit and truth. 25 The woman saith unto him, I know that Messiah cometh (he that is called Christ): when he is come, he will declare unto us all things. 26 Jesus saith unto her, I that speak unto thee am he.

27 And upon this came his disciples; and they marvelled that he was speaking with a woman; yet no man said, What seekest thou? or, Why speakest thou with her? 28 So the woman left her waterpot, and went away into the city, and saith to the people, 29 Come, see a man, who told me all things that *ever* I did: can this be the Christ?

¹ Gr. *spring:* and so in ver. 14; but not in ver. 11, 12.　　　² Or, *as he was* Comp. ch. 13. 25.
³ Some ancient authorities omit *For Jews have no dealings with Samaritans.*
⁴ Or, *Lord*　⁵ Or, *for such the Father also seeketh*　　　⁶ Or, *God is spirit*

Note 32. Ordinarily the Jews in going from Judaea to Galilee or from Galilee to Judaea would not go through Samaria but would cross the Jordan River into Peraea and then would recross after the borders of Samaria had been passed. Jesus probably followed that custom also as a rule, although He did not personally share any of the prejudice of His fellow Jews against the Samaritans.* But apparently there were special reasons on this occasion that made it necessary, or at least advisable, for Him to take the shorter route.

Observe in Nicodemus and the Samaritan woman the contrasts in those with whom our Lord dealt spiritually: a Jew and a Samaritan; a man and a woman; a Pharisee and an open sinner.

Consider some things about Jesus' method of doing personal work. In the case of Nicodemus: (a) He aroused his interest first by the miracles and second by the shocking statement of the necessity of being born over, (b) He taught him concerning regeneration, the love or grace of God in salvation, the atonement as the ground of salvation, faith as the application of salvation, justification received in salvation, doing the truth as a consequence of salvation, and (c) He awaited God's time for a decision. In the case of the Samaritan woman: (a) He broke down prejudice, (b) He gave her something to think about (water that satisfies thirst forever, God to be worshiped anywhere in spirit and truth), (c) He spoke to her conscience, and (d) He addressed her will.

Mount Gerizim had been a very ancient place of worship (Joshua 8:3—35). In saying that the Samaritan fathers worshiped in that

*George Ernest Wright and Floyd Vivian Filson, *The Westminster Historical Atlas to the Bible* (Philadelphia: The Westminster Press, 1945), p. 86; cf. Broadus, *Commentary on Matthew,* p. 395; Edersheim, *Life and Times of Jesus,* Vol. I, p. 394.

mountain the woman had reference to the temple which Sanballat (Neh. 2:10, et al.) built there about 400 B.C. (See paragraph on Samaritans, pp. 18f).

b. Winning the people of Sychar
#30
JOHN 4:30-42
30 They went out of the city, and were coming to him. 31 In the mean while the disciples prayed him, saying, Rabbi, eat. 32 But he said unto them, I have meat to eat that ye know not. 33 The disciples therefore said one to another, Hath any man brought him *aught* to eat? 34 Jesus saith unto them, My meat is to do the will of him that sent me, and to accomplish his work. 35 Say not ye, There are yet four months, and *then* cometh the harvest? behold, I say unto you, Lift up your eyes, and look on the fields, that they are [1]white already unto harvest. 36 He that reapeth receiveth wages, and gathereth fruit unto life eternal; that he that soweth and he that reapeth may rejoice together. 37 For herein is the saying true, One soweth, and another reapeth. 38 I sent you to reap that whereon ye have not labored: others have labored, and ye are entered into their labor.

39 And from that city many of the Samaritans believed on him because of the word of the woman, who testified, He told me all things that *ever* I did. 40 So when the Samaritans came unto him, they besought him to abide with them: and he abode there two days. 41 And many more believed because of his word; 42 and they said to the woman, Now we believe, not because of thy speaking: for we have heard for ourselves, and know that this is indeed the Saviour of the world.

[1] Or, *white unto harvest. Already he that reapeth &c.*

Note 33. We know that Jesus made two later journeys through Samaria: (1) from Galilee to Jerusalem for the Feast of Tabernacles at the beginning of the Fifth Period (Luke 9:52, #142), (2) on a circuit through Samaria, Galilee, and Peraea in making His last journey to Jerusalem (Luke 17:11, #180).

c. Departure for Galilee
#31
JOHN 4:43-44
43 And after the two days he went forth from thence into Galilee. 44 For Jesus himself testified, that a prophet hath no honor in his own country.

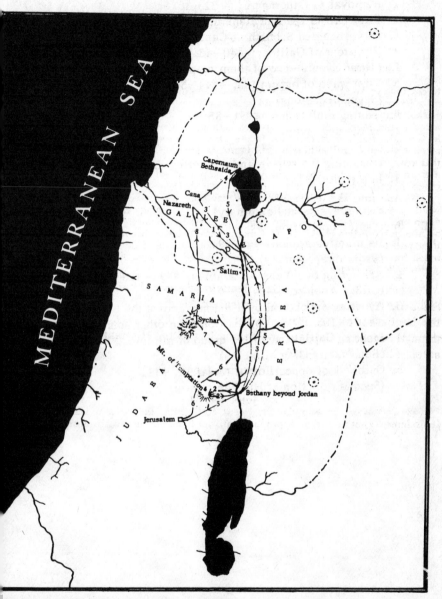

JURNEYS OF JESUS IN THE SECOND PERIOD
- From Nazareth to Bethany beyond Jordan to be baptized (#18).   2 - To the wilderness and the Mount of Tempta-
lon and return to Bethany (##19—21).   3 - To Cana to attend a marriage, first miracle (#23).   4 - To Capernaum
#24).   5 - To Jerusalem for first Passover of His ministry (#25).   6 - To the land of Judaea, where He carried on
irst Judaean ministry (#27).   7 - To Sychar (#29).   8 - To Nazareth (##31—33).
* Traditional location.   ⊙ A city of the Decapolis League)

A PREVIEW OUTLINE OF PERIOD THREE (Abbreviated), ##32–111

I. Beginnings ##32–50
1. Removal to Capernaum, ## 32 – 35
2. First call of the four fishermen, #36
3. First recorded Sabbath at Capernaum, ##37–39
4. First tour of Galilee, ##40–43
(Three events—two of them preparatory—and summary)
5. First wave of opposition, ##44–50
(Seven occasions)

II. Increasing multitudes, ##51–85
1. By the sea shore, #51
2. On the mountain, ##52–77
(Choosing the twelve and delivering the Sermon on the Mount)
3. In the city, #78
4. Touring the country, ##79–85
(Three events and summary)

III. Increasing opposition, ##86–111
1. Its manifestations ##86–89
(From three sources)
2. Answering by means of parables, ##90–103
(Group of ten parables)
3. Avoiding opposition by a journey across the Sea of Galilee,
##104–105   (Note opposition from other sources)
4. Meeting opposition with a group of miracles, ##106–110
(Four outstanding miracles)
5. Outbreak of opposition in Nazareth, #111
(Second rejection at His home town)

Ministry to the Multitudes in Galilee

(## 32 - 111)

Note 34. The third period was probably the longest in point of time of the suggested periods after the entrance of Jesus into public life. Just how long it was we have no way of knowing, because we do not know how long after the first Passover of His public life it began, nor how long before the third Passover it ended. But it lacked only the duration of the early Judaean ministry and the short stay in Samaria (##27–31), plus the duration of the practice trip of the Disciples (##113–117) lasting two years. Probably a conservative estimate of its duration would be a year and a half; possibly a little longer. It is to be noticed that I do not include all of His labors in Galilee in this period, because I regard the practice trip of the disciples as part of the fourth period (Special Ministry to the Twelve Disciples).

In this period our Lord acquired great publicity and gained high popularity. He gave Himself largely to the performance of miracles and setting forth of great social principles. These last brought Him into conflict with the temple and synagogue officials, but their opposition was at this time in the background. During this period He made no open claim that He was the Son of God and no open statement that it was His purpose to die for the salvation of men—though there were a few veiled allusions to this purpose.

Observe that after the introductory section all the material for this period was taken from the Synoptic Gospels except ##34, 47, 48.

I. Beginnings, ##32--50
   1. Removal to Capernaum (cf. #24), ##32–35
     (1) Arrival in Galilee, introductory summary
#32

MATT. [4:12]	MARK 1:14-15	LUKE 4:14-15	JOHN 4:45
[12 Now when he heard that John was delivered up, he withdrew into Galilee;] 4:17 17 From that time began Jesus to preach, and to say, Repent ye; for the kingdom of heaven is at hand.	14 Now after John was delivered up, Jesus came into Galilee, preaching the ¹gospel of God, 15 and saying, The time is fulfilled, and the kingdom of God is at hand: repent ye, and believe in the ¹gospel. ¹ Or, *good tidings:* and so elsewhere.	14 And Jesus returned in the power of the Spirit into Galilee: and a fame went out concerning him through all the region round about. 15 And he taught in their synagogues, being glorified of all.	45 So when he came into Galilee, the Galilaeans received him, having seen all the things that he did in Jerusalem at the feast: for they also went unto the feast.

77

Note 35. Notice how each of the Gospel writers gives a summary of the labors of Jesus during this period that is different from the others.
(2) Stopover at Nazareth, first rejection by His fellow-townsmen

#33
LUKE 4:16-30

16 And he came to Nazareth, where he had been brought up: and he entered as his custom was, into the synagogue on the sabbath day, and stood up to read. 17 And there was delivered unto him [1]the book of the prophet Isaiah. And he opened the [2]book, and found the place where it was written,
18 [3]The Spirit of the Lord is upon me,
[4]Because he anointed me to preach [5]good tidings to the poor:
He hath sent me to proclaim release to the captives,
And recovering of sight to the blind,
To set at liberty them that are bruised,
19 To proclaim the acceptable year of the Lord.
20 And he closed the [6]book, and gave it back to the attendant, and sat down: and the eyes of all in the synagogue were fastened on him. 21 And he began to say unto them, To-day hath this scripture been fulfilled in your ears. 22 And all bare him witness, and wondered at the words of grace which proceeded out of his mouth: and they said, Is not this Joseph's son? 23 And he said unto them, Doubtless ye will say unto me this parable, Physician, heal thyself: whatsoever we have heard done at Capernaum, do also here in thine own country. 24 And he said, Verily I say unto you, No prophet is acceptable in his own country 25 But of a truth I say unto you, There were many widows in Israel in the days of Elijah, when the heaven was shut up three years and six months, when there came a great famine over all the land; 26 and unto none of them was Elijah sent, but only, to [7]Zarephath, in the land of Sidon, unto a woman that was a widow. 27 And there were many lepers in Israel in the time of Elisha the prophet; and none of them was cleansed, but only Naaman the Syrian. 28 And they were all filled with wrath in the synagogue, as they heard these things; 29 and they rose up, and cast him forth out of the city, and led him unto the brow of the hill whereon their city was built, that they might throw him down headlong. 30 But he passing through the midst of them went his way.

| [1] Or, a roll | [2] Or, roll | [3] Is. lxi. 1 f. | [4] Or, Wherefore |
| [5] Or, the gospel | [6] Or. roll | [7] Gr. Sarepta. | |

Note 36. The third period in the life of Jesus began and closed with a rejection of Him at Nazareth (cf. #111). It was natural for Him, on His return from Judaea, to visit His mother and the other members of His family and to let the disciples who were with Him return to their homes and their business. The unsavory reputation of Nazareth (cf. John 1: 46, #22) is evidenced by its people's jealousy of the publicity which His program of miracles was bringing to Capernaum. Even His half brothers, with whom He had left the carpentry business, did not at this time believe on Him or have any sympathy for His program (cf. John 7: 5, #141).

See page 10 for the order of worship in the synagogues of Jesus' time. The Scripture that Jesus read and applied to Himself was Isa. 61: 1-2.

(3) A visit to Cana, healing the nobleman's son

#34
JOHN 4:46-54

46 He came therefore again unto Cana of Galilee, where he made the water wine. And there was a certain [1]nobleman, whose son was sick at Capernaum. 47
[1] Or, king's officer

78

John 4

When he heard that Jesus was come out of Judaea into Galilee, he went unto him, and besought *him* that he would come down, and heal his son; for he was at the point of death. 48 Jesus therefore said unto him, Except ye see *signs* and wonders, ye will in no wise believe. 49 The [1]nobleman saith unto him, [2]Sir, come down ere my child die. 50 Jesus saith unto him, Go thy way; thy son liveth. The man believed the word that Jesus spake unto him, and he went his way. 51 And as he was now going down, his [3]servants met him, saying, that his son lived. 52 So he inquired of them the hour when he began to amend. They said therefore unto him, Yesterday at the seventh hour the fever left him. 53 So the father knew that *it was* at that hour in which Jesus said unto him, Thy son liveth: and himself believed, and his whole house. 54 This is again the second sign that Jesus did, having come out of Judaea into Galilee.

[1] Or, *king's officer*   [2] Or, *Lord*   [3] Gr. *bondservants.*

Note 37. Since Cana was situated on the road from Nazareth to Capernaum, the natural order was for Him to visit Nazareth first on His return from Judaea and Samaria and then to stop at Cana on His way to Capernaum—not to go to Cana first and then back to Nazareth, as Robertson suggests.* We wonder if He was visiting the couple whose marriage He had attended some months before—or possibly Nathaniel. At any rate, He was not ready to go on to Capernaum when the nobleman implored Him to come down. This, the second miracle at Cana, was the first recorded miracle of healing, but likely there had been others of which we have no record, possibly at Capernaum (cf. Luke 4:23), and almost surely at Jerusalem (cf. John 2:23; 4:45). This is the first of four instances of healing in absentia.

(4) Arrival at Capernaum, setting up headquarters there
#35

MATT. 4:13-16	LUKE 4:31

13 And leaving Nazareth, he came and dwelt in Capernaum, which is by the sea, in the borders of Zebulun and Naphtali: 14 that it might be fulfilled which was spoken through Isaiah the prophet, saying,
15 [1]The land of Zebulun and the land of Naphtali,
  [2]Toward the sea, beyond the Jordan,
  Galilee of the [3]Gentiles,
16 The people that sat in darkness
  Saw a great light,
And to them that sat in the region
  and shadow of death,
To them did light spring up.
[1] Is. ix. 1, 2.
[2] Gr. *The way of the sea.*
[3] Gr. *nations:* and so elsewhere.
	31 And he came down to Capernaum, a city of Galilee.

Note 38. See Note 27. The quotation was Isa. 9:1—2, which is part of a familiar Messianic prophecy.

*A. T. Robertson, *Harmony of the Gospels*, ##38, 39, pp. 31f.

2. Calling the four fishermen (the first call to follow Him)
#36

MATT. 4:18-22

18 And walking by the sea of Galilee, he saw two brethren, Simon who is called Peter, and Andrew his brother, casting a net into the sea; for they were fishers. 19 And he saith unto them, Come ye after me, and I will make you fishers of men. 20 And they straightway left the nets, and followed him. 21 And going on from thence he saw two other brethren, ¹James the *son* of Zebedee, and John his brother, in the boat with Zebedee their father, mending their nets; and he called them. 22 And they straightway left the boat and their father, and followed him.

¹ Or, *Jacob*

MARK 1:16-20

16 And passing along by the sea of Galilee, he saw Simon and Andrew the brother of Simon casting a net in the sea; for they were fishers. 17 And Jesus said unto them, Come ye after me, and I will make you to become fishers of men. 18 And straightway they left the nets, and followed him. 19 And going on a little further, he saw ¹James the *son* of Zebedee, and John his brother, who also were in the boat mending the nets. 20 And straightway he called them: and they left their father Zebedee in the boat with the hired servants, and went after him.

¹ Or, *Jacob*

Note 39. It appears that until this time the four fishermen had not been challenged by the Lord Jesus to be His constant followers. Their presence with Him in Jerusalem and "the land of Judaea" and Samaria (##23, 24, 25, 27, 28, 29, 30) was doubtless spontaneous, because of their interest in the things that He did and said. But on arrival at Capernaum to inaugurate the Galilean ministry He invited them to be His daily companions in order that He might teach them the art of "men-fishing." The readiness with which they responded is probably explained by the fellowship that they had already had with Him in Judaea in making and baptizing disciples (cf. John 3:22; 4:1--2).

3. First recorded Sabbath at Capernaum, ##37--39
(1) At the Synagogue, healing a demoniac
#37

MARK 1:21-28

21 And they go into Capernaum; and straightway on the sabbath day he entered into the synagogue and taught. 22 And they were astonished at his teaching: for he taught them as having authority, and not as the scribes. 23 And straightway there was in their synagogue a man with an unclean spirit; and he cried out, 24 saying, What have we to do with thee, Jesus thou Nazarene? art thou come to destroy us? I know thee who thou art, the Holy One of God. 25 And Jesus rebuked ¹him, saying, Hold thy peace, and come out of him. 26 And the unclean spirit, ²tearing him and crying with a loud voice, came out of him. 27 And they were all amazed, insomuch that they questioned among themselves, saying, What is this? a new teaching! with authority he commandeth even the unclean spirits, and they obey him. 28

¹ Or, *it*   ² Or, *convulsing*

LUKE 4:31b-37

31b And he was teaching them on the sabbath day: 32 and they were astonished at his teaching; for his word was with authority. 33 And in the synagogue there was a man, that had a spirit of an unclean demon; and he cried out with a loud voice, 34 ¹Ah! what have we to do with thee, Jesus thou Nazarene? art thou come to destroy us? I know thee who thou art, the Holy One of God. 35 And Jesus rebuked him, saying, Hold thy peace, and come out of him. And when the demon had thrown him down in the midst, he came out of him, having done him no hurt. 36 And amazement came upon all, and they spake together, one with another, saying, What is ²this word? for with authority and power he commandeth the unclean spirits, and they come out. 37 And there went forth a rumor concerning him

¹ Or, *Let alone*
² Or, *this word, that with authority . . . come out?*

Mark 1	Luke 4
And the report of him went out straight-way everywhere into all the region of Galilee round about.	into every place of the region round about.

Note 40. At this point in His career Jesus seems to have been welcomed—even invited—to speak in the synagogues. Later this would change.

In this section we have the first record of our Lord's casting out demons. In the King James Version they are frequently called devils; but the New Testament speaks of one devil, (diabolos), frequently called Satan, the enemy of God and of all that is good; and these beings are in the American Standard Version rightly called demons (daimones or daimonia)—sometimes they are called unclean spirits. Seven such miracles are described in the Gospels in more or less detail (cf. ##37, 87, 105, 110, 124, 135, 153). Mention is also made of the case of Mary Magdalene, besides four other references to the cure of demonized persons (##39, 40, 51, 85). Moreover, in the Gospels the apostles, the seventy who were sent forth by Jesus, and an unknown person are said to have cast out demons (##114, 135, 148), and four references to such cures occur in the book of Acts. Many questions have been raised about these demons:

(1) Were the people described in these records troubled by outside powers, or spiritual personages, who had invaded their personalities and deprived them of the independent use of their faculties, or were they merely victims of some natural mental malady? It is admitted that the ancients generally attributed insanity to the work of supernatural (or infra-mundane) powers. It is possible also that Jesus found it necessary at times to accomodate Himself to the unscientific ideas of His day (though frankly there is no record of a certain instance when He did). But observe the following:

a. Jesus regarded the demons as real spiritual persons who had no bodies of their own, but who had taken possession of the physical faculties of their victims. He addressed them as such (Mark 1: 25, et al.), and spoke of them as such (Matt. 12: 26—30, 43—45; Luke 11: 18—26).

b. On three occasions the demons recognized Jesus and called Him "The Holy One of God" or "The Christ, the Son of God: or "Jesus, thou Son of the Most High God" (##37, 39, 105). Frequently demonized persons showed an acquaintance with the spirit world which cannot be explained on the ground of natural insanity. This is noticeable also of the two demonized persons told about in Acts—the girl at Philippi (Acts 16: 16) and the man of Ephesus (Acts 19: 15). Our Lord did not care for the testimony of demons and always made them hush, but the fact that they could recognize Him before His deity was confessed by the disciples is significant.

c. In answer to the accusation that Beelzebub was inspiring and authorizing and empowering Him to cast out demons, (cf. #87), Jesus used the expression, "if Satan cast out Satan," identifying the prince of demons (Beelzebub) with Satan or the Devil. On another occasion He spoke of the Devil and His angels (Matt. 25: 41); and mention of fallen angels is made elsewhere in the New Testament (II Pet. 2: 4; Jude 6). We wonder if these fallen angels are to be identified with demons. Many Bible interpreters do so identify them.

d. The sinful angels were cast down into Tartaros (Greek in II Pet. 2: 4; this word is not found elsewhere in the New Testament). The demons possessing the man of Gergasa asked Jesus if He had come to torment them "before the time" (Matt. 8: 29). Then they begged Him not to send them "into the deep" (Luke 8: 31), using a word for "deep," (abussos) that is translated "bottomless pit" (Rev. 20: 3), into which the Devil will be cast during the visible Kingdom of God. We do not know whether or not these utterances mean that Satan and the demons together await with dread a time when they will be transferred from Tartaros to the bottomless pit. In fact, one might wonder if Tartaros is the same as the bottomless pit. I am persuaded, indeed, that such is an idle question, and that we should not be any better off if we had the answer.

(2) What was the connection between demoniacal possession and sin? Did demons take possession of a person's faculties because of previous great sinfulness on his part? There is no hint in any of the records of the New Testament that such was the case. On the other hand, did demon-possession cause a person to live an especially wicked life? The works of Satan are always bad; however, the actions of these demonized persons resemble those of individuals who were irresponsible rather than morally blameable. In at least three cases the demonized suffered physical maladies (all of these involving dumbness) along with demon-possession, (##87, 110, 153).

(3) Are there demonized persons today? I do not know. There have been reports from widely scattered sources of suspected or asserted cases, but not enough publicity was given to them, or there was not enough opportunity for competent and unbiased investigation for us catagorically to affirm or deny them as such.

(2) At Simon Peter's home, healing Peter's wife's mother

#38

MATT. 8:14-15	MARK 1:29-31	LUKE 4:38-39
14 And when Jesus was come into Peter's house, he	29 And straightway, [1]when they were come out of the synagogue, they came into the house of Simon and Andrew, with [2]James and John. 30 Now	38 And he rose up from the synagogue, and entered into the house of Simon.
	[1] Some ancient authorities read *when he was come* out of the synagogue, he *came &c.* [2] Or, *Jacob*	

82

Matt. 8	Mark 1	Luke 4
saw his wife's mother lying sick of a fever. 15 And he touched her hand, and the fever left her; and she arose, and ministered unto him.	Simon's wife's mother lay sick of a fever; and straightway they tell him of her: 31 and he came and took her by the hand, and raised her up; and the fever left her, and she ministered unto them.	And Simon's wife's mother was holden with a great fever; and they besought him for her. 39 And he stood over her, and rebuked the fever; and it left her: and immediately she rose up and ministered unto them.

(3) After sunset, healing many
#39

MATT. 8:16-17	MARK 1:32-34	LUKE 4:40-41
16 And when even was come, they brought unto him many [1]possessed with demons: and he cast out the spirits with a word, and healed all that were sick: 17 that it might be fulfilled which was spoken through Isaiah the prophet, saying, [2]Himself took our infirmities, and bare our diseases. [1] Or, *demoniacs* [2] Is. liii. 4.	32 And at even, when the sun did set, they brought unto him all that were sick, and them that were [1]possessed with demons. 33 And all the city was gathered together at the door. 34 And he healed many that were sick with divers diseases, and cast out many demons; and he suffered not the demons to speak, because they knew him.[2] [1] Or, *demoniacs* [2] Many ancient authorities add *to be Christ.* See Lk. 4. 41.	40 And when the sun was setting, all they that had any sick with divers diseases brought them unto him; and he laid his hands on every one of them, and h e a l e d them. 41 And demons also came out from many, crying out, and saying, Thou art the Son of God. And rebuking them, he suffered them not to speak, because they knew that he was the Christ.

Note 41. No one complained because Jesus had healed Peter's wife's mother on the Sabbath day, as the synagogue authorities later complained and criticized Him for healing on the Sabbath. And we do not know how the news of that act of healing spread over the town. But we notice that those who had loved ones to heal waited until after sunset, when the Sabbath was officially ended, before they brought them to Peter's house. This shows the high regard that the common people had for the Sabbath.

4. First tour of Galilee (with the four fishermen), ##40—43
(1) Jesus at prayer, the tour announced
#40

MARK 1:35-39	LUKE 4:42-44
35 And in the morning, a great while before day, he rose up and went out, and departed into a desert place, and there prayed. 36 And Simon and they that were with him followed after him; 37 and they found him, and say unto him, All are seeking thee. 38 And he saith unto them, Let us go elsewhere into the next towns, that I may preach there also; for to this end came I forth. 39 And he· went into their synagogues throughout all Galilee, preaching and casting out demons.	42 And when it was day, he came out and went into a desert place: and the multitudes sought after him, and came unto him, and would have stayed him, that he should not go from them. 43 But he said unto them, I must preach [1]the good tidings of the kingdom of God to the other cities also: for therefore was I sent. 44 And he was preaching in the synagogues of [2]Galilee. [1] Or, *the gospel* [2] Very many ancient authorities read *Judaea.*

83

Note 42. Why was it necessary for Jesus to pray, since He was the Son of God and had the power to work the many miracles ascribed to Him? It should be remembered that for the time of His life in the flesh He had emptied Himself (Note 12), or divested Himself of the independent exercise of divine prerogatives and attributes. Moreover, it has been suggested (Note 26, (4), d.) that during His life in the flesh Jesus surely performed His miracles in dependence on the Holy Spirit or the Father. This meant that when He came to be the world's Saviour, though divine in essence and eternally self-existent, Jesus subjected Himself to essentially the same limitations as other human beings. Praying therefore was both befitting to Him, and necessary for Him, in order that He might obtain wisdom and guidance and power, as it is in the experience of all normal human beings. And surely to Him, more than to anyone else, prayer was a refreshing and enjoyable experience, a source of fellowship with God the Father. A study of the Gospel records will reveal fifteen occasions when He prayed: ##18 (Luke 3: 21), 40, 42 (Luke 5:16), 52 (Luke 6: 12), 83 (Matt. 11: 25--26, again in Luke 10: 21, #148), 119 (Matt. 14: 23), 130 (Luke 9: 18), 133 (Luke 9: 28--29), 152 (Luke 11: 1), 178 (John 11: 41f), 199 (John 12: 28), 233 (Luke 22: 32), 237, 238, 251 (Luke 23: 34), 252 (Matt. 27: 46, Luke 23: 46).

(2) The second call of the four fishermen to be His followers

#41

LUKE 5:1-11

1 Now it came to pass, while the multitude pressed upon him and heard the word of God, that he was standing by the lake of Gennesaret; 2 and he saw two boats standing by the lake: but the fishermen had gone out of them, and were washing their nets. 3 And he entered into one of the boats, which was Simon's, and asked him to put out a little from the land. And he sat down and taught the multitudes out of the boat. 4 And when he had left speaking, he said unto Simon, Put out into the deep, and let down your nets for a draught. 5 And Simon answered and said, Master, we toiled all night, and took nothing: but at thy word I will let down the nets. 6 And when they had done this, they inclosed a great multitude of fishes; and their nets were breaking; 7 and they beckoned unto their partners in the other boat, that they should come and help them. And they came, and filled both the boats, so that they began to sink. 8 But Simon Peter, when he saw it, fell down at Jesus' knees, saying, Depart from me; for I am a sinful man, O Lord. 9 For he was amazed, and all that were with him, at the draught of the fishes which they had taken; 10 and so were also ¹James and John, sons of Zebedee, who were partners with Simon. And Jesus said unto Simon, Fear not; from henceforth thou shalt ²catch men. 11 And when they had brought their boats to land, they left all, and followed him.

¹ Or, Jacob   ² Gr. take alive.

Note 43. I do not believe that this passage should be considered as parallel to the passages in #36, because the event described here is so different from the one described in that section by Matthew and Mark, and because, when we combine Mark and Luke, we have the order which I have given. I am convinced that after the call related in #36, and after "they left their nets" to follow Him, they must have taken them out again, probably to obtain a little more income. This was possibly on the night after the busy Sabbath at Capernaum. Doubtless the Lord meant to impress on them, especially on Simon Peter, that men-fishing was a full-time calling, and to them it meant to cease being fish-fishers. They must leave the fishing business for good and trust God to provide the things needed to support them and their families. Peter needed to have this lesson repeated, even after the resurrection of Jesus (cf. John 21, #268 and Note 274).

Look for other instances of teaching by the seaside (##45, 51, 90).

(3) A sample miracle of this tour, healing a leper
#42

MATT. 8:2-4	MARK 1:40-45	LUKE 5:12-16
2 And behold, there came to him a leper and [1]worshipped him, saying, Lord, if thou wilt, thou canst make me clean. 3 And he stretched forth his hand, and touched him, saying, I will; be thou made clean. And straightway his leprosy was cleansed.	40 And there cometh to him a leper, beseeching him, [1]and kneeling down to him, and saying unto him, If thou wilt, thou canst make me clean. 41 And being moved with compassion, he stretched forth his hand, and touched him, and saith unto him, I will; be thou made clean. 42 And straightway the leprosy departed from him, and he was made clean. 43 And he [2]strictly charged him, and straightway sent him out, 44 and saith unto	12 And it came to pass, while he was in one of the cities, behold, a man full of leprosy: and when he saw Jesus, he fell on his face, and besought him, saying, Lord, if thou wilt, thou canst make me clean. 13 And he stretched forth his hand, and touched him, saying, I will; be thou made clean. And straightway the leprosy departed from him.
4 And Jesus saith unto him, [2]See thou tell no man; but go, show thyself to the priest, and offer the gift that Moses commanded, for a testimony unto them. [1] See marginal note on ch. 2. 2. [2] Lev. xiii. 49; xiv. 2 ff.	him, See thou say nothing to any man: but go show thyself to the priest, and offer for thy cleansing the things which Moses [3]commanded, for a testimony unto them. 45 But he went out, and began to publish it much, and to spread abroad the [4]matter, insomuch that [5]Jesus could no more openly enter into [6]a city, but was without in desert places: and they came to him from every quarter. [1] Some ancient authorities omit *and kneeling down to him.* [2] Or, *sternly* [3] Lev. xiii. 49; xiv. 2 ff. [4] Gr. *word.* [5] Gr. *he.* [6] Or, *the city*	14 And he charged him to tell no man: but go thy way, and show thyself to the priest, and offer for thy cleansing, [1]according as Moses commanded, for a testimony unto them. 15 But so much the more went abroad the report concerning him: and great multitudes came together to hear, and to be healed of their infirmities. 16 But he withdrew himself in the deserts, and prayed. [1] Lev. xiii. 49; xiv. 2 ff.

Note 44. Leprosy was the most dreaded disease of Bible times. There was no known cure for it. See Lev. 13:45—46 for the law concerning the isolation of lepers. Even those who touched a leper were unclean (Lev. 15:7, et al.). This man manifested a faith that was commendable in every respect in that he had no doubt about the power of Jesus to cleanse him, though he was not so sure of His willingness. Jesus revealed His full sympathy for him by touching him as He healed him.

It has often been asked: "Why did Jesus command the cleansed leper—and others on other occasions—not to tell about the miracles of healing?" Doubtless the answer may be learned from the consequences of the former leper's disobedience to this command (Mark 1:45). It must be remembered that Jesus did not come to earth merely to be a free physician, whose cures were immediate and always effective, but to bring to the world salvation from sin. Stirred by the former leper's report of the miracle, the multitudes came thronging Jesus for physical cures and thus hindered Him in those labors which of necessity must precede His work of redemption. Therefore, after this and four other miracles Jesus commanded the beneficiaries not to make known the miraculous nature of their blessing (cf. Mark 5:43, #108; Matt. 9:30, #109; Mark 7:36, #125; Mark 8:26, #129;- also Matt. 12:16, #51; Matt. 16:20, #130; Matt. 17:9, #134.

(4) A summary of the tour
#43
Matt. 4:23-25

23 And [1]Jesus went about in all Galilee, teaching in their synagogues, and preaching the [2]gospel of the kingdom, and healing all manner of disease and all manner of sickness among the people. 24 And the report of him went forth into all Syria: and they brought unto him all that were sick, holden with divers diseases and torments, [3]possessed with demons, and epileptic, and palsied; and he healed them. 25 And there followed him great multitudes from Galilee and Decapolis and Jerusalem and Judaea and *from* beyond the Jordan.

[1] Some ancient authorities read *he*.   [2] Or, *good tidings:* and so elsewhere.   [3] Or, *demoniacs*

Note 45. Matthew was the only Gospel writer that summarized this tour. Those who accompanied Him were the four fishermen, and possibly Philip and Nathaniel. We have no way of knowing how long this tour lasted, or what cities were visited.

5. The first wave of opposition, ##44—50
   (1) Because He claimed authority to forgive sins, healing a paralytic

#44

Matt. 9:2-8	Mark 2:1-12	Luke 5:17-26
	1 And when he entered again into Capernaum after some days, it was noised that he was [1]in the house. 2 And many were gathered together, so that there was no longer room *for them*, no, not even about the door: and he spake the word unto them. 3 And they come, bringing unto him a man sick of the palsy, borne of four. 4 And when they could not [2]come nigh unto him for the crowd, they uncovered the roof	17 And it came to pass on one of those days, that he was teaching; and there were Pharisees and doctors of the law sitting by, who were come out of every village of Galilee and Judaea and Jerusalem: and the power of the Lord was with him [1]to heal. 18 And behold, men bring on a bed a man that was palsied: and they sought to bring him in, and to lay him before him. 19 And not finding by what *way* they
2 And behold, they brought to him a man sick of the palsy, lying on a bed:		
	[1] Or, *at home* [2] Many ancient authorities read *bring him unto him.*	[1] Gr. *that he should heal.* Many ancient authorities read *he should heal them.*

86

Matt. 9	Mark 2	Luke 5
	where he was: and when they had broken it up, they let down the [3]bed whereon the sick of the palsy lay.	might bring him in because of the multitude, they went up to the housetop, and let him down through the tiles with his couch into the
and Jesus seeing their faith said unto the sick of the 'palsy, Son, be of good cheer; thy sins are forgiven. 3 And behold, certain of the scribes said within themselves, This man blasphemeth.	5 And Jesus seeing their faith saith unto the sick of the palsy, [4]Son, thy sins are forgiven. 6 But there were certain of the scribes sitting there, and reasoning in their hearts, 7 Why doth this man thus speak? he blasphemeth: who can forgive sins but one, even	midst before Jesus. 20 And seeing their faith, he said, Man, thy sins are forgiven thee. 21 And the scribes and the Pharisees began to reason, saying, Who is this that speaketh blasphemies? Who can forgive sins, but
4 And Jesus [2]knowing their thoughts said, Wherefore think ye evil in your hearts? 5 For which is easier, to say, Thy sins are forgiven; or to say, Arise, and walk? 6 But that ye may know that the Son of man hath authority on earth to forgive sins (then saith he to the sick of the palsy), Arise, and take up thy bed, and go unto thy house.	God? 8 And straightway Jesus, perceiving in his spirit that they so reasoned within themselves, saith unto them, Why reason ye these things in your hearts? 9 Which is easier, to say to the sick of the palsy, Thy sins are forgiven; or to say, Arise, and take up thy [3]bed, and walk? 10 But that ye may know that the Son of man hath authority on earth to forgive sins (he saith to the sick of the palsy), 11 I say unto thee, Arise, take up thy [3]bed, and go unto thy house. 12 And	God alone? 22 But Jesus perceiving their [2]reasonings, answered and said unto them, [3]Why reason ye in your hearts? 23 Which is easier, to say, Thy sins are forgiven thee; or to say, Arise and walk? 24 But that ye may know that the Son of man hath authority on earth to forgive sins (he said unto him that was palsied), I say unto thee, Arise, and take up thy couch, and go unto thy house. 25 And immediately he rose up before them,
7 And he arose, and departed to his house. 8 But when the multitudes saw it, they were afraid, and glorified God, who had given such authority unto men.	he arose, and straightway took up the [3]bed, and went forth before them all; insomuch that they were all amazed, and glorified God, saying, We never saw it on this fashion.	and took up that whereon he lay, and departed to his house, glorifying God. 26 And amazement took hold on all, and they glorified God; and they were filled with fear, saying, We have seen strange things to-day.
[1] Gr. Child. [2] Many ancient authorities read seeing.	[3] Or, pallet [4] Gr. Child.	[2] Or, questionings [3] Or, What

Note 46. Present in the crowd when Jesus healed the paralytic, after speaking forgiveness of his sins, were the Pharisees and doctors of the law from Judaea and Jerusalem (Luke 5: 17). They probably either had an interest in the sale of sacrificial animals and the activities of the money-changers in the temple and were enraged because Jesus had expelled the traders from the temple courts, or they were dominated by those who controlled that traffic. At any rate, they followed Him into Galilee, apparently in order that they might obtain some charge which they could bring against Him.

Observe that Jesus did not deny their contention that only God had authority to forgive sins. However, by the miracle which followed He proved His own claim of such authority; because, if He had promised the man forgiveness of sins without authority to make good His promise, God would surely not have honored His attempt to perform the miracle.

The only conclusion possible, therefore, was that Jesus was approved of God, even in His claim of a divine prerogative.

(2) Because He associated with publicans, the call of Matthew and the feast which that one gave for Jesus and disciples

#45

MATT. 9:9-13

MARK 2:13-17

LUKE 5:27-32

9 And as Jesus passed by from thence, he saw a man, called Matthew, sitting at the place of toll: and he saith unto him, Follow me. And he arose, and followed him.
10 And it came to pass, as he ¹sat at meat in the house, behold, many ²publicans and sinners came and sat down with Jesus and his disciples. 11 And when the Pharisees saw it, they said unto his disciples, Why eateth your Teacher with the ²publicans and sinners? 12 But when he heard it, he said, They that are ³whole have no need of a physician, but they that are sick. 13 But go ye and learn what *this* meaneth, ⁴I desire mercy, and not sacrifice: for I came not to call the righteous, but sinners.
¹ Gr. *reclined:* and so always.
² See marginal note on ch. 5. 46.
³ Gr. *strong.*　　⁴ Hos. vi. 6.

13 And he went forth again by the sea side; and all the multitude resorted unto him, and he taught them. 14 And as he passed by, he saw Levi the *son* of Alphaeus sitting at the place of toll, and he saith unto him, Follow me. And he arose and followed him.
15 And it came to pass, that he was sitting at meat in his house, and many ¹publicans and sinners sat down with Jesus and his disciples: for there were many, and they followed him. 16 And the scribes ²of the Pharisees, when they saw that he was eating with the sinners and ¹publicans, said unto his disciples, ³*How is it* that he eateth ⁴and drinketh with ¹publicans and sinners? 17 And when Jesus heard it, he saith unto them, They that are ⁵whole have no need of a physician, but they that are sick: I came not to call the righteous, but sinners.
¹ That is, *collectors or renters. of Roman taxes.*
² Some ancient authorities read *and the Pharisees.*
³ Or, *He eateth . . . sinners.*
⁴ Some ancient authorities omit *and drinketh.*
⁵ Gr. *strong.*

27 And after these things he went forth, and beheld a ¹publican, named Levi, sitting at the place of toll, and said unto him, Follow me. 28 And he forsook all, and rose up and followed him.
29 And Levi made him a great feast in his house: and there was a great multitude of ¹publicans and of others that were sitting at meat with them. 30 And ²the Pharisees and their scribes murmured against his disciples, saying, Why do ye eat and drink with the ¹publicans and sinners? 31 And Jesus answering said unto them, They that are ³in health have no need of a physician; but they that are sick. 32 I am not come to call the righteous but sinners to repentance.
¹ See marginal note on ch. 3. 12.
²'Or, *the Pharisees and the scribes among them*
³ Gr. *sound.*

Note 47. See page 18 in the introduction for the reasons why the Publicans were so bitterly hated.

Note 48. Parables. In this section we have the parable of The Physician, which of our Lord's many parables, was probably the first of those on record. It is well here to state certain principles about parables and their interpretation.

1. Definition. A parable is an illustrative comparison, with or without narrative, used to teach or impress religious truth, in which something that is well known is placed beside something that one desires to make known or to clarify.

2. Sources from which Jesus drew His parables:

(1) Sometimes He used incidents which had taken place among

the people to illustrate the truth He was teaching. The parables of the Good Samaritan, the Prodigal Son, and the Rich Man and Lazarus, and others seem to fall in this class.

(2) Sometimes He would refer to a custom in common practice in His day or to a well known truth, as the parable of the Physician, or of the Lamp (lighted candle).

(3) Sometimes He would make use of invented or supposed incidents or stories. The parables of the Shepherd and the Lost Sheep, of the Importunate Neighbor, and others would fall into this class.

(4) Occasionally He would use a historical incident to illustrate the truth, as Moses lifting the serpent in the wilderness or Jonah in the belly of the whale for three days and nights.

Jesus regularly drew his parables from sources with which the people were familiar, and the conditions described in them were always true to reality.

3. Purpose of Jesus in using parables:

(1) To illustrate moral and spiritual truth by comparing it with things physical and social.

(2) To put things which, for the time being, were imperfectly understood in such form that they could be easily remembered until they should be better understood.

(3) To state truths likely to give offense in such a way that those who were spiritually disposed, and who sincerely desired to know the truth, could understand, while those who sought only to criticize would not see the point, and, therefore, would not be greatly disturbed.

(4) As a judgment against those who were wilfully blind.

4. Rules for interpreting parables. Because of careless or mechanical interpretation of parables, many erroneous conclusions have been reached. Especially should one hesitate to prove a religious doctrine just by the interpretation of a single parable. The following principles will be helpful.

(1) Be careful to understand the language of the parable itself. Know its reference to Palestinian life and customs.

(2) Determine what subject it is intended to illustrate. This is important. Sometimes Jesus or the Gospel writer would state it just before or after the parable; sometimes one must gather it from the connection.

(3) Then see just how the parable illustrates that subject. Look at the parable as a whole and do not begin by attempting to assign meaning to particular items.

(4) Finally one may determine to what extent separate details are significant, but frequently for the purpose of interpretation many of the details may not have any significance at all. An object does not necessarily represent the same thing every time it is used in a parable; in the parable of the Sower the seed represent the Word of God spoken by Christians, but in the parable of the Tares the good seed represented the Christians themselves.

Sometimes our Lord spoke two or more parables on the same occasion to teach the same truth, or at least truths very closely connected; as for example, the parable of the Patched Garment and the parable of the Wine Skins. Sometimes also the same parable was repeated on a later occasion, as the parable of the Lamp (##55, 94, 153) and the parable of the Lost Sheep (##139, 171). Jesus also spoke very similar parables on different occasions, as the parable of the Great Supper (#169) and that of the Marriage Feast of the King's Son (#210) or the parable of the Pounds (#194) and that of the Talents (#224).

(3) Because He did not observe the many religious fasts

#46

MATT. 9:14-17	MARK 2:18-22	LUKE 5:33-39
14 Then come to him the disciples of John, saying, Why do we and the Pharisees fast [1]oft, but thy disciples fast not? 15 And Jesus said unto them, Can the [2]sons of the bride-chamber mourn, as long as the bridegroom is with them? but the days will come, when the bridegroom shall be taken away from them, and then will they fast. 16 And no man putteth a piece of undressed cloth upon an old garment; for that which should fill it up taketh from the garment, and a worse rent is made. 17 Neither do *men* put new wine into old [3]wine-skins: else the skins burst, and the wine is spilled, and the skins perish: but they put new wine into fresh wine-skins, and both are preserved. [1] Some ancient authorities omit *oft* [2] That is, *companions of the bridegroom.* [3] That is, *skins used as bottles.*	18 And John's disciples and the Pharisees were fasting: and they come and say unto him, Why do John's disciples and the disciples of the Pharisees fast, but thy disciplies fast not? 19 And Jesus said unto them, Can the [1]sons of the bridechamber fast, while the bridegroom is with them? as long as they have the bridegroom with them, they cannot fast. 20 But the days will come, when the bridegroom shall be taken away from them, and then will they fast in that day. 21 No man seweth a piece of undressed cloth on an old garment: else that which should fill it up taketh from it, the new from the old, and a worse rent is made. 22 And no man putteth new wine into old [2]wine-skins; else the wine will burst the skins, and the wine perisheth, and the skins: but *they put* new wine into fresh wine-skins. [1] That is, *companions of the bridegroom.* [2] That is, *skins used as bottles.*	33 And they said unto him, The disciples of John fast often, and make supplications; likewise also the *disciples* of the Pharisees; but thine eat and drink. 34 And Jesus said unto them, Can ye make the [1]sons of the bride-chamber fast, while the bridegroom is with them? 35 But the days will come; and when the bridegroom shall be taken away from them, then will they fast in those days. 36 And he spake also a parable unto them: No man rendeth a piece from a new garment and putteth it upon an old garment; else he will rend the new, and also the piece from the new will not agree with the old. 37 And no man putteth new wine into old [2]wine-skins; else the new wine will burst the skins, and itself will be spilled, and the skins will perish. 38 But new wine must be put into fresh wine-skins. 39 And no man having drunk old *wine* desireth new; for he saith, The old is [3]good. [1] That is, *companions of the bridegroom.* [2] That is, *skins used as bottles.* [3] Many ancient authorities read *better.*

Note 49. Notice four parables in this section: (1) The Children of the Bride Chamber, (2) The Patched Garment, (3) The Wine Skins, and (4) Preference of Old Wine over New.

Our Lord did not condemn fasting as such. But fasting should be spontaneous, the expression of such earnestness in prayer that one does not desire to eat. Many of the Pharisees observed weekly fasts, and some fasted twice a week (Luke 18:12, #185). These were either to call forth the praise of men, or they were sort of an ascetic self-punishment. In neither case did one's fasting commend him to God; therefore in Matt. 6:16—18 (#66) Jesus did condemn that kind of fasting. But observe that He Himself fasted forty days in the wilderness, #19. In the law of Moses the only fast required was in connection with the Day of Atonement (cf. pp. 13f).

(4) Because He healed a man on the Sabbath and bade him carry his bed (at pool of Bethesda, in Jerusalem)
#47
JOHN 5:1-16

1 After these things there was [1]a feast of the Jews; and Jesus went up to Jerusalem.
2 Now there is in Jerusalem by the sheep *gate* a pool, which is called in Hebrew [2]Bethesda, having five porches. 3 In these lay a multitude of them that were sick, blind, halt, withered[3]. 5 And a certain man was there, who had been thirty and eight years in his infirmity. 6 When Jesus saw him lying, and knew that he had been now a long time *in that case,* he saith unto him, Wouldest thou be made whole? 7 The sick man answered him, 'Sir, I have no man, when the water is troubled, to put me into the pool: but while I am coming, another steppeth down before me. 8 Jesus saith unto him, Arise, take up thy [5]bed and walk. 9 And straightway the man was made whole, and took up his [5]bed and walked.
Now it was the sabbath on that day. 10 So the Jews said unto him that was cured, It is the sabbath, and it is not lawful for thee to take up thy [5]bed. 11 But he answered them, He that made me whole, the same said unto me, Take up thy [5]bed, and walk. 12 They asked him, Who is the man that said unto thee, Take up *thy [5]bed,* and walk? 13 But he that was healed knew not who it was; for Jesus had conveyed himself away, a multitude being in the place. 14 Afterward Jesus findeth him in the temple, and said unto him, Behold, thou art made whole: sin no more, lest a worse thing befall thee. 15 The man went away, and told the Jews that it was Jesus who had made him whole. 16 And for this cause the Jews persecuted Jesus, because he did these things on the sabbath.

[1] Many ancient authorities read *the feast.* (Comp. ch. 2. 13?)
[2] Some ancient authorities read *Bethsaida,* others *Bethzatha.*
[3] Many ancient authorities insert, wholly or in part, *waiting for the moving of the water: 4 for an angel of the Lord went down at certain seasons into the pool, and troubled the water: whosoever then first after the troubling of the water stepped in was made whole, with whatsoever disease he was holden.*   [4] Or, *Lord*   [5] Or, *pallet*

Note 50. It is not known for certain which of the feasts this was. Dr. Robertson* and many other Bible students hold that it was a Passover, and we follow their lead. We note that only John mentioned the first Passover (#25), and he alone of the Gospel writers mentioned this feast, which was probably second. At the first Passover Jesus aroused the ire of the temple authorities by cleansing the temple; and while attending this feast a year later He made them angry again by violating a rule of the rabbis against healing on the Sabbath, and by His claims of divine sonship, which we shall see in the next section. These temple authorities became His most determined enemies, so that after this, every time He returned to Jerusalem, they stirred up unrelenting opposition, (##145, 147, 163—165, 179, 197, 227). Already Jerusalem

*A. T. Robertson, *Harmony of the Gospels,* p. 42.

scribes had begun to hound His steps in Galilee (#44), and we shall see that they kept it up (##87, 123).

It will be observed that verse 4 is omitted from the text of the American Standard Version but found in the margin (footnote). It is omitted from all the more recent translations because it is not found in any of the most ancient six manuscripts of John's gospel. Moreover, the work of the angel which this verse describes does not resemble God's way of bestowing blessings (cf. Note 26 (4) a). Most students of the New Testament, therefore, have concluded that it was not part of the Gospel as it came from the hand of John.*

(5) Because He spoke of God as His Father and claimed divine prerogatives

#48

John 5:17-47

17 But Jesus answered them, My Father worketh even until now, and I work. 18 For this cause therefore the Jews sought the more to kill him, because he not only brake the sabbath, but also called God his own Father, making himself equal with God.

19 Jesus therefore answered and said unto them, Verily, verily, I say unto you, The Son can do nothing of himself, but what he seeth the Father doing: for what things soever he doeth, these the Son also doeth in like manner. 20 For the Father loveth the Son, and showeth him all things that himself doeth: and greater works than these will he show him, that ye may marvel. 21 For as the Father raiseth the dead and giveth them life, even so the Son also giveth life to whom he will. 22 For neither doth the Father judge any man, but he hath given all judgment unto the Son, 23 that all may honor the Son even as they honor the Father. He that honoreth not the Son honoreth not the Father that sent him. 24 Verily, verily, I say unto you, He that heareth my word, and believeth him that sent me, hath eternal life, and cometh not into judgment, but hath passed out of death into life. 25 Verily, verily, I say unto you, the hour cometh, and now is, when the dead shall hear the voice of the Son of God; and they that [1]hear shall live. 26 For as the Father hath life in himself, even so gave he to the Son also to have life in himself: 27 and he gave him authority to execute judgment, because he is a son of man. 28 Marvel not at this: for the hour cometh, in which all that are in the tombs shall hear his voice, 29 and shall come forth; they that have done good, unto the resurrection of life; and they that have [2]done evil, unto the resurrection of judgment.

30 I can of myself do nothing: as I hear, I judge: and my judgment is righteous; because I seek not mine own will, but the will of him that sent me. 31 If I bear witness of myself, my witness is not true. 32 It is another that beareth witness of me; and I know that the witness which he witnesseth of me is true. 33 Ye have sent unto John, and he hath borne witness unto the truth. 34 But the witness which I receive is not from man: howbeit I say these things, that ye may be saved. 35 He was the lamp that burneth and shineth; and ye were willing to rejoice for a season in his light. 36 But the witness which I have is greater than *that of* John; for the works which the Father hath given me to accomplish, the very works that I do, bear witness of me, that the Father hath sent me. 37 And the Father that sent me, he hath borne witness of me. Ye have neither heard his voice at any time, nor seen his form. 38 And ye have not his word abiding in you: for whom he sent, him ye believe not. 39 [3]Ye search the scriptures, because ye think that in them ye have eternal life; and these are they which bear witness of me; 40 and ye will

[1] Or, *hearken*   [2] Or, *practised*   [3] Or, *Search the scriptures*

*A manuscript of a large part of the Gospel of John, which was produced as early as the year 200 was photographed and microfilmed in 1950 and published toward the end of 1956. It is called "Papyrus 66," or "Papyrus Bohmer II." This manuscript is at least 125 years older than any previously known text; and it, like the oldest of the other manuscripts, does not contain this verse. (R. Scripps, Th.D., "A New Johanine Manuscript" in *Christianity Today*, June 10, 1957), p. 16.

not come to me, that ye may have life. 41 I receive not glory from men. 42 But I know you, that ye have not the love of God in yourselves. 43 I am come in my Father's name, and ye receive me not: if another shall come in his own name, him ye will receive. 44 How can ye believe, who receive glory one of another, and the glory that *cometh* from ⁴the only God ye seek not? 45 Think not that I will accuse you to the Father: there is one that accuseth you, *even* Moses, on whom ye have set your hope. 46 For if ye believed Moses, ye would believe me; for he wrote of me. 47 But if ye believe not his writings, how shall ye believe my words?

Note 51. The foregoing section is the first of six rather lengthy discourses of Jesus recorded in John in which He defended Himself against the criticism of His opponents (cf. chs. 6: 26—71; 7: 15—44; 8: 12—59; 10: 1—39; 12: 29—36). All of these took place at Jerusalem except the one in chapter 6.

(6) Because He defended His disciples for plucking off heads of grain on the Sabbath and eating the grains (cf. Note 52)

#49

MATT. 12:1-8	MARK 2:23-28	LUKE 6:1-5
1 At that season Jesus went on the sabbath day through the grainfields; and his disciples were hungry and began to pluck ears and to eat. 2 But the Pharisees, when they saw it, said unto him, Behold, thy disciples do that which it is not lawful to do upon the sabbath. 3 But he said unto them, ¹Have ye not read what David did, when he was hungry, and they that were with him; 4 how he entered into the house of God, and ²ate the show-bread, which it was not lawful for him to eat, neither for them that were with him, but only for the priests? 5 Or have ye not read in the law, ³that on the sabbath day the priests in the temple profane the sabbath, and are guiltless? 6 But I say unto you, that ⁴one greater than the temple is here. 7 But if ye had known what this meaneth, ⁵I desire mercy, and not sacrifice, ye would not have condemned the guiltless. 8 For the Son of man is lord of the sabbath.	23 And it came to pass, that he was going on the sabbath day through the grainfields; and his disciples ¹began, as they went, to pluck the ears. 24 And the Pharisees said unto him, Behold, why do they on the sabbath day that which is not lawful? 25 And he said unto them, ²Did ye never read what David did, when he had need, and was hungry, he, and they that were with him? 26 How he entered into the h o u s e of God ³when Abiathar was high priest, and ate the show-bread, which it is not lawful to eat save for the priests, and gave also to them that were with him?	1 Now it came to pass on a ¹sabbath, that he was going through the grainfields; and his disciples plucked the ears, and did eat, rubbing them in their hands. 2 But certain of the Pharisees said, Why do ye that which it is not lawful to do on the sabbath day? 3 And Jesus answering them said, ²Have ye not read even this, what David did, when he was hungry, he, and they that were with him; 4 how he entered into the house of God and took and ate the show-bread, and gave also to them that were with him; which it is not lawful to eat save for the priests alone?
	27 And he said unto them, The sabbath was made for man, and not man for the sabbath: 28 so that the Son of man is lord even of the sabbath.	5 And he said unto them, The Son of man is lord of the sabbath.
¹ 1 S. xxi. 6. ² Some ancient authorities read *they ate.* ³ Num. xxviii. 9, 10. ⁴ Gr. *a greater thing.* ⁵ Hos. vi. 6.	¹ Gr. *began to make* their *way plucking.* ² 1 S. xxi. 6. ³ Some ancient authorities read *in the days of Abiathar the high priest.*	¹ Many ancient authorities insert *second-first.* ² 1 S. xxi. 6.

(7) Because in a synagogue, He healed a man whose hand was withered

#50

MATT. 12:9-14

9 And he departed thence, and went into their synagogue: 10 and behold, a man having a withered hand. And they asked him, saying, Is it lawful to heal on the sabbath day? that they might accuse him. 11 And he said unto them, What man shall there be of you, that shall have one sheep, and if this fall into a pit on the sabbath day, will he not lay hold on it, and lift it out? 12 How much then is a man of more value than a sheep! Wherefore it is lawful to do good on the sabbath day. 13 Then saith he to the man, Stretch forth thy hand. And he stretched it forth; and it was restored whole, as the other. 14 But the Pharisees went out, and took counsel against him, how they might destroy him.

MARK 3:1-6

1 And he entered again into the synagogue; and there was a man there who had his hand withered. 2 And they watched him, whether he would heal him on the sabbath day; that they might accuse him. 3 And he saith unto the man that had his hand withered, ¹Stand forth. 4 And he saith unto them, Is it lawful on the sabbath day to do good, or to do harm? to save a life, or to kill? But they held their peace. 5 And when he had looked round about on them with anger, being grieved at the hardening of their heart, he saith unto the man, Stretch forth thy hand. And he stretched it forth; and his hand was restored. 6 And the Pharisees went out, and straightway with the Herodians took counsel against him, how they might destroy him.

¹ Gr. Arise into the midst.

LUKE 6:6-11

6 And it came to pass on another sabbath, that he entered into the synagogue and taught: and there was a man there, and his right hand was withered. 7 And the scribes and the Pharisees watched him, whether he would heal on the sabbath; that they might find how to accuse him. 8 But he knew their thoughts; and he said to the man that had his hand withered, Rise up, and stand forth in the midst. And he arose and stood forth. 9 And Jesus said unto them, I ask you, Is it lawful on the sabbath to do good, or to do harm? to save a life, or to destroy it? 10 And he looked round about on them all, and said unto him, Stretch forth thy hand. And he did so: and his hand was restored. 11 But they were filled with ¹madness; and communed one with another what they might do to Jesus.

¹ Or, foolishness

Note 52. We have just studied the first three of the six Sabbath controversies in the public life of Jesus. In the law of Moses, desecration of the Sabbath was made a capital offense (Exod. 35:2; Num. 15:32—36). If, therefore, the enemies of Jesus could get a clear case of Sabbath breaking against Him they could call for His death. Let us observe first, their accusations against Him and second, the defense He made for His actions.

1. Why the Pharisees accused Him:

(a) He healed a man on the Sabbath day and bade him to take up his pallet and walk (#47). (b) With approval He permitted His disciples to pull the heads of grain from the stalks, rub out the kernels, blow off the chaff, and eat the grains (#49). This was permitted on weekdays under Mosaic law (Deut. 23:25); so the Pharisees did not complain of the damage done the field of grain. But they said this entailed labor and was, therefore, unlawful on the Sabbath day—pulling off the heads of grain was harvesting, rubbing out the kernels was threshing, and blowing off the chaff was winnowing.* Some of them may have said also

*Edersheim, *Life and Times of Jesus*, Vol. II, p. 56.

94

at chewing raw grain was grinding. (c) On a Sabbath day He healed man who had come to the synagogue with a withered, useless hand #50). In this instance Jesus did not apply a remedy or even touch the man, and so outwardly He had not broken any law. Possibly this fact only angered His enemies the more.

2. In His defense against their accusations:

(a) He appealed to the example of God His Father whose work of sustaining the universe has continued to the present, after He finished his work of creation (John 5: 17, #48). (b) He appealed to the uncensured act of David, who, though n o t a priest, ate the shew-bread at the tabernacle to meet his needs (I Sam. 21: 6; Matt. 12: 3, #49). This was not a violation of the Sabbath law, but of another law just as strict. (c) He appealed to the actions of the priests, who even on the Sabbath prepared animals for sacrifice and offered them (Matt. 12: 5, #49—cf. Num. 28: 9, 18—19); and then He quoted Hos. 6: 6 to show that a merciful effort to relieve suffering or hunger is more pleasing to God than the sacrifices made in the temple (Matt. 12: 7, #49). (d) He stated that God instituted the Sabbath of rest to be a blessing to man; and that He did not create mankind just to be a race of Sabbath-keepers (Mark : 27, #49). (e) He declared that His own Messianic authority included jurisdiction even over the Sabbath day. This meant that His interpretation of what constitutes a violation of the Sabbath law was more authoritative than that of the learned scribes of His day (Matt. 12: 8, #49). (f) He maintained that doing good to one's fellow man is right any time, and relieving suffering is lawful even on the Sabbath (Mark 3: 4, #50). This was an extension of one of their regulations, which said that a physician might on the Sabbath day do that which would actually save life.* (g) He appealed to their own habits in caring for valuable animals on the Sabbath day, stating that since a man is more valuable than a sheep, there is more reason to relieve human suffering than to rescue a fallen sheep or to supply its ordinary needs (Matt. 12: 11, #50).

Jesus honored the Sabbath—honored it as a day of worship and a day of rest (cf. Luke 4: 16); but the foolish and unmerciful demands of the rabbinical interpretations aroused His anger as well as His grief (Mark 3: 5). To Him the rest on the Sabbath was intended for others as well as for one's self; and when occasion arose to bring someone rest from suffering and affliction and humiliation, it was both permissible and proper to give it.

II. Increasing multitudes—first steps toward an organization ##51-85

Note 53. Increasing Multitudes. In spite of the wave of opposition on the part of the Pharisees and synagogue authorities, the common people came to Jesus in increasing numbers. Possibly some came only to receive the benefits of His miraculous power in healing for themselves or for their loved ones, and others may have come out of mere

*Ibid., pp. 59ff.

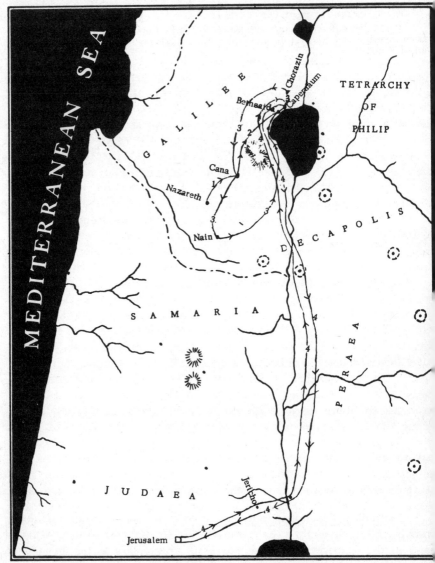

JOURNEYS OF JESUS IN THE FIRST HALF OF THE THIRD PERIOD
1 - From Nazareth to Cana (#34). 2 - From Cana to Capernaum (#35). 3 - The
first tour of Galilee (##40—43). 4 - From Capernaum to Jerusalem to attend a
feast, possibly the second Passover (and return to Capernaum, #47).

⊙ A city of the Decapolis league.

uriosity—to see what He would do or hear what He would say. But whatever their motive for coming, the number of those who thronged around Him continued to grow.

1. By the seashore, healing, teaching from a boat
#51

MATT. 12:15-21

15 And Jesus perceiving *it* withdrew from thence: and many followed him; and he healed them all,

16 and charged them that they should not make him known: 17 that it might be' fulfilled which was spoken through Isaiah the prophet, saying,
[1]18 Behold, my [2]servant whom I have chosen;
My beloved in whom my soul is well pleased:
I will put my Spirit upon him,
And he shall declare judgment to the [3]Gentiles.
19 He shall not strive, nor cry aloud;
Neither shall any one hear his voice in the streets.
20 A bruised reed shall he not break, and smoking flax shall he not quench,
Till he send forth judgment unto victory.
21 And in his name shall the [3]Gentiles hope.

[1] Is. xlii. 1 ff.
[2] See marginal note on Acts 3. 13. (Or, *child*)
[3] See marginal note on ch. 4. 15.

MARK 3:7-12

7 And Jesus with his disciples withdrew to the sea; and a great multitude from Galilee followed; and from Judaea, 8 and from Jerusalem, and from Idumaea, and beyond the Jordan, and about Tyre and Sidon, a great multitude, hearing [1]what great things he did, came unto him. 9 And he spake to his disciples, that a little boat should wait on him because of the crowd, lest they should throng him: 10 for he had healed many; insomuch that as many as had [2]plagues [3]pressed upon him that they might touch him. 11 And the unclean spirits, whensoever they beheld him, fell down before him, and cried, saying, Thou art the Son of God. 12 And he charged them much that they should not make him known.

[1] Or, *all the things that he did*
[2] Gr. *scourges.*   [3] Gr. *fell.*

Note 54. Teaching from the boat (the second time, cf. #41). Probably after Jesus on a Sabbath day healed the man with a withered hand in the Capernaum synagogue (#50), the rulers of that synagogue denied Him the privilege of teaching there any more. But on one occasion already, He had taught the people from Peter's fishing boat (#41), and hither, according to Mark, He went again. He seems to have established a regular place by the sea where He would meet the multitudes who came to Him. The Old Testament passage quoted in Matthew is from Isa. 42: 1--4, where it is said that "Neither shall any man hear his voice in the streets." Matthew likely had in mind that He did not at

97

this time join the issue with the synagogue authorities, and He did not go up and down the streets to attract a following.

2. On a mountain ##52-57
(1) After a night of prayer, choosing the twelve apostles
#52

MARK 3:13-19a	LUKE 6:12-16
13 And he goeth up into the mountain, and calleth unto him whom he himself would; and they went unto him. 14 And he appointed twelve,[1] that they might be with him, and that he might send them forth to preach, 15 and to have authority to cast out demons: 16 [2]and Simon he surnamed Peter; 17 and [3]James the *son* of Zebedee, and John the brother of [3]James; and them he surnamed Boanerges, which is, Sons of thunder: 18 and Andrew, and Philip, and Bartholomew, and Matthew, and Thomas, and [3]James, the *son* of Alphaeus, and Thaddaeus and Simon the [4]Cananaean, 19 and Judas Iscariot, who also [5]betrayed him.	12 And it came to pass in these days, that he went out into the mountain to pray; and he continued all night in prayer to God. 13 And when it was day, he called his disciples; and he chose from them twelve, whom also he named apostles: 14 Simon, whom he also named Peter, and Andrew his brother, and [1]James and John, and Philip and Bartholomew, 15 and Matthew and Thomas, and [1]James, *the son* of Alphaeus, and Simon who was called the Zealot, 16 and Judas *the* [2]*son* of [1]James, and Judas Iscariot, who became a traitor;
[1] Some ancient authorities add *whom also he named apostles.* See Lk. 6. 13; comp. ch. 6. 30. [2] Some ancient authorities insert *and he appointed twelve.* [3] Or, *Jacob* [4] Or, *Zealot* See Lk. 6. 15; Acts 1. 13. [5] Or, *delivered him up* [6] Or, *home*	[1] Or, *Jacob* [2] Or, *brother.* See Jude 1.

Note 55. First steps toward an Organization.

1. Why launch an organization? It must be remembered that our Lord did not come to earth to win popular favor, or merely to perform cures on the sick and afflicted, or just to deliver the multitudes of His day from tyranny—either the political tyranny of the Romans or the religious tyranny of the scribes—or even to inaugurate a movement for the improvement of social conditions of His day. He came to accomplish redemption for sinning humanity—to accomplish it by dying in the place of sinners and victoriously rising from the dead in victory over the Devil, the instigator of all sin. He did plan to inaugurate a movement, but it would be a movement of proclamation of redemption, to be begun after the redemption activities should have been accomplished; that is, after He would die and rise from the dead.

But He could not make known to the motley multitude who followed Him the real purpose of His earthly life; nor, at this time, even to any of the growing number of His sincere disciples. So He determined to choose certain ones from the multitude of His disciples to whom He would commit leadership in proclaiming this redemption, and whom He would weld into a simple organization. Then He would so teach them that, at a later time, He could make known the nature of His mission on earth; and He would give them special training in dealing with the mass of sinful humanity, so that on His departure from the earth He might commit to them their own important mission.

98

2. **Probable movements of Jesus at this time.** We cannot know how long the sea-side campaign of the Lord Jesus continued. The vivid account in the passage from Mark in #51 impresses one as a summary of His labors for many days. No doubt He at length invited or challenged those who cared to do so, to go with Him to the summit of a mountain not too far away and to spend a night under the stars of the sky. Tradition has long identified this mountain as the Horns of Hattin, frequently spoken of as the "Mount of Beatituaes." Although there is no word in the gospel records to substantiate this tradition, modern travelers say that this "mountain" with its two summits and the plateau between them perfectly satisfies the conditions named by the Gospel writers, Matthew and Luke. Jesus Himself spent the night in prayer, surely in some secluded spot nearby, undoubtedly seeking the guidance of God the Father in the momentous choices which He knew He must make the next day. Early the next morning He called together the group of disciples who had accompanied Him, and from them He chose the twelve apostles. Afterward, He descended to a level place (possibly the plateau between the summits of Hattin), where, in the presence of an increased multitude that had pursued Him to this retreat, He delivered the Sermon on the Mount as a sort of ordination sermon for the apostles whom He had chosen.

3. **The Twelve listed.** Four lists of the apostles are found. Besides those by Mark and Luke in this section, Matthew gives one in connection with their being sent forth on a practice trip (Matt. 10: 2--4; #113), and Luke gives in Acts 1: 13 a list of the eleven who remained after the ascension. A study of these four lists will reveal that they were named in three groups of four in each group (except, of course, that in the last group of the list in Acts there are only three names, since Judas Iscariot had committed suicide). The same name is at the head of each group in all the lists, and the names of those in each group are the same, though the order for the names in the group varies. Thus, Simon Peter comes first in each of the lists, Philip fifth, and James son of Alpheus ninth. We do not know whether this arrangement had any significance or not, but it may indicate that during the time they went around with Jesus, He made Peter, Philip and James son of Alpheus kind of "squad leaders." Bartholomew was probably the same as Nathaniel (John 1: 45ff and 21: 2), and Judas, the brother of James, was the same as Thadeus or Lebbius. During the time Jesus was with them Peter, James son of Zebedee, and John seem to have formed a sort of inner circle, since on three occasions He took them for experiences which were denied to the others (##108, 133, 238).

4. **The Work of the Apostles.** Mark lists two purposes for which He chose the twelve: (1) That they might be with Him, and (2) that He might send them forth. And in this sending forth He was also to have two ends in view: (a) to preach and (b) to have authority to heal sicknesses and cast out devils. The benefits which He had in mind to impart to them during their association together were surely two-fold:

(a) From His teaching. For almost two years, they were to be constant companions of Jesus, the Master Teacher. They would hear the teachings that He directed toward others; and, especially during the last year of their association with Him, He would direct many lessons specifically to them. In particular, they were to learn of the higher standard of living which Jesus taught—higher than that required by the law of Moses, especially as the Scribes interpreted the law. Also, they would hear many things about the coming Kingdom and about His impending death and resurrection, which they would be able to understand only after those events took place. (b) From observation of His labors and an opportunity to follow His example. They were to be sent on practice tours during their period of tutorage, for which they would receive power to work miracles, and would be charged with responsibility of using it. He was getting ready to send them forth after He would be taken out of the world in order that they might preach the salvation which He, through His death and resurrection, was going to accomplish. Doubtless He purposed to make them conscious of the mighty power of God, on which they might call whenever the occasion arose.

(2) Delivering their ordination address, ##53-77

a. Occasion and place

#53

MATT. 5:1-2	LUKE 6:17-20a
	17 And he came down with them, and stood on a level place, and a great multitude of his disciples, and a great number of the people from all Judaea and Jerusalem, and the sea coast of Tyre and Sidon, who came to hear him, and to be healed of their diseases; 18 and they that were troubled with unclean spirits were healed.
1 And seeing the multitudes, he went up into the mountain: and when he had sat down, his disciples came unto him: 2 and he opened his mouth and taught them saying,	19 And all the multitude sought to touch him; for power came forth from him, and healed them all. 20 And he lifted up his eyes on his disciples, and said,

Note 56. The first chapter of the training of the apostles was their ordination sermon, the memorable address that we call the SERMON ON THE MOUNT. It was delivered primarily to them, but in the hearing of the multitude. In it is not much about the way of salvation, but a great deal about the standard of Christian living. Therefore we give it the theme: "The Standard of Righteousness in the Messiah's Kingdom." It is more law than gospel, but law as Jesus had in mind to "fulfill" the Mosaic Code (cf. Note 59). In it He set forth principles by which their labors at Kingdom propagation would succeed and warned them of evils which, if practiced, would impede such success.

It is noticed that this address is found with variations in Matthew and in Luke. Matthew has thirteen paragraphs not found in Luke as part of the "Sermon," but Luke has recorded many of these sayings as spoken at other times under different circumstances. And Luke has seven verses not found here in Matthew, though at least two of them

100

are found in that Gospel in another connection. But even in the face of these variations, I believe that we must conclude that the ordination address of the apostles included all this material, and that Jesus repeated some of it on other occasions.

b. The address:

THE SERMON ON THE MOUNT

The theme: The Standard of Righteousness in the Messiah's Kingdom

(The outline of these sections is independent of the outline of the book.)

I. INTRODUCTORY STATEMENT CONCERNING THE SUBJECTS OF THE KINGDOM, ##54—55

1. Some of their essential characteristics, notice the sources of their happiness and woes (the Beatitudes)

#54

MATT. 5:3-10	LUKE 6:20b-26
3 Blessed are the poor in spirit: for theirs is the kingdom of heaven. 4 ¹Blessed are they that mourn: for they shall be comforted. 5 Blessed are the meek: for they shall inherit the earth. 6 Blessed are they that hunger and thirst after righteousness: for they shall be filled. 7 Blessed are the merciful: for they shall obtain mercy. 8 Blessed are the pure in heart: for they shall see God. 9 Blessed are the peacemakers: for they shall be called sons of God. 10 Blessed are they that have been persecuted for righteousness' sake: for theirs is the kingdom of heaven. ¹ Some ancient authorities transpose ver. 4 and 5.	20b Blessed *are* ye poor: for yours is the kingdom of God. 21 Blessed *are* ye that hunger now: for ye shall be filled. Blessed *are* ye that weep now: for ye shall laugh. 22 Blessed are ye, when men shall hate you, and when they shall separate you *from their company,* and reproach you, and cast out your name as evil, for the Son of man's sake. 23 Rejoice in that day, and leap *for joy:* for behold, your reward is great in heaven; for in the same manner did their fathers unto the prophets. 24 But woe unto you that are rich! for ye have received your consolation. 25 Woe unto you, ye that are full now! for ye shall hunger. Woe *unto you,* ye that laugh now! for ye shall mourn and weep. 26 Woe *unto you,* when all men shall speak well of you! for in the same manner did their fathers to the false prophets.

Note 57. The Beatitudes in relation to the rest of the Sermon on the Mount. The verses of the foregoing section (Matt. 5: 3—10 and the parallel verses in Luke) are known as the Beatitudes, because in the Latin version of the Bible they begin with the word beati (happy). They set forth conditions of true and lasting happiness, or blessedness. These eight beatitudes, as they appear in Matthew, seem to set before us the main topics that are discussed in this memorable address, but the order is reversed. Thus, in verses 11--16 (#55) the blessedness promised to those persecuted for the cause of righteousness is made

101

specific in the experiences of the apostles; the peacemakers are described in verses 21--26 (#57) as those who are quick to make peace between themselves and their adversaries, who will themselves be reconciled to their brethren before offering their sacrifice; the pure in heart are seen in verses 27--37 (##58, 59) as those who spurn to look on a woman to lust after her, and accordingly are pure and faithful in deed and in speech; the merciful are described in verses 38--47 and the parallel passages in Luke (##60, 61) as the ones who do not demand the eye for an eye or the tooth for a tooth as was permitted by the Mosaic law, but will rather turn the other cheek or go the second mile. Those hungering and thirsting after righteousness certainly will insist on genuine righteousness and will not be satisfied with that done merely to be seen of men (Matt. 6: 1--18, ##63 --66). That the meek will inherit the earth was promised in Psalm 37: 11. Therefore, our Lord enjoined the apostles in Matt. 6: 19—34 (##67--68) not to live their lives laying up treasures on earth or worrying about even the necessities of life. In pronouncing a blessing on the mourning ones, Jesus did not mean to put a premium on "long-faced-ness," but in Matt. 7: 13--14 (#73) He did say literally that the gate and the road which lead to spiritual life are narrow and hard-pressed. True repentance involves genuine sorrow for one's guilt and his depraved condition. The ones poor in spirit are those who realize that they have no acceptable price to offer in the day of judgment in payment for entrance into the heavenly Kingdom. They are in contrast with those described in Matt. 7: 21-23 (#75) who thought to offer their service of prophesying, casting out demons, and doing many other works of like nature. It is true that other matters are included in the Sermon on the Mount, but the connection between the Beatitudes and the paragraphs which I have cited seems to be more than accidental.

Another feature observed about the Beatitudes in Matthew's list is that the first four set forth the conditions of coming to God for Salvation, and the last four some prerequisites of effective service to God. Thus, confession of one's poverty before God and contrition of heart are elements of repentance, while meekness, a willingness to conform one's will to the will of God,* and a desire for, and acceptance of, the promised righteousness of God (cf. Matt. 6: 33) are elements of faith. On the other hand, a merciful attitude toward one's fellowman—even toward those who have wronged him, and purity in thought and word and deed, and a disposition to live peaceably, and a willingness to endure persecution are necessary if one will be a successful herald of "the Kingdom of God and His righteousness.

*The Greek word is *praus,* which was used to describe horses that had been broken, to conform their actions to the will of their drivers, cf. Henry George Liddell and Robert Scott, *Greek English Lexicon* (New York: Harper and Brothers, publishers, 1858), p. 1232.

2. Their function and their responsibility
#55
MATT. 5:11-16

11 Blessed are ye when *men* shall reproach you, and persecute you, and say all manner of evil against you falsely, for my sake. 12 Rejoice, and be exceeding glad: for great is your reward in heaven: for so persecuted they the prophets that were before you.

13 Ye are the salt of the earth: but if the salt have lost its savor, wherewith shall it be salted? it is thenceforth good for nothing, but to be cast out and trodden under foot of men. 14 Ye are the light of the world. A city set on a hill cannot be hid. 15 Neither do *men* light a lamp, and put it under the bushel, but on the stand; and it shineth unto all that are in the house. 16. Even so let your light shine before men; that they may see your good works, and glorify your Father who is in heaven.

Note 58. Salt and light were two of the most important items of everyday life in Jesus' day—and in any day. No more telling metaphor, therefore, could have been used to describe the labors which He was entrusting to these apostles and to all the heralds of salvation who would come after them. Therefore they must at all costs guard against becoming like savorless salt or lamps under a bushel. This is the first of three times that Jesus used this parable of a lamp (cf. ##94, 153).

II. KINGDOM RIGHTEOUSNESS IN RELATION TO THE LAW OF MOSES, ##56—62

1. General statement of the higher or fuller standard of righteousness in the kingdom of God

#56
MATT. 5:17-20

17 Think not that I came to destroy the law or the prophets: I came not to destroy, but to fulfil. 18 For verily I say unto you, Till heaven and earth pass away, one jot or one tittle shall in no wise pass away from the law, till all things be accomplished. 19 Whosoever therefore shall break one of these least commandments, and shall teach men so, shall be called least in the kingdom of heaven: but whosoever shall do and teach them, he shall be called great in the kingdom of heaven. 20 For I say unto you, that except your righteousness shall exceed *the righteousness* of the scribes and Pharisees, ye shall in no wise enter into the kingdom of heaven.

Note 59. When in verse 17 Jesus said that He came to fulfill the law, He did not refer to His life of perfect conformity to the law so that His death for sinners would be a sin offering without blemish. That truth is undeniably taught elsewhere in the New Testament (e. g. II Cor. 5: 21; Rom. 10: 4, et al.); but here our Lord meant that He would bring the law of God, as revealed in the Old Testament, to its fullness—in other words, that He would fill up its requirements. Examples of what He meant are seen in the things He had to say in the subsequent paragraphs about violations of the laws against murder, adultery, and like sins. He showed that God's true law not only forbids the outward act, but it also warns against the impulses and intents of the heart which lead to open violations of the law. On the other hand, Jesus did assert in this connection (verse 20) that a righteousness exceeding that of the scrupulous scribes and Pharisees is necessary for entrance into the Kingdom of Heaven. He doubtless had reference in that statement to the righteousness of God, which He exhorted the people to seek after (Matt. 6: 33), and with which those hungering after righteousness will be satisfied (Matt. 5: 6). It is the perfect righteousness of Jesus, which is imputed to those who believe on Him, and which does involve a perfect fulfilling on His part of all the law's demands. (cf. Rom. 10: 4; II Cor. 5: 21; Phil 3: 9).

2. Some specific comparisons of Kingdom standard with Mosaic standards, ##57—61

(1) In regard to murder and its cause (cf. Exod. 20: 13; Deut. 5: 17), the sanctity of human life

#57

MATT. 5:21-26

21 Ye have heard that it was said to them of old time, [1]Thou shall not kill; and whosoever shall kill shall be in danger of the judgment: 22 but I say unto you, that every one who is angry with his brother [2]shall be in danger of the judgment; and whosoever shall say to his brother, [3]Raca, shall be in danger of the council; and whosoever shall say, [4]Thou fool, shall be in danger [5]of the [6]hell of fire. 23 If therefore thou art offering thy gift at the altar, and there rememberest that thy brother hath aught against thee, 24 leave there thy gift before the altar, and go thy way, first be reconciled to thy brother, and then come and offer thy gift. 25 Agree with thine adversary quickly, while thou art with him in the way; lest haply the adversary deliver thee to the judge, and the judge [7]deliver thee to the officer, and thou be cast into prison. 26 Verily I say unto thee, Thou shalt by no means come out thence, till thou have paid the last farthing.

[1] Ex. xx. 13; Dt. v. 17. [2] Many ancient authorities insert *without cause.*
[3] An expression of contempt. [4] Or, *Moreh*, a Hebrew expression of condemnation.
[5] Gr. *unto* or *into.* [6] Gr. *Gehenna of fire.* [7] Some ancient authorities omit *deliver thee.*

Note 60. Those who quickly make peace with their adversaries will "be called children of God," because in this they are like God. He took the initiative in making peace between Himself and a sinful world (cf. Rom. 5: 1, 8; Isa. 53: 5c).

(2) In regard to adultery and divorce (cf. Exod. 20:14; Deut. 5:18, 24:1), the sanctity of the human home.

#58

MATT. 5:27-32

27 Ye have heard that it was said, [1]Thou shalt not commit adultery: 28 but I say unto you, that every one that looketh on a woman to lust after her hath committed adultery with her already in his heart. 29 And if thy right eye causeth thee to stumble, pluck it out, and cast it from thee: for it is profitable for thee that one of thy members should perish, and not thy whole body be cast into [2]hell. 30 And if thy right hand causeth thee to stumble, cut it off, and cast it from thee: for it is profitable for thee that one of thy members should perish, and not thy whole body go into [2]hell. 31 It was said also, [4]Whosoever shall put away his wife, let him give her a writing of divorcement: 32 but I say unto you, that every one that putteth away his wife, saving for the cause of fornication, maketh her an adulteress: and whosoever shall marry her when she is put away committeth adultery.

[1] Ex. xx. 14; Dt. v. 18. [2] Gr. *Gehenna.* [3] Dt. xxiv. 1, 3.

Note 61. Did Jesus intend for the disciples to take literally the injunction about amputating those portions of the body which might be the occasion of offense, or of moral stumbling? In answer, we observe that we have no account of an instance when any of the disciples ever

104

lid so. Amputating portions of one's body would not change the con-
lition of his heart from which all sins spring (cf. Matt. 15: 19). What
Jesus meant to emphasize was surely that it is better for one to live
impaired physically than to be a willing victim of repeated temptation.
Notice that the warning about the offending eye is in the verse following
the one describing the lustful look. This warning was repeated in #139
(Matt. 18: 9; Mark 9: 43, 45, 47). Jesus meant that those in the Kingdom must break with evil at any cost. Failure to do so is evidence that
one has not repented of sin and therefore is still under condemnation of
eternal death.

The teaching of Jesus concerning divorce was repeated in fuller
form during the closing weeks of His ministry (cf. Matt. 19: 3–9;
Mark 10: 2–12; Luke 16: 18, #175, and Note 176).

(3) In regard to oaths (cf. Lev. 19:12; Num. 30:2; Deut. 23:21;
see also Isa. 66:1; Ps. 48:2), the sanctity of human speech

#59

MATT. 5:33-37

33 Again, ye have heard that it was said to them of old time, [1]Thou shalt not
forswear thyself, but shalt perform unto the Lord thine oaths: 34 but I say unto
you, Swear not at all; neither by the heaven, for it is the throne of God; 35 nor
by the earth, for it is the footstool of his feet; nor [2]by Jerusalem, for it is the city
of the great King. 36 Neither shalt thou swear by thy head, for thou canst not make
one hair white or black. 37 [3]But let your speech be, Yea, yea; Nay, nay: and whatsoever is more than these is of [4]the evil *one.*

[1] Lev. xix. 12; Num. xxx. 2; Dt. xxiii. 21.   [2] Or, *toward*
[3] Some ancient authorities read *But your speech shall be.*   [4] Or, *evil:* as in ver. 39; vi. 13.

Note 62. Jesus would have His followers, particularly the heralds
of His Kingdom, to tell the truth so consistently that they would not
need to resort to an oath to get people to believe them. He did not imply that Christians must refuse to "be put on oath" if civil authorities
demand it. On a later occasion, when Jesus Himself was "adjured" by
the High Priest (required to answer on oath) to tell if He was the Messiah,
He answered without raising an objection (Matt. 26: 63, #241). Certainly, however, He would condemn resorting to an oath unnecessarily
or thoughtlessly in order to reinforce one's speech. With this agrees
the exhortation of James, a half brother of Jesus, who became a leader
in the Jerusalem Church (James 5: 12).

(4) In regard to retaliation (cf. Ex. 21:24; Lev. 24:20; Deut.
19:21)

#60

MATT. 5:38-42

38 Ye have heard that it was said,
An [1]eye for an eye, and a tooth for a
tooth: 39 but I say unto you, Resist not
[2]him that is evil: but whosoever smiteth
thee on thy right cheek, turn to him the
other also. 40 And if any man would

[1] Ex. xxi. 24; Lev. xxiv. 20; Dt. xix. 21.
[2] Or, *evil*

LUKE 6:29-30

29 To him that smiteth thee on the
one cheek offer also the other; and from
him that taketh away thy cloak withhold
not thy coat also.

Matt. 5	Luke 6
go to law with thee, and take away thy coat, let him have thy cloak also. 41 And whosoever shall [3]compel thee to go one mile, go with him two. 42 Give to him that asketh thee, and from him that would borrow of thee turn not thou away. [3] Gr. *impress*.	30 Give to every one that asketh thee; and of him that taketh away thy .goods ask them not again.

Note 63. Did our Lord mean for His followers to take literally the matter of turning the other cheek? It may be noted that Jesus Himself did not literally do so when struck by an officer of the High Priest (John 18: 22--23, #240), nor did Paul under similar circumstances (Acts 23: 2--3). But even so, it is better to turn the other cheek literally than to seek revenge, or to be embroiled in a brawl. The Mosaic law permitted a m a n t o e x a c t vengeance (Exod. 21: 24; Lev. 24: 20; Deut. 19: 21); but Jesus commanded His disciples to forego that right.

(5) In regard to treatment of enemies (cf. Lev. 19: 18), the sanctity of human friendship

#61

MATT. 5:43-47	LUKE 6:27-28, 32-36
43 Ye have heard that it was said, [1]Thou shalt love thy neighbor, and hate thine enemy: 44 but I say unto you, Love your enemies, and pray for them that persecute you; 45 that ye may be sons of your Father who is in heaven: for he maketh his sun to rise on the evil and the good, and sendeth rain on the just and the unjust. 46 For. if ye love them that love you, what reward have ye? do not even the [2]publicans the same? 47 And if ye salute your brethren only, what do ye more *than others?* do not even the Gentiles the same? [1] Lev. xix. 18. [2] That is, *collectors or renters of Roman taxes.*	27 But I say unto you that hear, Love your enemies, do good to them that hate you, 28 bless them that curse you, pray for them that despitefully use you. 32 And if ye love them that love you, what thank have ye? for even sinners love those that love them. 33 And if ye do good to them that do good to you, what thank have ye? for even sinners do the same. 34 And if ye lend to them of whom ye hope to receive, what thank have ye? even sinners lend to sinners, to receive again as much. 35 But love your enemies, and do *them* good, and lend, [1]never despairing; and your reward shall be great, and ye shall be sons of the Most High: for he is kind toward the unthankful and evil. 36 Be ye merciful, even as your Father is merciful.

Note 64. It is noteworthy that our Lord complied literally with the instructions that He gave to the disciples in the foregoing section. When Peter, in a rash effort to protect his Lord, cut off the right ear of a member of the band that had come to arrest Him, Jesus not only rebuked Peter, but touched the man's ear and healed it (Luke 22: 51, #239). Also He prayed for forgiveness to be granted to those who were in the act of crucifying Him (Luke 23: 34, #251).

3. The highest possible goal set for kingdom righteousness
#62

MATT. 5:48

48 Ye therefore shall be perfect, as your heavenly Father is perfect.

Note 65. The foregoing verse is capable of either of three interpretations: (1) It may be a promise of the imputed perfection of the Saviour which is reckoned to every believer (cf. Note 59). (2) It may be a promise of the flawless perfection which His followers will experience in the end (cf. Rom. 8: 29; I John 3: 2). Jesus measured the Christian's final perfection by that of the Father; Paul and John measured by that of Jesus. If our Lord had this meaning in mind here, He certainly implied that assurance of future perfection should inspire the disciples to strive toward perfection now. (3) Most probably He meant to impress on the disciples that they must make unceasing effort to attain toward perfection of living. The followers of Jesus are not to be satisfied or complacent with wrong of any kind in their lives. To be sure, though it is not so stated in this verse, the power by which Christians are to strive toward this perfection is in the Holy Spirit who is given to be with them (cf. Rom. 8: 13).

III. KINGDOM RIGHTEOUSNESS IN RELATION TO PERSONAL RELIGION, ##63—66

1. A general statement
#63

MATT. 6:1

1 Take heed that ye do not your righteousness before men, to be seen of them: else ye have no reward with your Father who is in heaven.

Note 66. Observe that the foregoing verse in the American Standard Version reads "righteousness" instead of "alms," as in the King James Version. "Righteousness" is the literal translation of the word which appears in the oldest copies (manuscripts) of Matthew at this place. Righteousness is a general term of which almsgiving and prayer and fasting are specific examples. The Revised Standard has the word "piety,"* and Williams and Montgomery each have the words "good deeds."**

Jesus had promised to those who hunger and thirst after righteousness the satisfaction of their hunger (Matt. 5: 6). But the hungry soul will certainly not be satisfied with insincere righteousness, performed only or chiefly to be seen of men. This is at least one respect in which the righteousness of a Christian exceeds that of the scribes and Pharisees (cf. Matt. 5: 20, #56, and Note 59; also Matt. 23: 5).

*The Revised Standard Version of the New Testament (New York: Thomas Nelson and Son, 1946), ad loc.
**Charles B. Williams, The New Testament, A Translation in the Language of People (Chicago: The Moody Press, 1937) ad loc. Helen Barrett Montgomery, The New Testament in Modern English (Philadelphia: American Baptist Publications Society, 1924), ad loc.

2. Its application to alms-giving
#64
MATT. 6:2-4

2 When therefore thou doest alms, sound not a trumpet before thee, as the hypocrites do in the synagogues and in the streets, that they may have glory of men. Verily I say unto you, They have received their reward. 3 But when thou doest alms, let not thy left hand know what thy right hand doeth: 4 that thine alms may be in secret: and thy Father who seeth in secret shall recompense thee.

Note 67. Teachings of Jesus on Giving. Jesus surely did not mean that one must deliberately keep his gifts a secret; but in admonishing His disciples to give alms in secret, He certainly had in mind giving in sincerity, and not for show. He promised that the Heavenly Father who sees even in secret will reward such givers. Observe that He commanded the disciples to lay up such rewards from the Heavenly Father as treasures in Heaven (vs. 20, #67). More specifically He said in Luke 12:33 (#156) that those who sell their possessions in order to give alms would be providing treasures in Heaven. To the rich young ruler He definitely promised Heavenly treasures if that one would sell his possessions and distribute to the poor (#187). Our Lord commended the sacrificial giving on the part of the widow (#217); and in the parable of the Unjust Steward (#174) He assured His disciples that worldly possessions (mammon) may, by a benevolent use, be made to be friends, who will welcome the givers into the Heavenly home.

3. Its application to one's prayer life
#65
MATT. 6:5-15

5 And when ye pray, ye shall not be as the hypocrites: for they love to stand and pray in the synagogues and in the corners of the streets, that they may be seen of men. Verily I say unto you, they have received their reward. 6 But thou, when thou prayest, enter into thine inner chamber, and having shut thy door, pray to thy Father who is in secret, and thy Father who seeth in secret shall recompense thee. 7 And in praying use not vain repetitions, as the Gentiles do: for they think that they shall be heard for their much speaking. 8 Be not therefore like unto them: for [1]your Father knoweth what things ye have need of, before ye ask him. 9 After this manner therefore pray ye: Our Father who art in heaven, Hallowed be thy name. 10 Thy kingdom come. Thy will be done, as in heaven, so on earth. 11 Give us this day [2]our daily bread. 12 And forgive us our debts, as we also have forgiven our debtors. 13 And bring us not into temptation, but deliver us from [3]the evil one.[4] 14 For if ye forgive men their trespasses, your heavenly Father will also forgive you. 15 But if ye forgive not men their trespasses, neither will your Father forgive your trespasses.

[1] Some ancient authorities read God your Father.
[2] Gr. our bread for the coming day. Or, our needful bread.   [3] Or, evil.
[4] Many authorities, some ancient, but with variations, add For thine is the kingdom, and the power, and the glory, for ever. Amen.

Note 68. In the foregoing paragraph Jesus taught about prayer from four view-points: (1) The motive should be a sincere desire to experience communion with God—to lay our petitions before God or to express our appreciation for the blessings which we have received from Him. This is taught by contrast with the hypocritical practice of pretending to pray, while in reality one is merely seeking to attract attention to himself as a person of great piety (verses 5--6). (2) In manner

108

a prayer should be simple and direct rather than high-sounding and long-drawn-out (verses 7--8). Using words or phrases in prayers manifestly because they are customarily so used is vain repetition—so also is a too frequent calling upon God by the same name or title. (3) In a suggestive model He set forth in small compass and simple language the wide range of prayer (verses 9--13). (4) A merciful attitude on the part of a person at prayer, prompting him to forgive his debtors, would qualify him to ask for the mercies of God.

The "Lord's Prayer" was not given to be used as a ritual, but to serve as a model in guiding one in his prayer life. Its use as a ritual borders on the vain repetitions which Jesus forbade in verse 7. A simple outline of the model prayer which should help one to understand our Lord's ideal of prayer is as follows:

1. The approach (verse 9)
    (1) Reverent address
    (2) Humble adoration
2. Petitions
    (1) Altruistic - praying for the coming of the Kingdom (involving a supplication for blessings on the labors of those who strive to extend the spiritual Kingdom and a yearning for the appearance of the visible Kingdom)
    (2) Egoistic - involving four petitions for one's self
        a. Needful temporal prosperity (daily bread)
        b. Forgiveness of sins so that one can enjoy fellowship with God
        c. Providential guiding of one's life so as to avoid as many temptations as possible
        d. Victory over the temptations which one must encounter.
4. Its application to the practice of fasting (cf. Note 49).

#66

MATT. 6:16-18

16 Moreover when ye fast, be not, as the hypocrites, of a sad countenance: for they disfigure their faces, that they may be seen of men to fast. Verily I say unto you, They have received their reward. 17 But thou, when thou fastest, anoint thy head, and wash thy face; 18 that thou be not seen of men to fast, but of thy Father who is in secret: and thy Father, who seeth in secret, shall recompense thee.

IV. KINGDOM RIGHTEOUSNESS IN RELATION TO EARTHLY POSSESSIONS, ##67--68

1. Concerning ambitions for treasures

#67

MATT. 6:19-24

19 Lay not up for yourselves treasures upon the earth, where moth and rust consume, and where thieves ¹break through and steal: 20 but lay up for yourselves treasures in heaven, where neither moth nor rust doth consume, and where thieves do not ¹break through nor steal: 21 for where thy treasure is, there will thy heart be also. 22 The lamp of the body is the eye: if therefore thine eye be single, thy whole body shall be full of light. 23 But if thine eye be evil, thy whole body shall be full of darkness. If therefore the light that is in thee be darkness, how great is the darkness! 24 No man can serve two masters: for either he will hate the one,

¹ Gr. dig through.

109

and love the other; or else he will hold to one, and despise the other. Ye cannot serve God and mammon.

Note 69. The Lord Jesus sought to warn the heralds of salvation and the Kingdom of God against the "money heart." They should not seek to pile up earthly possessions at the expense of attention to, and labor in, the Kingdom of God. Earthly possessions have a tendency to steal away the heart of the Christian from his interests in God's Kingdom. Heavenly treasures are more lasting and more satisfactory. For other teachings of Jesus about heavenly treasures see Luke 12: 33—34; #156; 16: 9, #174; Matt. 19: 21, #187.

2. Concerning anxiety for necessities
#68

MATT. 6:25-34

25 Therefore I say unto you, Be not anxious for your life, what ye shall eat, or what ye shall drink; nor yet for your body, what ye shall put on. Is not the life more than the food, and the body than the raiment? 26 Behold the birds of the heaven, that they sow not, neither do they reap, nor gather into barns; and your heavenly Father feedeth them. Are not ye of much more value than they? 27 And which of you by being anxious can add one cubit unto [1]the measure of his life? 28 And why are ye anxious concerning raiment? Consider the lilies of the field, how they grow; they toil not, neither do they spin: 29 yet I say unto you, that even Solomon in all his glory was not arrayed like one of these. 30 But if God doth so clothe the grass of the field, which to-day is, and to-morrow is cast into the oven, *shall he* not much more *clothe* you, O ye of little faith? 31 Be not therefore anxious, saying, What shall we eat? or, What shall we drink? or, Wherewithal shall be we clothed? 32 For after all these things do the Gentiles seek; for your heavenly Father knoweth that ye have need of all these things. 33 But seek ye first his kingdom, and his righteousness; and all these things shall be added unto you. 34 Be not therefore anxious for the morrow: for the morrow will be anxious for itself. Sufficient unto the day is the evil thereof.

[1] Or, *his stature.*

Note 70. Our Lord says to those dedicated to the propagation of His Gospel that anxiety over temporal necessities is:

1. Unnecessary, because (arguing from the lesser to the greater), since God supplies food for fowls and raiment for flowers, He will certainly supply the needs of His servants (verses 26, 28--30).

2. Unavailing, because just as being anxious will not add a measure to one's stature, it will not produce any other needful benefit (verse 27).

3. Unseemly, because to the Christian, life should mean more than food, and the body more than an object for adornment. Moreover, by being anxious about these matters the Christian puts himself in a class with the unevangelized heathen peoples (verses 25, 32).

V. KINGDOM RIGHTEOUSNESS IN RELATION TO SOCIAL BEHAVIOR, ##69--72
1. Concerning a censorious attitude toward others
#69

MATT. 7:1-5	LUKE 6:37-42
1 Judge not, that ye be not judged.	37 And judge not, and ye shall not

Matt. 7

2 For with what judgment ye judge, ye shall be judged: and with what measure ye mete, it shall be measured unto you.

3 And why beholdest thou the mote that is in thy brother's eye, but considerest not the beam that is in thine own eye? 4 Or how wilt thou say to thy brother, Let me cast out the mote out of thine eye; and lo, the beam is in thine own eye? 5 Thou hypocrite, cast out first the beam out of thine own eye; and then shalt thou see clearly to cast out the mote out of thy brother's eye.

Luke 6

be judged: and condemn not, and ye shall not be condemned: release, and ye shall be released: 38 give, and it shall be given unto you; good measure, pressed down, shaken together, running over, shall they give into your bosom. For with what measure ye mete it shall be measured to you again.

39 And he spake also a parable unto them, Can the blind guide the blind? shall they not both fall into a pit? 40 The disciple is not above his teacher: but every one when he is perfected shall be as his teacher. 41 And why beholdest thou the mote that is in thy brother's eye, but considerest not the beam that is in thine own eye? 42 Or how canst thou say to thy brother, Brother, let me cast out the mote that is in thine eye, when thou thyself beholdest not the beam that is in thine own eye? Thou hypocrite, cast out first the beam out of thine own eye, and then shalt thou see clearly to cast out the mote that is in thy brother's eye.

Note 71. Did Jesus ever exaggerate? Did He ever make His hearers laugh? Certainly He never sought to deceive anyone about anything, but in this passage He certainly did use extreme language to impress His audience, likely amusing them. The beam mentioned was a timber for the support of the roof of a house, certainly too large an object to be in one's eye. Other examples of such usage are Matthew 19: 24 (#188); 23: 24 (#215); and probably Luke 14: 26 (#170).

The giving referred to in Luke 6:38 certainly was more than the giving of money (though that was included); it involved the giving of love and service as well.

2. Concerning wise employment of endowments and opportunities

#70
MATT. 7:6

6 Give not that which is holy unto the dogs, neither cast your pearls before the swine, lest haply they trample them under their feet, and turn and rend you.

Note 72. According to the usual interpretation, the foregoing verse is an admonition not to waste one's labors giving the gospel message to unlikely or impossible prospects. But undoubtedly Jesus taught in the Parable of the Sower that the gospel sowers are to sow the seed on all types of soil, the wayside, the stony ground, and the thorny ground as well as the good ground (##90, 92, Note 95). Surely what Jesus meant to teach in the metaphor was that His servants should not cast the pearls of their holy endowments and opportunities before the swine of indulgence and self-glorification. As chosen disciples of His they enjoyed holy privileges which must not be given to the dogs of greed and self-glory.

111

3. Illustrated in the democracy of prayer and God's wisdom in answering it

#71

MATT. 7:7-11

7 Ask, and it shall be given you; seek, and ye shall find; knock, and it shall be opened unto you: 8 for every one that asketh receiveth; and he that seeketh findeth; and to him that knocketh it shall be opened. 9 Or what man is there of you, who, if his son shall ask him for a loaf, .will give him a stone; 10 or if he shall ask for a fish, will give him a serpent? 11 If ye then, being evil, know how to give good gifts unto your children, how much more shall your Father who is in heaven give good things to them that ask him?

4. The "Golden Rule" an all-inclusive social principle

#72

MATT. 7:12	LUKE 6:31
12 All things therefore whatsoever ye would that men should do unto you, even so do ye also unto them: for this is the law and the prophets.	31 And as ye would that men should do to you, do ye also to them likewise.

VI. TRUE KINGDOM RIGHTEOUSNESS CONTRASTED WITH COUNTERFEIT, ##73—77

1. As to the effort required

#73

MATT. 7:13-14

13 Enter ye in by the narrow gate: for wide [1] is the gate, and broad is the way, that leadeth to destruction, and many are they that enter in thereby. 14 [2] For narrow is the gate, and straitened the way, that leadeth unto life, and few are they that find it.

[1] Some ancient authorities omit *is the gate.*
[2] Many ancient authorities read *How narrow is the gate, &c.*

Note 73. Notice that the word describing the gate into eternal life is "strait," which means narrow, not "straight," which means not crooked. Verse 14 literally translated would read, "narrow the gate, and hard-pressed the road leading away into life, and few are the ones finding it." Indeed it is found only by contrition of heart and true repentence on the part of a sinner. We wonder if Jesus had reference to this state of mind when He spoke the second Beatitude, "Blessed are they that mourn..." (Matt. 5: 4).

2. As to the results produced

#74

MATT. 7:15-20	LUKE 6:43-45
15 Beware of false prophets, who come to you in sheep's clothing, but inwardly are ravening wolves. 16 By their fruits ye shall know them. Do *men* gather grapes of thorns, or figs of thistles? 17 Even so every good tree bringeth forth good fruit; but the corrupt tree bringeth forth evil fruit. 18 A good tree cannot bring forth evil fruit, neither can a corrupt tree bring forth good fruit. 19 Every tree that bringeth not forth good fruit is hewn down, and	43 For there is no good tree that bringeth forth corrupt fruit; nor again a corrupt tree that bringeth forth good fruit. 44 For each tree is known by its own fruit. For of thorns men do not gather figs, nor of a bramble bush gather they grapes. 45 The good man out of the

Matt. 7

cast into the fire. 20 Therefore by their fruits ye shall know them.

Luke 6

good treasure of his heart bringeth forth that which is good; and the evil *man* out of the evil *treasure* bringeth forth that which is evil: for out of the abundance of the heart his mouth speaketh.

Note 74. Those whom Jesus compared to wolves in sheep's clothing are surely those who in their teaching and preaching mix philosophies of men with the God-given gospel message, as well as those who compromise with evil in their behavior. Our Lord warns His chosen heralds of salvation and of the Kingdom of God against entering into partnership with such teachers as fellow-workers. They are false prophets, and in the end the fruits of their labors will be like thorns and thistles.

3. As to the destiny attained
#75
MATT. 7:21-23

21 Not every one that saith unto me, Lord, Lord, shall enter into the kingdom of heaven; but he that doeth the will of my Father who is in heaven. 22 Many will say to me in that day, Lord, Lord, did we not prophesy by thy name, and by thy name cast out demons, and by thy name do many [1]mighty works? 23 And then will I profess unto them, I never knew you: depart from me, ye that work iniquity.
[1] Gr. *powers.*

Note 75. The paupers in spiritual things (cf. Matt. 5: 3). Having prophesied or cast out demons or done many mighty works will not buy a ticket into the glorious visible Kingdom which will be manifest "in that day." Therefore, "Blessed are the poor in spirit." A sinner saved by grace does not offer any works of his own as a price for entrance; others offer a wealth of mighty works, but it is a counterfeit wealth.

4. The contrast illustrated by the parable of The Two Builders
#76

MATT. 7:24-27

24 Every one therefore that heareth these words of mine, and doeth them, shall be likened unto a wise man, who built his house upon the rock: 25 and the rain descended, and the floods came, and the winds blew, and beat upon that house; and it fell not: for it was founded upon the rock. 26 And every one that heareth these words of mine, and doeth them not, shall be likened unto a foolish man, who built his house upon the sand: 27 and the rain descended, and the floods came, and the winds blew, and smote upon that house; and it fell: and great was the fall thereof.

LUKE 6:46-49

46 And why call ye me, Lord, Lord, and do not the things which I say? 47 Every one that cometh unto me, and heareth my words, and doeth them, I will show you to whom he is like: 48 he is like a man building a house, who digged and went deep, and laid a foundation upon the rock: and when a flood arose, the stream brake against that house, and could not shake it: [1]because it had been well builded. 49 But he that [2]heareth, and [3]doeth not, is like a man that built a house upon the earth without a foundation; against which the stream brake, and straightway it fell in; and the ruin of that house was great.
[1] Many ancient authorities read *for it had been founded upon the rocks:* as in Mt. 7. 25.
[2] Gr. *heard.*　　　[3] Gr. *did not.*

113

Note 76. In the parable of the Two Builders, Jesus warned the newly chosen apostles, whom He was ordaining to be heralds of salvation and of participation in His Kingdom, that to disregard the things He had said in this great discourse would endanger the success of their labors like disregarding the importance of a foundation endangers the lasting usefulness of a house. The same may also be said of those who disregard any of the words of Jesus, as these words are relayed to them by His messengers.

(At this point the outline of Period Three is resumed, see p. 101).

c. Effect of the address on the hearers
#77
MATT. 7:28 — 8:1

28 And it came to pass, when Jesus had finished these words, the multitude were astonished at his teaching: 29 for he taught them as *one* having authority and not as their scribes.

1 And when he was come down from the mountain, great multitudes followed him.

Note 77. The people of Capernaum had said the same thing about His teaching in their synagogue (cf. Mark 1: 22, #37).

3. In the city, healing a centurion's servant
#78

MATT. 8:5-13

5 And when he was entered into Capernaum, there came unto him a centurion, beseeching him, 6 and saying, Lord, my [1]servant lieth in the house sick of the palsy, grievously tormented. 7 And he saith unto him, I will come and heal him. 8 And the centurion answered and said, Lord, I am not [2]worthy that thou shouldest come under my roof; but only say [3]the word, and my [1]servant shall be healed. 9 For I also am a man [4]under authority, having under myself soldiers: and I say to this one, Go, and he goeth; and to another, Come, and he cometh; and to my [5]servant, Do this, and he doeth it. 10 And when Jesus heard it, he marvelled, and said to them that followed, Verily I say unto you, [6]I have not found so great faith, no, not in Israel. 11 And I say unto you, that many shall come from the east and the west, and shall [7]sit down with Abraham, and Isaac, and Jacob, in the kingdom of heaven: 12 but the sons of the kingdom shall be cast forth into the outer darkness: there shall be the weeping and the gnashing of teeth.

[1] Or, *boy*   [2] Gr. *sufficient.*
[3] Gr. *with a word.*
[4] Some ancient authorities insert *set:* as in Lk. 7. 8.   [5] Gr. *bondservant.*
[6] Many ancient authorities read *With no man in Israel have I found so great faith.*
[7] Gr. *recline.*

LUKE 7:1-10

1 After he had ended all his sayings in the ears of the people, he entered into Capernaum.

2 And a certain centurion's [1]servant, who was [2]dear unto him, was sick and at the point of death. 3 And when he heard concerning Jesus, he sent unto him elders of the Jews, asking him that he would come and save his [1]servant. 4 And they, when they came to Jesus, besought him earnestly, saying, He is worthy that thou shouldst do this for him; 5 for he loveth our nation, and himself built us our synagogue. 6 And Jesus went with them. And when he was now not far from the house, the centurion sent friends to him, saying unto him, Lord, trouble not thyself; for I am not [3]worthy that thou shouldest come under my roof: 7 wherefore neither thought I myself worthy to come unto thee: but say [4]the word, and my [5]servant shall be healed. 8 For I also am a man set under authority, having under myself soldiers: and I say to this one, Go, and he goeth; and to another, Come, and he cometh; and to my [1]servant, Do this, and he doeth it. 9 And when Jesus heard these things, he marvelled at him, and turned

[1] Gr. *bondservant.*
[2] Or, *precious to him* Or, *honorable with him*
[3] Gr. *sufficient.*
[4] Gr. *with a word.*   [5] Or, *boy*

114

Matt. 8 | Luke 7

Matt. 8	Luke 7
13 And Jesus said unto the centurion, Go thy way; as thou hast believed, *so* be it done unto thee. And the ¹servant was healed in that hour. ¹ Or, *boy*	and said unto the multitudes that follow-ed him, I say unto you, I have not found so great faith, no, not in Israel. 10 And they that were sent, returning to the house, found the ¹servant whole. ¹ Gr. *bondservant.*

Note 78. Healing the servant of the Roman centurion was the second instance of healing in absentia in the labors of the Lord Jesus (cf. #34). There will be two more (##124, 181). The miracle suggests three divine attributes: (1) omnipotence seen in the power to perform the cure, (2) omnipresence suggested by His operating beyond His physical presence, (3) goodness in His concern for other races besides the Jews. The humanity of Jesus also is evident in His marvelling, or being surprised at the centurion's faith. This is the first two times when this was said about Jesus (cf. Mark 6:6, #111).

4. Touring the country, (with the twelve disciples, second tour of Galilee), ##79—85

Note 79. The Second Tour of Galilee. On the "First Tour of Galilee" (#40) our Lord was accompanied by the four fishermen—Andrew and Simon Peter, James and John. Others (possibly Philip and Nathaniel) may have joined the company before the first tour was finished. On the "Second tour of Galilee" He took with Him the newly chosen apostles (Luke 8:1, #85). After choosing those to whom He would entrust the fruits of the work which He was doing and of the sacrifice which He had in mind to make, it was natural that He should set about to train them; and the first step in their training after their ordination sermon was to have them accompany Him on a tour of the country. Thus they would hear what He said to the people and see the miracles that He performed. This was a trip of observation; the practice trip would come later—and their main work still later.

(1) At Nain, raising the widow's son

#79

LUKE 7:11-17

11 And it came to pass ¹soon afterwards, that he went to a city called Nain; and his disciples went with him, and a great multitude. 12 Now when he drew near to the gate of the city, behold, there was carried out one that was dead, the only son of his mother, and she was a widow: and much people of the city was with her. 13 And when the Lord saw her, he had compassion on her, and said unto her, Weep not. 14 And he came nigh and touched the bier: and the bearers stood still. And he said, Young man, I say unto thee, Arise. 15 And he that was dead sat up, and began to speak. And he gave him to his mother. 16 And fear took hold on all: and they glorified God, saying, A great prophet is arisen among us: and, God hath visited his people. 17 And this report went forth concerning him in the whole of Judaea, and all the region round about.
¹ Many ancient authorities read *on the next day.*

Note 80. This was the first of three occasions when Jesus raised a dead person to life (cf. ##108, 178). Such miracles had been performed in Old Testament times by Elijah and Elisha (I Kings 17:17--24;

II Kings 4: 32–37); and, after the ascension of Jesus, by Peter and Paul (Acts 9: 26–41; 20: 9–12). It was surely regarded as a more wonderful work than healing the sick, but it was not so great as the resurrection of Jesus Himself from the dead. All those whom He and the others brought back to life died again (though there is no record of when or how they died the second time), but Jesus was raised to be alive forever (cf. Rev. 1:18).

(2) Replying to the messengers from John the Baptist ##80—83
a. The inquiry and answer
#80

MATT. 11:2-6	LUKE 7:18-23
2 Now when John heard in the prison the works of the Christ, he sent by his disciples 3 and said unto him, Art thou he that cometh, or look we for another? 4 And Jesus answered and said unto them, Go and tell John the things which ye hear and see: 5 the blind receive their sight, and the lame walk, the lepers are cleansed, and the deaf hear, and the dead are raised up, and the poor have ¹good tidings preached to them. 6 And blessed is he, whosoever shall find no occasion of stumbling in me. ¹ Or, *the gospel*	18 And the disciples of John told him of all these things. 19 And John calling unto him ¹two of his disciples sent them to the Lord, saying, Art thou he that cometh, or look we for another? 20 And when the men were come unto him, they said, John the Baptist hath sent us unto thee, saying, Art thou he that cometh, or look we for another? 21 In that hour he cured many of diseases and ²plagues and evil spirits; and on many that were blind he bestowed sight. 22 And he answered and said unto them, Go and tell John the things which ye have seen and heard; the blind receive their sight, the lame walk, the lepers are cleansed, and the deaf hear, the dead are raised up, the poor have ³good tidings preached to them. 23 And blessed is he, whosoever shall find no occasion of stumbling in me. ¹ Gr. *certain two.* ² Gr. *scourges.* ³ Or, *the gospel*

Note 81. Why did John question the Messiahship of Jesus? After he had witnessed the sign which the Lord had given him (John 1: 33, #21), and after he had identified Jesus as the one greater than he who would come after him, why would he send these disciples with their inquiry?

The imprisonment of John, which was related in #28, had by this time most certainly lasted several months. The place of his confinement was most probably Machaerus, east of the Dead Sea, where the palace of Herod Antipas was located. Very probably he expected Jesus to hasten to his aid, miraculously to set him free from prison, and to visit punishment on Herod. He may have been impatient because Jesus had not yet begun, with fan in hand, thoroughly to purge the world's threshing floor—or even national Israel's, nor had the ax, which he had declared to be at the root of the trees, cut down any of them bringing forth the fruit of wickedness. Like the disciples of Jesus, He apparently was expecting an immediate appearance of the visible Kingdom.

In the reply of Jesus to this inquiry, He told these messengers to testify of the indisputable evidences of His divine mission and person which they had seen.

b. Eulogy of John
#81

<table>
<tr><td>

MATT. 11:7-15

7 And as these went their way, Jesus began to say unto the multitudes concerning John, What went ye out into the wilderness to behold? a reed shaken with the wind? 8 But what went ye out to see? a man clothed in soft *raiment?* Behold, they that wear soft *raiment* are in kings' houses. 9 ¹But wherefore went ye out? to see a prophet? Yea, I say unto you, and much more than a prophet. 10 This is he, of whom it is written.
²Behold, I send my messenger before thy face,
Who shall prepare thy way before thee.
11 Verily I say unto you, Among them that are born of women there hath not arisen a greater than John the Baptist: yet he that is ³but little in the kingdom of heaven is greater than he. 12 And from the days of John the Baptist until now the kingdom of heaven suffereth violence, and men of violence take it by force. 13 For all the prophets and the law prophesied until John. 14 And if ye are willing to receive ⁴it, this is Elijah, that is to come. 15 He that hath ears ⁵to hear, let him hear.
¹ Many ancient authorities read *But what went ye out to see? a prophet?* ² Mal. iii. 1.
³ Gr. *lesser.* ⁴ Or, *him.*
⁵ Some ancient authorities omit *to hear.*

</td><td>

LUKE 7:24-30

24 And when the messengers of John were departed, he began to say unto the multitudes concerning John, What went ye out into the wilderness to behold? a reed shaken with the wind? 25 But what went ye out to see? a man clothed in soft raiment? Behold, they that are gorgeously apparelled, and live delicately, are in kings' courts. 26 But what went ye out to see? a prophet? Yea, I say unto you, and much more than a prophet. 27 This is he of whom it is written,
¹Behold, I send my messenger before thy face,
Who shall prepare thy way before thee.
28 I say unto you, Among them that are born of women there is none greater than John: yet he that is ²but little in the kingdom of God is greater than he. 29 And all the people when they heard, and the ³publicans, justified God, ⁴being baptized with the baptism of John. 30 But the Pharisees and the lawyers rejected for themselves the counsel of God, ⁵being not baptized of him.
¹ Mal. iii. 1. ² Gr. *lesser.*
³ See marginal note on ch. 3. 12.
⁴ Or, *having been* ⁵ Or, *not having been*

</td></tr>
</table>

Note 82. Jesus declared His appreciation of John in impressive terms: (1) In spite of the question that John had raised about Jesus, he was no mere "reed shaken by the wind," any more than he was one clothed in soft garments. (2) He was a prophet and more than a prophet. (3) He was the messenger sent before the face of God's Anointed; he was that Elijah who was scheduled to come (cf. Mal. 3:1 and 4:5). To the Jerusalem deputation John had denied that he was Elijah personally come back to earth or one of the prophets risen from the dead (cf. Note 22). Jesus, of course, did not identify John literally with these Old Testament characters, but He affirmed that the prophecies in Malachi were fulfilled in him. And He asserted that among the prophets, there had not arisen one greater than John. Among the prophets up to John's day, he had the most vital message for the world—that the Kingdom of God was near at hand, and the most momentous mission—that of introducing to the world the King of the Kingdom, who was anointed of God, even God's Son. But what about the assertion that "he that is least in the Kingdom of Heaven is greater than John the Baptist"? If the least in the Kingdom is greater than John, the only logical conclusion

possible is that although John the Baptist was the first to herald the approach of the Kingdom of Heaven, he was not himself in the Kingdom in the same way as were the disciples of Jesus. His relation to God was similar to that of the saints of Old Testament times. Moreover, John's prophetic message to sinners, like that of Old Testament prophets, was a stern warning to repent; but it did not contain the gospel, or good news, of atonement for sin in the death of Jesus or of the glorious victory of His resurrection. But it is the privilege of the humblest Christian to announce this inspiring gospel. A Christian witnessing for Jesus is therefore greater than John the Baptist in prophetic opportunity (cf. Matt. 13: 17, #91).

c. Rebuking the generation of unbelievers
#82

MATT. 11:16-24

16 But whereunto shall I liken this generation? It is like unto children sitting in the marketplaces, who call unto their fellows 17 and say, We piped unto you, and ye did not dance; we wailed, and ye did not [1]mourn. 18 For John came neither eating nor drinking, and they say, He hath a demon. 19 The Son of man came eating and drinking, and they say, Behold, a gluttonous man and a winebibber, a friend of [2]publicans and sinners! And wisdom [3]is justified by her [4]works.

20 Then began he to upbraid the cities wherein most of his [5]mighty works were done, because they repented not. 21 Woe unto thee, Chorazin! woe unto thee, Bethsaida! for if the [5]mighty works had been done in Tyre and Sidon which· were done in you, they would have repented long ago in sackcloth and ashes. 22 But I say unto you, it shall be more tolerable for Tyre and Sidon in the day of judgment, than for you. 23 And thou, Capernaum, shalt thou be exalted unto heaven? thou shalt [6]go down unto Hades: for if the [5]mighty works had been done in Sodom which were done in thee, it would have remained until this day. 24 But I say unto you that it shall be more tolerable for the land of Sodom in the day of judgment, than for thee.

[1] Gr. beat the breast.
[2] See marginal note on ch. 5. 46.   [3] Or, was
[4] Many ancient authorities read children: as in Lk. 7. 35.   [5] Gr. powers.
[6] Many ancient authorities read be brought down.

LUKE 7:31-35

31 Whereunto then shall I liken the men of this generation, and to what are they like? 32 They are like unto children that sit in the marketplace, and call one to another; who say, We piped unto you, and ye did not dance; we wailed, and ye did not weep. 33 For John the Baptist is come eating no bread nor drinking wine; and ye say, He hath a demon. 34 The Son of man is come eating and drinking; and ye say, Behold, a gluttonous man, and a winebibber, a friend of [1]publicans and sinners! 35 And wisdom [2]is justified of all her children.

[1] See marginal note on ch. 3. 12.   [2] Or, was

Note 83. John and Jesus were very different in temperament and in method of presenting the coming Messianic Kingdom. But each of them attracted multitudes of hearers. The crowds would gather to hear John preach, but evidently the larger part did not repent; and throngs

118

came to hear Jesus and to see His miracles, but comparatively few of those would commit themselves to Him and His way of life. Jesus likened these multitudes to children in the market place who did not want to play with the other children. They would not respond to piping for a jolly game or to mourning for a sad one. Because, therefore, the people of Galilee would not repent, He pronounced the woes on the cities of that district which had been given the greatest opportunity. Observe that Jesus describes the judgment of God as taking into account an individual's opportunities in this life. Note that Luke does not record the woes in this connection, but he does record them as being spoken early in the Judaean ministry after Jesus had departed from the Galilean cities of opportunity never to return (#148).

d. The Universal invitation
#83
MATT. 11:25-30

25 At that season Jesus answered and said, I [1]thank thee, O Father, Lord of heaven and earth, that thou didst hide these things from the wise and understanding, and didst reveal them unto babes: 26 yea, Father, [2]for so it was well-pleasing in thy sight. 27 All things have been delivered unto me of my Father: and no one knoweth the Son, save the Father; neither doth any know the Father, save the Son, and he to whomsoever the Son willeth to reveal *him*. 28 Come unto me, all ye that labor and are heavy laden, and I will give you rest. 29 Take my yoke upon you, and learn of me; for I am meek and lowly in heart: and ye shall find rest unto your souls. 30 For my yoke is easy, and my burden is light.

[1] Or, *praise*.   [2] Or, *that*

Note 84. Did Jesus utter verse 25 above as an explanation of why so few had repented for John or for Himself? At any rate the universal invitation is for those who know themselves to be "babes" (cf. Luke 7: 29--30, #81).

(3) Dining with a Pharisee, being annointed by a sinful woman
#84
LUKE 7:36-50

36 And one of the Pharisees desired him that he would eat with him. And he entered into the Pharisee's house, and [1]sat down to meat. 37 And behold, a woman who was in the city, a sinner; and when she knew that he was [2]sitting at meat in the Pharisee's house, she brought [3]an alabaster cruse of ointment, 38 and standing behind at his feet, weeping, she began to wet his feet with her tears, and wiped them with the hair of her head, and [4]kissed his feet, and anointed them with the ointment. 39 Now when the Pharisee that had bidden him saw it, he spake within himself, saying, This man, if he were [5]a prophet, would have perceived who and what manner of woman this is that toucheth him, that she is a sinner. 40 And Jesus answering said unto him, Simon, I have somewhat to say unto thee. And he saith, Teacher, say on. 41 A certain lender had two debtors: the one owed five hundred [6]shillings, and the other fifty. 42 When they had not *wherewith* to pay, he forgave them both. Which of them therefore will love him most? 43 Simon answered and said, He, I suppose, to whom he forgave the most. And he said unto him, Thou hast rightly judged. 44 And turning to the woman, he said unto Simon, Seest thou this woman? I entered into thy house, thou gavest me no water for my feet: but she hath wetted my feet with her tears, and wiped them with her hair. 45 Thou gavest me no kiss: but she, since the time I came in, hath not

[1] Or, *reclined at table*   [2] Or, *reclining at table*   [3] Or, *a flask*   [4] Gr. *kissed much*
[5] Some ancient authorities read *the prophet*. See Jn. 1. 21, 25.
[6] The word in the Greek denotes a coin worth about eight pence half-penny, or nearly seventeen cents.

119

ceased to [7]kiss my feet. 46 My head with oil thou didst not anoint: but she hath anointed my feet with ointment. 47 Wherefore I say unto thee, Her sins, which are many, are forgiven; for she loved much: but to whom little is forgiven, *the same* loveth little. 48 And he said unto her, Thy sins are forgiven. 49 And they that [8]sat at meat with him began to say [9]within themselves, Who is this that even forgiveth sins? 50 And he said unto the woman, Thy faith hath saved thee; go in peace.

[7] Gr. *kiss much*   [8] Gr. *reclined.*   [9] Or, *among*

Note 85. The concern of Jesus for all classes of people may be observed in His willingness to dine both with the publicans and the Pharisees, the two groups furthest apart in the Jewish social order of that day. Three times He ate with publicans and was criticised for so doing (##45, 171, 193), and three times He dined with Pharisees (see ##154 and 168 for the other two). Without doubt it was to publicans and to the sinners like the woman of this section that Jesus referred as "babes" in #83 while the Pharisees were the "wise and prudent."

The identity of the sinful woman who anointed Jesus in the home of the Pharisee is unknown. There is no evidence that she was Mary Magdalene, although she is mentioned for the first time in the next section. This anointing is certainly not to be confused with the anointing by Mary of Bethany during the last week of His earthly life (#196).

Observe how Jesus answered the criticism in the mind of the Pharisee by revealing that He not only knew the character of the woman, but He knew also what was in the Pharisee's mind. And by means of the parable of The Two Debtors He both explained the action of the woman and set forth His attitude toward all penitent sinners.

(4) The second tour completed
#85
LUKE 8:1-3

1 And it came to pass soon afterwards, that he went about through cities and villages, preaching and bringing the [1]good tidings of the kingdom of God, and with him the twelve, 2 and certain women who had been healed of evil spirits and infirmities: Mary that was called Magdalene, from whom seven demons had gone out, 3 and Joanna the wife of Chuzas Herod's steward, and Susanna, and many others, who ministered unto [2]them of their substance.

[1] Or, *gospel*   [2] Many ancient authorities read *him.*

III. Increasing opposition, ##86–111

Note 86. Increasing Opposition. The increasing multitudes that were following Jesus naturally intensified the jealousy of His old enemies—the scribes from Jerusalem (cf. John 2: 18, #25; Luke 5: 17, #44; and Mark 3: 22, #87). And as we observed in Note 83, the multitudes themselves were not altogether sympathetic with Jesus and the way of life which He advocated. They came either to bring their afflicted loved ones and acquaintances for Jesus to heal or out of idle curiosity to hear what He said or see His miracles, and probably by this time His enemies were beginning to turn the sentiment of the crowds against Him.

1. Its manifestations (from three sources), ##86–89

(1) Alarm of some of His "friends" and their effort to take Him from before the public

#86
MARK 3:19b-21

19b And he cometh [1]into a house. 20 And the multitude cometh together again, so that they could not so much as eat bread. 21 And when his friends heard it, they went out to lay hold on him: for they said, He is beside himself.

[1] Or, *home*

Note 87. With the increased activities of the enemies of our Lord, and with His own selfless devotion to His work, it is not surprising that some of His "friends" began to fear for His safety and even for His sanity. And they wanted to take Him away by force, probably for a period of enforced rest, or possibly to silence Him until the determined opposition of the Jerusalem scribes should subside somewhat. This was probably what the enemies hoped would happen, but it did not deter Him from His labors, because these self-styled friends never did accomplish their purpose.

(2) Actions of His open enemies, ##87—88
a. Effort to discredit Him before the people by charging that His power over demons is the power of "Beelzebub"

#87

MATT. 12:22-37

22 Then was brought unto him [1]one possessed with a demon, blind and dumb: and he healed him, insomuch that the dumb man spake and saw. 23 And all the multitudes were amazed, and said, Can this be the son of David? 24 But when the Pharisees heard it, they said, This man doth not cast out demons, but [2]by [3]Beelzebub the prince of the demons. 25 And knowing their thoughts he said unto them, Every kingdom divided against itself is brought to desolation; and every city or house divided against itself shall not stand: 26 and if Satan casteth out Satan, he is divided against himself; how then shall his kingdom stand? 27 And if I [2]by [3]Beelzebub cast out demons, [2]by whom do your sons cast them out? therefore shall they be your judges. 28 But if I [2]by the Spirit of God cast out demons, then is the kingdom of God come upon you. 29 Or how can one enter into the house of the strong *man*, and spoil his goods, except he first bind the strong *man*? and then he will spoil his house. 30 He that is not with me is against me; and he that gathereth not with me scattereth. 31 Therefore I say unto you, Every sin and blasphemy shall be forgiven unto men; but the blasphemy against the Spirit shall not be forgiven.

[1] Or, *a demoniac*   [2] Or, *in*
[3] Gr. *Beelzebul*

MARK 3:22-30

22 And the scribes that came down from Jerusalem said, He hath [1]Beelzebub, and, [2]By the prince of the demons casteth he out the demons. 23 And he called them unto him, and said unto them in parables, How can Satan cast out Satan? 24 And if a kingdom be divided against itself, that kingdom cannot stand. 25 And if a house be divided against itself, that house will not be able to stand. 26 And if Satan hath risen up against himself, and is divided, he cannot stand, but hath an end.

27 But no one can enter into the house of the strong *man*, and spoil his goods, except he first bind the strong *man*; and then he will spoil his house. 28 Verily I say unto you, All their sins shall be forgiven unto the sons of men, and their blasphemies wherewith soever they shall blaspheme: 29 but whosoever shall blaspheme against the Holy Spirit hath

[1] Gr. *Beelzebul*   [2] Or, *In*

Matt. 12

32 And whosoever shall speak a word against the Son of man, it shall be forgiven him; but whosoever shall speak against the Holy Spirit, it shall not be forgiven him, neither in this ⁴world, nor in that which is to come. 33 Either make the tree good, and its fruit good; or make the tree corrupt, and its fruit corrupt: for the tree is known by its fruit. 34 Ye offspring of vipers, how can ye, being evil, speak good things? for out of the abundance of the heart the mouth speaketh. 35 The good man out of his good treasure bringeth forth good things: and the evil man out of his evil treasure bringeth forth evil things. 36 And I say unto you, that every idle word that men shall speak, they shall give account thereof in the day of judgment. 37 For by thy words thou shalt be justified, and by thy words thou shalt be condemned.

⁴ Or, age

Mark 3

never forgiveness, but is guilty of an eternal sin: 30 because they said, He hath an unclean spirit.

Note 88. The Blasphemous Accusation. The insane hatred which the enemies of Jesus bore toward Him knew no limits. From Mark 3: 22 we learn that on this occasion His slanderous critics were again "the scribes which came down from Jerusalem" (cf. Luke 5: 17, #44). These had been His unrelenting enemies since the cleansing of the temple at the beginning of His ministry (John 2: 14ff, #25). In the foregoing section He had just delivered an unfortunate victim from demon possession and thus had given him sanity and sight and speech. Although this was a good work, those enemies declared that He had received the power for the deed from Beelzebub, whom Jesus identified with Satan. Their reasoning seems to have been that, since Jesus with authority commanded the unclean spirits and they obeyed Him (cf. Mark 1: 27, #37), He must have that authority from Beelzebub, the "ruler of the unclean spirits." We find five answers that He made to this blasphemous charge:

(1) With the parabolic saying of a divided kingdom He declared that if Satan was tearing down his own kingdom—if he was beginning to do good in the world instead of bad, his own kingdom is destined to fall; and Jesus implied that Satan knows better than to do that (Matt. 12:25-26).

(2) He threw the argument back on His accusers, because some of their own people or sons were claiming to cast out demons. "If you say that the power of Beelzebub is necessary before anyone is able to cast out demons, you will have to accuse your own sons of being in league with Beelzebub; that is, if they do what they claim" (Matt. 12:27). Of course, Jesus did not admit that those "sons" (possibly pupils) were actually casting out demons, but the question had the same force as though they did.

122

(3) He suggested that there is another One whose power and command over-awes the demons, including Beelzebub Himself, and puts them to flight; and that One is the Spirit of God. If Jesus in casting out demons was empowered by that One (as, indeed He was, compare Acts 10:38), then the Kingdom of God, dispelling the rule of Satan, had come upon the people of that day, including His critics, before they expected it (Matt. 12:28). He emphasized this by the parable of the burglar in which the burglar represents Jesus who is able to bind the Devil, the strong man, and spoil his goods.

(4) At this point Jesus disclosed to His critics the gravity of their sin in making this accusation against Him. They had ascribed a blessing that was clearly from God, and therefore the work of the Holy Spirit, to the agency of the Devil. And they did it deliberately out of malice against Him who had done only good among the people. This ascribing to the agency of Satan that which clearly can only be accomplished in the power of the Spirit of God, and doing it in malice, is blasphemy. To blaspheme against the Holy Spirit is to make statements about Him or His work which are known to be false, and which drag Him down on a level with the Devil. For this sin there is no forgiveness; the one committing such "hath never forgiveness, but is guilty of an eternal sin" (Mark 3:29). The critics of Jesus seem already to have reached that horrible state. *

(5) After so momentous a pronouncement it would be natural for some in the crowd to say that they did not seriously mean the things that they had said. Therefore Jesus warned them that for even one's idle words he must give an account in the day of judgment (Matt. 12: 36--37).

b. Challenge that He perform some spectacular miracle before them all merely as a sign

#88

MATT. 12:38-45

38 Then certain of the scribes and Pharisees answered him, saying, Teacher, we would see a sign from thee. 39 But he answered and said unto them, An evil and adulterous generation seeketh after a sign; and there shall no sign be given to it but the sign of Jonah the prophet: '40 for as Jonah was three days and three nights in the belly of the ¹whale; so shall the Son of man be three days and three nights in the heart of the earth. 41 The men of Nineveh shall stand up in the judgment with this generation, and shall condemn it: for they repented at the preaching of Jonah; and behold, ²a greater than Jonah is here. 42 The queen of the south shall rise up in the judgment with this generation, and shall condemn it: for she came from the ends of the earth to hear the wisdom of Solomon; and behold, ²a greater than Solomon is here. 43 But the unclean spirit, when ³he is gone out of the man, passeth through waterless places, seeking rest, and findeth it not. 44 Then ³he saith,

¹ Gr. sea-monster   ² Gr. more than   ³ Or, it

* Broadus, *Commentary on Matthew*, p. 272, maintains that this sin can only be committed in the presence of miracles such as were performed during the New Testament times. Reference is also made in the New Testament to other sins against the Holy Spirit: (1) resisting the Holy Spirit (Acts 7:51), (2) grieving the Holy Spirit of God (Eph. 4:30), and (3) quenching the Holy Spirit; that is, suppressing Him (I Thess. 5:19).

Matt. 12

I will return into my house whence I came out; and when [3]he is come, [3]he findeth it empty, swept, and garnished. 45 Then goeth [3]he, and taketh with [4]himself seven other spirits more evil than [4]himself, and they enter in and dwell there: and the last state of that man becometh worse than the first. Even so shall it be also unto this evil generation.

[3] Or, it   [4] Or, itself

Note 89. The Demand for a Sign. After the first cleansing of the temple, on being confronted with a demand for a sign of His authority in that deed, our Lord answered with a veiled reference to His resurrection (John 2: 18—22, #25). Observe that His answer in the foregoing passage has a clearer reference to the resurrection; but, since this was before the first definite announcement of His impending death, (#131) His words were not understood even by His disciples. On two subsequent occasions, when His critics repeated their demand for a sign, He again gave the "sign of Jonah" as a reference to His coming resurrection. The resurrection of Jesus was, and will be until the end of this age, the sign of His divine sonship (cf. Rom. 1: 4). The demand in Luke 11: 16 was for a sign from Heaven, and it is of interest that in Matt. 24: 30 our Lord described His reappearing as "the sign of the Son of Man in Heaven" (#219). Observe what Paul said in I Cor. 1: 22 about the Jews seeking after a sign.

It is interesting to observe that both the blasphemous charge of the preceding section (#87) and the demand for a sign were repeated together during the later Judaean ministry (#153). In the parable of the Unclean Spirit, which was spoken on both occasions, the reference was undoubtedly to the Jewish religious leaders (scribes and Pharisees). These had purged every vestige of idol worship, the besetting sin of their fathers, from their national life, but they were guilty of censorious hypocrisy and rebellion against God. These were like seven new demons in their lives.

(3) The call from His mother and half brothers
#89

MATT. 12:46-50	MARK 3:31-35	LUKE 8:19-21
46 While he was yet speaking to the multitudes, behold, his mother and his brethren stood without, seeking to speak to him. 47 [1]And one said unto him, Behold, thy mother and thy brethren stand without, seeking to speak to thee. 48 But he answered and said unto him that told him, Who is my mother? and who are my brethren? 49 And he stretched forth his	31 And there come his mother and his brethren; and, standing without, they sent unto him, calling him. 32 And a multitude was sitting about him; and they say unto him, Behold, thy mother and thy brethren without seek for thee. 33 And he answereth them, and saith, Who is my mother and my brethren? 34 And looking round on them that sat round about him,	19 And there came to him his mother and brethren, and they could not come at him for the crowd. 20 And it was told him, Thy mother and thy brethren stand without, desiring to see thee.

[1] Some ancient authorities omit ver. 47.

Matt. 12	Mark 3	Luke 8
hand towards his disciples, and said, Behold, my mother and my brethren! 50 For whosoever shall do the will of my Father who is in heaven, he is my brother, and sister, and mother.	he saith, Behold, my mother and my brethren! 35 For whosoever shall do the will of God, the same is my brother, and sister, and mother.	21 But he answered and said unto them, My mother and my brethren are these that hear the word of God, and do it.

Note 90. Why were the mother of Jesus and His brothers seeking an audience with Him? And He seems to have assumed an indifferent attitude toward them—why? We do not know that He even went out to meet them.

Probably they were seeking to persuade Him to return with them to Nazareth. His mother may have been moved by the same misgivings that caused His "friends" to want to take Him away by force (#86). As for His brothers, we know that they did not believe on Him at this time— or some months later (John 7: 5, #141). They probably wanted Him to return with them and again take over management of the carpenter shop. The profits had probably fallen off during the months while He had been away.

2. Answering opposition by means of parables, ##90—103

Note 91. This is the first group of several parables coming together (cf. Luke 14 and 15, ##169—173; Matt. 21: 28—22: 10, ##208—210; 24: 42—25: 30, ##220—224 In this group there were ten, all spoken the same day and doubtless all for the encouragement of the apostles. We sometimes call this "the day of ten parables," but Jesus had already spoken four parables or parabolic sayings that day in answering the charges and questions of His critics (##87–88).

(1) Parables delivered from a boat to the multitudes on the sea shore, ##90—98

Note 92. Jesus was probably back at His regular place where He had taught the increasing multitudes after being denied the privilege of the Capernaum synagogue. This, then, makes three times He is said to have taught by the seaside (cf. ##41, 51).

a. Parables concerning His opponents, ##90—92

(a) Parable of the sower, illustrating the four classes of hearers

#90

MATT. 13:1-9	MARK 4:1-9	LUKE 8:4-8
1 On that day went Jesus out of the house, and sat by the sea side. 2 And there were gathered unto him great multitudes, so that he entered into a boat, and sat; and all the multitude stood on the beach.	1 And again he began to teach by the sea side. And there is gathered unto him a very great multitude, so that he entered into a boat, and sat in the sea; and all the multitude were by the sea on the land. 2 And he	4 And when a great multitude came together, and they of every city resorted unto him, he spake

125

Matt. 13   Mark 4   Luke 8

3 And he spake to them many things in parables, saying, Behold, the sower went forth to sow; 4 and as he sowed, some *seeds* fell by the way side, and the birds came and devoured them: 5 and others fell upon the rocky places, where they had not much earth: and straightway they sprang up, because they had no deepness of earth: 6 and when the sun was risen, they were scorched, and because they had no root, they withered away. 7 And others fell upon the thorns; and the thorns grew up and choked them: 8 and others fell upon the good ground, and yielded fruit, some a hundredfold, some sixty, some thirty. 9 He that hath ears[1], let him hear.

[1] Some ancient authorities add here, and in ver. 43, *to hear:* as in Mk. 4. 9; Lk. 8. 8.

taught them many things in parables, and said unto them in his teaching, 3 Hearken: Behold, the sower went forth to sow: 4 and it came to pass, as he sowed, some *seed* fell by the way side, and the birds came and devoured it. 5 And other fell on the rocky *ground,* where it had not much earth; and straightway it sprang up, because it had no deepness of earth: 6 and when the sun was risen, it was scorched; and because it had no root, it withered away. 7 And other fell among the thorns, and the thorns grew up, and choked it, and it yielded no fruit. 8 And others fell into the good ground, and yielded fruit, growing up and increasing; and brought forth, thirtyfold, and sixtyfold, and a hundredfold. 9 And he said, Who hath ears to hear, let him hear.

by a parable: 5 The sower went forth to sow his seed: and as he sowed, some fell by the way side; and it was trodden under foot, and the birds of the heaven devoured it. 6 And other fell on the rock; and as soon as it grew, it withered away, because it had no moisture. 7 And other fell amidst the thorns; and the thorns grew with it, and choked it. 8 And other fell into the good ground, and grew, and brought forth fruit a hundredfold. As he said these things, he cried, He that hath ears to hear, let him hear.

Note 93. In the foregoing parable the wayside was a path or roadway that ran along the edge of the field or through it, in which the plowed soil had been packed so hard that the seed would not be covered. The stony ground was a patch in the field where the solid rock was covered by only a few inches of soil, not a field with many stones mixed in the soil (Mark 4:5). Travelers from Palestine report that there are many places where the soil has been washed or blown away leaving the bare rock. When we consider the primitive plow tools of those days, we are not surprised that there were thorn or briar patches in the field or encroaching on it from the borders.

(b) Why Jesus spoke in parables that day
#91

MATT. 13:10-17   MARK 4:10-12   LUKE 8:9-10

10 And the disciples came, and said unto him, Why speakest thou unto them in parables? 11 And he answered and said unto them, Unto you it is given to know the mysteries of the kingdom of heaven, but to them it is not given. 12 For whosoever hath, to him shall be given, and he shall

10 And when he was alone, they that were about him with the twelve asked of him the parables. 11 And he said unto them, Unto you is given the mystery of the kingdom of God: but unto them that are without, all things are done in parables:

9 And his disciples asked him what this parable might be. 10 And he said, Unto you it is given to know the mysteries of the kingdom of God: but to the rest in parables:

Matt. 13	Mark 4	Luke 8

ave abunaance: but who-
soever hath not, from him
shall be taken away even
hat which he hath. 13
Therefore speak I to them
n parables; because seeing
hey see not, and hearing
hey hear not, neither do
hey understand. 14 And
unto them is fulfilled the
prophecy of Isaiah, which
aith,

¹By hearing ye shall
hear, and shall in no
wise understand;
And seeing ye shall see,
and shall in no wise
perceive:

15 For this people's heart
is waxed gross,
And their ears are dull
of hearing,
And their eyes they
have closed;
Lest haply they should
perceive with their
eyes,
And hear with their
ears,
And understand with
their heart,
And should turn again,
And I should heal them.
16 But blessed are your
eyes, for they see; and your
ears, for they hear. 17 For
verily I say unto you, that
many prophets and right-
eous men desired to see the
things which ye see, and
saw them not; and to hear
he things which ye hear,
and heard them not.
Is. vi. 9, 10.

12 that
seeing they may see, and
not perceive; and hearing
they may hear, and not
understand; lest haply they
should turn again, and it
should be forgiven them.

that seeing
they may not see, and hearing they may not under-
stand.

Note 94. All of the purposes of Jesus for using parables suggested
n Note 48 are illustrated in the parables of this group, especially those
numbered (3) and (4). He was setting forth truths which the disciples
the twelve and the others who were willing to learn, cf. verse 10 in
Mark) were permitted to know, but which were withheld from others. In
hat sense they were like "mysteries." This word "mystery" to the
people of that day signified information to be imparted to some and
withheld from others, like the secrets of a fraternal order. These
truths were not made known plainly to the majority of those gathered by
he sea side, because Jesus knew that under the leadership of the Jer-
salem scribes they would distort them and misuse them.

(c) Interpretation of the parable of The Sower, indicating the group of hearers

#92

MATT. 13:18-23	MARK 4:13-20	LUKE 8:11-15
18 Hear then ye the parable of the sower. 19 When any one heareth the word of the kingdom, and understandeth it not, *then* cometh the evil *one*, and snatcheth away that which hath been sown in his heart. This is he that was sown by the way side. 20 And he that was sown upon the rocky places, this is he that heareth the word, and straightway with joy receiveth it; 21 yet hath he not root in himself, but endureth for a while; and when tribulation or persecution ariseth because of the word, straightway he stumbleth. 22 And he that was sown among the thorns, this is he that heareth the word; and the care of the ¹world, and the deceitfulness of riches, choke the word, and he becometh unfruitful.	13 And he saith unto them, Know ye not this parable? and how shall ye know all the parables? 14 The sower soweth the word. 15 And these are they by the way side, where the word is sown; and when they have heard, straightway cometh Satan, and taketh away the word which hath been sown in them. 16 And these in like manner are they that are sown upon the rocky *places*, who, when they have heard the word, straightway receive it with joy; 17 and they have no root in themselves, but endure for a while; then, when tribulation or persecution ariseth because of the word, straightway they stumble. 18 And others are they that are sown among the thorns; these are they that have heard the word, 19 and the cares of the ¹world, and the deceitfulness of riches, and the lusts of other things entering in, choke the word, and it becometh unfruitful. 20 And those are they that were sown upon the good ground; such as hear the word, and accept it, and bear fruit, thirtyfold, and sixtyfold, and a hundred-fold.	11 Now the parable is this: The seed is the word of God. 12 And those by the way side are they that have heard; then cometh the devil, and taketh away the word from their heart, that they may not believe and be saved. 13 And those on the rock *are* they who, when they have heard, receive the word with joy; and these have no root, who for a while believe, and in time of temptation fall away. 14 And that which fell among the thorns, these are they that have heard, and as they go on their way they are choked with cares and riches and pleasures of *this* life, and bring no fruit to perfection.
23 And he that was sown upon the good ground, this is he that heareth the word, and understandeth it; who verily beareth fruit, and bringeth forth, some a hundredfold, some sixty, some thirty. ¹ Or, *age*	¹ Or, *age*	15 And that in the good ground, these are such as in an honest and good heart, having heard the word, hold it fast, and bring forth fruit with ¹patience. ¹ Or, *stedfastness*

Note 95. The disciples doubtless needed for their encouragement at this time just the truths that Jesus taught in these parables. While they were on the second tour of Galilee, they probably wondered why so few in the multitudes that saw the miracles of Jesus almost daily and heard His teachings (many of them being blessed by those miracles, became true disciples (cf. #82). Then on their return to Capernaum they were doubtless astonished at the determined opposition of His enemies. Jesus, knowing that in time the disciples would have the responsibility for making known the gospel, determined to warn them of the kind of hearing they would receive. In the audience gathered to hear Jesus that day were four kinds of hearers: (1) the hostile hearers, His

open enemies who had accused Him of being under the power or influence of Beelzebub, and who challenged Him to show them some spectacular sign; (2) the disappointing hearers (cf. John 2: 23ff, #26), His fearful "friends" who wanted to take Him away; (3) the hearers preoccupied with other interests, His half brothers who desired Him to return to the carpenter shop so that the profits would increase to the point where they had been before He went away; and (4) the interested hearers, the disciples and others who listened to His teachings with open hearts and were ready to commit themselves to Him. The application of the Parable of The Sower, describing four kinds of soil, to the four kinds of hearers, as Jesus Himself distinguished them in His interpretation of the parable, is obvious. Surely our Lord spoke this parable to warn the disciples that in their labors they would encounter all these classes of hearers, and to admonish them not to give up or quit, because the number of interested hearers would always be sufficient to make their labors worthwhile.

Observe that in this parable the seed represents the "word of God" (Luke) or the "word of the Kingdom" (Matthew) as it is delivered by Jesus or by any of His disciples.

(d) Parable of The Tares, illustrating source and end of opposition

#93
MATT. 13:24-30

24 Another parable set he before them, saying, The kingdom of heaven is likened unto a man that sowed good seed in his field: 25 but while men slept, his enemy came and sowed [1]tares also among the wheat, and went away. 26 But when the blade sprang up and brought forth fruit, then appeared the tares also. 27 And the [2]servants of the householder came and said unto him, Sir, didst thou not sow good seed in thy field? whence then hath it tares? 28 And he said unto them, An enemy hath done this. And the [2]servants say unto him, Wilt thou then that we go and gather them up? 29 But he saith, Nay; lest haply while ye gather up the tares, ye root up the wheat with them. 30 Let both grow together until the harvest: and in the time of the harvest I will say to the reapers, Gather up first the tares, and bind them in bundles to burn them; but gather the wheat into my barn.

[1] Or, *darnel*   [2] Gr. *bondservants*.   [3] Gr. *A man that is an enemy*.

Note 96. The tares were the stalks of a darnel plant, which in the early stages of its growth is indistinguishable from wheat. Travelers in the East tell us that unless the grains, or seed, of the tares are separated from the wheat before it is ground into flour, bread made from the flour frequently causes dizziness to those who eat it.* In the parable the presence of the tares became evident after the blade (stalks) had both sprung up and brought forth fruit; that is, after the heads of grain had formed on the stalks, from which the difference between wheat and tares was detected. The care with which the farmer had selected "good seed" and the preponderance of tares in the field made it evident that they had been sown by an enemy, or "his enemy," (the farmer's) as in verse 25. In the same verse, "among" in the phrase "among the wheat" is a translation of two words which literally mean "all through the midst."

*Broadus, *Commentary on Matthew*, p. 295.

129

Hence, with roots of wheat and tares so intertwined that it was impossible to pull out the tares without injury to the wheat.

b. Parables concerning the triumph of the kingdom over opposition, ##94—97

(a) Parable of The Lamp (repeated)

#94

MARK 4:21-25	LUKE 8:16-18
21 And he said unto them, Is the lamp brought to be put under the bushel, or under the bed, *and* not to be put on the stand? 22 For there is nothing hid, save that it should be manifested; neither was *anything* made secret, but that it should come to light. 23 If any man hath ears to hear, let him hear. 24 And he said unto them, Take heed what ye hear: with what measure ye mete it shall be measured unto you; and more shall be given unto you. 25 For he that hath, to him shall be given: and he that hath not, from him shall be taken away even that which he hath.	16 And no man, when he hath lighted a lamp, covereth it with a vessel, or putteth it under a bed; but putteth it on a stand, that they that enter in may see the light. 17 For nothing is hid, that shall not be made manifest; nor *anything* secret, that shall not be known and come to light. 18 Take heed therefore how ye hear: for whosoever hath, to him shall be given; and whosoever hath not, from him shall be taken away even that which he ¹thinketh he hath. ¹ Or, *seemeth to have*

Note 97. In the Parable of The Lamp our Lord doubtless meant to say to the disciples that they had been chosen to disseminate the redemption propaganda, just as a lamp is lighted to give forth light; and for them to let fear or discouragement stop their efforts is as foolish as it would be to put a lighted lamp under a bushel or under a bed. This parable illustrates the undiscouraged labors of the disciples as the means of triumph. Observe that the Parable of The Lamp had been spoken before at #55. It will be spoken again at #153.

(b) Parable of The Seed Growing to Fruit

#95

MARK 4:26-29

26 And he said, So is the kingdom of God, as if a man should cast seed upon the earth; 27 and should sleep and rise night and day, and the seed should spring up and grow, he knoweth not how. 28 The earth ¹beareth fruit of herself; first the blade, then the ear, then the full grain in the ear. 29 But when the fruit ²is ripe, straightway he ³putteth forth the sickle, because the harvest is come.

¹ Or, *yieldeth*   ² Or, *alloweth*   ³ Or, *sendeth forth*

Note 98. In the foregoing parable the Lord Jesus admonished His disciples to expect ultimate success to attend their labors. He would impress them that "in due season ye shall reap if ye faint not" (cf. Gal. 6: 9; Eccles. 11: 6). It therefore warns against discouragement in Christian work caused by impatience (cf. I Cor. 3: 6). The lesson of this parable naturally follows that of the preceding one, and is an apt introduction to the two which follow.

(c) Parable of The Mustard Seed

#96

MATT. 13:31-32	MARK 4:30-32
	30 And he said, How shall we liken the kingdom of God? or in what parable

Matt. 13

31 Another parable set he before them, saying, The kingdom of heaven is like unto a grain of mustard seed, which a man took, and sowed in his field: 32 which indeed is less than all seeds; but when it is grown, it is greater than the herbs, and becometh a tree, so that the birds of the heaven come and lodge in the branches thereof.

Mark 4

shall we set it forth? 31 [1]It is like a grain of mustard seed, which, when it is sown upon the earth, though it be less than all the seeds that are upon the earth, 32 yet when it is sown, groweth up, and becometh greater than all the herbs, and putteth out great branches; so that the birds of the heaven can lodge under the shadow thereof.

[1] Gr, As unto.

Note 99.   In the Parable of the Mustard Seed our Lord assured His disciples that the success of their labors would be gratifying beyond their fondest expectation—that the movement which He was inaugurating, and which He would carry on through their labors would grow to unimaginable proportions.   This parable and the next will be repeated in Luke 13: 19, #160.

(d) Parable of The Leaven
#97
MATT. 13:33

33 Another parable spake he unto them; The kingdom of heaven is like unto leaven, which a woman took, and hid in three [1]measures of meal, till it was all leavened.

[1] The word in the Greek denotes the Hebrew seah, a measure containing nearly a peck and a half

Note 100.   Surely in the Parable of the Leaven our Lord had the permeating power of leaven in mind, rather than its corrupting effect. He taught in this parable that the Kingdom of God would permeate the life of an individual who receives it into his heart, and through individuals the social units into which it is introduced.   This does not mean that the social order will ever be perfectly transformed before the return of Jesus, but that the presence of the spiritual Kingdom in society will have a telling effect upon it.

c.   General statement about His teaching in parables
#98

MATT. 13:34-35

34 All these things spake Jesus in parables unto the multitudes; and without a parable spake he nothing unto them: 35 that it might be fulfilled which was spoken through the prophet, saying, [1]I will open my mouth in parables; I will utter things hidden from the foundations [2]of the world.

[1] Ps. lxxviii. 2.
[2] Many ancient authorities omit of the world.

MARK 4:33-34

33 And with many such parables spake he the word unto them, as they were able to hear it; 34 and without a parable spake he not unto them: but privately to his own disciples he expounded all things.

(2) Parables delivered to the disciples in a house (on the same day), ##99—103

Note 101.   Observe that the parables spoken from the boat in the hearing of the multitudes were all on agricultural pursuits except the parable of the Lamp and that of the Leaven, which were drawn from peasant home life. Those spoken in the house to the disciples have the background of the market place, the fishers' work, and the home life of a wealthy person. Note also that these are recorded only by Matthew.

a. Interpretation of the Parable of the Tares
#99
MATT. 13:36-43

36 Then he left the multitudes, and went into the house: and his disciples came unto him, saying, Explain unto us the parable of the tares of the field. 37 And he answered and said, He that soweth the good seed is the Son of man; 38 and the field is the world; and the good seed, these are the sons of the kingdom; and the tares are the sons of the evil *one*; 39 and the enemy that sowed them is the devil: and the harvest is [1]the end of the world; and the reapers are angels. 40 As therefore the tares are gathered up and burned with fire; so shall it be in the [1]end of the world. 41 The Son of man shall send forth his angels, and they shall gather out of his kingdom all things that cause stumbling, and them that do iniquity, 42 and shall cast them into the furnace of fire: there shall be the weeping and the gnashing of teeth. 43 Then shall the righteous shine forth as the sun in the kingdom of their Father. He that hath ears[2], let him hear.

[1] Or, *the consummation of the age*   [2] See ver. 9.

Note 102. This parable was likely given to answer the unexpressed question in the minds of the disciples as to why they must encounter the hostile or disappointing or indifferent hearers anyway. In our Lord's interpretation He set forth both the source and the end of this opposition. The Devil was its source (verse 39), and the end of those who persist in their opposition will be in the fires of eternity (verse 42, cf. Rev. 20: 10, 15). In this parable, not the disciples are the sowers of the seed, but the "Son of Man." The disciples, along with other Christians, figure only as being among the "good seed;" that is, "the sons of the Kingdom." This is different from the meaning of the seed in the parable of the Sower (cf. Note 95).

Observe that this is a parable of the "Kingdom of Heaven," and that "the field is the world." In the interpretation by the Lord Jesus no mention is made of a church. And He did not in His interpretation take any notice of the orders of the householder that the wheat and the tares were to grow together, in the same field, until the time of the harvest. If that injunction in the parable is to be interpreted at all, it is certainly to be taken to mean that "the children of the Kingdom" and "the children of the wicked one" are to live together in the world until the end of the age. Very clearly it is not, as some interpreters teach, an injunction on a church to retain in its membership those that live disorderly or those who are manifestly unbelievers.*

b. Parables concerning the value of Kingdom participation,
##100—103
(a) Parable of The Hidden Treasure
#100
MATT. 13:44

44 The kingdom of heaven is like unto a treasure hidden in the field; which a

*I believe that the teaching of Jesus in this matter is found in Matthew 18:17 That is one of the only two passages in which Jesus is recorded to have spoken of a church, the other being Matthew 16:18.

132

nan found, and hid; and [1]in his joy he goeth and selleth all that he hath, and
buyeth that field.
[1] Or, *for joy thereof*

(b) Parable of The Pearl of Great Price
#101

MATT. 13:45-46
45 Again, the kingdom of heaven is like unto a man that is a merchant seek-
ng goodly pearls: 46 and having found one pearl of great price, he went and
old all that he had, and bought it.

(c) Parable of Valuable and Worthless Fishes
#102

MATT. 13:47-50
47 Again, the kingdom of heaven is like unto a [1]net, that was cast into the sea,
and gathered of every kind: 48 which, when it was filled, they drew up on the
beach; and they sat down, and gathered the good into vessels, but the bad they
cast away. 49 So shall it be in [2]the end of the world: the angels shall come forth,
and sever the wicked from among the righteous, 50 and shall cast them into the
urnace of fire: there shall be the weeping and the gnashing of teeth.
[1] Gr. *drag-net.*   [2] Or, *the consummation of the age*

Note 103. As suggested in the outline, the last three parables
above emphasize the value to an individual of participation in the Messiah's Kingdom. Just as the chief character of the parable of the
Hidden Treasure and in that of the Pearl of Great Price each sold all that
he had to buy a coveted possession, so the benefits of participation in
the Kingdom which our Lord was offering surpass in value all other
possessions, privileges, and attainments; and these might well be
sacrificed for those benefits. Jesus did not give approval to the shrewd,
almost dishonest, way in which the finder of the treasure obtained possession of it, but He used his eagerness in the transaction to illustrate
the great value of Kingdom benefits to the individual who participates in
them. The parable of the Pearl of Great Price seems also to portray a
person of a deep unfulfilled yearning, which at length is satisfied through
receiving Jesus as Saviour and King. The objective sought in one pagan
religion (Buddhism) has been to be rid of desire; but what the Lord Jesus
proposes to give, and what the disciples would be commanded to publish, would be satisfaction of a soul's desire. Another reason for the
surpassing value of Kingdom participation is suggested in the parable of
the Fish in the Net. Just as the fish caught in a seine are separated,
some to be kept and others to be thrown away, so people will be separated at the end of the world; and it is clearly implied that the basis of
separation will be the way they have received or rejected the gospel of
the Kingdom of Heaven as it is proclaimed by Jesus and the disciples.
Therefore, because they were destined to deal with that which is most
valuable in a person's experience, Jesus in these parables gave encouragement to the disciples for their future work.

c. Parable of The Householder's Treasure, illustrating the use of parables

#103

MATT. 13:51-52

51 Have ye understood all these things? They say unto him, Yea. 52 And he said unto them, Therefore every scribe who hath been made a disciple to the kingdom of heaven is like unto a man that is a householder, who bringeth forth out of his treasure things new and old.

Note 104. It is possible that there were individuals of the scribal class in the audience when Jesus spoke the ten parables, and that He had a recognized scribe in mind in verse 52 above. There probably were some scribes among them who were impressed by the teachings and works of Jesus, and who were among the disciples in the early Jerusalem church, (cf. Nicodemus and the man mentioned in Matt. 8: 19, #104). However, He may have been comparing the disciples themselves to scribes, implying that just as the scribes were the teachers of the law, so He was instructing the disciples to be the teachers of the Kingdom of Heaven. They probably very vaguely understood the things that He had been saying to them; but one day, after they should have experience in setting forth the message of the Kingdom, all these parables would have a new meaning to them. And further, all that they had learned about the Old Testament, and all they were yet to learn, would also take on new meaning in the light of the things that He had been saying. From the treasures of their memories they would, therefore, in after years be able to bring forth "things new and old."

3. Avoiding opposition by a journey across the lake, ##104—105
   (1) Stilling a storm, demonstrating power to quell the opposition of the elements

#104

MATT. 13:53; 8:18-27	MARK 4:35-41	LUKE 8:22-25
53 And it came to pass, when Jesus had finished these parables, he departed thence. MATT. 8 18 Now when Jesus saw great multitudes about him, he gave commandment to depart unto the other side. 19 And there came ¹a scribe, and said unto him, Teacher, I will follow thee whithersoever thou goest. 20 And Jesus saith unto him, The foxes have holes, and the birds of the heaven *have* ²nests; but the Son of man hath not where to lay his head. 21 And another of the disciples said unto	35 And on that day, when even was come, he saith unto them, Let us go over unto the other side. 36 And leaving the multitude, they take him with them, even as he was, in the boat. And other boats were with him.	22 Now it came to pass on one of those days, that he entered into a boat, himself and his disciples; he said unto them, Let us go over unto the other side of the lake: and they launched forth.

¹ Gr. *one scribe.*
² Gr. *lodging places.*

134

Matt. 8	Mark 4	Luke 8
him, Lord, suffer me first to go and bury my father. 22 But Jesus saith unto him, Follow me; and leave the dead to bury their own dead. 23 And when he was entered into a boat, his disciples followed him. 24 And behold, there arose a great tempest in the sea, insomuch that the boat was covered with the waves: but he was asleep. 25 And they came to him, and awoke him, saying, Save, Lord; we perish. 26 And he saith unto them, Why are ye fearful O ye of little faith? Then he arose, and rebuked the winds and the sea; and there was a great calm. 27 And the men marvelled, saying, What manner of man is this, that even the winds and the sea obey him?	37 And there ariseth a great storm of wind, and the waves beat into the boat, insomuch that the boat was now filling. 38 And he himself was in the stern, asleep on the cushion: and they awake him, and say unto him, Teacher, carest thou not that we perish? 39 And he awoke, and rebuked the wind, and said unto the sea, Peace, be still. And the wind ceased, and there was a great calm. 40 And he said unto them, Why are ye fearful? have ye not yet faith? 41 And they feared exceedingly, and said one to another, Who then is this, that even the wind and the sea obey him?	23 But as they sailed he fell asleep: and there came down a storm of wind on the lake; and they were filling with water, and were in jeopardy. 24 And they came to him, and awoke him, saying, Master, master, we perish. And he awoke, and rebuked the wind and the raging of the water: and they ceased, and there was a calm. 25 And he said unto them, Where is your faith? And being afraid they marvelled, saying one to another, Who then is this, that he commandeth even the winds and the water, and they obey him?

Note 105. This was the first of four journeys that Jesus made to the country east of the Sea of Galilee; that is, into the region of Decapolis or of Itruraea (cf. #118, 125, 128). It was also the first of two occasions when He stilled a raging storm on this sea (cf. #120). It is one of the best attested of the miracles of Jesus, being related in all the Synoptic Gospels, as well as one of the most impressive.

Drs. Broadus and Robertson in their Harmonies of the Gospels* place Matt. 8: 19—22 parallel with Luke 9: 57—60 (#143), which relates events much later in the ministry of Jesus. But probably more than one person came to Jesus with the offer to follow, and Jesus may have repeated this answer at least on these two occasions.** To make these verses parallel with the ones in Luke would make them come between the eighteenth and the nineteenth chapters of Matthew. But beginning with the fourteenth chapter, Matthew is in the same order as Mark, and in the same order as Luke so far as he and Luke recorded the same things. Therefore, I conclude that the passages relate distinct but similar events, and place them in the Harmony in what seems to be the logical order for each.

*John A. Broadus, Harmony of the Gospels in the Revised Version (New York: A. C. Armstrong and Son, 1906), p. 101; Robertson, Harmony of the Gospels, p. 112.
**Cf. Broadus, Commentary on Matthew, p. 184.

135

(2) Healing the Gergesene (Gadarene) demoniac (or demoniacs) — overcoming opposition from the spirit world, meeting opposition for economic reasons

#105

MATT. 8:28-34	MARK 5:1-20	LUKE 8:26-39
28 And when he was come to the other side into the country of the Gadarenes, there met him two [1]possessed with demons, coming forth out of the tombs, exceeding fierce, so that no man could pass by that way.	1 And they came to the other side of the sea, into the country of the Gerasenes. 2 And when he was come out of the boat, straightway there met him out of the tombs a man with an unclean spirit, 3 who had his dwelling in the tombs: and no man could any more bind him, no, not with a chain; 4 because that he had been often bound with fetters and chains, and the chains had been rent asunder by him, and the fetters broken in pieces: and no man had strength to tame him. 5 And always, night and day, in the tombs and in the mountains, he was crying out, and cutting himself with stones. 6 And when he saw Jesus from afar, he ran and [1]worshipped him;	26 And they arrived at the country of the [1]Gerasenes, which is over against Galilee. 27 And when he was come forth upon the land, there met him a certain man out of the city, who had demons; and for a long time he had worn no clothes, and abode not in *any* house, but in the tombs.
29 And behold, they cried out, saying, What have we to do with thee, thou Son of God? art thou come hither to torment us before the time?	7 and crying out with a loud voice, he saith, What have I to do with thee, Jesus, thou Son of the Most High God? I adjure thee by God, torment me not. 8 For he said unto him, Come forth, thou unclean spirit, out of the man. 9 And he asked him, What is thy name? And he saith unto him, My name is Legion; for we are many. 10 And he besought him much that he would not send them away out of the country. 11 Now there was there on the mountain side a great herd of swine feeding. 12 And they besought him, saying, Send us into the swine, that we may enter into them. 13 And he gave them leave. And the unclean spirits came	28 And when he saw Jesus, he cried out, and fell down before him, and with a loud voice said, What have I to do with thee, Jesus, thou Son of the Most High God? I beseech thee, torment me not. 29 For he was commanding the unclean spirit to come out from the man. For [2]oftentimes it had seized him: and he was kept under guard, and bound with chains and fetters; and breaking the bands asunder, he was driven of the demon into the deserts. 30 And Jesus asked him, What is thy name? And he said, Legion; for many demons were entered into him. 31 And they entreated him that he would not command them to depart into the abyss. 32 Now there was there a herd of many swine feeding on the moun-
30 Now there was afar off from them a herd of many swine feeding. 31 And the demons besought him, saying, If thou cast us out, send us away into the herd of swine. 32 And he said unto them, Go. And they came		

[1] Or, *demoniacs*

[1] The Greek word denotes an act of reverence, whether paid to a creature (see Mt. 4. 9; 18. 26) or to the Creator (see Mt. 4. 10).

[1] Many ancient authorities read *Gergesenes;* others, *Gadarenes:* and so in ver. 37.
[2] Or, *of a long time*

136

Matt. 8	Mark 5	Luke 8
out, and went into the swine: and behold, the whole herd rushed down the steep into the sea, and perished in the waters. 33 And they that fed them fled, and went away into the city, and told everything, and what was befallen to them that were ¹possessed with demons.	out, and entered into the swine: and the herd rushed down the steep into the sea, *in number* about two thousand; and they were drowned in the sea. 14 And they that fed them fled, and told it in the city, and, in the country. And they came to see what it was that had come to pass. 15 And they come to Jesus, and behold ²him that was possessed with demons sitting, clothed and in his right mind, *even* him that had the legion: and they were afraid. 16 And they that saw it declared unto them how it befell ²him that was possessed with demons, and concerning the swine. 17 And they began to beseech him to depart from their borders. 18 And as he was entering into the boat, ²he that had been possessed with demons besought him that he might be with him. 19 And he suffered him not, but saith unto him, Go to thy house unto thy friends, and tell them how great things the Lord hath done for thee, and *how* he had mercy on thee. 20 And he went his way,.and began to publish in Decapolis how great things Jesus had done for him: and all men marvelled.	tain: and they entreated him that he would give them leave to enter into them. And he gave them leave. 33 And the demons came out from the man, and entered into the swine: and the herd rushed down the steep into the lake, and were drowned. 34 And when they that fed them saw what had come to pass, they fled, and told it in the city and in the country. 35 And they went out to see what had come to pass; and they came to Jesus, and found the man, from whom the demons were gone out, sitting, clothed and in his right mind, at the feet of Jesus: and they were afraid. 36 And they that saw it told them how he that was possessed with demons was ³made whole. 37 And all the people of the country of the Gerasenes round about asked him to depart from them; for they were holden with great fear: and he entered into a boat, and returned. 38 But the man from whom the demons were gone out prayed him that he might be with him: but he sent him away, saying, 39 Return to thy house, and declare how great things God hath done for thee. And he went his way, publishing throughout the whole city how great things Jesus had done for him.
34 And behold, all the city came out to meet Jesus: and when they saw him, they besought *him* that he would depart from their borders.		

¹ Or, *demoniacs*   ² Or, *the demoniac*
³ Or, *saved*

Note 106. In the King James Version the destination of this trip is named in Matthew as "the country of the Gergesenes" and in Mark and Luke "the country of the Gadarenes." Textual critics (those who give special study to the ancient copies of the New Testament) tell us that in the most ancient manuscripts it is the other way around: the word being "Gerasenes" (rather than "Gergesenes") in Mark and Luke, and "Gadarenes" in Matthew; and thus it appears in the American Standard Version. Gerasa (or Gergesa) which was probably a village on the east shore of the Sea of Galilee, ruled in the time of Jesus by Gadara, one of the free cities of Decapolis. It is not to be confused with Gerasa, a larger city some forty or more miles to the southeast, which was itself one of the cities of Decapolis. The inhabitants were prevailingly Greek, or otherwise Gentile, which fact may account for the swine-raising industry there.

See Note 40 for comment on demoniacal possession and this case in particular. Matthew mentions two demoniacs, while Mark and Luke mention only one. Most interpreters* suggest that there were two, but the one described in Mark and Luke was the most violent. It is to be noted also that in #192 Matthew mentions two blind men, and Mark and Luke mention only one, calling him by name—Bartimaeus.

4. Returning to Capernaum, meeting His opponents with a group of outstanding miracles, ##106—110
   (1) Being entreated by Jairus, a Synagogue ruler, to come to heal his sick daughter

#106

MATT. 9:1; 18-19	MARK 5:21-24	LUKE 8:40-42
1 And he entered into a boat, and crossed over, and came into his own city. 18 While he spake these things unto them, behold, there came ¹a ruler, and ²worshipped him, saying, My daughter is even now dead: but come and lay thy hand upon her, and she shall live. 19 And Jesus arose, and followed him, and *so did* his disciples.	21 And when Jesus had crossed over again in the boat unto the other side, a great multitude was gathered unto him; and he was by the sea. 22 And there cometh one of the rulers of the synagogue, Jairus by name; and seeing him, he falleth at his feet, 23 and beseecheth him much, saying, My little daughter is at the point of death: I *pray thee*, that thou come and lay thy hands on her, that she may be ¹made whole, and live. 24 And he went with him; and a great multitude followed him, and they thronged him.	40 And as Jesus returned, the multitude welcomed him; for they were all waiting for him. 41 And behold, there came a man named Jairus, and he was a ruler of the synagogue: and he fell down at Jesus' feet, and besought him to come into his house; 42 for he had an only daughter, about twelve years of age, and she was dying. But as he went the multitudes thronged him.
¹ Gr. *one ruler*. ² See marginal note on ch. 2. 2.	¹ Or, *saved*	

Note 107. Broadus, following the order in Matthew, places the material of ##106--108 after the material in #46.** In this he was governed by the words,"While He spake these things," of Matt. 9:18 (the things about fasting in the preceding paragraph). But we know that chs. 5--13 of Matthew are not in chronological order; and, although recognizing the difficulty in the clause quoted above, it seems best to follow the order of Mark and Luke. Broadus in a note remarks, "The question of the position (of this material) in the Harmony cannot be settled, and it makes no difference as to understanding the content of the section."

*Including Broadus, *Commentary on Matthew*, p. 189, and A. B. Bruce *The Synoptic Gospels* in *The Expositor's Greek Testament*, ed. W. Robertson Nicoll (New York: Hodd and Straughton, 1917), Vol. I, p. 145.

**Harmony of the Gospels, p. 36.

Nothing is known about Jairus, other than what is related in these paragraphs. We could wish we knew something of his later life.

(2) Thronging multitude, delay caused by healing a woman who only touched his garment

#107

MATT. 9:20-22	MARK 5:25-34	LUKE 8:43-48
20 And behold, a woman, who had an issue of blood twelve years, came behind him, and touched the border of his garment:	25 And a woman, who had an issue of blood twelve years, 26 and had suffered many things of many physicians, and had spent all that she had, and was nothing bettered, but rather grew worse, 27 having heard the things concerning Jesus, came in the crowd behind, and touched his garment. 28 For she said, If I touch but his garments, I shall be [1]made whole. 29 And straightway the fountain of her blood was dried up; and she felt in her body that she was healed of her [2]plague. 30 And straightway Jesus, perceiving in himself that the power *proceeding* from him had gone forth, turned him about in the crowd, and said, Who touched my garments? 31 And his disciples said unto him, Thou seest the multitude thronging thee, and sayest thou, Who touched me? 32 And he looked round about to see her that had done this thing. 33 But the woman fearing and trembling, knowing what had been done to her, came and fell down before him, and told him all the truth. 34 And he said unto her, Daughter, thy faith hath [3]made thee whole; go in peace, and be whole of thy [2]plague.	43 And a woman having an issue of blood twelve years, who [1]had spent all her living upon physicians, and could not be healed of any, 44 came behind him, and touched the border of
21 for she said within herself, If I do but touch his garment, I shall be [1]made whole.		his garment: and immediately the issue of her blood stanched. 45 And Jesus said, Who is it that touched me? And when all denied, Peter said, [2]and they that were with him, Master, the multitudes press thee and crush *thee*. 46 But Jesus said, Some one did touch me; for I perceived that power had gone forth from me. 47 And When the woman saw that she was not hid, she came trembling, and falling down before him declared in the presence of all the people for what cause she touched him, and how she was healed immediately. 48 And he said unto her, Daughter, thy faith hath [3]made thee whole; go in peace.
22 But Jesus turning and seeing her said, Daughter, be of good cheer; thy faith hath [2]made thee whole. And the woman was [1]made whole from that hour. [1] Or, *saved* [2] Or, *saved thee*	[1] Or, *saved* [2] Gr. *scourge.* [3] Or, *saved thee*	[1] Some ancient authorities omit *had spent all her living upon physicians, and.* [2] Some ancient authorities omit *and they that were with him.* [3] Or, *saved thee*

Note 108. Did Jesus know before the woman was healed that she was troubled with her malady? Surely not; but her condition and her faith were certainly in the knowledge of God the Father and the Holy Spirit, on whom Jesus in His incarnate life depended for power to work miracles (cf. John 14:10; Matt. 12:28); and the healing was accomplished by the same divine power which had enabled Him to perform so many cures. The woman's faith was surely not in the garment Jesus wore but in

Jesus; and touching His garment was her way of expressing her faith. Her timid faith was rewarded of God and commended by Jesus.

(3) Tidings of the death of the synagogue ruler's daughter, Jesus raising her to life

#108

MATT. 9:23-26	MARK 5:35-43	LUKE 8:49-56
	35 While he yet spake, they come from the ruler of the synagogue's *house*, saying, Thy daughter is dead: why troublest thou the Teacher any further? 36 But Jesus, [1]not heeding the word spoken, saith unto the ruler of the synagogue, Fear not, only believe. 37 And he suffered no man to follow with him, save Peter, and [2]James, and John the brother of [2]James. 38 And they come to the house of the ruler of the synagogue; and he beholdeth a tumult, and *many* weeping and wailing greatly. 39 And when he was entered in, he saith unto them, Why make ye a tumult, and weep? the child is not dead, but sleepeth. 40 And they laughed him to scorn. But he, having put them all forth, taketh the father of the child and her mother and them that were with him, and goeth in where the child was. 41 And taking the child by the hand, he saith unto her, Talitha cumi; which is, being interpreted, Damsel, I say unto thee, Arise. 42 And straightway the damsel rose up, and walked; for she was twelve years old. And they were amazed straightway with a great amazement. 43 And he charged them much that no man should know this: and he commanded that *something* should be given her to eat.	49 While he yet spake, there cometh one from the ruler of the synagogue's *house*, saying, Thy daughter is dead; trouble not the Teacher. 50 But Jesus hearing it, answered him, Fear not: only believe, and she shall be [1]made whole. 51 And when he came to the house, he suffered not any man to enter in with him, save Peter, and John, and James, and the father of the maiden and her mother. 52 And all were weeping, and bewailing her: but he said, Weep not; for she is not dead, but sleepeth. 53 And they laughed him to scorn, knowing that she was dead.
23 And when Jesus came into the ruler's house, and saw the flute-players, and the crowd making a tumult, 24 he said, Give place: for the damsel is not dead, but sleepeth. And they laughed him to scorn. 25 But when the crowd was put forth, he entered in,		
and took her by the hand; and the damsel arose. 26 And [1]the fame hereof went forth into all that land.		54 But he, taking her by the hand, called, saying Maiden, arise. 55 And her spirit returned, and she rose up immediately: and he commanded that *something* be given her to eat. 56 And her parents were amazed: but he charged them to tell no man what had been done.
[1] Gr. *this fame.*	[1] Or, *Overhearing* [2] Or, *Jacob*	[1] Or, *saved*

Note 109. This was the second time Jesus raised a person from death; there will be one more (cf. ##79, 178). It was the first of three occasions when He took Peter, James, and John to witness special events (cf. ##133, 238).

140

(4) Healing two blind men
#109
MATT. 9:27-31

27 And as Jesus passed by from thence, two blind men followed him, crying out, and saying, Have mercy on us, thou son of David. 28 And when he was come into the house, the blind men came to him: and Jesus saith unto them, Believe ye that I am able to do this? They say unto him, Yea, Lord. 29 Then touched he their eyes, saying, According to your faith be it done unto you. 30 And their eyes were opened. And Jesus [1]strictly charged them, saying, See that no man know it. 31 But they went forth, and spread abroad his fame in all that land.

[1] Or, *sternly*

(5) Restoring a dumb demoniac, blasphemous charge repeated
#110
MATT. 9:32-34

32 And as they went forth, behold, there was brought to him a dumb man possessed with a demon. 33 And when the demon was cast out, the dumb man spake: and the multitudes marvelled, saying, It was never so seen in Israel. 34 But the Pharisees said, [1]By the prince of the demons casteth he out demons.

[1] Or, *In*

Note 110. This was the second occasion of the blasphemous accusation. See Note 88 for the answers that Jesus had made to this accusation.

5. Outbreak of opposition on His last visit to Nazareth, second rejection at Nazareth
#111

MATT. 13:54-58

54 And coming into his own country he taught them in their synagogue, insomuch that they were astonished, and said, Whence hath this man this wisdom, and these [1]mighty works? 55 Is not this the carpenter's son? is not his mother called Mary? and his brethren, [2]James, and Joseph, and Simon, and Judas? 56 And his sisters, are they not all with us? Whence then hath this man all these things? 57 And they were [3]offended in him. But Jesus said unto them, A prophet is not without honor, save in his own country, and in his own house. 58 And he did not many [1]mighty works there because of their unbelief.

[1] Gr. *powers.*　　[2] Or, *Jacob*
[3] Gr. *caused to stumble.*

MARK 6:1-6a

1 And he went out from thence; and he cometh into his own country; and his disciples follow him. 2 And when the sabbath was come, he began to teach in the synagogue: and [1]many hearing him were astonished, saying, Whence hath this man these things? and, What is the wisdom that is given unto this man, and *what mean* such [2]mighty works wrought by his hands? 3 Is not this the carpenter, the son of Mary, and brother of [3]James, and Joses, and Judas, and Simon? and are not his sisters here with us? And they were [4]offended in him. 4 And Jesus said unto them, A prophet is not without honor, save in his own country, and among his own kin, and in his own house. 5 And he could there do no [5]mighty work, save that he laid his hands upon a few sick folk, and healed them. 6a And he marvelled because of their unbelief.

[1] Some ancient authorities insert *the.*
[2] Gr. *powers.*　　[3] Or, *Jacob*
[4] Gr. *caused to stumble.*　　[5] Gr. *power.*

Note 111. We wonder if Jesus made this visit to Nazareth because of the coming of His mother and brothers to Him as related in #89. So far as the Gospel accounts go, this was the second and last visit that He made to His home town after He began His public ministry. On both

141

visits He was rejected by His former neighbors and fellow-townsmen (cf. #33). They might have been glad for Him to return as a noted Wonder-worker, but they were not interested in Him as a Teacher or as a Saviour. And He marveled because of their unbelief; that is, He was disappointed and likely puzzled at the reception He received. This is the second time it was said that He "marveled" (cf. #78).

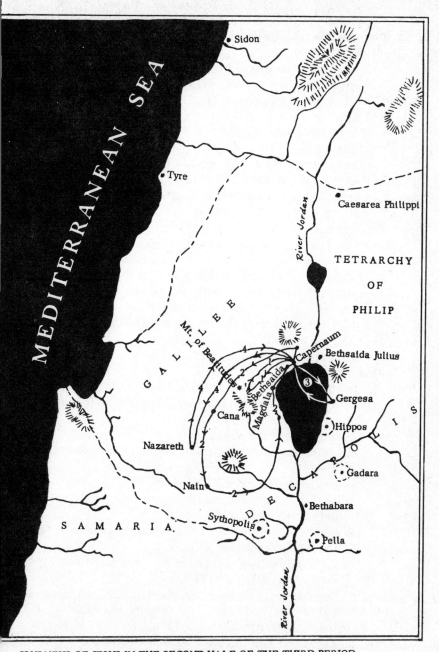

JOURNEYS OF JESUS IN THE SECOND HALF OF THE THIRD PERIOD
1 - From Capernaum to the Mount of Beatitudes and return (##52—78). 2 - The
second tour of Galilee (##79—85). 3 - From Capernaum to Gergesa (land of
Gergesenes or Gadarenes) and return (##104—106). 4 - From Capernaum to Nazareth and return to Capernaum (#111).

*Traditional location. ⟨•⟩ A city of the Decapolis league.

A PREVIEW OUTLINE OF PERIOD FOUR, ##112-140

I. The apostles practice tours and Jesus' third tour of Galilee, ##112--117
   1. Introductory summary, #112
   2. Instruction to the twelve, #113
   3. Work of the disciples, #114
   4. Third tour of Galilee, #115
   5. Beheading of John the Baptist, #116
   6. Return of the twelve, #117
II. The first retirement—across the Sea of Galilee, ##118-120
   1. Feeding the five thousand, #118
   2. Dispelling the multitude, retirement for prayer, #119
   3. Walking on the water, stilling a storm, #120
III. Treatment received on return to Galilee, ##121-123
   1. Deserted by the multitude at Capernaum, remaining in Galilee during Passover season, #121
   2. Sought by people of Gennesaret, #122
   3. Criticized by Pharisees from Jerusalem, #123
IV. The second retirement—to Phoenicia, #124
V. The third retirement—to Decapolis, ##125--126
   1. Miracles of healing, #125
   2. Feeding four thousand, #126
VI. Return to Magdala, #127
VII. The fourth retirement—to Caesarea Philippi, ##128--136
   1. Lesson about evil teachings and example of Pharisees, Sadducees, and Herod, #128
   2. Healing a blind man, #129
   3. Important events in neighborhood of Caesarea Philippi, ##130--135
     (1) Confession of Peter, #130
     (2) Definite announcement by Jesus of His forthcoming death and resurrection, #131
     (3) A solemn warning and an encouraging promise, #132
     (4) The Transfiguration, #133
     (5) The resurrection again foretold, interpretation of prophecy concerning Elijah, #134
     (6) Healing the demoniac boy, #135
   4. Second foretelling of His impending death, #136
VIII. Last teaching in Galilee, ##137-140
   1. In connection with payment of Temple tax, #137
   2. In regard to pre-eminence in the Kingdom, #138
   3. In regard to treatment of weak disciples, #139
   4. In regard to forgiveness, #140

Special Ministry to the Twelve Disciples
(## 1 1 2 - 1 4 0)

Note 112. <u>Some</u> <u>Introductory</u> <u>Observations</u>. We have reached the point in the study of our Lord's earthly life a little more than a year from the dark day when He would "give His life a ransom for many" (Mark 10: 45). However, up to this time He had not clearly revealed the sacrificial purpose that was in His heart, although on several occasions He had said some things which we can now understand to have referred to it. In order that the salvation which He intended to procure might be set forth before the people of the world, He chose the twelve to be leaders in a proclamation movement. The training of that group came more and more to occupy His attention. Up to this point the training process had included the following:

1. Almost immediately after His baptism and temptation He encouraged five—Andrew and Simon Peter, Philip and Nathaniel, or Bartholomew, and one unnamed, likely John—to follow Him voluntarily. For some months these—at least some of them and likely James, brother of John—accompanied Him more or less intermittently, returning to their homes and businesses after each trip. They went with Him to Jerusalem for the first Passover (of His ministry) and at least some of them remained with Him during the early Judaean ministry, administering baptism for Him, and accompanied Him on the journey through Samaria back to Galilee (John 2: 17; 3: 22; 4: 2, 8, 27, ##25--29).

2. At the beginning of His "Ministry to the Multitudes in Galilee" He challenged Andrew and Simon, James and John, the four fishermen, to follow Him and learn to be fishers of men, whereupon these accompanied Him on the First Tour of Galilee. Philip and Nathaniel may also have joined them, and later Matthew was invited to follow.

3. Not long after the Second Passover He made the formal choice of the twelve, "that they might be with Him, and that He might send them forth" (Mark 3: 14).

4. One of His first acts after choosing the twelve was to lead them on the Second Tour of Galilee during which they might observe more closely His mighty works and listen to His teaching. Also, for their benefit and encouragement primarily, He spoke the first great group of parables (##90--103), and by His marvelous miracles He surely impressed them with His power to overcome opposition of every kind.

But up to this point the training of the apostles for their future work appears to have been incidental in the labors of Jesus. He seems to have given His chief attention to the people at large—relieving their

145

suffering by His miracles, and impressing them with social ideals and standards which were new to them, and infinitely higher than those taught by the scribes. However, after His last visit to Nazareth, at least for some months, the emphasis appears to have been reversed— He gave His chief attention to the schooling of the apostles, and His ministrations to the multitudes seem to have been incidental. Two constituent features in the education of the twelve which were achieved during the period before us were: (1) They were given some practical experience in preaching and working miracles without the presence of Jesus. This was in the practice tours on which Jesus sent them as related in ##113, 114, 117. The reporting of their experiences on these tours probably occupied their attention for several weeks after their return. (2) After carefully preparing them to hear it, Jesus announced to them that His mission on earth would involve a tragic death at the hands of His enemies, followed by a victorious resurrection from death. This period is sometimes called the "season of retirement," because during it Jesus made four journeys with the disciples outside of Jewish territory to get away from the Jewish multitudes. It was on the last of these journeys that He informed them of the death which He must die.

I. The Practice Tours of the Apostles and Jesus' Third Tour of Galilee, ##112–117

1. Introductory summary

#112

MATT. 9:35-38	MARK 6:6b
35 And Jesus went about all the cities and the villages, teaching in their synagogues, and preaching the ¹gospel of the kingdom, and healing all manner of disease and all manner of sickness. 36 But when he saw the multitudes, he was moved with compassion for them, because they were distressed and scattered, as sheep not having a shepherd. 37 Then saith he unto his disciples, The harvest indeed is plenteous, but the laborers are few. 38 Pray ye therefore the Lord of the harvest, that he send forth laborers into his harvest.	6b And he went round about the villages teaching.

Note 113. Without doubt the foregoing passages are a preview summary of the labors of Jesus for some weeks at the beginning of this period (cf. Matthew's summary of the first tour of Galilee, Matt 4:23--25, #43). Verses 36--38 in Matthew reveal both the reaction of Jesus to the condition of the multitude and how he laid that condition on the hearts of the apostles.

2. Instruction to the twelve for their practice trip

#113

MATT. 10:1-42	MARK 6:7-11	LUKE 9:1-5
1 And he called unto him his twelve disciples, and	7 And he calleth unto him the twelve, and began to	1 And he called t[ ] twelve together, and ga[ ]

146

Matt. 10	Mark 6	Luke 9
gave them authority over unclean spirits, to cast them out, and to heal all manner of disease and all manner of sickness.	send them forth by two and two; and he gave them authority over the unclean spirits;	them power and authority over all demons, and to cure diseases. 2 And he sent them forth to preach the kingdom of God, and to heal ¹the sick.

Matt. 10

gave them authority over unclean spirits, to cast them out, and to heal all manner of disease and all manner of sickness.

2 Now the names of the twelve apostles are these: The first, Simon, who is called Peter, and Andrew his brother; ¹James the *son* of Zebedee, and John his brother; 3 Philip, and Bartholomew; Thomas, and Matthew the ²publican; ¹James the *son* of Alphaeus, and Thaddaeus; 4 Simon the ³Cananaean, and Judas Iscariot, who also ⁴betrayed him.

5 These twelve Jesus sent forth, and charged them, saying, Go not into *any* way of the Gentiles, and enter not into any city of the Samaritans; 6 but go rather to the lost sheep of the house of Israel. 7 And as ye go, preach, saying, The kingdom of heaven is at hand. 8 Heal the sick, raise the dead, cleanse the lepers, cast out demons: freely ye received, freely give. 9 Get you no gold, nor silver, nor brass in your ⁵purses; 10 no wallet for *your* journey, neither two coats, nor shoes, nor staff: for the laborer is worthy of his food. 11 And into whatsoever city or village ye shall enter, search out who in it is worthy; and there abide till ye go forth. 12 And as ye enter into the house, salute it. 13 And if the house be worthy, let your peace come upon it: but if it be not worthy, let your peace return to you. 14 And whosoever shall not receive you, nor hear your words, as ye go forth out of that house or that city, shake off the dust of your

¹ Or, *Jacob*
² See marginal note on ch. 5. 46.
³ Or, *Zealot*. See Lk. 6. 15;
   Acts 1. 13.
⁴ Or, *delivered him up*
⁵ Gr. *girdles*.

Mark 6

8 and he charged them that they should take nothing for *their* journey, save a staff only; no bread, no wallet, no ¹money in their ²purse; 9 but *to go* shod with sandals: and, *said he*, put not on two coats.

10 And he said unto them, Wheresoever ye enter into a house, there abide till ye depart thence. 11 And whatsoever place shall not receive you, and they hear you not, as ye go forth thence, shake off the dust that is under your feet for a testimony unto them.

¹ Gr. *brass*   ² Gr. *girdle*.

Luke 9

3 And he said unto them, Take nothing for your journey, neither staff, nor wallet, nor bread, nor money; neither have two coats.

4 And into whatsoever house ye enter, there abide, and thence depart. 5 And as many as receive you not, when ye depart from that city, shake off the dust from your feet for a testimony against them.

¹ Some ancient authorities omit *the sick*.

147

Matt. 10

feet. 15 Verily I say unto
you, It shall be more tolerable for the land of Sodom
and Gomorrah in the day
of judgment, than for that
city.

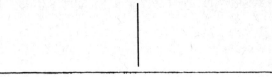

MATT. 10:16-42

16 Behold, I send you forth as sheep in the midst of wolves: be ye therefore wise as serpents, and [1]harmless as doves. 17 But beware of men: for they will deliver you up to councils, and in their synagogues they will scourge you; 18 yea and before governors and kings shall ye be brought for my sake, for a testimony to them and to the Gentiles. 19 But when they deliver you up, be not anxious how or what ye shall speak: for it shall be given you in that hour what ye shall speak. 20 For it is not ye that speak, but the Spirit of your Father that speaketh in you. 21 And brother shall deliver up brother to death, and the father his child: and children shall rise up against parents, and [2]cause them to be put to death. 22 And ye shall be hated of all men for my name's sake: but he that endureth to the end, the same shall be saved. 23 But when they persecute you in this city, flee into the next: for verily I say unto you, Ye shall not have gone through the cities of Israel, till the Son of man be come.

24 A disciple is not above his teacher, nor a [3]servant above his lord. 25 It is enough for the disciple that he be as his teacher, and the [3]servant as his lord. If they have called the master of the house [4]Beelzebub, how much more them of his household! 26 Fear them not therefore: for there is nothing covered, that shall not be revealed; and hid, that shall not be known. 27 What I tell you in the darkness, speak ye in the light; and what ye hear in the ear, proclaim upon the house-tops. 28 And be not afraid of them that kill the body, but are not able to kill the soul: but rather fear him who is able to destroy both soul and body in [5]hell. 29 Are not two sparrows sold for a penny? and not one of them shall fall on the ground without your Father: 30 but the very hairs of your head are all numbered. 31 Fear not therefore: ye are of more value than many sparrows. 32 Every one therefore who shall confess [6]me before men, [7]him will I also confess before my Father who is in heaven. 33 But whosoever shall deny me before men, him will I also deny before my Father who is in heaven.

34 Think not that I came to [8]send peace on the earth: I came not to [8]send peace, but a sword. 35 For I came to set a man at variance against his father, and the daughter against her mother, and the daughter in law against her mother in law: 36 and a man's foes *shall be* they of his own household. 37 He that loveth father or mother more than me is not worthy of me; and he that loveth son or daughter more than me is not worthy of me. 38 And he that doth not take his cross and follow after me, is not worthy of me. 39 He that [9]findeth his life shall lose it; and he that [10]loseth his life for my sake shall find it.

40 He that receiveth you receiveth me, and he that receiveth me receiveth him that sent me. 41 He that receiveth a prophet in the name of a prophet shall receive a prophet's reward: and he that receiveth a righteous man in the name of a righteous man shall receive a righteous man's reward. 42 And whosoever shall give to drink unto one of these little ones a cup of cold water only, in the name of a disciple, verily I say unto you he shall in no wise lose his reward.

[1] Or, *simple*   [2] Or, *put them to death*   [3] Gr. *bondservant.*   [4] Gr. *Beelzebul.*
[5] Gr. *Gehenna.*   [6] Gr. *in me.*   [7] Gr. *in him.*   [8] Gr. *cast.*
[9] Or, *found.*   [10] Or. *lost.*

Note 114. The journeys of the apostles in pairs were indeed practice tours, and the instructions which Jesus gave for them, as related by Mark and Luke and in verses 1--14 of the Matthew passage, were intended definitely for these journeys. In at least three particulars these instructions were different from those which He would later give them for their life service in what we call "The Great Commission"; (1) On these practice tours they were not to go among the Gentiles, or even into any city of the Samaritans, but only "to the lost sheep of the house of Israel" (Matt. 10: 5—6). But in the commission to their life's work, Jesus sent them among all nations (Matt. 28: 19, #269; Luke 24: 47, #271), or into all the world (Mark 16: 15, #271). (2) On the practice tours all that they were commissioned to preach was that "the Kingdom of Heaven is at hand," but in their life's work they were instructed to "preach the gospel" of "repentence and remission of sins" on the basis of Christ's suffering and resurrection (Mark 16: 15; Luke 24: 46). (3) For their practice tours they were sent out without purse or wallet, nor were they to take along extra clothing. They were expected to subsist on the generosity of the people among whom they would minister.* But for their life's work Jesus instructed them to take their purse and their wallet; in other words, to make use of such possessions and advantages as they could rightfully claim (Luke 22: 36, #233).

However, we are bound to conclude that many of the hardships of which Jesus forewarned them in Matt. 10: 16—42 were those which the disciples, and the Christians generally, would encounter in their work after the ascension of Jesus. It is not likely that the apostles suffered all those things on the short practice tours. Many of the things included in these verses of Matthew will be found repeated on later occasions; for instance, compare Matt. 10: 19 with Mark 13: 11 and Luke 12: 4—5; also Matt. 10: 32—33 with Mark 8: 38 and Luke 9: 56; also Matt. 10: 39; with Matt. 16: 25; Mark 8: 35; Luke 9: 24; 17: 33; and John 12: 25. Also compare the whole passage with Luke 12: 1—12. Those were important warnings which Jesus would keep before the disciples from that time forth.

3. The Work of the Disciples
#114

MARK 6:12-13
12 And they went out, and preached that *men* should repent. 13 And they cast out many demons, and anointed with oil many that were sick, and healed them.

LUKE 9:6
6 And they departed, and went throughout the villages, preaching the ¹gospel, and healing everywhere.
¹ Or, *good tidings*

Note 115. Evidently the pairs of apostles had the cities where they were to labor assigned to them. Their preaching while on these tours must have been like that of John the Baptist. Jesus had instructed them to proclaim that "the Kingdom of Heaven is at hand," and Mark related that they preached that all men should repent. John's preaching (and the early preaching of Jesus) consisted of both these proclamations (cf. Matt. 3: 2; 4: 17).

4. Jesus' Third Tour of Galilee
#115

MATT. 11:1
1 And it came to pass when Jesus had finished commanding his twelve disciples, he departed thence to teach and preach in their cities.

*The "wallet" ("scrip" in the King James Version) probably corresponded to our present day hand bag or shoulder pouch. These journeys would not last long, and the people would doubtless gladly give them lodging and food.

149

Note 116. Seemingly, while the pairs of apostles were on their missions, Jesus went alone on this the third tour of Galilee, visiting cities not assigned to the apostles. The tour narrated in the foregoing verse is probably the same as the one described in Matt. 9: 35, #112.

5. Fears of Herod Antipas, who about this time beheaded John the Baptist, aroused by the success of Jesus and the twelve

#116

MATT. 14:1-12	MARK 6:14-29	LUKE 9:7-9
1 At that season Herod the tetrarch heard the report concerning Jesus, 2 and said unto his servants, This is John the Baptist; he is risen from the dead; and therefore do these powers work in him.	14 And king Herod heard *thereof*; for his name had become known: and ¹he said, John the Baptizer is risen from the dead, and therefore do these powers work in him. 15 But others said, It is Elijah. And others said, *It is* a prophet, *even* as one of the prophets. 16 But Herod, when he heard *thereof*, said, John, whom I beheaded, he is risen. 17 For Herod himself had sent forth and laid hold upon John, and bound him in prison for the sake of Herodias, his brother Philip's wife; for he had married her. 18 For John said unto Herod, It is not lawful for thee to have thy brother's wife. 19 And Herodias set herself against him, and desired to kill him; and she could not; 20 for Herod feared John, knowing that he was a righteous and holy man, and kept him safe. And when he heard him, he ²was much perplexed; and he heard him gladly. 21 And when a convenient day was come, that Herod on his birthday made a supper to his lords, and the ³high captains, and the chief men of Galilee; 22 and when ⁴the daughter of Herodias herself came in and danced, ⁵she pleased	7 Now Herod the tetrarch heard of all that was done: and he was much perplexed, because that it was said by some, that John was risen from the dead; 8 and by some, that Elijah had appeared; and by others, that one of the old prophets was risen again. 9 And Herod said, John I beheaded: but who is this, about whom I hear such things? And he sought to see him.
3 For Herod had laid hold on John, and bound him, and put him in prison for the sake of Herodias, his brother Philip's wife. 4 For John said unto him, It is not lawful for thee to have her. 5 And when he would have put him to death, he feared the multitude, because they counted him as a prophet.		
6 But when Herod's birthday came, the daughter of Herodias danced in the midst, and pleased Herod. 7 Whereupon he promised with an oath to give her whatsoever she should ask.		

¹ Some ancient authorities read *they.*
² Many ancient authorities read *did many things.*
³ Or, *military tribunes.* Gr. *chiliarchs.*
⁴ Some ancient authorities read *his daughter Herodias.*
⁵ Or, *it*

150

Matt. 14   Mark 6

Herod and them that sat at meat with him; and the king said unto the damsel, Ask of me whatsoever thou wilt, and I will give it thee. 23 And he sware unto her, Whatsoever thou shalt ask of me, I will give it thee, unto the half of my kingdom.

8 And she, being put forward by her mother, saith, Give me here on a platter the head of John the Baptist.

24 And she went out, and said unto her mother, What shall I ask? And she said, The head of John the Baptizer. 25 And she came in straightway with haste unto the king, and asked, saying, I will that thou forthwith give me on a platter the head of John the Baptist.

9 And the king was grieved; but for the sake of his oaths, and of them that sat at meat with him, he commanded it to be given; 10 and he sent and beheaded John in the prison. 11 And his head was brought on a platter, and given to the damsel: and she brought it to her mother. 12 And his disciples came, and took up the corpse, and buried him; and they went and told Jesus.

26 And the king was exceeding sorry; but for the sake of his oaths, and of them that sat at meat, he would not reject her. 27 And straightway the king sent forth a soldier of his guard, and commanded to bring his head: and he went and beheaded him in the prison, 28 and brought his head on a platter, and gave it to the damsel; and the damsel gave it to her mother. 29 And when his disciples heard *thereof*, they came and took up his corpse, and laid it in a tomb.

Note 117. The student should reread the paragraph on page 5 naming the successors of Herod the Great, who was ruler in Palestine when Jesus was born. The Herod of the foregoing section is known in history as Herod Antipas, who was tetrarch* in Galilee and Peraea. The elder Herod (Herod the Great) had children by as many as seven of his ten wives, and their relations among themselves were considerably intertwined. Antipas was half brother to Philip, the first husband of Herodias and father of Salome, the girl who danced at Antipas' birthday feast; and the father of Herodias (Aristobulus) was half brother of both Philip and Antipas. This Philip lived in Rome and was not ruler over any territory; but there was another Philip, half brother to all the above mentioned, who was tetrarch of the territory east of the Sea of Galilee

*This term originally meant one of four rulers among whom a kingdom or country was divided. Later it came to designate a hereditary ruler of a small principality whose power and prestige did not justify the title "king," however, Mark consistently calls Antipas "king," also Matthew in vs. 9.

151

(Ituraea and Trachonitis, cf. Luke 3:1), and who later married Salome, the daughter of Herodias mentioned above. Incestuous marriages
and utter disregard for human life in their unceasing efforts to further
their own power and station characterize the members of the Herod family
in all their history. Probably John's criticism of Antipas merely echoed
the sentiments with which all devout Jews regarded the tetrarch, because his actions in this matter flagrantly violated the Mosaic code
(Lev. 18:16).

John had probably been kept in tortuous confinement in the prison
connected with Herod's palace in Machaerus for more than a year, until
he was sacrificed to the hatred of the unscrupulous Herodias. For a re-
view of the life of John the Baptist see ##4, 7, 17, 18, 21, 22, 27
28, 80, and 116. Mention is also made of him by Josephus in his
Antiquities of the Jews (XVIII, v, 2).

We wonder just when the murder of John took place or how long it
was before the fame of Jesus made Herod believe that Jesus was John
come back to life. Very probably the death of John occurred about the
time of the beginning of practice tours, or before; and the disciples of
John came to Jesus with their sorrow while He was journeying alone
Probably it was a good while later when the news of the combined successes of Jesus and of the disciples aroused the superstitious fears o
Herod and the speculations of many of the people. Compare Mark
6:14--16 and Luke 9:7--9 with Matt. 16:14 and parallels in #130.

6. The return of the jubilant apostles
#117

MARK 6:30	LUKE 9:10
30 And the apostles gather them-selves together unto Jesus; and they told him all things, whatsoever they had done, and whatsoever they had taught.	10 And the apostles, when they were returned, declared unto him what things they had done.

Note 118. Surely there was an understanding about the time and
the place for Jesus and the apostles to meet after the practice tours
Naturally the apostles would be excited and enthusiastic over their successes. But their gladness was certainly mingled with grief on learning
about the death of John the Baptist. To give comfort to the sorrowing
disciples of John and to give the returning apostles opportunity to repor
their experiences and successes, Jesus suggested withdrawing for seclusion and rest.

II. Second journey across the Sea of Galilee (the first retirement),
##118--120
1. Feeding the five thousand
#118

MATT. 14:13-21	MARK 6:31-44	LUKE 9:10 - 17	JOHN 6:1-13
	31 And he saith unto them, Come ye yourselves apart into a desert place, and rest a while. For		1 After these things Jesus went away to the other side of the sea of Galilee, which is the

Matt. 14	Mark 6	Luke 9	John 6
	there were many coming and going, and they had no leisure so much as to eat. 32 And they went away in the boat to a desert place apart. 33 And *the people* saw them going, and many knew *them*, and they ran together there ¹on foot from all the cities, and outwent them. 34 And he came forth and saw a great multitude, and he had compassion on them, because they were as sheep not having a shepherd: and he began to teach them many things. 35 And when the day was now far spent, his disciples came unto him, and said, The place is desert, and the day is now far spent; 36 send them away, that they may go into the country and villages round about, and buy themselves somewhat to eat. 37 But he answered and said unto them, Give ye them to eat. And they say unto him, Shall we go and buy two hundred ²shillings' worth of bread, and give them to eat? 38 And he saith unto them, How many loaves have ye? go *and* see. And when they knew, they say, Five, and two fishes. 39 And he commanded them		*sea* of Tiberias. 2 And a great multitude followed him, because they beheld the signs which he did on them that were sick. 3 And Jesus went up into the mountain, and there he sat with his disciples. 4 Now the passover, the feast of the Jews, was at hand.
13 Now when Jesus heard it, he withdrew from thence in a boat, to a desert place apart: and when the multitudes heard *thereof*, they followed him ¹on foot from the cities. 14 And he came forth, and saw a great multitude, and he had compassion on them, and healed their sick.		10b And he took them, and withdrew apart to a city called Bethsaida. 11 But the multitudes perceiving it followed him: and he welcomed them, and spake to them of the kingdom of God, and them that had need of healing he cured.	
15 And when even was come, the disciples came to him, saying, The place is desert, and the time is already past; send the multitudes away, that they may go into the villages, and buy themselves food.		12 And the day began to wear away; and the twelve came, and said unto him, Send the multitude away, that they may go into the villages and country round about, and lodge, and get provisions: for we are here in a desert place. 13 But he said unto them, Give ye them to eat.	5 Jesus therefore lifting up his eyes, and seeing that a great multitude cometh unto him, saith unto Philip, Whence are we to buy ¹bread, that these may eat? 6 And this he said to prove him: for he himself knew what he would do. 7 Philip answered him, Two hundred ²shillings' worth of ¹bread is not sufficient for them, that every one may take a little. 8 One of his disciples, Andrew, Simon Peter's brother, saith unto him, 9 There is a lad here, who hath five barley loaves, and two fishes: but what are
16 But Jesus said unto them, They have no need to go away; give ye them to eat.			
17 And they say unto him, We have here but five loaves, and two fishes. 18 And he said, Bring them hither to me.		And they said, We have no more than five loaves and two fishes; except we should go and buy food for all this people. 14 For they were about five thousand men.	
¹ Or, *by land*	¹ Or, *by land* ² The word in the Greek denotes a coin worth about eight pence half-penny, or nearly seventeen cents.		¹ Gr. *loaves.* ² The word in the Greek denotes a coin worth about eight pence halfpenny, or nearly seventeen cents.

Matt. 14	Mark 6	Luke 9	John 6
19 And he commanded the multitudes to ²sit down on the grass; and he took the five loaves, and the two fishes, and looking up to heaven, he blessed, and brake and gave the loaves to the disciples, and the disciples to the multitudes. 20 And they all ate, and were filled: and they took up that which remained over of the broken pieces, twelve baskets full. 21 And they that did eat were about five thousand men, besides women and children.	that all should ³sit down by companies upon the green grass. 40 And they sat down in ranks, by hundreds, and by fifties. 41 And he took the five loaves and the two fishes, and looking up to heaven, he blessed, and brake the loaves; and he gave to the disciples to set before them; and the two fishes divided he among them all. 42 And they all ate, and were filled. 43 And they took up broken pieces, twelve basketfuls, and also of the fishes. 44 And they that ate the loaves were five thousand men.	And he said unto his disciples, Make them ¹sit down in companies, about fifty each. 15 And they did so, and made them all ¹sit down. 16 And he took the five loaves and the two fishes, and looking up to heaven, he blessed them, and brake; and gave to the disciples to set before the multitude. 17 And they ate, and were all filled: and there was taken up that which remained over to them of broken pieces, twelve baskets.	these among so many? 10 Jesus said, Make the people sit down. Now there was much grass in the place. So the men sat down, in number about five thousand. 11 Jesus therefore took the loaves; and having given thanks, he distributed to them that were set down; likewise also of the fishes as much as they would. 12 And when they were filled, he saith unto his disciples, Gather up the broken pieces which remain over, that nothing be lost. 13 So they gathered them up, and filled twelve baskets with broken pieces from the five barley loaves, which remained over unto them that had eaten.
² Gr. recline.	³ Gr. recline.	¹ Gr. recline.	

Note 119. Except the resurrection of Jesus from death, the feeding of the five thousand is the only miracle narrated in all four gospels.

Was Jesus disappointed that He and His company did not get a day of rest and quiet? Or did He know when He suggested "come ye yourselves apart...and rest" (Mark 6:31) that the multitudes would meet them, and that the only rest they would get would be while they were crossing the lake in the boat? Surely He did not begrudge the multitude a day of healing and teaching and feeding, but was He surprised that the multitude followed? We have seen that Jesus could be surprised (Matt. 8:10; Luke 7:9, #78 and Mark 6:6, #111); so it is not doubting His deity if one should say that He was both surprised and in a measure disappointed at this time. We remember that during His earthly life He "emptied Himself" (Phil. 2:6 A.S.V.). Probably it was because He did not have opportunity that day to be alone with the disciples that He led them on a longer journey of retirement.

We know from John 6:4 that it was the Passover season of the year. This is the third Passover of our Lord's ministry (if the feast of John 5 was a Passover) and just a year before He would die.

This was the first of two miraculous feedings of the multitudes (cf. #126). It is significant that although our Lord refused to make bread out of stones for Himself (Matt. 4:3—4, #19), He did not hesitate to

154

multiply the loaves for the multitude. But He would not be their king and keep on multiplying their loaves.

2. Dispelling the multitude, retirement for prayer

#119

MATT. 14:22-23	MARK 6:45-46	JOHN 6:14-17
22 And straightway he constrained the disciples to enter into the boat, and to go before him unto the other side, till he should send the multitudes away. 23 And after he had sent the multitudes away, he went up into the mountain apart to pray: and when even was come, he was there alone.	45 And straightway he constrained his disciples to enter into the boat, and to go before *him* unto the other side to Bethsaida, while he himself sendeth the multitude away. 46 And after he had taken leave of them, he departed into the mountain to pray.	14 When therefore the people saw the ¹sign which he did, they said, This is of a truth the prophet that cometh into the world. 15 Jesus therefore, perceiving that they were about to come and take him by force, to make him king, withdrew again into the mountain himself alone. 16 And when evening came, his disciples went down unto the sea; 17 and they entered into a boat, and were going over the sea unto Capernaum.

¹ Some ancient authorities read *signs*.

Note 120. Jesus saw in the intention of the multitude to "take Him by force to make Him a king" (John 6:14) a recurrence of the temptation in which the Devil promised to give Him all the kingdoms of the world if He would worship that one who was the source of all evil (Matt. 4:8-9, #19). Probably the disciples shared and approved the purpose of the multitude. If He had yielded to their demands, He would have established the visible Kingdom before He made possible redemption from sin, and the era of the spiritual Kingdom would have been eliminated from His program (cf. Note 18). But to establish His visible Kingdom without redemption would have been nothing short of letting sin and death continue to reign (Rom. 5:14; 6:12), which, in turn, was equivalent to worshiping the Devil. However, Jesus knew that God's program was:

First, that He should pay the price of redemption in His death and resurrection, also that He should inaugurate the spiritual Kingdom with the redeemed ones as His subjects.

Second, that during the present age the disciples would proclaim the provision for redemption for all who will accept it, and thus advance the spiritual Kingdom.

Then third, that when this age is fulfilled, He should come to earth a second time to transform the spiritual Kingdom into the visible one.

Therefore, to forestall this purpose, which was becoming a plan of action, Jesus instructed the disciples to get into the boat at once and return to the western shore. Then, after dispersing the multitude, He hurried to a convenient place on the nearby mountain side to pray. In an hour of such temptation, even Jesus needed special strength from the Father to keep Him steadfast in the eternal program.

3. Walking on the water to overtake the twelve on their return to Capernaum, stilling the storm

#120

MATT. 14:24-33	MARK 6:47-52	JOHN 6:17b-21
24 But the boat ¹was now in the midst of the sea, distressed by the waves; for the wind was contrary. 25 And in the fourth watch of the night he came unto them, walking upon the sea. 26 And when the disciples saw him walking on the sea, they were troubled, saying, It is a ghost: and they cried out for fear. 27 But straightway Jesus spake unto them, saying, Be of good cheer; it is I; be not afraid. 28 And Peter answered him and said, Lord, if it be thou, bid me come unto thee upon the waters. 29 And he said, Come. And Peter went down from the boat, and walked upon the waters ²to come to Jesus. 30 But when he saw the ³wind, he was afraid; and beginning to sink, he cried out, saying, Lord, save me. 31 And immediately Jesus stretched forth his hand, and took hold of him, and saith unto him, O thou of little faith, wherefore didst thou doubt? 32 And when they were gone up into the boat, the wind ceased. 33 And they that were in the boat ⁴worshipped him, saying, Of a truth thou art the Son of God.	47 And when even was come, the boat was in the midst of the sea, and he alone on the land. 48 And seeing them distressed in rowing, for the wind was contrary unto them, about the fourth watch of the night he cometh unto them, walking on the sea; and he would have passed by them: 49 but they, when they saw him walking on the sea, supposed that it was a ghost, and cried out; 50 for they all saw him, and were troubled. But he straightway spake with them, and saith unto them, Be of good cheer: it is I; be not afraid.

51 And he went up unto them into the boat; and the wind ceased: and they were sore amazed in themselves; 52 for they understood not concerning the loaves, but their heart was hardened. | 17b And it was now dark, and Jesus had not yet come to them. 18 And the sea was rising by reason of a great wind that blew. 19 When therefore they had rowed about five and twenty or thirty furlongs, they behold Jesus walking on the sea, and drawing nigh unto the boat: and they were afraid. 20 But he saith unto them, It is I; be not afraid.

21 They were willing therefore to receive him into the boat: and straightway the boat was at the land whither they were going. |

¹ Some ancient authorities read *was many furlongs distant from the land.*
² Some ancient authorities read *and came.*
³ Many ancient authorities add *strong.*
⁴ See marginal note on ch. 2. 2.

Note 121. Observe three miracles, all manifesting His power over the external world, which Jesus performed during the day and night while He was on this trip across the lake: (1) increasing the loaves and fishes to feed the multitude, (2) walking on the water, and (3) stilling a storm. This was the second time when Jesus calmed a storm on the sea. On the former occasion, He was in the boat with the disciples when the storm arose (#104), and they knew that He was available to their call; but this time when it began to rage, He was miles away.

Yet, from His place of prayer He saw them and observed their struggles (Mark 6:48); and He did not hesitate to perform a miracle in order to come to them. What better preparation could these future missionaries have had for the time when they would be deprived of His physical presence? Not very long before His death He warned these disciples that the time was coming when they would wish in vain for a day in His bodily presence (Luke 17:22, #183). Nevertheless, after the resurrection, when He commissioned them for their world-wide labors, He assured them that He would be with them (and with their successors) all the days until the end of this age (Matt. 28:20, #269). Remembering the experience of this night, the disciples were prepared to trust that promise.

III. Treatment received on return to the coasts of Galilee, ##121—123

   1. Deserted by the multitude at Capernaum (after discourse on the Bread of Life), remaining in Galilee during Passover season

#121

JOHN 6:22—7:1

22 On the morrow the multitude that stood on the other side of the sea saw that there was no other [1]boat there, save one, and that Jesus entered not with his disciples into the boat, but *that* his disciples went away alone 23 (howbeit there came [2]boats from Tiberias nigh unto the place where they ate the bread after the Lord had given thanks): 24 when the multitude therefore saw that Jesus was not there, neither his disciples, they themselves got into the [2]boats, and came to Capernaum, seeking Jesus. 25 And when they found him on the other side of the sea, they said unto him, Rabbi, when camest thou hither? 26 Jesus answered them and said, Verily, verily, I say unto you, Ye seek me, not because ye saw signs, but because ye ate of the loaves, and were filled. 27 Work not for the food which perisheth, but for the food which abideth unto eternal life, which the Son of man shall give unto you: for him the Father, *even* God, hath sealed. 28 They said therefore unto him, What must we do, that we may work the works of God? 29 Jesus answered and said unto them, This is the work of God, that ye believe on him whom [3]he hath sent. 30 They said therefore unto him, What then doest thou for a sign, that we may see, and believe thee? what workest thou? 31 Our fathers ate the manna in the wilderness; as it is written, He [4]gave them bread out of heaven to eat. 32 Jesus therefore said unto them, Verily, verily, I say unto you, It was not Moses that gave you the bread out of heaven; but my Father giveth you the true bread out of heaven. 33 For the bread of God is that which cometh down out of heaven, and giveth life unto the world. 34 They said therefore unto him, Lord, evermore give us this bread. 35 Jesus said unto them, I am the bread of life: he that cometh to me shall not hunger, and he that believeth on me shall never thirst. 36 But I said unto you, that ye have seen me, and yet believe not. 37 All that which the Father giveth me shall come unto me; and him that cometh to me I will in no wise cast out. 38 For I am came down from heaven, not to do mine own will, but the will of him that sent me. 39 And this is the will of him that sent me, that of all that which he hath given me I should lose nothing, but should raise it up at the last day. 40 For this is the will of my Father, that every one that beholdeth the Son, and believeth on him, should have eternal life: and [5]I will raise him up at the last day.

41 The Jews therefore murmured concerning him, because he said, I am the bread which came down out of heaven. 42 And they said, Is not this Jesus, the son of Joseph, whose father and mother we know? how doth he now say, I am come down out of heaven? 43 Jesus answered and said unto them, Murmur not among yourselves. 44 No man can come to me, except the Father that sent me

---

[1] Gr. *little boat.*   [2] Gr. *little boats.*   [3] Or, *he sent*

[4] Neh. ix. 15; Ex. xvi. 4, 15; Ps. lxxviii. 24; cv. 40.   [5] Or, *that I should raise him up*

draw him: and I will raise him up in the last day. 45 It is written in the prophets, ⁶And they shall all be taught of God. Every one that hath heard from the Father, and hath learned, cometh unto me. 46 Not that any man hath seen the Father, save he that is from God, he hath seen the Father. 47 Verily, verily, I say unto you, He that believeth hath eternal life. 48 I am the bread of life. 49 Your fathers ate the manna in the wilderness, and they died. 50 This is the bread which cometh down out of heaven, that a man may eat thereof, and not die. 51 I am the living bread which came down out of heaven: if any man eat of this bread, he shall live for ever: yea and the bread which I will give is my flesh, for the life of the world.

52 The Jews therefore strove one with another, saying, How can this man give us his flesh to eat? 53 Jesus therefore said unto them, Verily, verily, I say unto you, Except ye eat the flesh of the Son of man and drink his blood, ye have not life in yourselves. 54 He that eateth my flesh and drinketh my blood hath eternal life; and I will raise him up at the last day. 55 For my flesh is ⁷meat indeed, and my blood is ⁸drink indeed. 56 He that eateth my flesh and drinketh my blood abideth in me, and I in him. 57 As the living Father sent me, and I live because of the Father; so he that eateth me, he also shall live because of me. 58 This is the bread which came down out of heaven: not as the fathers ate, and died; he that eateth this bread shall live forever. 59 These things said he in ⁹the synagogue, as he taught in Capernaum.

60 Many therefore of his disciples, when they heard this, said, This is a hard saying; who can hear ¹⁰it? 61 But Jesus knowing in himself that his disciples murmured at this, said unto them, Doth this cause you to stumble? 62 What then if ye should behold the Son of man ascending where he was before? 63 It is the spirit that giveth life; the flesh profiteth nothing: the words that I have spoken unto you are spirit, and are life. 64 But there are some of you that believe not. For Jesus knew from the beginning who they were that believed not, and who it was that should ¹¹betray him. 65 And he said, For this cause have I said unto you, that no man can come unto me, except it be given unto him of the Father.

66 Upon this many of his disciples went back, and walked no more with him. 67 Jesus said therefore unto the twelve, Would ye also go away? 68 Simon Peter answered him, Lord, to whom shall we go? thou ¹²hast the words of eternal life. 69 And we have believed and know that thou art the Holy One of God. 70 Jesus answered them, Did not I choose you the twelve, and one of you is a devil? 71 Now he spake of Judas the son of Simon Iscariot, for he it was that should ¹¹betray him, being one of the twelve.

1 And after these things Jesus walked in Galilee: for he would not walk in Judaea, because the Jews sought to kill him.

⁶ Is. liv. 13; (Jer. xxxi. 34?).　　　　⁷ Gr. true meat.　　　⁸ Gr. true drink.
⁹ Or, a synagogue　　　¹⁰ Or, him　　　¹¹ Or, deliver him up　　　¹² Or, hast words

Note 122. This was a turning point in the life of the Lord Jesus. The key verse of the passage is doubtless verse 66: "Many of His 'disciples' went back, and walked no more with Him." This was the last Galilean multitude to gather around Him, there were to be others in Decapolis and Judaea and Peraea, but no more in Galilee. It should be remembered that these were the same people who were so intent the day before, on compelling Jesus to be their king. He knew that they were seeking Him to obtain more loaves and fishes, not because they were impressed by His miracles. And because of that fact, doubtless, Jesus was willing to let the multitude go away, so that He might in the months ahead give His attention to the twelve.

In this discourse with them He set forth the following in rather veiled figures: (1) the surpassing value of spiritual benefits over the physical food, (2) His own heavenly origin and the necessity for divine enlightenment in order to exercise true faith in Him, (3) the blessings bestowed on those who submit themselves to Him to be (a) eternal life and (b) being raised up on the last day, and (4) the means by which He would bestow these blessings to be His coming down from Heaven in a human (flesh and blood) manner of life in which He was destined to experience death and a resurrection. But those people did not understand what He was talking about, and they were not interested in such things anyway. They merely wanted a king who could supply their physical needs. Therefore they went away.

2. Sought by the people of Gennesaret
#122

Matt. 14:34-36	Mark 6:53-56
34 And when they had crossed over, they came to the land, unto Gennesaret. 35 And when the men of that place knew him, they sent into all that region round about, and brought unto him all that were sick; 36 and they besought him that they might only touch the border of his garment: and as many as touched were made whole.	53 And when they had [1]crossed over, they came to the land unto Gennesaret, and moored to the shore. 54 And when they were come out of the boat, straightway *the people* knew him, 55 and ran round about that whole region, and began to carry about on their [2]beds those that were sick, where they heard he was. 56 And wheresoever he entered, into villages, or into cities, or into the country, they laid the sick in the marketplaces, and besought him that they might touch if it were but the border of his garment: and as many as touched [3]him were made whole.

[1] Or, *crossed over to the land, they came unto Gennesaret*   [2] Or, *pallets*   [3] Or, *it*

3. Criticized by the Pharisees from Jerusalem for disregarding Rabbinical Tradition, or the Oral Law
#123

Matt. 15:1-20	Mark 7:1-23
1 Then there come to Jesus from Jerusalem Pharisees and scribes, saying, 2 Why do thy disciples transgress the tradition of the elders? for they wash not their hands when they eat bread.	1 And there are gathered together unto him the Pharisees, and certain of the scribes, who had come from Jerusalem, 2 and had seen that some of his disciples ate their bread with [1]defiled, that is, unwashen, hands. 3 (For the Pharisees, and all the Jews, except they wash their hands [2]diligently, eat not, holding the tradition of the elders; 4 and *when they come* from the marketplace, except they [3]bathe themselves, they eat not; and many other things there are, which they have received to hold, [4]washings of cups, and pots, and brasen vessels[5].) 5 And the Pharisees and the scribes ask him, Why walk not thy disciples according to the tradition of the elders, but eat their bread with [1]defiled hands? 6 And he said unto them, Well did Isaiah prophesy of you hypocrites, as it is written.
3 And he answered and said unto them, Why do ye also transgress the commandment of God because of your tradition? 4 For God said, [1]Honor thy father and thy mother: and, [2]He that speaketh evil	

[1] Ex. xx. 12; Dt. v. 16.
[2] Ex. xxi. 17; Lev. xx. 9.

[1] Or, *common*
[2] Or, *up to the elbow*. Gr. *with the fist*.
[3] Gr. *baptize*. Some ancient authorities read *sprinkle themselves*.   [4] Gr. *baptizings*.
[5] Many ancient authorities add *and couches*.

159

Matt. 15

of father or mother, let him [3]die the death. 5 But ye say, Whosoever shall say to his father or his mother, That wherewith thou mightest have been profited by me is given to God; 6 he shall not honor his father[4]. And ye have made void the [5]word of God because of your tradition. 7 Ye hypocrites, well did Isaiah prophesy of you, saying,

8 [6]This people honoreth me with their lips;
But their heart is far from me.
9 But in vain do they worship me,
Teaching as their doctrines the precepts of men.

10 And he called to him the multitude, and said unto them, Hear, and understand: 11 Not that which entereth into the mouth defileth the man; but that which proceedeth out of the mouth, this defileth the man. 12 Then came the disciples, and said unto him, Knowest thou that the Pharisees were [7]offended, when they heard this saying? 13 But he answered and said, Every [8]plant which my heavenly Father planted not, shall be rooted up. 14 Let them alone: they are blind guides. And if the blind guide the blind, both shall fall into a pit. 15 And Peter answered and said unto him, Declare unto us the parable. 16 And he said, Are ye also even yet without understanding? 17 Perceive ye not, that whatsoever goeth into the mouth passeth into the belly, and is cast out into the draught? 18 But the things which proceed out of the mouth come forth out of the heart; and they defile the man. 19 For out of the heart come forth evil thoughts, murders, adulteries, fornications, thefts, false witness, railings: 20 these are the things which defile the man; but to eat with unwashen hands defileth not the man.

3 Or, surely die
4 Some ancient authorities add or his mother.
5 Some ancient authorities read law.
6 Is. xxix.13.   7 Gr. caused to stumble.
8 Gr. planting.

Mark 7

6 This people honoreth me with their lips,
But their heart is far from me.
7 But in vain do they worship me,
Teaching as their doctrines the precepts of men.

8 Ye leave the commandment of God, and hold fast the tradition of men. 9 And he said unto them, Full well do ye reject the commandment of God, that ye may keep your tradition. 10 For Moses said, [7]Honor thy father and thy mother; and, He that speaketh evil of father or mother, let him [8]die the death: 11 but ye say, If a man shall say to his father or his mother, That wherewith thou mightest have been profited by me is Corban, that is to say, Given to God; 12 ye no longer suffer him to do aught for his father or his mother; 13 making void the word of God by your tradition, which ye have delivered: and many such like things ye do. 14 And he called to him the multitude again, and said unto them, Hear me all of you, and understand: 15 there is nothing from without the man, that going into him can defile him; but the things which proceed out of the man are those that defile the man.[9] 17 And when he was entered into the house from the multitude, his disciples asked of him the parable. 18 And he saith unto them, Are ye so without understanding also? Perceive ye not, that whatsoever from without goeth into the man, it cannot defile him; 19 because it goeth not into his heart, but into his belly, and goeth out into the draught? This he said, making all meats clean. 20 And he said, That which proceedeth out of the man, that defileth the man. 21 For from within, out of the heart of men, [10]evil thoughts proceed, fornications, thefts, murders, adulteries, 22 covetings, wickednesses, deceit, lasciviousness, an evil eye, railing, pride, foolishness: 23 all these evil things proceed from within, and defile the man.

6 Is. xxix. 13.
7 Ex. xx. 12; Dt. v. 16; Ex. xxi. 17; Lev. xx. 9.
8 Or, surely die
9 Many ancient authorities insert ver. 16
If any man hath ears to hear, let him hear.
See ch. 4. 9. 23.
10 Gr. thoughts that are evil.

Note 123. At this point Jesus encountered again His old enemies, the scribes from Jerusalem (Matt. 15: 1; Mark 7: 1). This was their third attack on Him in Galilee (cf. ##44 and 87 and notes following).

The point of criticism this time was His disregard for the traditional regulation for washing one's hands before eating. With these scribes this was not a matter of cleanliness or sanitation, but of ritual; and not a ritual commanded in the law of Moses either, but one imposed by the scribes. For centuries Jewish scribes and Rabbis had been rendering decisions and interpretations on their law. As these decisions grew into a sizable body, they came to be known as the Tradition, or the Oral Law, which in time came to be regarded as of equal authority with the written law given by Moses.*

The Tradition referred to in the foregoing section was probably the rabbinical comment on Leviticus 15 et al., which had to do with the cleansing of those who had become ceremonially unclean; though no passage in the law says anything about bathing before ordinary, every-day meals. But the tradition gave rise to a whole system of ablutions, which in Heb. 6:2 is called "the doctrine of baptisms." We wonder if the criticism was lodged against Jesus at this time because He had recently permitted more than five thousand people to eat the bread and fish which He provided without directing them first to cleanse themselves according to the precepts of the tradition.

Jesus gave a two-fold answer to this criticism: (1) To the scribes who voiced it He showed how their traditions and the importance which they attached to them overshadowed the law of God itself and destroyed its force. As an example He pointed to the practice of avaricious sons who took advantage of a tradition in order to evade the commandment to honor one's father and mother and contribute to their support when such was needed. The tradition provided that one might declare that his possessions were dedicated to God (that is "corban") and therefore were not available for the support of his parents who might be in need. The Tradition was thus the means of evading the law. (2) To the people at large He asserted that it is not what a person eats that defiles him in the sight of God, but the sins of his depraved heart which show themselves in his actions. Notice the list of these which Jesus gave in verses 19--20 of Matthew and 21--23 of Mark.

The last phrase in verse 19 of Mark ("purging all meats") was regarded by the translators of the American Standard Version as a comment by Mark on this saying of Jesus; that is, it had the effect of removing the distinction between the meat of "clean" and "unclean" animals (cf. Leviticus 11 and Acts 10:15). Certainly Jesus assured those who had partaken of the loaves and fishes which He provided that they did not sin against God by eating that food with unwashed hands.

IV. The second retirement, going north into Phoenicia, delivering the Syrophoenician woman's daughter from a demon

#124

MATT. 15:21-28	MARK 7:24-30
21 And Jesus went out thence, and	24 And from thence he arose, and

*Compare page 16 in the Introduction. Broadus, *Commentary on Matthew*, p. 332, quotes three rabbis as affirming that the Tradition was more authoritative and more important than the law.

161

#124, continued

Matt. 15	Mark 7
withdrew into the parts of Tyre and Sidon. 22 And behold, a Canaanitish woman came out from those borders, and cried, saying, Have mercy on me, O Lord, thou Son of David; my daughter is grievously vexed with a demon. 23 But he answered her not a word. And his disciples came and besought him, saying, Send her away; for she crieth after us. 24 But he answered and said, I was not sent but unto the lost sheep of the house of Israel. 25 But she came and [1]worshipped him, saying, Lord, help me. 26 And he answered and said, it is not meet to take the children's [2]bread and cast it to the dogs. 27 But she said, Yea, Lord: for even the dogs eat of the crumbs which fall from their masters' table. 28 Then Jesus answered and said unto her, O woman, great is thy faith: be it done unto thee even as thou wilt. And her daughter was healed from that hour.	went away into the borders of Tyre [1]and Sidon. And he entered into a house, and would have no man know it; and he could not be hid. 25 But straightway a woman, whose little daughter had an unclean spirit, having heard of him, came and fell down at his feet. 26 Now the woman was a [2]Greek, a Syrophoenician by race. And she besought him that he would cast forth the demon out of her daughter. 27 And he said unto her, Let the children first be filled: for it is not meet to take the children's [3]bread and cast it to the dogs. 28 But she answered and saith unto him, Yea, Lord; even the dogs under the table eat of the children's crumbs. 29 And he said unto her, For this saying go thy way; the demon is gone out of thy daughter. 30 And she went away unto her house, and found the child laid upon the bed, and the demon gone out.
[1] See marginal note on ch. 2. 2. [2] Or, *loaf*	[1] Some ancient authorities omit *and Sidon.* [2] Or, *Gentile* [3] Or, *loaf*

Note 124. At this time Jesus was surely shunning the multitudes in order that He might give special instructions to the twelve. He was preparing them for His momentous announcement to them that it was going to be necessary for Him to suffer death and rise again. On His second journey across the Sea of Galilee He was doubtless attempting to withdraw with the disciples away from the crowds; but the people followed, with the result He miraculously fed the five-thousand. Although Passover (the third during His public ministry) was at hand, He and the disciples did not go up to Jerusalem to celebrate the feast; but instead He led them on a second journey out of the Jewish country, going in an opposite direction from Jerusalem into the country of Tyre and Sidon. But even there, although "He would have no man know it," still "He could not be hid" (Mark 7: 24).

V. Going east and south into Decapolis (the third retirement), ##125-126

1. Healing a deaf and dumb man

#125

MATT. 15:29-31	MARK 7:31-37
29 And Jesus departed thence, and came nigh unto the sea of Galilee; and he went up into the mountain, and sat there. 30 And there came unto him great multitudes, having with them the lame, blind, dumb, maimed, and many others, and they cast them down at his feet; and he healed them:	31 And again he went out from the borders of Tyre, and came through Sidon unto the sea of Galilee, through the midst of the borders of Decapolis. 32 And they bring unto him one that was deaf, and had an impediment in his speech; and they beseech him to lay his hand upon him. 33 And he took him aside from the multitude privately, and put his fingers into his ears, and he spat, and touched his tongue; 34 and

162

Matt. 15   #125, continued   Mark 7

Mark 7

looking up to heaven, he sighed, and saith unto him, Ephphatha, that is, Be opened. 35 And his ears were opened, and the bond of his tongue was loosed, and he spake plain. 36 And he charged them that they should tell no man: but the more he charged them, so much the more a great deal they published it. 37 And they were beyond measure astonished, saying, He hath done all things well; he maketh even the deaf to hear, and the dumb to speak.

31 insomuch that the multitude wondered, when they saw the dumb speaking, the maimed whole, and the lame walking, and the blind seeing: and they glorified the God of Israel.

Note 125. On withdrawing from Phoenicia, Jesus apparently turned south east and crossed the upper Jordan without returning to Capernaum. He probably made His way past the place where He had fed the five-thousand (#118), into the neighborhood of the free cities of Decapolis. This portion of His tour is usually spoken of as the third retirement, although it was part of the same circuit as the second retirement (#124). He was near to the place where He had permitted the demons, on being cast out of a man (or two men), to enter into the swine (#105); and the man, whom Jesus had bidden to tell how great things the Lord had done for Him, must have accomplished a good part (Mark 5: 19—20), because, when Jesus came again into that vicinity, multitudes flocked to Him to be benefited by His miracles, or merely to see Him perform them. And it is noticeable that this time no one invited Him to leave the country (cf. Mark 5: 17).

2. Feeding the four thousand (second miracle of this kind, cf. #118)

#126

MATT. 15:32-39a
32 And Jesus called unto him his disciples, and said, I have compassion on the multitude, because they continue with me now three days and have nothing to eat: and I would not send them away fasting, lest haply they faint on the way. 33 And the disciples say unto him, Whence should we have so many loaves in a desert place as to fill so great a multitude? 34 And Jesus said unto them, How many loaves have ye? And they said, Seven, and a few small fishes. 35 And he commanded the multitude to sit down on the ground; 36 and he took the seven loaves and the fishes; and he gave thanks and brake, and gave to the disciples, and the disciples to the multitudes..

MARK 8:1-9
1 In those days, when there was again a great multitude, and they had nothing to eat, he called unto him his disciples, and saith unto them, 2 I have compassion on the multitude, because they continue with me now three days, and have nothing to eat: 3 and if I send them away fasting to their home, they will faint on the way; and some of them are come from far. 4 And his disciples answered him, Whence shall one be able to fill these men with ¹bread here in a desert place? 5 And he asked them, How many loaves have ye? And they said, Seven. 6 And he commandeth the multitude to sit down on the ground: and he took the seven loaves, and having given thanks, he brake, and gave to his disciples, to set before them; and they set them before the multitude. 7 And they had a few small fishes: and having blessed them, he commanded to set these also before
¹ Gr. loaves.

163

#126, continued

Matt. 15	Mark 8
37 And they all ate, and were filled: and they took up that which remained over of the broken pieces, seven baskets full. 38 And they that did eat were four thousand men, besides women and children. 39a And he sent away the multitudes,	them. 8 And they ate, and were filled: and they took up, of broken pieces that remained over, seven baskets. 9 And they were about four thousand: and he sent them away.

Note 126. This is the second instance of a miraculous feeding of a multitude. Note that both miracles are recorded in both Matthew and Mark, and that Jesus Himself in #128 made reference to them both. Those, therefore, who hold that these are just different accounts of the same event have no ground for such conclusion. Several differences in the accounts may be observed. They were at different locations; although they were performed east of the Sea of Galilee, the latter miracle was at a place several miles south of the site of the former one. There was a different number fed; the people had been with Jesus a different duration of time; Jesus had a different amount of food with which to feed them; they gathered up a different number of baskets full of uneaten pieces; and the Greek words used to designate the baskets were different—the baskets used after the feeding of the four thousand were probably larger than those used after the feeding of the five thousand. These differences are observed both in Matthew and in Mark, and both in the accounts of the miracles and in the reference to them by Jesus as related in #128.

VI. Return to Dalmanutha (Magdala), answering a second demand for a sign (cf. #88)

#127

MATT. 15:39b - 16:4a	MARK 8:10-12
39b and entered into the boat, and came into the borders of Magadan. 1 And the Pharisees and Sadducees came, and trying him asked him to show them a sign from heaven. 2 But he answered and said unto them, ¹When it is evening, ye say, It will be fair weather: for the heaven is red. 3 And in the morning, It will be foul weather to-day: for the heaven is red and lowering. Ye know how to discern the face of the heaven; but ye cannot discern the signs of the times. 4a An evil and adulterous generation seeketh after a sign; and there shall no sign be given unto it, but the sign of Jonah.	10 And straightway he entered into the boat with his disciples, and came into the parts of Dalmanutha. 11 And the Pharisees came forth, and began to question with him, seeking of him a sign from heaven, trying him.
¹ The following words, to the end of ver. 3, are omitted by some of the most ancient and other important authorities.	12 And he sighed deeply in his spirit, and saith, Why doth this generation seek a sign? verily I say unto you, There shall no sign be given unto this generation.

Note 127. This was the second time the critics of Jesus asked for "a sign" (cf. #88). And Jesus answered, as before, with a referenc to Jonah; but, probably because the hypocritical inquirers were the same

or at least included some of the same as on the former occasion, He did not bother to explain the significance of Jonah's experience as a sign.

VII. The fourth retirement, via Bethsaida Julias to the regions of Caesarea Philippi and Mt. Hermon, ##128—136

1. En route to Bethsaida Julias, warning the disciples concerning the teachings (leaven) of the Pharisees and the Sadducees

#128

MATT. 16:4b-12

4b And he left them, and departed. 5 And the disciples came to the other side and forgot to take ¹bread. 6 And Jesus said unto them, Take heed and beware of the leaven of the Pharisees and Sadducees. 7 And they reasoned among themselves, saying, ²We took no ¹bread. 8 And Jesus perceiving it said, O ye of little faith, why reason ye among yourselves, because ye have no ¹bread? 9 Do ye not yet perceive, neither remember the five loaves of the five thousand, and how many ³baskets ye took up? 10 Neither the seven loaves of the four thousand, and how many ³baskets ye took up? 11 How is it that ye do not perceive that I spake not to you concerning ¹bread? But beware of the leaven of the Pharisees and Sadducees. 12 Then understood they that he bade them not beware of the leaven of ¹bread, but of the teaching of the Pharisees and Sadducees.

¹ Gr. loaves.
² Or, it is because we took no bread
³ Basket in ver. 9 and 10 represents different Greek words.

MARK 8:13-21

13 And he left them, and again entering into the boat departed to the other side.

14 And they forgot to take bread; and they had not in the boat with them more than one loaf. 15 And he charged them, saying, Take heed, beware of the leaven of the Pharisees and the leaven of Herod. 16 And they reasoned one with another, ¹saying, ²We have no bread. 17 And Jesus perceiving it saith unto them, Why reason ye, because ye have no bread? do ye not yet perceive, neither understand? have ye your heart hardened? 18 Having eyes, see ye not? and having ears, hear ye not? and do ye not remember? 19 When I brake the five loaves among the five thousand, how many ³baskets full of broken pieces took ye up? They say unto him, Twelve. 20 And when the seven among the four thousand, how many ³basketfuls of broken pieces took ye up? And they say unto him, Seven. 21 And he said unto them, Do ye not yet understand?

¹ Some ancient authorities read because they had no bread.
² Or, It is because we have no bread
³ Basket in ver. 19 and 20 represents different Greek words.

Note 128. The emphasis in this metaphor about leaven was on the corrupting effect it was supposed to have upon that of which it is made a part (cf. Note 100). The leaven of the Pharisees is named in Luke 12:1 as hypocrisy. The leaven of the Sadducees might well be named as rationalism or skepticism in religion and willingness to compromise one's scruples to obtain political or economic favors. The leaven of Herod must have been a cunning and utter disregard for the principles of right and wrong in order to advance one's personal ends. Could it be that the last warning was spoken for the benefit of Judas Iscariot?

2. Healing a blind man

#129

MARK 8:22-26

22 And they come unto Bethsaida. And they bring to him a blind man, and beseech him to touch him. 23 And he took hold of the blind man by the hand, and brought him out of the village; and when he had spit on his eyes, and laid his hands upon him, he asked him, Seest thou aught? 24 And he looked up, and said, I see men; for I behold them as trees, walking. 25 Then again he laid his

hands upon his eys; and he looked stedfastly, and was restored, and saw all things clearly. 26 And he sent him away to his home, saying, Do not even enter into the village.

Note 129. This is the only miracle of healing performed by our Lord in which relief came gradually.

3. Great Lessons in and around Caesarea Philippi, ##130—136

Note 130. Importance of events at Caesarea Philippi. At Caesarea Philippi the Lord Jesus passed through the greatest crisis of His earthly life after His baptism and before His triumphant entry into Jerusalem. Four things occured there and on nearby Mt. Hermon which made this a most important occasion in His career, namely: (1) For the first time He encouraged one of His followers formally to confess His Messiahship and deity. (2) For the first time He made known in plain terms His purpose to submit to humiliation and death at the hands of His enemies and His expectation to achieve a victory over death in a resurrection (3) For the first time He foretold His second coming to earth by announcing that He expected to "come in the glory of His Father with His angels." (4) In the transfiguration He experienced the only glorifying of His physical person during His life on earth, and He was accorded the only period of fellowship with Old Testament faithful ones who were permitted to visit earth from Heaven. At the same time He received the second commendation from the Father spoken in the hearing of men.

(1) Formal Confession by Simon Peter of the messiahship and divine sonship of Jesus

#130

MATT. 16:13-20	MARK 8:27-30	LUKE 9:18-21
13 Now when Jesus came into the parts of Caesarea Philippi, he asked his disciples, saying, Who do men say 'that the Son of man is? 14 And they said, Some say John the Baptist; some, Elijah; and others, Jeremiah, or one of the prophets. 15 He saith unto them, But who say ye that I am? 16 And Simon Peter answered and said, Thou art the Christ, the Son of the living God. 17 And Jesus answered and said unto him, Blessed art thou, Simon Bar-Jonah: for flesh and blood hath not revealed it unto thee, but my Father who is in heaven. 18 And I also say unto thee, that thou art ²Peter, and upon this ³rock I will	27 And Jesus went forth, and his disciples, into the villages of Caesarea Philippi: and on the way he asked his disciples, saying unto them, Who do men say that I am? 28 And they told him, saying, John the Baptist; and others, Elijah; but others, One of the prophets. 29 And he asked them, But who say ye that I am? Peter answereth and saith unto him, Thou art the Christ.	18 And it came to pass, as he was praying apart, the disciples were with him: and he asked them, saying, Who do the multitudes say that I am? 19 And they answering said, John the Baptist; but others say, Elijah; and others, that one of the old prophets is risen again. 20 And he said unto them, But who say ye that I am? And Peter answering said, The Christ of God.

¹ Many ancient authorities read *that I the Son of man am.* See Mk. 8. 27; Lk. 9. 18.
² Gr. *Petros.*   ³ Gr. *petra.*

166

Matt. 16	Mark 8	Luke 9
build my church; and the gates of Hades shall not prevail against it. 19 I will give unto thee the keys of the kingdom of heaven: and whatsoever thou shalt bind on earth shall be bound in heaven; and whatsoever thou shalt loose on earth shall be loosed in heaven. 20 Then charged he the disciples that they should tell no man that he was the Christ.	30 And he charged them that they should tell no man of him.	21 But he charged them, and commanded *them* to tell this to no man;

Note 131. Peter's Great Confession and the Response of Jesus. As was stated in Note 130, this was the first time Jesus encouraged one of His disciples deliberately and formally to confess His Messiahship and His deity. But it was not the first time that He was called the Son of God, as may be seen by referring to ##18, 21, 39, 105, 120, and 121. Moreover, He had Himself repeatedly called God His Father (cf. Luke 2: 49, #15; John 5: 17—18, #48; Matt. 10: 33, #113).

To prepare the way for asking the disciples to state their own conclusion about Him, He first inquired what popular opinion concerning Him they had picked up. Besides the superstitious delusion that He might be John the Baptist returned to life, which, as we saw in #155, represented the disquietude of conscience-stricken Herod, the other rumors identified Him with personages expected in the Messianic program as the scribes taught it: (1) Elijah, promised in Mal. 4: 5, expected to appear in person before the Messiah (John 1: 21; #20; Matt. 17: 10, #134), but identified by Jesus with John the Baptist (Matt. 11: 14; 17: 13, ##81, #134), (2) Jeremiah (Matt. 16: 14) popularly expected to return to earth to reveal where on Mt. Nebo he had hidden the Ark of the Covenant and the altar of incense at the time of the destruction of Solomon's temple,* (3) or one of the old prophets arisen again (Luke 9:19) expected as a fulfillment of Deut. 18: 18. It will be observed that this program agreed in general with that reflected in the inquiries which the deputation from Jerusalem made of John the Baptist (cf. #20 and Note 22), except Jeremiah was not then suggested as the prophet expected.

This transition was natural from popular opinion to their own studied conviction, which conviction was affirmed by Simon Peter. The importance which Jesus attached to this confession by Simon Peter is learned from the response which He made to it. Concerning this response two questions arise in the mind of almost every student of this passage.

First Question: What was the rock on which Jesus said He would build His church?

*II Maccabees 2:5-8. cf. Broadus, *Commentary on Matthew*, p. 353. Edersheim, *Life and Times of Jesus*, Vol. II. p. 79.

167

Before attempting to answer this question it is well to have in mind what the term "church" signified to Jesus and to New Testament Christians. In the light of the only other passage in which Jesus used the word "church" (Matt. 18:17, #140), and in the light of its usage throughout the New Testament, I define a church in general terms as: A group of believers in Jesus Christ united in receiving by faith the truths taught in His Word, dedicated to the practice of the ordinances and duties which He enjoined, and organized for worship and for propagating those teachings and ordinances. In all probability our Lord here used the word "church" in a generic sense referring to any church patterned in essential characteristics like the one which He built with His true followers as members, and which He left when He ascended back to Heaven, at least in rudimentary constitution.

What, then, was the rock on which He said He would build this church?

1. Surely Jesus did not mean that Simon Peter personally would be the foundation of the first church or of any church, or of all churches. He did not name Peter as the base of a whole column of absolute rulers of any church, as Roman Catholics contend. We must reject such a proposition because:

(1) Peter never did claim such authority, either in anything that he said or that he did, as recorded in the book of Acts or in his epistles. Indeed, he was content to call himself a fellow-elder with the other elders (I Pet. 5:1).

(2) He was never accorded such authority by the other Christians of his day. He wielded predominant influence in the Jerusalem church, but the members never did regard him as the ruler. They did not hesitate to criticize him or take him to task when his actions did not meet with their approval (cf. Acts 11:1—3 and Gal. 2:11). Such action or attitude would have been altogether out of place if directed toward one of "papal authority." When, as related in Acts 15, the church was considering an important matter in conference, Peter took part in the discussion, but he did not dictate the action of the church. Indeed, it was James, who was not an apostle, that suggested the plan of action taken by the church.

(3) There is no evidence that the rank or prerogative of any of the apostles were transmitted to successors at their death; and certainly no priority of influence which Peter may have had was thus transmitted, either by His own designation or by a choice of his contemporaries.

(4) It is sometimes argued that the Greek word translated "Peter" (petros) means a stone or a rock; and since Jesus said, "On this rock I will build my church" immediately after He had designated Simon as a petros, very naturally, they say, He meant that He would build it on Simon as a rock. But the words are not the same. Petros (the word translated "Peter") is a masculine form, and the word translated "rock" (in the clause, "On this rock I will build...") is the feminine form, petra. A study of the usage of these words in the New Testament brings

168

out that petra always signified a rock formation, or a stratum or ledge of rock, and that petros meant a stone, a detached piece of rock. Surely, if Jesus had meant that Simon Peter would be the foundation of His church, He would have used the same word in both places.

2. It has often been said that in this assertion Jesus referred to Himself personally, meaning that He would build His church on Himself as the foundation. But this is not likely, because such an interpretation mixes the figure, in that it makes the Builder of the house and the foundation on which the house is built to be the same. It is admitted that Jesus is named in the New Testament as the foundation for the hope of a Christian (I Cor. 3: 11; Eph. 3: 20; I Pet. 2: 4); but we must not confuse the church, an organized body, with an individual Christian or the experience of a Christian. Moreover, according to this interpretation, there is no connection between the declaration by Simon Peter and the response of Jesus.

3. I am convinced that our Lord meant that the truth affirmed in Peter's confession was the rock on which He would build the church—the truth that Jesus was and is Christ (or Messiah) and the divine Son of God. There was surely a connection between the confession by Simon Peter and the response by the Lord Jesus, and this interpretation recognizes that connection. Faith in Jesus as Saviour and as God incarnate is fundamental in the experience of every Christian and was the essential prerequisite for membership in the church which Jesus built. It should be observed that Matthew quoted Peter as making two assertions in his confession: (1) that Jesus was the Messiah, and (2) that the Messiah was and is Son of God. However, the latter assertion is not found in Mark and Luke; but certainly Matthew was inspired to record it. This is all the more significant, since Matthew wrote for Jewish readers; for it was because of His claims of divine sonship that the Jews condemned Him for blasphemy (John 5: 17—18, #48; Matt. 26: 63--66, #241).

Some have held that Jesus referred to the regeneration of character in Christian experience of which Peter was an example. But regeneration of character is a work of God which takes place in connection with an individual's believing personally in Jesus as the Christ, or Saviour, and as the Son of the living God; in other words, accepting the truth which Peter confessed and relying on it.

Our Lord promised that the gates of Hades would not prevail against His church thus founded; that is, in the conflict against the forces of Hades, the church founded on this fundamental truth will be victorious.

Second Question: What prerogative or privilege did Jesus bestow on Peter in giving him "the keys of the Kingdom of Heaven"?

At this point one would do well to restudy the phrase "Kingdom of Heaven" (or "Kingdom of God"), as it is discussed in Note 18, and to notice especially the definition suggested and the two senses in which Jesus and the gospel writers used the phrase. Participation in the Kingdom was rated in the teaching of Jesus as the highest privilege accorded any individual and the blessing of greatest worth. Possession of the "keys of the Kingdom" carried the prerogative to open the gates of the Kingdom to let people go in. The weighty responsibility of such prerogative may be perceived in the added statement, "whatsoever thou shalt bind on earth shall be bound in Heaven, and whatsoever thou shalt loose on earth shall be loosed in Heaven." In answering our question it is well to observe:

1. Peter was not the only one charged with the responsibility of binding and loosing. The actions of a church carry the same responsibility (Matt. 18:18, #140). The risen Jesus imposed on the whole group of apostles the responsibility of remitting or retaining sins (John 20:23). This was doubtless to impress them with the importance of being faithful in carrying out the commission which He had just given them when He announced, "As my Father hath sent me, even so send I you" (John 20:21).

2. We must infer, therefore, that the responsibility of remitting or retaining sins, of binding or loosing, is involved in the commission to make known the conditions of salvation. I conclude then that the keys of the Kingdom of Heaven are the grace to know and the commission to declare the conditions of entrance into the Kingdom, and that these are the privilege and the responsibility of every disciple of Jesus. The prerogative is not official (as some would ascribe to Peter and his so-called "successors") but declaratory. By declaring the conditions of entrance into the Kingdom, one is unlocking the doors thereto, and by neglecting or failing to declare these conditions he was leaving the doors locked.

Most surely the reference here is to the Kingdom in its spiritual manifestation, the Kingdom as it now operates. People enter the Kingdom through faith in Jesus as the Christ (Saviour) and the Son of the living God. However, those who enter the spiritual Kingdom will be in the visible Kingdom, and this statement of Jesus is true with respect to both manifestations of the Kingdom. But it must be admitted that at this time Peter and the other disciples had not perceived the idea of a spiritual Kingdom (cf. Luke 19:11, #194; Acts 1:6, #272).

3. But Peter was accorded one distinction in this matter which the other apostles did not share, in that he was to be the first to declare in a gospel sermon the conditions of entrance into the Kingdom. He was the first thus to unlock, as it were, the doors of the Kingdom, both to the Jews on the "Day of Pentecost" (Acts 2:14--43), and later to the Gentiles in the house of Cornelius (Acts 10:24--43, cf. Acts 15:7).

(2) The first definite announcement by Jesus of His coming death at Jerusalem and His resurrection

#131

MATT. 16:21-23	MARK 8:31-33	LUKE 9:22
21 From that time began 'Jesus to show unto his dis- ' Some ancient authorities read *Jesus Christ*.	31 And he began to teach them, that the Son	22 saying, The Son of man must suffer many

170

Matt. 16	Mark 8	Luke 9
ciples, that he must go unto Jerusalem, and suffer many things of the elders and chief priests and scribes, and be killed, and the third day be raised up. 22 And Peter took him, and began to rebuke him, saying, ²Be it far from thee, Lord: this shall never be unto thee. 23 But he turned, and said unto Peter, Get thee behind me, Satan: thou art a stumbling-block unto me: for thou mindest not the things of God, but the things of men. ² Or, God *have mercy on thee*	of man must suffer many things, and be rejected by the elders, and the chief priests, and the scribes, and be killed, and after three days rise again. 32 And he spake the saying openly. And Peter took him, and began to rebuke him. 33 But he turning about, and seeing his disciples, rebuked Peter, and saith, Get thee behind me, Satan; for thou mindest not the things of God, but the things of men	things, and be rejected of the elders and chief priests and scribes, and be killed, and the third day be raised up.

Note 132. Although the Lord Jesus did not until this conversation at Caesarea Philippi, clearly reveal His purpose to submit to death and then to achieve mastery over death in the resurrection, it had been His steady intention all al⌐ ϧ. In baptism He formally dedicated Himself to such experiences as His mission on earth (cf. Note 20). On a later occasion He asserted that "the Son of Man came...to give His life a ransom" (Matt. 20:28, #191); and just five days before the dark hour of His sacrificial suffering He affirmed, "For this cause came I unto this hour" (John 12:28, #199). Even before this discourse to the disciples He had as many as five times made statements in which we can see a reference to His death, though the people who heard them did not so understand them (cf. John 2:19, #25; John 3:14--15, #26; Matt. 9:15, #46, Matt. 12:40, #88, Matt. 10:38, #113). Having revealed His purpose to the disciples, the purpose itself was strengthened. From this time to the end He repeated time and again this solemn announcement.

It is not surprising that the words of Jesus brought surprise and dismay to the disciples, particularly Simon Peter. That disciple, in his assertion, "This shall not be unto Thee," seems to have set himself to keep the announced intention of his Lord from coming to pass. Very naturally all the disciples, because of their love for Jesus and loyalty to Him, were deeply grieved; and too, they were baffled in their expectation of an early inauguration of the visible Messianic Kingdom. To the end, therefore, they were unable to accept these statements of Jesus.

(3) A solemn warning and an encouraging promise
#132

MATT. 16:24-28	MARK 8:34 - 9:1	LUKE 9:23-27
24 Then said Jesus unto his disciples, If any man would come after me, let him deny himself, and take up his cross, and follow me.	34 And he called unto him the multitude with his disciples, and said unto them, If any man would come after me, let him deny himself, and take up his cross, and follow me.	23 And he said to all, If any man would come after me, let him deny himself, and take up his cross daily, and follow me.

171

Matt. 16   Mark 8, 9   Luke 9

Matt. 16

25 For whosoever would save his life shall lose it: and whosoever shall lose his life for my sake shall find it. 26 For what shall a man be profited, if he shall gain the whole world, and forfeit his life? or what shall a man give in exchange for his life? 27 For the Son of man shall come in the glory of his Father with his angels; and then shall he render unto every man according to his ¹deeds. 28 Verily I say unto you, There are some of them that stand here, who shall in no wise taste of death, till they see the Son of man coming in his kingdom.
¹ Gr. *doing.*

Mark 8, 9

35 For whosoever would save his life shall lose it; and whosoever shall lose his life for my sake and the ¹gospel's shall save it. 36 For what doth it profit a man, to gain the whole world, and forfeit his life? 37 For what should a man give in exchange for his life? 38 For whosoever shall be ashamed of me and of my words in this adulterous and sinful generation, the Son of man also shall be ashamed of him, when he cometh in the glory of his Father with the holy angels.
1 And he said unto them, Verily I say unto you, There are some here of them that stand *by,* who shall in no wise taste of death, till they see the kingdom of God come with power.
¹ See marginal note on ch. 1. 1.

Luke 9

24 For whosoever would save his life shall lose it; but whosoever shall lose his life for my sake, the same shall save it. 25 For what is a man profited, if he gain the whole world, and lose or forfeit his own self? 26 For whosoever shall be ashamed of me and of my words, of him shall the Son of man be ashamed, when he cometh in his own glory, and *the glory* of the Father, and of the holy angels. 27 But I tell you of a truth, There are some of them that stand here, who shall in no wise taste of death, till they see the kingdom of God.

Note 133. This (Matt. 16: 27 and parallels) was the first clear prediction by our Lord of His second coming. Jesus most surely referred in Mark 9: 1 and parallels to the events on what we call "the Day of Pentecost," when active propagation of Christianity was begun. At that time the Kingdom of God in the spiritual manifestation began its powerful march throughout the world, and it is today the most potent social force on earth. He assured these disciples in Matt. 16: 27 that the visible Kingdom will one day be realized, but in the next verse they were told that the Kingdom will operate and advance spiritually until the King visibly returns.

(4) The Transfiguration — encouragement from Heaven for the Lord Jesus and a solemn warning to the disciples

#133

Matt. 17:1-8

1 And after six days Jesus taketh with him Peter, and ¹James, and John his brother, and bringeth them up into a high mountain apart: 2 and he was transfigured before them; and his face did shine as the sun, and his garments became white as the light. 3 And behold,
¹ Or, *Jacob*

Mark 9:2-8

2 And after six days Jesus taketh with him Peter, and ¹James, and John, and bringeth them up into a high mountain apart by themselves: and he was transfigured before them; 3 and his garments became glistering, exceeding white, so as no fuller on earth can whiten them.
¹ Or, *Jacob*

Luke 9:28-36

28 And it came to pass about eight days after these sayings, that he took with him Peter and John and James, and went up ·into the mountain to pray. 29 And as he was praying, the fashion of his countenance was altered, and his raiment *became* white *and* dazzling. 30 And behold, there talked with him two

Matt. 17	Mark 9	Luke 9
there appeared unto them Moses and Elijah talking with him.	4 And there appeared unto them Elijah with Moses: and they were talking with Jesus.	men, who were Moses and Elijah; 31 who appeared in glory, and spake of his ¹decease which he was about to accomplish at Jerusalem. 32 Now Peter and they that were with him were heavy with sleep: but ²when they were fully awake, they saw his glory, and the two men that stood with him. 33 And it came to pass, as they were parting from him, Peter said
4 And Peter answered, and said unto Jesus, Lord, it is good for us to be here: if thou wilt, I will make here three ²tabernacles; one for thee, and one for Moses, and one for Elijah. 5 While he was yet speaking, behold, a bright cloud overshadowed them: and behold, a voice out of the cloud, saying. This is my beloved Son, in whom I am well pleased; hear ye him. 6 And when the disciples heard it, they fell on their face, and were sore afraid. 7 And Jesus came and touched them and said, Arise, and be not afraid. 8 And lifting up their eyes, they saw no one, save Jesus only.	5 And Peter answereth and saith to Jesus, Rabbi, it is good for us to be here: and let us make three ²tabernacles; one for thee, and one for Moses, and one for Elijah. 6 For he knew not what to answer; for they became sore afraid. 7 And there came a cloud overshadowing them: and there came a voice out of the cloud, This is my beloved Son: hear ye him. 8 And suddenly looking round about, they saw no one any more, save Jesus only with themselves.	unto Jesus, Master, it is good for us to be here: and let us make three ³tabernacles; one for thee, and one for Moses, and one for Elijah: not knowing what he said. 34 And while he said these things, there came a cloud, and overshowed them: and they feared as they entered into the cloud. 35 And a voice came out of the cloud, saying, This is ⁴my Son, my chosen: hear ye him. 36 And when the voice ⁵came, Jesus was found alone. And they held their peace, and told no man in those days any of the things which they had seen.
² Or, booths	² Or, booths	¹ Or, departure ² Or, having remained awake ³ Or, booths ⁴ Many ancient authorities read my beloved Son. See Mt. 17. 5; Mk. 9. 7. ⁵ Or, was past

Note 134. The transfiguration is one of the best attested events in the life of Jesus. It is described in each of the three Synoptic Gospels; Peter, who was present, unquestionably referred to it in II Pet. 1:16--18; and so very probably did John, who was also present, in John 1:14. This glorious experience granted our Lord doubtless served the following ends:

(1) God the Father expressed His own approval of the action of Jesus in revealing to the disciples that He was destined to undergo death and to achieve a resurrection.

(2) The Father also encouraged Him at a time when the disciples misunderstood and were unsympathetic.

(3) Also God bade the disciples, especially Peter, who had taken his Lord to task when the announcement was made, to hear and believe and accept this prediction which Jesus had spoken.

The voice from Heaven had previously been heard at the baptism of Jesus, which as we saw in Note 20 was a self-dedication to His mission involving sacrificial death and a resurrection; likewise at the transfiguration it followed soon after his first open avowal of that self-dedication. It was to be heard once more, #199.

(5) The resurrection again foretold, interpretation of prophecy concerning Elijah

#134

Matt. 17:9-13	Mark 9:9-13
9 And as they were coming down from the mountain, Jesus commanded them, saying, Tell the vision to no man, until the Son of man be risen from the dead. 10 And his disciples asked him, saying, Why then say the scribes that Elijah must first come? 11 And he answered and said, Elijah indeed cometh, and shall restore all things: 12 but I say unto you, that Elijah is come already, and they knew him not, but did unto him whatsoever they would. Even so shall the Son of man also suffer of them. 13 Then understood the disciples that he spake unto them of John the Baptist.	9 And as they were coming down from the mountain, he charged them that they should tell no man what things they had seen, save when the Son of man should have risen again from the dead. 10 And they kept the saying, questioning among themselves what the rising again from the dead should mean. 11 And they asked him, saying, ¹*How is it* that the scribes say that Elijah must first come? 12 And he said unto them, Elijah indeed cometh first, and restoreth all things: and how is it written of the Son of man, that he should suffer many things and be set at nought? 13 But I say unto you, that Elijah is come, and they have also done unto him whatsoever they would, even as it is written of him. ¹ Or, *The scribes say . . . come.*

Note 135. Jesus had already identified the promised Elijah with John the Baptist before a crowd including the disciples (see Note 82, cf. Notes 22 and 131); but since these disciples had seen the Elijah of the Old Testament in the Transfiguration, they were puzzled because the Messiah came before Elijah appeared. In reply Jesus again identified John as the fulfillment of the prophecy about the sending of Elijah (cf. Mal. 4: 5, also Luke 1: 17). In making the explanation He again by inference foretold His own death and resurrection; but we know from verse 10 of Mark that they could not believe that there would be a resurrection, because they refused to believe, until after it occurred, that He would die.

(6) Healing a demoniac boy, a lesson in prayer and faith

#135

Matt. 17:14-21	Mark 9:14-29	Luke 9:37-43a
	14 And when they came to the disciples, they saw a great multitude about them, and scribes questioning with them. 15 And straightway all the multitude, when they saw him, were greatly amazed, and running to him saluted him. 16 And he asked them, What question ye	37 And it came to pass, on the next day, when they were come down from the mountain, a great multitude met him.

174

Matt. 17	Mark 9	Luke 9

Matt. 17

14 And when they were come to the multitude, there came to him a man, kneeling to him, and saying, 15 Lord, have mercy on my son: for he is epileptic, and suffereth grievously; for oft-times he falleth into the fire, and oft-times into the water. 16 And I brought him to thy disciples, and they could not cure him. 17 And Jesus answered and said, O faithless and perverse generation, how long shall I be with you? how long shall I bear with you? bring him hither to me.

18 And Jesus rebuked him; and the demon went out of him: and the boy was cured from that hour.

Mark 9

with them? 17 And one of the multitude answered him, Teacher, I brought unto thee my son, who hath a dumb spirit; 18 and wheresoever it taketh him, it ¹dasheth him down: and he foameth, and grindeth his teeth, and pineth away: and I spake to thy disciples that they should cast it out; and they were not able. 19 And he answereth them and saith, O faithless generation, how long shall I be with you? how long shall I bear with you? bring him unto me. 20 And they brought him unto him: and when he saw him, straightway the spirit ²tare him grievously; and he fell on the ground, and wallowed foaming. 21 And he asked his father, How long time is it since this hath come unto him? And he said, From a child. 22 And oft-times it hath cast him both into the fire and into the waters, to destroy him: but if thou canst do anything, have compassion on us, and help us. 23 And Jesus said unto him, If thou canst! All things are possible to him that believeth. 24 Straightway the father of the child cried out, and said³, I believe; help thou mine unbelief. 25 And when Jesus saw that a multitude came running together, he rebuked the unclean spirit, saying unto him, Thou dumb and deaf spirit, I command thee, come out of him, and enter no more into him. 26 And having cried out, and ⁴torn him much, he came out: and *the boy* became as⁴ one dead; insomuch that the more part said, He is dead.

¹ Or, *rendeth him*   See Mt. 7.6.
² Or, *convulsed*   See ch. 1. 26.
³ Many ancient authorities add *with tears.*
⁴ Or, *convulsed*   See ch. 1. 26.

Luke 9

38 And behold, a man from the multitude cried, saying, Teacher, I beseech thee to look upon my son; for he is mine only child: 39 and behold, a spirit taketh him, and he suddenly crieth out; and it ¹teareth him that he foameth, and it hardly departeth from him, bruising him sorely. 40 And I besought thy disciples to cast it out; and they could not. 41 And Jesus answered and said, O faithless and perverse generation, how long shall I be with you, and bear with you? bring hither thy son.

42 And as he was yet a coming, the demon ²dashed him down, and ³tare *him* grievously. But Jesus rebuked the unclean spirit, and healed the boy, and gave him back to his father. 43 And they were all astonished at the majesty of God.

¹ Or, *convulseth*   ² Or, *rent him*
³ Or, *convulsed*

175

Matt. 17

19 Then came the disciples to Jesus apart, and said, Why could not we cast it out? 20 And he saith unto them, Because of your little faith: for verily I say unto you, If ye have faith as a grain of mustard seed, ye shall say unto this mountain, Remove hence to yonder place; and it shall remove; and nothing shall be impossible unto you.[1]

[1] Many authorities, some ancient, insert ver. 21 *But this kind goeth not out save by prayer and fasting.* See Mk. 9 29.

Mark 9

27 But Jesus took him by the hand, and raised him up; and he arose. 28 And when he was come into the house, his disciples asked him privately, [5]*How is it* that we could not cast it out? 29 And he said unto them, This kind can come out by nothing, s a v e by prayer.[6]

[5] Or, saying, *We could not cast it out.*
[6] Many ancient authorities add *and fasting.*

Note 136. Because the disciples had cast out many demons on their practice tours (#114), they confidently expected to deliver this boy from the evil spirit that was oppressing and tormenting him. But their confidence evidently was in their own power or in the words or methods they had used, rather than in God who had given them power to work the miracles. Jesus told them according to Matthew, verse 20, that they had not been able to cast it o u t because of their unbelief, and according to Mark, verse 29, that that kind would not come out but by prayer. The two accounts together probably mean that they were overly self-confident rather than consciously God-confident.

The words "and fasting" of verse 29 of Mark and all of verse 21 of Matthew are omitted from the American Standard Version and all other later translations, because they are not found in the oldest manuscripts, or copies of these Gospels.

It is interesting to compare the entreaty of this distracted father with that of the leper of #42. The father questioned the power of Jesus to bestow the blessing and was sharply rebuked, while the leper, though he questioned His willingness to heal but not His power, received the blessing forthwith.

4. Second definite prediction of His death and resurrection while returning through Galilee

#136

MATT. 17:22-23

22 And while they [1]abode in Galilee, Jesus said unto them, The Son of man shall be [2]delivered up into the hands of men;

[1] Some ancient authorities read *were gathering themselves together.*
[2] See ch. 10. 4.

MARK 9:30-32

30 And they went forth from thence, and passed through Galilee; and he would not that any man should know it. 31 For he taught his disciples, and said unto them, The Son of man is [1]delivered up into

[1] See ch. 3. 19.

LUKE 9:43b-45

43b But while all were marvelling at all the things which he did, he said unto his disciples, 44 Let these words sink into your ears for the Son of man shall be [1]delivered up into the hands of men. 45 But the

[1] Or, *betrayed*

176

Matt. 17	Mark 9	Luke 9
23 and they shall kill him, and the third day he shall be raised up. And they were exceeding sorry.	the hands of men, and they shall kill him; and when he is killed, after three days he shall rise again. 32 But they understood not the saying, and were afraid to ask him.	understood not this saying, and it was concealed from them, that they should not perceive it; and they were afraid to ask him about this saying.

VIII. Some further teachings in Galilee, probably the last in that province, ##137—140

1. In connection with payment of the temple tax

#137
MATT. 17:24-27

24 And when they were come to Capernaum, they that received the [1]half-hekel came to Peter, and said, Doth not your teacher pay the [1]half-shekel? 25 He saith, Yea. And when he came into the house, Jesus spake first to him, saying, What thinkest thou, Simon? the kings of the earth, from whom do they receive toll or tribute? from their sons, or from strangers? 26 And when he said, From strangers, Jesus said unto him, Therefore the sons are free. 27 But, lest we cause them to stumble, go thou to the sea, and cast a hook, and take up the fish that first cometh up; and when thou hast opened his mouth, thou shalt find a [2]shekel: that take, and give unto them for me and thee.

[1] Gr. didrachma.　　　　　[2] Gr. stater.

Note 137. "They that received tribute money" in this passage were not the publicans. This tribute was without doubt the temple tax, a Jewish levy (cf. Exod. 30: 11--16). It had to be paid with Jewish shekels. It was for this tribute that the money-changers would change Roman money into Jewish shekels (cf. ##25, 202)— for a consideration, of course.

2. In regard to pre-eminence in the Kingdom

#138

MATT. 18:1-5	MARK 9:33-37	LUKE 9:46-48
1 In that hour came the disciples unto Jesus, saying, Who then is [1]greatest in the kingdom of heaven? 2 And he called to him a little child, and set him in the midst of them, 3 and said, Verily I say unto you, Except ye turn, and become as little children, ye shall in no wise enter into the kingdom of heaven. 4 Whosoever therefore shall humble himself as this little child, the same is the [1]greatest in the kingdom of heaven. 5 And whoso shall receive one such little child in my name receiveth me:	33 And they came to Capernaum: and when he was in the house he asked them, What were ye reasoning on the way? 34 But they held their peace: for they had disputed one with another on the way, who was the [1]greatest. 35 And he sat down, and called the twelve; and he saith unto them, If any man would be first, he shall be last of all, and [2]servant of all. 36 And he took a little child, and set him in the midst of them: and taking him in his arms, he said unto them, 37 Whosoever shall receive one of such little children in my name, receiveth me: and whoso-	46 And there arose a [1]reasoning among them, which of them was the [2]greatest. 47 But when Jesus saw the [1]reasoning of their heart, he took a little child, and set him by his side, 48 and said unto them, Whosoever shall receive this little child in my name receiveth me: and whosoever shall receive me receiveth him that sent me: for he that is [3]least among you all, the same is great.
[1] Gr. greater.	[1] Gr. greater.　[2] Or, minister	[1] Or, questioning　[2] Gr. greater.　[3] Gr. lesser.

ever receiveth me, re-
ceiveth not me, but him
that sent me.

Note 138. It shocks our sense of propriety that the disciples, so soon after Jesus told them of His coming sufferings, should begin to dispute about who would have the highest place in a political kingdom. Thinking only of an early setting up of the visible Kingdom, they fondled their ambitions and heeded not the solemn declaration that He had so recently made to them. Indeed, this was just the first of four times when Jesus had to warn them about self-seeking ambition (cf. #191; Matt. 23: 8--12, #215; Luke 22: 24--27,#230).

3. In regard to treatment of weak or misguided disciples and occasion of stumbling

#139

MATT. 18:6-14	MARK 9:38-50	LUKE 9:49-50
	38 John said unto him, Teacher, we saw one casting out demons in thy name; and we forbade him, because he followed not us. 39 But Jesus said, Forbid him not: for there is no man who shall do a ¹mighty work in my name, and be able quickly to speak evil of me. 40 For he that is not against us is for us. 41 For whosoever shall give you a cup of water to drink, ²because ye are Christ's, verily I say unto you, he shall in no wise lose his reward. 42 And whosoever shall cause one of these little ones that believe ³on me to stumble, it were better for him if ⁴a great millstone were hanged about his neck, and he were cast into the sea. 43 And if thy hand cause thee to stumble, cut it off: it is good for thee to enter into life maimed, rather than having thy two hands to go into ⁵hell, into	49 And John answered and said, Master, we saw one casting out demons in thy name; and we forbade him, because he followeth not with us. 50 But Jesus said unto him, Forbid him not: for he that is not against you is for you.
6 but whoso shall cause one of these little ones that believe on me to stumble, it is profitable for him that ¹a great millstone should be hanged about his neck, and that he should be sunk in the depth of the sea. 7 Woe unto the world because of occasions of stumbling! for it must needs be that the occasions come; but woe to that man through whom the occasion cometh! 8 And if thy hand or thy foot causeth thee to stumble, cut it off, and cast it from thee: it is good for thee to enter into life maimed or halt, rather than having two hands or two feet to be cast into		

¹ Gr. *power.*
² Gr. *in name that ye are.*
³ Many ancient authorities omit *on me.*
⁴ Gr. *a millstone turned by an ass.*   ⁵ Gr. *Gehenna.*

Matt. 18   Mark 9

the eternal fire. 9 And if thine eye causeth thee to stumble, pluck it out, and cast it from thee: it is good for thee to enter into life with one eye, rather than having two eyes to be cast into the [1]hell of fire.

the unquenchable fire.[6] 45 And if thy foot cause thee to stumble, cut it off: it is good for thee to enter into life halt, rather than having thy two feet to be cast into [5]hell. 47 And, if thine eye cause thee to stumble, cast it out: it is good for thee to enter into the kingdom of God with one eye, rather than having two eyes to be cast into [5]hell; 48 where their worm dieth not, and the fire is not quenched. 49 For every one shall be salted with fire[7]. 50 Salt is good: but if the salt have lost its saltness, wherewith will ye season it? Have salt in yourselves, and be at peace one with another.

10

See that ye despise not one of these little ones: for I say unto you, that in heaven their angels do always behold the face of my Father who is in heaven.[3] 12 How think ye? If any man have a hundred sheep, and one of them be gone astray, doth he not leave the ninety and nine, and go unto the mountains, and seek that which goeth astray? 13 And if so be that he find it, verily I say unto you, he rejoiceth over it more than over the ninety and nine which have not gone astray. 14 Even so it is not [4]the will of your Father who is in heaven, that one of these little ones should perish.

[1] Gr. *a millstone turned by an ass.*   [2] Gr. *Gehenna of fire.*
[3] Many authorities, some ancient, insert ver. 11 *For the Son of man came to save that which was lost.* See Lk. 19. 10.
Gr. *a thing willed before your Father.*
Some ancient authorities read *my.*

[5] Gr. *Gehenna.*
[6] Ver. 44 and 46 (which are identical with ver. 48) are omitted by the best ancient authorities.
[7] Many ancient authorities add *and every sacrifice shall be salted with salt.* See Lev. 2. 13.

Note 139. The material of ##139, 140 was probably all spoken in Capernaum as Jesus and the disciples were resting from their journey to Caesarea Philippi, before setting out for Jerusalem to be at the Feast of

Tabernacles. All these things were said to the disciples only, with none of the former Galilean multitude present.

We wish we knew more about the man of whom John was speaking in his remark to the Lord Jesus. He seems to have been a true believer in Jesus, and not a counterfeit, as were the sons of Sceva some years later during Paul's labors at Ephesus (Acts 19: 13--16). But he was not willing to go all the way as a disciple. Likely our Lord had him in mind when He spoke of causing little ones who believe in Him to stumble.

Notice that the words about the offending hand or foot had already been spoken in the Sermon on the Mount (#58). Ordinarily Mark described the deeds of Jesus in detail and did not quote His sayings at length. But in this section Mark preserved more of what Jesus said about eternal punishment than did Matthew (cf. Note 175). Matthew included the parable of the lost sheep in this connection, which Luke related as spoken later (#171). Without doubt Jesus spoke the parable on both occasions. Although the material of verse 11 of Matthew ("For the Son of Man is come to save that which was lost") is omitted from the oldest copies of Matthew, and for that reason omitted here from the American Standard Version, there is no doubt that Jesus spoke these words later in the home of Zacchaeus (cf. Luke 19: 10. #193).

4. In regard to proper treatment toward an offending brother, duty of forgiveness

#140

MATTHEW 18:15-35

15 And if thy brother sin [1]against thee, go, show him his fault between thee and him alone: if he hear thee, thou hast gained thy brother. 16 But if he hear *thee* not, take with thee one or two more, that at the mouth of two witnesses or three every word may be established. 17 And if he refuse to hear them, tell it unto the [2]church: and if he refuse to hear the [2]church also, let him be unto thee as the Gentile and the [3]publican. 18 Verily I say unto you, What things soever ye shall bind on earth shall be bound in heaven; and what things soever ye shall loose on earth shall be loosed in heaven. 19 Again I say unto you, that if two of you shall agree on earth as touching anything that they shall ask, it [4]shall be done for them of my Father who is in heaven. 20 For where two or three are gathered together in my name, there am I in the midst of them.

21 Then came Peter and said to him, Lord, how oft shall my brother sin against me, and I forgive him? until seven times? 22 Jesus saith unto him, I say not unto thee, Until seven times; but, Until [5]seventy times seven. 23 Therefore is the kingdom of heaven likened unto a certain king, who would make a reckoning with his [6]servants. 24 And when he had begun to reckon, one was brought unto him, that owed him ten thousand [7]talents. 25 But forasmuch as he had not *wherewith* to pay his lord commanded him to be sold, and his wife, and children, and all that he had, and payment to be made. 26 The [8]servant therefore fell down and [9]worshipped him, saying, Lord, have patience with me, and I will pay thee all. 27 And the lord of that [8]servant, being moved with compassion, released him, and forgave him the [10]debt. 28 But that [8]servant went out, and found one of his fellow-servants, who owed him a hundred [11]shillings: and he laid hold on him, and took *him* by the throat

[1] Some ancient authorities omit *against thee.* [2] Or, *congregation*
[3] See marginal note on ch. 5. 46. [4] Gr. *shall become.*
[5] Or, *seventy times and seven* [6] Gr. *bondservants.*
[7] This talent was probably worth about £200, or $1000. [8] Gr. *bondservant.*
[9] See marginal note on ch. 2. 2. [10] Gr. *loan.*
[11] The word in the Greek denotes a coin worth about eight pence half-penny, or nearly seventeen cents.

saying, Pay what thou owest. 29 So his fellow-servant fell down and besought him, saying, Have patience with me, and I will pay thee. 30 And he would not: but went and cast him into prison, till he should pay that which was due. 31 So when his fellow-servants saw what was done, they were exceeding sorry, and came and told unto their lord all that was done. 32 Then his lord called him unto him, and saith to him, Thou wicked [8]servant, I forgave thee all that debt, because thou besoughtest me: 33 shouldest not thou also have had mercy on thy fellow-servant, even as I had mercy on thee? 34 And his lord was wroth, and delivered him to the tormentors, till he should pay all that was due. 35 So shall also my heavenly Father do unto you, if ye forgive not every one his brother from your hearts.

[8] Gr. *bondservant.*

Note 140. In section 139 Jesus had something to say about the sin of offending a weak believer (Matt. 18: 6, Mark 9: 42); in this section He took up the problem from the viewpoint of one offended. We wonder if something that one or more of the disciples had said in their dispute about who should be the greatest (Mark 9: 33—34) was the occasion of this lesson on seeking reconciliation. And we wonder also, since Peter raised the question, if he was the one "trespassed against."

Notice that Peter considered forgiveness from the standpoint of legalistic duty, a duty that in time might be altogether fulfilled. That was the viewpoint of the Pharisees concerning duties. In His answer Jesus did not merely increase the number of times one ought to forgive his brother from seven to seventy times seven, or exactly four hundred-ninety times, but He taught that a truly forgiving heart will go on forgiving indefinitely. This is illustrated by a parable about a forgiven but unforgiving debtor. A comparison of the debt that the first servant owed the king with that which a fellow-servant owed him* suggests the greatness of a Christian's debt of gratitude to God for remission of sins, as compared to anything the Christian may be called on to forgive in a fellow Christian—or in any other person, as to that.

*Broadus, *Commentary on Matthew,* p. 392, assumes that the comparison was $12,000,000 to $17.00.

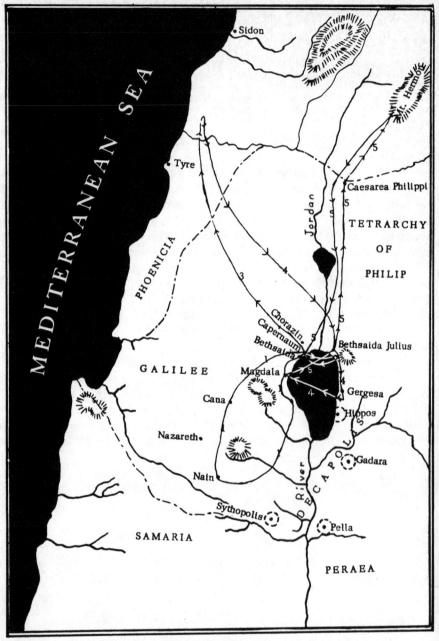

JOURNEYS OF JESUS IN THE FOURTH PERIOD

1 - Third tour of Galilee, beginning and ending at Capernaum (#115). 2 - Across the Sea of Galilee, feeding the 5,000 and return to Capernaum (##118—120). 3 - To regions of Tyre and Sidon (#124). 4 - Into Decapolis, feeding the 4,000, thence by ship to Magdala (##125—127). 5 - To Bethsaida Julius, thence to Caesaraea Philippi and Mount Hermon, and return to Capernaum (##128—136).

⟨⦿⟩ A city of the Decapolis league.

A PREVIEW OUTLINE OF PERIOD FIVE (Abbreviated), ##141-194

I.   Judaean Ministry, ##141-165
     1. The Feast of Tabernacles, ##141-150
        (1) Going to the feast (three incidents: (a) suggestion by unbelieving half brothers of Jesus, and His reply, (b) inhospitable Samaritan village and His response, (c) offers of superficial followers and His answer), ##141-143
        (2) At the feast (two points of interest: (a) different opinions about Him, (b) unsuccessful attempt to arrest Him), ##144-145
        (3) Lingering in Jerusalem after the feast (five incidents: (a) His judgment concerning the adulterous woman, (b) prolonged controversy with Pharisees and their attempt to stone Him, (c) sending out seventy, (d) answering lawyer's questions with parable of Good Samaritan, (e) healing man born blind), ##146-150
     2. Journeys in Judaea (twelve incidents: (1) visit in home of Martha and Mary, (2) lessons on prayer, (3) casting out demon and lessons therefrom, (4) dining with Pharisee and denouncing Pharisaism, (5) teaching disciples concerning hypocrisy and other matters, (6) teaching multitude concerning covetousness, (7) assurance and warnings of His second coming, (8) teachings on sufferings for the cause of the Kingdom, (9) declaration of universal need of repentance, (10) healing and teaching in Judaean synagogue, (11) teaching concerning the number to be saved, (12) experiences in Jerusalem during the absence of Jesus of the man healed of blindness), ##151-162
     3. At the Feast of Dedication, befriending the man formerly blind, the allegory of the Good Shepherd, in three parts, ##163-165
II. Peraean Ministry, ##166-194
     1. First sojourn in Peraea (five incidents: (1) withdrawal of Jesus across Jordan, (2) answering those trying to frighten Him of Herod, (3) lessons taught while dining with a Pharisee: about His healing on the Sabbath, and about hospitality and the invitation into the Kingdom, (4) parables spoken to multitude illustrating phases of discipleship—two showing total consecration required and three showing the unlimited invitation extended, (5) teaching disciples and Pharisees about stewardship and divorce—three parables), ##166-177
     2. A brief visit to Bethany (raising Lazarus to life), ##178-179
     3. Circling through Samaria, Galilee, Peraea, and back to Bethany (ten incidents: (1) withdrawal to Ephraim and borders of Galilee, (2) healing ten lepers, (3) teaching on spiritual and visible Kingdom of God, (4) two parables on prayer, (5) blessing little children, (6) Rich Young Ruler's inquiry and lessons therefrom, (7) third announcement of His approaching death and resurrection, (8) ambitious request of James and John, (9) healing blind Bartimaeus and his companion, (10) lessons on stewardship in conversion of Zachaeus and parable of The Pounds), ##180-194

Closing Ministry in Judaea and Peraea

(##141--194)

Note 141. The fifth period in the life of our Lord was six months in duration, lasting approximately from the Feast of Tabernacles (probably of A.D. 29) until the following Passover (see circle on page 12). It is roughly divided into halves: (1) the Judaean ministry, including and from the Feast of Tabernacles until and including the Feast of Dedication, and (2) the Peraean ministry, after the Feast of Dedication until Jesus arrived in Bethany six days before the day for eating the Passover (John 12: 1, #195). The Peraean ministry was itself divided into two parts, that which came before the raising of Lazarus, and that which came after that miracle.

We are largely dependent on Luke and John for our information about the events of this period, and these Gospels tell about altogether different events. We are therefore faced with the problem of placing the events related in John in the most probable relation to those related in Luke. I take it that the statement in Luke 9: 51, that Jesus "steadfastly set His face to go to Jerusalem," refers to His going to the Feast of Tabernacles; the statement in Luke 13: 22 about His "journeying toward Jerusalem" refers to His going to the Feast of Dedication; and the statement in Luke 17: 11, that He passed along the borders of Samaria and Galilee as He went to Jerusalem, refers to His going up for His last Passover. These passages guide us in determining when to break in on Luke's narrative for the feasts of Tabernacles and of Dedication—(John 7th and 8th chapters, and 10th chapter). But harmonists and writers on the Life of Christ seemingly have all differed on when, in relation to the narratives in Luke, the raising of Lazarus occurred. Considering all things that seem to have a bearing on it, I have set that miracle just before Luke 17: 11, which appears to be the most probable time; but I confess that the question is problematical.

I. The Judaean Ministry, ##141—165
  1. The Feast of Tabernacles, ##141—150
    (1) Preparations for and journey to the Feast, ##141—143
      a. Rejecting the suggestion of His half brothers that He go to this feast to gain publicity
        #141
        JOHN 7:2-9

2 Now the feast of the Jews, the feast of tabernacles, was at hand. 3 His brethren therefore said unto him, Depart hence, and go into Judaea, that thy disciples also may

John 7
behold thy works which thou doest. 4 For no man doeth anything in secret, [1]and himself seeketh to be known openly. If thou doest these things, manifest thyself to the world. 5 For even his brethren did not believe on him. 6 Jesus therefore saith unto them, My time is not yet come; but your time is always ready. 7 The world cannot hate you; but me it hateth, because I testify of it, that its works are evil. 8 Go ye up unto the feast: I go not up [2]unto this feast; because my time is not yet fulfilled. 9 And having said these things unto them, he abode *still* in Galilee.

[1] Some ancient authorities read *and seeketh it to be known openly.*
[2] Many ancient authorities add *yet*

Note 142. The half brothers of Jesus, who were named in #111, did not at this time believe in Him; but we find them after the ascension of Jesus gathered in the upper room with the disciples (Acts 1: 14). Paul wrote (I Cor. 15: 7) that the risen Jesus appeared to James—certainly the James who was his half-brother. We wonder if at the same time He did not also appear to His mother or even to all His brothers. That appearance, whether just to James or to them all, seems to have been so convincing that from that time His brothers were among His disciples.

b. Belated journey through Samaria to Jerusalem for the feast

#142

MATT. 19:1-2	MARK 10:1	LUKE 9:51-56	JOHN 7:10
1 And it came to pass when Jesus had finished these words, he departed from Galilee, and came into the borders of Judaea beyond the Jordan; 2 and great multitudes followed him; and he healed them there.	1 And he arose from thence, and cometh into the borders of Judaea and beyond the Jordan: and multitudes come together unto him again; and, as he was wont, he taught them again.	51 And it came to pass, when the days [1]were well-nigh come that he should be received up, he stedfastly set his face to go to Jerusalem, 52 and sent messengers before his face: and they went, and entered into a village of the Samaritans, to make ready for him. 53 And they did not receive him, because his face was *as' though he were* going to Jerusalem. 54 And when his disciples James and John saw *this,* they said, Lord, wilt thou that we bid fire to come down from heaven, and consume them[2]? 55 But he turned, and rebuked	10 But when his brethren were gone up unto the feast, then went he also up, not publicly, but as it were in secret.

[1] Gr. *were being fulfilled.*
[2] Many ancient authorities add *even as Elijah did.* Comp. 2 K. 1. 10-12.

185

#142, continued
Luke 9

them³. 56 And they went to another village.

³ Some ancient authorities add *and said, Ye know not what manner of spirit ye are of.* Some, but fewer, add also *For the Son of man came not to destroy men's lives but to save them.* Comp. ch. 19. 10; Jn. 3. 17; 12. 47.

Note 143. In the verses from Matthew and Mark in the foregoing section the writers probably meant to give a one-sentence summary of the activities of Jesus during this period. In them it is stated that on His departure from Galilee He "came into the coasts of Judaea," and "beyond the Jordan." Since Judaea did not extend "beyond the Jordan," we conclude that these gospel writers indicated that "when Jesus had finished these words (that is, the teachings delivered in Galilee), He departed" from that province for a ministry in the regions of Judaea and in those beyond Jordan. It is noteworthy that although Matthew and Mark both assert that Jesus went into Judaea at this time, neither one of those writers related that part of the period which we call the "Judaean Ministry" (## 141 — 165). Indeed, they related less than one third of the part which we call the "Peraean Ministry" (##166 —194).

Ordinarily in going from Galilee to Judaea, Jesus would follow the route usually taken by the other Jews, although He did not share the prejudices of His fellow Jews against the Samaritans (cf. Note 32); but He did not hesitate to take the shorter route through Samaria whenever the situation made such a course advisable. Probably the reason for doing so on this occasion was that the feast had already begun before He departed from Galilee. This lateness in departing for the feast may also have been the reason for His sending messengers before Him to prepare accomodations for the journey. Of course, we do not know the name of the village that would not receive Him and His company, but action of its inhabitants is evidence that the prejudice between the Jews and the Samaritans was mutual. The suggestion of James and John probably represents the early natural disposition of these brothers (cf. Mark 3: 17, #52). What a contrast with John, the apostle of love, in later years! The response of Jesus was in full accord, not only with His teachings of non-resistance, but also with the instructions He had given the disciples to flee, when persecuted in one city, to the next (Matt. 10: 3, #113).

    c. Giving would-be followers some important lessons in consecration

#143
LUKE 9:57-62
57 And as they went on the way, a certain man said unto him, I will follow

186

thee whithersoever thou goest. 58 And Jesus said unto him, The foxes have holes, and the birds of the heaven have ¹nests; but the Son of man hath not where to lay his head. 59 And he said unto another, Follow me. But he said, Lord, suffer me first to go and bury my father. 60 But he said unto him, Leave the dead to bury their own dead; but go thou and publish abroad the kingdom of God. 61 And another also said, I will follow thee, Lord; but first suffer me to bid farewell to them that are at my house. 62 But Jesus said unto him, No man, having put his hand to the plow, and looking back, is fit for the kingdom of God.

¹Gr. *lodging places.*

Note 144. The events of the foregoing section may have taken place as Jesus was preparing to leave Capernaum for Jerusalem, and therefore before the incident related in verses 54—56 of the preceding section, or they may have occurred somewhere on the way to Jerusalem. According to Matt. 8: 19—22, two men had already come to Jesus with proposals similar to those of verses 57 and 59 and had received the same answer (#104). Many harmonists put the Matthew passage here, as parallel to this paragraph from Luke. However, to me it seems probable, if not certain, that more than once superficial or overenthusiastic hearers would offer to accompany Him on His journeys (cf. Note 105).

By the parable of The Ploughman (vs. 62) Jesus taught that singleness of purpose and unqualified devotion are necessary characteristics of those that would be His followers.

(2) At the feast, ##144—145

a. Various opinions about Him expressed before His arrival

#144
JOHN 7:11-13

11 The Jews therefore sought him at the feast, and said, Where is he? 12 And there was much murmuring among the multitudes concerning him: some said, He is a good man; others said, Not so, but he leadeth the multitude astray. 13 Yet no man spake openly of him for fear of the Jews.

Note 145. So far as the gospel records go, Jesus had not attended any feast at Jerusalem for eighteen months; that is, since the feast of John 5 (#47), which we concluded was a Passover. For the six months just past He had seemingly avoided Jewish multitudes, leading the disciples into retirement in non-Jewish districts. It would be natural, therefore, for the crowds to inquire where He was at that time, and to look for Him among those coming to the feast—just in case He might come. It is instructive to observe how the crowds were beginning definitely to align themselves for or against Him.

b. After the "midst of the feast" teaching in the temple concerning His mission and His relation to the Father, unsuccessful efforts of His enemies to arrest Him

#145
JOHN 7:14-52

14 But when it was now the midst of the feast Jesus went up into the temple, and taught. 15 The Jews therefore marvelled, saying, How knoweth this man letters, having never learned? 16 Jesus therefore answered them, and said, My teaching is

not mine, but his that sent me. 17 If any man willeth to do his will, he shall know of the teaching, whether it is of God, or *whether* I speak from myself. 18 He that speaketh from himself seeketh his own glory: but he that seeketh the glory of him that sent him, the same is true, and no unrighteousness is in him. 19 Did not Moses give you the law, and *yet* none of you doeth the law? Why seek ye to kill me? 20 The multitude answered, Thou hast a demon: who seeketh to kill thee? 21 Jesus answered and said unto them, I did one work, and ye all marvel because thereof. 22 Moses hath given you circumcision (not that it is of Moses, but of the fathers); and on the sabbath ye circumcise a man. 23 If a man receiveth circumcision on the sabbath, that the law of Moses may not be broken; are ye wroth with me, because I made [1]a man every whit whole on the sabbath? 24 Judge not according to appearance, but judge righteous judgment.

25 Some therefore of them of Jerusalem said, Is not this he whom they seek to kill? 26 And lo, he speaketh openly, and they say nothing unto him. Can it be that the rulers indeed know that this is the Christ? 27 Howbeit we know this man whence he is: but when the Christ cometh, no one knoweth whence he is. 28 Jesus therefore cried in the temple, teaching and saying, Ye both know me, and know whence I am; and I am not come of myself, but he that sent me is true, whom ye know not. 29 I know him; because I am from him, and he sent me. 30 They sought therefore to take him: and no man laid his hand on him, because his hour was not yet come. 31 But of the multitude many believed on him; and they said, When the Christ shall come, will he do more signs than those which this man hath done? 32 The Pharisees heard the multitude murmuring these things concerning him; and the chief priests and the Pharisees sent officers to take him. 33 Jesus therefore said, Yet a little while am I with you, and I go unto him that sent me. 34 Ye shall seek me, and shall not find me: and where I am, ye cannot come. 35 The Jews therefore said among themselves, Whither will this man go that we shall not find him? will he go unto the Dispersion [2]among the Greeks, and teach the Greeks? 36 What is this word that he said, Ye shall seek me, and shall not find me; and where I am, ye cannot come?

37 Now on the last day, the great *day* of the feast, Jesus stood and cried, saying, If any man thirst, let him come unto me and drink. 38 He that believeth on me, as the scripture hath said, [3]from within him shall flow rivers of living water. 39 But this spake he of the Spirit, which they that believed on him were to receive: [4]for the Spirit was not yet *given;* because Jesus was not yet glorified. 40 *Some* of the multitude therefore, when they heard these words, said, This is of a truth the prophet. 41 Others said, This is the Christ. But some said, What, doth the Christ come out of Galilee? 42 [5]Hath not the scripture said that the Christ cometh of the seed of David, and from Bethlehem, the village where David was? 43 So there arose a division in the multitude because of him. 44 And some of them would have taken him; but no man laid hands on him.

45 The officers therefore came to the chief priests and Pharisees; and they said unto them, Why did ye not bring him? 46 The officers answered, Never man so spake. 47 The Pharisees therefore answered them, Are ye also led astray? 48 Hath any of the rulers believed on him, or of the Pharisees? 49 But this multitude that knoweth not the law are accursed. 50 Nicodemus saith unto them (he that came to him before, being one of them), 51 Doth our law judge a man, except it first hear from himself and know what he doeth? 52 They answered and said unto him, Art thou also of Galilee? Search, and [6]see that out of Galilee ariseth no prophet.

[1] Gr. *a whole man sound.*   [2] Gr. *of.*   [3] Gr. *out of his belly.*
[4] Some ancient authorities read *for the Holy Spirit was not yet given.*
[5] 2 S. vii. 12 ff.; Mic. v. 2.   [6] Or, *see: for out of Galilee &c.*

Note 146. The reader is referred to the paragraph on the Feast of Tabernacles on page 14 for the significance of this feast and the practices engaged in during the celebration.

The purpose of this work does not require, nor will its limits permit, us to take notice of all the interesting points in this passage. But observe the following:

(1) The words of Jesus in verse 37 probably reflect the custom of bringing a pitcher of water from the pool of Siloam and pouring it out with much ceremony at the foot of the altar, celebrating the two occasions when God gave to their Israelite forefathers water from the rocks (Exod. 17: 5—6; Num. 20: 7—11). We wonder if this had just taken place when Jesus spoke the words of that verse. The meaning of the metaphor as Jesus used it, was that, as the water from the rocks satisfied the thirst of the Israelites, so the Holy Spirit will satisfy the deepest desires of those who believe on Jesus, and that these in turn will become a source of blessing to others.

(2) His long-time enemies, the Jerusalem Pharisees, undertook to arrest Him, but were strangely unable. He was going to be in and around Jerusalem much of the time until the end, and it is interesting to notice how futile were their efforts, either to take Him or to stone Him to death.

(3) The loyalty of Nicodemus is refreshing.

(4) We wonder if verse 42 reflects an acquaintance on the part of John the author with the circumstances of Jesus' birth. He possibly knew them better than did even Matthew or Luke; but since those writers had already left accounts of that event, he chose not to leave a third one (cf. page 31 for the historical purpose of John in writing). Possibly the ignorance of that group of sanhedrists about the birth of Jesus was amusing to him as he set down their words—or more probably, a cause of grief.

(3) In Jerusalem after the close of the Feast of Tabernacles, ##146—150
    a. Account of the adulteress who was brought to Jesus
#146

JOHN 7:53—8:11

53 [1][And they went every man unto his own house: 1 but Jesus went unto the mount of Olives. 2 And early in the morning he came again into the temple, and all the people came unto him; and he sat down, and taught them. 3 And the scribes and the Pharisees bring a woman taken in adultery; and having set her in the midst, 4 they say unto him, Teacher, this woman hath been taken in adultery, in the very act. 5 [2]Now in the law Moses commanded us to stone such: what then sayest thou of her? 6 And this they said, trying him, that they might have *whereof* to accuse him. But Jesus stooped down, and with his finger wrote on the ground. 7 But when they continued asking him, he lifted up himself, and said unto them, He that is without sin among you, let him first cast a stone at her. 8 And again he stooped down, and with his finger wrote on the ground. 9 And they, when they heard it, went out one by one, beginning from the eldest, *even* unto the last: and Jesus was left alone, and the woman, where she was, in the midst. 10 And Jesus lifted up himself, and said unto her, Woman, where are they? did no man condemn thee? 11 And she said, No man, Lord. And Jesus said, Neither do I condemn thee: go thy way; from henceforth sin no more.]

[1] Most of the ancient authorities omit John 7. 53-8. 11. Those which contain it vary much from each other.   [2] Lev. xx. 10; Dt. xxii. 22 f.

Note 147. This paragraph (John 7: 53—8: 11) is not found in any of the oldest known copies (manuscripts) of the Gospel of John. The later ones which do include it differ sharply in the readings, and in a few manuscripts this narrative is made to follow the material in Luke

21:37—38. We are told also that the diction and style of writing in this paragraph is quite different from that in the rest of this Gospel. Most New Testament scholars, therefore, conclude that it was not a part of the Gospel as John wrote it. But many of them, probably a majority, agree that it is surely a true account of an incident in the life of Jesus, though some say it may not have happened just at this time. Although the textual evidence is against regarding it as the work of John, I am convinced, not only that it is a true account of an event which occurred, but also that the writer, whoever he was, was divinely inspired to record it. He probably received the narrative from John and inserted it in the Gospel at this point with the knowledge and approval of the aged apostle after one or more copies of the Gospel had been made without this story.

Therefore I hold that this incident most probably occurred at the time in which it is placed in John's record; that is, on the day after the close of the Feast of Tabernacles. The things related in the closing verses of the seventh chapter of John occurred on the last day of the feast; and, according to verse 53, the people began to depart for their homes. But Jesus did not plan to return to Galilee; instead, it was His purpose to spend some time in Judaea. It is possible that He had already sent out the seventy into the cities and villages where He had in mind to come; or, if not already, surely it was His intention to send them out at once. He repaired therefore, to a place on the Mount of Olives, just outside the city, where it was convenient and comfortable for Him and the disciples to spend the nights in open air. We remember that the Mosaic law instructed the people to dwell in booths during the Feast of Tabernalces (Lev. 23: 40—43); and probably a pavilion of some kind on the Mount was made available to Jesus and His disciples to serve as their booth during the feast—and doubtless at any time afterward when He wanted to use it. He probably did use it further as a sort of an out-door lodging. On the next day, when He returned to the temple early in the morning, those who came to hear Him teach were some who lingered in Jerusalem after the feast, or else some who lived in or near the city. Probably the servants of the temple were, as we would say, cleaning up after the feast.

In such a situation the scribes and Pharisees brought to Jesus the woman taken in adultery. Their insincerity is manifest in that they did not bring also the man who was her partner in sin; for according to the law of Moses, they both were to be stoned to death (cf. Lev. 20: 10, Deut. 22: 22—24). They merely sought occasion against Jesus. But in His answer He: (1) upheld the law of Moses, (2) stipulated that execution should be by innocent hands, (3) awakened the conscience of the accusers, and (4) when no one appeared who was qualified to cast the first stone (as Jesus knew all the time that no one would), He pronounced forgiveness on the woman, after having led her to the point where forgiveness would be truly beneficial.

b. Further teaching concerning His mission and His relation to the Father, prolonged controversy with the Pharisees and their efforts to stone Him

#147
JOHN 8:12-59

12 Again therefore Jesus spake unto them, saying, I am the light of the world: he that followeth me shall not walk in the darkness, but shall have the light of life. 13 The Pharisees therefore said unto him, Thou bearest witness of thyself; thy witness is not true. 14 Jesus answered and said unto them, Even if I bear witness of myself, my witness is true; for I know whence I came, and whither I go; but ye know not whence I come, or whither I go. 15 Ye judge after the flesh; I judge no man. 16 Yea and if I judge, my judgment is true; for I am not alone, but I and the Father that sent me. 17 Yea and in your law it is written, [1]that the witness of two men is true. 18 I am he that beareth witness of myself, and the Father that sent me beareth witness of me. 19 They said therefore unto him, Where is thy Father? Jesus answered, Ye know neither me, nor my Father: if ye knew me, ye would know my Father also. 20 These words spake he in the treasury, as he taught in the temple: and no man took him; because his hour was not yet come.

21 He said therefore again unto them, I go away, and ye shall seek me, and shall die in your sin: whither I go, ye cannot come. 22 The Jews therefore said, Will he kill himself, that he saith, Whither I go, ye cannot come? 23 And he said unto them, Ye are from beneath; I am from above: ye are of this world; I am not of this world. 24 I said therefore unto you, that ye shall die in your sins: for except ye believe that I am *he,* ye shall die in your sins. 25 They said therefore unto him, Who art thou? Jesus said unto them, [2]Even that which I have also spoken unto you from the beginning. 26 I have many things to speak and to judge concerning you: howbeit he that sent me is true; and the things which I heard from him, these speak I unto the world. 27 They perceived not that he spake to them of the Father. 28 Jesus therefore said, When ye have lifted up the Son of man, then shall ye know that [3]I am *he,* and *that* I do nothing of myself, but as the Father taught me, I speak these things. 29 And he that sent me is with me; he hath not left me alone; for I do always the things that are pleasing to him. 30 As he spake these things, many believed on him.

31 Jesus therefore said to those Jews that had believed him, If ye abide in my word, *then* are ye truly my disciples; 32 and ye shall know the truth, and the truth shall make you free. 33 They answered unto him, We are Abraham's seed, and have never yet been in bondage to any man: how sayest thou, Ye shall be made free? 34 Jesus answered them, Verily, verily, I say unto you, Every one that committeth sin is the bondservant of sin. 35 And the bondservant abideth not in the house for ever: the son abideth for ever. 36 If therefore the Son shall make you free, ye shall be free indeed. 37 I know that you are Abraham's seed; yet ye seek to kill me, because my word [4]hath not free course in you. 38 I speak the things which I have seen with [5]my Father: and ye also do the things which ye heard from *your* father. 39 They answered and said unto him, Our father is Abraham. Jesus saith unto them, If ye [6]were Abraham's children, [7]ye would do the works of Abraham. 40 But now ye seek to kill me, a man that hath told you the truth, which I heard from God: this did not Abraham. 41 Ye do the works of your father. They said unto him, We were not born of fornication; we have one Father, *even* God. 42 Jesus said unto them, If God were your Father, ye would love me: for I came forth and am come from God; for neither have I come of myself, but he sent me. 43 Why do ye not [8]understand my speech? *Even* because ye cannot hear my word. 44 Ye are of *your* father the devil, and the lusts of your father it is your will to do. He was a murderer from the beginning, and standeth not in the truth, because there is no truth in him. [9]When he speaketh a lie, he speaketh of his own: for he is a liar, and the father thereof. 45 But because I say the truth, ye believe me not. 46 Which of you convicteth me of sin? If I say truth, why do ye not believe me?

[1] Comp. Dt. xix. 15; xvii. 6.   [2] Or, *Altogether that which I also speak unto you*
[3] Or, *I am he: and I do*   [4] Or, *hath no place in you*
[5] Or, *the Father: do ye also therefore the things which ye heard from the Father*   [6] Gr. *are.*
[7] Some ancient authorities read *ye do the works of Abraham.*   [8] Or, *know*
[9] Or, *When one speaketh a lie, he speaketh of his own: for his father also is a liar.*

47 He that is of God heareth the words of God: for this cause ye hear *them* no
because ye are not of God. 48 The Jews answered and said unto him, Say we no
well that thou art a Samaritan, and hast a demon? 49 Jesus answered, I have no
a demon; but I honor my Father, and ye dishonor me. 50 But I seek not mine ow
glory: there is one that seeketh and judgeth. 51 Verily, verily, I say unto yo
If a man keep my word, he shall never see death. 52 The Jews said unto hin
Now we know that thou hast a demon. Abraham died, and the prophets; and tho
sayest, If a man keep my word, he shall never taste of death. 53 Art thou great.
than our father, Abraham, who died? and the prophets died: whom makest the
thyself? 54 Jesus answered, If I glorify myself, my glory is nothing: it is my Fath
that glorifieth me: of· whom ye say, that he is your God; 55 and ye have not know
him: but I know him; and if I should say, I know him not, I shall be like un
you, a liar: but I know him, and keep his word. 56 Your father Abraham rejoice
[10]to see my day; and he saw it, and was glad. 57 The Jews therefore said unto hin
Thou art not yet fifty years old, and hast thou seen Abraham? 58 Jesus said un
them, Verily, verily, I say unto you, Before Abraham was born, I am. 59 They too
up stones therefore to cast at him: but Jesus [11]hid himself, and went out of th
temple[12].

[10] Or, *that he should see*   [11] Or, *was hidden, and went &c.*
[12] Many ancient authorities add *and going through the midst of them went his way and so passed by*

Note 148. If we were justified in assuming that John 7: 53--8: 1
(#146) is inserted in the right place in the narrative, even if it was no
written by John, all of the discourse in this section took place on th
day (or possibly days) after the close of the feast. Verse 12 is surel
a reflection of their custom of erecting and lighting great candelabra i
the Court of the Women during the Feast of Tabernacles, in commem
òration of the pillar of fire, which, along with the pillar of cloud, guide
the Israelites on their journeys through the wilderness (Exod. 13: 21—22)
On the day after the feast the workmen at the temple certainly would b
called on for some labor in connection with the great lampstands, pos
sibly putting them away until they should be needed for the feast nex
year, thus attracting the attention of those gathered around Jesus. H
therefore declared that, just as the Israelites followed the pillar of fir
in safety, so those following Him would have the light of life. Jesu
is called light elsewhere in Luke 2: 32; John 1: 4—5, 9; 3: 19; 9: 5
12: 35--36, 46.

Again we must confine our remarks on this interesting discours
to the topics discussed:

(1) Jesus set before His critics how His claims were atteste
(claims to supply "living water"—7: 38, and to be the light of the world-
8: 12)—verses 13--19.

(2) He explained why the officers had not been able to arrest Him-
verses 20--22.

(3) He discussed divine sonship, which He claimed, and Abra
hamic sonship which His critics claimed, but asserted Satanic sonshi
to be their true spiritual state (cf. Matt. 13: 38b, #99)— verses 23--5:

(4) As the Son of God He claimed eternity of life—verses 51--58
The "I am" of verse 58 and of verse 24 (where "he" is printed in italics because it is not in John's original) should be compared with Exod
3: 14, and verse 25 with John 5: 17--18).

The attempt to stone Him related in verse 59 is the first of two such attempts (cf. John 10:31ff, #165).

c. Sending forth the seventy and their joyous return
#148
Luke 10:1-24

1 Now after these things the Lord appointed seventy[1] others, and sent them two and two before his face into every city and place, whither he himself was about to come. 2 And he said unto them, The harvest indeed is plenteous, but the laborers are few: pray ye therefore the Lord of the harvest, that he send forth laborers into his harvest. 3 Go your ways; behold, I send you forth as lambs in the midst of wolves. 4 Carry no purse, no wallet, no shoes; and salute no man on the way. 5 And into whatsoever house ye shall [2]enter, first say, Peace be to this house. 6 And if a son of peace be there, your peace shall rest upon [3]him: but if not, it shall turn to you again. 7 And, in that same house remain, eating and drinking such things as they give: for the laborer is worthy of his hire. Go not from house to house. 8 And into whatsoever city ye enter, and they receive you, eat such things as are set before you: 9 and heal the sick that are therein, and say unto them, The kingdom of God is come nigh unto you. 10 But into whatsoever city ye shall enter, and they receive you not, go out into the streets thereof and say, 11 Even the dust from your city, that cleaveth to our feet, we wipe off against you: nevertheless know this, that the kingdom of God is come nigh. 12 I say unto you, It shall be more tolerable in that day for Sodom, than for that city. 13 Woe unto thee, Chorazin! woe unto thee, Bethsaida! for if the [4]mighty works had been done in Tyre and Sidon, which were done in you, they would have repented long ago, sitting in sackcloth and ashes. 14 But it shall be more tolerable for Tyre and Sidon in the judgment, than for you. 15 And thou, Capernaum, shalt' thou be exalted unto heaven? thou shalt be brought down unto Hades. 16 He that heareth you heareth me: and he that rejecteth you rejecteth me; and he that rejecteth me rejecteth him that sent me.

17 And the seventy returned with joy, saying, Lord, even the demons are subject unto us in thy name. 18 And he said unto them, I beheld Satan fallen as lightning from heaven. 19 Behold, I have given you authority to tread upon serpents and scorpions, and over all the power of the enemy: and nothing shall in any wise hurt you. 20 Nevertheless in this rejoice not, that the spirits are subject unto you; but rejoice that your names are written in heaven.

21 In that same hour he rejoiced [5]in the Holy Spirit, and said, I [6]thank thee, O Father, Lord of heaven and earth, that thou didst hide these things from the wise and understanding, and didst reveal them unto babes: yea, Father, [7]for so it was well-pleasing in thy sight. 22 All things have been delivered unto me of my Father: and no one knoweth who the Son is, save the Father; and who the Father is, save the Son, and he to whomsoever the Son willeth to reveal him. 23 And turning to the disciples, he said privately, Blessed are the eyes which see the things that ye see: 24 for I say unto you, that many prophets and kings desired to see the things which ye see, and saw them not; and to hear the things which ye hear, and heard them not.

Many ancient authorities add and two: and so in ver. 17.   [2] Or, enter first, say
[1] Or, it   [4] Gr. powers.   [5] Or, by   [6] Or, praise   [7] Or, that

Note 149. The sending of the seventy messengers was surely for a different purpose from the earlier sending out of the twelve apostles. The apostles were sent on practice tours; and these were followed by seasons of retirement, on which doubtless they gave reports to Jesus of their experiences. But the mission of the seventy was more like that of the messengers whom He sent before Him when He set His face to go to Jerusalem (Luke 9:51—52, #142). Like those messengers, these seventy were sent "unto every city and place whither He Himself" was planning to come. Our Lord apparently had in mind to do in Judaea and Peraea in less than six months a work which had required a year and a half in Galilee, and He sent these seventy ahead of Him as, what would be called today, His "advance agents." However, He gave them practically the same instructions as He had given the twelve; He directed them to heal the sick and to preach that the Kingdom of God is come nigh just as He had instructed the twelve (cf. #113).

When were they sent out? Luke said, "after these things;" that is, after sending the messengers to prepare for His journey to Jerusalem (Luke 9:52, #142), and after the offer of service on the part of the three portrayed in #143. It was probably after His arrival in Jerusalem for the feast of Tabernacles, but before the end of the conflict with the authorities there. The mission may not have taken a great deal of time, as each pair of messengers was probably sent to only one city or village. It is possible, also, that Jesus began His journeys into the villages of Judaea before all of the seventy returned.

In the study of this period we shall observe a repetition in Luke of many sayings of Jesus which are found in Matthew in earlier connections. For example, compare verse 2 above with Matt. 9:37--38, #112; verses 3--12 with Matt. 10:5--16, #113; verses 13--16 with Matt. 11:20--24, #82; verses 21--22 with Matt. 11:25--27, #83. Other such repetitions will be observed in the study of the chapters of Luke that will follow, and there will also be sayings which Matthew quoted in connection with occasions later than those in which they are related in Luke. In an effort to account for these repetitions, some students of the Gospels assume that Matthew and Luke put in different connections the words of Jesus which they obtained from a common documentary list of quotations from Him. Many maintain that this document was the Logia ("Sayings of Jesus"), written by Matthew in Hebrew before he composed in Greek the Gospel as we have it (cf. Introduction, p. 23). Luke admits that he obtained his material from others "who from the beginning were eyewitnesses and ministers of the Word" (Luke 1:2, #2), and one source of his material may have been Matthew's Logia; but he certainly had many other sources of information, which he followed in putting these quotations where he did. Without doubt, the Lord Jesus repeated some of these statements on more than one occasion; and I see no reason for supposing that either Matthew or Luke got them in the wrong place. We might well expect Him to repeat before audiences in Judaea and Peraea some of the things He had said to Galilean throngs.

d. Answering a lawyer's question, parable of the Good Samaritan

#149
LUKE 10:25-37

25 And behold, a certain lawyer stood up and made trial of him, saying, Teacher what shall I do to inherit eternal life? 26 And he said unto him, What is written in the law? how readest thou? 27 And he answering said, [1]Thou shalt love the Lord thy God [2]with all thy heart, and with all thy soul, and with all thy strength, and with all thy mind; [3]and thy neighbor as thyself, 28 And he said unto him, Thou hast answered right: this do, and thou shalt live. 29 But he, desiring to justify himself, said unto Jesus, And who is my neighbor? 30 Jesus made answer and said, A certain man was

[1] Dt. vi 5.   [2] Gr. from.   [3] Lev. xix. 18.

going down from Jerusalem to Jericho; and he fell among robbers, who both stripped him and beat him, and departed, leaving him half dead. 31 And by chance a certain priest was going down that way: and when he saw him, he passed by on the other side. 32 And in like manner a Levite also, when he came to the place, and saw him, passed by on the other side. 33 But a certain Samaritan, as he journeyed, came where he was: and when he saw him, he was moved with compassion, 34 and came to him, and bound up his wounds, pouring on *them* oil and wine; and he set him on his own beast, and brought him to an inn, and took care of him. 35 And on the morrow he took out two 'shillings, and gave them to the host, and said, Take care of him; and whatsoever thou spendest more, I, when I come back again, will repay thee. 36 Which of these three, thinkest thou, proved neighbor unto him that fell among the robbers? 37 And he said, He that showed mercy on him. And Jesus said unto him, Go, and do thou likewise.

⁴ See marginal note on ch. 7. 41.

Note 150. Lawyers were learned scribes who were recognized as profound expositors of the law, but possibly not regarded quite so highly as the "doctors of the law." Though it is altogether conjecture on my part, I take it that the incident narrated in this section followed in close sequence after those of the preceding section, and that the lawyer was probably seated with those listening to Jesus at the time of the return of some of the seventy. From Luke's use of the words "and behold" (kai idou) we might gather that the lawyer's presence in the group and his rising to make his inquiry was a surprise to those present.* His question may have been occasioned by Jesus' assurance to the returning messengers that their names were written in Heaven, or by His prayer of thanksgiving which followed (vss. 20—22 in the preceding section).

This lawyer was the first of two who came to Jesus with this all-important question (cf. #187). We wonder why Jesus gave him an answer involving works rather than one involving faith, as He had given Nicodemus (John 3: 15, 16). In answer I would suggest: (1) This lawyer did not ask his question in sincerity. His purpose was to tempt or entangle Jesus. (2) The emphasis in the lawyer's question was on the matter of doing something, and Jesus gave an answer to fit the question. (3) The answer that Jesus gave required a perfect attitude toward God and man, which attitude would have led to acceptance of Jesus as Messiah and Saviour (cf. footnote on Note 188, p. 231).

Notice that this lawyer summed up the law in the same way that Jesus Himself did later in answer to another lawyer's question (cf. #213).

The parable of The Good Samaritan was spoken, not to answer what the lawyer must do to inherit eternal life, but to teach by illustration who was his neighbor. It is the first of sixteen parables spoken in this period of the life of Jesus which are found only in Luke.

*John Henry Thayer, *A Greek-English Lexicon of the New Testament* (Chicago: American Book Company, 1889), p. 297 (definition of *idou,* particularly where this passage among others is cited with the comment "when a thing is specified which is unexpected yet sure").

e. On a Sabbath day giving sight to a man who had been born blind   #150

1 And as he passed by, he saw a man blind from his birth. 2 And his disciples asked him, saying, Rabbi, who sinned, this man, or his parents, that he should be born blind? 3 Jesus answered, Neither did this man sin, nor his parents: but that the works of God should be made manifest in him. 4 We must work the works of him that sent me, while it is day: the night cometh, when no man can work. 5 When I am in the world, I am the light of the world. 6 When he had thus spoken, he spat on the ground, and made clay of the spittle, ¹and anointed his eyes with the clay, 7 and said unto him, Go, wash in the pool of Siloam (which is by interpretation, Sent). He went away therefore, and washed, and came seeing. 8 The neighbors therefore, and they that saw him aforetime, that he was a beggar, said, Is not this he that sat and begged? 9 Others said, It is he: others said, No, but he is like him. He said, I am he. 10 They said therefore unto him, How then were thine eyes opened? 11 He answered, The man that is called Jesus made clay, and anointed mine eyes, and said unto me, Go to Siloam, and wash: so I went away and washed, and I received sight. 12 And they said unto him, Where is he? He saith, I know not.

¹ Or, and with the clay thereof anointed his eyes

Note 151. Did this miracle take place as Jesus was leaving the city to begin His tour in Judaea? It can be safely assumed, I think, that the events related in John 9: 35—10: 39 (##163—165) occurred in connection with the Feast of Dedication, which was celebrated about two and a half months after the Feast of Tabernacles (cf. calendar circle on page 12). The events of John 9: 8—34 (#162) surely were spread over several weeks. I take it, therefore, that Jesus very likely performed the miracle of giving sight to this man as He "passed by" from His place of sojourn in Jerusalem, or on the Mount of Olives, enroute to some village in Judaea. Since it was the Sabbath, His destination must have been nearby; for, although he did not hesitate to violate the regulations set by the scribes in the matter of healing, He did not needlessly defy the accepted usage just for His own convenience. In the next section we shall find Him at Bethany (the village of Martha and Mary), which was near Jerusalem and nearer still to the Mount of Olives about a Sabbath day's journey (cf. Luke 24: 50 with Acts 1: 12, also John 11: 18). Furthermore, according to the maps, if He and the disciples encountered the blind man on the road to Bethany, the pool of Siloam was not very far away. We wonder, therefore, if He were passing by, enroute to Bethany for synagogue worship. When the neighbors inquired of the man recently blind where Jesus was, he did not know (John 9: 12), which fact indicates that Jesus was out of the city on the Judaean tour.

We wonder why Jesus put the clay mixed with spittle on the man's eyes. Possibly to encourage his faith and to give him an incentive to go to the Pool of Siloam as Jesus directed. This is the third time He used spittle in effecting a cure (cf. Mark 7: 33, #125, and 8: 23, #129).

This miracle occasioned the fourth Sabbath controversy (cf. ##47, 49, 50). However, only the man who had received sight was involved in the controversy.

2. Journeys in Judaea, ##151—161

(1) Resting in the home of Martha and Mary

#151

LUKE 10:38-42

38 Now as they went on their way, he entered into a certain village: and a certain woman named Martha received him into her house. 39 And she had a sister called Mary, who also sat at the Lord's feet, and heard his word. 40 But Martha was [1]cumbered about much serving; and she came up to him, and said, Lord, dost thou not care that my sister did leave me to serve alone? bid her therefore that she help me. 41 But the Lord answered and said unto her, [2]Martha, Martha, thou art anxious and troubled about many things: 42 [3]but one thing is needful: for Mary hath chosen the good part, which shall not be taken away from her.

[1] Gr. distracted.
[2] A few ancient authorities read Martha, Martha, thou art troubled; Mary hath chosen &c.
[3] Many ancient authorities read but few things are needful, or one.

Note 152. Without doubt the clause "on their way as they went," in verse 38 above refers to journeys of Jesus and the disciples in Judaea. It is inserted to indicate that the itinerary was begun for which He had sent the seventy to prepare the way (Luke 10: 1, #148). Luke does not designate the village of Martha and Mary by the name of Bethany, but we know from John 11 that these sisters lived at Bethany. The family of Martha and Mary (and Lazarus) appears in John in two later connections (John 11—12, ##178, 196).

When Jesus said that Mary had chosen the "good part which shall not be taken away from her," He evidently meant that she had chosen that benefit accruing from His visit in the home which would result in the greatest blessing—the benefit of fellowship with Him and of hearing His words. However, the "good part" which Mary had chosen is not to be regarded as identical with the "one thing" which Jesus said was needful. Observe that the marginal note to that verse says that "many ancient authorities" (very old copies, or manuscripts, of the New Testament) read, "But few things are needful, or one." If that is the true quotation of what Jesus said,[*] He undoubtedly had reference to articles of food. He was saying to Martha that she was anxious and distressed about many things to eat in the meal which she was preparing, when a few would be sufficient, indeed one was all that was necessary. Martha was missing the best blessing of having Jesus in the home because she was preparing so many things for the meal, when one was all that was necessary. But Mary was obtaining that blessing, and Jesus said He was not going to deprive her of it.

(2) Teaching the disciples to pray

#152

LUKE 11:1-13

1 And it came to pass, as he was praying in a certain place, that when he ceased, one of his disciples said unto him, Lord, teach us to pray, even as John also taught his disciples. 2 And he said unto them, When ye pray, say, [1]Father, Hallowed be thy

[1] Many ancient authorities read Our Father, who art in heaven. See Mt. 6. 9.

[*]It is the reading adopted both in The Greek New Testament distributed by the British and Foreign Bible Society (London: 1934), prepared by Eberhard Nestle, p. 190; and in Westcott and Hort, The New Testament in the Original Greek, p. 148.

197

name. Thy kingdom come.² 3 Give us day by day ³our daily bread. 4 And forgive us our sins; for we ourselves also forgive every one that is indebted to us. And bring us not into temptation⁴.

5 And he said unto them, Which of you shall have a friend, and shall go unto him at midnight, and say to him, Friend, lend me three loaves; 6 for a friend of mine is come to me from a journey, and I have nothing tó set before him; 7 and he from within shall answer and say, Trouble me not: the door is now shut, and my children are with me·in bed; I cannot rise and give thee? 8 I say unto you, Though he will not rise and·give him because he is his friend, yet because of his importunity he will arise and give him ⁵as many as he needeth. 9 And I say unto you, Ask, and it shall be given you; seek, and ye shall find; knock, and it shall be opened unto you. 10 For every one that asketh receiveth; and he that seeketh findeth; and to him that knocketh it shall be opened. 11 And of which of you that is a father shall his son ask ⁶a loaf, and he give him a stone? or a fish, and he for a fish give him a serpent? 12 Or *if* he shall ask an egg, will he give him a scorpion? 13 If ye then, being evil, know how to give good gifts unto your children, how much more shall *your* heavenly Father give the Holy Spirit to them that ask him?

² Many ancient authorities add· *Thy will be done, as in heaven, so on earth.* See Mt. 6. 10.
³ Gr. *our bread for the coming day.* Or, *our needful bread:* as in Mt. 6. 11.
⁴ Many ancient authorities add *but deliver us from the evil* one (or, *from evil*). See Mt. 6. 13.
⁵ Or, *whatsoever things*　　⁶ Some ancient authorities omit *a loaf, and he give him a stone? or.*

Note 153. The version of the Model Prayer in Luke is shorter than that in Matthew (cf. #65), and the occasion when Jesus is reported to have given it is altogether different. The parable of The Importunate Neighbor is found only in Luke. In it Jesus meant to teach continuance in prayer, not in order to "tease" God into giving the blessings sought, but out of a continuing faith. In verse 9 Jesus gave an interpretation of the parable, the words for "ask," "seek," and "knock," being present imperatives, indicating that our Lord enjoined continued asking or seeking or knocking.

The parable of The Father Giving Good Gifts to his Son is found also in Matthew as a part of the Sermon on the Mount, but not in connection with the Model Prayer (#71). In all Jesus spoke four parables on prayer, all found in Luke and three of them in Luke only (cf. ##184, 185).

(3) Casting out a demon, repetition of blasphemous charge against Him, repetition of warnings and teachings formerly spoken in Galilee

#153

LUKE 11:14-36

14 And he was casting out a demon *that was* dumb. And it came to pass, when the demon was gone out, the dumb man spake; and the multitudes marvelled. 15 But some of them said, ¹By ²Beelzebub the prince of the demons casteth he out demons. 16 And others, trying *him,* sought of him a sign from heaven. 17 But he, knowing their thoughts, said unto them, Every kingdom divided against itself is brought to desolation; ³and a house *divided* against a house falleth. 18 And if Satan also is divided against himself, how shall his kingdom stand? because ye say that I cast out demons ¹by ²Beelzebub. 19 And if I ¹by ²Beelzebub cast out demons, by whom do your sons cast them out? therefore shall they be your judges. 20 But if I by the finger of God cast out demons, then is the kingdom of God come upon you. 21 When the strong *man* fully armed guardeth his own court, his goods are in peace:

¹ Or, *In*　　　　² Gr. *Beelzebul.*　　　³ Or, *and house falleth upon house*

Luke 11

22 but when a stronger than he shall come upon him, and overcome him, he taketh from him his whole armor wherein he trusted, and divideth his spoils. 23 He that is not with me is against me; and he that gathereth not with me scattereth. 24 The unclean spirit when ⁴he is gone out of the man, passeth through waterless places, seeking rest, and finding none, ⁴he saith, I will turn back unto my house whence I came out. 25 And when ⁴he is come, ⁴he findeth it swept and garnished. 26 Then goeth ⁴he, and taketh to *him* seven other spirits more evil than ⁵himself; and they enter in and dwell there: and the last state of that man becometh worse than the first.

27 And it came to pass, as he said these things, a certain woman out of the multitude lifted up her voice, and said unto him, Blessed is the womb that bare thee, and the breasts which thou didst suck. 28 But he said, Yea rather, blessed are they that hear the word of God, and keep it.

29 And when the multitudes were gathering together unto him, he began to say, This generation is an evil generation: it seeketh after a sign; and there shall no sign be given to it but the sign of Jonah. 30 For even as Jonah became a sign unto the Ninevites, so shall also the Son of man be to this generation. 31 The queen of the south shall rise up in the judgment with the men of this generation, and shall condemn them: for she came from the ends of the earth to hear the wisdom of Solomon; and behold, ⁶a greater than Solomon is here. 32 The men of Nineveh shall stand up in the judgment with this generation, and shall condemn it: for they repented at the preaching of Jonah: and behold, ⁶a greater than Jonah is here.

33 No man, when he hath lighted a lamp, putteth it in a cellar, neither under the bushel, but on the stand, that they which enter in may see the light. 34 The lamp of thy body is thine eye: when thine eye is single, thy whole body also is full of light; but when it is evil, thy body also is full of darkness. 35 Look therefore whether the light that is in thee be not darkness. 36 If therefore thy whole body be full of light, having no part dark, it shall be wholly full of light, as when the lamp with its bright shining doth give thee light.

⁴ Or. *it*   ⁵ Or, *itself*   ⁶ Gr. *more than.*

Note 154. In the foregoing section is the account of the last occasion, so far as the record goes, when Jesus cast out a demon from its victim, the only such miracle performed in Judaea. And He was accused for the third time of being in league with Beelzebub (Satan) in working the miracle (cf. ##87, 110). In the defense of Himself here He made use of three points of the defense which He had made on the occasion of the first such accusation including the parable of The Burglar (cf. Note 88). However, the warning against blaspheming the Holy Spirit, which was a part of His defense on the former occasion, was not repeated at this time; but a similar warning was spoken in another connection very soon thereafter (cf. Luke 12: 10, #155), and probably to an audience which included many who heard these words. As in connection with the first such blasphemous accusation, He was again challenged to show a sign from Heaven (cf. #88, also #127); and, as formerly, He replied with a reference to the experience of Jonah as a sign of His authority, enforcing His words with the parable of the Unclean Spirit (cf. Matt. 12: 29, 43—45, and Note 89). This was the third time Jesus spoke the parable of The Lamp (cf. ##55, 94), but this time the meaning is different; it illustrates how one's ability to see a truth is affected by his willingness to look at it in the proper light (cf. Matt. 6: 22—23, #67).

(4) Dining with a Pharisee (a second time), denouncing Pharisees and lawyers as a class, aggravating their enmity (cf. ##84, 123, also 215

#154

LUKE 11:37-54

37 Now as he spake, a Pharisee asketh him to ¹dine with him: and he went in, and sat down to meat. 38 And when the Pharisee saw it, he marvelled that he had not first bathed himself before ¹dinner. 39 And the Lord said unto him, Now ye the Pharisees cleanse the outside of the cup and of the platter; but your inward part is full of extortion and wickedness. 40 Ye foolish ones, did not he that made the outside make the inside also? 41 But give for alms those things which ²are within; and behold, all things are clean unto you.

42 But woe unto you Pharisees! for ye tithe mint and rue and every herb, and pass over justice and the love of God: but these ought ye to have done, and not to leave the other undone. 43 Woe unto you Pharisees! for ye love the chief seats in the synagogues, and the salutations in the marketplaces. 44 Woe unto you! for ye are as the tombs which appear not, and the men that walk over *them* know it not.

45 And one of the lawyers answering saith unto him, Teacher, in saying this thou reproachest us also. 46 And he said, Woe unto you lawyers also! for ye load men with burdens grievous to be borne, and ye yourselves touch not the burdens with one of your fingers. 47 Woe unto you! for ye build the tombs of the prophets, and your fathers killed them. 48 So ye are witnesses and consent unto the works of your fathers: for they killed them, and ye build *their tombs.* 49 Therefore also said the wisdom of God, I will send unto them prophets and apostles; and *some* of them they shall kill and persecute; 50 that the blood of all the prophets, which was shed from the foundation of the world, may be required of this generation; 51 from the blood of Abel unto the blood of Zachariah, who perished between the altar and the ³sanctuary: yea, I say unto you, it shall be required of this generation. 52 Woe unto you lawyers! for ye took away the key of knowledge: ye entered not in yourselves, and them that were entering in ye hindered.

53 And when he was come out from thence, the scribes and the Pharisees began to ⁴press upon him vehemently, and to provoke him to speak of ⁵many things; 54 laying wait for him, to catch something out of his mouth.

¹ Gr. *breakfast.*　　　² Or, *ye can*　　　³ Gr. *house.*
⁴ Or, *set themselves vehemently against* him　　　⁵ Or, *more*

Note 155. This was the second time, so far as the record goes, that Jesus dined with a Pharisee (cf. #84); there will be another (Luke 14: 1, #168). It was the second time they found fault with Him for eating without the ceremonial washing (cf. #123). This time it seems He was expected to bathe Himself thoroughly before the meal (Greek, "be immersed," baptisthē). His answer to their criticism this time was a counter criticism and a general denunciation of the Pharisees and lawyers for their ostentation and hypocrisy. Was He an ungracious guest in the Pharisee's home? Probably if we would consider that the scribes and Pharisees of Jerusalem and Judaea were His unrelenting enemies, we should suspect, if not fully conclude, that this Judaean Pharisee invited Jesus to this meal in order that he and his fellow Pharisees might find a feasible ground of accusation against Him. Such a view is in agreement with verses 53—54. Accordingly, any pretension of friendship that went with the invitation was sheer hypocrisy, just as was their pretension of complying with the Levitical law of purification, and He, therefore, had sufficient reason for exposing and denouncing their hypocrisy. We shall find later He repeated these denunciations, and added to them, in the oration of Matthew 23 (#215).

(5) Teachings concerning the hypocrisy of the Pharisees

#155
LUKE 12:1-12

1 In the mean time, when [1]the many thousands of the multitude were gathered together, insomuch that they trod one upon another, he began to [2]say unto his disciples first of all, Beware ye of the leaven of the Pharisees, which is hypocrisy. 2 But there is nothing covered up, that shall not be revealed; and hid, that shall not be known. 3 Wherefore whatsoever ye have said in the darkness shall be heard in the light; and what ye have spoken in the ear in the inner chambers shall be proclaimed upon the housetops. 4 And I say unto you my friends, Be not afraid of them that kill the body, and after that have no more that they can do. 5 But I will warn you whom ye shall fear: Fear him, who after he hath killed hath [3]power to cast into [4]hell; yea, I say unto you, Fear him. 6 Are not five sparrows sold for two pence? and not one of them is forgotten in the sight of God. 7 But the very hairs of your head are all numbered. Fear not: ye are of more value than many sparrows. 8 And I say unto you, Every one who shall confess [5]me before men, [6]him shall the Son of man also confess before the angels of God: 9 but he that denieth me in the presence of men shall be denied in the presence of the angels of God. 10 And every one who shall speak a word against the Son of man, it shall be forgiven him: but unto him that blasphemeth against the Holy Spirit it shall not be forgiven. 11 And when they bring you before the synagogues, and the rulers, and the authorities, be not anxious how or what ye shall answer, or what ye shall say: 12 for the Holy Spirit shall teach you in that very hour what ye ought to say.

[1] Gr. the myriads of.
[2] Or, say unto his disciples, First of all beware ye
[3] Or, authority
[4] Gr. Gehenna.
[5] Gr. in me.
[6] Gr. in him.

Note 156. The Lord Jesus had already, while He was in Galilee, spoken the warnings and promises of this section (compare verse 1 with Matt. 16:6 and Mark 8:15; verses 2—9 with Matt. 10:26—33; verses 8—9 also with Mark 8:38; verse 10 with Matt. 12:31—32, Mark 3:28—30; and verses 11—12 with Matt. 10:19—20, ##87, 113, 128). Very probably it was because of the manifest insincerity and hypocrisy on the part of the Pharisee with whom He had dined (#154) and of the others present, and their increased hostility, that He repeated these admonitions to the disciples. The words in verse 1 translated "in the mean time" literally mean "in which circumstances." Therefore, it is entirely possible that the gathering crowds, including His disciples and all His followers, knew what had taken place in the Pharisee's house.

(6) Teachings concerning worldly wealth, the parable of The Rich Fool (cf. ##67--68)

#156
LUKE 12:13-34

13 And one out of the multitude said unto him, Teacher, bid my brother divide the inheritance with me. 14 But he said unto him, Man, who made me a judge or a divider over you? 15 And he said unto them, Take heed, and keep yourselves from all covetousness: [1]for a man's life consisteth not in the abundance of the things which he possesseth. 16 And he spake a parable unto them, saying, The ground of a certain rich man brought forth plentifully: 17 and he reasoned within himself, saying, What shall I do, because I have not where to bestow my fruits? 18 And he said, This will I do: I will pull down my barns, and build greater; and there will I bestow all my grain and my goods. 19 And I will say to my [2]soul, [2]Soul, thou hast much goods laid up for many years; take thine ease, eat, drink, be merry. 20 But God said unto him, Thou foolish one, this night [3]is thy [2]soul required of thee; and the things which thou hast prepared, whose shall they be? 21 So is he that layeth up treasure for himself, and is not rich toward God.

[1] Or, for even in a man's abundance his life is not from the things which he possesseth
[2] Or, life
[3] Gr. they require thy soul.

201

22 And he said unto his disciples, Therefore I say unto you, Be not anxious for *your* [4]life, what ye shall eat; nor yet for your body, what ye shall put on. 23 For the [4]life is more than the food, and the body than the raiment. 24 Consider the ravens, that they sow not, neither reap; which have no store-chamber nor barn; and God feedeth them: of how much more value are ye than the birds! 25 And which of you by being anxious can add a cubit unto [5]the measure of his life? 26 If then ye are not able to do even that which is least, why are ye anxious concerning the rest? 27 Consider the lilies, how they grow: they toil not, neither do they spin; yet I say unto you, Even Solomon in all his glory was not arrayed like one of these. 28 But if God doth so clothe the grass in the field, which to-day is, and to-morrow is cast into the oven; how much more *shall he clothe* you, O ye of little faith? 29 And seek not ye what ye shall eat, and what ye shall drink, neither be ye of doubtful mind. 30 For all these things do the nations of the world seek after: but your Father knoweth that ye have need of these things. 31 Yet seek ye [6]his kingdom, and these things shall be added unto you. 32 Fear not, little flock; for it is your Father's good pleasure to give you the kingdom. 33 Sell that which ye have, and give alms; make for yourselves purses which wax not old, a treasure in the heavens that faileth not, where no thief draweth near, neither moth destroyeth. 34 For where your treasure is, there will your heart be also.

[4] Or, *soul*   [5] Or, *his stature*   [6] Many ancient authorities read *the kingdom of God.*

Note 157. Apparently Jesus h a d said nothing to encourage the dissatisfied heir to bring his complaint to Him. Perhaps, this man, like many more, was expecting the Messiah to set up the visible Kingdom in short order, and was making his request subject to the realization of such expectation. But the answer of Jesus gave him no comfort. Not only was the setting up of the visible Kingdom at that time foreign to the purpose of Jesus, but this man's quarrelsome attitude toward earthly wealth was contrary to everything which He had taught on that subject (cf. Matt. 5: 40ff, #60). Doubtless He spoke the parable of the Rich Fool to warn the complaining brother not to attach too much importance to earthly possessions, apparently using as an example the father of the contending brothers, or whosever estate it was that they were quarrelling over. That one had yielded up his soul to God after a life of exhausting toil; and now the fruits of his labors, instead of being a source of pleasure to himself, as he had planned, had become a bone of contention between the brothers. In verse 19 the word "soul" is probably used as an equivalent to one's whole personality. This was in accord with the Hebrew understanding of the word.

From this point Jesus proceeded to repeat for this company of Judaean followers the s a m e lessons concerning worldly possessions which He had given to the apostles and the assembled Galilean crowds in the Sermon on the Mount (cf. ##67, 68). In the former discourse (Matt. 6: 20) He admonished His hearers to lay (or "treasure") up treasures in Heaven without suggesting how the heavenly treasures are to be stored up; but in this address He specified the method and means of opening and maintaining a heavenly savings account to be selling one's possessions and giving alms. On a later occasion He promised heavenly treasures to the "Rich Young Ruler" on the same condition (#187).

(7) Teachings concerning the need of constant preparedness for His second coming

#157

LUKE 12:35-48

35 Let your loins be girded about, and your lamps burning; 36 and be ye yourselves like unto men looking for their lord, when he shall return from the marriage feast; that, when he cometh and knocketh, they may straightway open unto him. 37 Blessed are those [1]servants, whom the lord when he cometh shall find watching: verily I say unto you, that he shall gird himself, and make them sit down to meat, and shall come and serve them. 38 And if he shall come in the second watch, and if in the third, and find *them* so, blessed are those *servants*. 39 [2]But know this, that if the master of the house had known in what hour the thief was coming, he would have watched, and not have left his house to be [3]broken through. 40 Be ye also ready: for in an hour, that ye think not the Son of man cometh.

41 And Peter said, Lord, speakest thou this parable unto us, or even unto all? 42 And the Lord said, Who then is [4]the faithful and wise steward, whom his lord shall set over his household, to give them their portion of food in due season? 43 Blessed is that [5]servant, whom his lord when he cometh shall find so doing. 44 Of a truth I say unto you, that he will set him over all that he hath. 45 But if that [5]servant shall say in his heart, My lord delayeth his coming; and shall begin to beat the menservants and the maidservants, and to eat and drink, and to be drunken; 46 the lord of that [5]servant shall come in a day when he expecteth not, and in an hour when he knoweth not, and shall [6]cut him asunder, and appoint his portion with the unfaithful. 47 And that [5]servant, who knew his lord's will, and made not ready, nor did according to his will, shall be beaten with many *stripes;* 48 but he that knew not, and did things worthy of stripes, shall be beaten with few *stripes.* And to whomsoever much is given, of him shall much be required: and to whom they commit much, of him will they ask the more.

[1] Gr. *bondservants.*   [2] Or, *But this ye know*   [3] Gr. *digged through.*
[4]Or, *the faithful steward, the wise* man *whom &c*
[5] Gr. *bondservant.*   [6] Or, *severely scourge him*

Note 158.   The foregoing section is our Lord's second mention of His coming (vs. 40), which we interpret to be His coming again to earth (cf. #132).   The warnings and promises of this section were a logical sequence of the exhortation in the preceding section to seek the Kingdom of God, and of the assurance to the "little flock" that the Father is pleased to give them the Kingdom (vss. 31--32). The hearers on that day (including the disciples) had no conception of any manifestation of the Kingdom other than the visible Kingdom, which Jesus knew would be inaugurated at the time of His return to earth.   The greatest rewards in the visible Kingdom will be for those who shall have been faithful to the King during the time of the spiritual Kingdom, and who will not be caught off guard when He appears to transform the spiritual into the visible (cf. Note 18).   Observe the four parables: (1) The Door-Keeper (vss. 36--38), and (2) The Thief in the Night (vs. 39), in both of which Jesus warned the disciples against being caught unprepared at His return.   Then (3) The Steward, or the Household Manager (vss. 42--46), which emphasizes the importance that the disciples be found at His coming faithfully engaged in the service which He shall assign to them (and to us, their successors), And finally, (4) the Servants Disobedient Knowingly and those Disobedient Ignorantly (vss. 47--48), in which He warned those who had opportunity to know His will that they will be held under more weighty responsibility, and that disobedience by them will involve heavier penalty.

(8) Warning concerning His own approaching suffering and death and of sufferings to be endured for the sake of the Kingdom   #158

LUKE 12:49-59

49 I came to cast fire upon the earth; and ¹what do I desire, if it is already kindled? 50 But I have a baptism to be baptized with; and how am I straitened till it be accomplished! 51 Think ye that I am come to give peace in the earth? I tell you, Nay; but rather division: 52 for there shall be from henceforth five in one house divided, three against two, and two against three. 53 They shall be divided, father against son, and son against father; mother against daughter, and daughter against her mother; mother in law against her daughter in law, and daughter in law against her mother in law.

54 And he said to the multitudes also, When ye see a cloud rising in the west, straightway ye say, There cometh a shower; and so it cometh to pass. 55 And when *ye see* a south wind blowing, ye say, There will be a ²scorching heat; and it cometh to pass. 56 Ye hypocrites, ye know how to ³interpret the face of the earth and the heaven; but how is it that ye know not how to ³interpret this time? 57 And why even of yourselves judge ye not what is right? 58 For as thou art going with thine adversary before the magistrate, on the way give diligence to be quit of him; lest haply he drag thee unto the judge, and the judge shall deliver thee to the ⁴officer, and the ⁴officer shall cast thee into prison. 59 I say unto thee, Thou shalt by no means come out thence, till thou have paid the very last mite.

¹ Or, *how would I that it were already kindled!*   ² Or, *hot wind*   ³ Gr. *prove.*   ⁴ Gr. *exactor.*

Note 159. In the paragraph of this section Jesus returned to the tone of discourse with which this chapter began (#155):

(1) He set forth (vss. 49--53) the need for steadfast loyalty on the part of His people in their service to Him in a hostile world. In this, the standard for them (and for their successors to the end of the age) would be His own steadfastness in the sufferings which awaited Him in connection with His approaching death. To express this, He used the figure of baptism, which is usually taken to mean that He would be overwhelmed, immersed, in torture and anguish. True as this was, the figure was also appropriate in view of the literal burial which would follow His death. As His being baptized was prophetic of His death and resurrection, so these experiences would reflect His baptism.

(2) He chided His unbelieving hearers (vss. 54--57) because they did not see in His life among them (as they were not going to see in the wonders which accompanied His death and His victorious resurrection) a sign that He truly was the Messiah, that He was God's Son, and that He was the world's Saviour.

(3) Possibly turning His thoughts back to the dissatisfied heir, He spoke another word of warning about strife and law suits over earthly possessions (vss. 58—59).

As related by Matthew and Mark, Jesus had spoken all these things, except verses 49 and 50, in Galilee earlier but in different connections (Matt. 10:34-36, #113; Matt. 16:2-3, #127; Matt. 5:25-26, #57).

(9) Teachings concerning the universal need of repentance #159

LUKE 13:1-9

1 Now there were some present at that very season who told him of the Galilaeans, whose blood Pilate had mingled with their sacrifices. 2 And he answered and said unto them, Think ye that these Galilaeans were sinners above all the Galilaeans,

204

because they have suffered these things? 3 I tell you, Nay: but, except ye repent, ye shall all in like manner perish. 4 Or those eighteen, upon whom the tower in Siloam fell, and killed them, think ye that they were ¹offenders above all the men that dwell in Jerusalem? 5 I tell you, Nay: but, except ye repent, ye shall all likewise perish.

6 And he spake this parable; A certain man had a fig tree planted in his vineyard; and he came seeking fruit thereon, and found none. 7 And he said unto the vinedresser, Behold, these three years I come seeking fruit on this fig tree, and find none: cut it down; why doth it also cumber the ground? 8 And he answering saith unto him, Lord, let it alone this year also, till I shall dig about it, and dung it: 9 and if it bear fruit thenceforth, well; but if not, thou shalt cut it down.

¹ Gr. debtors.

Note 160. History does not throw any light on either of the tragedies spoken of in the foregoing section. It is interesting, if not significant, that people in Judaea took pains to inform, or remind, Jesus about the massacre of the Galileans. We wonder why Pilate had them slain as they were offering sacrifices. Were they fomenting a rebellion against Rome? Were they dedicating themselves in a burnt offering to the carrying out of such a rebellion? If not guilty, did Pilate suspect them of seditious activity? And was there a slur at Galileans on the part of those Judaeans, with the insinuation that, if He, a Galilean should remain the center of large gatherings of the people in Judaea, He might suffer the same fate? In answer, Jesus (1) indicated that we cannot judge the guilt of an individual by what he suffers, and (2) declared that all of them, Galileans and Judaeans alike, were such sinners that the only hope of escaping punishment just as horrible as that of the Galileans was God's mercy, which would be exercised only as they repented.

Then Jesus turned from the Galileans to men of Jerusalem (Judaeans),whose tragic death, caused by the falling of the Tower of Siloam,* proved, according to public opinion, that they were guilty of sin greater than that of most people. In this regard Jesus declared again that the only hope that any of those present might escape God's wrath would be God's mercy, which He would exercise only as they repented.

The parable of The Barren Fig Tree, spared for years when it should have borne fruit, pictures God's long-suffering and mercy; but it also teaches that there is a limit to God's mercy if the guilty ones do not repent.

This whole paragraph may have reference to the rebellion of the Jewish people against God, and their rebellion against Rome also, which would be punished within forty years after these events in the destruction of Jerusalem and the ravishing of the country. But surely the application was and is primarily to individuals rather than to the race at large.

*Where this tower was located, or when or why it fell is not known.

(10) On a Sabbath healing a crippled woman in a Judaean synagogue, answering the complaint of the synagogue ruler, repeating the parables of The Mustard Seed and of The Leaven
#160

LUKE 13:10-21

10 And he was teaching in one of the synagogues on the sabbath day. 11 And behold, a woman that had a spirit of infirmity eighteen years; and she was bowed together, and could in no wise lift herself up. 12 And when Jesus saw her, he called her, and said to her, Woman, thou art loosed from thine infirmity. 13 And he laid his hands upon her: and immediately she was made straight, and glorified God. 14 And the ruler of the synagogue, being moved with indignation because Jesus had healed on the sabbath, answered and said to the multitude, There are six days in which men ought to work: in them therefore come and be healed, and not on the day of the sabbath. 15 But the Lord answered him, and said, Ye hypocrites, doth not each one of you on the sabbath loose his ox or his ass from the ¹stall, and lead him away to watering? 16 And ought not this woman, being a daughter of Abraham, whom Satan had bound, lo, *these* eighteen years, to have been loosed from this bond on the day of the sabbath? 17 And as he said these things, all his adversaries were put to shame: and all the multitude rejoiced for all the glorious things that were done by him.

18 He said therefore, Unto what is the kingdom of God like? and whereunto shall I liken it? 19 It is like unto a grain of mustard seed, which a man took, and cast into his own garden; and it grew, and became a tree; and the birds of the heaven lodged in the branches thereof.

20 And again he said, Whereunto shall I liken the kingdom of God? 21 It is like unto leaven, which a woman took and hid in three ²measures of meal, till it was all leavened.

¹ Gr. *manger*.   ² See marginal note on Mt. 13. 33.

Note 161. Just as Jesus went regularly into the synagogues while on the tours in Galilee, so also in Judaea. And just as in the earlier ministry His teaching and His activities in the synagogue aroused wonder and praise on the part of some and criticism from others, so in the Judaean ministry. At the worship service in this section He (1) healed a woman of an eighteen-year crippling and disfiguring malady, (2) answered the criticism lodged against Him for this action, and (3) spoke concerning the growth of the Kingdom.

The healing of the crippled woman reminds one of the healing of the man with a withered hand (#50). This was the fifth Sabbath controversy. In defending His deed of mercy Jesus compared His action in delivering the woman from her malady with their customary actions of untying an animal to lead it to water. To make the contrast more evident He designated the woman as a "daughter of Abraham," thus appealing to their race pride.

Likely He repeated the parables of the mustard seed and of the leaven because of the favor with which the people had received the miracle and His words (v. 17). The parables mean the same as when spoken earlier (##96, 97). Notice that in Luke 12:1 (#155) He used leaven to represent hypocrisy, something evil; but here (as in Matt. 13:33, #97) it represents the Kingdom of God, something good.

(11) Going to the Feast of Dedication, teaching the multitude concerning the number to be saved

#161

LUKE 13:22-30

22 And he went on his way through cities and villages, teaching, and journeying on unto Jerusalem. 23 And one said unto him, Lord, are they few that are saved? And he said unto them, 24 Strive to enter in by the narrow door: for many, I say unto you, shall seek to enter in, and shall not be ¹able. 25 When once the master of the house is risen up, and hath shut to the door, and ye begin to stand without, and to knock at the door, saying, Lord, open to us; and he shall answer and say to you, I know you not whence ye are; 26 then shall ye begin to say, We did eat and drink in thy presence, and thou didst teach in our streets; 27 and he shall say, I tell you, I know not whence ye are; depart from me, all ye workers of iniquity. 28 There shall be the weeping and the gnashing of teeth, when ye shall see Abraham, and Isaac, and Jacob, and all the prophets, in the kingdom of God, and yourselves cast forth without. 29 And they shall come from the east and west, and from the north and south, and shall ²sit down in the kingdom of God. 30 And behold, there are last who shall be first, and there are first who shall be last.

¹ Or, *able, when once*   ² Gr. *recline.*

Note 162. In the foregoing section the journey to Jerusalem (v. 22) was surely for the Feast of Dedication (John 10: 22, #165). The question about the number to be saved may have been raised by one who had heard Jesus speak of universal necessity for repentance and then about the marvelous growth of the Kingdom, and who had trouble reconciling these assertions. In His reply Jesus warned them, the inquirer and those with him, that the important objective for them was, not to speculate on the comparative number that will be saved, but to make sure that they themselves would enter into the Kingdom and into Heaven. In this connection Jesus made use of sayings which we have met in other connections in Matthew (7: 13, 21--23, ##73, 75; 8: 11-12, #78).

(12) Persecution by the Pharisees of the man born blind

#162

JOHN 9:13-34

13 They bring to the Pharisees him that aforetime was blind. 14 Now it was the sabbath on the day when Jesus made the clay, and opened his eyes. 15 Again therefore the Pharisees also asked him how he received his sight. And he said unto them, He put clay upon mine eyes, and I washed, and I see. 16 Some therefore of the Pharisees said, This man is not from God, because he keepeth not the sabbath. But others said, How can a man that is a sinner do such signs? And there was a division among them. 17 They say therefore unto the blind man again, What sayest thou of him, in that he opened thine eyes? And he said, He is a prophet. 18 The Jews therefore did not believe concerning him, that he had been blind, and had received his sight, until they called the parents of him that had received his sight, 19 and asked them, saying, Is this your son, who ye say was born blind? how then doth he now see? 20 His parents answered and said, We know that this is our son, and that he was born blind: 21 but how he now seeth, we know not; or who opened his eyes, we know not: ask him; he is of age; he shall speak for himself. 22 These things said his parents, because they feared the Jews: for the Jews had agreed already, that if any man should confess him *to be* Christ, he should be put out of the synagogue. 23 Therefore said his parents, He is of age; ask him. 24 So they called a second time the man that was blind, and said unto him, Give glory to God: we know that this man is a sinner. 25 He therefore answered, Whether he is a sinner, I know not: one thing I know, that, whereas I was blind, now I see. 26 They said therefore unto him, What did he to thee? how opened he thine eyes? 27 He answered them, I told you even now, and ye did not hear; wherefore would ye hear

#162, continued
John 9

it again? would ye also become his disciples? 28 And they reviled him, and said, Thou art his disciple; but we are disciples of Moses. 29 We know that God hath spoken unto Moses: but as for this man, we know not whence he is. 30 The man answered and said unto them, Why, herein is the marvel, that ye know not whence he is, and *yet* he opened mine eyes. 31 We know that God heareth not sinners: but if any man be a worshipper of God, and do his will, him he heareth. 32 Since the world began it was never heard that any one opened the eyes of a man born blind. 33 If this man were not from God, he could do nothing. 34 They answered and said unto him, Thou wast altogether born in sins, and dost thou teach us? And they cast him out.

Note 163. As suggested in Note 151, Jesus very probably healed this man of his blindness as He set forth on the tour of the cities of Judaea. The agitation among those who had known the man and among the Pharisees and synagogue authorities, caused by the fact that the miracle was performed on a ' Sabbath, took place while Jesus was out of the city. This was the fourth Sabbath controversy; and unlike the others, it was the man who had been benefited by the miracle who suffered from the displeasure of the Jewish authorities. The clause, "and they cast him out" (vs. 34) is understood by some interpreters* to mean merely that they drove him from their presence. However, because of the threat which the Jerusalem Jews made against anyone who should acknowledge Jesus as the Messiah (vs. 22), I think it most probably means that they expelled him from membership in the synagogue, an action involving the infliction of very humiliating social restrictions.**

3. At the Feast of Dedication, ##163-165
   (1) Befriending the man healed, first part of the allegory of
   The Good Shepherd

#163
JOHN 9:35 – 10:6

35 Jesus heard that they had cast him out; and finding him, he said, Dost thou believe on ¹the Son of God? 36 He answered and said, And who is he, Lord, that I may believe on him? 37 Jesus said unto him, Thou hast both seen him, and he it is that speaketh with thee. 38 And he said, Lord, I believe. And he ²worshipped him. 39 And Jesus said, For judgment came I into this world, that they that see not may see; and that they that see may become blind. 40 Those of the Pharisees who were with him heard these things, and said unto him, Are we also blind? 41 Jesus said unto them, If ye were blind, ye would have no sin: but now ye say We see: your sin remaineth.

1 Verily, verily, I say unto you, He that entereth not by the door into the fold of the sheep, but climbeth up some other way, the same is a thief and a robber 2 But he that entereth in by the door is ³the shepherd of the sheep. 3 To him the porter openeth; and the sheep hear his voice: and he calleth his own sheep by name, and leadeth them out. 4 When he hath put forth all his own, he goeth before

¹ Many ancient authorities read *the Son of Man*.
² The Greek word denotes an act of reverence, whether paid to a creature (as here) or to the Creator (see ch. 4, 20.).　　　　³ Or, *a shepherd*

*Hovey, *Commentary on John*, p. 210, and Westcott, *The Gospel According to St. John*, p. 149.
**From Edersheim, *Life and Times of Jesus*, Vol. II, p. 184, I quote "Hence forth he (one excluded from the synagogue) was as one dead. He was not allowed to study with others, no intercourse was to be held with him, he was not even to be shown the road. He might indeed buy the necessities of life, but it was for bidden to eat and drink with such an one."

208

hem, and the sheep follow him: for they know his voice. 5 And a stranger will
hey not follow, but will flee from him: for they know not the voice of strangers.
This ⁴parable spake Jesus unto them: but they understood not what things they
vere which he spake unto them.
⁴ Or, *proverb*

Note 164. Notice that the marginal note at verse 6 suggests the
word "proverb" instead of "parable." This is because John used a word
here (paroimia), which is different from the one usually translated parable (parabolē).* The figure of the Good Shepherd is in reality an extended metaphor, or allegory, manifestly setting forth a plurality of
truths; but a true parable was usually used to teach or illustrate only
one truth (cf. Note 48). The allegory of the Good Shepherd is in three
parts, probably spoken on three different days of the Feast of Dedication
(vs. 22, #165). In the first part Jesus portrayed some differences between Himself, the true Shepherd of distressed souls, and the Pharisees and synagogue authorities (scribes and rabbis), depicted as thieves
and robbers. These latter had driven the erst-while blind man from
their presence and doubtless expelled him from the synagogue because
he would not join them in hating Jesus, who had bestowed on him the
greatest blessing of his life. In contrast Jesus not only gave him sight,
but befriended him when he was in need.

(2) The second part of the allegory of The Good Shepherd
#164

JOHN 10:7-18
7 Jesus therefore said unto them again, Verily, verily, I say unto you, I am the
door of the sheep. 8 All that came ¹before me are thieves and robbers: but the
sheep did not hear them. 9 I am the door; by me if any man enter in, he shall be
saved, and shall go in and go out, and shall find pasture. 10 The thief cometh
not, but that he may steal, and kill, and destroy: I came that they may have life,
and may ²have *it* abundantly. 11 I am the good shepherd: the good shepherd layeth
down his life for the sheep. 12 He that is a hireling, and not a shepherd, whose
own the sheep are not, beholdeth the wolf coming, and leaveth the sheep, and fleeth,
and the wolf snatcheth them, and scattereth *them*: 13 he *fleeth* because he is a
hireling, and careth not for the sheep. 14 I am the good shepherd; and I know
mine own, and mine own know me, 15 even as the Father knoweth me, and I know
the Father; and I lay down my life for the sheep. 16 And other sheep I have, which
are not of this fold: them also I must ³bring, and they shall hear my voice; and
they shall become one flock, one shepherd. 17 Therefore doth the Father love me,
because I lay down my life, that I may take it again. 18 No one ⁵taketh it away
from me, but I lay it down of myself. I have ⁶power to lay it down, and I have
power to take it again. This commandment received I from my Father.
¹ Some ancient authorities omit *before me.*   ² Or, *have abundance*   ³ Or, *lead*
⁴ Or, *there shall be one flock*   ⁵ Some ancient authorities read *took it away.*   ⁶ Or, *right*

Note 165. There was surely an interval between the first part of
this allegory and the second, at least long enough for it to be evident

*In the American Standard Version the word (paroimia) is translated "dark
saying" in John 16:25, 29, and "proverb" in II Pet. 2:22. In the King James Version
it is translated "parable" in this passage but "proverb" in the other two. In the
Revised Standard Version it is translated "figures" in all the passages.

209

that the listeners generally did not understand what Jesus meant in the first part, and long enough that, when He spoke the second part, He was speaking to them "again" (vs. 7). In this part He contrasted the ills which the Pharisees, like thieves (vs. 10) or hirelings (vs. 12), impose on their followers with the blessings that He bestows on those who trust and follow Him. Repeatedly also He stated that for Him the cost of bestowing these blessings was going to be the laying down of His own life and taking it again. Nowhere in the Bible is there a clearer statement of the willingness with which He died, or of the sufficiency of power by which He came back to life, than in verse 18.

(3) The divided multitude, the third part of the allegory of
The Good Shepherd, the second attempt to stone Jesus
#165

JOHN 10:19-39
19 There arose a division again among the Jews because of these words. 20 And many of them said, He hath a demon, and is mad; why hear ye him? 21 Others said, These are not the sayings of one possessed with a demon. Can a demon open the eyes of the blind?
22 ¹And it was the feast of the dedication at Jerusalem: 23 it was .winter; and Jesus was walking in the temple in .Solomon's ²porch. 24 The Jews therefore came round about him, and said unto him, How long dost thou hold us in suspense? If thou art the Christ, tell us plainly. 25 Jesus answered them, I told you, and ye believe not: the works that I do in my Father's name, these bear witness of me 26 But ye believe not, because ye are not of my sheep. 27 My sheep hear my voice and I know them, and they follow me: 28 and I give unto them eternal life; and they shall never perish, and no one shall snatch them out of my hand. 29 ³My Father who hath given *them* unto me, is greater than all; and no one is able to snatch ⁴them out of the Father's hand. 30 I and the Father are one. 31 The Jews took up stones again to stone him. 32 Jesus answered them, Many good works have showed you from the Father; for which of those works do ye stone me? 33 The Jews answered him, For a good work we stone thee not, but for blasphemy; and because that thou, being a man, makest thyself God. 34 Jesus answered them, Is it not written in your law, ⁵I said, Ye are gods? 35 If he called them gods, unto whom the word of God came (and the scripture cannot be broken), 36 say ye of him whom the Father ⁶sanctified and sent into the world, Thou blasphemest; because said, I am *the* Son of God? 37 If I do not the works of my Father, believe me not 38 But if I do them, though ye believe not me, believe the works: that ye may know and understand that the Father is in me, and I in the Father. 39 They sough again to take him: and he went forth out of their hand.
¹ Some ancient authorities read *At that time was the feast.*   ².Or, *portico*
³ Some ancient authorities read *That which my Father hath given unto me.*
⁴ Or, aught   ⁵ Ps. lxxxii. 6.   ⁶ Or, *consecrated*

Note 166. The Feast of Dedication (cf. pp. 7 and 17) was observed eight days. Without doubt, Jesus spoke the third part of the allegory of the Good Shepherd on a later day of the feast week, after He had spoken the first and second parts. In this part Jesus affirmed His perfect competence as a Shepherd in a four-fold statement of the security of those who are His sheep (vss. 28--29), and He asserted His own unity with His Father (v. 30). Notice that the Jews were incited by this last claim to try again to stone Him, just as they had done at the Feast of Tabernacles when He made His claim of eternal existence (John 8:58--59, #147). But again, as by a miracle, He made His escape.

II. The Peraean Ministry, ##166--194
1. A brief sojourn in that province, ##166--177
(1) Withdrawing "beyond Jordan"
#166
JOHN 10:40-42

40 And he went away again beyond the Jordan into the place where John was at the first baptizing; and there he abode. 41 And many came unto him; and they said, John indeed did no sign: but all things whatsoever John spake of this man were true. 42 And many believed on him there.

Note 167. Although the only definite assertion that Jesus went at this time into Peraea (beyond Jordan) is in John, each of the Synoptics makes reference to His labors in t h a t part of the country (cf. Matt. 19: 1--2; Mark 10: 1, #142, and the comment in Note 168 on the account of His arrival there given in Luke).

(2) Answering those that would warn Him against Herod Antipas
#167
LUKE 13:31-35

31 In that very hour there came certain Pharisees, saying to him, Get thee out, and go hence: for Herod would fain kill thee. 32 And he said unto them, Go and say to that fox, Behold, I cast out demons and perform cures to-day and to-morrow, and the third *day* I [1]am perfected. 33 Nevertheless I must go on my way to-day and to-morrow and the *day* following: for it cannot be that a prophet perish out of Jerusalem. 34 O Jerusalem, Jerusalem, that killeth the prophets, and stoneth them that are sent unto her! how often would I have gathered thy children together, even as a hen *gathereth* her own brood under her wings, and ye would not! 35 Behold, your house is left unto you *desolate:* and I say unto you, Ye shall not see me, until ye shall say, Blessed *is* he that cometh in the name of the Lord.

[1] Or, *end my course*

Note 168. The Herod mentioned in the section above was Herod Antipas, who was tetrarch in Galilee and Peraea. The King James Version reads in verse 31, "The same day," by which it would seem that the incident related in this section occurred on the day when Jesus answered the inquiry about the number that will be saved (#161). But the order of the Greek words demands that they be translated, "on the day itself." The most ancient copies (manuscripts) of the Gospel have the word for "hour" instead of the one for "day," and so the American Standard reads, "In t h a t very hour." However, the insertion of the word "that" (for which there is no equivalent Greek in this clause) still leaves the impression that this warning about Herod Antipas came immediately after the question and answer concerning the number that will be saved. But when that question was raised, Jesus was enroute to Jerusalem after a tour of the villages and towns of Judaea. Since it is asserted in John 10: 40 that, from the Feast of Dedication, He went away "beyond Jordan," which took Him into Herod's domain, it seems best to me to understand the phrase to mean that within the hour when Jesus crossed the Jordan into Herod's territory these Pharisees came advising Him to get out of Peraea. Probably they hoped to frighten Him away by the fate which John the Baptist had suffered from Herod.

Peraea was regarded as Jewish territory, the people being under the same religious and social laws as those of Galilee or Judaea. The

211

Pharisees did not welcome the coming of Jesus into their midst (which probably had been heralded by one or more of the pairs from among the seventy) because they feared a defection of the people from their teachings.

But Jesus did not scare easily, because He knew that His final sacrifice would be made in Jerusalem. His metaphor, calling Herod a fox, indicates that He knew that Herod did not have the courage to try to take Him. Herod was afraid that He was John the Baptist risen from the dead.

Jesus spoke the words of verses 34—35 later, as the climax of His great oration against the scribes and Pharisees (Matt. 23: 37—39, #215). The clause "and stonest..." is surely a reflection of the two attempts by the Jerusalem Jews to stone Him, one of them probably only a few hours before this incident (John 8: 59, #147, John 10: 31f, #165).

(3) Dining with a Pharisee on a Sabbath day, ##168—169
a. Healing a man of dropsy, defending His action
(the sixth and last Sabbath controversy)
#168

LUKE 14:1-6
1 And it came to pass, when he went into the house of one of the rulers of the Pharisees on a sabbath to eat bread, that they were watching him. 2 And behold, there was before him a certain man that had the dropsy. 3 And Jesus answering spake unto the lawyers and Pharisees, saying, Is it lawful to heal on the sabbath, or not? 4 But they held their peace. And he took him, and healed him, and let him go. 5 And he said unto them, Which of you shall have ¹an ass or an ox fallen into a well, and will not straightway draw him up on a sabbath day? 6 And they could not answer again unto these things.
¹ Many ancient authorities read *a son*. See ch. 13. 15.

Note 169. This is the third and last recorded occasion when Jesus dined with a Pharisee. Probably, since the Pharisees of the preceding section failed to disuade Him from His intended labors in Peraea, this man invited Him for a meal on the Sabbath and arranged to have the man afflicted with dropsy there in order that the Pharisees present might observe Him heal the man in disregard of their Sabbath regulations and so have occasion to accuse Him before the Sanhedrin. In this he resembled the other Pharisee who thus had invited Him a short time before, seemingly that he and his confederates might obtain evidence against Him (cf. #154, Note 155).

In verse 3 the word "answering" indicates His response to an unvoiced question implied in their watching Him. The question which Jesus put to them is similar to the one He raised with the synagogue rulers of Capernaum on the occasion of healing the man with a withered hand (Mark 3: 4, #50), and, as formerly, the Pharisee and his friends were afraid to answer Him. Also the defense which Jesus made for His action at this time is identical with that made on the earlier occasion except this time it was an ass or an ox that He pictured as fallen into a pit instead of a sheep as in Matt. 12: 11. Some of the ancient manuscripts have the word for "son" instead of the word for "ass." If that is the correct reading, the comparison was still more impressive.

b. Lessons suggested by what He observed at this meal, parable of The Great Supper
#169

LUKE 14:7-24

7 And he spake a parable unto those that were bidden, when he marked how they chose out the chief seats; saying unto them, 8 When thou art bidden of any man to a marriage feast, [1]sit not down in the chief seat; lest haply a more honorable man than thou be bidden of him, 9 and he that bade thee and him shall come and say to thee, Give this man place; and then thou shalt begin with shame to take the lowest place. 10 But when thou art bidden, go and sit down in the lowest place; that when he that hath bidden thee cometh, he may say to thee, Friend, go up higher: then shalt thou have glory in the presence of all that [2]sit at meat with thee. 11 For every one that exalteth himself shall be humbled; and he that humbleth himself shall be exalted.

12 And he said to him also that had bidden him, When thou makest a dinner or a supper, call not thy friends, nor thy brethren, nor thy kinsmen, nor rich neighbors; lest haply they also bid thee again, and a recompense be made thee. 13 But when thou makest a feast, bid the poor, the maimed, the lame, the blind: 14 and thou shalt be blessed; because they have not *wherewith* to recompense thee: for thou shalt be recompensed in the resurrection of the just.

15 And when one of them that [3]sat at meat with him heard these things, he said unto him, Blessed is he that shall eat bread in the kingdom of God. 16 But he said unto him, A certain man made a great supper; and he bade many: 17 and he sent forth his [4]servant at supper time to say to them that were bidden, Come; for *all* things are now ready. 18 And they all with one *consent* began to make excuse. The first said unto him, I have bought a field, and I must needs go out and see it; I pray thee have me excused. 19 And another said, I have bought five yoke of oxen, and I go to prove them; I pray thee have me excused. 20 And another said, I have married a wife, and therefore I cannot come. 21 And the [4]servant came, and told his lord these things. Then the master of the house being angry said to his [4]servant, Go out quickly into the streets and lanes of the city, and bring in hither the poor and maimed and blind and lame. 22 And the [4]servant said, Lord, what thou didst command is done, and yet there is room. 23 And the lord said unto the [4]servant, Go out into the highways and hedges, and constrain *them* to come in, that my house may be filled. 24 For I say unto you, that none of those men that were bidden shall taste of my supper.

[1] Gr. *recline not.*
[2] Gr. *recline.* Comp. ch. 7. 36, 37, marg.
[3] Gr. *reclined.* Comp. ch. 7. 36, 37, marg.
[4] Gr. *bondservant.*

Note 170. After silencing His watchful critics in the matter of healing on the Sabbath, Jesus proceeded to give some timely advice to the vain-glorious guests present at the Pharisee's dinner with Him (vss. 8—11). Then He gave some lessons in true hospitality to His host and others present, who undoubtedly had formed a circle of clannish hosts, entertaining each other in turn. The parable of The Great Supper was in response to the remark of a guest that it will be a blessed privilege to "eat bread in the Kingdom of God," which remark was doubtless prompted by the promise of Jesus that the host who would invite the poor to his feasts will "be recompensed in the resurrection of the just" (vss. 14—15). It is instructive that our Lord named only "the just" as participating in that resurrection. The only manifestation of the Kingdom which this guest conceived of was the visible Kingdom, which, in his

213

mind, would follow that resurrection. Jesus had said that people would come from the four points of the compass to sit down with the patriarchs in that Kingdom (cf. Luke 13: 29, #161). Through this parable He said to His fellow-guest that some people were foolishly passing up the privileges of the Kingdom for inferior blessings and satisfactions.

(4) Teaching in parables concerning discipleship, ##170--173
a. Parables of the Unfinished Tower and the Cautious King, emphasizing the cost of discipleship
#170

LUKE 14:25-35

Now there went with him great multitudes: and he turned, and said unto them, 26 If any man cometh unto me, and hateth not his own father, and mother, and wife, and children, and brethren, and sisters, yea, and his own life also, he cannot be my disciple. 27 Whosoever doth not bear his own cross, and come after me, cannot be my disciple. 28 For which of you, desiring to build a tower, doth not first sit down and count the cost, whether he have *wherewith* to complete it? 29 Lest haply, when he hath laid a foundation, and is not able to finish, all that behold begin to mock him, 30 saying, This man began to build, and was not able to finish. 31 Or what king, as he goeth to encounter another king in war, will not sit down first and take counsel whether he is able with ten thousand to meet him that cometh against him with twenty thousand? 32 Or else, while the other is yet a great way off, he sendeth an ambassage, and asketh conditions of peace. 33 So therefore whosoever he be of you that renounceth not all that he hath, he cannot be my disciple. 34 Salt therefore is good: but if even the salt have lost its savor, wherewith shall it be seasoned? 35 It is fit neither for the land nor for the dunghill: *men* cast it out. He that hath ears to ear, let him hear.

Note 171. Our Lord, of course, did not mean that His disciples should harbor malice against their fathers and mothers, or wives and children, or brothers and sisters. But He insisted that their love for Him should so overshadow the love for these members of their families that their love for their people would be as hatred in comparison. Thus, if they should have to choose between loyalty to Him or to their family, they are expected to choose to be loyal to Him, though this should involve taking one's stand against his loved ones (cf. His words to the twelve in Matt. 10: 34--37). He warned the multitude of would-be followers that they must count the cost of discipleship, a cost involving a possible forsaking of all that one has.

Jesus emphasized these warnings by repeating the Parable of Salt (vss. 34--35). A desire to follow Him is a good and admirable thing in an individual if that desire is rooted in a loyalty and dedication to Him to the point of forsaking all that one has for His sake. But if one lacks such loyalty, following Jesus will be a disappointment to the individual, and such a one will be as worthless in the Messiah's Kingdom as savorless salt. This was the third time that Jesus spoke of savorless salt (cf. Matt. 5: 13, #55; Mark 9: 50, #139).

b. Three great parables spoken to the Pharisees, all emphasizing the universal privilege of discipleship, ##171--173

214

(a) The criticism which occasioned them, and the parable of the Lost Sheep

#171

LUKE 15:1-7

1 Now all the [1]publicans and sinners were drawing near unto him to hear him. 2 And both the Pharisees and the scribes murmured, saying, This man receiveth sinners, and eateth with them.

3 And he spake unto them this parable, saying, 4 What man of you, having a hundred sheep, and having lost one of them, doth not leave the ninety and nine in the wilderness, and go after that which is lost, until he find it? 5 And when he hath found it, he layeth it on his shoulders, rejoicing. 6 And when he cometh home, he calleth together his friends and his neighbors, saying unto them, Rejoice with me, for I have found my sheep which was lost. 7 I say unto you, that even so there shall be joy in heaven over one sinner that repenteth, *more* than over ninety and nine righteous persons, who need no repentance.

[1] See marginal note on ch. 3. 12.

Note 172. The publicans were generally eager and receptive hearers of the Lord Jesus. Possibly the testimony of Matthew, a former publican but now an apostle, had something to do with it. From verse 2 we conclude that Jesus had lately had a meal witn one or more publicans; and, just as the Pharisees had criticized Him when He attended Matthew's feast (#45), so now they, as it were, raised their hands in holy horror. They did the same thing later when He dined with Zacchaeus (#193). Moreover, on the earlier occasion He answered their criticism with the parable of The Physician, so at this time He replied with three of the best-known parables of the Bible. According to Matthew, the parable of The Lost Sheep had already been spoken but with a different application (Matt. 18: 12--14, #139).

(b) The parable of The Lost Coin

#172

LUKE 15:8-10

8 Or what woman having ten [1]pieces of silver, if she lose one piece, doth not light a lamp, and sweep the house, and seek diligently until she find it? 9 And when she hath found it, she calleth together her friends and neighbors, saying, Rejoice with me, for I have found the piece which I had lost. 10 Even so, I say unto you, there is joy in the presence of the angels of God over one sinner that repenteth.

[1] Gr. *drachma*, a coin worth about eight pence, or sixteen cents.

Note 173. As was true of the parables of The Patched Garment and of The Wine Skins (#46), the parables of The Lost Sheep and of The Lost Coin illustrate one truth; namely, that God is pleased when a sinner repents; that is, when he turns from sin to God. And all those who profess to serve God ought to rejoice when they learn of such repentance on the part of any sinner, and to commend the one who induced him to take such action.

(c) The parable of The Prodigal Son (the Lost Boy)

#173

LUKE 15:11-32

11 And he said, A certain man had two sons: 12 and the younger of them said to his father, Father, give me the portion of [1]*thy* substance that falleth to me. And he divided unto them his living. 13 And not many days after, the younger son gathered all together and took his journey into a far country; and there he wasted

[1] Gr. *the.*

#173, continued
Luke 15

his substance with riotous living. 14 And when he had spent all, there arose a mighty famine in that country; and he began to be in want. 15 And he went and joined himself to one of the citizens of that country; and he sent him into his fields to feed swine. 16 And he would fain ²have filled his belly with ³the husks that the swine did eat: and no man gave unto him. 17 But when he came to himself he said, How many hired servants of my father's have bread enough and to spare, and I perish here with hunger! 18 I will arise and go to my father, and will say unto him, Father, I have sinned against heaven, and in thy sight: 19 I am no more worthy to be called thy son: make me as one of thy hired servants. 20 And he arose, and came to his father. But while he was yet afar off, his father saw him, and was moved with compassion, and ran, and fell on his neck, and ⁴kissed him. 21 And the son said unto him, Father, I have sinned against heaven, and in thy sight: I am no more worthy to be called thy son⁵. 22 But the father said to his ⁶servants, Bring forth quickly the best robe, and put it on him; and put a ring on his hand, and shoes on his feet: 23 and bring the fatted calf, *and* kill it, and let us eat, and make merry: 24 for this my son was dead, and is alive again; he was lost, and is found. And they began to be merry. 25 Now his elder son was in the field: and as he came and drew nigh to the house, he heard music and dancing. 26 And he called to him one of the servants, and inquired what these things might be. 27 And he said unto him, Thy brother is come; and thy father hath killed the fatted calf, because he hath received him safe and sound. 28 But he was angry, and would not go in: and his father came out, and entreated him. 29 But he answered and said to his father, Lo, these many years do I serve thee, and I never transgressed a commandment of thine; and *yet* thou never gavest me a kid, that I might make merry with my friends: 30 but when this thy son came, who hath devoured thy living with harlots, thou killedst for him the fatted calf. 31 And he said unto him, ⁷Son, thou art ever with me, and all that is mine is thine. 32 But it was meet to make merry and be glad: for this thy brother was dead, and is alive *again;* and *was* lost, and is found.

² Many ancient authorities read *have been filled.*
³ Gr. *the pods of the carob tree.*   ⁴ Gr. *kissed him much.* See ch. 7. 38, 45.
⁵ Some ancient authorities add *make me as one of thy hired servants.* See ver. 19.
⁶ Gr. *bondservants.*   ⁷ Gr. *Child.*

Note 174. The parable of The Prodigal Son is probably the most familiar, and doubtless the most loved, of all the parables. Thousands whose sin-wrecked lives have brought them to the brink of despair have been inspired by it to cast themselves on the mercy of God; and in so doing they have not only realized forgiveness and divine acceptance, but have also found power for victorious living. The question has often been asked: Does the prodigal son represent a lost person or a backslidden saved person? Some have reasoned that since the wandering, wasteful boy was a son of his father even in the far country, therefore he must represent a child of God who is straying from the path of righteousness and duty. All three parables spoken in succession on this occasion—The Lost Sheep, The Lost Coin, and The Lost Boy—without doubt illustrate the same truth. And since sheep in the allegory of The Good Shepherd in John 10 represent saved ones, and likewise in the description of the judgment in Matt. 25:31–46, some have argued that in the figurative language of the Bible sheep always represent saved people. But surely the sheep in Isa. 53:6 do not represent saved people. Indeed, what an object represents in a parable must be determined by its connection in that parable in the light of the evident purpose for which the parable was spoken. For example, seed does not represent the

216

same thing in the parable of The Sower that it does in the parable of The Tares (cf. ##92 and 99).

The sheep in the parable in #171 and the wandering boy in the parable of #173 must represent what the Lord Jesus intended them to represent. Certainly all three of these parables were spoken by our Lord in defense of His action of welcoming publicans and sinners as they drew nigh to hear Him, and eating with them when the occasion arose. It is not reasonable to suppose that these publicans and sinners had been disciples of Jesus and were now backslidden. In my opinion, the point of these parables is set forth in verses 7 and 10: "There is joy in Heaven over one sinner that repententh." In neither of these verses is a distinction made between one who for the first time turns to God in penitence and a trusting plea for mercy, and a backslidden one who comes back in penitence and rededication. God is pleased on either or both occasions. The prodigal son, therefore, represents any sinful one who comes in penitence and faith to God, either a lost person or a backslider.

(5) Parables on Stewardship, teaching concerning divorce, ##174—177

a. Parable of The Unjust Steward

#174
LUKE 16:1-13

1 And he said also unto the disciples, There was a certain rich man, who had a steward; and the same was accused unto him that he was wasting his goods. 2 And he called him, and said unto him, What is this that I hear of thee? render the account of thy stewardship; for thou canst be no longer steward. 3 And the steward said within himself, What shall I do, seeing that my lord taketh away the stewardship from me? I have not strength to dig; to beg I am ashamed. 4 I am resolved what to do, that, when I am put out of the stewardship, they may receive me into their houses. 5 And calling to him each one of his lord's debtors, he said to the first, How much owest thou unto my lord? 6 And he said, A hundred [1]measures of oil. And he said unto him, Take thy [2]bond, and sit down quickly and write fifty. 7 Then said he to another, And how much owest thou? And he said, A hundred [3]measures of wheat. He saith unto him, Take thy [2]bond, and write fourscore. 8 And his lord commended [4]the unrighteous steward because he had done wisely: for the sons of this [5]world are for their own generation wiser than the sons of the light. 9 And I say unto you, Make to yourselves friends [6]by means of the mammon of unrighteousness; that, when it shall fail, they may receive you into the eternal tabernacles. 10 He that is faithful in a very little is faithful also in much: and he that is unrighteous in a very little is unrighteous also in much. 11 If therefore ye have not been faithful in the unrighteous mammon, who will commit to your trust the true *riches*? 12 And if ye have not been faithful in that which is another's, who will give you that which is [7]your own? 13 No [8]servant can serve two masters: for either he will hate the one, and love the other; or else he will hold to one, and despise the other. Ye cannot serve God and mammon.

[1] Gr. *baths*, the bath being a Hebrew measure. See Ezek. 45. 10, 11, 14.
[2] Gr. *writings*.   [3] Gr. *cors*, the cor being a Hebrew measure. See Ezek. 45. 14.
[4] Gr. *the steward of unrighteousness*.
[5] Or, *age*   [6] Gr. *out of*.
[7] Some ancient authorities read *our own*.   [8] Gr. *household-servant*.

Note 175.   Notice that Jesus addressed the parable in this section to "His disciples." The point in the parable is the right use of mammon; that is, of earthly possessions. Although Jesus said of Himself, "The Son of Man hath not where to lay His head," there were among His

217

disciples men of some means. For example, the fishermen owned their equipment and were able to employ "hired servants" (Mark 1: 20). Matthew had doubtless accumulated something while he was a publican, and doubtless there were other publicans of some wealth among those who were drawing "near unto Him to hear Him" (Luke 15: 1, #171) that had begun to take their stand as disciples.

The parable itself at first thought is puzzling because the character from whom Jesus would have us learn the lesson was dishonest to the end. Our Lord meant to teach in the parable that, just as this dishonest steward was shrewd enough to use his last days of control over his lord's wealth so as to make friends for himself who would take care of him in his time of need, thus the followers of Jesus can use worldly possessions—even though they be the mammon of unrighteousness—so that at death they will be as friends to welcome the disciples into everlasting tabernacles. It was the lesson of laying up treasures in Heaven which Jesus taught on other occasions (cf. Note 157).

b. Answering inquiries of Pharisees concerning divorce
#175

MATT. 19:3-12	MARK 10:2-12	LUKE 16:14-18
		14 And the Pharisees, who were lovers of money, heard all these things; and they scoffed at him. 15 And he said unto them, Ye are they that justify yourselves in the sight of men; but God knoweth your hearts: for that which is exalted among men is an abomination in the sight of God. 16 The law and the prophets *were* until John: from that time the [1]gospel of the kingdom of God is preached, and every man entereth violently into it. 17 But it is easier for heaven and earth to pass away, than for one tittle of the law to fall.
3 And there came unto him [1]Pharisees, trying him, and saying, Is it lawful *for a man* to put away his wife for every cause? 4 And he answered and said, Have ye not read, [2]that he who [3]made *them* from the beginning made them male and female, 5 and said, [4]For this cause shall a man	2 And there came unto him Pharisees, and asked him, Is it lawful for a man to put away *his* wife? trying him. 3 And he answered and said unto them, [1]What did Moses command you? 4 And they said, Moses suffered to write a bill of divorcement, and to put her away.	
[1] Many authorities, some ancient, insert *the*. [2] Gen. i. 27; v. 2. [3] Some ancient authorities read *created*. [4] Gen. ii. 24.	[1] Dt. xxiv. 1, 3.	[1] Or, *good tidings*: comp. ch. 3. 18.

218

Matt. 19	Mark 10	Luke 16

leave his father and mother, and shall cleave to his wife; and the two shall become one flesh? 6 So that they are no more two, but one flesh. What therefore God hath joined together, let not man put asunder. 7 They say unto him, [5]Why then did Moses command to give a bill of divorcement, and to put *her* away? 8 He saith unto them, Moses for your hardness of heart suffered you to put away your wives: but from the beginning it hath not been so. 9 And I say unto you, Whosoever shall put away his wife, [6]except for fornication, and shall marry another, committeth adultery: [7]and he that marrieth her when she is put away committeth adultery. 10 The disciples say unto him, If the case of the man is so with his wife, it is not expedient to marry. 11 But he said unto them, Not all men can receive this saying, but they to whom it is given. 12 For there are eunuchs, that were so born from their mother's womb: and there are eunuchs, that were made eunuchs by men: and there are eunuchs, that made themselves eunuchs for the kingdom of heaven's sake. He that is able to receive it, let him receive it.

5 But Jesus said unto them, For your hardness of heart he wrote you this commandment. 6 But from the beginning of the creation, Male and female made he them. 7 For this cause shall a man leave his father and mother, [2]and shall cleave to his wife; 8 and the two shall become one flesh: so that they are no more two, but one flesh. 9 What therefore God hath joined together, let not man put asunder. 10 And in the house the disciples asked him again of this matter. 11 And he saith unto them, Whosoever shall put away his wife, and marry another, committeth adultery against her: 12 and if she herself shall put away her husband, and marry another, she committeth adultery.

18 Every one that putteth away his wife, and marrieth another, committeth adultery: and he that marrieth one that is put away from a husband committeth adultery.

[5] Dt. xxiv. 1-4.
[3] Some ancient authorities read *saving for the cause of fornication, maketh her an adulteress:* as in ch. 5. 32.
[7] The following words, to the end of the verse, are omitted by some ancient authorities.

[2] Some ancient authorities omit *and shall cleave to his wife.*

Note 176. Although the material of the preceding section was addressed to the disciples, including likely some of the publicans of #171, the money loving Pharisees were listening, and they "scoffed at," Jesus. The idea was repugnant to them that a publican would even go at death, to "the eternal habitations," much less that his money might so be used that it would be as friends to welcome him when he got there.

We wonder if some of these Pharisees who came inquiring about divorce were among those who met Jesus within an hour after He arrived in Peraea, urging Him to get out of that district for fear that Herod might kill Him (#167). And was their inquiry about divorce an effort to get Him to say something that would bring the wrath of Herod upon Him, as it had been brought on John the Baptist when that one publicly condemned Herod's marriage to Herodias? Notice that both Matthew and Mark say that in raising the question they were "tempting Him." They probably reasoned that, since the matter of divorce and remarriage was a tender subject with Herod and Herodias, the surest way to get rid of Jesus would be to induce Him to say something on the subject which would arouse the wrath of the tetrarch.

Jesus repeated on this occasion what He had said about divorce in the Sermon on the Mount (Matt. 5:32, #58). Notice that, according to the account in Matthew, He named fornication (marital unfaithfulness) as a possible cause, but the only cause, for divorce and remarriage. According to Mark and Luke Jesus did not name even this as a valid cause. But Broadus maintains* that this cause was universally admitted, and Mark and Luke did not deem it necessary to mention it. Observe that the only mention of a woman divorcing her husband is in Mark, and there was no excepting clause of cause. Again Broadus makes the timely suggestion** that in this Jesus had special reference to Herodias, who had divorced Philip, her first husband; and that Mark was careful to relate it because he was writing for Roman Christians. Also notice that Mark makes no mention of the one who marries a divorced woman, and that no exception is mentioned in either Matthew or Luke about the guilt of such a one. Are we to assume that the exception mentioned in Matthew (5:32 and 19:9) applies in every case? Such assumption would be natural, and most interpreters do so assume; but those who do so should confess that it is an assumption on their part.

c. Parable of The Rich Man and Lazarus
#176
LUKE 16:19-31

19 Now there was a certain rich man, and he was clothed in purple and fine linen, ¹faring sumptuously every day: 20 and a certain beggar named Lazarus was laid at his gate, full of sores, 21 and desiring to be fed with the *crumbs* that fell from the rich man's table; yea, even the dogs came and licked his sores. 22 And it came to pass, that the beggar died, and that he was carried away by the angels into Abraham's bosom: and the rich man also died, and was buried. 23 And in Hades he lifted up his eyes, being in torments, and seeth Abraham afar off, and Lazarus in his bosom. 24 And he cried and said, Father Abraham, have mercy on me, and send Lazarus, that he may dip the tip of his finger in water, and cool my tongue; for I am in anguish in this flame. 25 But Abraham said, ²Son, remember that thou in thy lifetime receivedst thy good things, and Lazarus in like manner evil things: but now here he is comforted, and thou art in anguish. 26 And ³besides all this, between us and you there is a great gulf fixed, that they that would pass from hence to you may not be able, and that none may cross over from thence to

¹ Or, *living in mirth and splendor every day*   ² Gr. *Child.*   ³ Or, *in all these things*

Commentary on Matthew, p. 399.
**Ibid.

us. 27 And he said, I pray thee therefore, father, that thou wouldest send him to my father's house; 28 for I have five brethren; that he may testify unto them, lest they also come into this place of torment. 29 But Abraham saith, They have Moses and the prophets; let them hear them. 30 And he said, Nay, father Abraham: but if one go to them from the dead, they will repent. 31 And he said unto him, If they hear not Moses and the prophets, neither will they be ·persuaded, if one rise from the dead.

Note 177. There is no need to say that the narrative of The Rich Man and Lazarus is not a parable, as some confidently assert, in order to conserve the accuracy of the description of future punishment that is found in it. A parable is an illustrative comparison, or narrative, used to teach or to impress religious truth (cf. Note 48). And it is not necessary that a story be fictitious for it to be called a parable. Likely many of the parables, including the one in this section, are accounts of incidents that actually occurred; and certainly the conditions described in all of them are true to life—in this case, true to the life to come. If one could prove that Jesus did "make up" this story (which no one can, or ever will) it would not lose its value as an accurate description of future punishment. The experiences of the rich man and of Lazarus, as Jesus described them, are the experiences of the people who die under the same circumstances. And Jesus was the only person who ever lived on earth who could describe the experiences of people after death or report a conversation between any two of them. When He was born, He came from a pre-existent life, so that even the demons knew Him. No one has passed through the gates of death and returned to earth to give an account of what he saw or felt in the world to come; even those who were miraculously restored to this life for a while apparently have left no description of the world after death. For information about that world we are dependent on the words of Jesus and the inspired writings of the apostles.

Jesus did not call the rich man in the parable Dives, as he is popularly designated. Dives is the Latin word for "rich," and in the Latin Testament the word dives is used, meaning "The rich one;" but neither in any English version, nor in Greek does the name Dives occur.

The word translated "Hell" in verse 23 is hades which to the Greeks and Greek-speaking Jews meant the abode of the souls of those who have died, both good and bad. This is in full accord with the words of Peter in Acts 2:31, where, in speaking of the resurrection of Jesus, he said that "He (the Christ) was not left in Hades" (A.S.V.). Peter, therefore, assumed that the soul of Jesus was in Hades between His death and His resurrection. We observe that the rich man in Hades was in torment, was tormented in a flame; but that Lazarus, also in Hades, was in "Abraham's bosom" and was comforted. Jesus said to the penitent thief being crucified at the same time with Him that they would be together that day "in Paradise" (Luke 23:43, #251). We conclude, therefore, that Paradise was the same as that part of Hades called

Abraham's bosom, and that between the comforts of Abraham's bosom and the torments of Hades which the rich man suffered there was the "great gulf fixed."

Jesus did not set forth a system of doctrine (either on future punishment or any other subject), and one must certainly use great care in arriving at general conclusions. It is clear, however, that he taught in this passage that the wicked pass at death into the torments of Hades; He taught in John 5: 29 that they will come forth in a resurrection of judgment, and He taught in Matthew 25:41 that after the judgment they will be consigned to "eternal fire." Jesus also used another word (gehenna) for Hell eleven times (all recorded in the Synoptic Gospels). He called it the "Hell of fire" (Matt. 5:22; 18:8), "the unquenchable fire" (Mark 9:43), the place "where their worm dieth not, and the fire is not quenched" (Mark 9:48). I take it that this is the "eternal fire" to which the wicked will be consigned after the judgment.

If it is objected that this was the popular belief of that day, I would agree. But I would observe that the Lord Jesus, who was God's Son, endorsed this much of the popular teaching of the day. When we inquire why He endorsed it, we must choose from three alternatives: (1) He did not know any better, or (2) He knew better but would not contradict or correct popular opinion, or (3) He knew it to be true. I choose the last alternative.

This parable is a continuation of the words of Jesus to money loving Pharisees (vs. 14, #175). The truth which He primarily sought to impress is that, though in this life one is able to enjoy all that money can procure, if he is not right with God, he is not as well off as the most abject beggar who is right with God. Certainly He did not mean to teach that the rich man went to the torments of Hades because he was rich, or that Lazarus went to the comforts of Abraham's bosom because he was poor.

d. Parable of The Unprofitable Servants
#177
Luke 17:1-10

1 And he said unto his disciples, It is impossible but that occasions of stumbling should come; but woe unto him, through whom they come! 2 It were well for him if a millstone were hanged about his neck, and he was thrown into the sea, rather than that he should cause one of these little ones to stumble. 3 Take heed to yourselves: if thy brother sin, rebuke him; and if he repent, forgive him. 4 And if he sin against thee seven times in the day, and seven times turn again to thee, saying, I repent; thou shalt forgive him.

5 And the apostles said unto the Lord, Increase our faith. 6 And the Lord said, If ye had faith as a grain of mustard seed, ye would say unto this sycamine tree, Be thou rooted up, and be thou planted in the sea; and it would obey you. 7 But who is there of you, having a [1]servant plowing or keeping sheep, that will say unto him, when he is come in from the field, Come straightway and sit down to meat; 8 and will not rather say unto him, Make ready wherewith I may sup, and gird thyself, and serve me, till I have eaten and drunken; and afterward thou shalt eat and drink? 9 Doth he thank the [1]servant because he did the things that were commanded? 10 Even so ye also, when ye shall have done all the things that are

[1] Gr. bondservant.

ommanded you, say, We are unprofitable ²servants; we have done that which it
vas our duty to do.
²'Gr. bondservants.

Note 178. In the above section, verses 1—4 are a repetition of
naterial in Matt. 18:9—10, 21—22 (##139, 140); but there is enough
variation to assure us that the two passages were spoken on different
occasions.

Verse 6 is a repetition of Matt. 17:20 (#135). Of course an in-
sensate grain of mustard seed is not capable of exercising faith; but,
planted, it makes room for its roots displacing whatever obstructs its
growth. It functions according to its God-given nature as though it ex-
pects God to supply what it needs. That is the kind of faith and dependence on God that Jesus would lead His disciples to exercise. And
the mountain may be a mountain of difficulty impeding the efforts of
God's people, not simply a pile of earth and stone. It is possible that
the Lord Jesus repeated the saying at this time to remind the disciples
of the circumstances under which He had previously used the comparison, and to impress the same lesson on them (cf. Note 136).

The parable of The Unprofitable Servants certainly was not spoken
to show our Lord's ideal for the treatment of servants. But from the
prevailing custom of dealing with servants, He taught the disciples that
they can never do enough service to bring God under obligation to them.

2. A brief visit to Judaea (Bethany), ##178—179
(1) Raising Lazarus from the dead
#178
JOHN 11:1-44

1 Now a certain man was sick. Lazarus of Bethany, of the village of Mary
and her sister Martha. 2 And it was that Mary who anointed the Lord with ointment, and wiped his feet with her hair, whose brother Lazarus was sick. 3 The
sisters therefore sent unto him, saying, Lord, behold, he whom thou lovest is sick.
4 But when Jesus heard it, he said, This sickness is not unto death, but for the
glory of God, that the Son of God may be glorified thereby. 5 Now Jesus loved
Martha, and her sister, and Lazarus. 6 When therefore he heard that he was sick,
he abode at that time two days in the place where he was. 7 Then after this he
saith to the disciples, Let us go into Judaea again. 8 The disciples say unto him,
Rabbi, the Jews were but now seeking to stone thee; and goest thou thither again?
9 Jesus answered, Are there not twelve hours in the day? If a man walk in the day,
he stumbleth not, because he seeth the light of this world. 10 But if a man walk
in the night, he stumbleth, because the light is not in him. 11 These things spake
he: and after this he saith unto them, Our friend Lazarus is fallen asleep; but I go,
that I may awake him out of sleep. 12 The disciples therefore said unto him, Lord,
if he is fallen asleep, he will ¹recover. 13 Now Jesus had spoken of his death: but
they thought that he spake of taking rest in sleep. 14 Then Jesus therefore said
unto them plainly, Lazarus is dead. 15 And I am glad for your sakes that I was not
there, to the intent ye may believe; nevertheless let us go unto him. 16 Thomas
therefore, who is called ²Didymus, said unto his fellow-disciples, Let us also go,
that we may die with him.

17 So when Jesus came, he found that he had been in the tomb four days
already. 18 Now Bethany was nigh unto Jerusalem, about fifteen furlongs off; 19
and many of the Jews had come to Martha and Mary, to console them concerning
¹ Gr. be saved.   ² That is, Twin.

their brother. 20 Martha therefore, when she heard that Jesus was coming, went and met him: but Mary still sat in the house. 21 Martha therefore said unto Jesus, Lord, if thou hadst been here, my brother had not died. 22 And even now I know that, whatsoever thou shalt ask of God, God will give thee. 23 Jesus saith unto her, Thy brother shall rise again. 24 Martha saith unto him, I know that he shall rise again in the resurrection at the last day. 25 Jesus said unto her, I am the resurrection, and the life: he that believeth on me, though he die, yet shall he live; 26 and whosoever liveth and believeth on me shall never die. Believest thou this? 27 She saith unto him, Yea, Lord: I have believed that thou art the Christ, the Son of God, *even* he that cometh into the world. 28 And when she had said this, she went away, and called Mary [3]her sister secretly, saying, The Teacher is here, and calleth thee. 29 And she, when she heard it, arose quickly, and went unto him. 30 (Now Jesus was not yet come into the village, but was still in the place where Martha met him.) 31 The Jews then who were with her in the house, and were consoling her, when they saw Mary, that she rose up quickly and went out, followed her supposing that she was going unto the tomb to [4]weep there. 32 Mary therefore, when she came where Jesus was, and saw him, fell down at his feet, saying unto him, Lord, if thou hadst been here, my bother had not died. 33 When Jesus therefore saw her [5]weeping, and the Jews *also* [5]weeping who came with her, he [6]groaned in the spirit, and [7]was troubled, 34 and said, Where have ye laid him? They say unto him, Lord, come and see. 35 Jesus wept. 36 The Jews therefore said, Behold how he loved him! 37 But some of them said, Could not this man, who opened the eyes of him that was blind, have caused that this man also should not die? 38 Jesus therefore again [8]groaning in himself cometh to the tomb. Now it was a cave, and a stone lay [9]against it. 39 Jesus saith, Take ye away the stone. Martha, the sister of him that was dead, saith unto him, Lord, by this time [10]the body decayeth; for he hath been *dead* four days. 40 Jesus saith unto her, Said I not unto thee, that, if thou believedst, thou shouldest see the glory of God? 41 So they took away the stone. And Jesus lifted up his eyes, and said, Father, I thank thee that thou heardest me. 42 And I knew that thou hearest me always: but because of the multitude that standeth around I said it, that they may believe that thou didst send me. 43 And when he had thus spoken, he cried with a loud voice, Lazarus, come forth. 44 He that was dead came forth, bound hand and foot with [11]grave-clothes; and his face was bound about with a napkin. Jesus saith unto them, Loose him, and let him go.

[3] Or, *her sister, saying secretly*   [4] Gr. *wail.*
[5] Gr. *wailing.*   [6] Or, *was moved with indignation in the spirit*   [7] Gr. *troubled himself.*
[8] Or, *being moved with indignation in himself*   [9] Or, *upon*   [10] Gr. *he stinketh.*
[11] Or, *grave-bands*

Note 179. There is nothing either in Luke or in John to indicate just where to break in on the narrative in Luke for the account of the raising of Lazarus. It must have been before the healing of the ten lepers, because at that time Jesus was at the border of Samaria and Galilee enroute back to Jerusalem (Luke 17: 11, #180). This is the third and last time in the life of Jesus when He raised to life one who had died (cf. ##79, 108). Observe that the accounts of these miracles are distributed among all of the gospel records, the first in Luke, the second in all three of the Synoptics, and this last one in John.

There is no doubt that these were the same sisters whose hospitality Jesus enjoyed when He set out on the tour of Judaea (Luke 10: 38ff; #151), although Lazarus is not mentioned in connection with that incident. Jesus interrupted His ministry in Peraea to answer the call of the sisters. It is idle to ask why he delayed two days before coming. In the end the sisters obtained what they would have gotten if Jesus had come to them promptly; that is, the restoration of their brother in health.

The literal translation of the words of Jesus in verses 25 and 26 would be, "The one believing on Me, even if he dies, he will live; and everyone living and believing on Me shall in no wise die unto the forever." Although I recognize that the rendering in our versions ("shall never die") is regarded to be according to the Greek idiom, it seems to me that the meaning of Jesus is here better expressed by the literal translation. Martha was assured that the believers in Christ who had died will live again; and that living believers, if and when they die, will not die to remain dead forever.

(2) Increasing hatred at Jerusalem
#179
JOHN 11:45-53
45 Many therefore of the Jews, who came to Mary and beheld [1]that which he did, believed on him. 46 But some of them went away to the Pharisees, and told them the things which Jesus had done.
47 The chief priests therefore and the Pharisees gathered a council, and said, What do we? for this man doeth many signs. 48 If we let him thus alone, all men will believe on him: and the Romans will come and take away both our place and our nation. 49 But a certain one of them, Caiaphas, being high priest that year, said unto them, Ye know nothing at all, 50 nor do ye take account that it is expedient for you that one man should die for the people, and that the whole nation perish not. 51 Now this he said not of himself: but being high priest that year, he prophesied that Jesus should die for the nation; 52 and not for the nation only, but that he might also gather together into one the children of God that are scattered abroad. 53 So from that day forth they took counsel that they might put him to death.

[1] Many ancient authorities read *the things which he did.*

Note 180. The reaction of the Jews of Jerusalem to the raising of Lazarus accords with their efforts to stone Jesus following the Feast of Tabernacles (John 8:59, #147) and during the Feast of Dedication (John 10:31, #165). Added to their hatred of long standing was now a fear lest His rising popularity might cause the Romans to put tighter restrictions on the nation and possibly deprive the Sanhedrin of what power it had been able to retain. So in a council of priests (predominantly Sadducees) and Pharisees they definitely determined to be rid of Him. It seems that such a miracle as the raising of Lazarus ought to have convinced them, but Jesus surely described their attitude when He quoted Abraham as saying to the rich man, "neither will they be persuaded though one rise from the dead" (Luke 16:31, #176).

3. Last tour of the country, circling through Samaria, Galilee, and Peraea, and back to Bethany, ##180-194
(1) Withdrawal to Ephraim and the border of Galilee
#180

LUKE 17:11	JOHN 11:54
	54 Jesus therefore walked no more openly among the Jews, but departed thence into the country near to the wilderness, into a city called Ephraim; and there he tarried with the disciples.
And it came to pass, [1]as they were on the way to Jerusalem, that he was	
[1] Or, *as he was*	

225

Luke 17

passing ²along the borders of Samaria
and Galilee.
² Or, *through the midst of &c.*

Note 181. After the raising of Lazarus, Jesus, knowing the determined hostility of the priests and Pharisees of Jerusalem, withdrew to
this city of Ephraim, which map-makers usually put between Jerusalem
and the border of Galilee, though its exact location is not known. Here
apparently, He rested some time with the disciples, and then proceeded farther north to the border of Galilee, to circle back through Peraea to
Bethany and Jerusalem in order to be present for the approaching Passover. In this way He joined groups from Galilee who were going up fo
the feast. Jesus knew that at that Passover season He would be arrested, mistreated, and put to death, but He did not shrink or seek to evade
the suffering, because for it He had come to earth.

(2) Healing the ten lepers, commending the thankful one,
     a Samaritan
#181
LUKE 17:12-19

12 And as he entered into a certain village, there met him ten men that wer
lepers, who stood afar off: 13 and they lifted up their voices, saying, Jesus, Master
have mercy on us. 14 And when he saw them, he said unto them, Go and show your
selves unto the priests. And·it came to pass, as they went, they were cleansed
15 And one of them, when he saw that he was healed, turned back, with a loud
voice glorifying God; 16 and he fell upon his face at his feet, giving him thanks
and he was a Samaritan. 17 And Jesus answering said, Were not the ten cleansed
but where are the nine? 18 ¹Were there none found that returned to give glory to
God, save this ²stranger? 19 And he said unto him, Arise, and go thy way: thy fait
hath ³made thee whole.
    ¹ Or, *There were none found . . . save this stranger.*   ² Or, *alien*   ³ Or, *saved the*

Note 182. This miracle occurred near the boundary between Samaria and Galilee as Jesus was on His last journey to Jerusalem (cf
Note 181). This was the fourth and last instance of healing in absentia
(cf. ##34, 78, 124). It may not be significant, but it is interesting to
notice that in the first three instances the persons thus healed were all
Gentiles, and at least one of the ten lepers was a Samaritan. Does this
mean that to members of His own race Jesus bestowed His blessings
with a closer personal affinity than to outsiders? Or does it signify that
Gentiles and Samaritans were capable of exercising more faith than the
Jews? These are questions about which one should not be too dogmatic.

(3) Teachings concerning the Kingdom of God, ##182—183
     a. The Kingdom in its present manifestation
#182
LUKE 17:20-21

20 And being asked by the Pharisees, when the kingdom of God cometh, h
answered them and said, The kingdom of God cometh not with observation: 2
neither shall they say, Lo, here! or, There! for lo, the kingdom of God is ¹within
you.
    ¹ Or, *in the midst of you*

Note 183. These Pharisees probably raised their question (vs. 20 above) as a thrust of sarcasm. Since both John the Baptist and Jesus proclaimed the Kingdom of God to be near at hand and had aroused the hopes of the people, and since these Pharisees saw no outward signs of the Kingdom's being set up as an outward monarchy, they taunted Jesus with the question: "When is the Kingdom of God that you have been talking about going to come?" Of course they had the visible Kingdom in mind, for at that time not even the disciples conceived of the spiritual Kingdom. In reply Jesus made reference to both manifestations of the Kingdom: to the visible Kingdom in the last sentence of verse 20 and the first one of verse 21, and to the spiritual Kingdom in the last sentence of verse 21.

By asserting that "the Kingdom of God cometh not with observation," Jesus closed the book on all the efforts to foretell, by comparing prophecies with contemporary events, the time of His return to earth for the inauguration of the visible Kingdom. By saying that "the Kingdom of God is within you" He may have meant "in your hearts," signifying that the loyal allegiance of an individual to Jesus as supreme King is the spiritual Kingdom. In that case the pronoun "you" was used indefinitely, denoting people in general. More probably, though, He was saying that the Kingdom (meaning the spiritual Kingdom) had already been established among them, or within their social order; in other words, that there were already individuals among them who were in the spiritual Kingdom, because in their hearts they had enthroned Jesus as King.

b. Some things preceding and attending the visible
    manifestation of the Kingdom
#183
LUKE 17:22-37

22 And he said unto the disciples, The days will come, when ye shall desire to see one of the days of the Son of man, and ye shall not see it. 23 And they shall say to you, Lo, there! Lo, here! go not away, nor follow after *them*: 24 for as the lightning, when it lighteneth out of the one part under the heaven, shineth unto the other part under heaven; so shall the Son of man be [1]in his day. 25 But first must he suffer many things and be rejected of this generation. 26 And as it came to pass in the days of Noah, even so shall it be also in the days of the Son of man. 27 They ate, they drank, they married, they were given in marriage, until the day that Noah entered into the ark, and the flood came, and destroyed them all. 28 Likewise even as it came to pass in the days of Lot; they ate, they drank, they bought, they sold, they planted, they builded; 29 but in the day that Lot went out from Sodom it rained fire and brimstone from heaven, and destroyed them all: 30 after the same manner shall it be in the day that the Son of man is revealed. 31 In that day, he that shall be on the housetop, and his goods in the house, let him not go down to take them away: and let him that is in the field likewise not return back. 32 Remember Lot's wife. 33 Whosoever shall seek to gain his life shall lose it: but whosoever shall lose his life shall [2]preserve it. 34 I say unto you, In that night there shall be two men on one bed; the one shall be taken, and the other shall be left. 35 There shall be two women grinding together; the one shall be taken, and the other shall be left.[3] 37 And they answering say unto him, Where, Lord? And he said unto them, Where the body *is*, thither will the [4]eagles also be gathered together.

[1] Some ancient authorities omit *in his day.*   [2] Gr. *save it alive.*
[3] Some ancient authorities add ver. 36 *There shall be two men in the field; the one shall be taken, and the other shall be left.* Mt. 24. 40.   [4] Or, *vultures*

227

Note 184. In the foregoing section, the words about the revealing of the Son of Man (vs. 30) and the setting up of the visible Kingdom were doubtless in response to the surprise aroused in the minds of the disciples at what Jesus told the Pharisees in the preceding section about the Kingdom of God. Not only will people not be able to calculate when the Son of Man will be revealed to inaugurate the visible Kingdom, but they, the disciples, were going to long for that time to come. Note three impressive truths: (1) The return of Jesus to earth will be public; that is, it will be seen and recognized by all; it will not be private and secret (vss. 23—24). (2) Before the realization of the visible Kingdom, Jesus Himself would be rejected by the Jewish people and would suffer at their hands (vs. 25). We can see in this a repeated prediction of His death, to be followed by His resurrection and the progress of the spiritual Kingdom, but the disciples did not understand it. And we know that the rejection by the Jewish people as a whole has continued through the centuries. (3) People generally, including some Christians and many professing Christians, will be so engrossed in their temporal plans that they will not be expecting the return of Christ or the trans-mutation ("regeneration" in Matt. 19:28) of the Kingdom.

The parable of The Vultures (vs. 37), answering the inquiry of the disciples about the destination of those taken so suddenly from their fellows, teaches that, just as vultures are attracted by a carcass, so at the coming of Jesus His presence will be the center of attraction for His people.

This is the second passage in Luke in which Jesus announced some conditions that will prevail at His return and the importance of being prepared (cf. Luke 12:35--48, #157). Some of these things will be repeated in the great prophecy of ##219--225.

(4) Two parables on prayer, ##184—185
    a. The parable of The Courageous Widow
        #184
        LUKE 18:1-8

1 And he spake a parable unto them to the end that they ought always to pray, and not to faint; 2 saying, There was in a city a judge, who feared not God, and regarded not man: 3 and there was a widow in that city; and she came oft unto him, saying, ¹Avenge me of mine adversary. 4 And he would not for a while: but afterward he said within himself, Though I fear not God, nor regard man; 5 yet because this widow troubleth me, I will avenge her, ²lest she ³wear me out by her continual coming. 6 And the Lord said, Hear what ⁴the unrighteous judge saith 7 And shall not God avenge his elect, that cry to him day and night, ⁵and yet he is longsuffering over them? 8 I say unto you, that he will avenge them speedily. Nevertheless, when the Son of man cometh, shall he find ⁶faith on the earth?

¹ Or, Do me justice of: and so in ver. 5, 7, 8,   ² Or, lest at last by her coming she wear me out
³ Gr. bruise.   ⁴ Gr. the judge of unrighteousness.
⁵ Or, and is he slow to punish on their behalf?   ⁶ Or, the faith

Note 185. I am sure that the foregoing parable will be better understood if one will observe its connection with the preceding paragraph. In the perilous times which will prevail just before the return of the Lord, people will be so engrossed with temporal matters, or so

228

vainly self-confident in their scientific accomplishments, that they will underrate God's power to work in His world or His willingness to do so in answer to prayer. Or else they will be so burdened by the oppressions and the wickedness of the day that they will disparage the efficacy of prayer. In this parable Jesus taught that Christians ought to have sufficient faith in God to inspire them to pray even in circumstances that are most unpromising. The lesson is summarized by Luke in verse 1 and by the Lord Jesus in verse 8.

b. The parable of The Pharisee and The Publican
#185
LUKE 18:9-14

9 And he spake also this parable unto certain who trusted in themselves that they were righteous, and set ¹all others at nought: 10 Two men went up into the temple to pray; the one a Pharisee, and the other a ²publican. 11 The Pharisee stood and prayed thus with himself, God, I thank thee, that I am not as the rest of men, extortioners, unjust, adulterers, or even as this ²publican. 12 I fast twice in the week; I give tithes of all that I get. 13 But the ²publiean, standing afar off, would not lift up so much as his eyes unto heaven, but smote his breast, saying, God, ³be thou merciful to me ⁴a sinner. 14 I say unto you, This man went down to his house justified rather than the other: for every one that exalteth himself shall be humbled; but he that humbleth himself shall be exalted.

¹ Gr. the rest.
² See marginal note on ch. 3. 12.
³ Or, be thou propitiated
⁴ Or, the sinner

Note 186. Doubtless some of the Pharisees who had sarcastically inquired when the Kingdom of God would come (#182) were still in the group listening to Jesus. Their vanity and overconfidence in their moral accomplishments are evidenced by the prayer that Jesus quoted from the Pharisee in the temple. In contrast He cited the prayer of a despised publican, one who was at the opposite extreme of the Jewish social order. In his self-confidence the Pharisee did not recognize any need that God could supply; but the publican confessed his poverty in spiritual values (cf. Matt. 5: 3, #54), his need for forgiveness, and he had faith to ask God to grant the blessing needed.

Observe from the footnote that the word translated "be merciful" literally means "be propitiated." Jesus probably implied that these prayers were uttered in the temple while the sin offering was being sacrificed. And this may reflect the overshadowing realization that His own death, by which He would make the true atonement for sins, awaited Him during the approaching Passover season. This is the last of the four parables on prayer (cf. #152 and Note 153).

(5) Blessing little children
#186

MATT. 19:13-15	MARK 10:13-16	LUKE 18:15-17
13 Then were there brought unto him little children, that he should lay his hands on them, and pray: and the disciples rebuked them. 14 But Jesus said, Suffer the little chil-	13 And they were bringing unto him little children, that he should touch them: and the disciples rebuked them. 14 But when Jesus saw it, he was moved with indignation, and said unto	15 And they were bringing unto him also their babes, that he should touch them: but when the disciples saw it, they rebuked them. 16 But Jesus called them unto him, saying

229

Luke 18	Mark 10	Matt. 19
dren ,and forbid them not, to come unto me: for ¹to such belongeth the kingdom of heaven. 15 And he laid his hands on them, and departed thence. ¹ Or, of such is	them, Suffer the little children to come unto me; forbid them not: for ¹to such belongeth the kingdom of God. 15 Verily I say unto you, Whosoever shall not receive the kingdom of God as a little child, he shall in no wise enter therein. 16 And he took them in his arms, and blessed them, laying his hands upon them. ¹ Or, of such is	Suffer the little children to come unto me, and forbid them not: for ¹to such belongeth the kingdom of God. 17 Verily I say unto you, Whosoever shall not receive the kingdom of God as a little child, he shall in no wise enter therein. ¹ Or, of such is

Note 187. The pronoun "such" in verse 14 of Matthew and parallels refers to those who come to Jesus, including little children if and when they come to Him. I believe also that the translation suggested in the footnote ("of such is the Kingdom") is preferred to that of the text, because Jesus was doubtless teaching that the Kingdom of God is composed of those who come to Him. In Matt. 5:3 (#54) Jesus had said that the poor in spirit are the ones who compose the Kingdom of Heaven. Coming to Jesus, therefore, involves humility and poverty of spirit. A place in the Kingdom is the privilege even of the little child who comes to Jesus, and to forbid or hinder little children from coming to Him is to deprive them of the blessings of the Kingdom. Moreover, everyone who desires to share the blessedness of the Kingdom must receive it just as a little child receives it; that is, by coming to Jesus. It is clear that Jesus transferred the idea from a physical coming to Him, as the children in this passage were coming, to the spiritual coming in faith.

(6) Further teachings concerning discipleship, ##187—189
   a. Occasion of this teaching, question by
      the rich young ruler

#187

Matt. 19:16-22	Mark 10:17-22	Luke 18:18-23
16 And behold, one came to him and said, ¹Teacher, what good thing shall I do, that I may have eternal life? 17 And he said unto him, ²Why askest thou me concerning that which is good? One there is who is good: but if thou wouldest ¹ Some ancient authorities read Good Teacher. See Mk. 10. 17; Lk. 18. 18. ² Some ancient authorities read Why callest thou me good? None is good save one, even God. See Mk. 10. 18; Lk. 18. 19.	17 And as he was going forth ¹into the way, there ran one to him, and kneeled to him, and asked him, Good Teacher, what shall I do that I may inherit eternal life? 18 And Jesus said unto him, Why callest thou me good? none is good save one, even God. 19 Thou knowest the commandments, ²Do not kill, Do not commit adultery, Do not steal, Do not bear ¹ Or, on his way ² Ex. xx. 12-16; Dt. v. 16-20.	18 And a certain ruler asked him, saying, Good Teacher, what shall I do to inherit eternal life? 19 And Jesus said unto him, Why callest thou me good? none is good, save one, even God. 20 Thou knowest the commandments, ¹Do not commit adultery, Do not kill, Do not steal, Do not bear false witness, Honor thy father and mother. ¹ Ex. xx. 12-16; Dt. v. 16-20.

Matt. 19	Mark 10	Luke 18
enter into life, keep the commandments. 18 He saith unto him, Which? And Jesus said, ³Thou shalt not kill, Thou shalt not commit adultery, Thou shalt not steal, Thou shalt not bear false witness, 19 Honor thy father and mother; and, ⁴Thou shalt love thy neighbor as thyself. 20 The young man saith unto him, All these things have I observed: what lack I yet? 21 Jesus said unto him, If thou wouldest be perfect, go, sell that which thou hast, and give to the poor, and thou shalt have treasure in heaven: and come, follow me. 22 But when the young man heard the saying, he went away sorrowful; for he was one that had great possessions.	false witness, Do not defraud, Honor thy father and mother. 20 And he said unto him, Teacher, all these things have I observed from my youth. 21 And Jesus looking upon him loved him, and said unto him, One thing thou lackest: go, sell whatsoever thou hast, and give to the poor, and thou shalt have treasure in heaven: and come, follow me. 22 But his countenance fell at the saying, and he went away sorrowful: for he was one that had great possessions.	21 And he said, All these things have I observed from my youth up. 22 And when Jesus heard it, he said unto him, One thing thou lackest yet: sell all that thou hast, and distribute unto the poor, and thou shalt have treasure in heaven: and come, follow me. 23 But when he heard these things, he became exceeding sorrowful; for he was very rich.

³ Ex. xx. 12-16; Dt. v. 16-20.
⁴ Lev. xix. 18.

Note 188. The inquirer in this section is generally known as the "Rich Young Ruler." Matthew twice referred to him as young, Luke called him a ruler, and all three accounts assert that he was rich. He was the second to inquire of Jesus what to do to inherit eternal life (cf. #149). Notice that in reply Jesus referred both of them to the law. In this instance Matthew relates that He included in the list of commandments the comprehensive precept from Lev. 19:18: "Thou shalt love thy neighbor as thyself;" and on the previous occasion He led the lawyer to quote both this and the other comprehensive precept of Deut. 6:5. Doubtless His purpose was to awaken in them a realization of their insufficiency before God.* We judge that this young man was a Pharisee, since he claimed to have kept the law from his youth up; that is, those commandments dealing with one's duties to his fellowman. But Jesus, by instructing him to sell his possessions and give the proceeds to the poor, proved to him that he had not kept all the commandments as he had claimed.

The question arises, Why did Jesus impose this hard requirement on this young man, especially since, as Mark asserts, He loved Him? The same requirement was not made of the four fishermen or of Matthew. But the fishermen did forsake their boats and nets, and Matthew

*Broadus, *Commentary on Matthew*, p. 406 quotes Bengel, a writer of the eighteenth century, thus: "Those who feel secure Jesus refers to the law; the contrite he consoles with the gospel." The same quotation is cited in Latin in *A Critical and Exegetical Commentary on the Gospel According to St. Luke*. In the *International Critical Commentary* (New York: Charles Scribner's Sons, 1920), p. 432.

ιorsook the lucrative tax-collecting position. Doubtless Jesus saw that in the case of the rich young ruler nothing short of such drastic action would be forsaking "all that he hath" (cf. Luke 14: 33, #170). We hear no more of this young man. We wish we knew if he ever changed his mind—if he was among those mentioned in Acts 2: 45 or 4: 34--35 who sold their goods that distribution might be made to those who had need.

b. The need of self-denial on the part of the disciples of Jesus

#188

MATT. 19:23-26	MARK 10:23-27	LUKE 18:24-27
23 And Jesus said unto his disciples, Verily I say unto you, It is hard for a rich man to enter into the kingdom of heaven.	23 And Jesus looked round about, and saith unto his disciples, How hardly shall they that have riches enter into the kingdom of God! 24 And the disciples were amazed at his words. But Jesus answereth again, and saith unto them, Children, how hard is it ¹for them that trust in riches to enter into the kingdom of God! 25 It is easier for a camel to go through a needle's eye, than for a rich man to enter into the kingdom of God. 26 And they were astonished exceedingly, saying ²unto him, Then who can be saved? 27 Jesus looking upon them saith, With men it is impossible, but not with God: for all things are possible with God.	24 And Jesus seeing him said, How hardly shall they that have riches enter into the kingdom of God!
24 And again I say unto you, It is easier for a camel to go through a needle's eye, than for a rich man to enter into the kingdom of God. 25 And when the disciples heard it, they were astonished exceedingly, saying, Who then can be saved? 26 And Jesus looking upon *them* said to them, With men this is impossible; but with God all things are possible.		25 For it is easier for a camel to enter in through a needle's eye, than for a rich man to enter into the kingdom of God. 26 And they that heard it said, Then who can be saved? 27 But he said, The things which are impossible with men are possible with God.

¹ Some ancient authorities omit *for them that trust in riches.*
² Many ancient authorities read *among themselves.*

Note 189. In the foregoing section the words "How hardly" in the opening verses of Mark and Luke m e a n "with what difficulty." The translation in the American Standard ("It is hard for a rich man to enter...) expresses the meaning better than that in the King James ("a rich man shall hardly enter...")· Jesus was surely solicitous for the Rich Young Ruler and made the remark about his difficulty, not in criticism, but with understanding. Nothing is gained by trying to tone down the comparison that He made in verse 24 of Matthew and parallels. The camel that Jesus spoke of was the beast of burden (not a cable or rope, as some have suggested); and the needle's eye was the hole in their sewing instrument (not a small gate in the wall of Jerusalem, as others have assumed). Our Lord would have the disciples imagine the largest domestic animal that they knew going through the smallest usable opening (cf. the comparison of the mote and the beam #69). Clearly it was humanly impossible, as Jesus Himself confessed (vs. 26 of Matthew and parallels); and this impossibility was what so amazed the disciples. But Jesus also asserted that it is possible for God, both to put a camel through a needle's eye, and to change the heart of a rich man.

c. Simon Peter's question about rewards and three answers from Jesus

#189

MATT. 19:27-30	MARK 10:28-31	LUKE 18:28-30
27 Then answered Peter and said unto him, Lo, we have left all, and followed thee; what then shall we have? 28 And Jesus said unto them, Verily I say unto you, that ye who have followed me, in the regeneration when the Son of man shall sit on the throne of his glory, ye also shall sit upon t w e l v e thrones, judging the twelve tribes of Israel. 29 And every one that hath left houses, or brethren, or sisters, or father, or mother, [1]or children, or lands, for my name's sake, shall receive [2]a hundredfold, and shall inherit eternal life.	28 Peter began to say unto him, Lo, we have left all, and have followed thee.	28 And Peter said, Lo, we have left [1]our own, and followed thee.
	29 Jesus said, Verily I say unto you, There is no man that hath left house, or brethren, or sisters, or mother, or father, or children, or lands, for my sake, and for the [1]gospel's sake, 30 but he shall receive a hundredfold now in this time, houses, and brethren, and sisters, and mothers, and children, and lands, with persecutions; and in the [2]world to come eternal life. 31 But many that are first shall be last; and the last first.	29 And he said unto them, Verily I say unto you, There is no man that hath left house, or wife, or brethren, or parents, or children, for the kingdom of God's sake, 30 who shall not receive manifold more in this time, and in the [2]world to come eternal life.
30 But many shall be last that are first; and first that are last.		
[1] Many ancient authorities add or wife: as in Lk. 18. 29. [2] Some ancient authorities read manifold.	[1] See marginal note on ch. 1. 1. [2] Or, age	[1] Or, our own homes. See Jn. 19. 27. [2] Or, age

MATT. 20:1-16

1 For the kingdom of heaven is like unto a man that was a householder, who went out early in the morning to hire laborers into his vineyard. 2 And when he had agreed with the laborers for a [1]shilling a day, he sent them into his vineyard. 3 And he went out about the third hour, and saw others standing in the market-place idle; 4 and to them he said, Go ye also into the vineyard, and whatsoever is right I will give you. And they went their way. 5 Again he went out about the sixth and the ninth hour, and did likewise. 6 And about the eleventh *hour* he went out, and found others standing; and he saith unto them, Why stand ye here all the day idle? 7 They say unto him, Because no man hath hired us. He saith unto them, Go ye also into the vineyard. 8 And when even was come, the lord of the vineyard saith unto his steward, Call the laborers, and pay them their hire, beginning from the last unto the first. 9 And when they came that *were hired* about the eleventh hour, they received every man a [1]shilling. 10 And when the first came, they supposed that they would receive more; and they likewise received every man a

[1] See marginal note on ch. 18. 28.

¹shilling. 11 And when they received it, they murmured against the householder, 12 saying, These last have spent *but* one hour, and thou hast made them equal unto us, who have borne the burden of the day and the ²scorching heat. 13 But he answered and said to one of them, Friend, I do thee no wrong: didst not thou agree with me for a ¹shilling? 14 Take up that which is thine, and go thy way; it is my will to give unto this last, even as unto thee. 15 Is it not lawful for me to do what I will with mine own? or is thine eye evil, because I am good? 16 So the last shall be first, and the first last.

¹ See marginal note on ch. 18. 28.   ² Or, *hot wind*

Note 190. The demand made of the Rich Young Ruler and that one's going away without acceding to that demand, and the remarks of Jesus about the difficulty which rich people experience in entering the Kingdom of God doubtless prompted Peter to speak of the sacrifices which he and the other disciples had made in order that they might follow Jesus and to inquire about the rewards that they would receive. Possibly he was mindful also that Jesus had said a short time before to a multitude following Him that one must forsake all that he has to be His disciple (Luke 14: 26, 33, #170). To Peter's question Jesus gave a three-fold answer: (1) In the future age they will share in His glory (Matt. 19: 28). Here the word "regeneration" certainly means the time of the visible Kingdom of God (cf. Luke 21: 31, 22: 30), the age usually spoken of as the "millennium," when the Lord Jesus will be visibly present, sitting on the throne of His glory as the world's Ruler (cf. Note 18, "The Visible Kingdom"). (2) In this life the satisfaction and joys which the disciples would receive from following Him would compensate them a hundred-fold for any loss of the possessions which they had given up, and for the necessity of forsaking loved ones; and besides this, they would inherit eternal life in the world to come, the blessing for which the Rich Young Ruler had come inquiring (Matt. 19: 29--30 and parallels). (3) Peter and the other disciples would do well to trust God completely in the matter of rewards (Matt. 19: 30—20: 16). The teaching of the parable of The Laborers in The Vineyard is not that the person who serves Jesus only a short period late in life will be rewarded the same as the one who renders life-long service, as may appear from a superficial reading, but that He who serves without thought of compensation, or in complete confidence in the Lord to reward him fairly, will be surprised at the magnificence of his reward.

(7) Third definite announcement concerning His approaching death
#190

MATT. 20:17-19	MARK 10:32-34	LUKE 18:31-34
17 And as Jesus was going up to Jerusalem, he took the twelve disciples apart, and on the way he said unto them,	' 32 And they were on the way, going up to Jerusalem; and Jesus was going before them: and they were amazed; and they that fol-	31 And he took unto him the twelve, and said unto them,

Matt. 20	Mark 10	Luke 18
	lowed were afraid. And he took again the twelve, and began to tell them the things that were to happen	
18 Behold, we go up to Jerusalem; and the Son of .man shall be ¹delivered unto the chief priests and scribes; and they shall condemn him to death, 19 and shall deliver him unto the Gentiles to mock, and to scourge, and to crucify: and the third day he shall be raised up.	unto him, 33 *saying*, Behold, we go up to Jerusalem; and the Son of man shall be delivered unto the chief priests and the scribes; and they shall condemn him to death, and shall deliver him unto the Gentiles: 34 and they shall mock him, and shall spit upon him, and shall scourge him, and shall kill him; and after three days he shall rise again.	Behold, we go up to Jerusalem, and all the things that are written through the prophets shall be accomplished unto the Son of man. 32 For he shall be ¹delivered up unto the Gentiles, and shall be mocked, and shamefully treated, and spit upon: 33 and they shall scourge and kill him: and the third day he shall rise again. 34 And they understood none of these things; and this saying was hid from them, and they perceived not the things that were said.
¹ See ch. 10. 4.		¹ Or, *betrayed*

Note 191. This was the third positive and distinct announcement by Jesus to the disciples concerning the certainty of His impending death and resurrection (cf. ##131, 136), besides two statements which clearly implied such expectation (Matt. 17:12, #134 and Luke 17:25; #183). This time He was more specific as to the time and the manner of His death. It would take place in connection with this trip to Jerusalem, He would be betrayed to His enemies the Sanhedrin leaders, they would condemn Him and deliver Him to the Gentiles (Romans), these would humiliate and torture Him, and His death would be by crucifixion. And He added, as He had done on both the previous occasions, that He would rise from the dead on the third day. But the disciples, although some of them had been solemnly enjoined by the Voice of transfiguration, "Hear ye Him" (#133), could not understand or believe His words to them.

(8) Ambitious request of James and John
#191

MATT. 20:20-28	MARK 10:35-45
20 Then came to him the mother of the sons of Zebedee with her sons, ¹worshipping *him*, and asking a certain thing of him. 21 And he said unto her, What wouldest thou? She saith unto him, Command that these my two sons may sit, one on thy right hand, and one on thy left hand, in thy kingdom. 22 But Jesus answered and said, Ye know not what ye ask. Are ye able to drink the cup that I am about to drink? They	35 And there come near unto him ¹James and John, the sons of Zebedee, saying unto him, Teacher, we would that thou shouldest do for us whatsoever we shall ask of thee. 36 And he said unto them, What would ye that I should do for you? 37 And they said unto him, Grant unto us that we may sit, one on thy right hand, and one on *thy* left hand, in thy glory. 38 But Jesus said unto them, Ye know not what ye ask. Are ye
¹ See marginal note on ch. 2. 2.	¹ Or, *Jacob*

Matt. 20   Mark 10

say unto him, We are able. 23 He saith unto them, My cup indeed ye shall drink: but to sit on my right hand, and on *my* left hand, is not mine to give; but *it is for them* for whom it hath been prepared of my Father. 24 And when the ten heard it, they were moved with indignation concerning the two brethren. 25 But Jesus called them unto him, and said, Ye know that the rulers of the Gentiles lord it over them, and their great ones exercise authority over them. 26 Not so shall it be among you: but whosoever would become great among you shall be your ²minister;

27 and whosoever would be first among you shall be your ³servant: 28 even as the Son of man came not to be ministered unto, but to minister, and to give his life a ransom for many.

² Or, *servant*   ³ Gr. *bondservant.*

able to drink the cup that I drink? or to be baptized with the baptism that I am baptized with? 39 And they said unto him, We are able. And Jesus said unto them, The cup that I drink ye shall drink; and with the baptism that I am baptized withal shall ye be baptized: 40 but to sit on my right hand or on *my* left hand is not mine to give; but *it is for them* for whom it hath been prepared. 41 And when the ten heard it, they began to be moved with indignation concerning ¹James and John. 42 And Jesus called them to him, and saith unto them, Ye know that they who are accounted to rule over the Gentiles lord it over them; and their great ones exercise authority over them. 43 But it is not so among you: but whosoever would become great among you, shall be your ²minister; 44 and whosoever would be first among you, shall be ³servant of all. 45 For the Son of man also came not to be ministered unto, but to minister, and to give his life a ransom for many.

² Or, *servant*   ³ Gr. *bondservant.*

Note 192. In all probability this ambitious request on the part of James and John was prompted by the promise which Jesus made just a short time before, that in the visible Kingdom the apostles would sit on twelve thrones (Matt. 19:28, #189). Notice that in Matthew it is said that the mother of these disciples came to Jesus with the petition, and Mark has it that they themselves made the request. Their mother was probably a sister of Mary, the mother of Jesus (cf. Note 17, 7). We wonder if these cousins of Jesus tried to use their mother to plead for the preferred places, for their thrones on the basis of kinship. We do not wonder that the other ten disciples "were displeased with the two brethren." And when we consider that the request came immediately after a solemn prediction of His sufferings and death, we do not wonder that Jesus so sharply rebuked them. This may have been an echo of the strife in the apostolic group that arose some months previously, soon after Jesus had made the first announcement of His coming death and resurrection (cf. #138).

Jesus illustrated the limit of self-abasement and service that He desired the disciples to manifest by calling attention to His own life of service and stating that the climax of His service to others would be His giving "His life as a ransom for many" (Matt. vs. 28; Mark vs. 45). This was the clearest statement of the purpose of His coming death that He had made up to this time.

(9) Restoring sight to blind Bartimaeus (and his companion)

#192

MATT. 20:29-34	MARK 10:46-52	LUKE 18:35-43
29 And as they went out from Jericho, a great multitude followed him. 30 And behold, two blind men sitting by the way side, when they heard that Jesus was passing by, cried out, saying, Lord, have mercy on us, thou son of David. 31 And the multitude rebuked them, that t h e y should hold their peace: but they cried out the more, saying, Lord, have mercy on us, thou son of David. 32 And Jesus stood still, and called them, and said, What will ye that I should do unto you? 33 They say unto him, Lord, that our eyes may be opened. 34 And Jesus, being moved with compassion, touched their eyes; and straightway they received their sight, and followed him.	46 And they come to Jericho: and as he went out from Jericho, with his disciples and a great multitude, the son of Timaeus, Bartimaeus, a blind beggar, was sitting by the way side. 47 And when he heard that it was Jesus the Nazarene, he began to cry out, and say, Jesus, thou son of David, have mercy on me. 48 And many rebuked him, that he should hold his peace: but he cried out the more a great deal, Thou son of David, have mercy on me. 49 And Jesus stood still, and said, Call ye him. And they call the blind man, saying unto him, Be of good cheer: rise, he calleth thee. 50 And he, casting away his garment, sprang up, and came to Jesus. 51 And Jesus answered him, and said, What wilt thou that I should do unto thee? And the blind man said unto him, [1]Rabboni, that I may receive my sight. 52 And Jesus said unto him, Go thy way: thy faith hath [2]made thee whole. And straightway he received his sight, and followed him in the way. [1] See John 20. 16. [2] Or, saved thee	35 And it came to pass, as he drew nigh unto Jericho, a certain blind man sat by the way side begging: 36 and hearing a multitude going by, he inquired what this meant. 37 And they told him, that Jesus of Nazareth passeth by. 38 And he cried, saying, Jesus, thou son of David, have mercy on me. 39 And they that went before rebuked him, that he should hold his peace: but he cried out the more a great deal, Thou son of David, have mercy on me. 40 And Jesus stood, and commanded him to be brought unto him: and when he was come near, he asked him, 41 What wilt thou that I should do unto thee? And he said, Lord, that I may receive my sight. 42 And Jesus said unto him, Receive thy sight: thy faith hath [1]made thee whole. 43 And immediately he received his sight, and followed him, glorifying God: and all the people, when they saw it, gave praise unto God. [1] Or, saved thee

Note 193. Two blind men are mentioned in Matthew, but in Mark and Luke only one. We observed in #105 that Matthew told of two demoniacs who met Jesus in the land of the Gergesenes, and Mark and Luke told of only one. The most likely explanation in both instances is that there were two men in each case, but one attracted more attention. In Mark alone is either of them identified as Bartimaeus.

(10) Further teaching concerning stewardship, ##193—194

a. Occasion of this teaching, the conversion of Zacchaeus

#193

LUKE 19:1-10

1 And he entered and was passing through Jericho. 2 And behold, a man called by name Zacchaeus; and he' was a chief publican, and he was rich. 3 And he sought to see Jesus who he was; and could not for the crowd, because he was little of

stature. 4 And he ran on before, and climbed up into a sycomore tree to see him: for he was to pass that way. 5 And when Jesus came to the place, he looked up, and said unto him, Zacchaeus, make haste, and come down; for to-day I must abide at thy house. 6 And he made haste, and came down, and received him joyfully. 7 And when they saw it, they all murmured, saying, He is gone in to lodge with a man that is a sinner. 8 And Zacchaeus stood, and said unto the Lord, Behold, Lord, the half of my goods I give to the poor; and if I have wrongfully exacted aught of any man, I restore four-fold. 9 And Jesus said unto him, Today is salvation come to this house, forasmuch as he also is a son of Abraham. 10 For the Son of man came to seek and to save that which was lost.

Note 194. This was the third and last time when Jesus dined with a publican (cf. ##45, 171). So He dined three times with Pharisees (cf. ##84, 154, 168) and three times with publicans, the opposite extremes in the Jewish social order.

Observe that, though Jesus had said that it is easier for a camel to go through the eye of a needle than for a rich man to enter the Kingdom of God (#188), Zacchaeus, a rich man, did enter that day the spiritual Kingdom, since he experienced salvation. But Jesus had also reminded the disciples that with God all things are possible, even preparing the heart of a rich man to enter the Kingdom (cf. Note 189).

b. Parable of The Pounds, illustrating the relation of stewardship to the visible Kingdom of God
#194
LUKE 19:11-28

11 And as they heard these things, he added and spake a parable, because he was nigh to Jerusalem, and *because* they supposed that the kingdom of God was immediately to appear. 12 He said therefore, A certain nobleman went into a far country, to receive for himself a kingdom, and to return. 13 And he called ten ¹servants of his, and gave them ten ²pounds, and said unto them, Trade ye *herewith* till I come. 14 But his citizens hated him, and sent an ambassage after him, saying, We will not that this man reign over us. 15 And it came to pass, when he was come back again, having received the kingdom, that he commanded these ¹servants, unto whom he had given the money, to be called to him, that he might know what they had gained by trading. 16 And the first came before him, saying, Lord, thy pound hath made ten pounds more. 17 And he said unto him, Well done, thou good ³servant: because thou wast found faithful in a very little, have thou authority over ten cities. 18 And the second came, saying, Thy pound, Lord, hath made five pounds. 19 And he said unto him also, Be thou also over five cities. 20 And ⁴another came, saying, Lord, behold, *here is* thy pound, which I kept laid up in a napkin: 21 for I feared thee, because thou art an austere man: thou takest up that which thou layedst not down, and reapest that which thou didst not sow. 22 He saith unto him, Out of thine own mouth will I judge thee, thou wicked ³servant. Thou knewest that I am an austere man, taking up that which I laid not down, and reaping that which I did not sow; 23 then wherefore gavest thou not my money into the bank, and ⁵I at my coming should have required it with interest? 24 And he said unto them that stood by, Take away from him the pound, and give it unto him that hath the ten pounds. 25 And they said unto him, Lord, he hath ten pounds. 26 I say unto you, that unto every one that hath shall be given; but from him that hath not, even that which he hath shall be taken away from him. 27 But these mine enemies, that would not that I should reign over them, bring hither, and slay them before me.

28 And when he had thus spoken, he went on before, going up to Jerusalem.

¹ Gr. *bondservants.*
² Mina, here translated a pound, is equal to one hundred drachmas. See ch. 15. 8.
⁴ Gr. *the other.*　　　³ Gr. *bondservant.*　　　⁵ Or, *I should have gone and required*

Note 195. Jesus spoke the parable of The Pounds to warn the disciples and others who expected Him to set up the visible Kingdom upon His arrival in Jerusalem, or at least some time during the coming Passover week (vs. 11). He sought to get it over to them that He must go away and return before the visible Kingdom could be set up. And He endeavored to impress that, while He is away, He was leaving a task for them to perform; and they (and all His followers) are to be rewarded according to their faithfulness in that task. We know that the task was, and is, to proclaim the gospel and thus to spread the spiritual Kingdom.

Some students of the New Testament have suggested that this parable was based on experience and actions of Archelaus (cf. Matt. 2:22, #14), who was named by Herod the Great in his will to succeed him as king of Judaea. It was necessary for Archelaus to go to Rome because his father's will was subject to confirmation or annulment by the Roman senate.* Some of his experiences may be reflected in the details of this parable, but history does not relate that he committed any money to his servants as capital with which to trade in his absence.

Do not confuse the parable of The Pounds with the parable of The Talents, which was spoken on the Mount of Olives not many days later (cf. #222).

*George R. Bliss, *Commentary on the Gospel of Luke* in *The American Commentary on the New Testament,* ed., Alvah Hovey (Philadelphia: American Baptist Publications Society, 1884), p. 279. Bruce, *The Synoptic Gospels in The Expositor's Greek Testament,* Vol. I, p. 605. Josephus, *Antiquities of the Jews,* XVII. ix. 1.

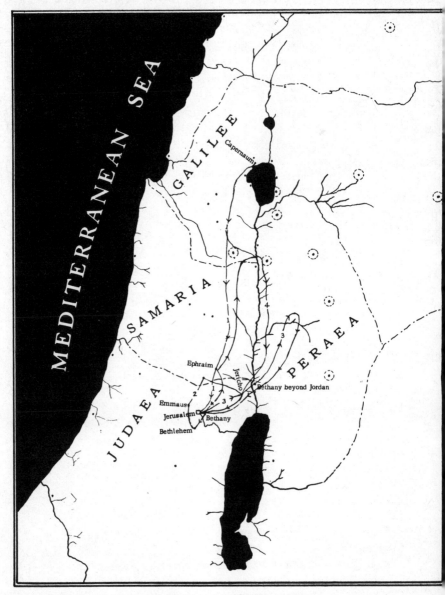

JOURNEYS OF JESUS IN THE FIFTH PERIOD
1 - From Capernaum to Jerusalem for the Feast of Tabernacles (#142).   2 - Tour of Judaea, beginning and endin
at Jerusalem—Feast of Dedication (##151—161).   3 - Journeys in Peraea and return to Bethany or raising c
Lazarus (##166—178).   4 - Circuit through Samaria, the border of Galilee, Peraea, and back to Bethany (##180—194
        (⊙ City of the Decapolis League)

A PREVIEW OUTLINE OF PERIOD SIX (Abbreviated), ##195-255

. Friday of week before—arrival of Jesus at Bethany, #195
I. Saturday—two incidents: (1) supper at Bethany and anointing of Jesus by Mary, (2) plot against Lazarus, ##196-197
II. Sunday—three incidents: (1) Triumphant Entry into Jerusalem, (2) request of Greeks to see Him, (3) return to Bethany, ## 198-200
V. Monday—four incidents: (1) curse on the barren fig tree, (2) the (second) cleansing of the temple (3) healing and teaching in the temple, (4) return to Bethany, ##201-204
. Tuesday—seven incidents: (1) lessons from the withered fig tree, (2) challenge of Jesus' authority and His (four) replies, (3) contest of questions (four questions), (4) last public words of Jesus (5) commendation of widow's gift to the temple, (6) The Great Prophecy concerning destruction of temple and His coming again, (7) plot of Judas with Sanhedrin leaders, ##205-227
I. Wednesday: No record
II. Thursday
   1. Observance of Passover—four incidents: (1) preparation by Peter and John, (2) arrival at upper room, (3) lessons in humility, (4) Judas' plot and that one's departure, ##228-231
   2. Last words of Jesus with the disciples before His death (four incidents: (1) institution of Memorial Supper, (2) prediction of Peter's denials, (3) discourses of comfort, (4) intercessory prayer), ##232-237
   3. Arrival at the Garden of Gethsemane, 238
III. Friday: ##239-254
   1. Betrayal, arrest, Peter's effort at defense, #239
   2. "Trials," ##240-247
     (1) Three Jewish: before Annas, before Caiaphas and a select few, before assembled Sanhedrin (also denials of Peter and suicide of Judas), ##240-244
     (2) Three Roman: before Pilate, before Herod, before Pilate again, imposing death sentence, ##245-247
   3. Crucifixion, ##248-253
     (1) Preliminary tortures, #248
     (2) Journey to Golgotha, comforting friends, #249
     (3) Arrival and attendant events, #250
     (4) Jesus on the cross, #251-252
       a. Hours of physical suffering (three sayings), #251
       b. Hours of darkness and of spiritual anguish added to physical sufferings (four sayings), #252
       c. Some things occurring in connection with the death of Jesus, #253
   4. Entombment of Jesus, #254
X. Saturday: A guard stationed at the tomb, #255

Ministry of the Last Week and the Cross

(## 195—254)

Note 196. Any study of the life of the Lord Jesus that neglects to take into account the primary purpose of His coming to live on earth misses the mark altogether. And He had a purpose in His earthly living, which purpose was evidently in His own consciousness from the time of His baptism to the end. As the second Person of the Godhead He had lived from eternity past, but He chose to be born and live a human life, in order that He might "give His life as a ransom" for sinners. Because of its very nature, He could not at first disclose this purpose even to His closest friends or most ardent admirers; and to the end, He made it known only to a small group, the twelve and possibly a few others; and these did not take seriously His prediction of a tragic and sacrificial death.

We have noticed the rising tide of enmity against Him. It began at the first Passover after His baptism, when He drove the licensed traders and money changers from the courts of the temple (#25). Two things about this enmity are noticeable: (1) It always erupted afresh whenever He visited Jerusalem (cf. John 5: 16, 18, #47, 48; 7: 42, #145; 8: 59, #147; 10: 31, 39, #165; 11: 53, #179), and (2) the scribes from Jerusalem frequently stirred it up outside of Judaea. (cf. Luke 5: 17, #44; Mark 3: 22, #87; Matt. 15: 1 and Mark 7: 1, #123). Although not all the opposition to Him came from Jerusalem and Judaea, that city and section were the center of the most active and most bitter agitation against Him.

In the period before us we shall see Him come to Jerusalem for the fourth Passover of His ministry, with the full consciousness that during this Passover season His enemies would take Him, subject Him to a mock trial, deliver Him to the Romans, and press for a sentence of death. We shall see the seeming triumph of the forces of evil as His lifeless body hung limp on the cross. But in it all we shall see the unconquerable, self-sacrificing spirit of our Lord; and then we shall see Him in glorious victory over the powers of death and wickedness.

I have followed the common custom of outlining the activities of this last week in Bethany and Jerusalem, commonly called Passion week by days, following the modern weekly calendar.

I. Friday (a week before Passover day) arrival at Bethany, near Jerusalem, where He spent some of the nights of this week
#195

JOHN 11:55 — 12:1

55 Now the passover of the Jews was at hand: and many went up to Jerusalem out of the country before the passover, to purify themselves. 56 They sought therefore for Jesus, and spake one with another, as they stood in the temple, What think ye? That he will not come ot the feast? 57 Now the chief priests and the Pharisees had given commandment, that, if any man knew where he was, he should show it, that they might take him.

1 Jesus therefore six days before the passover came to Bethany, where Lazarus was, whom Jesus raised from the dead.

Note 197. Two circumstances likely led to the questioning among the early-comers to the Passover about whether or not Jesus would come to the feast: (1) Although He did not attend the Passover the previous year, He had been a conspicuous figure at two more recent feasts, Tabernacles and Dedication (##145, 163ff); and they probably reasoned that, since He had begun to attend feasts, He would surely attend the Passover. (2) Notwithstanding the truth which Jesus sought to impress in the parable of The Pounds (#194 and Note 195), many still expected the visible Kingdom to be set up and proclaimed at this Passover. They must have reasoned that, if Jesus did come to this feast, the controversy between Him and the temple authorities would surely come to a crisis. Had there not been an effort to stone Him to death at each of those recent feasts which He had attended? And after the miracle of raising Lazarus from the dead, had not Caiaphas decreed that it was "expedient," therefore necessary, for Jesus to die? Doubtless they reasoned—and rightly so—that things could not go on much longer as they were.

We are tempted to laugh at the instructions of the Sanhedrin group as related in verse 57. Jesus Himself came to the feast early by six days. On the first day after the Sabbath He made an appearance in that city, not furtively or secretly, but publicly in a triumphant entry both into the city and into the temple. The next day He boldly entered the temple and repeated the cleansing of the house of God, an act which three years before had so furiously enraged the temple authorities. And the third day He spent in a contest of questions and answers with these priests and Pharisees; and having bested them at their own game, He delivered in an outburst of oratory, a scathing denunciation against them. No one had to point Him out to them; they had plenty of opportunities to take Him, but they did not until He was ready for them to do so.

II. Saturday, ##196—197
1. Jesus and His disciples and His friends likely observed the Sabbath until sunset, though this fact is not mentioned in the Gospels

243

2. The supper at Bethany in the home of Simon the leper, annointed by Mary of Bethany

#196

MATT. 26:6-13

6 Now when Jesus was in Bethany, in the house of Simon the leper, 7 there came unto him a woman having ¹an alabaster cruse of exceeding precious ointment, and she poured it upon his head, as ²he sat at meat. 8 But when the disciples saw it, they had indignation, saying, To what purpose is this waste? 9 For this *ointment* might have been sold for much, and given to the poor.

10 But Jesus perceiving it said unto them, Why trouble ye the woman? for she hath wrought a good work upon me. 11 For ye have the poor always with you; but me ye have not always. 12 For in that she ³poured this ointment upon my body, she did it to prepare me for burial. 13 Verily I say unto you, Wheresoever ⁴this gospel shall be preached in the whole world, that also which this woman hath done shall be spoken of for a memorial of her.

¹ Or, *a flask*
² Or, *reclined at table*
³ Gr. *cast*.
⁴ Or, *these good tidings*

MARK 14:3-9

3 And while he was in Bethany in the house of Simon the leper, as he sat at meat, there came a woman having ¹an alabaster cruse of ointment of ²pure nard very costly; *and* she brake the cruse, and poured it over his head. 4 But there were some that had indignation among themselves, *saying*, To what purpose hath this waste of the ointment been made? 5 For this ointment might have been sold for above three hundred ³shillings, and given to the poor. And they murmured against her. 6 But Jesus said, Let her alone; why trouble ye her? she hath wrought a good work on me. 7 For ye have the poor always with you, and whensoever ye will ye can do them good: but me ye have not always. 8 She hath done what she could; she hath anointed my body beforehand for the burying. 9 And verily I say unto you, Wheresoever the ⁴gospel shall be preached throughout the whole world, that also which this woman hath done shall be spoken of for a memorial of her.

¹ Or, *a flask*   ² Or, *liquid nard*
³ See marginal note on ch. 6. 37.
⁴ See marginal note on ch. 1. 1.

JOHN 12:2-8

2 So they made him a supper there: and Martha served; but Lazarus was one of them that ¹sat at meat with him. 3 Mary therefore took a pound of ointment of ²pure nard, very precious, and anointed the feet of Jesus, and wiped his feet with her hair: and the house was filled with the odor of the ointment. 4 But Judas Iscariot, one of his disciples, that should ³betray him, saith, 5 Why was not this ointment sold for three hundred ⁴shillings, and given to the poor? 6 Now this he said, not because he cared for the poor; but because he was a thief, and having the ⁵bag ⁶took away what was put therein. 7 Jesus therefore said, ⁷Suffer her to keep it against the day of my burying 8 For the poor ye have always with you; but me ye have not always.

¹ Gr. *reclined*. ² Or, *liquid nard*
³ Or, *deliver him up*
⁴ See marginal note on ch. 6. 7.
⁵ Or, *box*
⁶ Or, *carried what was put therei*
⁷ Or, *Let her alone: it was tha she might keep it*

Note 198. It should be observed that in Matthew and Mark the accounts of the supper at Bethany and the anointing of Jesus are found after the accounts of the events on Tuesday. Probably for that reason, this incident is placed on Tuesday night in Broadus' and Robertson's harmonies of the Gospels.* But it should be noticed that both of these Gospel records simply state that this event occurred while He was at Bethany. But in John it is related that the triumphant entry into Jerusalem, which undoubtedly took place on Sunday, .was "on the morrow" after the supper (John 12: 12, #198). I conclude, therefore, that this

*Broadus, *Harmony of the Gospels*, p. 170. Robertson, *A Harmony of the Gospels*, p. 187. On the other hand William Arnold Stevens and Ernest DeWit Burton, *A Harmony of the Gospels for Historical Study* (New York: Charles Scribner' Sons, 1932), pp. 166ff., place this incident before the Triumphant Entry.

supper was given for Jesus on Saturday after sunset; that is, after the close of the Sabbath. It would be natural for this family—Martha, Mary, and Lazarus, on whom Jesus had bestowed so great a blessing—to want to show its appreciation as early as possible after his return to their village.

It is observed that Luke did not give an account of this supper, but he (and he alone) gave an account of a previous anointing of our Lord by a woman in the home of a Pharisee in Galilee (Luke 7: 36—50, #84). The two incidents should not be confused. The time, the place, the personnel, and the attendant circumstances are all different. Notice that at this supper the sisters are shown in their true light—Martha still careful about the serving, and Mary, who had loved to sit at Jesus' feet, impulsively pouring out a heart of love in the sacrifice of the alabaster box and its costly contents.

Doubtless Judas was so stung by the rebuke from Jesus that his decision to sell out to the Sanhedrin group was reached at that time or soon afterward. This was probably the reason why the account of this incident is found in Matthew and Mark just before that of his agreement with the chief priests.

3. Plot of the Sanhedrin leaders to destroy Lazarus that the people might not believe on Jesus
#197
JOHN 12:9-11

9 The common people therefore of the Jews learned that he was there: and they came, not for Jesus' sake only, but that they might see Lazarus also, whom he had raised from the dead. 10 But the chief priests took counsel that they might put Lazarus also to death; 11 because that by reason of him many of the Jews went away, and believed on Jesus.

Note 199. The insane jealousy of the Sanhedrin group—chief priests—is evidenced by their plan to have Lazarus put to death, and that for no crime whatever except that of being alive after he had died, and thus being a living testimony to the power of Jesus. We wonder how much good it would have done to kill Lazarus; he had been dead once, and Jesus had brought him back to life; could He have not done so again? And they were to learn that it did not help their cause to put Jesus to death either; for He came back to life also.

III. Sunday, ##198—200
1. Triumphant Entry into Jerusalem
#198

MATT. 21:1-11	MARK 11:1-11a	LUKE 19:29-44	JOHN 12:12-19
1 And when they drew nigh unto Jerusalem, and came unto Bethphage, unto the mount of Olives, then Jesus sent two disciples, 2 saying unto them,	1 And when they draw nigh unto Jerusalem, unto Bethphage and Bethany, at the mount of Olives, he sendeth two of his disciples, 2 and saith unto	29 And it came to pass, when he drew nigh unto Bethphage and Bethany, at the mount that is called Olivet, he sent two of the disciples, 30 saying, Go your way	12 On the morrow ¹a great multitude that had come to the feast, when they heard that Jesus was coming to Jerusalem, ¹ Some ancient authorities read *the common people*. See ver. 9.

245

Matt. 21   Mark 11   Luke 19   John 12

Go into the village that is over against you, and straightway ye shall find an ass tied, and a colt with her: loose *them*, and bring *them* unto me. 3 And if any one say aught unto you, ye shall say, The Lord hath need of them; and straightway he will send them. 4 Now this is come to pass, that it might be fulfilled which was spoken through the prophet, saying, 5. [1]Tell ye the daughter of Zion,

Behold, thy King cometh unto thee,

Meek, and riding upon an ass,

And upon a colt the foal of an ass.

6 And the disciples went, and did even as Jesus appointed them, 7 and brought the ass, and the colt, and put on them their garments; and he sat thereon. 8 And the most part of the multitude spread their garments in the way; and others cut branches from the trees, and spread them in the way. 9 And the multitudes that went before him, and that followed, cried, saying, Hosanna to the son of David: Blessed *is* he that cometh in the name of the Lord; Hosanna in the highest.

them, Go your way into the village that is over against you: and straightway as ye enter into it, ye shall find a colt tied, whereon no man ever yet sat; loose him, and bring him. 3 And if any one say unto you, Why do ye this? say ye, The Lord hath need of him; and straightway he [1]will send him [2]back hither. 4 And they went away, and found a colt tied at the door without in the open street; and they loose him. 5 And certain of them that stood there said unto them, What do ye, loosing the colt? 6 And they said unto them even as Jesus had said: and they let them go. 7 And they bring the colt unto Jesus, and cast on him their garments; and he sat upon him. 8 And many spread their garments upon the way; and others [3]branches, which they had cut from the fields. 9 And they that went before and they that followed, cried, Hosanna; Blessed *is* he that cometh in the name of the Lord: 10 Blessed *is* the kingdom that cometh, *the kingdom* of our father David: Hosanna in the highest.

into the village over against you; in which as ye enter ye shall find a colt tied, whereon no man ever yet sat: loose him, and bring him. 31 And if any one ask you, Why do ye loose him? thus shall ye say, The Lord hath need of him. 32 And they that were sent went away, and found even as he had said unto them. 33 And as they were loosing the colt, the owners thereof said unto them, Why loose ye the colt? 34 And they said, The Lord hath need of him. 35 And they brought him to Jesus: and they threw their garments upon the colt, and set Jesus thereon. 36 And as he went, they spread their garments in the way. 37 And as he was now drawing nigh, *even* at the descent of the mount of Olives, the whole multitude of the disciples began to rejoice and praise God with a loud voice for all the [1]mighty works which they had seen; 38 saying, Blessed *is* the King that cometh in the name of the Lord: peace in heaven, and glory in the highest. 39 And some of the Pharisees from the multitude said unto him, Teacher, rebuke thy disciples. 40 And he answered and said, I tell you that, if these shall hold

13 took the branches of the palm trees, and went forth to meet him, and cried out, Hosanna: Blessed *is* he that cometh in the name of the Lord, even the King of Israel. 14 And Jesus, having found a young ass, sat thereon; as it is written, 15 [2]Fear not, daughter of Zion: behold, thy King cometh, sitting on an ass's colt. 16 These things understood not his disciples at the first: but when Jesus was glorified, then remembered they that these

---

[1] Is. lxii. 11; Zech. ix. 9.

[1] Gr. *sendeth.*
[2] Or, *again*
[3] Gr. *layers of leaves.*

[1] Gr. *powers.*

[2] Zech. ix. 9.

Matt. 21	Mark 11	Luke 19	John 12
		their peace, the stones will cry out.	things were written of him, and that they had done these things unto him. 17 The multitude therefore that was with him when he called Lazarus out of the tomb, and raised him from the dead, bare witness. 18 For this cause also the multitude went and met him, for that they heard that he had done this sign. 19 The Pharisees therefore said among themselves, ³Behold how ye prevail nothing; lo, the world is gone after him.
		41 And when he drew nigh, he saw the city and wept over it, 42 saying, ²If thou hadst known in ³this day, even thou, the things which belong unto ⁴peace! but now they are hid from thine eyes. 43 For the days shall come upon thee, when thine enemies shall cast up a ⁵bank about thee, and compass thee round, and keep thee in on every side, 44 and shall dash thee to the ground, and thy children within thee; and they shall not leave in thee one stone upon another: because thou knewest not the time of thy visitation.	
10 And when he was come into Jerusalem, all the city was stirred, saying, Who is this? 11 And the multitudes said, This is the prophet, Jesus, from Nazareth of Galilee.	11 And he entered into Jerusalem, into the temple;		

² Or, *O that thou hadst known*
³ Some ancient authorities read *this thy day.*
⁴ Some ancient authorities read *thy peace.*
⁵ Gr. *palisade.*

³ Or, *Ye behold*

Note 200. I have often wondered why Jesus permitted and even encouraged this acclamation of His kingly messiahship on the part of the people. He had refused to let the multitude make Him King after the feeding of the five thousand (cf. John 6:15, #119 and Note 120). Just a few days before this He had spoken the parable of The Pounds to correct the notion that "the Kingdom of God (in its visible manifestation) should immediately appear" (Luke 19: 11, #194). Possibly, knowing that the chief priests and Pharisees had passed out the word that, if anyone should know where He was, that one was to report it (John 11: 57), He was challenging them by entering the city and the temple as the center of a public procession. But it is noticeable that the ever-watchful Romans, who were always quick to put down any move that might threaten their rule in the provinces, did not take any notice of this Triumphant Entry into the capital city. Therefore it was clearly evident that He had no intention of setting up a new visible Kingdom at that time— even though the people acclaimed Him as "the Son of David," (Matt. vs. 9), or as "the King that cometh in the name of the Lord" (Luke vs. 38). The lamentation over Jerusalem and the prophecy of its utter destruction (Luke 19: 41—44) would certainly have been out of place in a political or military triumphant entrance into the capital city. This prophecy was to be repeated and enlarged two days later (##218-219).

2. Request of the Greeks to see Him and His response
#199
JOHN 12:20-36a

20 Now there were certain Greeks among those that went up to worship at the feast: 21 these therefore came to Philip, who was of Bethsaida of Galilee, and asked him saying, Sir, we would see Jesus. 22 Philip cometh and telleth Andrew: Andrew cometh, and Philip, and they tell Jesus. 23 And Jesus answereth them, saying, The hour is come, that the Son of man should be glorified. 24 Verily, verily, I say unto you, Except a grain of wheat fall into the earth and die, it abideth by itself alone; but if it die, it beareth much fruit. 25 He that loveth his ¹life loseth it; and he that hateth his ¹life in this world shall keep it unto ²life eternal. 26 If any man serve me, let him follow me; and where I am, there shall also my servant be: if any man serve me, him will the Father honor. 27 Now is my soul troubled; and what shall I say? Father, save me from this ³hour. But for this cause came I unto this hour. 28 Father, glorify thy name. There came therefore a voice out of heaven, saying, I have both glorified it, and will glorify it again. 29 The multitude therefore, that stood by, and heard it, said that it had thundered: others said, An angel hath spoken to him. 30 Jesus answered and said, This voice hath not come for my sake, but for your sakes. 31 Now is ⁴the judgment of this world: now shall the prince of this world be cast out. 32 And, I, if I be lifted up ⁵from the earth, will draw all men unto myself. 33 But this he said, signifying by what manner of death he should die. 34 The multitude therefore answered him, We have heard out of the law that the Christ abideth for ever: and how sayest thou, The Son of man must be lifted up? who is this Son of man? 35 Jesus therefore said unto them, Yet a little while is the light ⁶among you. Walk while ye have the light, that darkness overtake you not: and he that walketh in the darkness knoweth not whither he goeth, 36 While ye have the light, believe on the light, that ye may become sons of light.

¹ ² *life* in these places represents two different Greek words.   ³ Or, *hour?*
⁴ Or, *a judgment*   ⁵ Or, *out of*   ⁶ Or, *in*   ⁷ Or, *was hidden from them*

Note 201. To me it seems probable that the request of the Greeks to see Jesus and His response occurred on the same day with the Triumphant Entry; that is, on Sunday of the last week.* Verse 23 seems to

*Broadus, *A Harmony of the Gospels*, p. 144 and Robertson, *A Harmony of the Gospels*, pp. 157f. each has the Greeks coming on Monday. Stevens and Burton, *A Harmony of the Gospels for Historical Study*, p. 185 place this incident at the

(continued on next page)

indicate that the excitement of the public parade had not subsided. These were Greeks, not merely Grecian Jews. They were probably "proselytes of the gate," but uncircumcised nevertheless. Therefore, they could go no further in the temple than the Court of the Gentiles. Jesus had probably passed on into the Court of the Women or the Court of the Israelites (cf. Mark 11:11, #198). Therefore, the Greeks brought their request to Philip, who had a Greek name, and who may have been known personally to some of them. He lived in the same town with Andrew (John 1:44, #22), and the two may have been close friends.* Knowing that the Greeks could not go further into the temple, these disciples carried their request to Jesus, probably expecting Him to come with them back to the Court of the Gentiles to meet and talk to the Greeks, which He probably did in the end.

It was a glorious day for Jesus. Not only had many Jews in gala procession just proclaimed Him to be the "Son of David"; that is, the Messianic king, but this coming of the Greeks was doubtless prophetic of a turning to Him by the Gentiles. He saw in both these events—the Triumphant Entry and the request of the Greeks—the beginning of "the hour...when the Son of Man shall be glorified." But there is always a price of glory, which Jesus illustrated in the parable of The Grain of Wheat. This price is the same, whether for the grain of wheat, or for the Saviour of the world, or for the followers of the Saviour of the world; it is a willingness to sacrifice one's own life to the point of falling into the ground and dying.

3. Return to Bethany
#200

MARK 11:11b	JOHN 12:36b
11b and when he had looked round about upon all things, it being now eventide, he went out unto Bethany with the twelve.	36b These things spake Jesus, and he departed and ¹hid himself from them. ¹ Or, *was hidden from them*

Note 202. Jesus had arrived in Bethany on Friday, six days before the Passover (John 12:1, #195). He spent Friday night, Saturday night, Sunday night, and Monday night (Matt. 21:17, #200) in that village, probably in the home of Martha and Mary and Lazarus. But surely not all the disciples shared with Him the hospitality of the sisters. That would have been a burden which Jesus certainly would not have imposed on them. We know that John had lodging quarters in the city or somewhere in the vicinity, which he doubtless shared with his mother Salome, and Mary the mother of Jesus, who was probably a sister to Salome (cf. John 19:25, 27, #251 and Note 255). The other disciples possibly had their lodging places, or they may have begun to

(continued from preceding page)
close of His activities in the temple on Tuesday; Hovey, *Commentary on John*, p. 252 and Westcott, *The Gospel According to St. John*, p. 180 also understood it to have occurred as late as Tuesday.

*They are mentioned together in connection with three incidents, in ##22, 118, and this one.

249

spend the nights at their regular place on the Mount of Olives (cf. Note 147).

IV. Monday, ##201—204
1. The barren fig tree
#201

MATT. 21:18-19a	MARK 11:12-14
18 Now in the morning as he returned to the city, he hungered. 19a And seeing ¹a fig tree by the way side, he came to it, and found nothing thereon, but leaves only; and he saith untó it, Let there be no fruit from thee henceforward for ever. ¹ Or, *a single*	12 And· on the morrow, when they were come out from Bethany, he hungered. 13 And seeing a fig tree afar off having leaves, he came, if haply he might find anything thereon: and when he came to it, he found nothing but leaves; for it was not the season of figs. 14 And he answered and said unto it, No man eat fruit from thee henceforward for ever. And his disciples heard it.

Note 203.   In Matthew the account of Jesus and the barren fig tree reads as though the entire incident occurred on Tuesday, and as though the withering was noticeable from the time when Jesus pronounced on it the curse of perpetual fruitlessness.   Indeed the account i n Matthew reads as though the cleansing of the temple occurred on the day of the Triumphant Entry, without an intervening night and a trip to Bethany and return to Jerusalem.   Mark is more specific in relating the return t o Bethany after the Triumphant Entry, indicating that the first part of the fig tree incident and the cleansing of the temple occurred the next day (Monday).   We doubtless do well to follow Mark's order and to understand Matthew to mean (vs. 19b, #205) that immediately the fig tree was caused to begin to wither away.

I have often wondered why the Lord Jesus pronounced this curse on the fig tree, especially since "it was not the season of figs" (vs. 13 of Mark).   We are told* that in Palestine the trees of certain varieties of figs which are going to bear a crop of fruit will put on early small figs along with the leaves, not many of which will grow to maturity.   But the immature fruit is often eaten by the natives as it falls from the tree. Doubtless it was with this fruit that our Lord sought to satisfy His hunger.   But since He found nothing on this tree but leaves, it was evident that it would not bear fruit at all, at least not that year.   This incident has been spoken of as a parable in action.   Whether Jesus meant it as such or not, it is a forcible illustration of the end which did come to the Sanhedrin and the priesthood, the Pharisaic and the Sadducaic elements of Judaism.

2. The second cleansing of the temple and the reaction of the Sanhedrin leaders
#202

MATT. 21:12-13	MARK 11:15-18	LUKE 19:45-48
12 And Jesus entered	15 And they come to	45 And he entered into

*Masterman, E. W. G., "Fig, Fig Tree," in *International Standard Bible Encyclopedia*, Vol. II, pp. 1108f.

Matt. 21	Mark 11	Luke 19
into the temple [1]of God, and cast out all them that sold and bought in the temple, and overthrew the tables of the .m o n e y-changers, and the seats of them that sold the doves;	Jerusalem: and he entered into the temple, and began to cast out them. that sold and them that bought in the temple, and overthrew the tables of the money-changers, and the seats of them that sold the doves; 16 and he would not suffer that any man should carry a vessel through the temple.	the temple, and began to cast out them that sold,
13 and he saith unto them, It is written, [2]My house shall be called a house of prayer: [3]but ye make it a den of robbers.	17 And he taught, and said unto them, Is it not written, [1]My house shall be called a house of prayer for all the nations? [2]but ye have made it a den of robbers. 18 And the chief priests and the scribes heard it, and sought how they might destroy him: for they feared him, for all the multitude was astonished at his teaching.	46 saying unto them, It is written, [1]And my house shall be a house of prayer: but [2]ye have made it a den of robbers. 47 And he was teaching daily in the temple. But the chief priests and the scribes and the principal men of the people sought to destroy him: 48 and they could not find what they might do; for the people all hung upon him, listening.
[1] Many ancient authorities omit *of God.* [2] Is. lvi. 7. [3] Jer. vii. 11.	[1] Is. lvi. 7. [2] Jer. vii. 11.	[1] Is. lvi. 7. [2] Jer. vii. 11.

Note 204. In John 2: 13—22 (#25) is the record of a cleansing of the temple which Jesus made during the first Passover of His ministry, three years earlier. Early in His messianic labors our Lord set about to correct the extortionate practices permitted and abetted by the temple authorities, who doubtless shared in the profits of this traffic (cf. Note 28). Since Jesus did not attend the Passover next preceding this one (cf. Note 124), and because their hatred of Him had burned to the point of utterly disregarding His drastic action of three years before, they were emboldened to establish again the traffic in sacrificial animals and in the Jewish coins for the temple tax. He probably observed that provision was made for the unholy traffic when He was in the temple on the preceding day (Sunday), and on His arrival Monday He vigorously repeated His action of the former occasion.

The effect of the two cleansings was the same. The first one made the Jerusalem scribes His unrelenting enemies, so that on His every visit to that city afterward they stirred up a controversy with Him. This second act of interference with the traffic which they had established—or at least permitted—intensified their determination to put Him to death at their first opportunity.

3. Healing and Teaching in the Temple
#203
MATT. 21:14-16

14 And the blind and the lame came to him in the temple; and he healed them. 15 But when the chief priests and the scribes saw the wonderful things that he did, and the children that were crying in the temple and saying, Hosanna to the son of

David; they were moved with indignation„ 16 and said unto him, Hearest thou what these are saying? And Jesus saith unto them, Yea: did ye never read, [1]Out of the mouth of babes and sucklings thou hast perfected praise?

[1] Ps. viii. 2.

Note 205. These were probably the last miracles of healing which Jesus performed, except at the time of His arrest, the healing of the high priest's servant's ear, which Peter had cut off (Luke 22:51, #239). They were also, so far as is recorded, the only ones performed in the temple.

The shouts of praise by the children in the temple were doubtless echoes of the words of the people during the Triumphant Entry the day before, but they may have been inspired also by the show of authority and power on Jesus' part in driving from the temple those who were desecrating its courts. Those priests and scribes, already angered by the cleansing of the temple, were completely frustrated at the sight of the miracles and were all the more enraged by the shouting of the youngsters. Their futile appeal to Jesus was a repetition of the request which some of them made the day before (cf. Luke 19:39—40, #198). The quotation in the reply of Jesus is from Psalm 8:2.

4. Return to Bethany
#204

MATT. 21:17	MARK 11:19
17 And he left them, and went forth out of the city to Bethany, and lodged there.	19 And every [1]evening [2]he went forth out of the city.
	[1] Gr. whenever evening came.
	[2] Some ancient authorities read they.

V. Tuesday, ##205—227

Note 206. This was the last day of our Lord's public ministry; and it was one of the busiest and most strenuous days of His entire life, including all the things related in ##205—227.* Before departing from Bethany that morning He probably bespoke His appreciation of His friends' hospitality and signified His intention to spend the remaining nights of the week with the disciples in the open at their favorite spot on the Mount of Olives.

1. The barren fig tree observed to be withered, a lesson on prayer
#205

MATT. 21:19b-23	MARK 11:20-26
19b And immediately the fig tree withered away. 20 And when the disciples saw it, they marvelled, saying, How did the fig tree immediately wither away? 21 And Jesus answered and said unto them, Verily I say unto you, If ye have faith, and doubt not, ye shall not only do what is done to the fig tree, but even if ye shall say unto this mountain, Be thou taken up and cast into the sea,	20 And as they passed by in the morning, they saw the fig tree withered away from the roots. 21 And Peter calling to remembrance saith unto him, Rabbi, behold, the fig tree which thou cursedst is withered away. 22 And Jesus answering saith unto them, Have faith in God. 23 Verily I say unto you, Whosoever shall say unto this mountain, Be thou taken up and cast into the sea; and

*The "day of parables by the sea side" was also a "busy day," recorded in #86—103.

252

Matt. 21

Mark 11

it shall be done. 22 And all things, whatsoever ye shall ask in prayer, believing, ye shall receive.

shall not doubt in his heart, but shall believe that what he saith cometh to pass; he shall have it. 24 Therefore I say unto you, All things whatsoever ye pray and ask for, believe that ye [1]receive them, and ye shall have them. 25 And whensoever ye stand praying, forgive, if ye have aught against any one; that your Father also who is in heaven may forgive you your trespasses.[2]

[1] Gr. *received.*

[2] Many ancient authorities add ver. 26 *But if ye do not forgive, neither will your Father who is in heaven forgive your trespasses.* Comp. Mt. 6. 15; 18. 35.

Note 207. Whether the incident of the barren fig tree was intended to be a "parable in action" or not (cf. Note 203), it was certainly the occasion of impressing on the disciples some important lessons concerning faith and prayer. This was the third time that Jesus spoke of removing obstacles—a mountain or a sycamine tree—through faith in God (cf. ##135, 177). Such faith in the power of God, and in His wisdom as well, ought to prompt the prayers of a Christian. Mark alone relates in this connection His words about willingness to forgive and its bearing on the effectiveness of prayer. We cannot know whether this reflects a continued strife among the disciples, or whether it implied an injunction for them to forgive even those who were doing, and were yet to do, so great wrongs to Him (cf. Luke 23:34, #251; Acts 3:17f).

2. The challenge of His authority and His replies, ##206—209

(1) The challenge issued

#206

MATT. 21:23

23 And when he was come into the temple, the chief priests and the elders of the people came unto him as he was teaching, and said, By what authority doest thou these things? and who gave thee this authority?

MARK 11:27-28

27 And they come again to Jerusalem: and as he was walking in the temple, there come to him the chief priests, and the scribes, and the elders; 28 and they said unto him, By what authority doest thou these things? or who gave thee this authority to do these things?

LUKE 20:1-2

1 And it came to pass, on one of the days, as he was teaching the people in the temple, and preaching the [1]gospel, there came upon him the chief priests and the scribes with the elders; 2 and they spake, saying unto him, Tell us: By what authority doest thou these things? or who is he that gave thee this authority?

[1] Or, *good tidings:* comp. ch. 3. 18.

Note 208. After Jesus so high-handedly cleansed the temple court on the day before, the Sanhedrin leaders were more determined than ever to get Him out of the way. But they dared not move against Him directly because of His great influence with the people, which was demonstrated by the enthusiasm with which they accompanied Him with shouts and applause into the city in the triumphant entry (cf. Mark 11:9f and Luke 19: 47--48, #202; John 12: 19, #198). So they set about to discredit Him with the people. Accordingly, a deputation from their number met Him to challenge His authority when He arrived in the temple. "These things" of their question doubtless included (1) teaching the people publicly, (2) permitting a throng of the people to escort Him into the city and temple two days before in a triumphant—even a royal—ovation, acclaiming Him the "Son of David," and (3) presuming to drive from the temple the dealers in sacrificial animals and the money changers who surely had been licensed by the temple authorities. Jesus spent most of this busy day in controversy with these leaders of the Sanhedrin; and in the end, without doubt, He stood higher with the people than at the beginning.

(2) The first answer, a counter question (observe their dilema)

#207

MATT. 21:24-27	MARK 11:29-33	LUKE 20:3-8
24 And Jesus answered and said unto them, I also will ask you one ¹question, which if ye tell me, I likewise will tell you by what authority I do these things. 25 The baptism of John, whence was it? from heaven or from men? And they reasoned with themselves, saying, If we shall say, From heaven; he will say unto us, Why then did ye not believe him? 26 But if we shall say, From men; we fear the multitude; for all hold John as a prophet. 27 And they answered Jesus, and said, We know not. He also said unto them, Neither tell I you by what authority I do these things. ¹ Gr. *word.*	29 And Jesus said unto them, I will ask of you one ¹question, and answer me, and I will tell you by what authority I do these things. 30 The baptism of John, was it from heaven, or from men? answer me. 31 And they reasoned with themselves, saying, If we shall say, From heaven; he will say, Why then did ye not believe him? 32 ²But should we say, From men—they feared the people: ³for all verily held John to be a prophet. 33 And they answered Jesus and say, We know not. And Jesus saith unto them, Neither tell I you by what authority I do these things. ¹ Gr. *word.* ² Or, *But shall we say, From men?* ³ Or, *for all held John to be a prophet indeed*	3 And he answered and said unto them, I also will ask you a ¹question; and tell me: 4 The baptism of John, was it from heaven, or from men? 5 And they reasoned with themselves, saying, If we shall say, From heaven; he will say, Why did ye not believe him? 6 But if we shall say, from men; all the people will stone us: for they are persuaded that John was a prophet. 7 And they answered, that they knew not whence *it was.* 8 And Jesus said unto them, Neither tell I you by what authority I do these things. ¹ Gr. *word.*

Note 209. The authority of Jesus to do what He was doing did not depend on the authority of John the Baptist, although John had definitely and repeatedly borne testimony to Jesus (cf. Matt. 3: 11 and parallels, #17, also John 1: 30ff, #21). But because of this testimony, if these priests and elders had been able or willing to answer Jesus' question to them, they would have had the answer to their own question. Notice the dilemma in which He had them; that is, their inability to give either possible answer to His question without embarassing themselves before the very ones with whom they were trying to discredit Him.

(3) The second answer, the parable of The Two Sons
#208
MATT. 21:28-32

28 But what think ye? A man had two [1]sons; and he came to the first, and said, [2]Son, go work today in the vineyard. 29 And he answered and said, I will not: but afterward he repented himself, and went. 30 And he came' to the second, and said likewise. And he answered and said, I go, sir: and went not. 31 Which of the two did the will of his father? They say, The first. Jesus saith unto them, Verily I say unto you, that the [3]publicans and the harlots go into the kingdom of God before you. 32 For John came unto you in the way of righteousness, and ye believed him not; but the [3]publicans and the harlots believed him: and ye, when ye saw it, did not even repent yourselves afterward, that ye might believe him.

[1] Gr. *children*   [2] Gr. *Child.*   [3] See marginal note on ch. 5. 46.

Note 210. Since the antagonists of Jesus had made themselves the judges of His authority, He proceeded to show in three parables how they, as representatives and leaders of God's covenant race and nation, were utterly failing in their mission. The two sons in the parable above most probably represent the different elements within the Jewish race— the common people, including the publicans and the sinners, as contrasted with the scribes and Pharisees and the leaders of the Sanhedrin, as is evidenced by the groups mentioned in verse 32.

(4) The third answer, the parable of The Wicked Husbandmen
#209

MATT. 21:33-46	MARK 12:1-12	LUKE 20:9-19
33 Hear another parable: There was a man that was a householder, who planted a vineyard, and set a hedge about it, and digged a winepress in it, and built a tower, and let it out to husbandmen, and went into another country. 34 And when the season of the fruits drew near, he sent his [1]servants to the husbandmen, to receive [2]his fruits. 35 And the husbandmen took his [1]servants, and beat one, and killed another, and stoned another. 36 Again, he sent other [1]servants more than the first: and they did unto them in like manner. 37 But afterward he sent unto them his son, saying, They will reverence my son. 38 But the husbandmen, when they saw the son, said among themselves, This is the heir; come, let us kill him, and take his inheritance.	1 And he began to speak unto them in parables. A man planted a vineyard, and set a hedge about it, and digged a pit for the winepress, and built a tower, and let it out to husbandmen, and went into another country. 2 And at the season he sent to the husbandmen a [1]servant, that he might receive from the husbandmen of the fruits of the vineyard. 3 And they took him, and beat him, and sent him away empty. 4 And again he sent unto them another [1]servant; and him they wounded in the head, and handled shamefully. 5 And he sent another; and him they killed: and many others; beating some, and killing some. 6 He had yet one, a beloved son: he sent him last unto them, saying, They will reverence my son. 7 But those husbandmen said among themselves, This is the heir; come, let us kill him, and the inheritance shall be	9 And he began to speak unto the people this parable: A man planted a vineyard, and let it out to husbandmen, and went into another country for a long time. 10 And at the season he sent unto the husbandmen a [1]servant, that they should give him of the fruit of the vineyard: but the husbandmen beat him, and sent him away empty. 11 And he sent yet another [1]servant: and him also they beat, and handled him shamefully, and sent him away empty. 12 And he sent yet a third: and him also they wounded, and cast him forth. 13 And the lord of the vineyard said, What shall I do? I will send my beloved son; it may be they will reverence him. 14 But when the husbandmen saw him, they reasoned one with another, saying, This is the heir; let us kill him, that the inheritance may be ours.
[1] Gr. *bondservants.* [2] Or, *the fruits of it*	[1] Gr. *bondservant.*	[1] Gr. *bondservant.*

Matt. 21   Mark 12   Luke 20

39 And they took him, and cast him forth out of the vineyard, and killed him. 40 When therefore the lord of the vineyard shall come, what will he do unto those husbandmen? 41 They say unto him, He will miserably destroy those miserable men, and will let out the vineyard unto other husbandmen, who shall render him the fruits in their seasons. 42 Jesus saith unto them, Did ye never read in the scriptures:

[3]The stone which the
   builders rejected,
The same was made the
   head of the corner;
This was from the Lord,
And it is marvellous in
our eyes? 43 Therefore say I unto you, The kingdom of God shall be taken away from you, and shall be given to a nation bringing forth the fruits thereof. 44 [4]And he that falleth on this stone shall be broken to pieces: but on whomsoever it shall fall, it will scatter him as dust. 45 And when the chief priests and the Pharisees heard his parables, they perceived that he spake of them. 46 And when they sought to lay hold on him, they feared the multitudes, because they took him for a prophet.

[3] Ps. cxviii. 22 f.
[4] Some ancient authorities omit ver. 44.

ours. 8 And they took him, and killed, and cast him forth out of the vineyard. 9 What therefore will the lord of the vineyard do? he will come and destroy the husbandmen, and will give the vineyard unto others. 10 Have ye not read even this scripture:

[2]The stone which the
   builders rejected,
The same was made the
   head of the corner;
11 This was from the Lord,
And it is marvellous in
   our eyes?
12 And they sought to lay hold on him; and they feared the multitude; for they perceived that he spake the parable against them: and they left him, and went away.

[2] Ps. cxviii. 22 f.

15 And they cast him forth out of the vineyard, and killed him. What therefore will the lord of the vineyard do unto them? 16 He will come and destroy these husbandmen, and will give the vineyard unto others. And when they heard it, they said, [2]God forbid. 17 But he looked upon them, and said, What then is this that is written,

[3]The stone which the
   builders rejected,
The same was made the
   head of the corner?
18 Every one that falleth on that stone shall be broken to pieces; but on whomsoever it shall fall, it will scatter him as dust.

19 And the scribes and the chief priests sought to lay hands on him in that very hour; and they feared the people: for they perceived that he spake this parable against them.

[2] Gr. Be it not so. [3] Ps. cxviii. 22.

Note 211. In the parable of The Wicked Husbandmen Jesus denounced these Sanhedrin leaders for using their opportunity for world religious leadership to enrich and glorify themselves. In consequence, they were rejecting the Messiah who had long been promised them in their Scriptures. And He foretold that in time this distinction and responsibility will be taken from them and from the Jewish people and will be given to others. So it has been through the centuries since their day that the knowledge and worship of the one true God, which until that time had been the practice of the Israelitish, or Jewish, people, have been proclaimed and propagated by Gentile Christians.

(5) The fourth answer, the parable of The Marriage Feast of the King's Son

#210

1 And Jesus answered and spake again in parables unto them, saying, 2 The kingdom of heaven is likened unto a certain king, who made a marriage feast for his son, 3 and sent forth his [1]servants to call them that were bidden to the marriage feast: and they would not come. 4 Again he sent forth other [1]servants, saying, Tell them that are bidden, Behold, I have made ready my dinner; my oxen and my fatlings are killed, and all things are ready: come to the marriage feast. 5 But they made light of it, and went their ways, one to his own farm, another to his merchandise; 6 and the rest laid hold on his [1]servants, and treated them shamefully, and killed them. 7 But the king was wroth; and he sent his armies, and destroyed those murderers, and burned their city. 8 Then saith he to his [1]servants, The wedding is ready, but they that were bidden were not worthy. 9 Go ye therefore unto the partings of the highways, and as many as ye shall find, bid to the marriage feast. 10 And those [1]servants went out into the highways, and gathered together all as many as they found, both bad and good: and the wedding was filled with guests. 11 But when the king came in to behold the guests, he saw there a man who had not on a wedding-garment: 12 and he saith unto him, Friend, how camest thou in hither not having a wedding-garment? And he was speechless. 13 Then the king said to the [2]servants, Bind him hand and foot, and cast him out into the outer darkness; there shall be the weeping and the gnashing of teeth. 14 For many are called, but few chosen.

[1] Gr. bondservants.   [2] Or, ministers

Note 212. We must not confuse the parable of the Marriage Feast of the King's Son with the parable of The Great Supper, which was spoken several weeks earlier, while Jesus was dining with a Pharisee (Luke 14: 16—24, #169). That parable illustrates the folly of anyone who discounts the invitation to participate in the blessings of the Kingdom (to "eat bread in the Kingdom of God"); but this one was spoken to illustrate the wickedness of the Jewish people—particularly the Sanhedrin group—in rejecting Him, and the plight which would overtake them. As the peculiar objects of God's love and care and the recipients of His special revelations, they were given first the offer of salvation and the first opportunity to become heralds of the Kingdom. But they were declining these privileges with scorn, and in the years ahead they were going to scorn them more. For this shameful action their city was destined to be destroyed, and they were to be scattered and persecuted.

But this is a double parable. Verses 11—14 were doubtless spoken for the benefit of a different group from those to whom verses 1—10 were addressed. Listening to Jesus as He replied to the challenge from these Sanhedrin leaders were groups of common people, some of the same ones who on the occasion of the Triumphant Entry cried, "Hosanna to the Son of David," probably including publicans and sinners. In these verses Jesus warned this group that, if they would benefit by His offer of salvation and the invitation to partake of Kingdom blessings, they must do so on His terms, just as those who would partake of the wedding feast must put on the wedding garment.

3. The great contest of questions

Note 213. The second effort of that day to discredit Jesus before the common people was made in a series of hard or tricky questions, which different groups of His enemies propounded to Him. They doubtless hoped also to lead Him to say something which they could use as evidence in condemning Him. These groups were the Pharisees, the Sadducees, and the Herodians—sects who sharply opposed each other in contending for their claims, but now united against Jesus, because each sect regarded Him as dangerous to its claims or objectives.

(1) A question raised jointly by the Pharisees and the Herodians —"Is it lawful to pay tribute to Caesar?"
#211

MATT. 22:15-22	MARK 12:13-17	LUKE 20:20-26
15 Then went the Pharisees, and took counsel how they might ensnare him in *his* talk. 16 And they send to him their disciples, with the Herodians, saying, Teacher, we know that thou art true, and teachest the way of God in truth, and carest not for any one: for thou regardest not the person of men. 17 Tell us therefore, What thinkest thou? Is it lawful to give tribute unto Caesar, or not? 18 But Jesus perceived their wickedness, and said, Why make ye trial of me, ye hypocrites? 19 Show me the tribute money. And they brought unto him a [1]denarius. 20 And he saith unto them, Whose is this image and superscription? 21 They say unto him, Caesar's. Then saith he unto them, Render therefore unto Caesar the things that are Caesar's; and unto God the things that are God's. 22 And when they heard it, they marvelled, and left him, and went away. [1] See marginal note on ch. 18. 28.	13 And they send unto him certain of the Pharisees and of the Herodians, that they might catch him in talk. 14 And when they were come, they say unto him, Teacher, we know that thou art true, and carest not for any one; for thou regardest not the person of men, but of a truth teachest the way of God: Is it lawful to give tribute unto Caesar, or not? 15 Shall we give, or shall we not give? But he knowing their hypocrisy, said unto them, Why make ye trial of me? bring me a [1]denarius, that I may see it. 16 And they brought it. And he saith unto them, Whose is this image and superscription? And they said unto him, Caesar's. 17 And Jesus said unto them, Render unto Caesar the things that are Caesar's, and unto God the things that are God's. And they marvelled greatly at him. [1] See marginal note on ch. 6. 37.	20 And they watched him, and sent forth spies, who feigned themselves to be righteous, that they might take hold of his speech, so as to deliver him up to the [1]rule and to the authority of the governor. 21 And they asked him, saying, Teacher, we know that thou sayest and teachest rightly, and acceptest not the person *of any*, but of a truth teachest the way of God; 22 Is it lawful for us to give tribute unto Caesar, or not? 23 But he perceived their craftiness, and said unto them, 24 Show me a [2]denarius. Whose image and superscription hath it? And they said, Caesar's. 25 And he said unto them, Then render unto Caesar the things that are Caesar's, and unto God the things that are God's. 26 And they were not able to take hold of the saying before the people: and they marvelled at his answer, and held their peace. [1] Or, *ruling power* [2] See marginal note on ch. 7. 41.

Note 214. Jesus had that morning caught the deputation of priests and elders in a dilemma (#207); so at this time the Pharisees and Herodians joined forces in an effort to entrap Him in the same way. They evidently thought that they had a question with inescapable answers, either of which would prove to be embarrassing, if not fatal, to Jesus. Many of the Pharisees were sympathizers of the zealots who regarded

paying tax to the heathen Romans, not only a badge of slavery, but an act of disloyalty to the Lord God, whom they claimed as their only Ruler and Lord. If, therefore, Jesus should say that it was lawful and right to pay the tax to Caesar, as the Roman emperor was called, the Pharisees might say to the common people that He was merely a collaborator of the Romans, seeking to bring the people into complete subjection. This, they hoped, would turn the people against Him. On the other hand, the Herodians, being partizans of the Herod family, some of whom were appointed by the Romans to positions of high honor and power, counseled payment of the tribute. If, therefore, Jesus should say that it was not right to pay the tax, these might make it appear that He was urging the people to rebel; and they would thus have ground to accuse Him before the governor (procurator) and secure His arrest, and perhaps His death. But Jesus "took the dilemma by the horns," saying in effect that it was right to pay the tribute to Caesar; but He proved that this did not violate one's obligation to God, since one ought also to render unto God the things that are due to Him. And with His historic answer He laid the foundation for the Christian principle of separation of church and state.

It is interesting that, when the Sanhedrin leaders later brought Jesus before Pilate, the Roman governor, some of them did accuse Him of "forbidding to give tribute to Caesar" (Luke 23:2, #245), but this accusation seemingly had little weight in securing sentence against Him.

(2) Question raised by the Sadducees about marriage and the resurrection

#212

MATT. 22:23-33	MARK 12:18-27	LUKE 20:27-40
23 On that day there came to him Sadducees, [1]they that say that there is no resurrection: and they asked him, 24 saying, Teacher, Moses said, [2]If a man die, having no children, his brother [3]shall marry his wife, and raise up seed unto his brother. 25 Now there were with us seven brethren: and the first married and deceased, and having no seed left his wife unto his brother; 26 in like manner the second also, and the third, unto the [4]seventh. 27 And after them all, the woman died. 28 In the res-	18 And there come unto him Sadducees, who say that there is no resurrection; and they asked him, saying, 19 Teacher, Moses wrote unto us, [1]If a man's brother die, and leave a wife behind him, and leave no child, that his brother should take his wife, and raise up seed unto his brother. 20 There were seven brethren: and the first took a wife, and dying left no seed; 21 and the second took her, and died, leaving no seed behind him; and the third likewise: 22 and the seven left no seed. Last of all the woman also died. 23 In the resurrection whose wife shall she be of them? for the	27 And there came to him certain of the Sadducees, they that say that there is no resurrection; 28 and they asked him, saying, Teacher, [1]Moses wrote unto us, that if a man's brother die, having a wife, and he be childless, his brother should take the wife, and raise up seed unto his brother. 29 There were therefore seven brethren: and the first took a wife, and died childless; 30 and the second: 31 and the third took her; and likewise the seven also left no children, and died. 32 Afterward the woman also died. 33 In the resurrection therefore whose wife of them shall she be? for the

[1] Many ancient authorities read *saying.*
[2] Dt. xxv. 5.
[3] Gr. *shall perform the duty of a husband's brother to his wife.*
[4] Gr. *seven.*

[1] Dt. xxv. 5.

[1] Dt. xxv. 5.

Matt. 22	Mark 12	Luke 20
urrection therefore whose wife shall she be of the seven? for they all had her. 29 But Jesus answered and said unto them, Ye do err, not knowing the scriptures, nor the power of God. 30 For in the resurrection they neither marry, nor are given in marriage, but are as angels[5] in heaven. 31 But as touching the resurrection of the dead, have ye not read that which was spoken unto you by God, saying, 32 [6]I am the God of Abraham, and the God of Isaac, and the God of Jacob? God is not *the God* of the dead, but of the living. 33 And when the multitudes heard it, they were astonished at his teaching.	seven had her to wife. 24 Jesus said unto·them, Is it not for this cause that ye err, that ye know not the scriptures, nor the power of God? 25 For when they shall rise from the dead, they neither marry, nor are given in marriage; but are as angels in heaven. 26 But as touching the dead, that they are raised; have ye not read in the book of Moses, in *the place concerning* the Bush, how God spake unto him, saying, [2]I am the God of Abraham, and the God of Isaac, and the God of Jacob? 27 He is not the God of the dead, but of the living: ye do greatly err.	seven had her to wife. 34 And Jesus said unto them, The sons of this [2]world marry, and are given in marriage: 35 but they that are accounted worthy to attain to that [2]world, and the resurrection from the dead, neither marry, nor are given in marriage: 36 for neither can they die any more: for they are equal unto the angels; and are sons of God, being sons of the resurrection. 37 But that the dead are raised, even Moses showed, in [3]*the place concerning* the Bush, when he calleth the Lord the God of Abraham, and the God of Isaac, and the God of Jacob. 38 Now he is not the God of the dead, but of the living: for all live unto him. 39 And certain of the scribes answering said, Teacher, thou hast well said. 40 For they durst not any more ask him any question.
[5] Many ancient authorities add *of God.* [6] Ex. iii. 6.	[2] Ex. iii. 6.	[2] Or, *age* [3] Ex. iii. 6.

Note 215. The Sadducees seem to have been the "free-thinkers" among the Jews (cf. paragraph about them on page 18 , also Acts 23: 6). Since many of the priests were of that sect, and control of the temple was largely by the priests, the Sadducees were especially angry with Him for cleansing the temple. And too, if the Romans should become suspicious of His rising popularity (cf. Note 180), they stood a chance of losing more than any other group. Moreover, since Jesus had taken the part of the Pharisees in the controversy over a resurrection of the dead (cf. Luke 13: 29, #161; 14: 14, #169; John 5: 28--29, #48), they reasoned that if they should baffle Him with a question about the resurrection, they would both discredit Him before the people and also win a victory over their old rivals, the Pharisees.

The question that they raised with Him may have been one with which they had often confounded the Pharisees, involving the seldom-used law of "levirate marriage" (cf. Deut. 25: 5--6; also Gen. 38: 8; Ruth 4: 11). Jesus gave a clear proof of immortality from their Scripture, which was regarded as proof of the resurrection. As a syllogism, it may be stated as follows:

Major Premise: God is the God of living people, not dead people.

Minor Premise: But to Moses God said, "I am...the God of Abraham,...of Isaac, and...of Jacob," after the patriarchs had died.

Therefore: Abraham, Isaac, and Jacob must be living after they died.

(3) Question raised by a lawyer (a Pharisee)⌐ "Which is the greatest commandment of the law?"

#213

MATT. 22:34-40

34 But the Pharisees, when they heard that he had put the Sadducees to silence, gathered themselves together. 35 And one of them, a lawyer, asked him a question, trying him: 36 Teacher, which is the great commandment in the law? 37 And he said unto him, [1]Thou shalt love the Lord thy God with all thy heart, and with all thy soul, and with all thy mind. 38 This is the great and first commandment. 39 [2]And a second like *unto it* is this, [3]Thou shalt love thy neighbor as thyself. 40 On these two commandments the whole law hangeth, and the prophets.

[1]Dt. vi. 5.
[2] Or, *And a second is like unto it, Thou shalt love &c.*   [3] Lev. xix. 18.

MARK 12:28-34

28 And one of the scribes came, and heard them questioning together, and knowing that he had answered them well, asked him, What commandment is the first of all? 29 Jesus answered, The first is, [1]Hear, O Israel; [2]The Lord our God, the Lord is one: 30 and thou shalt love the Lord thy God [3]with all thy heart, and [3]with all thy soul, and [3]with all thy mind, and [3]with all thy strength. 31 The second is this, [4]Thou shalt love thy neighbor as thyself. There is none other commandment greater than these. 32 And the scribe said unto him, Of a truth, Teacher, thou hast well said that he is one; and there is none other but he: 33 and to love him with all the heart, and with all the understanding, and with all the strength, and to love his neighbor as himself, is much more than all whole burnt-offerings and sacrifices. 34 And when Jesus saw that he answered discreetly, he said unto him, Thou art not far from the kingdom of God. And no man after that durst ask him any question.

[1] Dt. vi. 4 ff.
[2] Or, *The Lord is our God; the Lord is one*   [3] Gr. *from.*   [4] Lev. xix. 18.

Note 216. Matthew calls this questioner a lawyer; Mark simply calls him a scribe. The lawyers were scribes who had gained distinction in their study of the law. They would naturally be of the party of Pharisees rather than the Sadducees. Matthew says that the question, "Which is the great commandment of the law?" came out of consultation of the Pharisees, and that it was raised to tempt or trick Jesus; Mark does not mention these details. In reply Jesus summarized the law with two injunctions which are not found in the Ten Commandments; but in Deut. 6: 4—5 and Lev. 19: 18. The first of these references is a summary of the first four of the Ten Commandments, setting forth duties to God; and the latter a summary of the last six, setting forth duties to one's fellow man. Doubtless some of the scribes had already observed these two commandments as comprehending the whole law, since some months earlier when Jesus had asked another lawyer, "What is written in the Law?" that one replied by quoting the same verses, (Luke 10: 26—27, #149). Paul in two of his epistles (Rom. 13: 9 and

261

Gal. 5:14) set forth the second of these ("Thou shalt love thy neighbor as thyself") as fulfilling all the law governing our relations to each other; and in James 2:8 this injunction is called "the royal law according to the Scripture."

On the whole, Mark gives a more favorable picture of this scribe (lawyer) than does Matthew. He voiced his own approval and commendation of the answer that Jesus gave; whereupon Jesus replied, "Thou art not far from the Kingdom of God." We wish we knew his attitude toward Christianity in later days, whether or not on the Day of Pentecost or later he came all the way into the Kingdom.

(4) Question from the Lord Jesus to His enemies—"What think ye of Christ?"

#214

Matt. 22:41-46	Mark 12:35-37a	Luke 20:41-44
41 Now while the Pharisees were gathered together, 42 saying, What think ye of the Christ? whose son is he? They say unto him, *The son* of David. 43 He saith unto them, How then doth David in the Spirit call him Lord, saying, 44 ¹The Lord said unto my Lord, Sit thou on my right hand, Till I put thine enemies underneath thy feet? 45 If David then calleth him Lord, how is he his son? 46 And no one was able to answer him a word, neither durst any man from that day forth ask him any more questions. ¹ Ps. cx. 1.	And Jesus answered and said, as he taught in the temple, How say the scribes that the Christ is the son of David? 36 David himself said in the Holy Spirit. ¹The Lord said unto my Lord, Sit thou on my right hand, Till I make thine enemies ²the footstool of thy feet. 37 David himself calleth him Lord; and whence is he his son? ¹ Ps. cx. 1. ² Some ancient authorities read *underneath thy feet.*	41 And he said unto them, How say they that the Christ is David's son? 42 For David himself saith in the book of Psalms, ¹The Lord said unto my Lord, Sit thou on my right hand, 43 Till I make thine enemies the footstool of thy feet. 44 David therefore calleth him Lord, and how is he his son? ¹ Ps. cx. 1.

Note 217. Of course we are not to understand that Jesus was asking those Pharisees what they thought of Him, Jesus of Nazareth. They looked on Him as a deceiver of the people, because He had led the people to regard Him as the promised Messiah or Christ (John 7:12, 47, #144; Matt. 27:63, #255). It was concerning their idea of the Christ whom they were expecting that Jesus asked. (See section on "The Messianic Hope" in the Introduction, pages 20f).

One of the fundamental articles in their belief about the coming Messiah, or Christ, as gathered from Old Testament prophecies, was that He was to be a descendant of David (cf. I Sam. 7:12; Psalm 89:3f 132:11; Isa. 9:7; 11:1; Jer. 23:5; 30:9). And the people who accepted Jesus as the Christ addressed Him, or referred to Him, as "the Son of

262

David" (cf. Matt. 12:23, #87; 9:27, #109; 15:22, #124; 20:30 et al. #192; 21:9, #198; 21:15, #203). Furthermore, we know that Jesus did fulfill that messianic condition (Matt. 1:1; Rom. 1:3—4), because both Joseph, His legal father, and Mary, His true mother, were descendants of David (cf. #3); but doubtless those priests and scribes did not know it (John 7:42, #145).

In raising this question Jesus did not imply that the scribes were in error in saying that the Christ was to be a descendant of David; but He indicated that He was and is also the eternal Son of God, and therefore of a higher rank than David and to be honored as the Lord of His royal ancestors. The idea that the Christ would be One essentially divine, as well as human, probably had not occurred to the Jewish interpreters. To set this forth Jesus quoted from Psalm 110:1, which is ascribed to David, and which the Jewish people generally regarded to be a promise of the Messiah. Consequently, it was quoted effectively in Peter's sermon on the Day of Pentecost (Acts 2:34—35) and several times in the Epistle to the Hebrews (Heb. 1:13; 5:6; 7:17, 21).

With this question by the Lord Jesus the contest of hard questions came to a close. His antagonists had asked Jesus three questions which He answered clearly and readily; He asked them one, and with it He silenced them. They hated Him none the less, but they were afraid to ask Him any more questions. On the other hand, the common people, with whom they tried to discredit Him, were all the more impressed with His superior ability.

4. The last public words of Jesus, ##215—216
(1) Denunciation against the scribes and Pharisees
#215

MATT. 23:1-4	MARK 12:37b-40	LUKE 20:45-47
	37b And ¹the common people heard him gladly.	
1 Then spake Jesus to the multitudes and to his disciples, 2 saying, The scribes and the Pharisees sit on Moses' seat: 3 all things therefore whatsoever they bid you, *these* do and observe: but do not ye after their works: for they say, and do not. 4 Yea, they bind heavy burdens ¹and grievous to be borne, and lay them on men's shoulders; but they themselves will not move them with their finger.	38 And in his teaching he said, Beware of the scribes, who desire to walk in long robes, and *to have* salutations in the marketplaces, 39 and chief seats in the synagogues, and chief places at feasts: 40 they that devour widows' houses, ²and for a pretence make long prayers; these shall receive greater condemnation.	45 And in the hearing of all the people he said unto his disciples, 46 Beware of the scribes, who desire to walk in long robes, and love salutations in the marketplaces, and chief seats in the synagogues, and chief places at feasts; 47 who devour widows' houses, and for a pretence make long prayers: these shall receive greater condemnation.
¹ Many ancient authorities omit *and grievous to be borne.*	¹ Or, *the great multitude* ² Or, *even while for a pretence they make*	

MATT. 23:5-39

5 But all their works they do to be seen of men: for they make broad their phylacteries, and enlarge the borders *of their garments,* 6 and love the chief place at feasts, and the chief seats in the synagogues, 7 and the salutations in the marketplaces, and to be called of men, Rabbi   8 But be not ye called Rabbi: for one is

263

your teacher, and all ye are brethren. 9 And call no man your father on the earth: for one is your Father, [1]*even* he who is in heaven. 10 Neither be ye called masters: for one is your master, *even* the Christ. 11 But he that is [2]greatest among you shall be your [3]servant. 12 And whosoever shall exalt himself shall be humbled; and whosoever shall humble himself shall be exalted.

13 But woe unto you, scribes and Pharisees, hypocrites! because ye shut the kingdom of heaven [4]against men: for ye enter not in yourselves, neither suffer ye them that are entering in to enter.[5]

15 Woe unto you, scribes and Pharisees, hypocrites! for ye compass sea and land to make one proselyte; and when he is become so, ye make him twofold more a son of [6]hell than yourselves.

16 Woe unto you, ye blind guides, that say, Whosoever shall swear by the [7]temple, it is nothing; but whosoever shall swear by the gold of the [7]temple, he is a debtor. 17 Ye fools and blind: for which is greater, the gold, or the [7]temple that hath sanctified the gold? 18 And, Whosoever shall swear by the altar, it is nothing; but whosoever shall swear by the gift that is upon it, he is [8]a debtor. 19 Ye blind: for which is greater, the gift, or the altar that sanctifieth the gift? 20 He therefore that sweareth by the altar, sweareth by it, and by all things thereon. 21 And he that sweareth by the [7]temple, sweareth by it, and by him that dwelleth therein. 22 And he that sweareth by the heaven, sweareth by the throne of God, and by him that sitteth thereon.

23 Woe unto you, scribes and Pharisees, hypocrites! for ye tithe mint and [9]anise and cummin, and have left undone the weightier matters of the law, justice, and mercy, and faith: but these ye ought to have done, and not to have left the other undone. 24 Ye blind guides, that strain out the gnat, and swallow the camel!

25 Woe unto you, scribes and Pharisees, hypocrites! for ye cleanse the outside of the cup and of the platter, but within they are full from extortion and excess. 26 Thou blind Pharisee, cleanse first the inside of the cup and of the platter, that the outside thereof may become clean also.

27 Woe unto you, scribes and Pharisees, hypocrites! for ye are like unto whited sepulchres, which outwardly appear beautiful, but inwardly are full of dead men's bones, and of all uncleanness. 28 Even so ye also outwardly appear righteous unto men, but inwardly ye are full of hypocrisy and iniquity.

29 Woe unto you, scribes and Pharisees, hypocrites! for ye build the sepulchres of the prophets, and garnish the tombs of the righteous, 30 and say, If we had been in the days of our fathers, we should not have been partakers with them in the blood of the prophets. 31 Wherefore ye witness to yourselves, that ye are sons of them that slew the prophets. 32 Fill ye up then the measure of your fathers. 33 Ye serpents, ye offspring of vipers, how shall ye escape the judgment of [6]hell? 34 Therefore, behold, I send unto you prophets, and wise men, and scribes: some of them shall ye kill and crucify; and some of them shall ye scourge in your synagogues, and persecute from city to city: 35 that upon you may come all the righteous blood shed on the earth, from the blood of Abel the righteous unto the blood of Zachariah son of Barachiah, whom ye slew between the sanctuary and the altar. 36 Verily I say unto you, All these things shall come upon this generation.

37 O Jerusalem, Jerusalem, that killeth the prophets, and stoneth them that are sent unto her! how often would I have gathered thy children together, even as a hen gathereth her chickens under her wings, and ye would not! 38 Behold, your house is left unto you [10]desolate. 39 For I say unto you, Ye shall not see me henceforth, till ye shall say, Blessed *is* he that cometh in the name of the Lord.

[1] Gr. *the heavenly.* [2] Gr. *greater.* [3] Or, *minister* [4] Gr. *before.*
[5] Some authorities insert here, or after ver. 12, ver. 14 *Woe unto you, scribes and Pharisees, hypocrites! for ye devour widows' houses, even while for a pretence ye make long prayers: therefore ye shall receive greater condemnation.* See Mk. 12. 40; Lk. 20. 47.
[6] Gr. *Gehenna.* [7] Or, *sanctuary:* as in ver. 35. [8] Or, *bound by his oath* [9] Or, *dill*
[10] Some ancient authorities omit *desolate.*

Note 218. The disputings between Jesus and the leaders of the Sanhedrin undoubtedly took place in the Court of the Women (cf. Mark 12:41, #217). As the disputation continued, very naturally there would be a growing crowd of those who had come to the Passover ahead of time as they gathered around to hear. And according to Mark 12:37b (literally translated), "the great multitude was hearing Him gladly;" and this crowd was inclined to exult in His victory over the arrogant rabbis and aristocratic priests. Since no more questions were forthcoming, Jesus took occasion to enhance His triumph by delivering a scathing denunciation of the scribes and Pharisees as a class. This discourse is reported more at length in Matthew than in either Mark or Luke, but in Luke there is an account of an earlier strong remonstrance against this group (Luke 11:39—52, #154). As we have it in Matthew, this address is the purest oration in which Jesus indulged during His whole ministry, I have wondered if He did not ascend to some vantage point that was nearby in the temple—possibly up three or four of the fifteen semicircular steps which led from the Court of the Women to the Court of the Israelites—where before the sea of upturned faces He delivered this philippic against His unrelenting critics.

Observe in the following outline how His eloquence rose to a climax:

(1) Conciliatory introduction, verses 2—3a
(2) Preliminary general accusation with warning to hearers, verses 3b—12
(3) The eight woes, verses 13—33
(4) The peroration, verses 34—39

Notice how this last public address of the Lord Jesus emphasized the elements of truth which had characterized all His ministry: (1) exposure and condemnation of hypocrisy and wrong in general, (2) a willingness, even a yearning, to show mercy, (3) a warning of the consequences of rejection.

(2) His words concerning the final rejection of the ruling class

#216

John 12:37-50

37 But though he had done so many signs before them, yet they believed not on him: 38 that the word of Isaiah the prophet might be fulfilled, which he spake,
[1]Lord, who hath believed our report?
And to whom hath the arm of the Lord been revealed?
39 For this cause they could not believe, for that Isaiah said again,
40 [2]He hath blinded their eyes, and he hardened their heart;
Lest they should see with their eyes, and perceive with their heart,
And should turn,
And I should heal them.
41 These things said Isaiah, because he saw his glory: and he spake of him. 42 Nevertheless even of the rulers many believed on him; but because of the Pharisees they did not confess [3]it, lest they should be put out of the synagogue: 43 for they loved the glory *that is* of men more than the glory *that is* of God.
44 And Jesus cried and said, He that believeth on me, believeth not on me, but on him that sent me. 45 And he that beholdeth me beholdeth him that sent me. 46 I am come a light into the world, that whosoever believeth on me may not

---

[1] Is. liii. 1.   [2] Is. vi. 10.   [3] Or, him

abide in the darkness. 47 And if any man hear my sayings, and keep them not, I judge him not: for I came not to judge the world, but to save the world. 48 He that rejecteth me, and receiveth not my sayings, hath one that judgeth him: the word that I spake, the same shall judge him in the last day. 49 For I spake not from myself; but the Father that sent me, he hath given me a commandment, what I should say, and what I should speak. 50 And I know that his commandment is life eternal; the things therefore which I speak, even as the Father hath said unto me, so I speak.

Note 219. It is impossible to determine just when during the last week the words of Jesus in the above paragraph from the Gospel of John were spoken. It is the only material in that Gospel between the events on the day of the Triumphant Entry (Sunday) and the eating of the Passover (Thursday evening). They would be a very fitting close for this day of controversy in the temple. His foes, having been foiled in their efforts to debase Him before the multitude, doubtless withdrew even before Jesus finished His oration. Verses 37—43 are John's observations, not only on the results of the day's disputation, but of the fruits of the labors of Jesus in general. The words of Jesus quoted in verses 44—50 were possibly spoken in the hearing of the disciples and other sympathizers as the crowds were scattering after the oration.

5. Commendation of the widow's gift of two mites
#217

MARK 12:41-44	LUKE 21:1-4
41 And he sat down over against the treasury, and beheld how the multitude cast [1]money into the treasury: and many that were rich cast in much. 42 And there came [2]a poor widow, and she cast in two mites, which made a farthing. 43 And he called unto him his disciples, and said unto them, Verily I say unto you, This poor widow cast in more than all they that are casting into the treasury: 44 for they all did cast in of their superfluity; but she of her want did cast in all that she had, *even* all her living.	1 And he looked up, [1]and saw the rich men that were casting their gifts into the treasury. 2 And he saw a certain poor widow casting in thither two mites. 3 And he said, Of a truth I say unto you, This poor widow cast in more than they all: 4 for all these did of their superfluity cast in unto the gifts; but she of her want did cast in all the living that she had.
[1] Gr. *brass.* [2] Gr. *one.*	[1] Or, *and saw them that . . . treasury, and they were rich.*

Note 220. After several hours of conflict with representatives from the Sanhedrin, and after His matchless oration, our Lord was doubtless exhausted physically. Finding a place to sit down from which He could look at the people coming and going in their preparation for sacred Passover, He had opportunity to observe them as they cast their gifts into the treasure chests. According to Edersheim* there were thirteen "trumpet-shaped boxes" in the Court of the Women into which the people would cast their contributions for various causes connected with the temple worship. "All her living" (vs. 44 in Mark, 4 in Luke) may mean all she had been able to save from her life's earnings (cf. Luke 8: 43, #107; 15: 12, 30, #173), or else all she had to live on that

*Life and Times of Jesus, Vol. II, p. 387.

day. According to all the authorities,* the two mites were worth about half a cent in American money, though the buying power in that day was higher than today.

6. The great prophecy, ##218—225
   (1) In the temple, prediction that the temple would be utterly destroyed

#218

MATT. 24:1-2	MARK 13:1-2	LUKE 21:5-6
1 And Jesus went out from the temple, and was going on his way; and his disciples came to him to show him the buildings of the temple. 2 But he answered and said unto them, See ye not all these things? verily I say unto you, There shall not be left here one stone upon another, that shall not be thrown down.	1 And as he went forth out of the temple, one of his disciples saith unto him, Teacher, behold, what manner of stones and what manner of buildings! 2 And Jesus said unto him, Seest thou these great buildings? there shall not be left here one stone upon another, which shall not be thrown down.	5 And as some spake of the temple, how it was adorned with goodly stones and offerings, he said, 6 As for these things which ye behold, the days will come, in which there shall not be left here one stone upon another, that shall not be thrown down.

Note 221. The temple was still in the process of being built. At the first Passover of our Lord's public life, three years earlier, the Jews said that construction on it had been going on forty-six years (John 2: 20, #25); by this time, therefore, forty-nine. Surely with each new addition there was a greater degree of splendor and beauty. Probably the disciples were pointing out some piece of work newly finished and remarking on the expected magnificence of the completed structure.

The statement of Jesus would surely have been true even if the destructive Jewish-Roman War had not come as early as it did, because all man-made edifices are subject to the ravages of natural forces or of future wars or to the whims of future builders. But the words of Jesus were fulfilled earlier than any one could naturally expect.

We are told that the work on the temple was not completed until A.D. 64,** just two years before war with the Romans broke out; and at the end of that conflict in 70 it was a total ruin.

(2) On the Mount of Olives, further predictions concerning the return of Jesus and the inauguration of the visible kingdom of God, ##219—225
   a. Graphic prophecy and impressive warnings

#219

MATT. 24:3-42	MARK 13:3-33	LUKE 21:7-36
3 And as he sat on the mount of Olives, the disciples came unto him pri-	3 And as he sat on the mount of Olives over against the temple, Peter	7 And they asked him, saying, Teacher, when therefore shall these things

*T. Lewis, "Mite" in International Standard Bible Encyclopedia, Vol. III, p. 2067 and others.

**W. Shaw Coldecott and James Orr, "Temple" in International Standard Bible Encyclopedia, Vol. V, p. 2937; T. W. Davis, "Temple" in Hasting's Dictionary of the Bible, Vol. IV, p. 712.

Matt. 24

vately, saying, Tell us, when shall these things be? and what *shall be* the sign of thy ¹coming, and of ²the end of the world? 4 And Jesus answered and said unto them, Take heed that no man lead you astray. 5 For many shall come in my name, saying, I am the Christ; and shall lead many astray. 6 And ye shall hear of wars and rumors of wars; see that ye be not troubled: for *these things* must needs come to pass; but the .end is not yet. 7 For nation shall rise against nation, and kingdom against kingdom; and there shall be famines and earthquakes in divers places. 8 But all these things are the beginning of travail. 9 Then shall they deliver you up unto tribulation, and shall kill you: and ye shall be hated of all the nations for my name's sake. 10 And then shall many stumble, and shall ³deliver up one another, and shall hate one another. 11 And many false prophets shall arise, and shall lead many astray. 12 And because iniquity shall be multipled, the love of the many shall wax cold. 13 But he that endureth to the end, the same shall be saved. 14 And ⁴this gospel of the kingdom shall be preached in the whole ⁵world for a testimony unto all the nations; and then shall the end come.

Mark 13

and ¹James and John and Andrew asked him privately, 4 Tell us, when shall these things be? and what *shall be* the sign when these things are all about to be accomplished? 5 And Jesus began to say unto them, Take heed that no man lead you astray. 6 Many shall come in my name, saying, I am *he;* and shall lead many astray. 7 And when ye shall hear of wars and rumors of wars, be not troubled: *these things* must needs come to pass; but the end is not yet. 8 For nation shall rise against nation, and kingdom against kingdom; there shall be earthquakes in divers places; there shall be famines: these things are the beginning of travail.

9 But take ye heed to yourselves: for they shall deliver you up to councils; and in synagogues shall ye be beaten; and before governors and kings shall ye stand for my sake, for a testimony unto them. 10 And the ²gospel must first be preached unto all the nations. 11 And when they lead you *to judgment,* and deliver you up, be not anxious beforehand what ye shall speak: but whatsoever shall be given you in that hour, that speak ye; for it is not ye that speak, but the Holy Spirit. 12 And brother shall ³deliver up brother to death, and the father his child; and children shall rise against parents, and ⁴cause them to be put to death. 13 And ye shall be hated of all men for my name's sake: but he that endureth to the end, the same shall be saved.

Luke 21

be? and what *shall be* the sign when these things are about to come to pass? 8 And he said, Take heed that ye be not led astray: for many shall come in my name, saying I am *he;* and, The time is at hand: go ye not after them. 9 And when ye shall hear of wars and tumults, be not terrified: for these things must needs come to pass first; but the end is not immediately.

10 Then said he unto them, Nation shall rise against nation, and kingdom against kingdom; 11 and there shall be great earthquakes, and in divers places famines and pestilences; and there shall be terrors and great signs from heaven. 12 But before all these things, they shall lay their hands on you, and shall persecute you, delivering you up to the synagogues and prisons, ¹bringing you before kings and governors for my name's sake. 13 It shall turn out unto you for a testimony 14 Settle it therefore in your hearts, not to meditate beforehand how to answer: 15 for I will give you a mouth and wisdom, which all your adversaries shall not be able to withstand or to gainsay. 16 But ye shall be ²delivered up even by parents, and brethen, and kinsfolk, and friends; and *some* of you ³shall they cause to be put to death. 17 And ye shall be hated of all men for my name's sake. 18 And not a hair of your head shall perish. 19 In your ⁴patience ye shall win your ⁵souls.

---

¹ Gr. *presence.*
² Or, *the consummation of the age*   ³ See ch. 10. 4.
⁴ Or, *these good tidings*
⁵ Gr. *inhabited earth.*

¹ Or, *Jacob*
² See marginal note on ch. 1. 1.
³ See ch. 3. 19.
⁴ Or, *put them to death*

¹ Gr. *you being brought.*
² Or, *betrayed*
³ Or, *shall they put to death*
⁴ Or, *stedfastness*   ⁵ Or, *lives*

Matt. 24	Mark 13	Luke 21

Matt. 24

15 When therefore ye see the abomination of desolation, which was [6]spoken of through Daniel the prophet, standing in [7]the holy place (let him that readeth understand), 16 then let them that are in Judaea flee unto the mountains: 17 let him that is on the housetop not go down to take out the things that are in his house: 18 and let him that is in the field not return back to take his cloak. 19 But woe unto them that are with child and to them that give suck in those days! 20 And pray ye that your flight be not in the winter, neither on a sabbath: 21 for then shall be great tribulation, such as hath not been from the beginning of the world until now, no, nor ever shall be. 22 And except those days had been shortened, no flesh would have been saved: but for the elect's sake those days shall be shortened.

23 Then if any man shall say unto you, Lo, here is the Christ, or, Here; believe [8]it not. 24 For there shall arise false Christs, and false prophets, and shall show great signs and wonders; so as to lead astray, if possible, even the elect. 25 Behold, I have told you beforehand. 26 If therefore they shall say unto you, Behold, he is in the wilderness; go not forth: Behold, he is in the inner chambers; believe [9]it not. 27 For as the lightning cometh forth from the east, and is seen even unto the west; so shall be the [10]coming of the Son of man. 28 Wheresoever the carcase is, there will the [11]eagles be gathered

[6] Dan. ix. 27; xi. 31; xii. 11.
[7] Or, a holy place
[8] Or, him   [9] Or, them
[10] Gr. presence.   [11] Or, vultures

Mark 13

14 But when ye see the abomination of desolation standing where he ought not (let him that readeth understand), then let them that are in Judaea flee unto the mountains: 15 and let him that is on the housetop not go down, nor enter in, to take anything out of his house: 16 and let him that is in the field not return back to take his cloak. 17 But woe unto them that are with child and to them that give suck in those days! 18 And pray ye that it be not in the winter. 19 For those days shall be tribulation, such as there hath not been the like from the beginning of the creation which God created until now, and never shall be. 20 And except the Lord had shortened the days, no flesh would have been saved; but for the elect's sake, whom he chose, he shortened the days.

21 And then if any man shall say unto you, Lo, here is the Christ; or, Lo, there; believe [5]it not: 22 for there shall arise false Christs and false prophets, and shall show signs and wonders, that they may lead astray, if possible, the elect. 23 But take ye heed: behold, I have told you all things beforehand.

[5] Or, him

Luke 21

20 But when ye see Jerusalem compassed with armies then know that her desolation is at hand. 21 Then let them that are in Judaea flee unto the mountains; and let them that are in the midst of her depart out; and let not them that are in the country enter therein. 22 For these are days of vengeance, that all things which are written may be fulfilled. 23 Woe unto them that are with child and to them that give suck in those days! for there shall be great distress upon the [6]land, and wrath unto this people. 24 And they shall fall by the edge of the sword, and shall be led captive into all the nations: and Jerusalem shall be trodden down of the Gentiles, until the times of the Gentiles be fulfilled.

[6] Or, earth

Matt. 24 | Mark 13 | Luke 21

together.

29 But immediately after the tribulation of those days the sun shall be darkened, and the moon shall not give her light, and the stars shall fall from heaven, and the powers of the heavens shall be shaken: 30 and then shall appear the sign of the Son of man in heaven: and then shall all the tribes of the earth mourn, and they shall see the Son of man coming on the clouds of heaven with power and great glory. 31 And he shall send forth his angels [12]with [13]a great sound of a trumpet, and they shall gather together his elect from the four winds, from one end of heaven to the other.

32 Now from the fig tree learn her parable: when her branch is now become tender, and putteth forth its leaves, ye know that the summer is nigh; 33 even so ye also, when ye see all these things, know ye that [14]he is nigh, *even* at the doors. 34 Verily I say unto you, This generation shall not pass away, till all these things be accomplished. 35 Heaven and earth shall pass away, but my words shall not pass away. 36 But of that day and hour knoweth no one, not even the angels of heaven, [15]neither the Son, but the Father only. 37 And as *were* the days of Noah, so shall be the [10]coming of the Son of man. 38 For as in those days which were before the flood they were eating and drinking, marry-

[12] Many ancient authorities read *with a great trumpet, and they shall gather &c.*
[13] Or, *a trumpet of great sound*
[14] Or, *it*
[15] Many authorities, some ancient, omit *neither the Son.*
[10] Gr. *presence.*

---

24 But in those days, after that tribulation, the sun shall be darkened, and the moon shall not give her light, 25 and the stars shall be falling from heaven, and the powers that are in the heavens shall be shaken. 26 And then shall they see the Son of man coming in clouds with great power and glory. 27 And then shall he send forth the angels, and shall gather together his elect from the four winds, from the uttermost part of the earth to the uttermost part of heaven.

28 Now from the fig tree learn her parable: when her branch is now become tender, and putteth forth its leaves, ye know that the summer is nigh; 29 even so ye also, when ye see these things coming to pass, know ye that [6]he is nigh, *even* at the doors. 30 Verily I say unto you, This generation shall not pass away, until all these things be accomplished. 31 Heaven and earth shall pass away: but my words shall not pass away. 32 But of that day or that hour knoweth no one, not even the angels in heaven, neither the Son, but the Father. 33 Take ye heed, watch [7]and pray: for ye know not when the time is.

[6] Or, *it*
[7] Some ancient authorities omit *and pray.*

---

25 And there shall be signs in sun and moon and stars; and upon the earth distress of nations, in perplexity for the roaring of the sea and the billows; 26 men [7]fainting for fear, and for expectation of the things which are coming on [8]the world: for the powers of the heavens shall be shaken. 27 And then shall they see the Son of man coming in a cloud with power and great glory. 28 But when these things begin to come to pass, look up, and lift up your heads; because your redemption draweth nigh.

29 And he spake to them a parable: Behold the fig tree, and all the trees: 30 when they now shoot forth, ye see it and know of your own selves that the summer is now nigh. 31 Even so ye also, when ye see these things coming to pass, know ye that the kingdom of God is nigh. 32 Verily I say unto you, This generation shall not pass away, till all things be accomplished. 33 Heaven and earth shall pass away: but my words shall not pass away.

34 But take heed to yourselves, lest haply your hearts be overcharged with surfeiting, and drunkenness, and cares of this life, and that day come on you suddenly as a snare: 35 for *so* shall it come upon all them that dwell on the face of all the earth. 36 But watch ye at every season, making supplication, that ye may prevail to escape all these things that shall come to pass, and to

[7] Or. *expiring*
[8] Gr. *the inhabited earth.*

#219, continued

Matt. 24

ing and giving in marriage, until the day that Noah entered into the ark, 39 and they knew not until the flood came, and took them all away; so shall be the [10]coming of the Son of man. 40 Then shall two men be in the field; one is taken, and one is left: 41 two women *shall be* grinding at the mill; one is taken, and one is left. 42 Watch therefore: for ye know not on what day your Lord cometh.

[10] Gr. *presence*.

Luke 21

stand before the Son of man.

Note 222. As has been said, Jesus apparently planned that He and the disciples would spend this spring night in the open at their regular place on the Mount of Olives. Before they began to "bed down" for the night, doubtless as they sat in full view of the temple area across the Kidron Valley, some of the disciples ("Peter and James and John and Andrew," vs. 3 in Mark) asked for more enlightenment on the prophecy which Jesus had made as they were departing from the temple. They wanted to know "when shall these things be?" (that is, the dismantling of the temple). Moreover, they wanted to know also the sign of His coming and of the end of the age (vs. 3 in Matt.; aiōn, the word translated "world," would be better translated "age"). Although Jesus had on previous occasions spoken of coming in glory and with the angels (Matt. 16: 27), coming "at an hour when ye think not," (Luke 12: 40, #157) and of "the day that the Son of Man is revealed," (Luke 17: 30, #183), and had described some circumstances attending that event, the disciples must certainly have had confused notions about this matter, since they still hoped that He was about to set up the visible Kingdom.

The reply of Jesus included prophecies concerning both the destruction of Jerusalem, involving the destruction of the temple, and His own return to earth at the end of the present age. But He did not tell them when either of those events would take place. Indeed, with reference to His coming, He gave them to understand that neither the angels of Heaven nor even Himself (in His state of self-emptying) knew when it would be. Even if He had known, He would doubtless not have told them; because, as He said to them on a later occasion, it was not theirs to know times or seasons (Acts 1: 6—8). But He warned them (and their successors, including ourselves) of the persecutions that would have to be endured and the labors that must be put forth before He would come, or the age would end. And He admonished them (and us) not to lose hope if things do not follow in just the order or sequence expected, and not to become victims of the false messiahs who would surely appear to prey upon the weak faith of some Christians. And He

271

commanded that they and we must be in such state of preparedness that we shall not be found off-guard when He does come.

But He did not give them a sign by which they, or Christians of any latter age, might calculate the time of His coming; indicating that it was as true for them as it had been for the inquiring Pharisees that the Kingdom of God (the visible Kingdom) "cometh not with observation" (Luke 17: 20, #182). The only sign that He spoke of was "the sign of the Son of Man in Heaven," which involves seeing "the Son of Man coming in the clouds of Heaven with power and great glory" (vs. 30 in Matthew and parallels). When the people of the world see that sign, they will not need to calculate when He will come; He will already be in the act of coming. But He did indicate that the setting up of the visible Kingdom will follow after His coming to earth (vs. 31 in Luke).

The following is a rather general outline of the section:

(1) Prophecies of hardships and labors in general that Christians may expect, including the rise of false messiahs, political upheavals, fiery persecutions, and withal the world-wide preaching of the gospel. None of these things is to be regarded as signs of His coming or of the end of the age. Indeed, some of them have already come to pass more than once, and may do so again before the end (Matt. 24: 4—14; Mark 13: 5—13; Luke 21: 8—10).

(2) Prophecies of hardships to be experienced in connection with the fall of Jerusalem and the destruction of the temple (Matt. 24: 15—22; Mark 13: 14—20; Luke 21 :20—24). There is evidence that the Christians living in Jerusalem at the outbreak of the war between the Jews and the Romans, or many of them, were acquainted with these prophecies; and, taking warning from them, they fled from the city to the town of Pella in Peraea, and thus escaped the most terrible hardships of the siege.*

(3) Repeated warning against f a l s e prophets, false signs, and false messiahs—a warning particularly against claims that the Messiah has come (returned) secretly (Matt. 24: 23—28; Mark 13: 21—23). Note that there is no material in Luke under this division; but in Luke 17: 23—37 (#183) is an account of an earlier discourse of Jesus, which included some of these warnings.

(4) Prophecies, for the most part, concerning events connected with the return of Christ (Matt. 24:29—31; Mark 13: 24—27; Luke 21: 25—28).

(5) Warnings concerning the need for preparedness (Matt. 24: 32—42; Mark 13: 28—33; Luke 21: 29—36).

*Cf. Broadus, *Commentary on Matthew*, pp. 486f. and Edersheim, *Life and Times of Jesus*, Vol. II, p. 448. These authors cite Eusebius, *Church History* (4th century) III, v. 2f; cf. Max L. Margolis and Alexander Marx, *A History of the Jewish People* (Philadelphia: The Jewish Publications Society of America, 1927), pp. 199f. The Christians were probably among those mentioned by Josephus as being permitted by Titus to flee from the beseiged city (*Wars of the Jews*, V,x,1).

I confess that the divisions in the outline may not be mutually exclusive. I have not been able to find assured answers to all the questions that we should like to raise about these passages. Undoubtedly, our Lord purposely arranged it thus lest His people become more interested in studying signs than in preaching the gospel, more interested in the approaching visible Kingdom than in their divinely-given task of extending (under the Holy Spirit) the present spiritual Kingdom.

A difficulty is met in Matt. 24:34, and parallels: "This generation shall not pass till all these things be fulfilled." We know that all who were living then have died; and many generations have been born and passed off the earth since Jesus spoke those words, and all of the things prophesied have not yet come to pass. Three interpretations have been suggested:

(1) The expression "all these things" in this verse may answer to "these things" in Matt. 24:3, and refer only to the events which transpired in connection with the destruction of the temple. But in each of the accounts this statement is in the midst of prophecies that clearly portray our Lord's return—in Luke it follows immediately the promise of the visible Kingdom of God.

(2) The reference may be to the generation that will be on the earth when the signs mentioned in Matt. 24:29ff begin to take place, and the verse may mean that, after those signs are first observed, a full generation will not pass until all the prophecies of this discourse are fulfilled. But if our Lord had reference to a generation many centuries in the future from His day, He would certainly have said "that generation" rather than "this generation." It is admitted that Peter (Acts 3:20--21; II Pet. 3:12) and Paul (I Thess. 4:15—17; I Cor. 15:51—52) and John (I John 2:28) and other first-century Christians at first expected the Lord to return during their lifetime. But, although the Lord Jesus confessed that He did not know the day or the hour of His coming again (vs. 32 in Mark), He surely knew it would not occur during the lifetime of the people then living, since He had spoken of many things that would take place during the centuries which have followed.

(3) To me it seems most probable that by "this generation" our Lord meant the Jewish race, and He taught that the Jewish people as a distinct race will not be obliterated or absorbed until all these prophecies will be fulfilled. One of the marvels of history is the way the Jewish people have maintained their racial identity. I recognize that genea, the word found here in all the Gospel accounts, usually means a single succession of natural descent, or a majority of the people alive at any given time. But in Luke 11:50--51 and Matt. 23:36 the Lord Jesus clearly spoke of the Jewish race as "this generation" (genea), and it seems best to understand His words to have the same meaning in these passages.

To me it seems certain that Jesus purposed in this prophecy to divert the minds of the disciples from signs and times to their task of

273

gospel witnessing, reminding them of some of the persecutions and temptations which would beset them in fulfilling that task. I am convinced, therefore, that it is futile for us to try to determine when these prophecies will be fulfilled. Rather it behooves us to be as faithful stewards and use well the talents committed to us, so that when He does return, we shall not be ashamed (cf. I John 2:28). This conclusion is borne out in the parables of ##220—225, with which the prophecy is concluded.

b. Some impressive parables emphasizing the importance of constant preparedness, ##220—225

(a) The parable of The Doorkeeper

#220

MARK 13:34-37

34 *It is* as *when* a man, sojourning in another country, having left his house, and given authority to his [1]servants, to each one his work, commanded also the porter to watch. 35 Watch therefore: for ye know not when the lord of the house cometh, whether at even, or at midnight, or at cockcrowing, or in the morning; 36 lest coming suddenly he find you sleeping. 37 And what I say unto you I say unto all, Watch.

[1] Gr. *bondservants.*

Note 223. Luke's account of our Lord's great prophetic discourse is concluded with a warning to the disciples that they watch and be prepared at any time for His coming. But to reinforce that warning the parable of The Door-keeper is added in Mark, and in Matthew four other parables, which are followed by a portrayal of the judgment involving the simile of The Sheep and the Goats, which also has been styled a parable. The parable of the Door-keeper in Mark and the first two parables in Matthew (The Thief in the Night and The Household Manager) are variations of similar parables recorded in Luke as spoken on a previous occasion (Luke 12:35--46, #157); and this fact may account for Luke's omitting them here. The last three paragraphs of Matthew's account of this prophecy (the parables of The Ten Virgins and of The Talents and the portrayal of the judgment) embrace some of our Lord's most impressive teachings.

(b) The parable of The Thief in the Night

#221

MATT. 24:43-44

43 [1]But know this, that if the master of the house had known in what watch the thief was coming, he would have watched, and would not have suffered his house to be [2]broken through. 44 Therefore be ye also ready; for in an hour that ye think not the Son of man cometh.

[1] Or, *but this ye know*   [2] Gr. *digged through*

(c) The parable of The Steward (household manager)

#222

MATT. 24:45-51

45 Who then is the faithful and wise [1]servant, whom his lord hath set over his household, to give them their food in due season? 46 Blessed is that [1]servant, whom his lord when he cometh shall find so doing. 47 Verily I say unto you, that he will set him over all that he hath. 48 But if that evil [1]servant shall say in his heart

[1] Gr. *bondservant*

My lord tarrieth; 49 and shall begin to beat his fellow-servants, and shall eat and drink with the drunken; 50 the lord of that [1]servant shall come in a day when he expecteth not, and in an hour when he knoweth not, 51 and shall [2]cut him asunder, and appoint his portion with the hypocrites: there shall be the weeping and the gnashing of teeth.

[1] Gr. bondservant   [2] Or, severely scourge him

(d) The parable of The Virgins celebrating a marriage
#223
MATT. 25:1-13

1 Then shall the kingdom of heaven be likened unto ten virgins, who took their [1]lamps, and went forth to meet the bridegroom. 2 And five of them were foolish, and five were wise. 3 For the foolish, when they took their [1]lamps, took no oil with them: 4 but the wise took oil in their vessels with their [1]lamps. 5 Now while the bridegroom tarried, they all slumbered and slept. 6 But at midnight there is a cry, Behold, the bridegroom! Come ye forth to meet him.· 7 Then all those virgins arose, and trimmed their [1]lamps. 8 And the foolish said unto the wise, Give us of your oil; for our [1]lamps are going out. 9 But the wise answered, saying, Peradventure there will not be enough for us and you: go ye rather to them that sell, and buy for yourselves. 10 And while they went away to buy, the bridegroom came; and they that were ready went in with him to the marriage feast: and the door was shut. 11 Afterward came also the other virgins, saying, Lord, Lord, open to us. 12 But he answered and said, Verily I say unto you, I know you not. 13 Watch therefore, for ye know not the day nor the hour.

[1] Or, torches

Note 224. All of Matthew 25 is a continuation of the discourse of Jesus to His disciples on the Mount of Olives. Whatever else the parable of The Ten Virgins teaches, to the disciples it was certainly a warning against setting a time for the Lord's return to earth. To do so would tend to lead them to make an inadequate preparation to meet Him, in consequence of which they would be caught unprepared.

Many details of the story are omitted from the parable; and indeed, if they had been supplied, they would not add anything to the lesson Jesus sought to impress. A few facts, however, are relevant. All the virgins hoped, and were expected, to participate in a meeting of the bridegroom and to share the festivities which followed. Whether the meeting was to take place as he approached the bride's home for the initial ceremonies* or as he returned with the bride and some friends to his own or his father's home for the festivities,** the parable does not say. But to participate in the procession and the festivity which followed each of the virgins was expected to carry a lighted torch or lamp. All the virgins with their lamps (presumably lighted) assembled at the meeting place. But in the parable the bridegroom was later in arriving than the virgins had expected, and they all went to sleep. Five of them, however, had brought oil in their vessels along with their lamps, presumably extra oil for such an emergency. These were wise in that they were ready to meet the bridegroom at such time as he saw fit to

*So Edersheim, Life and Times of Jesus, Vol. I, p. 455 and A. B. Bruce, The Synoptic Gospels in Expositor's Greek Testament, Vol. I, p. 299.
**So Broadus, Commentary on Matthew, p. 499.

arrive; the others were foolish in that they presumed that the bridegroom would arrive before their lamps should go out. Whether they were able to buy oil at that time of the night, or whether they attempted to get in without lighted lamps, the parable does not say. They were not prepared to meet the bridegroom when he did come, and they did not participate in the celebrations or festivities.

All that Jesus said to the disciples in the way of interpretation of this parable was, "Watch therefore; for ye know neither the day nor the hour." We know from other New Testament writings that the Christians of the apostolic age expected Jesus to return to earth during their lifetime (cf. Note 222). The truly loyal ones remained faithful until they were called to meet Him in death. But even in the days of Peter there were those who in derision would ask the Christians, "Where is the promise of His coming?" (II Pet. 3:4). Such an attitude leads to carelessness in Christian service and neglect of an adequate preparation for His return.

The question is often asked: Do the foolish virgins represent lost people? Certainly unbelievers are not prepared for His coming. Also, just as the foolish virgins found the door shut and were refused admission, likewise Jesus had described the fate of the unsaved in the parable of the Closed Door (Luke 13:25, #161). In this particular the two parables are alike. But I am sure that in this one Jesus meant to warn the disciples, to whom He spoke, that they should be prepared either for a delay in His coming, or for a sudden and unexpected coming.

(e) The parable of The Talents
#224
MATT. 25:14-30

14 For *it is* as *when* a man, going into another country, called his own [1]servants, and delivered unto them his goods. 15 And unto one he gave five talents, to another two, to another one; to each according to his several ability; and he went on his journey. 16 Straightway he that received the five talents went and traded with them, and made other five talents. 17 In like manner he also that *received* the two gained other two. 18 But he that received the one went away and digged in the earth, and hid his lord's money. 19 Now after a long time the lord of those [1]servants cometh, and maketh a reckoning with them. 20 And he that received the five talents came and brought other five talents, saying, Lord, thou deliveredst unto me five talents: lo, I have gained other five talents. 21 His lord said unto him, Well done, good and faithful [2]servant: thou hast been faithful over a few things, I will set thee over many things; enter thou into the joy of thy lord. 22 And he also that received the two talents came and said, Lord, thou deliveredst unto me two talents: lo, I have gained other two talents. 23 His lord said unto him, Well done, good and faithful [2]servant: thou hast been faithful over a few things, I will set thee over many things; enter thou into the joy of thy lord. 24 And he also that had received the one talent came and said, Lord, I knew thee that thou art a hard man, reaping where thou didst not sow, and gathering where thou didst not scatter; 25 and I was afraid, and went away and hid thy talent in the earth: lo, thou hast thine own. 26 But his lord answered and said unto him, Thou wicked and slothful [2]servant, thou knewest that I reap where I sowed not, and gather where I did not scatter; 27 thou oughtest therefore to have put my money to the bankers, and at my coming I should have received back mine own with interest. 28 Take ye away therefore the talent from him, and give it unto him that hath the ten talents. 29 For unto

[1] Gr. *bondservants*.　　　　[2] Gr. *bondservant*.

276

every one that hath shall be given, and he shall have abundance: but from him that hath not, even that which he hath shall be taken away. 30 And cast ye out the unprofitable ²servant into the outer darkness: there shall be the weeping and the gnashing of teeth.

² Gr. bondservant.

Note 225. Every Bible student observes similarities between the parable of The Talents and that of The Pounds, which Jesus had spoken a short time (likely not more than a week) earlier. Just as Jesus repeated some of His parables on more than one occasion,* so He would sometimes speak a parable which was a variation of one spoken earlier. Two outstanding examples are The Marriage Feast of the King's Son (#210), a variation of The Great Supper (#169), and The Talents in the section above, a variation of The Pounds (#194). The disciples, to whom our Lord addressed the parable of The Talents, must have recognized its close similarity to the parable of The Pounds; for they were in the group to whom He had spoken that parable, and it was surely fresh in their minds at this time.

But some important differences in these parables are noticeable. The parable of The Pounds is recorded only in Luke, that of The Talents only in Matthew. The parable of The Pounds was spoken to a considerable company of followers, including the disciples, as they were going up to Jerusalem for the Passover; that of The Talents was spoken on the Mount of Olives after a busy day of controversy in Jerusalem, and was addressed only to the disciples, possibly only to Peter and James and John and Andrew (Mark 13:3). There were differences in the details of the two parables; as in the number of servants employed (ten in the parable of The Pounds, three in that of The Talents), the amount of money involved (pounds in the earlier parable—minas, equivalent to about seventeen dollars each in American money; talents in the later parable, equivalent to about $1,500 or $22,500 each in American money, according to whether they were talents of silver or of gold), the comparative amount entrusted to each servant (in the earlier parable equal amounts, and in the later one in the ratio of five, two, and one), and in the way the enterprising and successful servants were rewarded or commended (in the earlier parable they were given as many cities as they had gained pounds, in the later one each servant who had doubled his capital was commended in the same language). Apparently Jesus implied in the parable of The Pounds that Christians of equal opportunity will be rewarded at His coming according to the fruits of their labors, and in the parable of The Talents that those of unequal opportunity will receive commendation according as they are faithful with what they have. Probably the greatest difference in the parables is in the points of emphasis. In the parable of The Pounds Jesus sought to

*For example, the parable of The Lamp in ##55, 94, and 153 and the parable of The Mustard Seed and that of The Leaven in ##96 and 97 and in #160, and the parable of The Lost Sheep, ##139, 171, and others.

correct the thought entertained by many that the visible Kingdom of God would be inaugurated during the coming Passover season. He endeavored to tell them that, before such expectation would be realized He (the nobleman) must go into a far (the heavenly) country and return. The primary emphasis was on His going away; the rewards on His return are seen as a consequence. But in the parable of The Talents He was impressing the disciples, who had inquired about a sign of His coming, that the best way to be ready for that coming would be through constant and faithful labors in the enterprise which He would entrust to them. The emphasis is on His return and the consequent rewards or commendation for labors, the going away being taken for granted.

(f) Simile of The Sheep and the Goats
#225
MATT. 25:31-46

31 But when the Son of man shall come in his glory, and all the angels with him, then shall he sit on the throne of his glory: 32 and before him shall be gathered all the nations: and he shall separate them one from another, as the shepherd separateth the sheep from the goats; 33 and he shall set the sheep on his right hand but the goats on the left. 34 Then shall the King say unto them on his right hand Come, ye blessed of my Father, inherit the kingdom prepared for you from the foundation of the world: 35 for I was hungry, and ye gave me to eat; I was thirsty and ye gave me drink; I was a stranger, and ye took me in; 36 naked, and ye clothed me; I was sick, and ye visited me; I was in prison, and ye came unto me 37 Then shall the righteous answer him, saying, Lord, when saw we thee hungry and fed thee? or athirst, and gave thee drink? 38 And when saw we thee a stranger and took thee in? or naked, and clothed thee? 39 And when saw we thee sick, or in prison, and came unto thee? 40 And the King shall answer and say unto them Verily I say unto you, Inasmuch as ye did it unto one of these my brethren, even these least, ye did it unto me. 41 Then shall he say also unto them on the left hand ¹Depart from me, ye cursed, into the eternal fire which is prepared for the devil and his angels: 42 for I was hungry, and ye did not give me to eat; I was thirsty and ye gave me no drink; 43 I was a stranger, and ye took me not in; naked and ye clothed me not; sick, and in prison, and ye visited me not. 44 Then shall they also answer, saying, Lord, when saw we thee hungry, or athirst, or a stranger, o naked, or sick, or in prison, and did not minister unto thee? 45 Then shall he answer them, saying, Verily I say unto you, Inasmuch as ye did it not unto one of these least, ye did it not unto me. 46 And these shall go away into eternal punishment but the righteous into eternal life.

¹ Or, Depart from me under a curse

Note 226. Our Lord climaxed His great prophetic discourse with a vivid delineation of a time of judgment involving all peoples. He had already spoken repeatedly of the judgment. Rewarding "every man according to his works" (Matt. 16: 27, #132) is undeniably an act of universal judgment. The parables of the Pounds (#194) and of the Talents (#224) imply a judgment of rewards for the servants of Christ. Implications or assertions of the judgment are found also in John 5: 22, 27 (#48), Matt. 7: 22, and other passages.

In the foregoing passage Jesus asserted that after His coming in glory, He will be seated on the throne of His glory, designating Himself as "the King." Since He previously had said (Matt. 19: 28, #189) that He will sit on the throne of His glory during the regeneration, or visible Kingdom, I take it that this judgment procedure will be during that period; or probably at its conclusion, since the wicked as well as the righteous will be present, and also since the people will be consigned to their everlasting destiny after the judgment.

Some students of the Bible understand this passage to describe a "judgment of nations" (that is, nationalities), because in our English versions the word "nations" is found in verse 32. Moreover, realizing that salvation is not a reward for good works, it seems odd to some interpreters that Jesus depicted the King as determining eternal destiny on the ground of the treatment accorded those whom He calls His brethren. Some say, therefore, that the nations of history will be called into account for the treatment which they have given to the Jewish people. But the word translated "nations" (genē) means primarily "races," or "peoples"—nations as aggregations of people, not as governmental units. And most probably the Lord Jesus was giving encouragement to the disciples, who would have to endure all these privations (hunger, thirst, loneliness, lack of clothing, sickness, and imprisonment) in the labors which He was committing to them. In that case, His brethren are all the heralds of salvation (cf. Matt. 12:50, also Heb. 2:11), rather than just the Jewish people. The treatment which any people accord the heralds of the gospel is indicative of their attitude toward the Lord Jesus. If they exercise faith in Him and are loyal to Him, they will undoubtedly be kindly disposed to His messengers who instruct them in the way of salvation.

7. Luke's summary of the movements of Jesus during the week

#226
LUKE 21:37-38
37 And every day he was teaching in the temple; and every night he went out, and lodged in the mount that is called Olivet. 38 And all the people came early in the morning to him in the temple, to hear him.

Note 227. The verses in the above section are a summary of the activities of Jesus during that week, probably beginning with the day of the Triumphant Entry. He was in the temple on Sunday, Monday, and Tuesday. He spent Sunday night and Monday night in Bethany (##200, 204), which was on the farther slope of the Mount of Olives from the city. But the word translated "lodged" in verse 37 (aulizomai) signifies "to pass the night in the open air;"* and this Jesus and the disciples undoubtedly did on Tuesday night and Wednesday night in a spot near the garden of Gethsamane. This may be how Judas knew where to lead his band of officers (cf. John 18:2, #239).

8. Plot formed to arrest and kill Him (Judas sells out)
#227

MATT. 26:1-5; 14-16	MARK 14:1-2; 10-11	LUKE 22:1-6
1 And it came ot pass, when Jesus had finished all these words, he said unto	1 Now after two days was *the feast* of the passover and the unleavened	1 Now the feast of unleavened bread drew nigh, which is called the Pass-

*Thayer, *A Greek English Lexicon of the New Testament.*

279

Matt. 26	Mark 14	Luke 22
his disciples, 2 Ye know that after two days the passover cometh, and the Son of man is ¹delivered up to be crucified. 3 Then were gathered together the chief priests, and the elders of the people, unto the court of the high priest, who was called Caiaphas; 4 and they took counsel together that they might take Jesus by subtlety, and kill him. 5 But they said, Not during the feast, lest a tumult arise among the people.	bread: and the chief priests and the scribes sought how they might take him with subtlety, and kill him: 2 for they said, Not during the feast, lest haply there shall be a tumult of the people.	over. 2 And the chief priests and the scribes sought how they might put him to death; for they feared the people.
14 Then one of the twelve, who was called Judas Iscariot, went unto the chief priests, 15 and said, What are ye willing to give me, and I will ¹deliver him unto you? And they weighed unto him thirty pieces of silver. 16 And from that time he sought opportunity to ¹deliver him *unto them*.	10 And Judas Iscariot, ¹he that was one of the twelve, went away unto the chief priests, that he might ²deliver him unto them. 11 And they, when they heard it, were glad, and promised to give him money. And he sought how he might conveniently ²deliver him *unto them*.	3 And Satan entered into Judas who was called Iscariot, being of the number of the twelve. 4 And he went away, and communed with the chief priests and captains, how he might ¹deliver him unto them. 5 And they were glad, and covenanted to give him money. 6 And he consented, and sought opportunity to ¹deliver him unto them ²in the absence of the multitude.

¹ See ch. 10. 4.

¹ Gr. *the one of the twelve.*
² See ch. 3. 19.

¹ Or, *betray*
² Or, *without tumult*

Note 228. I have included three incidents in the section above: (1) The statement of Jesus in regard to the approaching Passover and the treachery that He would suffer, (2) the called meeting of the Sanhedrin, or of its prominent leaders, to devise a way of taking Jesus without resentment of the multitude of common people who were in the city for the Passover, and (3) the defection of Judas in agreeing to deliver Jesus to His enemies for a price. The statement by Jesus is of help to us in dating His movements during this the last week of His earthly life. The called meeting of the Sanhedrin is no surprise to us after the miserable failure of their efforts all that day (Tuesday) to discredit Jesus before the multitude. It is possible that this meeting of priests and elders and scribes, before which Judas made his traitorous proposal, took place on Wednesday rather than Tuesday night. But if it did, the outline of the activities of Jesus during the week would not be changed, since He most probably rested on Wednesday.

VI. Wednesday

Note 229. Most students of the New Testament maintain that the Lord Jesus rested on Wednesday and a large part of Thursday. We know that He was crucified on the day before the Sabbath (Mark 15:42; John 19:31, #254), which was Friday. Therefore the eating of the Passover and the incidents that took place with it (##229-235) must have occurred on Thursday night. This accords with the words of Jesus spoken after the great prophecy (which was on Tuesday) that the Passover was then two days away (Matt. 26:2, #227). There is therefore no account of any activity of Jesus on Wednesday. With regard to the contention of some that the Passover was observed on Wednesday night and the crucifixion occurred Thursday see Note 260.

VII. Thurdsay, ##228-238
   1. Observance of the Passover by Jesus and His disciples
      ##228-231

Note 230. There are those who maintain that Jesus did not eat this Passover, but that the accounts we have are of another meal which He ate twenty-four hours earlier. Two reasons are generally set forth for this contention: (1) If Jesus in dying for the redemption of sinners is to be regarded as fulfillment of the Passover type (because the Passover lamb was slain for the redemption of the first-born Israelites), then it was proper, they say, for Jesus to die at the time when the Passover lambs were being slain; that is, in the afternoon of the fourteenth of Nisan. But it is presumptuous to set aside, merely for sentimental reasons, the plain records of the Synoptic Gospels that our Lord both had preparations made for the observance of the Passover (#228), and that He did observe the feast (Luke 22:15, #229). (2) They say that the phrase, "before the feast of the Passover," in John 13:1 indicates that the incidents related in that chapter occurred in connection with a meal before the Passover. But such conclusion is neither necessary, nor indeed probable. The verse merely says that before the feast Jesus realized that the hour had come for Him to return unto the Father (cf. Matt. 26:2, 18, ##227, 228), and that He loved His own with a love that endured to the end. It most probably described His emotions as He arrived at the upper room for the Passover observance, and while the disciples were hurrying to get the best places at the table. If the phrase in question means that all the incidents related in that chapter occurred before the Feast of the Passover, then John at this place is in conflict with the Synoptics. But certainly this is not the case; and truly Jesus did eat the Passover at the regular hour for the feast.

(1) Peter and John sent to make preparation
#228

MATT. 26:17-19	MARK 14:12-16	LUKE 22:7-13
17 Now on the first *day* of unleavened bread the disciples came to Jesus, saying, Where wilt thou that we make ready for thee to eat the passover?	12 And on the first day of unleavened bread, when they sacrificed the passover, his disciples say unto him, Where wilt thou that we go and make ready that	7 And the day of unleavened bread came, on which the passover must be sacrificed. 8 And he sent Peter and John, saying, Go and make ready for

Matt. 26	Mark 14	Luke 22
	thou mayest eat the pass-over? 13 And he sendeth two of his disciples, and saith unto them, Go into the city, and there shall meet you a man bearing a pitcher of water: follow him; 14 and wheresoever he shall enter in, say to the master of the house, The Teacher saith, Where is my guest-chamber, where I shall eat the passover with my disciples? 15 And he will himself show you a large upper room furnished *and* ready: and there make ready for us. 16 And the disciples went forth, and came into the city, and found as he had said unto them: and they made ready the passover.	us the passover, that we may eat. 9 And they said unto him, Where wilt thou that we make ready? 10 And he said unto them, Be-hold, when ye are entered into the city, there shall meet you a man bearing a pitcher of water; follow him into the house where-into he goeth. 11 And ye shall say unto the master of the house, The Teacher saith unto thee, Where is the guest-chamber, where I shall eat the passover with my disciples? 12 And he will show you a large upper room furnished: there make ready. 13 And they went, and found as he had said unto them: and they made ready the passover.
18 And he said, Go into the city to such a man, and say unto him, The Teacher saith, My time is at hand; I keep the passover at thy house with my disciples. 19 And the disciples did as Jesus appointed them; and they made ready the pass-over.		

Note 231. The day for slaughtering the Passover lamb was the fourteenth of Nisan, or Abib (cf. Exod. 12:6). The preparations which Peter and John were to make would be: securing a lamb, having it killed by a priest in the temple, attending to the roasting of it, and securing other items necessary such as the unleavened bread, the wine, the bitter herbs, and anything else needful. The instructions by which they would know where to make these preparations involved supernatural knowledge on the part of Jesus; and this was a miracle performed in the same pow-er as that by which He worked other miracles. This was not the first exercise of such supernatural knowledge by the Lord Jesus (as examples cf. Matt. 21:2 and parallels, John 11:11, 14). It has been suggested, and reasonably, that the purpose of Jesus in giving the instructions in such a way that they would know the location of the house only after they followed the instructions, was to keep Judas in the dark, so that he would not come with the arresting band of officers before the Passover was finished, or before Jesus had opportunity to speak farewell words of warning and encouragement to the loyal disciples. Probably the owner of the upper room was an admirer and disciple of Jesus and was expect-ing, or at least hoping, that Jesus might make this request. Indeed, Jesus may already have spoken to him about it. According to Mark's account, Jesus said that they would find the room "furnished and pre-pared." This likely means that it was supplied with the necessary table and couches, and that it was made ready, even to the removal of every-thing that would resemble or suggest leaven (cf. Exod. 12:15). This is interesting in view of the suggestion which some have made that this house was probably Mark's father's home.* After the resurrection, an

*Edersheim, *Life and Times of Jesus*, Vol. II, p. 485.

upper room—v e r y probably t h i s one—was the meeting place f o r the apostles (Acts 1: 13); and we know that later, when Peter's life was threatened, the home of Mark's mother was a meeting place for the Jerusalem church, where prayer was made for the apostle (Acts 12: 12).

(2) Arrival at the upper room, first passing of the Passover cup

#229

MATT. 26:20	MARK 14:17	LUKE 22:14	JOHN 13:1
			1 Now before the feast of the passover, Jesus knowing that his hour was come that he should depart out of this world unto the Father, having loved his own that were in the world, he loved them ¹unto the end.
20 Now when even was come, he was ¹sitting at meat with the twelve ²disciples; ¹ Or, *reclining at table* ² Many authorities, some ancient, omit *disciples*.	17 And when it was evening he cometh with the twelve.	14 And when the hour was come, he sat down, and the apostles with him.	¹ Or, *to the uttermost*

LUKE 22:15-18

15 And he said unto them, With desire I have desired to eat this passover with you before I suffer: 16 for I say unto you, I shall not eat it, until it be fulfilled in the kingdom of God. 17 And he received a cup, and when he had given thanks, he said, Take this, and divide it among yourselves: 18 for I say unto you, I shall not drink from henceforth of the fruit of the vine, until the kingdom of God shall come.

Note 232. The hour was about sunset, as the fourteenth of Nisan turned into the fifteenth. Jesus led the ten disciples from their camping place on the Mount of Olives to the house of the upper room, the location of which the disciples with Him did not know until they arrived. This was the first Passover that Jesus attended after choosing the twelve; and so it was His only opportunity of observing the feast with the apostles. When our Lord spoke of the Passover's being "fulfilled in the Kingdom of God" (vs. 16 in Luke) He evidently implied that the salvation of sinners in consequence of His atoning death would be the fulfillment of the Jewish memorial feast, since it was in consequence of the first Passover that the Israelites were delivered f r o m Egyptian slavery. Such fulfillment will be seen in its completion and consummation in the future visible manifestation of the Kingdom of God. That was certainly the manifestation of the Kingdom of which He spoke in verse 18. The passing of the cup in verse 17 is not to be confused with that at the institution of the Lord's Supper, which took place later (#232). This was doubtless the first of the four customary passings of the cup during the Passover.*

In ##229—232, I have followed the order given in Matthew, Mark, and John, which differs from that in Luke. Although Luke proposed in

Ibid., p. 496.

his preface (Luke 1:3, #2) "to write...in order," the order followed here not only has the weight of more witnesses, but seems the most natural for what Jesus did and said.

(3) The disciples rebuked for their covetous ambition, a lesson in humility (Jesus washing the feet of the disciples)
#230

LUKE 22:24-27

24 And there arose also a contention among them, which of them was accounted to be [1]greatest.

25 And he said unto them, The kings of the Gentiles have lordship over them; and they that have authority over them are called Benefactors. 26 But ye *shall* not *be* so: but he that is the greater among you, let him become as the younger; and he that is chief, as he that doth serve. 27 For which is greater, he that [2]sitteth at meat, or he that serveth? is not he that [2]sitteth at meat? but I am in the midst of you as he that serveth.

JOHN 13:2-17

2 And during supper, the devil having already put into the heart of Judas Iscariot, Simon's *son*, to [1]betray him, 3 *Jesus,* knowing that the Father had given all things into his hands, and that he came forth from God, and goeth unto God, 4 riseth from supper, and layeth aside his garments; and he took a towel, and girded himself. 5 Then he poureth water into the basin, and began to wash the disciples' feet, and to wipe them with the towel wherewith he was girded. 6 So he cometh to Simon Peter. He saith unto him, Lord, dost thou wash my feet? 7 Jesus answered and said unto him, What I do thou knowest not now; but thou shalt understand hereafter. 8 Peter saith unto him, Thou shalt never wash my feet. Jesus answered him, If I wash thee not, thou hast no part with me. 9 Simon Peter saith unto him, Lord, not my feet only, but also my hands and my head. 10 Jesus saith to him. He that is bathed needeth not [2]save to wash his feet, but is clean every whit: and ye are clean, but not all. 11 For he knew him that should [1]betray him; therefore said he, Ye are not all clean.

12 So when he had washed their feet, and taken his garments, and [3]sat down again, he said unto them, Know ye what I have done to you? 13 Ye call me, Teacher, and, Lord: and ye say well; for so I am.

14 If I then, the Lord and the Teacher, have washed your feet, ye also ought to wash one another's feet. 15 For I have given you an example, that ye also should do as I have done to you. 16 Verily, verily, I say unto you, A [4]servant is not greater than his lord; neither [5]one that is sent greater than he that sent him. 17 If ye know these things, blessed are ye if ye do them.

[1] Or, *deliver him up*
[2] Some ancient authorities omit *save,* and *his feet.*   [3] Gr. *reclined.*
[4] Gr. *bondservant.*   [5] Gr. *an apostle.*

[1] Gr. *greater.*   [2] Gr. *reclineth.*

284

Note 233. I have made the above passages from Luke and John parallel because they both are an account of how the Lord Jesus dealt that night with pride and personal ambition. Luke has set forth in verse 24 the wrong that Jesus sought to correct, followed by some words that He said in reproof. John showed how Jesus reproved them for this wrong by means of His example as well as his words. Compare what Jesus had already said to them about their ambition in Matt. 18: 1—5; 20: 25—28; 23: 10—12, ##138, 191, 215. Surely His words as recorded in verses 25—27 of Luke came somewhere among His teachings as recorded by John after the washing of the disciples' feet. The last clause of Luke 22: 26 indicated that He had already performed that service.

In verse 2 of John the translation "during supper" in the American Standard Version (also the Revised Standard) is a better representation of the Greek words than "supper being ended," which is found in the King James Version. A good literal translation would be, "supper being in progress." This was the situation after the passing of the first cup. Edersheim remarks that at this point in the feast it was customary for the head of the household to rise and wash his hands; and he suggests that, instead of washing His hands, Jesus laid aside His outer garment and prepared to wash the disciples' feet—possibly without their knowing what He had in mind until He came to the first one to be washed. This first one he (Edersheim) surmises to have been Peter.*

The use of sandals in New Testament times made washing of the feet a needful and common act of hospitality. Doubtless provision for such comfort was furnished by the average host, and in wealthier homes servants were usually provided to perform the courtesy for the guests. Peter and John in preparing for the Passover had provided the basin and water and towel, but evidently did not propose to perform the service of washing the feet of the others. Doubtless during the day they had all bathed themselves in preparation for observance of the feast (cf. vs. 10) so that physically and ceremonially they were clean except for their feet. But their hearts were fouled with jealousy and pride and personal ambition. The action of Jesus, therefore, not only removed the dust from the feet of the disciples, who were so anxious to obtain a high place in the Kingdom that they would not wash their own (or their brethern's) feet; but it would lead also to the cleansing of their hearts from jealousy and greed—that is, with the exception of that one into whose heart the devil had put the purpose to betray the Master. And Jesus knew about that one, and in His loving ministration He washed the dust off his feet also, but the heart of the traitor remained as foul as ever.

But I do not believe that our Lord meant that foot-washing should be practiced in the churches as an ordinance, for the following reasons: (1) The disciples certainly did not so understand it, since there is no evidence that any of the churches of the New Testament ever so practiced it as an ordinance. The earliest mention of such practice found in

*Ibid., p. 499.

285

church history is in the decrees by a council of bishops at Elvira, Spain, about 306 A.D. in which it was condemned.* (2) It does not set forth pictorially any great truth connected with the way of salvation as do the two recognized ordinances—the Lord's Supper depicting the atoning death of the Saviour and baptism His burial and victorious ressurrection. (3) To have given a command to observe the act as a church ordinance would have destroyed the force of a command to practice it when needed as a service. In verses 14—15 our Lord surely meant to enjoin this ministry on the disciples whenever a brother stood in need of such service.

(4) Prediction of treachery of Judas, his departure
#231

MATT. 26:21-25	MARK 14:18-21	LUKE 22:21-23	JOHN 13:18-32
			18 I speak not of you all: I know whom I ¹have chosen: but that the scripture may be fulfilled, ²He that eateth ³my bread lifted up his heel against me. 19 From henceforth I tell you before it come to pass, that, when it is come to pass, ye may believe that I am *he*. 20 Verily, verily, I say unto you, He that receiveth me receiveth him that sent me.
21 and as they were eating, he said, Verily I say unto you, that one of you shall ¹betray me. 22 And they were exceeding sorrowful, and began to say unto him every one, Is it I, Lord? 23 And he answered and said, He that dipped his hand with me in the dish, the same shall ¹betray me. 24 The Son of man goeth, even as it is written of him: but woe unto that man through whom the Son of man is ¹betrayed! ¹ See marginal note on ch. 10. 4.	18 And as they ¹sat and were eating, Jesus said, Verily I say unto you, One of you shall ²betray me, even he that eateth with me. 19 They began to be sorrowful, and to say unto him one by one, Is it I? 20 And he said unto them, *It is* one of the twelve, he that dippeth with me in the dish. 21 For the Son of man goeth, even as it is written of him: but woe unto that man through whom the ¹ Gr. *reclined.*	21 But behold, the hand of him that ¹betrayeth me is with me on the table. 22 For the Son of man indeed goeth, as it hath been determined: but woe unto that man through whom he is ¹betrayed! 23 And they began to question among themselves, which of them it was that should do this thing. ¹ See ver. 4.	21 When Jesus had thus said, he was troubled in the spirit, and testified, and said, Verily, verily, I say unto you, that one of you shall ⁴betray me. 22 The disciples looked one on another, doubting of whom he spake. 23 There was at the table reclining in Jesus' bosom one of his disciples, whom Jesus loved. 24 Simon Peter therefore beckoneth to him, and saith unto ¹ Or, *chose* ² Ps. xli. 9. ³ Many ancient authorities read *his bread with me.* ⁴ Or, *deliver me up*

*Albert Henry Newman, *A Manual of Church History* (Philadelphia: American Baptist Publications Society, 1904), Vol. I, p. 140.

Matt. 26	Mark 14	John 13
good were it [2]for that man if he had not been born.	Son of man is [2]betrayed! good were it [3]for that man if he had not been born.	him, Tell us who it is of whom he speaketh. 25 He leaning back, as he was, on Jesus' breast saith unto him, Lord, who is it? 26 Jesus therefore answereth, He it is, for whom I shall dip the sop, and give it him. So when he had dipped the sop, he taketh and giveth it to Judas, the son of Simon Iscariot. 27 And after the sop, then entered Satan into him. Jesus therefore saith unto him, What thou doest, do quickly. 28 Now no man at the table knew for what intent he spake this unto him. 29 For some thought, because Judas had the [5]bag, that Jesus said unto him, Buy what things we have need of for the feast; or, that he should give something to the poor. 30 He then having received the sop went out straightway: and it was night.
[25] And Judas, who [1]betrayed him, answered and said, Is it I, Rabbi? He saith unto him, Thou hast said.		31 When therefore he was gone out, Jesus saith, Now [6]is the Son of man glorified, and God [6]is glorified in him; 32 and God shall glorify him in himself, and straightway shall he glorify him.

[2] Gr. for him if that man.

[2] See marginal note on ch. 3. 19.
[3] Gr. for him if that man.

[5] Or, box   [6] Or, was

Note 234. The perfidy of Judas was deepened by his reclining at the table with Jesus and partaking of the same meal with Him. In eastern lands for two to eat together implied a covenant or pledge of friendship.* But Judas was calmly partaking of this sacred meal with the

*Marcus Dods, The Gospel of St. John in The Expositor's Greek Testament (op cit.) Vol. I, p. 818.

Master even after he had agreed with the enemies of Jesus to deliver Him to them for a price. Jesus knew this, and to call attention to his baseness He quoted (vs. 18 in John) from Psalm 41:9. When He announced plainly that one of them would betray Him, they all (that is, eleven of them) thought that He meant that one of them would unwittingly do something which would result in His being taken by His enemies. It is a bit difficult to give the exact order of all the sayings in all the gospel records in the above section. But we can be sure that Jesus let Judas know that He was aware of what that one had in mind. On the other hand, the disciples seemingly did not realize that Jesus had identified Judas as the traitor—possibly even John and Peter did not understand the sign that Jesus gave John (cf. vs. 28 in John). The fact that some of the disciples supposed that Jesus bade Judas to buy something for the feast (vs. 29 in John) has occasioned difficulty for some, since they were already in the act of eating the Passover feast. But "the feast" in their minds included also the feast of unleavened bread, which lasted a week. And indeed, we do not know how ample had been their provision for the whole occasion.

Of course, the disciples did not know what awaited Jesus. But Jesus knew it all—the treacherous arrest, the sham court trials by those who were determined to be rid of Him before the people generally could protest, the torture inflicted by the officers and soldiers, the excruciating death by crucifixion, and above all "bearing our sins in His own body on the tree" (cf. I Pet. 2:24)—He knew it all, and it is no wonder that "He was troubled in the spirit" (cf. vs. 21 in John). Doubtless He was troubled also for the disciples—was grieved because of the selfish ambition and pride which they had manifested that night. And He was pained beyond measure for Judas, who had submitted to feet-washing by the Master and afterward sat blandly partaking of the Passover while planning to deliver the Lord to His enemies at the first opportunity.

The saying of Jesus after the departure of Judas (vss. 31–32) reminds us of His words at the coming of the Greeks (John 12:23, #199; 17:1, #237). Jesus regarded the hour of His death as the hour of His glory, because His death was the climax of His service to the world (cf. Matt. 20:28, #191, Phil. 2:8–11; Rev. 5:9).

2. Last words of Jesus with His disciples (before His death) ##232—236

(1) Institution of the Memorial Supper

#232

MATT. 26:26-29	MARK 14:22-25	LUKE 22:19-20
26 And as they were eating, Jesus took [1]bread, and blessed, and brake it; and he gave to the disciples, and said, Take, eat; this is my body.	22 And as they were eating, he took [1]bread, and when he had blessed, he brake it, and gave to them, and said, Take ye: this is my body.	19 And he took [1]bread, and when he had given thanks, he brake it, and gave to them, saying, This
[1] Or, a loaf	[1] Or, a loaf	[1] Or, a loaf

Matt. 26	Mark 14	Luke 22
27 And he took a [2]cup, and gave thanks, and gave to them, saying, Drink ye all of it; 28 for this is my blood of the [3]covenant, which is poured out for many unto remission of sins. 29 But I say unto you, I shall not drink henceforth of this fruit of the vine, until that day when I drink it new with you in my Father's kingdom.	23 And he took a cup, and when he had given thanks, he gave to them: and they all drank of it. 24 And he said unto them, This is my blood of the [2]covenant, which is poured out for many. 25 Verily I say unto you, I shall no more drink of the fruit of the vine, until that day when I drink it new in the kingdom of God.	is my body [2]which is given for you: this do in remembrance of me. 20 And the cup in like manner after supper, saying, This cup is the new covenant in my blood, even that which is poured out for you.
[2] Some ancient authorities read *the cup.* [3] Many ancient authorities insert *new.*	[2] Some ancient authorities insert *new.*	[2] Some ancient authorities omit *which is given for you . . . which is poured out for you.*

Note 235. Besides these accounts of the institution of the Memorial Supper appearing in the Synoptic Gospels, one is found in I Cor. 11: 23–26, which Paul says he "received of the Lord." The question continues to arise in the minds of some Bible students: Had Judas departed from the upper room when Jesus instituted the Lord's Supper? According to the order in Matthew and Mark he had, but in Luke the account of the institution of the Supper precedes the account of the words of Jesus about Judas' treachery. John does not tell about the institution of the Lord's Supper, but he does say that Judas departed before the Passover supper was finished. Moreover, Luke states that the institution of the Lord's Supper came "after supper" (vs. 20 above, cf. I Cor. 11: 25); that is, after celebrating the Passover. I assume, therefore, that all the accounts imply that the traitor had withdrawn when Jesus instituted the Memorial Supper. Certainly Jesus realized that Judas was not interested in doing anything to perpetuate the memory of a broken body or shed blood which He Himself was preparing to break and to shed.

Notice how, according to Matthew, the Lord Jesus connected the shedding of His blood with the remission of sins. He had predicted His death many times; He had asserted that the laying down of His life would be "for the sheep" (John 10: 11, #164), that the giving of His life would be a ransom for many (Matt. 20:28, #191); but at this time, within less than twenty-four hours of its taking place, He spoke of it as the ground for remission of sins.

Luke was the only gospel writer who recorded our Lord's command to continue to observe the Supper (vs. 19), but he was joined in this by Paul, who under inspiration delivered to the Corinthians that which he had "received of the Lord" (I Cor. 11: 23). As the Passover meal, which this group had just eaten, commemorated the deliverance of the Israelites from slavery in Egypt—the event regarded as the most important in Israel's history—so the importance in the program of redemption which Jesus attached to His atoning death is shown by His command that His followers observe as a recurring ordinance this Supper, depicting His broken body and His shed blood. From I Cor. 11: 18—20 (American Standard Version) we conclude that the Supper was meant to be observed in church capacity.

(2) Prediction that Peter would deny Jesus
#233

MATT. 26:31-35	MARK 14:27-31	LUKE 22:28-38	JOHN 13:33-38
		28 But ye are they that have continued with me in my temptations; 29 and ¹I appoint unto you a kingdom, even as my Father appointed unto me, 30 that ye may eat and drink at my table in my kingdom; and ye shall sit on thrones judging the twelve tribes of Israel.	
			33 Little children, yet a little while I am with you. Ye shall seek me: and as I said unto the Jews, Whither I go, ye cannot come; so now I say unto you. 34 A new commandment I give unto you, that ye love one another; ¹even as I have loved you, that ye also love one another. 35 By this shall all men know that ye are my disciples, if ye have love one to another.
31 Then saith Jesus unto them, All ye shall be offended in me this night: for it is written, ¹I will smite the shepherd, and the sheep of the flock shall be scattered abroad. 32 But after I am raised up, I will go before you into Galilee. 33 But Peter answered and said unto him, If all shall be ²offended in thee, I will never be ²offended. 34 Jesus said unto him, Verily	27 And Jesus saith unto them, All ye shall be ¹offended: for it is written, ²I will smite the shepherd, and the sheep shall be scattered abroad. 28 Howbeit, after I am raised up, I will go before you into Galilee. 29 But Peter said unto him, Although all shall be ¹offended, yet will not I. 30 And Jesus saith unto him, Verily I say unto thee, that thou to-	31 Simon, Simon, behold, Satan ²asked to have you, that he might sift you as wheat: 32 but I made supplication for thee, that thy faith fail not; and do thou, when once thou hast turned again, establish thy brethren. 33 And he said unto him, Lord, with thee I am ready	36 Simon Peter saith unto him, Lord, whither goest thou? Jesus answered, Whither I go, thou canst not follow me now; but thou shalt follow afterwards. 37 Peter saith unto him, Lord, why cannot I follow thee even now? I will lay down my life for thee. 38 Jesus answereth, Wilt thou lay down thy life for me? Verily, verily, I say unto thee, The
¹ Zech. xiii. 7. ² Gr. *caused to stumble.*	¹ Gr. *caused to stumble.* ² Zech. xiii. 7.	¹ Or, *I appoint unto you, even as my Father appointed unto me a kingdom, that ye may eat and drink &c.* ² Or, *obtained you by asking*	¹ Or, *even as I loved you, that ye also may love one another.*

290

Matt. 26	Mark 14	Luke 22	John 13
I say unto thee, that this night, before the cock crow, thou shalt deny me thrice. 35 Peter saith unto him, Even if I must die with thee, *yet* will I not deny thee. Likewise also said all the disciples.	day, *even* this night, before the cock crow twice, shalt deny me thrice. 31 But he spake exceeding vehemently, If I must die with thee, I will not deny thee. And in like manner also said they all.	to go both to prison and to death. 34 And he said, I tell thee, Peter, the cock shall not crow this day, until thou shalt thrice deny that thou knowest me. 35 And he said unto them, When I sent you forth without purse, and wallet, and shoes, lacked ye anything? And they said, Nothing. 36 And he said unto them, But now, he that hath a purse, let him take it, and likewise a wallet; ³and he that hath none, let him sell his cloak, and buy a sword. 37 For I say unto you, that this which is written must be fulfilled in me, ⁴And he was reckoned with transgressors: for that which concerneth me hath ⁵fulfilment. 38 And they said, Lord, behold, here are two swords. And he said unto them, It is enough. ³ Or, *and he that hath no sword, let him sell his cloak, and buy one.* ⁴ Is. liii. 12. ⁵ Gr. *end.*	cock shall not crow, till thou hast denied me thrice.

Note 236. All the Gospel records relate that Jesus forewarned Peter that before daybreak he would deny his Master, and they all present this prediction following Peter's strong, even boastful, declaration of his loyalty to Jesus. But the occasion of Peter's strong statement was not set forth in them all as the same. The order which I have indicated seems to be the logical one: first verses 28–30 of Luke, then verses 33–37 of John, then verses 31–33 of Matthew and 27–29 in Mark, then verses 31–33 in Luke, and finally the definite prediction of Peter's denials. In verse 33 of John, Jesus referred to statements that He had made at the Feast of Tabernacles about six months earlier (cf. John 7: 34; 8: 31).

Verses 31–32 in Luke are frequently misunderstood because the reader does not notice the difference between the plural "you"* in verse

*In the language of the King James Version and of the American Standard Version "you" is used only in the plural number and objective case.

31 and the singulars "thee," "thou," and "thy" of verse 32. Satan had desired (literally, "asked") the privilege of sifting the group of apostles. Judas had already, as it were, fallen through the sieve. Would Peter be next? Possibly in the days that followed he came nearer deserting the company than we realize, and was kept from doing so only because Jesus prayed for him. After the removal of Judas, Simon Peter would sink the deepest of them all in spirit, but he would emerge the strongest. Thus he would be in position to strengthen the others. Probably it was with this in mind that Jesus gave in this connection the injunction for mutual love in verses 34—35 of John.

We do not know who volunteered the information that two swords were in the room; but, since Peter and John had made the preparations for the Passover, they were surely the ones who found them. Peter evidently carried one of them along with him when they left the room, intending to make good his promise of loyalty to Jesus, even if it meant imprisonment and death. As far back as the day at Caesarea Philippi, when Jesus first announced that it would be necessary for Him to suffer and die, Peter had protested, "Lord, this shall not be unto Thee." (Matt. 16:22, #131).

> (3) First section of parting discourse to the disciples—
>   in the upper room

Note 237. After the departure of Judas from the group in the upper room, and after the Passover supper was finished and the Memorial Supper was instituted, Jesus and the remaining disciples lingered around the table before singing the customary closing Psalm,* while He spoke to them final words of comfort and encouragement and warning. Then when they did sing the hymn and depart, He continued to address them as they made their way back to their accustomed place of encampment on the Mount of Olives. John alone has preserved those farewell words in chapters 14, 15, and 16 of his gospel. In these precious utterances and in the Intercessory Prayer which followed (John 17), the beloved disciple has given us an insight into the emotional life of the Lord Jesus found nowhere else in the gospels. We cannot but be touched by the Master's unselfish concern for the disciples who were soon to be bereft of His presence, especially when we realize that He knew the sufferings and the horrors which He Himself would endure during the next eighteen hours. These sayings of our Lord, in true Johannine style, defy our efforts at detailed analysis; but they are better appreciated when we feel their implications than when we subject them to logical analysis. He spoke repeatedly on each of the following topics: His intimate relation with the Father, the Holy Spirit and His work for and through Christians, the power in prayer to which they would have access, His leaving them and yet being still with them, the persecutions which they would have to endure, their love for Him as manifested in keeping

*Edersheim, *Life and Times of Jesus*, Vol. II, pp. 513, 533.

His commandments, and their love for each other. To the Christian overtaken in sorrow, or discouraged by failure, or facing opposition or persecution, or feeling the need of power, these chapters constitute a most precious part of the Bible.

#234

JOHN 14:1-31

1 Let not your heart be troubled: [1]believe in God, believe also in me. 2 In my Father's house are many [2]mansions; if it were not so, I would have told you; for I go to prepare a place for you. 3 And if I go and prepare a place for you, I come again, and will receive you unto myself; that where I am, *there* ye may be also. 4 [3]And whither I go, ye know the way. 5 Thomas saith unto him, Lord, we know not whither thou goest; how know we the way? 6 Jesus saith unto him, I am the way, and the truth, and the life: no one cometh unto the Father, but [4]by me. 7 If ye had known me, ye would have known my Father also: from henceforth ye know him, and have seen him. 8 Philip saith unto him, Lord, show us the Father, and it sufficeth us. 9 Jesus saith unto him, Have I been so long time with you, and dost thou not know me, Philip? he that hath seen me hath seen the Father; how sayest thou, Show us the Father? 10 Believest thou not that I am in the Father, and the Father in me? the words that I say unto you I speak not from myself: but the Father abiding in me doeth his works. 11 Believe me that I am in the Father, and the Father in me; or else believe me for the very works' sake. 12 Verily, verily, I say unto you, He that believeth on me, the works that I do shall he do also; and greater *works* than these shall he do; because I go unto the Father. 13 And whatsoever ye shall ask in my name, that will I do, that the Father may be glorified in the Son. 14 If ye shall ask [5]anything in my name, that will I do. 15 If ye love me, ye will keep my commandments. 16 And I will [6]pray the Father, and he shall give you another [7]Comforter, that he may be with you for ever, 17 *even* the Spirit of truth: whom the world cannot receive; for it beholdeth him not, neither knoweth him: ye know him; for he abideth with you, and shall be in you. 18 I will not leave you [8]desolate: I come unto you. 19 Yet a little while, and the world beholdeth me no more; but ye behold me: because I live, [9]ye shall live also. 20 In that day ye shall know that I am in my Father, and ye in me, and I in you. 21 He that hath my commandments, and keepeth them, he it is that loveth me: and he that loveth me shall be loved of my Father, and I will love him, and will manifest myself unto him. 22 Judas (not Iscariot) saith unto him, Lord, what is come to pass that thou wilt manifest thyself unto us, and not unto the world? 23 Jesus answered and said unto him, If a man love me, he will keep my word: and my Father will love him, and we will come unto him, and make our abode with him. 24 He that loveth me not keepeth not my words: and the word which ye hear is not mine, but the Father's who sent me.

25 These things have I spoken unto you, while *yet* abiding with you. 26 But the [7]Comforter, *even* the Holy Spirit, whom the Father will send in my name, he shall teach you all things, and bring to your remembrance all that I said unto you. 27 Peace I leave with you; my peace I give unto you: not as the world giveth, give I unto you. Let not your heart be troubled, neither let it be fearful. 28 Ye heard how I said to you, I go away, and I come unto you. If ye loved me, ye would have rejoiced, because I go unto the Father: for the Father is greater than I. 29 And now I have told you before it come to pass, that, when it is come to pass, ye may believe. 30 I will no more speak much with you, for the prince of the world cometh: and he hath nothing [10]in me; 31 but that the world may know that I love the Father, and as the Father gave me commandment, even so I do. Arise, let us go hence.

[1] Or, *ye believe in God*   [2] Or, *abiding-places*
[3] Many ancient authorities read *And whither I go ye know, and the way ye know.*
[4] Or, *through*   [5] Many ancient authorities add *me.*   [6] Gr. *make request of.*
[7] Or, *Advocate*   Or, *Helper*   Gr. *Paraclete.*   [8] Or, *orphans*   [9] Or, *and ye shall live*
[10]Or, *in me.*   31 *But that &c. . . . . I do, arise &c.*

(4) Departure for Gethsemane
#235

MATT. 26:30	MARK 14:26	LUKE 22:39
30 And when they had sung a hymn, they went out into the mount of Olives.	26 And when they had sung a hymn, they went out unto the mount of Olives.	39 And he came out, and went, as his custom was, unto the mount of Olives; and the disciples also followed him.

Note 238. At length Jesus suggested that the group should be going, and doubtless after rising and singing the hymn (or Psalm) with which the Jews usually closed their observance of the Passover, they departed for their lodging place on the Mount of Olives, in or near the Garden of Gethsemane. As they were leaving the upper room, Peter probably lingered behind the others to take one of the swords, which he and John had found, and to conceal it under his cloak. While they walked along, or as they paused here and there, Jesus continued to address them with the consoling and encouraging words found in John 15 and 16. Somewhere along the way He paused for the Prayer of report to the Father and presentation of the disciples as is related in John 17.

(5) Discourse spoken on the way to Gethsemane
#236
JOHN 15:1 — 16:33

1 I am the true vine, and my Father is the husbandman. 2 Every branch in me that beareth not fruit, he taketh it away: and every *branch* that beareth fruit, he cleanseth it, that it· may bear more fruit. 3 Already ye are clean because of the word which I have spoken unto you. 4 Abide in me, and I in you. As the branch cannot bear fruit of itself, except it abide in the vine; so neither can ye, except ye abide in me. 5 I am the vine, ye are the branches: He that abideth in me, and I in him, the same beareth much fruit: for apart from me ye can do nothing. 6 If a man abide not in me, he is cast forth as a branch, and is withered; and they gather them, and cast them into the fire, and they are burned. 7 If ye abide in me, and my words abide in you, ask whatsoever ye will, and it shall be done unto you. 8 Herein ¹is my Father glorified, ²that ye bear much fruit; and *so* shall ye be my disciples. 9 Even as the Father hath loved me, I also have loved you: abide ye in my love. 10 If ye keep my commandments, ye shall abide in my love: even as I have kept my Father's commandments, and abide in his love. 11 These things have I spoken unto you, that my joy may be in you, and *that* your joy may be made full. 12 This is my commandment, that ye love one another, even as I have loved you. 13 Greater love hath no man than this, that a man lay down his life for his friends. 14 Ye are my friends, if ye do things which I command you. 15 No longer do I call you ³servants; for the ⁴servant knoweth not what his lord doeth: but I have called you friends; for all things that I heard from my Father I have made known unto you. 16 Ye did not choose me, but I chose you, and appointed you, that ye should go and bear fruit, and *that* your fruit should abide: that whatsoever ye shall ask of the Father in my name, he may give it you. 17 These things I command you, that ye may love one another. 18 If the world hateth you, ⁵ye know that it hath hated me before *it hated* you. 19 If ye were of the world, the world would love its own: but because ye are not of the world, but I chose you out of the world, therefore the world hateth you. 20 Remember the word that I said unto you, A ⁴servant is not greater than his lord. If they persecuted me, they will also persecute you; if they kept my word, they will keep yours also. 21 But all these things will they do unto you for my name's sake, because they know not him that sent me. 22 If I had not come and spoken unto them, they had not had sin: but now they have no excuse for their sin. 23 He that hateth me hateth my Father also. 24 If I had not done among them the works which none other did, they had not had sin: but

¹ Or, *was*   ² Many ancient authorities read *that ye bear much fruit, and be my disciples.*
³ Gr. *bondservants.*   ⁴ Gr. *bondservant.*   ⁵ Or, *know ye*

now have they both seen and hated both me and my Father. 25 But *this cometh to pass*, that the word may be fulfilled that is written in their law, "They hated me without a cause. 26 But when the [7]Comforter is come, whom I will send unto you from the Father, *even* the Spirit of truth, which [8]proceedeth from the Father, he shall bear witness of me: 27 [9]and ye also bear witness, because ye have been with me from the beginning.

1 These things have I spoken unto you, that ye should not be caused to stumble. 2 They shall put you out of the synagogues: yea, the hour cometh, that whosoever killeth you shall think that he offereth service unto God. 3 And these things will they do, because they have not known the Father, nor me. 4 But these things have I spoken unto you, that when their hour is come, ye may remember them, how that I told you. And these things I said not unto you from the beginning, because I was with you. 5 But now I go unto him that sent me; and none of you asketh me, Whither goest thou? 6 But because I have spoken these things unto you, sorrow hath filled your heart. 7 Nevertheless I tell you the truth: It is expedient for you that I go away; for if I go not away, the [7]Comforter will not come unto you; but if I go, I will send him unto you. 8 And he, when he is come, will convict the world in respect of sin, and of righteousness, and of judgment: 9 of sin, because they believe not on me; 10 of righteousness, because I go to the Father, and ye behold me no more; 11 of judgment, because the prince of this world hath been judged. 12 I have yet many things to say unto you, but ye cannot bear them now. 13 Howbeit when he, the Spirit of truth, is come, he shall guide you into all the truth: for he shall not speak from himself; but what things soever he shall hear, these shall he speak: and he shall declare unto you the things that are to come. 14 He shall glorify me: for he shall take of mine, and shall declare *it* unto you. 15 All things whatsoever the Father hath are mine: therefore said I, that he taketh of mine, and shall declare *it* unto you. 16 A little while, and ye behold me no more; and again a little while, and ye shall see me. 17 *Some* of his disciples therefore said one to another, What is this that he saith unto us, A little while, and ye behold me not; and again a little while, and ye shall see me: and, Because I go to the Father? 18 They said therefore, What is this that he saith, A little while? We know not what he saith. 19 Jesus perceived that they were desirous to ask him, and he said unto them, Do ye inquire among yourselves concerning this, that I said, A little while, and ye behold me not, and again a little while, and ye shall see me? 20 Verily, verily, I say unto you, that ye shall weep and lament, but the world shall rejoice: ye shall be sorrowful, but your sorrow shall be turned into joy. 21 A woman when she is in travail hath sorrow, because her hour is come: but when she is delivered of the child, she remembereth no more the anguish, for the joy that a man is born into the world. 22 And ye therefore now have sorrow: but I will see you again, and your heart shall rejoice, and your joy no one taketh away from you. 23 And in that day ye shall [10]ask me no question. Verily, verily, I say unto you, If ye shall ask anything of the Father, he will give it you in my name. 24 Hitherto have ye asked nothing in my name: ask, and ye shall receive, that your joy may be made full.

25 These things have I spoken unto you in [11]dark sayings: the hour cometh, when I shall no more speak unto you in [11]dark sayings, but shall tell you plainly of the Father. 26 In that day ye shall ask in my name: and I say not unto you, that I will [12]pray the Father for you; 27 for the Father himself loveth you, because ye have loved me, and have believed that I came forth from the Father. 28 I came out from the Father, and am come into the world: again, I leave the world, and go unto the Father. 29 His disciples say, Lo, now speakest thou plainly, and speakest no [13]dark saying. 30 Now know we that thou knowest all things, and needest not that any man should ask thee: by this we believe that thou camest forth from God. 31 Jesus answered them, Do ye now believe? 32 Behold, the hour cometh, yea, is come, that ye shall be scattered, every man to his own, and shall leave me alone: and *yet* I am not alone, because the Father is with me. 33 These things have I

[6] Ps. xxxv. 19; lxix. 4.   [7] Or, *Advocate*   Or, *Helper*   Gr. *Paraclete*.   [8] Or, *goeth forth from*
[9] Or, *and bear ye also witness*   [10] Or, *ask me nothing*   Comp. ver. 26; ch. 14. 13, 20.
[11] Or, *parables*   [12] Gr. *make request of.*   [13] Or, *parable*

spoken unto you, that in me ye may have peace. In the world ye have tribulation: but be of good cheer; I have overcome the world.

(6) The Intercessory Prayer (or Prayer or Report to the Father)

#237

JOHN 17:1-26

1 These things spake Jesus; and lifting up his eyes to heaven, he said, Father, the hour is come; glorify thy Son, that the Son may glorify thee: 2 even as thou gavest him authority over all flesh, that ¹to all whom thou hast given him, he should give eternal life. 3 And this is life eternal, that they should know thee the only true God, and him whom thou didst send, *even* Jesus Christ. 4 I glorified thee on the earth, having accomplished the work which thou hast given me to do. 5 And now, Father, glorify thou me with thine own self with the glory which I had with thee before the world was. 6 I manifested thy name unto the men whom thou gavest me out of the world: thine they were, and thou gavest them to me; and they have kept thy word. 7 Now they know that all things whatsoever thou hast given me are from thee: 8 for the words which thou gavest me I have given unto them; and they received *them*, and knew of a truth that I came forth from thee, and they believed that thou didst send me. 9 I ²pray for them: I ²pray not for the world, but for those whom thou hast given me; for they are thine: 10 and all things that are mine are thine, and thine are mine: and I am glorified in them. 11 And I am no more in the world, and these are in the world, and I come to thee. Holy Father, keep them in thy name which thou hast given me, that they may be one, even as we *are*. 12 While I was with them, I kept them in thy name which thou hast given me: and I guarded them, and not one of them perished, but the son of perdition; ³that the scripture might be fulfilled. 13 But now I come to thee; and these things I speak in the world, that they may have my joy made full in themselves. 14 I have given them thy word; and the world hated them, because they are not of the world, even as I am not of the world. 15 I ²pray not that thou shouldest take them ⁴from the world, but that thou shouldest keep them ⁴from ⁵the evil *one*. 16 They are not of the world, even as I am not of the world. 17 ⁶Sanctify them in the truth: thy word is truth. 18 As thou didst send me into the world, even so ·sent I them into the world. 19 And for their sakes I ⁶sanctify myself, that they themselves also may be sanctified in truth. 20 Neither for these only do I ²pray, but for them also that believe on me through their word; 21 that they may all be one; even as thou, Father, *art* in me, and I in thee, that they also may be in us: that the world may believe that thou didst send me. 22 And the glory which thou hast given me I have given unto them; that they may be one, even as we *are* one; 23 I in them, and thou in me, that they may be perfected into one; that the world may know that thou didst send me, and lovedst them, even as thou lovedst me. 24 Father, ⁷I desire that they also whom thou hast given me be with me where I am, that they may behold my glory, which thou hast given me: for thou lovedst me before the foundation of the world. 25 O righteous Father, the world knew thee not, but I knew thee; and these knew that thou didst send me; 26 and I made known unto them thy name, and will make it known; that the love wherewith thou lovedst me may be in them, and I in them.

¹ Gr. *whatsoever thou hast given him, to them he &c.*   ² Gr. *make request.*
³ Ps. xli. 9?   ⁴ Gr. *out of.*   ⁵ Or, *evil*   ⁶ Or, *Consecrate*
⁷ Gr. *that which thou hast given me, I desire that where I am, they also may be with me, that &c.*

Note 239. The Intercessory Prayer is in the nature of a report by the Son of God to the Father concerning His work as Prophet and Teacher. For three and a half years He had labored teaching the people as "One having authority" (Mark 1:22, #37) or as "a Teacher come from God," (John 3:2, #26), winning disciples, a n d giving them special instruction to prepare them for proclaiming the salvation which He would achieve for the race of sinners in His death and resurrection. He had also wrought many miracles of healing and otherwise, which brought joy to many and evidenced God's approval of His labors and teaching. Our Lord had now finished this work (verse 4), concluding it with the words of encouragement just spoken to the disciples; and there remained only the suffering and the climactic victory—the dying for sin and the vanquishing of death in a resurrection.

In this prayer no fewer than eight times Jesus cited things which He had done in fulfilling the work that the Father had committed to Him. A major part of these labors was with the disciples, whom He invariably (six times) referred to in this prayer as those whom the Father had given Him. These He now presented to God as the products of His years of labor. The objective of His working with them was that He might send them into the world (vs. 18). Most of the petitions in this prayer were for the disciples. In verses 20—21 He included all that would become disciples until the end of time, but in verses 22 and 24 He reverted again to those with whom He had labored.

The one petition which He made for Himself was that God would glorify Him so that He in turn might glorify the Father. These words certainly are to be interpreted in the light of what He said in John 12:23ff (#199) and 13:31--32 (#231), in both of which passages He connected the hour of His glory with the hour of His death. His death for sinners and the salvation which He has procured through His death has been, and forever will be, the ground of His pre-eminent glory (Phil. 2:9—11; Rev. 5:9—10). No greater example of submission to God and dedication to a mission of labors and self-sacrifice can be found than in this Intercessory Prayer.

3. Arrival at the Garden of Gethsemane, His great agony of soul and His deeply earnest prayer
#238

MATT. 26:36-46	MARK 14:32-42	LUKE 22:40-46	JOHN 18:1
36 Then cometh Jesus with them unto a place called Gethsemane, and saith unto his disciples, Sit ye here, while I go yonder and pray. 37 And he took with him Peter and the two sons of Zebedee, and began to be sorrowful and sore troubled. 38 Then saith he unto them, My soul is exceeding sorrowful, even unto death: abide ye here, and watch. Gr. an enclosed piece of ground.	32 And they come unto ¹a place which was named Gethsemane: and he saith unto his disciples, Sit ye here, while I pray. 33 And he taketh with him Peter and ²James and John, and began to be greatly amazed, and sore troubled. 34 And he saith unto them, My soul is exceeding sorrowful even unto death: abide ye here, and watch. 35 And he ¹ Gr. an enclosed piece of ground. ² Or, Jacob	40 And when he was at the place, he said unto them, Pray that ye enter not into temptation. 41 And he was parted from them about a stone's cast; and he kneeled down and prayed, 42 saying, Father, if thou be willing, remove this cup from me: nevertheless not my will, but thine, be done. 43 ¹And there appeared unto him an angel from heaven, ¹ Many ancient authorities omit ver. 43, 44.	1 When Jesus had spoken these words, he went forth with his disciples over the ¹brook ²Kidron, where was a garden, into which he entered, himself and his disciples. ¹ Or, ravine Gr. winter-torrent. ² Or, of the Cedars

297

Matt. 26	Mark 14	Luke 22
with me. 39 And he went forward a little, and fell on his face, and prayed, saying, My Father, if it be possible, let this cup pass away from me: nevertheless, not as I will but as thou wilt. 40 And he cometh unto the disciples, and findeth them sleeping, and saith unto Peter, What, could ye not watch with me one hour? 41 ²Watch and pray, that ye enter not into temptation: the spirit indeed is willing, but the flesh is weak. 42 Again a second time he went away, and prayed, saying, My Father, if this cannot pass away, except I drink it, thy will be done. 43 And he came again and found them sleeping, for their eyes were heavy. 44 And he left them again, and went away, and prayed a third time, saying again the same words. 45 Then cometh he to the disciples, and saith unto them, ³Sleep on now, and take your rest: behold, the hour is at hand, and the Son of man is ⁴betrayed into the hands of sinners. 46 Arise, let us be going: behold, he is at hand that ⁴betrayeth me.	went forward a little, and fell on the ground, and prayed that, if it were possible, the hour might pass away from him. 36 And he said, Abba, Father, all things are possible unto thee; remove this cup from me: howbeit not what I will, but what thou wilt. 37 And he cometh, and findeth them sleeping, and saith unto Peter, Simon, sleepest thou? couldest thou not watch one hour? 38 ³Watch and pray, that ye enter not into temptation: the spirit indeed is willing, but the flesh is weak. 39 And again he went away, and prayed, saying the same words. 40 And again he came, and found them sleeping, for their eyes were very heavy; and they knew not what to answer him. 41 And he cometh the third time, and saith unto them, ⁴Sleep on now, and take your rest: it is enough; the hour is come; behold, the Son of man is ⁵betrayed into the hands of sinners. 42 Arise, let us be going: behold, he that ⁵betrayeth me is at hand.	strengthening him. 44 And being in an agony he prayed more earnestly; and his sweat became as it were great drops of blood falling down upon the ground. 45 And when he rose up from his prayer, he came unto the disciples, and found them sleeping for sorrow, 46 and said unto them, Why sleep ye? rise and pray, that ye enter not into temptation.

² Or, *Watch ye, and pray that ye enter not*
³ Or, *Do ye sleep on, then, and take your rest?*
⁴ See marginal note on ch. 10. 4.

³ Or, *Watch ye, and pray that ye enter not*
⁴ Or, *Do ye sleep on, then, and take your rest?*
⁵ See marginal note on ch. 3. 19.

Note 240. We are sometimes puzzled that the Intercessory Prayer of John 17 is followed so closely by the turbulent prayers of Gethsemane.

In the Intercessory Prayer, our Lord spoke of His coming death as His being glorified—indeed, He seemed rather to have looked altogether beyond the tortures of His death to His being reunited with the Father. But in the prayers in Gethsemane, He saw death as a bitter cup pressed to His lips, so bitter that He shrank from it and asked if it might not be removed. From the time of His baptism, some three and a half years before, He had faced, seemingly without flinching, this hour which He knew must come. We sometimes wonder why this sudden change in attitude. Why this exceeding sorrow? Why such stirring of His soul as to produce the bloody sweat? And especially why at this late hour the imploring that, if it were possible, the cup might be removed and He should be spared the experience of death and sin bearing? Of these questions I am sure we shall never know the full answer, because we shall never know the depth of humiliation and suffering and soul agony that Jesus endured. But I suggest three circumstances which might have had some bearing on it: (1) This was not the first time that He experienced this sorrow and dread of His death. At the time of the coming of the Greeks, when He spoke the parable of The Grain of Wheat He exclaimed that His soul was sorrowful, and He seems to have debated whether or not to ask for deliverance from the hour of death (John 12: 20—28, particularly vss. 23 and 27, #199). And the transfiguration experience was probably given Him to encourage and strengthen Him after He first clearly made known that death and a resurrection were involved in His earthly mission (#133 and Note 134). (2) Up to this point He had probably given Himself in such complete abandonment to the work He had been doing that He had never realized (in the state of His self-emptying) the depth of woe and agony to which He would descend in order to achieve salvation for sinners. This work, in a large measure, was making preparation to have the salvation proclaimed to the world. But now, having finished the work (John 17: 4), He began to consider the sacrificial part of His mission, the sufferings which were so near at hand. And it all came to Him with a disturbing, agitating shock. (3) The sufferings that loomed before Him were more than the shame and injustice of His arrest and the mock Jewish trials and the hurried Roman trial, more than the physical suffering of death by crucifixion, though that was the most painful manner of execution that the Romans could contrive. Through the centuries many martyrs have endured the tortures of the rack and death at the stake of burning with thanksgiving that they were permitted thus to suffer for Him. Jesus realized that, in addition to all these things which others have endured, He would give His life (His soul) as a ransom price for sinners (Matt. 20: 28, #191). This involved bearing their sins in His body (I Pet. 2: 24), being made sin for them (II Cor. 5: 21), enduring the curse of the law for those who have broken the law (Gal. 3: 13). He foresaw that in this suffering He would be deprived even of the sustaining presence of the Father (Matt. 27: 46, #252), because the Lord would lay on Him the iniquity of us all (cf. Isa. 53:6). This was suffering infinitely greater than that endured by any martyr or by any other person crucified. Probably He foresaw all this for the first time in the limitations of His human life, and it filled Him with such dread that it all but shook His purpose of many months.

But His steadfast faith in, and loyalty to, the Father saved Him in this His most trying hour. "Not as I will," He prayed, "but as Thou wilt" (vs. 39 in Matt.). And in the second prayer this loyal submissiveness to the Father is in the position of emphasis (vs. 42 in Matt.). After the third prayer and after the visit by the strengthening angel from Heaven (vs. 43 in Luke), the victory was complete. Could it be that He was given to see again something of the eternal plan by which salvation for sinners would be achieved without compromising the interests of Holiness? And was He promised the legions of angels to defend Him from His foes if He should ask for them (Matt. 26:53, #239)? But He did not—He would not—so pray. However, He who was Lord of angels, though now for a little while made lower than the angels for the suffering of death (Heb. 2:9), received strength from an angel; and in that strength He calmly faced all the shame and torture that was about to come upon Him.

VIII. Friday, ##239—254
1. Jesus betrayed and arrested, Peter's rash effort to defend Him

#239

MATT. 26:47-56	MARK 14:43-52	LUKE 22:47-53	JOHN 18:2-12
			2 Now Judas also, who ¹betrayed him, knew the place: for Jesus oft-times resorted thither with his disciples. 3 Judas then, having received the ²band *of soldiers*, and officers from the chief priests and the Pharisees, cometh thither with lanterns and torches and weapons.
47 And while he yet spake, lo, Judas, one of the twelve, came, and with him a great multitude with swords and staves, from the chief priests and elders of the people. 48 Now he that ¹betrayed him gave them a sign, saying, Whomsoever I shall kiss, that is he: take him. 49 And straightway he came to Jesus, and said, Hail, Rabbi; and ²kissed him. 50 And Jesus said unto him, Friend, *do* that for which thou art come.	43 And straightway, while he yet spake, cometh Judas, one of the twelve, and with him a multitude with swords and staves, from the chief priests and the scribes and the elders. 44 Now he that betrayed him had given them a token, saying, Whomsoever I shall kiss, that is he; take him, and lead him away safely. 45 And when he was come, straightway he came to him, and saith, Rabbi; and ¹kissed him.	47 While he yet spake, behold, a multitude, and he that was called Judas, one of the twelve, went before them; and he drew near unto Jesus to kiss him. 48 But Jesus said unto him, Judas, ¹betrayest thou the Son of man with a kiss?	
			4 Jesus therefore, knowing all the things that were coming upon him,
¹ See marginal note on ch. 10. 4.			¹ Or, *delivered him up*
² Gr. *kissed him much.*	¹ Gr. *kissed him much*	¹ See ver. 4.	² Or, *cohort*

300

Matt. 26	Mark 14	Luke 22	John 18
			went forth, and saith unto them, Whom seek ye? 5 They answered him, Jesus of Nazareth. Jesus saith unto them, I am *he*. And Judas also, who ¹betrayed him, was standing with them. 6 When therefore he said unto them, I am *he*, they went backward, and fell to the ground. 7 Again therefore he asked them, Whom seek ye? And they said, Jesus of Nazareth.
Then they came and laid hands on Jesus, and took him. 51 And behold, one of them that were with Jesus stretched out his hand, and drew his sword, and smote the ³servant of the high priest, and struck off his ear. 52 Then saith Jesus unto him, Put up again thy sword into its place: for all they that take the sword shall perish with the sword. 53 Or thinkest thou that I cannot beseech my Father, and he shall even now send me more than twelve legions of angels? 54 How then should the scriptures be fulfilled, that thus it must be? 55 In that hour said Jesus to the multitudes, Are ye come out as against a robber with swords and staves to seize me? I sat daily in the temple teaching, and ye took me not. 56 But all this is come to pass, that the scriptures of the	46 And they laid hands on him, and took him. 47 But a certain one of them that stood by drew his sword, and smote the ²servant of the high priest, and struck off his ear. 48 And Jesus answered and said unto them, Are ye come out, as against a robber, with swords and staves to seize me? 49 I was daily with you in the temple teaching, and ye took me not: but *this is done* that the scriptures might be fulfilled. 50 And they all left him, and fled. 51 And a certain young man followed with him, having a linen cloth cast about him, over *his* naked *body*: and they lay hold on him; 52 but he left the linen cloth, and fled naked.	49 And when they that were about him saw what would follow, they said, Lord, shall we smite with the sword? 50 And a certain one of them smote the ²servant of the high priest, and struck off his right ear. 51 But Jesus answered and said, Suffer ye *them* thus far. And he touched his ear, and healed him. 52 And Jesus said unto the chief priests, and captains of the temple, and elders, that were come against him, Are ye come out, as against a robber, with swords and staves? 53 When I was daily with you in the temple, ye	8 Jesus answered, I told you that I am *he;* if therefore ye seek me, let these go their way: 9 that the word might be fulfilled which he spake, Of those whom thou hast given me I lost not one. 10 Simon Peter therefore having a sword drew it, and struck the high priest's ³servant, and cut off his right ear. Now the ³servant's name was Malchus. 11 Jesus therefore said unto Peter, Put up the sword into the sheath: the cup which the Father hath given me, shall I not drink it? 12 So the ²band and the ⁴chief captain, and the officers of the Jews, seized Jesus and bound him,
³ Gr. *bondservant.*	² Gr. *bondservant.*	² Gr. *bondservant.*	³ Gr. *bondservant* ⁴ Or, *military tribune* Gr. *chiliarch.*

301

Matt. 26	Luke 22
prophets might be fulfilled. Then all the disciples left him, and fled.	stretched not forth your hands against me: but this is your hour, and the power of darkness.

Note 241. The calmness with which Jesus met the band of soldiers and arresting officers, the care He exercised to assure the safety of the loyal disciples, and His readiness to drink the cup of death which the Father was giving Him, along with His refusal to call for any of the twelve legions of defending angels, are all in sharp contrast with His troubled spirit in the prayer which He had just poured out to the Father. Indeed, all the actions of Jesus from this time until the outcry of spiritual anguish on the cross are characterized by a composure and calmness beyond our understanding. Was that composure the consequence of the strengthening ministry of the angel? Does it bespeak the sustaining presence of the Father with Him up to the hour of darkness and the outcry? His demeanor in these hours of stress, particularly His silence as He faced His accusers before the high priest, and later as He stood before Pilate, was surely a fulfillment of the prophecy in Isa. 53:7.

It is interesting to observe how each of the four Gospel writers told about Peter's wielding a sword and cutting off the high priest's servant's ear. Only John identified the assailant by name. Possibly that was because Peter did not like to talk about it; and the Synoptists, who doubtless wrote during that apostle's lifetime, had respect for his desires in the matter. Some interpreters have supposed that, as long as Peter lived, he was in danger of being charged with rebellion against Rome if it should be known that he used a sword in opposition to a band of Roman soldiers; and for that reason Matthew, Mark, and Luke would not, while he was living, relate who it was that drew the sword. But after the death of Peter, John saw no need of withholding any longer the name of the disciple who undertook to defend Jesus from the arresting band. Doubtless John called his name to show that his companion in Christian labors for many years, sincerely intended to make good his promise to go with Jesus even to prison and to death if necessary.

The rebuke which Jesus addressed to Peter is altogether different in each of the Gospel writings. Mark, who according to tradition traveled with Peter in later years as interpreter, did not relate at all the words of Jesus to the apostle. Luke, who had related that there were two swords in the upper room (vs. 38, #233), and who indicated in this connection that others were also ready to strike, seems to have summed up the response of Jesus in one sentence, "Suffer ye thus far." John, who did not relate the prayers of agony in the garden, nevertheless quoted Jesus as saying, "The cup that My Father hath given me, shall I not drink it?" Matthew, who wrote for Jewish readers, has the fullest account of this reprimand by Jesus, but altogether different from the others. Three points are included in it: (1) Entering into a conflict of force subjects one to the peril of destruction. Certainly in that instance, if Peter had persisted in resisting, he would, without a miracle from God, have brought destruction on the whole band. These words of Jesus were in accord with His teachings on non-resistance: (2) If Jesus had been minded to resist, the legions of angels would have been put at His command. A little while before He had prayed the Father: "If it be possible, let this cup pass..., nevertheless...as Thou wilt." But now, having gained the victory in prayer, He would not ask for the legions of angels. (3) To the members of the Sanhedrin who were present, Jesus showed that He regarded His death to be a fulfillment of Scripture, and Matthew was careful to preserve this for his Jewish readers. Certainly Jesus said all the things that each and all the Gospels ascribe to Him. The rebuke must have stung Peter very deeply, and doubtless it aroused a spirit of resentment.

If, as many have supposed, Mark was the young man mentioned in verses 51—52 of his Gospel, this was one incident in the life of Jesus which he could relate as an eyewitness.

2. The "trials" of Jesus, ##240—247
   (1) Those before Jewish "judges" and events connected with them, ##240—244

Note 242. After He was arrested in the garden, Jesus was brought three times before Jewish dignitaries and officers. For want of a better word we call those appearances before representatives of the law of that day "trials," though it is a travesty to do so. The first "trial" was a private examination by Annas, an ex-high priest; the second was also a preliminary examination by Caiaphas, the high priest, and picked members of the Sanhedrin gathered in unofficial capacity; and the third was before the Sanhedrin, hastily gathered in an official meeting to give sentence against Jesus.

These Jewish authorities were not in position to give Jesus a fair and impartial trial. They had secured His arrest by bribing one of the disciples. Moreover, Caiaphas, the high priest who would preside over the formal meeting of the Sanhedrin, had already expressed his verdict when he counseled some weeks previously that it was expedient for Jesus to die (John 11: 50, #179). Furthermore, they were in no temper for giving Him a fair trial, because on two occasions (one of them just four days earlier) Jesus had purged the temple courts of the dealers in animals for sacrifice and the money-changers, whom these priests had licensed, and from whose traffic they, particularly Annas, received a large income.

a. Preliminary questioning by Annas a former High
   Priest

#240
JOHN 18:13-14, 19-23
13 And led him to Annas first; for he was father in law to Caiaphas, who was

303

high priest that year. 14 Now Caiaphas was he that gave counsel to the Jews, that it was expedient that one man should die for the people.

19 The high priest therefore asked Jesus of his ,disciples, and of his teaching. 20 Jesus answered him, I have spoken openly to the world; I ever taught in ¹synagogues, and in the temple, where all the Jews come together; and in secret spake I nothing. 21 Why askest thou me? ask them that have heard *me*, what I spake unto them: behold, these know the things which I said. 22 And when he had said this, one of the officers standing by struck Jesus ²with his hand, saying, Answerest thou the high priest so? 23 Jesus answered him, If I have spoken evil, bear witness of the evil: but if well, why smitest thou me?

¹ Gr. *synagogue*.   ² Or, *with a rod*

Note 243. The Jewish high priests wielded so great an influence that the Roman rulers assumed the authority to appoint them and remove them from office. Annas had been the high priest from A. D. 7 to 14, and he continued to exercise tremendous influence after he was deposed. He was soon able to get a son of his appointed as high priest, and a little later his son-in-law, Caiaphas, who was the high priest at this time. Still later four other sons exercised at different times the office of high priest. Even while Caiaphas was the real high priest, Annas was sometimes called high priest. Thus in verse 19 of the above passage John probably referred to Annas rather than Caiaphas. He is definitely named as the high priest in Acts 4:6, and in Luke 3:2 both Annas and Caiaphas are mentioned together as the high priests. This probably meant that, during the twelve years when Caiaphas held the title and performed the outward functions of the position, Annas formed the policies and made the decisions of the office. He and his family are said to have been arrogant and rapacious, and immensely rich. Their wealth had largely come from the traffic in sacrificial animals and other requisites for the temple service, including the Jewish coins for the temple tax. They were hated by their fellow Jews.

It is probable that the purpose of this examination was to get some ground for accusing Jesus which would have a semblance of legality. But when he inquired about the disciples of Jesus and His teaching, Jesus merely challenged him to seek information from any who heard him; and the crafty priest got no advantage. The action of the officer in striking Jesus was outrageous.

b. Unofficial examination by the High Priest Caiaphas and some picked members of the Sanhedrin (First period of mockery)

#241

MATT. 26:57, 59-68	MARK 14:53, 55-65	LUKE 22:54a, 63-65	JOHN 18:24
57 And they that had taken Jesus led him away to *the house of* Caiaphas the high priest, where the scribes and the elders were gathered together.	53 And they led Jesus away to the high priest: and there come together with him all the chief priests and the elders and the scribes.	54 And they seized him, and led him *away*, and brought him into the high priest's house.	24 Annas therefore sent him bound unto Caiaphas the high priest.

Matt. 26   Mark 14   Luke 22

59 Now the chief priests and the whole council sought false witness against Jesus, that they might put him to death; 60 and they found it not, though many false witnesses came. But afterward came two, 61 and said, This man said, I am able to destroy the ¹temple of God, and to build it in three days. 62 And the high priest stood up, and said unto him, Answerest thou nothing? what is it which these witness against thee? 63 But Jesus held his peace. And the high priest said unto him, I adjure thee by the living God, that thou tell us whether thou art the Christ, the Son of God. 64 Jesus saith unto him, Thou hast said: nevertheless I say unto you, Henceforth ye shall see the Son of man sitting at the right hand of Power, and coming on the clouds of heaven. 65 Then the high priest rent his garments, saying, He hath spoken blasphemy: what further need have we of witnesses? behold, now ye have heard the blasphemy: 66 what think ye? They answered and said, He is ²worthy of death.

67 Then did they spit in his face and buffet him: and some smote him ³with the palms of their hands, 68 saying, Prophesy unto us, thou Christ: who is he that struck thee?

¹ Or, sanctuary: as in ch. 23. 35; 27. 5.
² Gr. liable to.   ³ Or, with rods

55 Now the chief priests and the whole council sought witness against Jesus to put him to death; and found it not. 56 For many bare false witness against him, and their witness agreed not together. 57 And there stood up certain, and bare false witness against him, saying, 58 We heard him say, I will destroy this ¹temple that is made with hands, and in three days I will build another made without hands. 59 And not even so did their witness agree together. 60 And the high priest stood up in the midst, and asked Jesus, saying, Answerest thou nothing? what is it which these witness against thee? 61 But he held his peace, and answered nothing. Again the high priest asked him, and saith unto him, Art thou the Christ, the Son of the Blessed? 62 And Jesus said, I am: and ye shall see the Son of man sitting at the right hand of Power, and coming with the clouds of heaven. 63 And the high priest rent his clothes, and saith, What further need have we of witnesses? 64 Ye have heard the blasphemy: what think ye? And they all condemned him to be ²worthy of death. 65 And some began to spit on him, and to cover his face, and to buffet him, and to say unto him, Prophesy: and the officers received him with ³blows of their hands.

¹ Or, sanctuary   ² Gr. liable to.
³ Or, strokes of rods

63 And the men that held ¹Jesus mocked him, and beat him. 64 And they blindfolded him, and asked him, saying, Prophesy: who is he that struck thee? 65 And many other things spake they against him, reviling him.

¹ Gr, him.

Note 244. The purpose of this examination was doubtless to induce Jesus to say something which the Sanhedrin leaders might use in accusing Him (cf. Luke 11: 53—54, #154). Their first tactic seems to have been to employ false witnesses who would accuse Him of some crime, expecting Jesus to deny their accusation; and from this denial they would formulate a charge. But, in the first place, the "witnesses"

305

did not agree in their "testimony." And in the second place, Jesus did not answer them, even when two of them perverted His words of three years before, that, if or when they should destroy the temple (and John said that He spoke of the temple of His body), He would raise it up in three days (John 2: 19, #25). The failure of the "witnesses" to agree and the dignified silence of Jesus were an embarrassment to the high priest and the others present. Therefore, in desperation they demanded of Him a confession of His messiahship and divine sonship, which confession they might make the basis of a charge of blasphemy. Though He had refused to answer their false accusations, He did not refuse to confess the nature of His mission on earth or His relation to the Father. And He added to the confession a prophecy that in due time they would see a glorious confirmation of His words, which prophecy enraged the members of the Sanhedrin all the more. The abuses and indignities heaped on Jesus at the close of this examination, while they were waiting for the dawn and full meeting of the Sanhedrin, were altogether uncalled-for. They were forbidden by the Jewish law of that time, but they revealed the temper and the character of the high priest who permitted them.

Observe that, in this "trial," the Great High Priest, who was about to offer Himself without blemish unto God as a Sin Offering, was facing one who disgraced the sacred office which, through the centuries since Aaron, had typified the true high priesthood. And it is a stroke of irony that Caiaphas, the titular high priest, in demanding the death of Him who was both the true High Priest and Sin Offering—this death being the true and effective atonement for sin—was doing that which would make the Jewish priesthood on earth unnecessary forever afterward.

c. Peter denying any connection with or knowledge of
   Jesus

#242

MATT. 26:58, 69-75	MARK 14:54, 66-72	LUKE 22:54b-62	JOHN 18:15-18, 25-27
58 But Peter followed him afar off, unto the court of the high priest, and entered in, and sat with the officers, to see the end.	54 And Peter had followed him afar off, even within, into the court of the high priest; and he was sitting with the officers, and warming himself in the light *of the fire.*	54b But Peter followed afar off. 55 And when they had kindled a fire in the midst of the court, and had sat down together, Peter sat in the midst of them.	15 And Simon Peter followed Jesus, and *so did* another disciple. Now that disciple was known unto the high priest, and entered in with Jesus into the court of the high priest; 16 but Peter was standing at the door without. So the other disciple, who was known unto the high priest, went out and spake unto her that kept the door, and brought in Peter. 17 The maid therefore
69 Now Peter was sitting without in the court: and a maid came unto him,	66 And as Peter was beneath in the court, there cometh one of the maids of	56 And a certain maid seeing him as he sat in the light *of the fire,* and look-	

306

Matt. 26	Mark 14	Luke 22	John 18

saying, Thou also wast with Jesus the Galilaean. 70 But he denied before them all, saying, I know not what thou sayest. 71 And when he was gone out into the porch, another *maid* saw him, and saith unto them that were there, This man also was with Jesus of Nazareth. 72 And again he denied with an oath, I know not the man. 73 And after a little while they that stood by came and said to Peter, Of a truth thou also art *one* of them; for thy speech maketh thee known. 74 Then began he to curse and to swear, I know not the man. And straightway the cock crew. 75 And Peter remembered the word which Jesus had said, Before the cock crow, thou shalt deny me thrice. And he went out, and wept bitterly.

the high priest; 67 and seeing Peter warming himself, she looked upon him, and saith, Thou also wast with the Nazarene, *even* Jesus. 68 But he denied, saying, [1] I neither know, nor understand what thou sayest: and he went out into the [2] porch; [3] and the cock crew. 69 And the maid saw him, and began again to say to them that stood by, This is *one* of them. 70 But he again denied it. And after a little while, again they that stood by said to Peter, Of a truth thou' art *one* of them: for thou art a Galilaean. 71 But he began to curse, and to swear, I know not this man of whom ye speak. 72 And straightway the second time the cock crew. And Peter called to mind the word; how that Jesus said unto him, Before the cock crow twice, thou shalt deny me thrice. [4]And when he thought thereon he wept.
[1] Or, *I neither know, nor understand: thou, what sayest thou?*
[2] Gr. *forecourt.*
[3] Many ancient authorities omit *and the cock crew.*
[4] Or, *And he began to weep*

ing stedfastly upon him, said, This man also was with him. 57 But he denied, saying, Woman, I know him not. 58 And after a little while another saw him, and said, Thou also art *one* of them. But Peter said, Man, I am not. 59 And after the space of about one hour another confidently affirmed, saying, Of a truth this man also was with him; for he is a Galilaean. 60 But Peter said, Man, I know not what thou sayest. And immediately, while he yet spake, the cock crew. 61 And the Lord turned, and looked upon Peter. And Peter remembered the word of the Lord, how that he said unto him, Before the cock crow this day thou shalt deny me thrice. 62 And he went out and wept bitterly.

that kept the door saith unto Peter, Art thou also *one* of this man's disciples? He saith, I am not. 18 Now the [1]servants and the officers were standing *there*, having made [2]a fire of coals; for it was cold; and they were warming themselves: and Peter also was with them, standing and warming himself.
[1] Gr. *bondservants.*
[2] Gr. *a fire of charcoal.*

25 Now Simon Peter was standing and warming himself. They said therefore unto him, Art thou also *one* of his disciples? He denied, and said, I am not. 26 One of the [1]servants of the high priest, being a kinsman of him whose ear Peter cut off, saith, Did not I see thee in the garden with him? 27 Peter therefore denied again: and straightway the cock crew.
[1] Gr. *bondservants.*

Note 245. Peter's first two denials of the Lord Jesus probably occurred during the unofficial examination of Jesus by Caiaphas and the other invited members of the Sanhedrin, and the third possibly after that examination and before the formal "trial" by the Sanhedrin—during the time while the officers and others were heaping abuse a n d insult on Jesus (#241).

Peter seems to have been late getting from the garden to the place where they had led Jesus; possibly he did not go to the house of Annas at all. Had he come by way of the upper room to leave the sword which he had taken to the garden? What thoughts were in his mind at this time? Was he blaming Jesus for not letting him use the sword more? Probably, in spite of what Jesus had repeatedly said, he still entertained hopes of an early inauguration of the visible Kingdom of God (cf. Luke 19: 11, #194); and he likely thought, when he was swinging the sword, that he was striking the first blow in its defense. But since Jesus had stopped him with the sharp rebuke, he was confused.

What motive led Peter to deny his Lord? Was it fear? If he had been afraid, he would not likely have drawn a sword in a group that included Roman soldiers, and even less likely would he have followed Jesus and the officers to the palace of the high priest where they were trying Him. More probably he was disappointed and confused, if not offended or angry, because Jesus would not let Peter defend Him. For around eight months (since they were at Caesarea Philippi) Jesus had been telling them that this was going to happen, but Peter, at the first mention of the matter, had taken Jesus to task about it; and in the end he seems to have set himself to keep it from coming to pass. Now, since he had been frustrated in that purpose, he probably felt "let down," and may even have contemplated really leaving Jesus and His band. Were the denials in accord with a line of action that Peter was really considering? Was Peter, like Judas, about to slip through Satan's sifter, out of the company of the disciples of Jesus? But to keep Peter from taking such a course Jesus had prayed for him; and in answer to that prayer Peter would yet declare his love for, and his loyalty to, his Lord (Luke 22: 32, #233; John 21: 15ff, #268).

d. Formal trial before the Sanhedrin, condemnation for blasphemy

#243

MATT. 27:1	MARK 15:1a	LUKE 22:66-71
1 Now when morning was come, all the chief priests and the elders of the people took counsel against Jesus to put him to death:	1 And straightway in the morning the chief priests with the elders and scribes, and the whole council, held a consultation,	66 And as soon as it was day, the assembly of the elders of the people was gathered together, both chief priests and scribes; and they led him away into their council, saying, 67 If thou art the Christ, tell us. But he said unto them, If I tell you, ye will not believe: 68 and if I ask *you*, ye will not answer. 69 But from henceforth shall the Son of man be seated at the right hand of the power of God. 70 And they all said, Art hou then the Son of God? And he said unto them, ¹Ye say that I am. 71 And they said,
		¹ Or, Ye say it, because I am

308

Luke 22
What further need have we
of witness? for we our-
selves have heard from his
own mouth.

Note 246. At this, the only Jewish "trial" which had any semblance of legality, no witnesses were introduced. The high priest and
those in charge began by demanding of Jesus that He repeat the confession which He had made earlier in the informal examination. His insight into their true motives and purpose is seen in His answer: "If I
tell you, ye will not believe. . . . " As a warning, as well as a vindication
of Himself, He repeated also the prophecy that they were going to see
Him in His Messianic and divine glory and power. As we know, this involved His resurrection from the death which they were about to inflict
on Him and His glorious exaltation and His return to the earth. They
pressed Him for a statement not only that He was Messiah, but also
that He was the Son of God, which to them were different propositions.
A claim to divine sonship to their minds was the most blatant blasphemy, and on a charge of blasphemy they condemned Him. Indeed,
for anyone except Jesus, such a statement would have been blasphemy,
but for Jesus it was simple truth; and they had had ample opportunity to
know it was truth.

Those who have studied Jewish law* of that day have found many
illegal features of the actions of the Sanhedrin. They tell us that Annas
had no right to try or even to question Jesus, that Caiaphas had no authority to call a meeting of the Sanhedrin at night, either in formal session or for informal consultation, that the Sanhedrin could not meet legally in the house of Caiaphas (and it was there that the death penalty
was first voted on Jesus), that capital punishment could not be inflicted
during the day on which the trial was held, and that a trial was not to be
held on the day before the sabbath or on a feast day. But a fair and legal trial was not the true objective of the priests and other members of
the Sanhedrin. They were determined to pronounce the death sentence
and sought only for a pretense of legality in doing so.

e. Judas in remorse and suicide
#244
MATT. 27:3-10

3 Then Judas, who [1]betrayed him, when he saw that he was condemned, repented himself, and brought back the thirty pieces of silver to the chief priests and
elders, 4 saying, I have sinned in that I [1]betrayed [2]innocent blood. But they said,
What is that to us? see thou *to it*. 5 And he cast down the pieces of silver into the
sanctuary, and departed; and he went away and hanged himself. 6 And the chief
priests took the pieces of silver, and said, It is not lawful to put them into the

[1] See marginal note on ch. 10. 4.   [2] Many ancient authorities read *righteous*.

Ibid., pp. 546, 556f.; Broadus, *Commentary on Matthew*, pp. 546ff. W. N. Clark,
Commentary on the Gospel of Mark in *An American Commentary on the New
Testament (op cit.)* pp. 222f. See also the paragraph on the Sanhedrin in the
Introduction.

³treasury, since it is the price of blood. 7 And they took counsel, and bought with them the potter's field, to bury strangers in. 8 Wherefore that field was called, the field of blood, unto this day. 9 Then was fulfilled that which was spoken through Jeremiah the prophet, saying, ⁴And ⁵they took the thirty pieces of silver, the price of him that was priced, ⁶whom *certain* of the children of Israel did price; 10 and ⁷they gave them for the potter's field, as the Lord appointed me.

³ Gr. *corbanas,* that is, *sacred treasury.* Comp. Mk. 7. 11. ⁴ Zech. xi. 12, 13. ⁵ Or, *I took*
⁶ Or, *whom they priced on the part of the sons of Israel* ⁷ Some ancient authorities read *I gave.*

Note 247. In Note 198 it was suggested that resentment as well as greed for money probably led Judas to commit his shameful treachery. If so, that resentment was stirred, or at least consummated, by the rebuke that Jesus dealt him when, at the supper at Bethany, he complained because Mary used the costly ointment to anoint Jesus, instead of making it available for the relief of the poor (#196). There may have been something in the tone or look of Jesus which revealed to Judas that Jesus knew that Judas was a thief (John 12: 6).* Probably, also he despaired of Jesus' ever setting up a visible kingdom; and certainly he realized that, if Jesus did know of his thievery, he would not be given a position of trust, even if the kingdom should be inaugurated at this time. Such thoughts as these may have entered, along with his covetousness, into the motive of Judas for selling out to the enemies of Jesus. But whatever it was that led him to make the deal with the murderous priests, it was not enough to compensate for the raucous voice, the unstilled conviction, of conscience—so soon after he received his thirty pieces of silver (valued by all authorities at about fifteen to eighteen dollars**) did he rue his bargain. The expression on the face of Jesus at the Passover supper, His reproving questions in the garden (Matt. 26: 50; Luke 22: 48), the calmness with which He submitted to arrest, and the look of dismay on the faces of the other apostles—all these and many other memories must have haunted the traitor during the remaining hours of the night and the early morning. And he had no place to go—the Jewish authorities would not accept him into their company or even show appreciation for his help in accomplishing their purpose, and certainly he could not go back to the group of apostles. Back to the temple he hastened, bolting into the restricted court of the priests in a vain effort to undo his deed. Meeting only sneers and mockery from the priests, he flung at them the only advantage that had accrued to him from his crime—the thirty pieces of silver—and ran out. Which direction he ran we do not know, probably to the south of the city to the potter's field, which the priests later bought with the pieces

*Broadus, *Commentary on Matthew,* p. 522 quotes from Jerome: "Unhappy Judas! the loss he thought he had incurred by the pouring out of the ointment, he wishes to make up by selling his Master."

**Broadus, *Commentary on Matthew,* p. 522; Edersheim, *Life and Times of Jesus,* Vol. II, p. 507; H. Porter, "Piece of Silver" in *International Standard Bible Encyclopedia,* Vol. IV, p. 2395.

of silver. Securing a rope and doubtless finding a tree extending over a precipice, he hanged himself. And even in death he was a most horrible spectacle. For some cause, either at the time of his suicide, or in connection with the removal of the body, the rope was severed "and he fell there face downward, and his body broke in two, and all his intestines poured out" (Acts 1: 18, Williams' translation).

(2) Those before Roman judges, ##245—247

Note 248. The Jewish Sanhedrin exercised only such authority in criminal cases as the Romans had seen fit to grant unto it. We know that at this time it did not have the authority to inflict the death penalty on any one (John 18: 31). Therefore, the sentence against Jesus, agreed on in the informal meeting in the house of Caiaphas (#241), and formally voted in the "official" meeting at daybreak (#243), could be no more than a recommendation to the Roman procurator ("governor" in our English versions) that Jesus be sentenced to die. Before that sentence was passed on Him, Jesus stood "trial" three times before Roman officials: first before Pilate the procurator, then before Herod Antipas, the tetrarch in Peraea and Galilee (where Jesus had been reared and where He had spent most of His active ministry), and finally before Pilate again.

a. First appearance before Pilate, the procurator
#245

MATT. 27:2, 11-14	MARK 15:1b-5	LUKE 23:1-5	JOHN 18:28-38
2 And they bound him, and led him away, and delivered him up to Pilate the governor.	1b And bound Jesus, and carried him away, and delivered him up to Pilate.	1 And the whole company of them rose up, and brought him before Pilate.	28 They lead Jesus therefore from Caiaphas into the ¹Praetorium: and it was early; and they themselves entered not into the ¹Praetorium, that they might not be defiled, but might eat the passover. 29 Pilate therefore went out unto them, and saith, What accusation bring ye against this man? 30 They answered and said unto him, If this man were not an evildoer, we should not have delivered him up unto thee. 31 Pilate therefore said unto them, Take him yourselves, and judge him according to your law. The Jews said unto him, ¹ Or, *palace*

311

Matt. 27	Mark 15	Luke 23	John 18
			It is not lawful for us to put any man to death: 32 that the word of Jesus might be fulfilled which he spake, signifying by what manner of death he should die.
		2 And they began to accuse him, saying, We found this man perverting our nation, and forbidding to give tribute to Caesar, and saying that he himself is Christ a king.	
11 Now Jesus stood before the governor: and the governor asked him, saying, Art thou the King of the Jews?	2 And Pilate asked him, Art thou the King of the Jews?	3 And Pilate asked him, saying, Art thou the King of the Jews?"	33 Pilate therefore entered again into the ¹Praetorium, and called Jesus, and said unto him, Art thou the King of the Jews? 34 Jesus answered, Sayest thou this of thyself, or did others tell it thee concerning me? 35 Pilate answered, Am I a Jew? Thine own nation and the chief priests delivered thee unto me: what hast thou done? 36 Jesus answered, My kingdom is not of this world: if my kingdom were of this world, then would my ²servants fight, that I should not be delivered to the Jews: but now is my kingdom not from hence. 37 Pilate therefore said unto
And Jesus said unto him, Thou sayest.	And he answering saith unto him, Thou sayest.	And he answered him and said, Thou sayest.	him, Art thou a king then? Jesus answered, ³Thou sayest that I am a king. To this end have I been born, and to this end am I come into the world, that I should bear witness unto the truth. Every one that is of the truth heareth my voice.

² Or, *officers*: as in ver. 3, 12, 18, 22.
³ Or, *thou sayest it, because I am a king.*

Matt. 27	Mark 15	Luke 23	John 18
			38 Pilate saith unto him, What is truth?
		4 And Pilate said unto the chief priests and the mul-	And when he had said this, he went out again unto the Jews, and saith unto
12 And when he was ac- cused by the chief priests and elders, he answered nothing. 13 Then saith Pilate unto him, Hearest thou not how many things they witness against thee? 14 And he gave him no answer, not even to one word: insomuch that the governor marvelled greatly.	3 And the chief priests accused him of many things. 4 And Pilate again asked him, saying, Answerest thou nothing? be- hold how many things they accuse thee of. 5 But Jesus no more answered anything; insomuch that Pilate marvelled.	titudes, I find no fault in this man. 5 But they were the more urgent, saying, He stirreth up the people, teaching throughout all Ju- daea, and beginning from Galilee even unto this place.	them, I find no crime in him.

Note 249. Pontius Pilate was the fifth procurator (governor) appointed to rule Judaea after Archelaus, the son of Herod the Great, was deposed in A.D. 6 from his office as "ethnarch." He ruled from 26 to 36. His seat of government was at Caesarea, but he frequently came to Jerusalem during important feasts to prevent or quell riots. References to him in history show that he was a harsh and merciless ruler, who did not hesitate needlessly to put to death numbers of his subjects or to desecrate their sacred religious feelings and practices. The incident related in Luke 13:1 (#159) about having Galilean worshipers slain so that their blood was mingled with the blood of their sacrifices, though not found in any other record, is representative of his character.

The accusers of Jesus at first thought they would induce Pilate to sentence Him to death on their recommendation without the trouble of a formal trial. But Pilate would not oblige them with such a summary sentence of death; he demanded to know the charge that they were bringing against Him (vss. 29—31 in John). In the Sanhedrin they condemned him for blasphemy, in that He said He was the Son of God; but realizing the contempt that Pilate had shown for their religious scruples in the past, they evidently reasoned that he would pay no attention to such a charge. Therefore, they made the charge of fomenting sedition against Rome, forbidding to pay tax to Caesar (the exact opposite of which was true, cf. #211 and Note 214), and claiming that He was Christ a King (vs. 2 in Luke; to a Roman their words would mean "an anointed king").

As procurator, Pilate would naturally be on the lookout for any individual who endeavored to stir up the people against the Romans or to set himself up as a king. Accordingly, he asked Jesus if He were the

313

King of the Jews; and it seems odd (reading from the Synoptic records) that, although Jesus answered in the affirmative, the governor at once rendered his verdict as "not guilty." However, according to the record in John (vss. 36—37), Jesus explained that "now" (for the present) His Kingdom was "not of this world,"—not one for which His servants would fight. Pilate therefore easily saw that their charge of sedition was groundless, and at once gave his judgment as "I find no fault in this man."

Some Bible students find a difficulty in verse 28 of John. If the Passover was eaten the night before (Thursday evening), why should these Jews be afraid that they might be so defiled by entering Pilate's judgment hall that they could not eat the Passover? But Edersheim relates that the word for "Passover" was often used to denote all the special sacrificial meals of the Feast of Unleavened Bread, which lasted a week. A very important sacrifice was scheduled to be offered and eaten on that the first day of the Passover week (which began at sundown the day before); and to have entered the house of a Gentile would have so defiled them that they could not lawfully eat that sacrifice.* They were straining at the gnat of Levitical defilement and swallowing the camel of plotting and securing the murder of One who had done good, and only good, in their land.

b. Appearance before Herod Antipas, the tetrarch
#246
LUKE 23:6-12

6 But when Pilate heard it, he asked whether the man were a Galilaean. 7 And when he knew that he was of Herod's jurisdiction, he sent him unto Herod, who himself also was at Jerusalem in these days.

8 Now when Herod saw Jesus, he was exceeding glad: for he was of a long time desirous to see him, because he had heard concerning him; and he hoped to see some ¹miracle done by him. 9 And he questioned him in many words; but he answered him nothing. 10 And the chief priests and the scribes stood, vehemently accusing him. 11 And Herod with his soldiers set him at nought, and mocked him, and arraying him in gorgeous apparel sent him back to Pilate. 12 And Herod and Pilate became friends with each other that very day: for before they were at enmity between themselves.

¹ Gr. sign.

Note 250. This was the Herod who had ordered John the Baptist beheaded, and who later was troubled by apprehension that Jesus was John risen from the dead (#116). When the Jews of Peraea tried to frighten Jesus out of their territory on the ground that Herod wanted to kill Him, He, knowing of Herod's fears, called that ruler a fox, implying that Herod would not risk getting near enough to Him to have Him arrested and brought to him for trial. It is true that at this time Herod had for some time wanted to see Jesus because he hoped to see Him perform a miracle. But Jesus did not work miracles for show, and surely He would not perform one to please such a dissolute, unprincipled person as Herod Antipas. What a contrast between the wretch on the throne of judg-

*Edersheim, Life and Times of Jesus, Vol. II, p. 568.

ment, clothed in royal purple but dissolute in heart, and the Prisoner who stood before him, disheveled in raiment and visage but as pure as Heaven in character! Foiled in his effort to induce Jesus to perform a miracle, and probably astonished at His complete silence in the face of the serious though doubtful accusations brought against Him, Herod found no satisfaction in this appearance of Jesus before him, other than seeing Him mockingly clothed in a gorgeous garment (likely a cast-off one of Herod's own) and otherwise ridiculed. Without pretending to render a decision, Herod sent Him back to Pilate, probably clothed in the gaudy garment.

c. Second appearance before Pilate, the procurator's unsuccessful attempt to release Jesus as a Passover favor, reluctant aquiescence in the death sentence

#247

MATT. 27:15-26	MARK 15:6-15	LUKE 23:13-25	JOHN 18:39 — 19:16a
		13 And Pilate called together the chief priests and the rulers and the people, 14 and said unto them, Ye brought unto me this man, as one that perverteth the people: and behold, I, having examined him before you, found no fault in this man touching those things whereof ye accuse him: 15 no, nor yet Herod: for ¹he sent him back unto us; and behold, nothing worthy of death hath been done by him. 16 I will therefore	
15 Now at ¹the feast the governor was wont to release unto the multitude one prisoner, whom they would. 16 And they had then a notable prisoner. called Barabbas. 17 When therefore they were gathered together, Pilate said unto them, Whom will ye that I release unto you? Barabbas, or Jesus who is called Christ?	6 Now at ¹the feast he used to release unto them one prisoner, whom they asked of him. 7 And there was one called Barabbas, *lying* bound with them that had made insurrection, men who in the insurrection had committed murder. 8 And the multitude went up and began to ask him *to do* as he was wont to do unto them. 9 And Pilate answered them, saying, Will	chastise him, and release him.² 18 But they cried out all together, saying, Away with this man, and release unto us Barabbas: —19 one who for a certain in-	39 But ye have a custom, that I should release unto you one at the passover: will ye therefore that I release unto you the King of the Jews? 40 They cried out therefore again, saying, Not this man, but Barabbas. Now Barabbas was a robber.
¹ Or, *a feast*	¹ Or, *a feast*	¹ Many ancient authorities read *I sent you to him.* ² Many ancient authorities insert ver. 17 *Now he must needs release unto them at the feast one* prisoner. Comp Mt. 27. 15; Mk. 15. 6; Jn. 18. 39. Others add the same words after ver. 19.	

315

Matt. 27	Mark 15	Luke 23	John 19

Matt. 27

18 For he knew that for envy they had delivered him up. 19 And while he was sitting on the judgment-seat, his wife sent unto him, saying, Have thou nothing to do with that righteous man; for I have suffered many things this day in a dream because of him. 20 Now the chief priests and the elders persuaded the multitudes that they should ask for Barabbas, and destroy Jesus. 21 But the governor answered and said unto them, Which of the two will ye that I release unto you? And they said, Barabbas. 22 Pilate saith unto them, What then shall I do unto Jesus who is called Christ? They all say, Let him be crucified. 23 And he said, Why, what evil hath he done? But they cried out exceedingly, saying, Let him be crucified.

Mark 15

ye that I release unto you the King of the Jews? 10 For he perceived that for envy the chief priests had delivered him up.

11 But the chief priests stirred up the multitude, that he should rather release Barabbas unto them.

12 And Pilate again answered and said unto them, What then shall I do unto him whom ye call the King of the Jews? 13 And they cried out again, Crucify him. 14 And Pilate said unto them, Why, what evil hath he done? But they cried out exceedingly, Crucify him.

Luke 23

surrection made in the city, and for murder, was cast into prison.

20 And Pilate spake unto them again, desiring to release Jesus; 21 but they shouted, saying, Crucify, crucify him. 22 And he said unto them the third time, Why, what evil hath this man done? I have found no cause of death in him: I will therefore chastise him and release him.

John 19

1 Then Pilate therefore took Jesus, and scourged him. 2 And the soldiers platted a crown of thorns, and put it on his head, and arrayed him in a purple garment; 3

John 19

and they came unto him, and said, Hail, King of the Jews! and they struck him [1]with their hands. 4 And Pilate went out again, and saith unto them, Behold, I bring him out to you, that ye may know that I find no crime in him. 5 Jesus therefore came out, wearing the crown of thorns and the purple garment. And *Pilate* saith unto them, Behold, the man! 6 When therefore the chief priests and the officers saw him, they cried out, saying, Crucify *him*, crucify *him*! Pilate saith unto them, Take him yourselves, and crucify him: for I find no crime in him. 7 The Jews answered him, We have a law, and by that law he ought to die, because he made himself the Son of God. 8 When Pilate therefore heard this saying, he was the more afraid; 9 and he entered into the [2]Praetorium again, and saith unto Jesus, Whence art thou? But Jesus gave him no answer. 10 Pilate therefore saith unto him, Speakest thou not unto me? knowest thou not that I have [3]power to release thee, and have [3]power to crucify thee? 11 Jesus answered him, Thou wouldest have no [3]power against me, except it were given thee from above: therefore he that delivered me unto thee hath greater sin. 12 Upon this Pilate sought to release him: but the Jews cried out, saying, If thou release this man, thou art not Caesar's friend: every one that maketh himself a king [4]speaketh against Caesar.

[1] Or, *with rods*   [2] Or, *palace*   [3] Or, *authority*   [4] Or, *opposeth Caesar*

Matt. 27	Mark 15	Luke 23	John 19
24 So when Pilate saw that he prevailed nothing, but rather that a tumult was arising, he took water, and washed his hands before the multitude, saying, I am innocent [2]of the blood of this righteous man; see ye *to it*. 25 And all the people answered and said, His blood *be* on us, and on our children.			13 When Pilate therefore heard these words, he brought Jesus out, and sat down on the judgment-seat at a place called The Pavement, but in Hebrew, Gabbatha. 14 Now it was the Preparation of the passover: it was about the sixth hour. And he saith unto the Jews, Behold, your King! 15 They therefore cried out, Away with *him*, away with *him*, crucify him! Pilate saith unto them, Shall I crucify your King? The chief priests answered, We have no king but Caesar. 16 Then therefore he delivered him unto them to be crucified.
		23 But they were urgent with loud voices, asking that he might be crucified. And their voices prevailed.	
26 Then released he unto them Barabbas; but Jesus he scourged and delivered to be crucified.	15 And Pilate, wishing to content the multitude, released unto them Barabbas, and delivered Jesus, when he had scourged him, to be crucified.	24 And Pilate gave sentence that what they asked for should be done. 25 And he released him that for insurrection and murder had been cast into prison, whom they asked for; but Jesus he delivered up to their will.	

[2] Some ancient authorities read *of this blood: see ye &c.*

Note 251. The appearance of Jesus before Herod (#246) is related only in Luke. In Matthew, Mark, and John the trial before Pilate is related as one appearance, continuing from the leading of Jesus to Pilate by the Sanhedrin leaders to the pronouncing of the final sentence. In harmonizing the account in Luke with those in the other Gospels, one cannot be sure just which statements in the others were made before Jesus was sent to Herod and which were made after. However, since Pilate's suggestion that he release Jesus as the customary Passover favor appears in all the accounts, and since in Luke it is related immediately after the return of Jesus from Herod to Pilate, we are justified in regarding everything narrated before that suggestion as taking place during the first appearance of Jesus before Pilate, and the suggestion and everything narrated after it as occurring after the appearance before Herod. According to John, Pilate made four appearances outside the judgment hall, and apparently one is given in Luke that is not found in John. Combining John and Luke, the following outline is probably a fair representation of these Roman "trials" involving five times when Pilate, with Jesus present, faced the chief priests and other Sanhedrin leaders outside the judgment hall (indicated by numerals and A), and four times when he took Jesus into the judgment hall or sent Him elsewhere (indicated by numerals and B). 1A and 1B and 2A and 2B have already been set forth in ##245, 246, and Notes 249, 250; and are, therefore, only briefly mentioned here.

1A. Pilate met the Sanhedrin leaders outside the judgment hall when they brought Jesus to him (John 18:29). Refusing to impose a sentence on their recommendation only, he heard the charge of sedition.

1B. He entered the judgment hall with Jesus and asked if He were the King of the Jews (John 18:33). Jesus gave the affirmative answer with explanation.

2A. He reappeared with Jesus before the Jewish leaders outside the judgment hall with his decision: "I find no fault in Him" (John 18:38). The priests and elders, in turn, accused Jesus of many things but Jesus kept silent, so that Pilate marveled. They mentioned in their accusations that Jesus had labored extensively in a district ruled by Herod (Luke 23:5).

2B. Learning that Jesus was a Galilean, Pilate sent Him to Herod, where He maintained complete silence (Luke 23:6ff).

3A. On the return of Jesus from Herod, Pilate met the priests and rulers, presumably outside the judgment hall (Luke 23:13). He repeated his verdict: "I...have found no fault in this Man touching those things whereof ye accuse Him, nor yet Herod." But in deference to the Jewish rulers, he agreed to chastise (scourge) Jesus and let Him go. Scourging, as terrible as it was, was not sufficient penalty for the crime of sedition; but Pilate knew that Jesus was not guilty of sedition in any form, and it was not for sedition that the Sanhedrin leaders had had Him arrested. He may have reasoned that scourging would be sufficient penalty for whatever infraction against the Sanhedrin regulations Jesus had committed. About this time a multitude had arrived, reminding Pilate of his custom of releasing a prisoner for them each year at the Passover, and demanding the favor at this time (Mark 15:8). When, in reply, he suggested that he might release for them Jesus, "the King of the Jews," the priests and elders persuaded the multitude, or its leaders, to call for the release of Barabbas. It is noteworthy that Barabbas had taken part in insurrection, the offense with which the rulers had charged Jesus. Probably he had been a leader in a recent uprising of which we have no account in history, and in it had been guilty of both murder and robbery. And yet he was probably a sort of popular hero.

3B. But Pilate had Jesus led away to be scourged, probably in a place connected with the judgment hall where this horrible punishment was usually inflicted (John 19:1). As practiced by the Romans, "so hideous was the punishment (by scourging) that the victim usually fainted and not rarely died under it."* The soldiers also mockingly crowned Him with a wreath of thorns and clothed Him with a cast-off purple robe, possibly merely replacing the one which Herod had put upon Him. Probably it was during this time also that Pilate received the disquieting message from his wife.

4A. After the scourging Pilate "went forth again" out of the judgment hall (John 19:4), accompanied by Jesus wearing the crown of thorns, probably with the full intention of releasing Him. When he again suggested this action, the multitude, led by the priests, insisted on the release of Barabbas; and they demanded that Jesus be crucified. Pilate insisted that they make a charge against Him which they could substantiate (Matt. 27:23), or else that they assume all responsibility for crucifying Him while he pronounced him innocent (John 19:6). Whereupon someone in the crowd responded, "...by our law He ought to die, because He made Himself the Son of God" (John 19:7). That was the original charge, the charge of blasphemy; and although Pilate had little regard for their religion, there was something in the charge that made him afraid. It is impossible that he had not heard something of the many miracles which Jesus had performed; and the saying probably brought to mind the message which he had received from his wife. Possibly in his superstition he was afraid that Jesus might be a sort of demigod, such a one as the legendary Hercules of Roman mythology, whose wrath Pilate dreaded to arouse.

4B. Accordingly, He led the wounded, humiliated Jesus back into the judgment hall for another private interview (John 19:9). But when he inquired about his origin, Jesus again became silent. Pilate remonstrated, reminding his Prisoner that he had authority to crucify or to release Him. To which Jesus replied that all the authority that the governor exercised was in reality granted to him from Heav-

*Henry E. Dosker, "Scourge," in the *International Standard Bible Encyclopedia*,). 2704.

en: and then He said, "He that delivered Me unto thee hath the greater sin." At this point the sentence was inevitable; Pilate could not now evade it; but even so, he was not sinning against as much light as was Caiaphas, who was responsible for bringing Jesus to Pilate for judgment. Apparently, the words that turned the tide were shouted on the outside, but were heard in the judgment hall: "If thou let this man go, thou art not Caesar's friend." Pilate was more afraid for his standing with Tiberius than for anything else; he could take no risk along that line.

5A. Finally the governor "brought Jesus forth and sat down in the judgment seat in a place that is called the Pavement" (John 19: 13). This was probably a special seat which he had a servant to move outside, from which he had in mind to pronounce the formal sentence. He raised the question with the Jewish rulers: "Shall I crucify a King?" Whether this was a final effort to evade the responsibility, or a jeer that he was casting at the Jewish rulers, it brought humiliating response: "We have no king but Caesar." Pilate dreaded a popular tumult, and it seemed that one was about to arise. Before pronouncing sentence, however, he again attempted to evade responsibility for the deed by ceremonially washing his hands before them (cf. Deut. 21: 6--9; Ps. 26: 6). When the priests responded, "His blood be on us and our children," they did not know how terrible was the curse that they called upon their nation, or with what fury it would come on them when, while doubtless some of them were still living, the Romans should destroy Jerusalem with great slaughter and furious vengeance. After the ceremony of washing his hands, Pilate pronounced the sentence of death on Jesus.

From the accounts in Matthew (vs. 26) and Mark (vs. 15), we would conclude that Pilate had Jesus scourged in connection with the sentence for crucifixion. Many authorities agree that it was the custom so to torture a condemned person before crucifying him.* However, Jesus had already been terribly scourged and crowned with thorns before Pilate yielded to the clamors of the Jews (John 19: 1--2); and it is not probable that this horrible punishment was repeated after so short an interval. The clause in Matthew and Mark that is translated "When he had scourged Jesus...," is more literally translated, "having scourged Jesus, he delivered Him that he might be crucified." Probably Matthew and Mark relate it here to indicate that the scourging was fully carried out.

The day before the Sabbath was usually designated as the "Preparation" (cf. Mark 15: 42; Luke 23: 54; John 19: 31; #254). That certainly was the meaning of "Preparation" in John 19: 14. Here it was doubtless called the "Preparation of the Passover" because it was the preparation for the Sabbath which came during Passover week. The

*Broadus, *Commentary on Matthew*, p. 565; Hovey, *Commentary on John*, p 365; Dosker, *op cit.*, James Stalker, *The Life of Jesus Christ* (Edinburgh: T. and T Clark, 1939), p. 127.

phrase here surely does not denote the day to prepare for the Passover, because we know that they had eaten the Passover the night before (##229—232).

As was stated in Note 24, John probably used a system of counting time that was similar to our own; that is, he counted a day from midnight to midnight. Therefore the sixth hour of verse 14 would be about six o'clock in the morning. This would not conflict with the statement in Mark 15: 25 (#251), where the Jewish reckoning is used, that the crucifixion was begun at the third hour, or about nine o'clock by our time. However, it is hard to see how there was enough time between "morning" of Matthew 27: 1 and Mark 15: 1 and six o'clock for the formal hearing of the Sanhedrin and the three Roman hearings. Yet we do not know just how early in the "morning" the Sanhedrin held its formal meeting before leading Jesus to Pilate. Hovey points out that the word which is translated "morning" in Matthew 27: 1 and Mark 15: 1 and "early" in John 18: 28 (it is the same Greek word, prōi) frequently denoted the fourth watch of the night, or from three to six in the morning.* He suggests a timing which supposes Jesus to have been brought to Pilate at around three-thirty, and the final sentence to have been passed around six-thirty. We observe that John said, "about (hōs) the sixth hour," which might have been as late as six-thirty, or even later. But whatever the timing, it is evident that the Sanhedrin leaders were anxious to get Jesus sentenced as early as possible, because (1) they wanted it over before the multitude of Jesus' admirers had opportunity to know about it (cf. Matt. 26: 4—5, #227 and Luke 19: 47—48, #202); and (2) this was a feast day and they desired to take part in the religious services and sacred meals of the day. In modern language, they "railroaded" the case through with all speed.

3. The crucifixion of Jesus, ##248—253

(1) Jesus humiliated and tortured by the soldiers while preparation was being made

#248

MATT. 27:27-30	MARK 15:16-19
27 Then the soldiers of the governor took Jesus into the [1]Praetorium, and gathered unto him the whole [2]band. 28 And they [3]stripped him, and put on him a scarlet robe. 29 And they platted a crown of thorns and put it upon his head, and a reed in his right hand; and they kneeled down before him, and mocked him, saying, Hail, King of the Jews! 30 And they spat upon him, and took the reed and smote him on the head.	16 And the soldiers led him away within the court, which is the [1]Praetorium; and they call together the whole [2]band. 17 And they clothe him with purple, and platting a crown of thorns, they put it on him; 18 and they began to salute him, Hail, King of the Jews! 19 And they smote his head with a reed, and spat upon him, and bowing their knees [3]worshipped him.
[1] Or, palace See Mk. 15. 16. [2] Or, cohort [3] Some ancient authorities read clothed.	[1] Or, palace [2] Or, cohort [3] See marginal note on ch. 5. 6.

Note 252. Some time was necessary to prepare for the execution of the sentence. Probably Pilate decided, after he pronounced sentence on Jesus, to have the two thieves crucified with Him. These doubtless,

*Commentary on John, p. 377f.

321

along with Barabbas, were in prison awaiting execution for their crimes in connection with an insurrection. While preparation was being made for the three crucifixions, the soldiers who were the governor's body guard, having led Jesus into the "common hall" (probably the barrack), invited "the whole band of soldiers" to join in a spree of taunting and deriding Him before they should lead Him away to be crucified. As was said in Note 251, Jesus had been scourged before Pilate actually pronounced sentence (John 19: 1), and it is not likely that that torturous deed was repeated. Also the crown of thorns mentioned in the above section was probably the same as that of John 19: 2. But the whole band of hardened soldiers took a savage delight in humiliating and mocking their innocent Victim as One who aspired to be King of the Jews. According to Matthew, they stripped Him, which may mean they took off the "gorgeous robe" with which Herod had arrayed Him and probably His own under coat, and threw around Him a coarse scarlet soldier's cloak. This was the fourth such period of mockery and indignity that Jesus endured after He was arrested in the garden (cf. Matt. 26: 67—68 et al. #241; Luke 23: 11, #246; John 19: 3, #247). And all the while "He opened not His mouth" (cf. Isa. 53: 7).

(2) Events on the way to the place of execution
#249

MATT. 27:31-32	MARK 15:20-21	LUKE 23:26-32	JOHN 19:17a
31 And when they had mocked him, they took off from him the robe, and put on him his garments, and led him away to crucify him.	20 And when they had mocked him, they took off from him the purple, and put on him his garments. And they lead him out to crucify him.		
		26 And when they led him away, they laid hold upon one Simon of Cyrene, coming from the country, and laid on him the cross, to bear it after Jesus.	17 They took Jesus therefore: and he went out, bearing the cross for himself,
32 And as they came out, they found a man of Cyrene, Simon by name: him they ¹compelled to go *with them*, that he might bear his cross.	21 And they ¹compel one passing by, Simon of Cyrene, coming from the country, the father of Alexander and Rufus, to go *with them*, that he might bear his cross.	27 And there followed him a great multitude of the people, and of women who bewailed and lamented him. 28 But Jesus turning unto them said, Daughters of Jerusalem, weep not for me, but weep for yourselves, and for your children. 29 For behold, the days are coming, in which they shall say, Bless-	

¹ Gr. *impressed*.   ¹ Gr. *impress*.

Luke 23

ed are the barren, and the wombs that never bare, and the breasts that never gave suck. 30 Then shall they begin to say to the mountains, Fall on us; and to the hills, Cover us. 31 For if they do these things in the green tree, what shall be done in the dry?

32 And there were also two others, malefactors, led with him to be put to death.

Note 253. According to John, Jesus went out bearing His cross. Ordinarily a condemned one was compelled to carry the cross on which he was to be put to death to the place of execution. All of the Synoptic Gospels, however, say that they (the soldiers in charge) compelled Simon of Cyrene to carry the cross. The general conclusion is that Jesus started out carrying it, but because of His exhausted condition (in His true humanity), He fell under its weight; and that Simon carried it the rest of the way. About Simon, Mark adds that he was the father of Alexander and Rufus. Apparently these sons of Simon were believers in Christ, well-known to the Roman Christians for whom Mark wrote (Rom. 16: 13). If Simon was not already a disciple of Jesus, he probably became a Christian later.

In the "great multitude of people" who followed to the place of execution (vs. 27 in Luke) were many who sympathized with His enemies, and who later participated in taunting Him; but there were also some who admired Him and were willing to be His followers (cf. Luke 24: 19—21; also 23: 48). Luke did not identify the loyal women, either in verse 27 or in verse 49. They surely were, or included, the four mentioned in John 19: 25. But Luke related how Jesus took occasion to console His weeping friends so far as His own sufferings were concerned. And in the same breath He warned them of the greater woes which would come upon the dwellers in Jerusalem of that generation and the next. In this He doubtless was predicting the horrible sufferings which came to the people during the siege and destruction of the city from A. D. 66 to 70.* In this saying the "green tree" meant Himself who was condemned of sedition on an accusation which the governor knew to be false; and the "dry tree" meant the next generation of Jews who would be openly guilty of that offense, and would actively prosecute a fanatical and bloody war with the Roman rulers.

* Cf. Josephus, *Wars of the Jews*, V, xi, 1.

(3) Arrival at Golgotha, Jesus refusing the wine and myrrh
#250

MATT. 27:33-34	MARK 15:22-23	LUKE 23:33a	JOHN 19:17b
33 And when they were come unto a place called Golgotha, that is to say, The place of a skull, 34 they gave him wine to drink mingled with gall: and when he had tasted it, he would not drink.	22 And they bring him unto the place, Golgotha, which is, being interpreted, The place of a skull. 23 And they offered him wine mingled with myrrh: but he received it not.	33 And when they came unto the place which is called [1]The skull,	17b unto the place called The place of a skull, which is called in Hebrew Golgotha:
		[1] According to the Latin, *Calvary*, which has the same meaning.	

Note 254. There has been much difference of opinion about the place of the crucifixion. The church of the Holy Sepulcher, erected in the fourth century within the city of Jerusalem, was for centuries thought to cover both the place of crucifixion and the place of the tomb. However, the true location was surely outside the city (Heb. 13:12). In recent times opinion has shifted to a site north and east of the city, called Gordon's Calvary from its modern discoverer. It is a hill which many travelers report to resemble a skull, and an empty tomb has been found nearby, which many regard to be the one in which the body of Jesus was laid.

(4) The hours of the crucifixion, Jesus on the cross, ##251—252
a. Three hours of physical suffering, from the third hour to the sixth hour (9 A.M. to 12 M.)
#251

MATT. 27:35-44	MARK 15:24-32	LUKE 23:33b-43	JOHN 19:18-27
35 And when they had crucified him, they parted his garments among them, casting lots; 36 and they sat and watched him there. 37 And they set up over his head his accusation written, THIS IS JESUS THE KING OF THE JEWS, 38 Then are there crucified with him two robbers, one on the right hand and one on the left.	24 And they crucify him, and part his garments among them, casting lots upon them, what each should take. 25 And it was the third hour, and they crucified him. And the superscription of his accusation was written over, THE KING OF THE JEWS. 27 And with him they crucify two robbers; one on his right hand, and one on his left.[1]	33b there they crucified him, and the malefactors, one on the right hand and the other on the left. 34 [1]And Jesus said, Father, forgive them; for they know not what they do. And parting his garments among them, they cast lots.	18 where they crucified him, and with him two others, on either side one, and Jesus in the midst. 19 And Pilate wrote a title also, and put it on the cross. And there was written, JESUS OF NAZARETH, THE KING OF THE JEWS. 20 This title therefore read many of the Jews, [1]for the place where Jesus was crucified was nigh to the city; and it was written in Hebrew, *and* in Latin, *and* in Greek. 21 The chief priests of the Jews there-
	[1] Many ancient authorities insert ver. 28 *And the Scripture was fulfilled, which saith, And he was reckoned with transgressors.* See Lk. 22.37.	[1] Some ancient authorities omit *And Jesus said, Father, forgive them; for they know not what they do.*	[1] Or, *for the place of the city where Jesus was crucified was nigh at hand*

Matt. 27	Mark 15	Luke 23	John 19

John 19 (continued)

fore said to Pilate, Write not, The King of the Jews; but, that he said, I am King of the Jews. 22 Pilate answered, What I have written I have written.

23 The soldiers therefore, when they had crucified Jesus, took his garments and made four parts, to every soldier a part; and also the ²coat: now the ²coat was without seam, woven from the top throughout. 24 They said therefore one to another, Let us not rend it, but cast lots for it, whose it shall be: that the scripture might be fulfilled, which saith,

> ³They parted my garments among them,
> And upon my vesture did they cast lots.

25 These things therefore the soldiers did. But there were standing by the cross of Jesus his mother, and his mother's sister, Mary the *wife* of Clopas, and Mary Magdalene.

Matt. 27

39 And they that passed by railed on him, wagging their heads, 40 and saying, Thou that destroyest the ¹temple, and buildest it in three days, save thyself: if thou art the Son of God, come down from the cross. 41 In like manner also the chief priests mocking *him*, with the scribes and elders, said, 42 He

Mark 15

29 And they that passed by railed on him, wagging their heads, and saying, Ha! thou that destroyest the ²temple, and buildest it in three days, 30 save thyself, and come down from the cross. 31 In like manner also the chief priests mocking *him* among themselves with the scribes said, He

Luke 23

35 And the people stood beholding. And the rulers also scoffed at him, saying, He saved others; let him save himself, if this is the Christ of God, his chosen. 36 And the soldiers also mocked him, coming to him, offering him vinegar, 37 and saying, If thou art the King of the Jews, save thyself.

John 19

26 When Jesus therefore saw his mother, and the disciple standing by whom he loved, he saith unto his mother, Woman, behold, thy son! 27 Then saith he to the disciple, Behold, thy mother! And from that hour the disciple took her unto his own *home*.

¹ Or, *sanctuary*

² Or, *sanctuary*

² Or, *tunic*
³ Ps. xxii. 18.

Matt. 27	Mark 15	Luke 23	John 19
saved others; [2]himself he cannot save. He is the King of Israel; let him now come down from the cross, and we will believe on him. 43 He trusteth on God; let him deliver him now, if he desireth him: for he said, I am the Son of God. 44 And the robbers also that were crucified with him cast upon him the same reproach.	saved others; [3]himself he cannot save. 32 Let the Christ, the King of Israel, now come down from the cross, that we may see and believe. And they that were crucified with him reproached him.	38 And there was also a superscription over him, THIS IS THE KING OF THE JEWS. 39 And one of the malefactors that were hanged railed on him, saying, Art not thou the Christ? save thyself and us. 40 But the other answered, and rebuking him said, Dost thou not even fear God, seeing thou art in the same condemnation? 41 And we indeed justly; for we receive the due reward of our deeds: but this man hath done nothing amiss. 42 And he said, Jesus, remember me when thou comest [2]in thy kingdom. 43 And he said unto him, Verily I say unto thee, To-day shalt thou be with me in Paradise.	

[2] Or, *can he not save himself?*

[3] Or, *can he not save himself?*

[2] Some ancient authorities read *into thy kingdom*.

Note 255. Crucifixion was the cruelest, the most tortuous, the most humiliating, and the most horrible manner of execution practiced in ancient times. Other nations may have originated it, but the Romans made wider use of it than any other people. The victim would be in extreme pain for hours, sometimes days, before death came as a welcome relief. We know from Mark (vs. 25 above) that the crucifixion of Jesus, the act of affixing Him on the cross, took place at the third hour of the day according to the Jewish reckoning (about nine o'clock in the morning by our time). He died at their ninth hour (about our three o'clock) or soon thereafter. Thus He was six hours in this great suffering. But from Mark 15:44 we learn that to Pilate, who doubtless had had experience with such executions, this was a surprisingly short time. In our studies, this six-hour period is naturally divided into two practically equal parts: that time before the miraculous darkness, which appeared at their sixth hour (about noon), and the time of the darkness, from their sixth hour to their ninth hour (mid afternoon). His death was probably hastened by the infinitely more intense spiritual agonies, which He surely underwent during the latter half.

The section above includes the Gospel accounts of the first half of this six-hour period. During those three hours Jesus suffered all the physical tortures which victims of crucifixion ordinarily would undergo, the same sufferings that the two robbers who were being crucified with Him were undergoing.

Probably His prayer for His executioners was uttered while they were nailing Him to the cross. A strange prayer it was to all who heard it—the hardened soldiers, His jeering foes, and even His loyal friends. But He had given an injunction many months before that was as startling to those who heard—"Pray for those that persecute you" (Matt. 5: 44).

Surely it was early in the ordeal that Jesus committed His mother to John's care. As suggested in Note 16, a comparison of John 19: 25 with Matt. 27: 56 and Mark 15: 40 leads us to conclude that Mary, mother of Jesus, and Salome, mother of John (a son of Zebedee), were probably sisters. Mary and Salome were doubtless lodging for the period of the Passover in the quarters which John had procured for them.* John probably accompanied both of them on the sad journey to Golgotha. The half brothers of Jesus were surely not present because (1) at that time they did not believe in Him (John 7: 5) and were out of sympathy with His work, and (2) they may have been afraid to take His part in any way. It was natural, therefore, for Jesus to commit His mother in this hour of sorrow to her nephew, "the disciple. . . whom He loved," rather than to her younger sons. When John went with Mary back to the city, Salome (possibly at Mary's request) remained at the scene, along with the two other Marys, but farther removed from the cross (Matt. 27: 55—56; Mark 15: 40).

During the first half of Jesus' stay on the cross, members of the Sanhedrin and others who were present, out of a fiendish desire to see Him suffer, taunted Him with every insult they could think of. Pilate doubtless wrote the superscription as an insult to the Jewish people, as though he would proclaim: "Look what the Romans do to this people's king!" But the mockers turned the burlesque against Jesus; they challenged Him to come down from the cross, mockingly promising to believe on Him if He would do so. But He did not accept their challenge for the same reason that He would not pray five days before, "Father,

---

*Notice that "home" in John 19:27 is printed in italics because the Greek word for "home" or "house" does not appear here. "His own" (neuter plural) likely means the quarters which he had rented. Probably this verse does not mean that John took Mary to live with Him the remainder of her life, as some commentators suppose, but only the rest of their stay in Jerusalem. In Acts 1:14 Mary is mentioned in connection with the brothers of Jesus, who by that time had become believers; and she was probably living with them at that time.

save me from this hour" (John 12:27, #199), and for the same reason that He did not in the garden call for the twelve legions of angels to defend Him (Matt. 26:53, #239). He was going to do something more wonderful than coming down from the cross—He came up from the grave; and even then those mocking priests did not believe on Him. The one bright spot in this scene of cruel jeering and mocking was the prayer of the penitent thief and Jesus' assuring answer thereto.

But at no time during those hours of such intense physical suffering and personal humiliation did Jesus utter a word of complaint or vindication. Truly "He was led as a lamb to the slaughter, yet He opened not His mouth" (Isa. 53:7). It is significant that each one of His utterances during this period looked toward the welfare of others: (1) He prayed for His tormentors. (2) He made provision for His mother. (3) He promised salvation to the penitent robber.

b. Three hours of darkness and spiritual agony, from the sixth hour to the ninth hour (12 m. to 3 p.m.), the death of Jesus

#252

Matt. 27:45-50	Mark 15:33-37	Luke 23:44, 45a, 46	John 19:28-30
45 Now from the sixth hour there was darkness over all the [1]land until the ninth hour. 46 And about the ninth hour Jesus cried with a loud voice, saying, [2]Eli, Eli, lama sabachthani? that is, My God, my God, [3]why hast thou forsaken me? 47 And some of them that stood there, when they heard it, said, This man calleth Elijah. 48 And straightway one of them ran, and took a sponge, and filled it with vinegar, and put it on a reed, and gave him to drink. 49 And the rest said, Let be; let us see whether Elijah cometh to	33 And when the sixth hour was come, there was darkness over the whole [1]land until the ninth hour. 34 And at the ninth hour Jesus cried with a loud voice, Eloi, Eloi, lama sabachthani? which is, being interpreted, [2]My God, my God, [3]why hast thou forsaken me? 35 And some of them that stood by, when they heard it, said, Behold, he calleth Elijah. 36 And one ran, and filling a sponge full of vinegar, put it on a reed, and gave him to drink, saying, Let be; let us see whether Elijah cometh to take him down.	44 And it was now about the sixth hour, and a darkness came over the whole [1]land until the ninth hour, 45a [2]the sun's light failing:	28 After this Jesus, knowing that all things are now finished, [1]that the scripture might be accomplished, saith, I thirst. 29 There was set there a vessel full of vinegar: so they put a sponge full of the vinegar upon hyssop, and brought it to his mouth. 30 When Jesus therefore had received the vinegar, he said, It is finished:

[1] Or, earth	[1] Or, earth		
[2] Ps. xxii. 1.	[2] Ps. xxii. 1.	[1] Or, earth	
[3] Or, why didst thou forsake me?	[3] Or, why didst thou forsake me?	[2] Gr. the sun failing.	[1] Ps. lxix. 21.

Matt. 27	Mark 15	Luke 23	John 19
save him.[4] 50 And Jesus cried again with a loud voice, and yielded up his spirit. [4] Many ancient authorities add *And another took a spear and pierced his side, and there came out water and blood.* See Jn. 19. 34.	37 And Jesus uttered a loud voice, and gave up the ghost.	46 [3]And Jesus, crying with a loud voice, said, Father, into thy hands I commend my spirit: and having said this, he gave up the ghost. [3] Or, *and when Jesus had cried with a loud voice, he said*	and he bowed his head, and gave up his spirit.

Note 256. The three hours set forth in the foregoing section were the most critical hours in the world's history after the entrance of sin into man's life. Three incidents (two set forth in this section and one in the next) bespeak the momentous significance of that time: (1) the darkness, (2) the cry of spiritual desolation and (3) the rending of the veil in the temple.

The darkness of that day cannot be accounted for naturally. It could not have been an eclipse, because it was at the wrong time of the moon-month. The only thing that can be said is that it was miraculous, that in some way God took away the light of the sun; and we waste our time and effort if we try to explain how it was done. At that time, when the Father would deal with the Son for us, it was fitting that a curtain of darkness should hide the suffering Saviour from His jeering tormentors and from His sorrowing friends. Indeed, the taunting and jeering doubtless subsided after the darkness enshrouded the land; and Jesus was left to suffer in silence. Most surely it was during those hours of darkness that God laid on Him the iniquity of us all (Isa. 53: 6), that He "bore our sins in His body on the tree" (I Pet. 2: 24), that He was made "to be sin for us" (II Cor. 5: 21), that God set Him forth "to be a propitiation...in His blood" (Rom. 3: 25). In some way He was experiencing the woes of the "outer darkness" (Matt. 8: 12) in order that He might impart "the light of life" to those who follow Him (John 8: 12). This was the deep suffering of which the agony in the garden was in anticipation.

Near to the end of this period Jesus broke the silence with the cry of desolation: "My God, My God, why has Thou forsaken Me?" These words are indeed a quotation from Psalm 22: 1 in Hebrew. The question has arisen: Did the Father really forsake the Son in the hour of His intensest suffering? I am convinced that our Lord would not have uttered such a cry of desolation if in some way during these hours of darkness there had not been a suspension of fellowship between the Father and Son. He had experienced such a fellowship with His Father throughout His life; and I am convinced that in answer to the agonizing prayer in Gethsemane, in a special way, He was granted the sustaining presence of God throughout that night and day of great and increasing humiliation and suffering. But at last the moment came when He must (since He purposed to be our Saviour, cf. Matt. 1: 21) bear the sins of a sinning race. That involved submitting to that which, when visited against guilty sinners, is the wrath of God (Rom. 1: 18), since it is from the wrath of God that we are saved by His death (Rom. 5: 10—11). Certainly God was not angry with Him; He was pleased with Him. The Father was pleased when Jesus in baptism dedicated Himself to this death as His mission on earth, and again when He first openly declared His steadfast purpose to submit to death (Matt. 3: 17; 17: 5); and certainly He was never more pleased with Him than when He was voluntarily enduring for earth's sinners that infliction which is the expression of God's wrath. For centuries it had been foretold: "He was bruised for our iniquities.... Yet it pleased the Lord to bruise Him, He hath put Him to grief" (Isa. 53: 5, 10). What He suffered, it was God's plan for Him to suffer; and Jesus Himself recognized and approved it when He said, "For this cause came I unto this hour" (John 12: 27, #199).

But since Jesus knew that He had come into the world for such an hour as this, the question arises: Why this outcry, which sounds s o much like a complaint? I do not know; but I am reminded that the Lord Jesus, the Second Person of the Godhead, was still in the state of His self-emptying. By his own statement, there were things which He did not know (cf. Mark 13: 32, #219). Was it that, in such a state, He did not know the fulness of the agony involved in the role of a Sin Offering until He was suffering it?

The cry of desolation came at the ninth hour, doubtless as the darkness was lifting. Both of the Gospel records which tell about this cry also tell how some of the crowd who did not understand the Hebrew in the outcry, but who did know that the scribes expected Elijah to appear in the Messianic age, erroneously inferred that Jesus was calling for Elijah. And both Matthew and Mark relate that immediately one from the group in pity gave Him to drink from the vinegar (probably sour wine mixed with water) which doubtless had been provided for the benefit of the soldiers.

In John it is stated that it was after Jesus had exclaimed, "I thirst," that the act of mercy was performed, and He uttered that exclamation because He knew that all things were finished that the Scripture might be accomplished (vs. 28). The same account tells (vs. 30) that after receiving the drink Jesus said, "It is finished," using the same word as in verse 28. This statement by Jesus, along with one above by John the writer, indicates that the undescribable agony for the sins of the world which He had suffered during the hours of darkness—the agony of Hell—was over. That was a cry of victory. In the Intercessory Prayer on the night before He had said to the Father, "I have finished the work..." (John 17: 4, #237), using the same word for "finished" as in the above verses. At that time the work was finished, but the atoning suffering remained to be endured. Now, after the hours of darkness, the suffering also was finished, except the closing moments of bodily torture and the experience of physical death. Except for His actually dying and entering into vanquishing conflict with the powers of death, the price of redemption had been paid.

John seems to indicate that the end came immediately after he said, "It is finished." But all the Synoptics tell that just before the end Jesus cried out with a loud voice, inferring that it was a wordless cry, a final struggle with bodily suffering. From Luke we learn that probably His last utterance on the cross was a calm commending of His spirit, His immortal personality, to the Father. It was a quotation from Ps. 31: 5, but to Him it had a more personal meaning than to the psalmist. With these words He died in faith, depending on the Father to bring Him forth in a powerful resurrection in victory over death (and over the Devil who had the power of death, Heb. 2: 14).

During the latter half of His stay on the cross, therefore, our Lord Jesus uttered four sayings, besides a loud wordless cry. They were: (1) the cry of desolation, "My God, My God, why hast Thou forsaken Me?" (2) the utterance of physical anguish, "I thirst," (3) the realization of victory, "It is finished," and (4) the expression of faith and resignation, "Father, into thy hands I commend my spirit." Just as all three of His sayings during the first three hours looked toward the welfare of others, so all of those during these latter three hours had to do with His own suffering or His own welfare.

(5) Some things occurring in connection with the death of Jesus

#253

MATT. 27:51-56	MARK 15:38-41	LUKE 23:45b, 47-49
51 And behold, the veil of the [1]temple was rent in two from the top to the bottom; and the earth did quake; and the rocks were rent; 52 and the tombs were opened; and many bodies of the saints that had fallen asleep were raised; 53 and coming forth out of the tombs after his resurrection they entered into the holy city and appeared unto many. 54 Now the centurion, and they that were with him watching Jesus, when they saw the earthquake, and the things that were done, feared exceedingly, saying, Truly this was [2]the Son of God. 55 And many women were there beholding from afar, who had followed	38 And the veil of the [1]temple was rent in two from the top to the bottom. 39 And when the centurion, who stood by over against him, saw that he [2]so gave up the ghost, he said, Truly this man was [3]the Son of God. 40 And there were also women beholding from afar: among whom were	45b And the veil of the [1]temple was rent in the midst. 47 And when the centurion saw what was done, he glorified God, saying, Certainly this was a righteous man. 48 And all the multitudes that came together to this sight, when they beheld the things that were done, returned smiting their breasts.
[1] Or, sanctuary [2] Or, a son of God	[1] Or, sanctuary [2] Many ancient authorities read so cried out, and gave up the ghost. [3] Or, a son of God	[1] Or, sanctuary

Matt. 27	Mark 15	Luke 23
Jesus from Galilee, ministering unto him: 56 among whom was Mary Magdalene, and Mary the mother of ³James and Joses, and the mother of the sons of Zebedee.	both Mary Magdalene, and Mary the mother of ⁴James the ⁵less and of Joses, and Salome; 41 who, when he was in Galilee, followed him, and ministered unto him; and many other women that came up with him unto Jerusalem.	49 And all his acquaintance, and the women that followed with him from Galilee, stood afar off, seeing these things.
⁴ Or, *Jacob* ⁵ Gr. *little*.	³ Or, *Jacob*	

Note 257. Besides the darkness, which preceded it, three other wonderful phenemona attended the death of Jesus. They were: the rending of the veil of the temple, the earthquake, and the opening of the graves and subsequent coming forth of the "bodies of the saints." Of these, the earthquake may have been from natural causes; but if so, it was certainly miraculously timed. The other two were clearly supernatural.

Like the darkness, the rending of the temple veil is related in each of the Synoptic Gospels. The veil which separated the Holy Place in the temple from the Holy of Holies was very heavy and very strong.* Only the high priest ever went behind it, and he only on the Day of Atonement with the blood of the sin offering (evidence of the death of the animal offered) to make figurative atonement for the sins of the people committed during the preceding year (see paragraph on the Day of Atonement, pp. 13f). The rending of the veil at the time of the death of Jesus was certainly direct action of God; and without doubt it signified that the true atonement for sin had been made. The way into the heavenly Holy of Holies has been opened to all that will come to it by Him who is the eternal High Priest and the true Offering for sin (Isa. 53: 10; Heb. 7: 25, 9: 8, 26b). From that day there has been no need for human priests to carry behind the veil the blood of animals that could not in reality bear the sins of a worshiper, because He who died on that day was truly "made to be sin for us"—"He bore our sins in His body on the tree" (II Cor. 5: 21; I Pet. 2: 24).

Whether the earthquake was from natural causes or not, it, along with the other wonders, certainly made a solemn impression on the officer who had been in charge of the executions, and probably on the other soldiers. As his confession appears in Luke, he at least realized that Jesus was not guilty of what the priests accused Him of, or of anything else worthy of death. As it appears in Matthew and Mark, he realized that the Man whom he had crucified was of divine origin. We wonder if, after the resurrection, this impression led him and any of the other soldiers to full discipleship.

The account of the opening of the graves and raising of the bodies of those "saints that had fallen asleep" is found only in Matthew, and

*Edersheim, *Life and Times of Jesus*, Vol. II, p. 611, cf. the paragraph on the temple in the Introduction.

there is no clear reference to any part of the incident anywhere else in the New Testament. Therefore I am unable to answer satisfactorily any of the many questions that have been raised about the incident. It was a way that God had of showing the significance of the events of that day.

4. The entombment of Jesus

#254

JOHN 19:31-37

31 The Jews therefore, because it was the Preparation, that the bodies should not remain on the cross upon the sabbath (for the day of that sabbath was a high *day*), asked of Pilate that their legs might be broken, and *that* they might be taken away. 32 The soldiers therefore came, and brake the legs of the first, and the other that was crucified with him: 33 but when they came to Jesus, and saw that he was dead already, they brake not his legs: 34 howbeit one of the soldiers with a spear pierced his side, and straightway there came out blood and water. 35 And he that hath seen hath borne witness, and his witness is true: and he knoweth that he saith true, that ye also may believe. 36 For these things came to pass, [1]that the scripture might be fulfilled, A bone of him shall not be [2]broken. 37 And again another scripture saith, [3]They shall look on him whom they pierced.

[1] Ex. xxii. 46; Num. ix. 12; Ps. xxxiv. 20. [2] Or, *crushed* [3] Zech. xii. 10.

MATT. 27:57-61	MARK 15:42-47	LUKE 23:50-56	JOHN 19:38-42
57 And when even was come, there came a rich man from Arimathaea, named Joseph, who also himself was Jesus' disciple:	42 And when even was now come, because it was the Preparation, that is, the day before the sabbath, 43 there came Joseph of Arimathaea, a councillor of honorable estate, who also himself was looking for the kingdom of God; and he	50 And behold, a man named Joseph, who was a councillor, a good and righteous man 5₺ (he had not consented to their counsel and deed), *a man* of Arimathaea, a city of the Jews, who was looking for the	38 And after these things Joseph of Arimathaea, being a disciple of Jesus, but secretly for fear of the Jews, asked of Pilate that he might take away the body of Jesus: and Pilate gave *him* leave.
58 this man went to Pilate, and asked for the body of Jesus. Then Pilate commanded it to be given up.	boldly went in unto Pilate, and asked for the body of Jesus. 44 And Pilate marvelled if he were already dead: and calling unto him the centurion, he asked him whether he [1]had been any while dead. 45 And when he learned it of the centurion, he granted the corpse to Joseph.	kingdom of God: 52 this man went to Pilate, and asked for the body of Jesus.	
59 And Joseph took the body, and wrapped it in	46 And he bought a linen cloth, [1] Many ancient authorities read *were already dead.*	53 And he took it down, and wrapped it in a linen cloth,	He came therefore, and took away his body. 39 And there came also Nicodemus, he who at the first came to him by night, bringing a [1]mixture of myrrh and aloes, about a hundred pounds. 40 So they took the body of [1] Some ancient authorities read *roll.*

333

Matt. 27	Mark 15	Luke 23	John 19
a clean linen cloth, 60 and laid it in his own new tomb, which he had hewn out in the rock: and he rolled a great stone to the door of the tomb, and departed.	and taking him down, wound him in the linen cloth, and laid him in a tomb which had been hewn out of a rock; and he rolled a stone against the door of the tomb.	and laid him in a tomb that was hewn in stone, where never man had yet lain.	Jesus, and bound it in linen cloths with the spices, as the custom of the Jews is to bury. 41 Now in the place where he was crucified there was a garden; and in the garden a new tomb wherein was never man yet laid. 42 There then because of the Jews' Preparation (for the tomb was nigh at hand) they laid Jesus.
		54 And it was the day of the Preparation, and the sabbath ¹ drew on. 55 And	
61 And Mary Magdalene was there, and the other Mary, sitting over against the sepulchre.	47 And Mary Magdalene and Mary the *mother* of Joses beheld where he was laid. ¹ Many ancient authorities read *were already dead.*	the women, who had come with him out of Galilee, followed after, and beheld the tomb, and how his body was laid. 56 And they returned, and prepared spices and ointments. And on the sabbath they rested according to the commandment. ¹ Gr. *began to dawn.*	

Note 258. The Sanhedrin leaders had been obstinate in demanding the death of Jesus on that day. But that was their day of Preparation, the day before the Sabbath; and it was doubly important that the executions should be finished, and that the bodies should be buried before the end of the day. It would have been (1) a defilement of the city and of the land of Judaea for the bodies to be left on the crosses during the Sabbath (cf. Deut. 21:23), and (2) a desecration of the Sabbath to take them from the crosses and bury them after sunset, and that Sabbath was doubly sacred because it was the one coming during Passover week. The Jewish leaders, therefore, petitioned Pilate to hasten the death of the victims on the crosses by having their legs broken. Such practice was not infrequent among the Romans. Breaking the legs of the victims would not, of itself, have hastened their death enough to permit the bodies to be taken from the cross that afternoon; but this wanton practice was generally followed by a death stroke with spear or sword, which put an end to what remained of life. Probably, the soldiers thrust their spears into the robbers also, as well as into the body of Jesus.

Jesus was manifestly dead already, and breaking His legs obviously could not cause any additional suffering for Him. But, doubtless to make sure that He was dead, the soldier did thrust his spear into the side of the lifeless body. Ordinarily, a wound in a dead body does not bleed, but from the opening in the side of the Lord Jesus there came out blood and water. We wonder if this was the result of internal bleeding; and if so, whether it is evidence that Jesus died from a rupture of the heart or of a great blood vessel. If such was the case, it might account for the wordless outcry which Jesus uttered just before He commended His spirit to the Father.

Observe that all four of the Gospel writers name Joseph of Arimathea as the one who took the initiative in giving Jesus an honorable burial. For that purpose, he furnished his own new tomb, which he had hewn in the rock, doubtless for himself and His family. This is the only connection in which he is mentioned in the Bible. Only in John is Nicodemus set forth as cooperating with Joseph, contributing a hundred pound weight of myrrh and aloes. In all, Nicodemus is mentioned three times in John (chs. 3: 1—21; 7: 50—52, ##26, 145, cf. Note 29). Both of these friends of Jesus were members of the Sanhedrin, who had previously kept their admiration and friendship for Him hidden from their fellow Sanhedrists; but the sufferings of Jesus seem to have inspired them to a m e a s u r e of boldness (vs. 43 in Mark). Observe that although the other members of the Sanhedrin would not enter the house of Pilate, lest they be so defiled that they could not legally eat of the feast of unleavened bread (John 18: 28), these two noble Sanhedrists did not hesitate to handle the dead body of Jesus, a deed which would defile them for seven days (Num. 19: 11). We wish we knew what was their attitude toward Christianity after the resurrection and after Pentecost, and what labors they expended for it.

It is interesting, though it may not be especially significant, to put together the statements about the women who were at the cross and what John said about himself, and thus to try to reconstruct their movements. We know that at first four women, along with John, were present a t the cross; Mary the mother of Jesus, Mary's sister Salome (John's mother), Mary Magdalene, and Mary, wife of Cleopas (mother of James and Joses). When Jesus died, three of these were still present: Mary Magdalene, Mary the mother of James and Joses, and Salome (Matt. 27: 56; Mark 15: 40). Only two of them, Mary Magdalene and Mary the mother of James and Joses, witnessed the burial (Mark 15: 47). Early in the ordeal John, at Jesus' request, had taken Mary, his aunt, to the lodging in the city which he had provided. Probably after Mary had calmed a bit and was resting, she sent John back to Golgotha, asking him to send Salome to her. He probably arrived by the cross not long before Jesus died—after the cry of desolation, and before the call of physical thirst. He maintains that he heard and saw what he has recorded (John 19: 35): Jesus' words, "I thirst," someone's giving Him a drink of vinegar from a sponge, His words, "It is finished," His bowing H i s head in death, and the soldier's piercing His side. Salome doubtless withdrew to the lodging to be with Mary as soon as Jesus died. John probably was present at the hurried embalming of the body and its entombment. Mary Magdalene and Mary the mother of James and Joses also viewed the burial; and, observing where the body was laid, returned to their lodging to prepare additional spices with which to anoint the body after the Sabbath should be past.

IX. Saturday, a guard stationed at the tomb
#255
MATT. 27:62-66

62 Now on the morrow, which is *the day* after the Preparation, the chief priests and the Pharisees were gathered together unto Pilate, 63 saying, Sir, we remember that that deceiver said while he was yet alive, After three days I rise again. 64 Command therefore that the sepulchre be made sure until the third day, lest haply his disciples come and steal him away, and say unto the people, He is risen from the dead: and the last error will be worse than the first. 65 Pilate said unto them, [1]Ye have a guard: go, [2]make it *as* sure as ye can. 66 So they went, and made the sepulchre sure, sealing the stone, the guard being with them.

[1] Or, *Take a guard*   [2] Gr. *make it sure, as ye know.*

Note 259. It is surprising that the enemies of Jesus recalled His statement that He was to rise from the dead; while His disciples and friends overlooked it, although to them He had repeatedly foretold it (##131, 134, 136, 190, 233). In spite of Jesus' many statements to the contrary, the disciples were still expecting an immediate inauguration of the visible Kingdom (Luke 19:11, #194). Since all their expectations revolved around His continuing to live, His death, though frequently predicted, so stunned them that everything He had said about a resurrection must have been forgotten. On the other hand, His enemies who did not believe in Him as a prophet, had repeatedly been so foiled and angered by His many miracles and irresistable wisdom in disputation that, having heard Him say that after giving up His life He would take it again (John 10:17—18, #164), they did not forget it. And Judas also may have mentioned His promise to rise from death some time in his negotiations with them. The irony of the situation is that the only Person who has ever come forth in victory over death is One whose tomb was guarded to keep His body in it.

Note 260. In the foregoing outline and notes I have followed the traditional timing of the last week of our Lord's life, holding that He observed the Passover on Thursday evening and was crucified on Friday, and that He rested on Wednesday and a large part of Thursday. According to the Jewish reckoning of that day, both the Passover meal and the crucifixion occurred on the fifteenth day of the month Nisan. But some Bible students, being influenced by the words of Jesus in Matt. 12:40 ("the Son of Man shall be three days and three nights in the heart of the earth") have sought to show that He was crucified earlier than Friday, and therefore He did not rest on Wednesday. But observe the following:

1. The accounts show that Jesus was tried, condemned, and crucified all on the "day of Preparation," which was the day before the Sabbath (Mark 15:42; Luke 23:54; John 19:14, 31, 42). The guard was

placed at the tomb on the day after the Preparation; that is, on the Sabbath day (Matt. 27:62). Early in the morning of the first day of the week (the day after the Sabbath, Matt. 28:1), while it was yet dark Mary Magdalene found the tomb open (John 20:1); and a little later, "when the sun was risen," the other women, on entering the open tomb, were informed by the angel that Jesus had risen (Mark 16:1, 6). The crucifixion, therefore, was on the day before the Sabbath and the resurrection on the day after the Sabbath.

2. Matthew, who was the only Gospel writer that quoted the statement of Jesus that He would be in the earth "three days and three nights," also quoted Him three times as saying that He would rise again "on the third day" after death (chs. 16:21; 17:23; 20:19). In Luke, every statement of Jesus foretelling His resurrection and every assertion about it after it occurred declares that it was "on the third day" (chs. 9:22; 18:33; 24:7, 46). In Mark, according to the American Standard Version, each of the three predictions of Jesus is that He would rise again "after three days" (chs. 8:31; 9:31; 10:34; but the King James Version has "on the third day" in 9:31 and 10:34). In John there is only one prediction about the event that indicates when it would be, and that the veiled reference to it in chapter 2:19--22 ("Destroy this temple and in three days I will raise it up"). Paul doubtless indicated what was the general understanding of Christians in A.D. 57, when he wrote, "he hath been raised from the dead on the third day according to the Scriptures" (I Cor. 15:4).

There are therefore three phrases: (1) "three days and three nights," used once in Matthew, (2) "after three days," used three times in Mark (American Standard Version) and "in three days," used once in John, and (3) "on the third day," used three times in Matthew, five times in Luke, and once by Paul. Do they mean the same thing? Probably the answer is in the words of the Sanhedrin leaders to Pilate (Matt. 27:63—64). They quoted Jesus as saying He would rise "after three days," and they asked for authority to have the tomb guarded "until the third day." In their minds, therefore, the two expressions must have been equivalent to each other.

3. The Jews of that day, so we are told,* in measuring time, counted any part of a day as a day. According to that custom, counting what was left of Friday, "the day of Preparation," after the death and hurried entombment of Jesus until sunset as the first day, and Saturday, the Sabbath day, as the second day, and the time after sunset Saturday until the time of the resurrection Sunday morning as the third day, Jesus is seen to have arisen on "the third day," which, according to the current understanding, was "after three days." Therefore, although we must conclude that Jesus was in the tomb only one full twenty-four hour day and a part of a day before it and a part of a day after it, this con-

---

*Robertson, *Harmony of the Gospels*, pp. 290f.; Broadus, *Commentary on Matthew*, p. 582; Edersheim, *Life and Times of Jesus*, pp. 630f.

clusion fulfilled in the minds of His hearers the prediction that He would be "in the heart of the earth three days and three nights." There is no need then to try to adjust the plain record in order to make it fit modern conception of days.

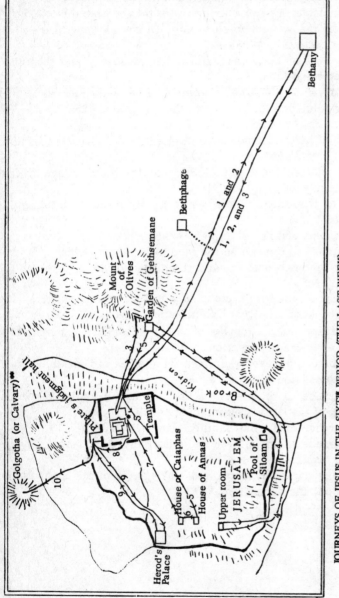

JOURNEYS OF JESUS IN THE SIXTH PERIOD (THE LAST WEEK)

1 - On Sunday (##198–200) and 2 - on Monday (##201–204) from Bethany to the temple in Jerusalem and return on each day. 3 - On Tuesday from Bethany to the temple, thence to the Mount of Olives, probably Gethsemane (##205–219). 4 - On Thursday from the Mount of Olives to the upper room and return to Gethsemane (##229–238). 5 - Friday from Mount of Olives to house of Annas (#240). Thence 6 - to house of Caiaphas (#241). Thence 7 - to the meeting place of the Sanhedrin (#244). Thence 8 - to Pilate's judgment hall (#245). Thence 9 - to house of Herod (Antipas) and return to Pilate's house (#246). 10 - From Pilate's hall of judgment to Golgotha (#249).

*"Hall of Hewn Stone," meeting place of the Sanhedrin   **Probable location.

A PREVIEW OUTLINE OF PERIOD SEVEN, ##256-272

I.   The faithful women and the risen Jesus, ##256-262
1.   Journey of the two Marys to the tomb on Sabbath afternoon, purchasing spices for further anointing of the body, #256
2.   Events occurring in connection with the resurrection, #257
3.   Visit of the women to the tomb on the morning of the first day of the week, ##258-259
     (1) Arrival of Mary Magdalene, her discovery and report to Peter and John, #258
     (2) Arrival of the other women, their encounter with the angels, and their report to the disciples, #259
4.   Visit of Peter and John to the tomb, #260
5.   Return of Mary Magdalene to the tomb, first appearance of the risen Jesus, #261
6.   Appearance of Jesus to the other women, the message to His brothers, #262

II. Reaction of His enemies to news of the resurrection, bribing the guard, #263

III. The risen Jesus and His disciples, ##264-272
1.   Appearance to the two on the road to Emmaus, #264
2.   Report of the two to the apostles, news of the appearance to Peter, #265
3.   First appearance to a group of apostles (ten in number), the first giving of the Great Commission, #266
4.   Second appearance to the apostles (eleven in number) one week after the resurrection, #267
5.   Appearance to seven disciples by the Sea of Galilee, three-fold confession of Peter, #268
6.   Appearance to the eleven on the mountain in Galilee, second giving of the Great Commission, #269
7.   Appearance to His half brother, James, #270
8.   Appearance to the eleven in Jerusalem, third giving of the Great Commission, #271
9.   Final appearance, fourth and final giving of the Great Commission, the ascension, #272

Ministry of the Resurrection Victory

(## 256 — 272)

Note 261. Readers of the Gospels always experience a thrill of joy and victory when they come to the resurrection accounts. Apart from the resurrection the ignominious death of Jesus was an irremissible tragedy; but together those two events constitute the ground for God's gift of salvation to sinners. Moreover, Jesus had repeatedly, before His death, indicated that the resurrection would be the sign of His authority for all that He did and taught. He had, therefore, staked the genuineness of His claims on this momentous event. It took both His death and His resurrection to fulfill the prophecy which He enacted when He was baptized (cf. Note 20).

After His resurrection, the body of Jesus possessed properties and exercised powers which it did not possess or exercise before His death. These are observed in His vanishing from the sight of the two at Emmaus (Luke 24: 31, #264), His entrance into the room where the disciples were gathered in spite of closed doors (John 20: 19, 26, ##266, 267), and the way He would appear to individuals or groups for short intervals, and remain unseen possibly for days before He would appear to someone else. These appearances were in a true body of flesh and bones, in which He consumed food; but in it He was not subject to the limitations which characterize men and women in this life—which, indeed, characterized Him before His death. These new properties and powers are doubtless marks of what Paul called a spiritual body (I Cor. 15: 44, cf. Phil. 3: 21).

After the resurrection we do not have accounts of any journeys that Jesus made with the disciples (except to the Mount of Olives for the ascension, probably from the upper room in Jerusalem, Luke 24: 50), but of detached appearances, which occurred in Jerusalem, on the Sea of Galilee, on a mountain in Galilee, and again in Jerusalem.

Some students of the Bible have held that the Gospel accounts of the resurrection and subsequent activities of Jesus are in hopeless conflict with one another; but I believe that a careful study of these accounts will show that they are altogether consistent with each other at this point, just as elsewhere. To be sure, the accounts are more or less fragmentary, and many details which we should like to know are omitted, but nothing in one account is in conflict with anything in any of the others.

I. The faithful women and the risen Jesus, ##256—262

1. Journey of the two Marys late on the Sabbath day to view the tomb, purchasing spices after the Sabbath was past (after sunset) for further anointing of the body of Jesus

#256

MATT. 28:1

1 Now late on the sabbath day, as it began to dawn toward the first *day* of the week, came Mary Magdalene and the other Mary to see the sepulchre.

MARK 16:1

1 And when the sabbath was past, Mary Magdalene, and Mary the *mother* of [1]James, and Salome, bought spices, that they might come and anoint him.
[1] Or, *Jacob*

Note 262. According to Matthew, the same two women who remained at the tomb on the crucifixion day until after the hasty burial returned "late on the Sabbath day, as it began to dawn toward the first day of the week." The word translated, "as it began to dawn" is fundamentally the same word as the one translated, "drew on" in Luke 23:54, in describing the close of the previous day ("it was the day of Preparation and the Sabbath drew on"). This journey seems to have been made just to see the tomb (possibly to make sure of its exact location) not long before sunset on the Sabbath day (Saturday), about twenty-four hours after they had departed from this place. After sunset, the shops in Jerusalem would be open, so that it was possible for the women to buy the spices with which to complete the anointing of the body the next morning. Salome joined them in making the purchases, and in such preparing of the spices as was necessary (Luke 24:1).

2. Things occurring in connection with the resurrection of Jesus

#257

MATT. 28:2-4

2 And behold, there was a great earthquake; for an angel of the Lord descended from heaven, and came and rolled away the stone, and sat upon it. 3 His appearance was as lightning, and his raiment white as snow: 4 and for fear of him the watchers did quake, and became as dead men.

Note 263. It is noteworthy that no one of the Gospel writers describes the resurrection itself—the greatest of all the miracles, the mightiest manifestation of God's power since creation, the most terrific struggle between opposing forces in all the history of the universe. The curtain is drawn on that most sacred scene.

We do not know at just what hour it occurred—certainly some time before Mary Magdalene who, of the women coming to anoint the body, was first to reach the tomb. Without doubt only the soldiers who were guarding the tomb saw the angel descend from Heaven and roll away the stone, and immediately they so fainted away that, for some time, they did not know what was going on. Matthew probably learned of the events

342

related in these verses from soldiers who were later converted to Christianity.

3. The women going to the tomb early in the morning of the first day of the week to anoint the body of Jesus further with the spices which they had prepared, ##258—259

(1) Mary Magdalene arriving before the others, her discovery and hasty withdrawal to report to Peter and John

#258
JOHN 20:1-2

1 Now on the first *day* of the week cometh Mary Magdalene early, while it was yet dark, unto the tomb, and seeth the stone taken away from the tomb. 2 She runneth therefore, and cometh to Simon Peter, and to the other disciple whom Jesus loved, and saith unto them, They have taken away the Lord out of the tomb, and we know not where they have laid him.

Note 264. Mary Magdalene evidently came ahead of the other women to the tomb, since she came "while it was yet dark" (John 20: 1), and the others came "when the sun was risen," though still "very early in the morning" (Mark 16: 2). Probably there were four or more who had agreed to meet at the tomb that they might anoint the body with the spices which they had prepared. Luke (vs. 10) names Mary Magdalene, Joanna, and Mary, the mother of James, and others. Though Salome, the mother of John, had participated in buying the spices, she may have felt that she was needed to stay with her sister Mary, the mother of Jesus.

Mary Magdalene, seeing the stone rolled away from the door of the tomb, came to a hasty conclusion that the body had been removed by hostile hands, and without bothering to investigate, ran to tell Peter and John. Since her report was to these two disciples only, the natural conclusion is that they were not at the same lodging place with the other nine disciples. Probably John was residing in the lodging that he had obtained for his mother Salome, and his aunt, Mary. Peter was probably lodging somewhere by himself.* He was bowed down, not only in grief because of the death of His Lord, but with remorse also because of his shameful denials when Jesus was on trial. Probably his place of lodging was not far from John's, who may have been more willing to sympathize than the others.

(2) Arrival of the other women, their encounter with the angels and their withdrawal to report to the nine disciples

#259

MATT. 28:5-8	MARK 16:2-8	LUKE 24:1-11
	2 And very early on the first day of the week, they	1 But on the first day of the week, at early dawn,

*The repetition of the preposition for "to" (*pros*) in vs. 2 ("to Simon Peter and to the other disciple") indicates that Mary went to each one separately.

343

Matt. 28 | Mark 16 | Luke 24

Matt. 28

5 And the angel answered and said unto the women, Fear not ye; for I know that ye seek Jesus, who hath been crucified. 6 He is not here; for he is risen, even as he said. Come, see the place [1]where the Lord lay. 7 And go quickly, and tell his disciples, He is risen from the dead; and lo, he goeth before you into Galilee; there shall ye see him: lo, I have told you. 8 And they departed quickly from the tomb with fear and great joy, and ran to bring his disciples word.

[1] Many ancient authorities read where he lay.

Mark 16

come to the tomb when the sun was risen. 3 And they were saying among themselves, Who shall roll us away the stone from the door of the tomb? 4 and looking up, they see that the stone is rolled back: for it was exceeding great. 5 And entering into the tomb, they saw a young man sitting on the right side, arrayed in a white robe; and t h e y w e r e amazed. 6 And he saith unto them, Be not amazed: ye seek Jesus, the Nazarene, who hath been crucified: he is risen; he is not here: behold, the place where they laid him! 7 But go, tell his disciples and Peter, He goeth before you into Galilee: there shall ye see him, as he said unto you. 8 And they went out and fled from the tomb; for trembling and astonishment had come upon them: and they said nothing to any one; for they were afraid.

Luke 24

they came unto the tomb, bringing the spices which they had prepared. 2 And they found the stone rolled away from the tomb. 3 And they entered in, and found not the body [1]of the Lord Jesus. 4 And it came to pass, while they were perplexed thereabout, behold, two men stood by them in dazzling apparel: 5 and as they were affrighted and bowed down their faces to the earth, they said unto them, Why seek ye [2]the living among the dead? 6 [3]He is not here, but is risen: remember how he spake unto you when he was yet in Galilee, 7 saying that the Son of man must be delivered up into the hands of sinful men, and be crucified, and the third day rise again. 8 And they remembered his words, 9 and returned [4]from the tomb, and told all these things to the eleven, and to all the rest. 10 Now they were Mary Magdalene, and Joanna, and Mary the *mother* of James: and the other women with them told these things unto the apostles. 11 And these words appeared in their sight as idle talk; and they disbelieved them.

[1] Some ancient authorities omit of the Lord Jesus.
[2] Gr. him that liveth.
[3] Some ancient authorities omit He is not here, but is risen.
[4] Some ancient authorities omit from the tomb.

Note 265. The other women came after Mary Magdalene's hasty departure from the tomb. These, seeing the stone rolled away, entered into the sepulcher, and were greeted by a "young man," dressed characteristically as a heavenly visitant, without doubt the angel who had rolled away the stone. Luke describes two such "men," and John tells of two who later appeared to Mary Magdalene; but in each of the records one was the spokesman. He bade the women to calm their fears, assured them that Jesus had come to life, as He Himself had promised, and sent them to bear this news to the disciples, along with a message that He would meet them in Galilee. This was a repetition of a promise that Jesus had made to them on the night of the Passover observance (Matt. 26:32, #233). Mary Magdalene had already reported to Peter and John that the tomb was empty; and they were doubtless on their way to the tomb. The other women, without doubt, made their report to the other nine disciples. But it seems that those who should have been the ones first to expect the resurrection were the ones hardest to convince. The report of the jubilant women "appeared in their sight as idle talk."

I recognize that Matthew 28:1—8 reads as though everything related in those verses occurred in a short time. But in view of the phrase, "late on the Sabbath day," we must conclude either that the resurrection occurred on the Sabbath (Saturday), or understand that some time—possibly eight hours or more—intervened between verses 1 and 2; and another period of time—probably not so long—intervened between verses 4 and 5. The latter understanding is necessary in view of statements in the other Gospels. It takes Matt. 28:1 and Mark 16:1 in their most natural meaning; and also it enables us naturally to relate the Gospel records to each other.

Verses 9 and 10 of Luke read as though the disciples were together and all of the women (Mary Magdalene included) reported the empty tomb and the message of the angel to the eleven as one group. However, the writer does not say that they were in one group; and we conclude that Mary Magdalene made her report to two disciples, and the other women to the other nine.

4. Visit of Peter and John to the tomb, their findings
#260

LUKE 24:12	JOHN 20:3-4
12 ¹But Peter arose, and ran unto the tomb; and stooping and looking in, he seeth the linen cloths by themselves; and he ²departed to his home, wondering at that which was come to pass. ¹ Some ancient authorities omit ver. 12. ² Or, *departed, wondering with himself*	3 Peter therefore went forth, and the other disciple, and they went toward the tomb. 4 And they ran both together: and the other disciple outran Peter, and came first to the tomb;

JOHN 20:5-10

5 and stooping and looking in, he seeth the linen cloths lying; yet entered he not in. 6 Simon Peter therefore also cometh, following him, and entered into the tomb; and he beholdeth the linen cloths lying, 7 and the napkin, that was upon his head, not lying with the linen cloths, but rolled up in a place by itself. 8 Then entered in therefore the other disciple also, who came first to the tomb, and he saw, and believed. 9 For as yet they knew not the scripture, that he must rise again from the dead. 10 So the disciples went away again unto their own home.

Note 266. Since it was the report of Mary Magdalene that moved Peter and John to run to the tomb, all they knew was that the tomb was open. They had not heard about the angels in the tomb, or the message which those personages sent to the disciples by the other women. John says of himself that he saw and believed, though he and Peter saw neither the risen Jesus nor the angels (cf. Luke 24:24). The rolled-back stone, the empty tomb, the orderly arrangement of the grave clothes, all together, convinced him that the body was not removed by anyone hostile to Jesus. We wonder if he recalled some of the announcements which his Lord had made about His dying and rising again. When he says that they (the disciples) "did not know the Scripture that He must rise again," he probably meant the Scriptures of the Old Testament. Later, Jesus would expound those Scriptures to the disciples (Luke 24: 45). Observe that all that Luke could say about Peter at this time, was that he wondered "at that which was come to pass" (Luke 24: 12). The angels, in giving their instructions to the women, had specifically included him as one to whom they must deliver their message (Mark 16: 7). The two disciples must have gone immediately from the empty tomb to report to the nine what they knew. They had not seen the angels, as did the women; and neither had they, or the women, as yet seen the risen Jesus. This fact impressed Cleopas and his companion, who were about to set out for Emmaus. After making their report, Peter and John doubtless departed—John to report to Mary and Salome what he had seen, and Peter to be by himself in his own lodging (cf. Luke 24: 12). There probably the special message from the angels to him was delivered by the women.

5. Mary Magdalene's return to the tomb, first appearance of the risen Jesus

#261

MARK 16:9-11

9 [1]Now when he was risen early on the first day of the week, he appeared first to Mary. Magdalene, from whom he had cast out seven demons.

10 She went and told them that had been with him, as they mourned and wept. 11 And they, when they heard that he was alive, and had been seen of her, disbelieved.

[1] The two oldest Greek manuscripts, and some other authorities, omit from ver. 9 to the end. Some other authorities have a different ending to the Gospel.

JOHN 20:11-18

11 But Mary was standing without at the tomb weeping: so, as she wept, she stooped and looked into the tomb; 12 and she beholdeth two angels in white sitting, one at the head, and one at the feet, where the body of Jesus had lain. 13 And they say unto her, Woman, why weepest thou? She saith unto them, Because they have taken away my Lord, and I know not where they have laid him. 14 When she had thus said, she turned herself back, and beholdeth Jesus standing, and knew not that it was Jesus. 15 Jesus saith unto her, Woman, why weepest thou? whom seekest thou? She, supposing him to be the gardener, saith unto him, Sir, if thou hast borne him hence, tell me where thou hast laid him, and I will take him away. 16 Jesus saith unto her, Mary. She turneth herself, and saith unto him in Hebrew, Rabboni; which is to say, Teacher. 17 Jesus saith to her, [1]Touch me not; for I am not yet ascended unto the Father: but go unto my brethren, and say to them, I ascend unto my Father and your Father, and my God and your God. 18 Mary Magdalene cometh and telleth the disciples, I have seen the Lord; and that he had said these things unto her.

[1] Or, Take not hold on me

Note 267. In the oldest two copies (manuscripts) of the New Testament, the Gospel of Mark comes to a close with verse 8 of this chapter, and some other manuscripts have a different ending from the one in our Bibles. For that reason, and because of differences in diction and style observed in verses 9—20 from that which characterize the rest of this Gospel, many students of the New Testament hold that Mark doubtless did not write those closing verses. But the passage occurs, though with variations, in many other manuscripts almost as old as the two mentioned above and in some of the oldest translations of the New Testament into the languages of people who did not speak Greek. A portion of it was quoted and ascribed to Mark by Irenaeus, a Christian writer who lived about 130—200 and wrote probably 150 years before those oldest copies of the New Testament mentioned above were produced. I recognize all these difficulties of interpretation; but since the inspiring Holy Spirit has, from the earliest days of the use of the New Testament, permitted this material to be included in Christian Bibles, it seems to me that it should be regarded as inspired and authentic, whether Mark himself later in life added it to his original work, or whether someone else added it during the apostolic age (See Introduction, p. 26). Certainly the Spirit was able to inspire the writing of the addition, whosever work it is, just as He inspired the rest.

In the foregoing section the Markan account merely summarizes an incident which John relates in more detail. Mary Magdalene doubtless missed the other women that morning altogether. They came to the tomb while she was away to tell Peter and John that the tomb was open, and had departed before Peter and John arrived. After these two went away, Mary returned, probably with no definite purpose except to indulge in weeping, not only because of the death of her Benefactor, but now over the loss of His body. On her first visit to the tomb, she did not see the angels nor had she heard their message about Jesus' coming to life again, but on this visit she was given both to see the angels and to be the first to see the risen Lord Himself.

The question is frequently asked: Why did Jesus tell Mary not to touch Him, but did not forbid the other women to hold Him by His feet (Matt. 28:9)? Later He invited the disciples to handle Him (Luke 24:39), and still later invited Thomas to put his finger in the nail prints in His hands and his hand in the opening in His side made by the spear (John 20:27). In the first place, Mary had no doubts about His identity, as the group of disciples had that night, and as Thomas had a week later. She did not need to touch Him to be convinced that He was real. In the second place, the word translated "touch" may mean "cling to;" and the tense of Jesus' negative command (present) indicates that He meant for her to stop doing what she had already begun. Mary was probably clinging to Him as though she thought that she would not let Him away from her again, now that she had Him back. He probably sought to emphasize that, in the future, His relations with her and with all others who had known Him must be of a more spiritual nature.

Observe that Jesus commissioned Mary Magdalene to take a message to His brothers, who before His death did not believe on Him. But Mary went, instead, to the disciples, probably arriving after Cleopas and his companion had departed for Emmaus. Although this was the third report that they had received, and was from one who had seen the risen Jesus, the disciples continued in their disbelief.

6. Appearance of Jesus to the other women, giving them a message for His brothers

#262

MATT. 28:9-10

9 And behold, Jesus met them, saying, All hail. And they came and took hold of his feet, and [1]worshipped him. 10 Then saith Jesus unto them, Fear not: go tell my brethren that they depart into Galilee, and there shall they see me.

[1] See marginal note on ch. 2:2.

Note 268. When Jesus appeared to Mary Magdalene, the other women had already hurried away on their errand to tell the disciples what they had seen and what the angels had said to them. The joyous enthusiasm inspired by their wonderful experiences of the morning may have been chilled somewhat because the disciples did not believe their story or share its hopes and joys. But soon it was stirred again when Jesus Himself met them with a glad salutation. With rapture they came reverently to Him and, falling down, they took Him by the feet and worshiped Him. He did not rebuke them for touching Him as He had done Mary Magdalene, probably because their actions were more reverent than hers had been. He calmed their natural fears and sent them also to His brothers, as He had sent Mary, with a message that they should go on back to Galilee and that He would meet them there also. Apparently He was planning to meet both His disciples and His family in the scenes where He had spent most of His labor and lived almost all of His life on earth.*

II. The reaction of the enemies of Jesus to the news of the resurrection, bribing the guard to tell an incredible falsehood about it   #263

MATT. 28:11-15

11 Now while they were going, behold, some of the guard came into the city, and told unto the chief priests all the things that were come to pass. 12 And when they were assembled with the elders, and had taken counsel, they gave much money unto the soldiers, 13 saying, Say ye, His disciples came by night, and stole him away while we slept. 14 And if this [1]come to the governor's ears, we will persuade him, and rid you of care. 15 So they took the money, and did as they were taught; and this saying was spread abroad among the Jews, *and continueth* until this day.

[1] Or, *come to a hearing before the governor*

*In placing the foregoing section after the report of these women to the disciples, I have followed Westcott, *The Gospel According to John*, p. 288, and J. W. Sheppard, *The Christ of the Gospels* (Grand Rapids: Wm. B. Erdman's Publishing Company), p. 616. The clause, "as they went to tell the disciples" in vs. 9 of the King James Version does not appear in the American Standard Version or in any other modern translation because it occurs only in a few very late manuscripts of the Greek Testament, and it was probably not in the Gospel as Matthew wrote it.

(continued on next page)

Note 269. The clause, "while they were going," indicates that members of the guard remained in their condition "as dead men" until both Mary Magdalene and the other women had come to the tomb and departed. The departure of the "watchers" is related after the account of the appearance of Jesus to the women, but they may have gone away earlier. Matthew probably was grouping all the experiences of the women together. The members of the guard may not have been around when Peter and John came to the tomb or when Mary Magdalene returned.

Observe that Matthew says, "Some of the guard came...," probably indicating that some of them did not go to the priests, or at least did not accept their bribe or tell the false story about the disciples stealing the body while they themselves were asleep. We do not know if any of these were among those who took part in the crucifixion; but when we remember the impression which the way Jesus died and the earthquake made on the centurion and those with him (Matt. 27:54, #253), it would be surprising if the resurrection, the wonder of wonders, did not lead some of them to full acceptance of the claims of Jesus and adherance later to the company of disciples.

The incident is evidence of the depraved and determined opposition of the Sanhedrin leaders to Jesus and to everything that would redound to His honor. From the beginning of His ministry to the end of His presence on earth, they shut their eyes to His powerful works and closed their hearts to His claims. Matthew says that the absurd report of the bribed soldiers was current among the Jews when he wrote the Gospel, probably between A.D. 60 and 65.*

III. The risen Christ and His disciples, ##264—272
1. Appearance to the two on the road to Emmaus
#264

MARK 16:12	LUKE 24:13
12 And after these things he was manifested in another form unto two of them, as they walked, on their way into the country.	13 And behold, two of them were going that very day to a village named Emmaus, which was three-score furlongs from Jerusalem.

LUKE 24:14-32
14 And they communed with each other of all these things which had happened. 15 And it came to pass, while they communed and questioned together, that Jesus himself drew near, and went with them. 16 But their eyes were holden that they should not know him. 17 And he said unto them, ¹What communications are these that ye have one with another, as ye walk? And they stood still, looking sad. 18

(continued from preceding page)

If, as the true text indicates, the meeting of Jesus with the women was after their report to the disciples, two difficulties are cleared up. (1) It was natural for the two enroute to Emmaus to say that the women, who had reported to the disciples before these departed from the group, had not seen Jesus. (2) We can understand why Jesus would send these women to His brothers with the message that they had already delivered to the disciples, especially since Mary Magdalene was going to the disciples with the message that He gave her, instead of to His brothers as He had instructed her.

*Edersheim says (*Life and Times of Jesus*, Vol. II, pp. 63f) that it is found in Jewish writings of the middle ages and early modern times.

Luke 24

And one of them, named Cleopas, answering said unto him, [2]Dost thou alone sojourn in Jerusalem and not know the things which are come to pass there in these days? 19 And he said unto them, What things? And they said unto him, The things concerning Jesus the Nazarene, who was a prophet mighty in deed and word before God and all the people: 20 and how the chief priests and our rulers delivered him up to be condemned to death, and crucified him. 21 But we hoped that it was he who should redeem Israel. Yea and besides all this, it is now the third day since these things came to pass. 22 Moreover certain women of our company amazed us, having been early at the tomb; 23 and when they found not his body, they came, saying, that they had also seen a vision of angels, who said that he was alive. 24 And certain of them that were with us went to the tomb, and found it even so as the women had said: but him they saw not. 25 And he said unto them, O foolish men, and slow of heart to believe [3]in all that the prophets have spoken! 26 Behooved it not the Christ to suffer these things, and to enter into his glory? 27 And beginning from Moses and from all the prophets, he interpreted to them in all the scriptures the things concerning himself. 28 And they drew nigh unto the village, whither they were going: and he made as though he would go further. 29 And they constrained him, saying, Abide with us; for it is toward evening, and the day is now far spent. And he went in to abide with them. 30 And it came to pass, when he had sat down with them to meat, he took the [4]bread and blessed; and breaking it he gave to them. 31 And their eyes were opened, and they knew him; and he vanished out of their sight. 32 And they said one to another, Was not our heart burning within us, while he spake to us in the way, while he opened to us the scriptures?

[1] Gr. *What words are these that ye exchange one with another.*
[2] Or, *Dost thou sojourn alone in Jerusalem, and knowest thou not the things*
[3] Or, *after*   [4] Or, *loaf*

Note 270. Cleopas and his companion certainly withdrew from the company of disciples after the arrival both of the women, and later of Peter and John, with their respective reports about what they had seen and heard at the tomb, but before the coming of Mary Magdalene with news that she had seen Jesus alive. All that the travelers to Emmaus knew of the day's events was that the tomb was empty of the body of Jesus, as reported by the women and confirmed by Peter and John, and the presence of the angels in the tomb and their message to the disciples, as reported by the women (vss. 22—24).

One task which the Lord Jesus faced during His post-resurrection stay on earth was to impress on the disciples that His true mission in the world involved just the experiences through which He had passed—His death and His resurrection. On at least two times before His death He had referred to prophecies about Himself which involved these experiences (Luke 18:31, #190, and 22:37, #233); but He did not on those occasions undertake to interpret the prophecies—indeed He could not have done so. But now He took occasion to teach these sorrowful followers of His that it was proper—even necessary—for the promised Messiah to suffer those things before He could enter into His glory. Their words indicate that they, like all others of their day, were looking for the Messiah to set up the visible Kingdom and to deliver Israel from the oppressing foreign rulers. And that was the only function of the coming Messiah which they recognized. He began to teach them something about the redemption of sinners which He came to accomplish.

He would later carry on these teaching labors more at length with the group of His disciples.

2. Report of the two Emmaus disciples to the apostles at Jerusalem, news of the appearance of Jesus to Simon Peter

#265

MARK 16:13	LUKE 24:33-35
13 And they went away and told it unto the rest: neither believed they them.	33 And they rose up that very hour, and returned to Jerusalem, and found the eleven gathered together, and them that were with them, 34 saying, The Lord is risen indeed, and hath appeared to Simon. 35 And they rehearsed the things *that happened* in the way, and how he was known of them in the breaking of the bread.

Note 271. The joyous reception accorded the two returning from Emmaus, as related by Luke, and the report to them by the group that the risen Jesus had appeared to Peter, seem at first to be out of line with the Markan account that the group of disciples did not believe the report of the two about their encounter with Jesus. I do not know the explanation because I do not know all the circumstances. It is possible that their disbelief of the two was merely their inability to understand how Jesus could be with the two so soon after (or possibly, before) He had been with Peter, or how He could vanish out of their sight as He did. The miracles of that day were more wonderful than they had seen even Him perform.

If Simon Peter ever told anyone what took place when the risen Lord Jesus met him (vs. 34 above, cf. I Cor. 15:5), we have no record of it. The experience was probably too sacred for him to talk about, and we do well not to try to pull aside the curtain drawn around that meeting. However, I have wondered if Jesus did not encourage the remorseful disciple to take his place again among the apostles and to join the others at their place of lodging. He seems to have been with them when Jesus appeared to them a little later.

3. First appearance of the risen Jesus to the apostles (ten in number), the first imposing of the Great Commission

#266

LUKE 24:36-43	JOHN 20:19-23
36 And as they spake these things, he himself stood in the midst of them, [1]and saith unto them, Peace *be* unto you. 37 But they were terrified and affrighted, and supposed that they beheld a spirit. 38 And he said unto them, Why are ye troubled? and wherefore do questionings arise in your heart? 39 See my hands and my feet, that it is I myself:	19 When therefore it was evening, on that day, the first *day* of the week, and when the doors were shut where the disciples were, for fear of the Jews, Jesus came and stood in the midst, and saith unto them, Peace *be* unto you. 20 And when he had said this, he showed unto them his hands and his side.

[1] Some ancient authorities omit *and saith unto them. Peace be unto you.*

351

handle me, and see; for a spirit hath not flesh and bones, as ye behold me having. 40 [2]And when he had said this, he showed them his hands and his feet. 41 And while they still disbelieved for joy, and wondered, he said unto them, Have ye here anything to eat? 42 And they gave him a piece of a broiled fish[3]. 43 And he took it, and ate before them.

The disciples therefore were glad, when they saw the Lord. 21 Jesus therefore said to them again, Peace be unto you: as the Father hath sent me, even so send I you. 22 And when he had said this, he breathed on them, and saith unto them, Receive ye the Holy Spirit: 23 whose soever sins ye forgive, they are forgiven unto them; whose soever sins ye retain, they are retained.

[2] Some ancient authorities omit ver. 40.
[3] Many ancient authorities add and a honeycomb.

Note 272. We wonder if the first appearance of Jesus to the group of disciples after the resurrection took place in the "upper room" where they had observed the Passover and He instituted the memorial Supper a few nights earlier (Luke 22: 12) and where Jesus spoke words of warning and comfort to them as they lingered. Might not that room have been the lodging place of the eleven (except Peter and John) since the crucifixion day? It is a fact that, after the ascension, they repaired to "the upper room" (Acts 1:13); and it is altogether possible that, with the owner's approval, they made it headquarters while they were in Jerusalem.*

Three points are observed in our Lord's words to the disciples at this appearance, as they are preserved for us in John: (1) He commissioned them to the task for which He had been training them for two years—He sent them on a mission similar to that on which the Father had sent Him (vs. 21, cf. ch. 17: 8). That was the first of four times after the resurrection when He imposed on them their world-wide task. (2) He assured them of power through which they would succeed in their task—the power of the Holy Spirit (vs. 22). (3) He revealed the objective to be sought in their labors—remission of sins for those with whom they should labor (vs. 23).

Certainly Jesus did not mean that the apostles would remit sins by their own word of authority; but that their work would be in the realm of gospel proclamation, in consequence of which people would receive remission of sins (cf. Luke 24:47, #271; also Matt. 16:19; 18:18 and Note 131, Second Question).

*The Greek words for "upper room" are different in the two passages, but doubtless they indicate the same place.

4. The second appearance of the risen Jesus to the apostles (eleven in number) one week after the resurrection

#267

MARK 16:14

14 And afterward he was manifested unto the eleven themselves as they sat at meat; and he upbraided them with their unbelief and hardness of heart, because they believed not them that had seen him after he was risen.

JOHN 20:24-31

24 But Thomas, one of the twelve, called ¹Didymus, was not with them when Jesus came. 25 The other disciples therefore said unto him, We have seen the Lord. But he said unto them, Except I shall see in his hands the print of the nails, and put my finger into the print of the nails, and put my hand into his side, I will not believe.

26 And after eight days again his disciples were within, and Thomas with them. Jesus cometh, the doors being shut, and stood in the midst, and said, Peace be unto you. 27 Then saith he to Thomas, Reach hither thy finger, and see my hands; and reach *hither* thy hand, and put it into my side: and be not faithless, but believing. 28 Thomas answered and said unto him, My Lord and my God. 29 Jesus saith unto him, Because thou hast seen me, ²thou hast believed: blessed *are* they that have not seen, and *yet* have believed.

30 Many other signs therefore did Jesus in the presence of the disciples, which are not written in this book: 31 but these are written, that ye may believe that Jesus is the Christ, the Son of God; and that believing ye may have life in his name.

¹ That is, *Twin.*   ² Or, *hast thou believed?*

Note 273. Thomas was probably an obstinate disbeliever, rather than a mere "doubter." He had surely been among those who would not believe the testimony of the women concerning their experience on the resurrection morning (though he was not present that evening when Jesus appeared to them). It was his attitude in particular that Jesus upbraided (vs. 14 in Mark). He had the outlook of a pessimist, but a rugged loyalty to Jesus, nevertheless (cf. John 11:16). This appearance and the challenge of Jesus, not only brought convincing proof of the resurrection, but inspired the obstinate apostle anew in loyal allegiance to his Lord and his God.

Apparently, John intended to conclude his Gospel with the material of this section. The emphasis in the closing paragraph is on belief of his stories from the life of Jesus. This is seen from: (1) the account of the convincing of Thomas, the hard to convince, that the resurrection was a fact, (2) the blessing that Jesus pronounced on those who would believe on the testimony of witnesses, without requiring physical evidence, and (3) a statement that his objective in writing these stories was faith in Jesus on the part of his readers so that they would have life through Him. John seems to have confessed acquaintances with the Gospels already written when he spoke of the other signs performed in the presence of the disciples which are not written in this book. As a casual notice will reveal, John's Gospel is largely made up of a record of incidents not related in the other accounts.

The disciples w e r e probably still in Jerusalem when this, the second meeting on record between them and the risen Jesus occurred. We do not know why they lingered in the city in spite of the instructions from Jesus to return to Galilee for a special meeting (Matt. 26: 32, #233; 28: 7, #259). Possibly it was because some of their number, Thomas in particular, had not been convinced that Jesus was risen from the dead.

5. Appearance to seven disciples beside the sea of Galilee, Peter's three-fold confession of his love for Jesus
#268
JOHN 21:1-25

1 After these things Jesus manifested himself again to the disciples at the sea of Tiberias; and he manifested *himself* on this wise. 2 There were together Simon Peter, and Thomas called [1]Didymus, and Nathanael of Cana in Galilee, and the *sons* of Zebedee, and two other of his disciples. 3 Simon Peter saith unto them, I go a fishing. They say unto him, We also come with thee. They went forth, and entered into the boat; and that night they took nothing. 4 But when day was now breaking, Jesus stood on the beach: yet the disciples knew not that it was Jesus. 5 Jesus therefore saith unto them, Children, have ye aught to eat? They answered him, No. 6 And he said unto them, Cast the net on the right side of the boat, and ye shall find. They cast therefore, and now they were not able to draw it for the multitude of fishes. 7 That disciple therefore whom Jesus loved saith unto Peter, It is the Lord. So when Simon Peter heard that it was the Lord, he girt his coat about him (for he [2]was naked), and cast himself into the sea. 8 But the other disciples came in the little boat (for they were not far from the land, but about two hundred cubits off), dragging the net *full* of fishes. 9 So when they got out upon the land, they see [3]a fire of coals there, and [4]fish laid thereon, and [5]bread. 10 Jesus saith unto them, Bring of the fish which ye have now taken. 11 Simon Peter therefore went [6]up, and drew the net to land, full of great fishes, a hundred and fifty and three: and for all there were so many, the net was not rent. 12 Jesus saith unto them, Come *and* break your fast. And none of the disciples durst inquire of him, Who art thou? knowing that it was the Lord. 13 Jesus cometh, and taketh the [5]bread, and giveth them, and the fish likewise. 14 This is now the third time that Jesus was manifested to the disciples, after that he was risen from the dead.

15 So when they had broken their fast, Jesus saith to Simon Peter, Simon, *son* of [7]John, [8]lovest thou me more than these? He saith unto him, Yea, Lord; thou knowest that I [9]love thee. He saith unto him, Feed my lambs. 16 He saith to him again a second time, Simon, son of [7]John, [8]lovest thou me? He saith unto him, Yea, Lord; thou knowest that I [9]love thee. He said unto him, Tend my sheep. 17 He saith unto him the third time. Simon, *son* of [7]John, [9]lovest thou me? Peter was grieved because he said unto him the third time, [9]Lovest thou me? And he said unto him, Lord, thou knowest all things; thou [10]knowest that I [9]love thee. Jesus saith unto him, Feed my sheep. 18 Verily, verily, I say unto thee, When thou wast young, thou girdest thyself, and walkedst whither thou wouldest: but when thou shalt be old, thou shalt stretch forth thy hands, and another shall gird thee, and carry thee whither thou wouldest not. 19 Now this he spake, signifying by what manner of death he should glorify God. And when he had spoken this, he saith unto him, Follow me. 20 Peter, turning about, seeth the disciple whom Jesus loved

[1] That is, Twin.   [2] Or, had on his undergarment only. Comp. ch. 13. 4; Is. 20. 2; Mic. 1. 8. 11.
[3] Gr. a fire of charcoal.   [4] Or, a fish   [5] Or, a loaf   [6] Or, aboard
[7] Gr. Joanes. See ch. 1. 42, margin.
[8] [9] Love in these places represents two different Greek words.
[10] Or, perceivest

following; who also leaned back on his breast at the supper, and said, Lord, who is he that [11]betrayeth thee? 21 Peter therefore seeing him saith to Jesus, Lord, [12]and what shall this man do? 22 Jesus saith unto him, If I will that he tarry till I come, what *is that* to thee? follow thou me. 23 This saying therefore went forth among the brethren, that that disciple should not die: yet Jesus said not unto him, that he should not die; but, If I will that he tarry till I come, what *is that* to thee?

24 This is the disciple that beareth witness of these things, and wrote these things: and we know that his witness is true.

25 And there are also many other things which Jesus did, the which if they should be written every one, I suppose that even the world itself would not contain the books that should be written.

[11] Or, *delivereth thee up*   [12] Gr. *and this man, what?*

Note 274. Without doubt, John originally brought his Gospel to a close with the material in chapter 20; and later he added the material in chapter 21. The addition was certainly made by John himself and probably before any copies of the original work were made.

Before the events of this chapter, the disciples had returned to Galilee. This was the second miraculous draught of fishes (cf. #41). John knew about the first such miracle, because he was there when it occurred; and he doubtless knew that the account of it was in the Gospel of Luke. It is noticeable that next to Jesus, Simon Peter was the most prominent person in both incidents. The divine purpose of the first one was to impress Peter of his call to full-time following of Jesus (cf. Note 43). And doubtless this second such experience was divinely brought about to impress the same disciple that he was still expected to live in undivided service to his Master. When he returned to Galilee, Peter was surely still chagrined because he had denied the Lord Jesus after he had so boastfully declared that he never would, and he was probably confused about future plans. He surely felt that neither Jesus nor the other disciples would be willing to accord him a place in whatever program Jesus had in mind. So he may have been thinking seriously of going back to the fishing profession, leaving the others to carry out the program of Jesus. When Jesus asked him, therefore, "Lovest thou me more than these?" He probably meant, "more than the equipment of the fisherman which you have been using."*

Most Bible students—even many who have not studied Greek—know that the word for "love" in the first and second questions which Jesus asked Peter is different from the word in Peter's answers. In those questions Jesus used a word (agapaō) reflecting reverence and loyalty as well as strong devotion. But Peter in his answers used a word (phileō) denoting merely a personal devotion, or strong human affection. Peter

* It has been suggested that He meant "more than the other disciples love" — an allusion to Peter's boastful attitude on the night of the Passover (cf. Matt. 26:33 and parallels, #233). My reasons for the above conclusion are: (1) Jesus never sought to inspire the disciples to try to excel each other — in fact He found it necessary constantly to discourage such a spirit of rivalry among them (cf. ##138, 191, 230); and (2) Peter in his discouragement probably thought that Jesus would have no more use for him, and he might as well return to his old profession.

had just given evidence of that kind of devotion when he leaped into the sea and swam to the shore to be with Jesus. But remembering how he had pledged to Jesus in the upper room his unwavering support, and then had denied Him after being stopped in giving Him support in the way that he (Peter) wanted to give it, he was afraid to delcare the love that involves loyalty. In His third question, Jesus, seeing that Peter had two times evaded a declaration of the love involving loyalty, used the word which Peter had been using in his answers and inquired about that one's personal affection for Him. This seems to be what grieved Peter—not that Jesus asked three times if he loved Him, but that in the third question He inquired even about the love of devotion that Peter felt for Him. Whereupon, in stronger t e r m s than before, Peter declared his devoted affection for his Lord.

Observe that in response to each of Peter's answers, Jesus issued a command to him: "Feed My lambs," "Tend My sheep," and "Feed My sheep (little sheep, or highly prized sheep)." In that way He let the erring disciple know that He still wanted him in the work for which He had been training Him—there was no occasion for Peter to go back to the fishing profession. So Satan did not get the second one of the disciples through his sifter (cf. Luke 22:31--32, #233); indeed, Peter was now in position to strengthen the others. And Jesus went on to assure His loving disciple, now restored in devotion and growing loyalty, that one day this devotion to, and loyalty for, his Master would cause him to let an executioner lead him away to death. Even yet he would have the opportunity to lay down his life for his Lord (cf. John 13:37, #233).

6. Appearance to the eleven apostles **on a mountain in Galilee** and probably to five hundred **others (I Cor. 15:6), second** imposing of the Great Commission

#269

Matt. 28:16-20

16 But the eleven disciples went into Galilee, unto the mountain where Jesus had appointed them. 17 And when they saw him, they [1]worshipped *him*; but some doubted. 18 And Jesus came to them and spake unto them, saying, All authority hath been given unto me in heaven and on earth. 19 Go ye therefore, and make disciples of all the nations, baptizing them into the name of the Father and of the Son and of the Holy Spirit: 20 teaching them to observe all things whatsoever I commanded you: and lo, I am with you [2]always, even unto [3]the end of the world.
[1] See marginal note on ch. 2. 2.   [2] Gr. *all the days.*   [3] Or, *the consummation of the age*

Note 275. This was doubtless the one meeting of Jesus and His disciples after the resurrection t h a t was definitely planned ahead of time. It took place on "the mountain where Jesus had appointed them." This appointment had been mentioned three recorded times: by Jesus to the disciples on the night before His death, just after instituting the memorial Supper (Matt. 26:32, #233), by the angels to the women in the message to the disciples (Matt. 28:7, #259), and by Jesus to the women in the message to His brothers (Matt. 28:10, #262). Jesus evidently regarded it as an important meeting; and very probably He

356

spoke of it during one of the earlier appearances to the disciples, possibly the one in which Thomas was convinced (John 20:26ff, #267). At some time He surely designated the time when, and the place where, the meeting was to be held. He did not charge the apostles or anyone else to keep the meeting secret, and it would be natural for them to tell other known disciples about it, and it was just as natural for these and other curious ones to be on the designated mountain at the appointed time. For these considerations many Bible students have concluded that this was the time when, as Paul relates (I Cor. 15:6), Jesus "appeared to above five hundred brethren at once." The paragraph in Matthew reads as though this appearance was exclusively to the eleven, but it does not definitely say so. The doubting ones present were surely not any of the apostles—not even Thomas, for that one had been convinced one week after the resurrection day. Possibly His brothers were among the doubters, if they were present. His next appearance was to His brother James, probably with the purpose of producing full conviction on the part of His brothers (cf. Note 276).

He doubtless made a longer address to the crowd than is reported in Matthew. What we have is surely the summary with which He climaxed His discourse. We call it The Great Commission. This was the second of four times when He imposed on His followers the task of world-wide evangelization, and its wording is the most inclusive of them all. It involves (1) a statement of His universal authority, (2) the commission to their world-wide task, and (3) the promise of His age-long spiritual presence. The commission itself embraced (a) making disciples from among all the nations, or peoples (b) baptizing the disciples in proclamation of their allegiance to Him as a Person of the triune God, and (c) teaching the disciples to comply with all His commandments, including this command to make, baptize, and teach disciples. Thus the commission is self-perpetuating until the end of the age.

7. Appearance to His half brother James
#270
I Cor. 15:7a

7 Then he appeared to ¹James.

¹ Or, *Jacob*

Note 276. It is generally assumed by Bible students that the James to whom Paul says Jesus appeared was our Lord's own half brother. Probably he was the one denoted every time the apostle mentioned a James. We do not know any of the circumstances of the appearance, but Paul indicates that it was after the appearance to more than five hundred. There is no record that the risen Jesus appeared to His mother; but since, as we have seen, He sent a message to His brothers that they should meet Him in Galilee (#262), I have often wondered if He appeared to all His brothers and to His mother in connection with the appearance to James. At any rate, we know that, immediately after the ascension, His brothers, who before His death did not believe on Him, were, along with His mother, associated with the disciples (Acts 1: 14). Very probably many, if not all, of "one-hundred twenty" of Acts 1: 15, including the family, were with Jesus and the disciples at Jerusalem just before the ascension.

8. Appearance to the eleven in Jerusalem, third imposing of the Great Commission

#271

MARK 16:15-18	LUKE 24:44-49	ACTS 1:4-5
15 And he said unto them, Go ye into all the world, and prea'ch the [1]gospel to the whole creation. 16 He that believeth and is baptized shall be saved; but he that disbelieveth shall be condemned. 17 And these signs shall accompany them that believe: in my name shall they cast out demons; they shall speak with [2]new tongues; 18 they shall take up serpents, and if they drink any deadly thing, it shall in no wise hurt them; they shall lay hands on the sick, and they shall recover. [1] See marginal note on ch. 1. 1. [2] Some ancient authorities omit *new*.	44 And he said unto them, These are my words which I spake unto you, while I was yet with you, that all things must needs be fulfilled, which are written in the law of Moses, and the prophets, and the psalms, concerning me. 45 Then opened he their mind, that they might understand the scriptures; 46 and he said unto them, Thus it is written, that the Christ should suffer, and rise again from the dead the third day; 47 and that repentance [1]and remission of sins should be preached in his name unto all the [2]nations, beginning from Jerusalem. 48 Ye are witnesses of these things. 49 And behold, I send forth the promise of my Father upon you: but tarry ye in the city, until ye be clothed with power from on high. [1] Some ancient authorities read *unto*. [2] Or, *nations. Beginning from Jerusalem, ye are witnesses*	4 and, [1]being assembled together with them, he charged them not to depart from Jerusalem, but to wait for the promise of the Father, which, *said he*, ye heard from me: 5 for John indeed baptized with water; but ye shall be baptized [2]in the Holy Spirit not many days hence. [1] Or, *eating with them* [2] Or, *with*

Note 277. From a casual reading of Luke 24: 36--53, one would naturally conclude that all the things related in that passage occurred on one occasion; that is, at the end of the day when He arose from death. But that would make the ascension take place on the night of the resurrection day, and we know that Jesus continued to appear to the disciples for forty days after the resurrection, before He ascended to the Father (Acts 1: 3). Therefore all of it could not have occurred on the same night. We also know that on the resurrection day Jesus instructed the disciples and His brothers to go into Galilee, where He would meet them (Matt. 28: 7, #259; John 20: 17, #261; Matt. 28: 10, #262); but it

358

is a matter of record that the ascension was from the Mount of Olives, and in verse 49 of Luke and verse 4 of Acts of the section above He charged them to remain in the city of Jerusalem. Since the events of ##268 and 269 occurred in Galilee, we conclude that they had made the journey to Galilee and had returned to Jerusalem some days before the Feast of Pentecost. For some of them, the resurrection had brought renewed hopes of an immediate inauguration of the visible Kingdom, and in their minds they had settled on Pentecost as the time when Jesus would probably set it up. I have included the paragraph from Acts in the foregoing section with the one from Luke because in both passages Jesus commanded the disciples not to depart from Jerusalem.

9. Final appearance, last giving of the Great Commission, the ascension

#272

MARK 16:19-20

19 So then the Lord Jesus, after he had spoken unto them, was received up into heaven, and sat down at the right hand of God.

20 And they went forth, and preached everywhere, the Lord working with them. and confirming the word by the signs that followed. Amen.

LUKE 24:50-53

50 And he led them out until *they were* over against Bethany: and he lifted up his hands, and blessed them.

51 And it came to pass, while he blessed them, he parted from them, [1]and was carried up into heaven.

52 And they [2]worshipped him, and returned to Jerusalem with great joy: 53 and were continually in the temple, blessing God.
[1] Some ancient authorities omit *and was carried up into heaven.*
[2] Some ancient authorities omit *worshipped him, and.* See marginal note on ch. 4. 7.

ACTS 1:6-12

6 They therefore, when they were come together, asked him, saying, Lord, dost thou at this time restore the kingdom to Israel? 7 And he said unto them, It is not for you to know times or seasons, which the Father hath [1]set within his own authority. 8 But ye shall receive power, when the Holy Spirit is come upon you: and ye shall be my witness both in Jerusalem, and in all Judaea and Samaria, and unto the uttermost part of the earth. 9 And when he had said these things, as they were looking, he was taken up; and a cloud received him out of their sight. 10 And while they were looking stedfastly into heaven as he went, behold two men stood by them in white apparel; 11 who also said, Ye men of Galilee, why stand ye looking into heaven? this Jesus, who was received up from you into heaven, shall so come in like manner as ye beheld him going into heaven. 12 Then returned they unto Jerusalem from the mount called Olivet, which is nigh unto Jerusalem, a sabbath day's journey off.
[1] Or, *appointed by*

359

Note 278. It is possible that some of the disciples were so filled with the thought of the visible Kingdom that they did not learn well the lesson of the important place which the death of Jesus and His resurrection occupied in His mission on earth. In their question in verse 6 of the Acts passage, "at this time" probably meant the time of the approaching feast of Pentecost, when another concourse of people would come to Judaea and Jerusalem, just as they had come for the Passover some weeks before. The rumor of the events during the recent Passover week would (and probably did) swell the number coming up for Pentecost. Replying to their question, Jesus gave them to understand that the time table of the future was not in the scope of their responsibility. The Father, He said, has reserved all this in His own authority, including the time when the Kingdom will be transformed from spiritual to visible. Moreover, He brought their attention back to their own responsibility—they were to bear witness of Him throughout the world. And He assured them again of power to succeed in that task, power which they would receive when the Holy Spirit would come to dominate their activities. And as they, and all the followers of Jesus, have been faithful in that task, they have enlarged the bounds and the influence of the Kingdom.

The place of ascension, according to tradition, was on the summit of the Mount of Olives; it was certainly somewhere on the mountain in sight of Bethany. The disciples surely did not know why Jesus was leading them to that place, and their question regarding the Kingdom may have been suggested as they passed along the route of the Triumphant Entry into Jerusalem. It is interesting, if not significant, that He gave the answer near the place, if not on the place, where two days before the Passover He had delivered the prophetic discourse, which was in reply to questions of the same general import as this one—and the same general conclusion is embraced in the reply.

In the last words of our Lord on earth in His body, He brushed aside the inquiry of His followers about the time for the inauguration of the visible Kingdom, and commissioned them again to give themselves to a program of bearing testimony of Him on a world-wide scale. This was the fourth and last giving of "the Great Commission." With this commission He departed from them bodily, but He had already promised (Matt. 28: 20, #269) that His unseen presence would be with them (and with us, their successors) until the end of the age. And, as the angels assured them, He will visibly and bodily return to "restore the Kingdom to Israel," even to the "Israel of God" (Gal. 6: 16).

INDEX

FOR FINDING IN THE HARMONY ANY PASSAGE OF THE GOSPELS

(References are to section numbers)

MATTHEW

JOHN